ORGANIZATIONAL
BEHAVIOR 2

ORGANIZATIONAL BEHAVIOR 2

ESSENTIAL THEORIES OF PROCESS AND STRUCTURE

JOHN B. MINER

M.E.Sharpe
Armonk, New York
London, England

Library of Congress Cataloging-in-Publication Data

Miner, John B.
  Organizational behavior 1. Essential theories of motivation and leadership.
  Organizational behavior 2. Essential theories of process and structure / by John B. Miner.
    p. cm.
  Includes bibliographical references and index.
   Vol. 1: ISBN 0-7656-1523-1 (cloth : alk. paper)
   Vol. 2: ISBN 0-7656-1525-8 (cloth : alk. paper)
  1. Employee motivation. 2. Leadership. 3. Organizational behavior. I. Title:
Organizational behavior two. Essential theories of process and structure. II. Title:
Organizational behavior. 2, Essential theories of process and structure. III. Title: Essential
theories of process and structure. IV. Title.

HF5549.5.M63M5638 2005
302.3'5--dc22   2005003746

DEDICATION

To the intellectual leaders who coined the ideas and much of the research that made this book possible:

Chris Argyris	James G. March
Lee Roy Beach	John W. Meyer
Peter M. Blau	Jeffrey Pfeffer
Tom Burns	Walter W. Powell
Glenn R. Carroll	Derek S. Pugh
Richard M. Cyert	Gerald R. Salancik
Paul J. DiMaggio	Edgar H. Schein
Fred E. Emery	W. Richard Scott
John Freeman	Herbert A. Simon
Michael T. Hannan	G. M. Stalker
David J. Hickson	Arnold S. Tannenbaum
C. Robert Hinings	James D. Thompson
Robert L. Kahn	Eric L. Trist
Daniel Katz	Max Weber
Paul R. Lawrence	Karl E. Weick
Jay W. Lorsch	Lynne G. Zucker

—and the many who worked with them.

CONTENTS

PART V. SOCIOLOGICAL CONCEPTS OF ORGANIZATION

LIST OF TABLES AND FIGURES

TABLES

ix

FIGURES

PREFACE

Essential Theories of Process and Structure is the third in a series of books dealing with macro-level organizational behavior theories, spread unevenly over a twenty-three-year period. The predecessors were *Theories of Structure and Process* (Dryden, 1982), and *Organizational Behavior: Foundations, Theories, and Analyses* (Oxford University Press, 2002).

All of these books presuppose some prior work in such fields as organizational behavior, management, and the like. Given an introduction of this kind, the reader should find little in this book that overlaps with his or her prior learning. The reason for this is that basic courses typically take a content- or problem-centered approach. In contrast, this book takes a different tack, focusing on the best theories in the field of macro-organizational behavior and the contributions these theories have made to understanding organizations. Dealing with these theories and the research on them requires not only some basic study in the area, but an introduction to statistics as well. With these kinds of preparation the reader should have no difficulty comprehending the material presented here, even though some of the theories are by their nature quite demanding.

WHY THEORY?

There are several advantages to being exposed to a book that focuses on theory, as this one does. The first is that theories become the nodes for ideas around which knowledge comes to concentrate. This concentration of knowledge surrounding theories makes for a comprehensive, yet more parsimonious, coverage of the subject matter of a field. Good theories tend to attract research and consequently, much of what we really know about the processes and structures of organizations is encompassed within the theoretical framework. In short, casting a net that catches only theories, and then only those theories that have been shown by research to be the better ones at the present time, provides an ideal perspective on organizational behavior subject matter.

A second advantage is that concentrating on theories permits a degree of insight into how organizational science really operates that is not possible otherwise. This is because the interplay between theory development and research is at the very heart of any scientific discipline. To understand this process one has to approach the subject matter of a field through its theories. This becomes particularly important for a field like organizational behavior where the ties between professional school education and practice are not as close as they are in medicine, for instance. To bring the educational process and actual practice closer together there needs to be a reciprocal relationship and thus mutual understanding. Much has been written on how academics need to understand the practitioner perspective better, and I applaud such efforts, but practitioners also need to understand how knowledge is generated in organizational behavior, if the relationship is to be truly reciprocal. This book, with its emphasis on theory, provides a window to the science of organizational behavior in a way that is not otherwise possible.

WHY THESE THEORIES?

The theories presented in this volume were selected from a larger listing of thirty-five theories of organizational processes and structure originally created to include the most significant theories of the field, if not necessarily the most valid. This larger listing was developed from existing books devoted to surveying the organizational behavior theoretical literature. These thirty-five were reduced to the twenty-one presented here by applying criteria specified as follows.

Importance Rating

The seventy-one organizational behavior experts who responded to a survey rated the thirty-five theories on a seven-point scale (with 7 as the high value) with regard to the theory's importance to the field. For the twenty-one selected theories, the mean such rating was 4.97, while the mean rating for the theories not included in this book was 3.81. The criterion applied to insure inclusion in this volume was a rating of 5.00 or above; twelve theories met this criterion.

Institutionalization

An institution may be defined as a cognitive, normative, or regulative structure or activity that provides stability and meaning to social behavior. Thus, theories that have the backing of institutionalization are widely known and endorsed. The distribution of importance ratings for each theory was analyzed to determine whether the frequencies in the upper half of the distribution departed from normal curve expectations, and if so, whether this deviation represented an exaggeration of the frequencies sufficient to produce statistical significance. Those theories that achieved significance were said to be institutionalized; all six of them are included in this book. Further detail on institutional theory is given in Chapter 20.

Estimated Validity

Validity was determined by the author based on an assessment of the research on the theory, as to both its quantity and the support it provided. The "goodness" of the theoretical statements was considered as well, as were evaluations by other reviewers, including meta-analyses. These summary ratings were made on a five-point scale (with 5 as the high point). The mean estimated validity for the twenty-one selected theories was 3.48, and for the theories not included here it was 2.29. Any theory with a rating of 4 or 5 was automatically selected, and there were ten of these.

Estimated Usefulness

Usefulness in practice was also established by the author, depending on the extent to which such applications existed, the extent of the research on these applications, and the support for practical use provided by this research. Endorsements by practitioners provided in the literature were considered too, but no attempt was made to establish the facts regarding the extent of actual use in practice; the latter were believed to be so subject to faddism as to be unreliable. Again, the estimated usefulness ratings were made on a five-point scale (with 5 as the high point). For the twenty-one theories included in this volume the mean such evaluation was 2.52, and for the fourteen theories excluded it was 2.21. The criterion for inclusion was a rating of 4 or 5, and there were three of these. Thus, the usefulness criterion contributed rather infrequently to inclusion in this book, at least in a unique sense.

In addition to the criteria for a labeling as "essential" provided from these four sources, any theory that consistently met the next highest rating category was included as well. Any such consistently "almost good enough" theory was judged to be worthy of inclusion, not on the basis of performance relative to any single criterion, but because of the total summed score. This kind of theory was not institutionalized, but had an importance rating in the 4.00–4.99 range, an estimated validity of 3, and an estimated usefulness of 3. There was one such theory.

Greater detail on the measures set forth above may be obtained from two sources: "The Rated Importance, Scientific Validity, and Practical Usefulness of Organizational Behavior Theories: A Quantitative Review" in the 2003 *Academy of Management Learning and Education,* Volume 2, pages 250–268; and "The Institutionalization of Organizational Behavior Theories: An Empirical Investigation" to be included in a subsequent volume of this *Organizational Behavior* series and also available from the author. The fourteen theories not selected for inclusion in this book are discussed in *Organizational Behavior: Foundations, Theories, and Analyses* (Oxford University Press, 2002). All of these sources were written by myself.

The estimated validity and usefulness ratings originally made in 2000 were updated as of 2004. The result was that four theories increased in value on one or both criteria, because either new research evidence was introduced in the interim, or because new theories and/or applications were published by the theory's author(s). In no case did these revisions produce an increase of more than one rating category, but in two instances the consequence was the designation of a theory as "essential," and thus its inclusion in this book.

A point needs to be made regarding the dates of origin of these theories. They extend back to the early 1900s and run to the 1980s; yet this is not a history book. Without exception these theories can be found cited in the current literature, and they will be found there many times. Several reasons exist for this situation. One consideration is that it takes a number of years for a theory to accumulate enough research to permit an adequate evaluation. Thus, theories of the 1990s and beyond are almost automatically excluded. Furthermore, during the 1960s and 1970s a large number of individuals came to organizational behavior from other disciplines, thus creating new combinations of knowledge and a particularly fertile ground for theory generation.

Perhaps more important than any other consideration, however, is that organizational behavior theorists tend to keep revising and developing their theories once they get started, and they typically do not stop much before they die. A few of those considered in this book have indeed stopped theorizing because they are no longer among us, but most are still at it. This means that many theories of organizational behavior that began decades ago are also very current and continue to dominate the field.

STRUCTURE OF THE BOOK

This book is divided into five parts. Part I includes two chapters intended to set the scene for what follows by providing background on scientific method, theory construction and evaluation, measurement considerations, research design, the nature of knowledge in organizational behavior, and other considerations needed to truly understand the theoretical discussions in the remaining parts. Perhaps some readers are sufficiently familiar with this material and feel they can skip the introduction and move directly to the theories themselves. Nevertheless, these two chapters contain a considerable amount of material that is new; more than 45 percent of the references cite publications dated 2000 or later. I recommend at least a quick skim, and for those who are reasonably new to the field, this should be the needed background to decipher what follows.

Parts II through V take up essential theories of organizational process and structure in different groupings. Decision making as an organizational process is considered in Part II. It is presented at an early point because many organizational behavior scholars view decision making as the framework on which the rest of the macro field is built. Part III takes up systems concepts, which, in their open systems version, deal with interactions between organizations and their environments. These theories derive about equally from the fields of both psychology and sociology. The early theory of Max Weber is central to the ideas presented in Parts IV and V. Part IV begins with theories that are of an essentially sociological origin, and that build upon Weber. It ends, however, with two theories that draw upon organization development, and in the process present what can only be construed as attacks upon bureaucracy theory and the structure it portrays. Finally, Part V considers three theories that represent the cornerstone of present-day organizational sociology; these differ in their sources of origin, but have substantial overlapping content and some common constructs as well.

STRUCTURE OF THE CHAPTERS

After the book's introductory material, the remaining chapters follow a generally consistent format. An outline covering the various headings of the chapter provides a road map facilitating progress through the discussion, and a guide to finding a way out should the reader get lost en route. The introductory material, including what is labeled "background," is intended to place the theory at hand in its context, both intellectual and historical. What are the sources of the theorist's ideas, and what sort of environment nurtured them? I have tried here to provide for the reader something of a biographical understanding of the theorists as people. Note that, with one exception, all of the theorists are males. There was little diversity of any kind among theorists of organizational behavior at the time these theories emerged. It is different now, and I assume that in the future a book such as this will possess a much more diversified cast of characters.

An important feature at the beginning of each chapter is the box (or, on occasion, boxes) that presents the ratings of the theory to be considered, and its decade of origin. The ratings are those discussed earlier in this preface—the importance rating; institutionalization, if appropriate; estimated validity; and estimated usefulness—each expressed using a set of stars. This information should prove helpful, going into the discussion, in guiding the reader as to what to expect with each theory.

Following the introductory material for each chapter, the theory is presented in developmental sequence. In a few instances this represents an early comprehensive statement with only a few changes subsequently, but much more frequently the development of the theory extends over years. Some theories are still in transition at this writing. This theoretical statement is followed by an evaluation and impact section, which considers the appropriate research, usually starting with the research conducted by the theory's author(s). In many cases these initial investigations by the theorists set the pattern for subsequent studies by others. In analyzing the research I am rarely able to consider all possible studies, but every effort is made to take up the more significant ones. Meta-analyses and evaluative reviews are relied upon heavily in reaching conclusions.

Applications, if there are any (and in a number of instances there are), are considered at appropriate points in the presentation. Usually there is less research, and less by way of evaluations by others, where applications are concerned, but I have presented whatever is available in both instances. In my opinion, in an applied field such as organizational behavior, it is as important to evaluate theories in terms of their relevance for practice as to consider their validity.

In the conclusions section of each chapter I attempt to explain and document how the estimated validity and estimated usefulness ratings were made for that particular theory. Thus, both positive and negative features are noted and then balanced to arrive at the final rating as reflected in the stars awarded in the box at the beginning of each chapter.

The chapter-end references are numerous, providing both a developmental chronology of theoretical statements and a record of significant research. This is partly to document statements made in the text, but it also provides a list of sources to use for follow-up should the reader wish to learn more about a particular theory. The total number of references runs to over a thousand, with an average of fifty per chapter. Some 30 percent of these were published in 2000 or more recently, supporting the contention that this is a thoroughly up-to-date volume.

STRUCTURE OF ORGANIZATIONAL BEHAVIOR

Essential Theories of Process and Structure is a sequel to *Essential Theories of Motivation and Leadership* (2005). Both books are prefaced with the title *Organizational Behavior* to indicate their common origin. While theories of organizational process and structure relate primarily to intergroup relationships, organizationwide concepts, and organization–environment interactions, theories of motivation and leadership focus on individual and small-group functioning within an organizational context. Together, theories of the two types constitute the theoretical input to the field of organizational behavior.

However, these two thrusts are not entirely independent of one another, and they have been merging increasingly in recent years. Concepts and constructs from one area tend to find their way into the other, thus bringing the two poles closer together and tending to unify organizational behavior. In a very real sense, the division into two areas represents an artificial distinction imposed because the study of organizations is too large for one book, or even for one course. Thus, to truly understand the discipline of organizational behavior as a whole, one must look into the theories of motivation and leadership as well as those theories considered here. This means knowing about such institutionalized theories as Kurt Lewin's social psychological views of leadership and change, Frederick Herzberg's motivation hygiene theory, Victor Vroom's expectancy theory, Stacy Adams's equity theory, and Edwin Locke and Gary Latham's goal setting theory at the very least, as well as the formulations presented in this book. Only then can a full understanding of organizational behavior be achieved.

John B. Miner
Eugene, Oregon
October 2004

ACKNOWLEDGMENTS

My major debt in preparing this book is acknowledged in the dedication. Without the efforts of the various theorists of organizational processes and structure there would have been nothing to write about. They have not only proved themselves to be very good theorists, but they have served in large part to carry the young field of organizational behavior through its formative years.

I am also indebted to Oxford University Press for giving me permission to use material from my *Organizational Behavior: Foundations, Theories, and Analyses* wherever in the present volume it proved appropriate. Harry Briggs at M.E. Sharpe has shown himself to be both a very helpful person and a highly proficient editor; it has been a pleasure to work with him. Amy Odum, my production editor, has been equally helpful.

Finally, in the absence of any university support, my wife, Barbara, has taken on all of the numerous tasks involved in the preparation of this book, other than writing it. I thank her not only for her dedication and efficiency, but for her support and love.

PART I

SCIENTIFIC INTRODUCTION

CHAPTER 1

SCIENCE AND ITS THEORY

What is *organizational behavior?* It is a social science discipline—much like cultural anthropology, economics, political science, psychology, and sociology. That means that it utilizes the scientific method to establish truth and to validate its theories. It is a discipline that historically has had its intellectual home in business schools. It is a new discipline relative to the other social sciences, having its origins in the middle twentieth century. The key points are that it is a science and that it has a history that, though short, has been quite turbulent.

Although the exact boundaries of the discipline are somewhat fuzzy (see Blood 1994), organizational behavior's focus is clearly on the world of organizations. The concern is first with the behavior and nature of people within organizations, and second with the behavior and nature of organizations within their environments. The term *organizational behavior* initially had reference only to the behavior and nature of people in organizations. Given the fuzziness of its boundaries, the discipline always had a tendency to stretch beyond that domain, however. By the time it was approaching twenty-five years of age, it clearly had staked a claim to incorporating the behavior and nature of organizations as well. This is historically consistent in that both the study of the behavior and nature of people and the study of the behavior and nature of organizations emerged in business schools in the same places at the same times. The focus of this volume, however, is on the latter, with the usual caveat regarding fuzzy boundaries.

In line with its professional school origins, organizational behavior is an applied discipline, concerned with matters of practice and application. Despite this orientation, it has relatively few members who actually devote their primary professional efforts to the practice of organizational behavior in business and other organizational settings; rather, most are concentrated in academia—teaching, writing, and conducting research. In my opinion this is unfortunate; the field would be better off, not by reducing its academic efforts, but by expanding its practitioner efforts. We will return to this theme in various ways throughout this book.

Several other terms have become intertwined with organizational behavior over the years, although none has achieved quite the same level of acceptance. One is *organization theory,* which has come to refer almost exclusively to the study of the behavior and nature of organizations in their environments. A second is *organization(al) science,* which appears to cover essentially the same ground as organizational behavior, and which in many respects I prefer as a designation for our field (see Miner 1984). However, right now organizational behavior has won the day. Finally, there is the term *organization studies,* which also has a broad connotation, extending, at least in the recent period, beyond the science of organizations to incorporate several different philosophic positions (see Clegg, Hardy, and Nord 1996).

Having explained what organizational behavior is, I need to say something about what it is not. It is not *strategic management,* a field that has emerged and achieved stature more recently than organizational behavior (see Schendel and Hofer 1979) and that has differentiated itself at the border that previously existed between organizational behavior and economics, borrowing from and overlapping with each. Also organizational behavior is not *economics,* although in recent years there has been some confounding of the two fields and some even foresee a possible future takeover of organizational behavior by economics (see, for example, Pfeffer 1995). However, economics was well established in business schools long before organizational behavior arrived, and organizational behavior was spawned, in large part at the behest of economists, as a separate and distinct discipline. Historically the two are clearly different entities with very different origins.

Finally, organizational behavior is not *philosophy.* That, however, is a rather complex story. As a science, our field is closely tied to, though separate from, the philosophy of science. In this respect it is like all other sciences, and the relationship can be expected to continue as long as organizational behavior defines itself as a social science. But philosophy has been threaded into organizational behavior in other respects from the very beginning, not always to the benefit of either field. Sometimes, in the hands of certain individuals, organizational behavior and philosophy have become almost indistinguishable from one another. Understanding what is involved here requires a background in the nature of science, scientific theory, scientific research, and in the history of science—in short in the scientific foundations of the field. It also requires a background in the ways in which philosophy has become threaded into organizational behavior at various points in time. These matters are considered in these introductory chapters of Part I.

The primary focus of this book, however, is on the major theories that have evolved within the broad field of organizational behavior that deal with the processes of organizational functioning and the structures of organizational forms. The goal is to provide an understanding of these theories and thus to determine what they can tell us that might prove useful to people who participate in organizations.

In point of fact we all participate in various organizations, such as schools, companies, and hospitals throughout our lives, and we devote a large percentage of our time to such participation. Most people would like to function more effectively in organizations and to contribute to more effective functioning of the organizations themselves. It seems logical that the more we know about organizations and the way they operate, the better our chances of coping with them adequately and of achieving our own goals within them and for them. Giving us this knowledge is what theories of organizational behavior attempt to do.

As a foundation for understanding these theories it is important to know what scientific theory is and what it is not, as well as how theory relates to research and how research either supports or fails to support theory. These are the concerns of this scientific introduction. The intent is to provide a basic understanding that can be drawn on as specific theories are discussed in the remainder of the book.

THEORY AND PRACTICE

Theory is the cornerstone of any science. It provides the ideas that fuel research and practice. Theories of organizational behavior are as potentially useful when applied to organizations as theories of physics and chemistry are when used in developing new manufacturing technologies and consumer products, or theories of biology are in advancing medical practice. However, the relationship between theory and practice (or application, or usefulness) in organizational behavior is often misunderstood. For many people the term *theory* evokes images of a speculative, ivory-towered world, far removed from reality. Theories do not sound helpful in understanding the practical facts of organizational life. Yet one hears such statements as that of the eminent psychologist Kurt Lewin (1945), who said that "nothing is so practical as a good theory." And this dictum continues to receive widespread acceptance today (see, for example, Van de Ven 1989).

Confusion on this score is in fact widespread; the subject requires consideration here at the outset because a particular reader's preconceptions regarding the theory–practice relationship (or the lack thereof) can color that person's thinking about the entire field. The idea that theory is somehow "ivory tower" while practice is "real world"—and that the two are distinct and separate—permeates much current discussion of business school education and of the role of the organizational behavior discipline (Das 2003, Donaldson 2002).

What then is the state of the situation at the interface between academic theory and research, and the world of application? What do studies tell us? One of the most comprehensive such studies deals with the research knowledge, much of it theory-based, of human resource managers (Rynes, Brown, and Colbert 2002; Rynes, Colbert, and Brown 2002). This investigation indicated that these managers were not very knowledgeable regarding the research evidence; they were only neutral on the value of research findings for practice, and most read very little in the research literature. Yet those few who were more conversant with the research worked for more financially successful companies. A difficulty appears to be that many HR managers rely almost entirely on the popular press for knowledge input (Mazza and Alvarez 2000), and often get wrong information from such sources. Not surprisingly, the popular press tends to pick up on temporary fads and fashions that are "hot" at the time, many of which are simply recycled versions of old ideas that had been discarded (Spell 2001).

Another study, focused on a specific theory, failed to find evidence of an understanding of this theory among managers, although M.B.A. students were better informed (Priem and Rosenstein 2000). Thus, practicing managers could not go in the directions prescribed because they lacked the knowledge to do so. Although value and motivational differences are involved here (Brooks, Grauer, Thornbury, and Highhouse 2003; Miner 2004), this in itself would not logically account for the academic-managerial gap found; the problem appears to be in not going to appropriate sources of information (Roehling, Cavanaugh, Moynihan, and Boswell 2000).

The data thus seem to indicate a substantial gap between theory and perceived usefulness in practice. Yet there are reasons to believe that this gap can be reduced under appropriate circumstances (Rynes, Bartunek, and Daft 2001). One objective of this volume is to facilitate this process and accordingly to narrow the gap so that practitioners will come away with a greater appreciation of the value that organizational behavior theory can bring to practice. Examples of recent academic–practitioner collaborations on research studies (Ford, Duncan, Bedeian, Ginter, Rousculp, and Adams 2003; Rynes and McNatt 2001) and of increasing concern about linking theory to practice (Cooper and Locke 2000) give reason for optimism in this regard.

In this context, let me return to Lewin's (1945) dictum. What Lewin meant by a good theory is one that is validated by adequate research. To be truly useful, a theory must be intimately intertwined with research, and to the extent that it is, it has the potential for moving beyond philosophic speculation to become a sound basis for action. Good theory is thus practical because it advances knowledge in a field, guides research to important questions, and enlightens practice in some manner (Van de Ven 1989).

Some theories are obviously more concerned with application than others. Some, at the time of inception, may fail to meet the test of usefulness, only to find their way to a juncture with practice later on. Some theories are never tested, or fail the test of research, and they are not very good theories, at least as far as anyone can tell. In any event a *good* theory has the potential for valid applications and thus can prove useful if correctly applied. A theory in an applied field, such as organizational behavior, that is so divorced from application (so ivory tower?) that it has no potential for speaking to practice is very unlikely to be a *good* theory. This is the viewpoint that guides the analyses and interpretations presented throughout this book.

SCIENCE DEFINED

Science is an enterprise by which a particular kind of ordered knowledge is obtained about natural phenomena by means of controlled observations and theoretical interpretations. Ideally, this science, of which organizational behavior is a part, lives up to the following:

1. The definitions are precise
2. The data-collecting is objective
3. The findings are replicable
4. The approach is systematic and cumulative
5. The purposes are understanding and prediction, plus, in the applied arena, control (Berelson and Steiner 1964).

The usually accepted goals of scientific effort are to increase understanding and to facilitate prediction (Dubin 1978). At its best, science will achieve both of these goals. However, there are many instances in which prediction has been accomplished with considerable precision, even though true understanding of the underlying phenomena is minimal; this is characteristic of much of the forecasting that companies do as a basis for planning, for example. Similarly, understanding can be far advanced, even though prediction lags behind. For instance, we know a great deal about the various factors that influence the level of people's work performance, but we do not know enough about the interaction of these factors in specific instances to predict with high accuracy exactly how well a certain individual will do in a particular position.

In an applied field, such as organizational behavior, the objectives of understanding and prediction are joined by a third objective—influencing or managing the future, and thus achieving control. An economic science that explained business cycles fully and predicted fluctuations precisely would represent a long step toward holding unemployment at a desired level. Similarly, knowledge of the dynamics of organizations and the capacity to predict the occurrence of particular structures and processes would seem to offer the possibility of engineering a situation to maximize organizational effectiveness. To the extent that limited unemployment or increased organizational effectiveness are desired, science then becomes a means to these goals. In fact much scientific work is undertaken to influence the world around us. To the extent applied science meets such objectives, it achieves a major goal.

THE ROLE OF THEORY IN SCIENCE

Scientific method evolves in ascending levels of abstractions (Brown and Ghiselli 1955). At the most basic level it portrays and retains experience in symbols. The symbols may be mathematical, but to date in organizational behavior they have been primarily linguistic. Once converted to symbols, experience may be mentally manipulated, and relationships may be established.

Description utilizes symbols to classify, order, and correlate events. It remains at a low level of abstraction and is closely tied to observation and sensory experience. In essence it is a matter of ordering symbols to make them adequately portray events. The objective is to answer "what" questions.

Explanation moves to a higher level of abstraction in that it attempts to establish meanings behind events. It attempts to identify causal, or at least concomitant, relationships so that observed phenomena make some logical sense.

Theory Defined

At its maximal point, explanation creates *theory*. Scientific theory is a patterning of logical constructs, or interrelated symbolic concepts, into which the known facts regarding a phenomenon, or theoretical domain, may be fitted. A theory is a generalization, applicable within stated boundaries, that specifies the relationships between factors. Thus it is an attempt to make sense out of observations that in and of themselves do not contain any inherent and obvious logic (Dubin 1976). The objective is to answer "how," "when," and "why" questions.

Since theory is so central to science, a certain amount of repetition related to this topic may be forgiven. Campbell (1990) defines theory as a collection of assertions, both verbal and symbolic, that identifies what variables are important for what reasons, specifies how they are interrelated and why, and identifies the conditions under which they should be related or not. Sutton and Staw (1995) place their emphasis somewhat differently, but with much the same result. For them theory is about the connections among phenomena, a story about why acts, events, structure, and thoughts occur. It emphasizes the nature of causal relationships, identifying what comes first as well as the timing of events. It is laced with a set of logically interconnected arguments. It can have implications that we have not previously seen and that run counter to our common sense.

How Theory Works

Figure 1.1 provides a picture of the components of a theory. A theory is thus a system of constructs and variables with the constructs related to one another by propositions and the variables by hypotheses. The whole is bounded by the assumptions, both implicit and explicit, that the theorist holds with regard to the theory (Bacharach 1989).

Figure 1.1   **The Components of Theories and How They Function**

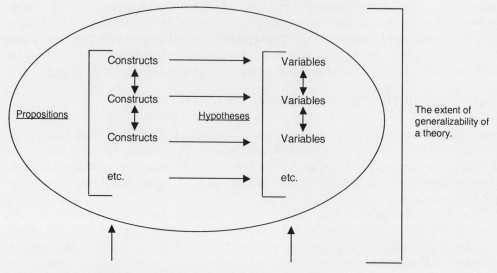

Constructs are "terms which, though not observational either directly or indirectly, may be applied or even defined on the basis of the observables" (Kaplan 1964, 55). They are abstractions created to facilitate understanding. Variables are observable, they have multiple values, and they derive from constructs. In essence they are operationalizations of constructs created to permit testing of hypotheses. In contrast to the abstract constructs, variables are concrete. Propositions are statements of relationships among constructs. Hypotheses are similar statements involving variables. Research attempts to refute or confirm hypotheses, not propositions, per se.

All theories occupy a domain within which they should prove effective and outside of which they should not. These domain-defining, bounding assumptions (see Figure 1.1) are in part a product of the implicit values held by the theorist relative to the theoretical content. These values typically go unstated and, if that is the case, they cannot be measured. Spatial boundaries restrict the effective use of the theory to specific units, such as types of organizations or kinds of people. Among these, cultural boundaries are particularly important for theory (Cheng, Sculli, and Chan 2001). Temporal boundaries restrict the effective use of the theory to specific time periods. To the extent they are explicitly stated, spatial and temporal boundaries can be measured and thus made operational. Taken together, they place some limitation on the generalizability of a theory. These boundary-defining factors need not operate only to specify the domain of a theory, however; all may serve in stating propositions and hypotheses as well. For example, *time* has recently received considerable attention as a variable that may enter into hypotheses (George and Jones 2000; Mitchell and James 2001).

Organizational behavior has often been criticized for utilizing highly ambiguous theoretical constructs—it is not at all clear what they mean (see, for example, Sandelands and Drazin 1989). This same ambiguity can extend to boundary definitions and domain statements. In a rather cynical vein, Astley and Zammuto (1992) even argue that this ambiguity is functional for a theorist in that it increases the conceptual appeal of a theory. Conflicting positions do not become readily apparent and the domain of application may appear much greater than the empirical reality. Such purposeful ambiguity creation can cause the constructs and ideas of a theory to be extended into the world of practice to an extent that is not empirically warranted. Not surprisingly, these views immediately met substantial opposition (see, for example, Beyer 1992). The important point, however, is that science does not condone this type of theoretical ambiguity. Precise definitions are needed to make science effective (Locke 2003), and a theory that resorts to ambiguity is to that extent a poor theory.

ASSUMPTIONS OF SCIENCE

Science must make certain assumptions about the world around us. These assumptions might not be factually true, and to the extent they are not, science will have less value. However, to the extent science operates on these assumptions and produces a degree of valid understanding, prediction, and influence, it appears more worthwhile to utilize the assumptions.

Science assumes, first, that certain natural groupings of phenomena exist, so that classification can occur and generalization within a category is meaningful. For some years, for instance, the field then called business policy, operating from its origins in the case method, assumed that each company is essentially unique. This assumption effectively blocked the development of scientific theory and research in the field. Increasingly, however, the assumption of uniqueness has been disappearing, and generalizations applicable to classes of organizations have emerged (see, for instance, Steiner and Miner 1986). As a result, scientific theory and research are burgeoning in the field of strategic management.

Second, science assumes some degree of constancy, or stability, or permanence in the world. Science cannot operate in a context of complete random variation; the goal of valid prediction is totally unattainable under such circumstances. Thus objects and events must retain some degree of similarity from one time to another. In a sense this is an extension of the first assumption, but now over time rather than across units (see McKelvey 1997 for a discussion of these premises). For instance, if organizational structures, once introduced, did not retain some stability, any scientific prediction of their impact on organizational performance would be impossible. Fortunately they do have some constancy, but not always as much as might be desired.

Third, science assumes that events are determined and that causes exist. This is the essence of explanation and theorizing. It may not be possible to prove a specific causation with absolute certainty, but evidence can be adduced to support certain causal explanations and reject others. In any event, if one does not assume some kind of causation, there is little point in scientific investigation; the assumption of determinism is what sparks scientific effort. If, for instance, one assumes that organizational role prescriptions do not influence individual performance, then the whole area of organizational design moves outside the realm of scientific inquiry. Organizational behavior must assume some kind of causal impact of the organization on its members. It then becomes the task of science to determine the nature of this impact.

Finally, because science is firmly rooted in observation and experience, it is necessary to assume some degree of trustworthiness for the human processes of perceiving, remembering, and reasoning. This trustworthiness is always relative, but it must exist to some degree. The rules under which science operates are intended to increase the degree of reliability with which scientific observation and recording operate. The purpose is to achieve an objective, rational, replicable result, which will be convincing to those who are knowledgeable in the area of study.

RULES OF SCIENTIFIC INQUIRY

If the findings of research are to be replicated and the generalizations from research are to be valid, concepts must be clearly defined in terms of the procedures used to measure them. This has been a problem in the field of organizational behavior. On occasion theoretical concepts are stated in such an ambiguous manner and the conditions for their measurement left so uncertain that the researcher is hard put to devise an adequate test of a theory.

Second, scientific observation must be controlled so that causation may be attributed correctly. The objective is to be certain that an outcome is in fact produced by what is believed to produce it and not by something else. Control of this kind is achieved through the use of various experimental designs, or through measurement and statistical adjustment, as discussed in Chapter 2. In the complex world of organizational functioning, establishing controls sufficient to pin down causation often has proved to be difficult.

Third, because science is concerned with generalization to contexts that extend far beyond a given experiment, it is essential that research utilize samples that are adequate in both size and conditions of their selection. One must have confidence that the results obtained are generalizable and can be put to use outside the research situation. The field of statistics becomes important for organizational behavior because of its potential for determining how much confidence can be placed in a particular research outcome.

Fourth, and this bears repeating, science requires that its propositions, hypotheses, and theories be stated in terms that can be tested empirically. This is where philosophy and science part company. Unfortunately, in the past organizational behavior has not always clearly separated scientific from philosophic statements. The result has been considerable confusion, and on occasion effort has been wasted on attempts to test theories that are not really testable as stated. Bacharach (1989) provides a good discussion of this falsifiability requirement.

THEORY BUILDING

A distinction is often made between deductive and inductive theory. In building a theory by deduction, one first establishes a set of premises. Then certain logical consequences of these premises are deduced and subsidiary concepts are established. The starting point is rational thought, and logical consistency is a major concern in development of the theory. Often such theories are stated in mathematical terms.

Inductive theory, in contrast, builds up from observation, often from research, rather than down from a set of premises. Essentially one puts together a theory that best seems to explain what is known in a given area at the present time. Then new tests of this theory, or of hypotheses derived from it, are carried out, just as they would be if the theory were developed deductively.

Gottfredson (1983) points to three ways in which inductive theory may be developed from research findings. First, one may immerse oneself in the data generated by past research, but with a healthy skepticism regarding the interpretations of the data by others. Second, one may pick one or more specific patterns of results to explain, thus narrowing the theory-building task to a more limited domain than general theory. Finally, one may try to resolve inconsistencies, anomalies, puzzling results, and incompatible points of view in the literature and in the data reported there.

A major pitfall in the use of the inductive approach in theory building is that the research from which the theory is induced may tend to become confused with an adequate test of the theory. Thus the same research is used twice for two different purposes, and a self-fulfilling prophecy results. In the case of truly deductive theories, this is not possible. When theories are developed inductively, it is crucial that they be tested on a new sample in a manner that is entirely independent of the pre-theory research. If one goes back to the prior sample or to data used in developing the theory, anything unique and ungeneralizable (attributable to chance fluctuation) in that particular situation is very likely to be confirmed. As a result, a theory that is erroneous insofar as generalization and practical usefulness are concerned may well be accepted.

It is actually more useful to think of theories as falling at points along a deductive–inductive continuum than as falling into distinct categories. Probably no theory is completely devoid of some inductive input. On the other hand, there are instances arising from entirely inductive processes. Such instances are often referred to as *dust-bowl empiricism,* implying that no theory is involved at all. However, the result may look very much like a theory.

An example of dust-bowl empiricism would be a study in which a great many measures, say several hundred, are obtained on a sample of organizations. These data are then put into a computer, and closely related measures are identified through the use of correlation techniques, factor analysis, or some similar procedure. What emerges is a set of hypothesized relationships among variables—a set of statements very much like an inductively derived theory. This "theory" is then tested on a new sample of organizations, using the appropriate measures to make sure that it does not incorporate relationships that represent mere chance fluctuations associated with the particular sample from which the theory was induced.

Any theory, irrespective of the method of construction and the extent of research confirmation, should always be treated as provisional in nature. Theories are constructed to be modified or replaced as new knowledge is developed; this is the way science advances. Furthermore, modification on the basis of research tends to be inductive rather than deductive. Findings emerge that do not quite fit the existing theory. Accordingly, the theory is changed so that these new data can be explained, and a test is then made of the revised theory. As a result of this kind of theoretical tinkering, even predominantly deductive theories may take on a strong inductive element over time; if they do not, they may well be replaced.

DEFINING A GOOD OR STRONG THEORY

In order to evaluate theories, science needs some criteria for deciding whether a theory is good or not so good. It is evident from what has been said already that some explanatory statements may not meet the requirements of scientific theory at all, and that what was good theory at one time may be not-so-good theory some years later.

First, theories should contribute to the goals of science. They should aid understanding, permit prediction, and facilitate influence. The more they do these things, the better they are. A theory that is comprehensive in its coverage of the phenomena that it explains is preferable to one that is limited in scope. However, broad scope alone is not enough. Many so-called grand theories attempt too much and fail simply because they do not really explain the wide range of phenomena they attempt to consider.

Second, there should be a clear delineation of the domain of the theory as indicated in Figure 1.1. The boundaries of application should be specified so that the theory is not utilized in situations for which it was never intended and is therefore useless. Definition of the coverage of a theory often has been neglected in the social sciences generally (Dubin 1978), and the field of organizational behavior is no exception.

Third, theory should direct research efforts to important matters. The number of research studies that could be done in the world is almost infinite. Yet most of these studies, even if the time and effort to carry them out were available, would not yield significant results in a statistical sense, and many of those that did would be trivial in terms of their usefulness. Good theory helps us focus research efforts on salient variables, identify important relationships, and come up with truly *significant* findings in every sense of the word. Basically, then, good theory protects the researcher from wasting time.

Fourth, theories at their best yield a kind of added value to research efforts. If several key hypotheses derived from a theory are confirmed by research, then the whole body of the theory becomes available for use. Thus theory-based research has the potential for yielding not just a few isolated facts, but powerful explanation and prediction across the whole domain of the theory. This aspect of good theory is one of its most practical consequences. Unfortunately, many theories do not have this cumulative character.

Fifth, theories should be readily testable. It should be clear exactly what must be done to either confirm or disconfirm them. On occasion, experimenters will carry out studies that they believe to be adequate tests of a theory, only to have the theorist say, "That is not what I meant." When theory is well formulated, this situation should rarely arise. Ideally the theorist will identify the variables of the theory in operational terms.

Sixth, good theory is not only confirmed by research derived from it, but is also logically consistent within itself and with other known facts. In the case of complex theories, it is entirely possible to develop propositions that would predict diametrically opposed outcomes in the same situation. This is particularly likely to happen when the theorist comes at the same subject matter from different directions, using different concepts and assumptions. Such internal, logical inconsistencies must be ironed out if the theory is to be of much use. Furthermore, theories do not exist in a vacuum; they are part of the total body of scientific knowledge. At any given time it may not be entirely clear how a particular theory fits into the larger scientific configuration, but a theory that from the outset quite obviously does not fit at all is to that degree deficient. Theories should build on what is known and fit consistently into the entire network of existing knowledge (Hartman 1988).

Seventh, the best theory is the one that is simplest in statement. If a given set of phenomena can be explained parsimoniously with a few variables, that theory should be preferred over one that achieves the same level of explanation with a much more complex set of variables and relationships. Science does not value complexity in its own right; there is enough of that all around us in nature. Highly complex and involved theories are often very difficult to put into practice. Thus, the ultimate objective must be to replace them with simpler explanations. Unfortunately, the process of inductive theory modification often demands that new constructs and variables be added continually as unanticipated findings emerge and need to be explained. Under such circumstances a theory may fall of its own weight, for it is just too cumbersome to be useful.

Theories that consistently fail to attain these criteria (and thus ultimately emerge as bad) can have negative consequences for science (Webster and Starbuck 1988). They can well sustain themselves for a considerable period of time and lead science in wrong directions.

They can also produce confusion and conflict that block scientific progress. All this argues for immediate testing of new theories so that their status can be established quickly. Without this the risk of impediment to scientific advance is substantial.

Writing in the *Harvard Business Review* in the article "Why Hard-Nosed Executives Should Care about Management Theory," Christensen and Raynor (2003) note that good theories are valuable in part because they help us make predictions; since reliable data are available only from the past, using strong theories of causality is the only way a manager can peer into the future with confidence. In addition, sound theories help us to interpret the present and thus understand what is happening, and why. Good theories make it possible to differentiate the signals that portend significant changes in the future from the noise that means nothing.

At a very high level of abstraction, the ultimate goal of science, and its theory as well, is to discover truth. This involves a firm belief that there is a reality out there external to the observer within which this truth exists. However, the ability to know this truth is plagued with uncertainty. Science seeks truth with the full recognition that it can never be known with absolute certainty—only approximations to certainty are possible. This view has been categorized as "scientific realism" or "organizational realism" (McKelvey 1997). Such a view reflects the predominant position in organizational behavior at the present time.

However, a minority position does exist. Such a position emphasizes the socially constructed nature of organizational phenomena and espouses a subjectivity that seems to deny the existence of outside reality altogether (see Weiss 2000 for an extended discussion of this view). Accordingly, truth takes a backseat to novelty, provocativeness, and uniqueness. In this view, the goal of theory construction and the basis for theory evaluation is not truth, but uniqueness (Mone and McKinley 1993). These are not the values of science, but they do reflect a current philosophic position. We will return to so-called "contra" views of this kind in Chapter 2, but for now it is sufficient to indicate that the fact that a theory is socially constructed does not make it incompatible with truth and objectivity—thus with the goals and methods of science (Meckler and Baillie 2003).

KINDS OF THEORIES

Theories can be good or bad, or more frequently somewhere in-between; they can seek truth, or some other goal. Many additional ways to classify theories exist as well. Although the labels that result are often self-evident, several approaches require more discussion.

Micro, Macro, and Meso

Micro theory in organizational behavior deals with the behaviors and nature of individuals and small groups in organizations. It has been strongly influenced by psychology, and many theorists of this kind were originally trained in that field. A good understanding of the micro approach can be had from a reading of Staw (1991). Motivation and leadership are essentially micro subjects, although theories in both areas may contain variables that extend beyond that designation.

Macro theory focuses on the behavior and nature of organizations, not of individuals and groups. Parts of the organization may be of concern as well, and so may the environment surrounding the organization. Sociology has played a role in the development of macro theory very similar to that played by psychology in micro theory. In a companion piece to the Staw (1991) article, Pfeffer (1991) offers a good example of how macro theorizing works. The theories discussed in this book represent predominantly the macro approach.

This distinction between micro and macro levels has been part of the organizational be-havior field since its early years (for a recent example of this distinction, see Wright and Boswell 2002). A more recent arrival, at least in terms of terminology, is meso theory. House, Rousseau, and Thomas-Hunt (1995) define the meso approach as concerning the simulta-neous study of at least two levels, where one level deals with individual or group processes or variables, one level deals with organizational processes or variables, and bridging or linking propositions are set forth to relate the two levels. An example of meso theorizing is presented in a book by Tosi (1992).

Tosi's (1992) book contains a number of theoretical propositions that may be used to illustrate the macro–micro–meso distinctions:

> The relevant environment of an organization is defined as external organizations or institu-tions which have direct effects on decisions and processes in the focal organization (29)—*macro.*

> The degree of volatility of the environmental sectors affects the structure of subsystem relationships in organizations (34)—*macro.*

> When individual personality manifests itself it usually does so with respect to interactions with others or toward the organization, not in terms of work patterns or levels of perfor-mance (82)—*micro.*

> A particular leader action is interpreted and attributions are made in the situational context. Different situations may result in different attributions about the same acts. It is the nature of the attribution, not the behavior itself which is related to effectiveness (196)—*micro.*

> The dominant form of conflict in organic organizations is rivalry. The bases for the rivalry will be

> 1. competition for resources for projects in process and/or
> 2. status-based competition between specialists from different disciplines.

> There will be moderate to low levels of vertical conflict in organic organizations (110)—*meso.*

> Power striving predispositions will lead to power striving and political behavior when orga-nizations are loosely coupled (128)—*meso.*

Typologies as Theory

A number of theories set forth various categories of organizations, environments, people, or groups, usually in the range of two to five. These formulations may deal with ideal types—sets of intellectual, hypothetical constructs created purely to study variety and change, which are not necessarily found in their complete form in the real world at all (Lammers 1988). At the other extreme are formulations that utilize only empirically derived clusters, based on real world data, which are created using the techniques of dust-bowl empiricism (Ketchen and Shook 1996). There are variants between these two as well.

The terms *typology* and *taxonomy* may be applied to these formulations, but they have not been used in a consistent manner, and there is no universal agreement on either definitions or appropriate approaches (Rich 1992). There are even those who decry the use of such classification systems entirely, viewing them as inherently unsound (Donaldson 1996). Given this situation, a working approach to theories of this kind is needed. In what follows I believe the discussion is consistent with the dominant position in the field of organizational behavior at the present time. If not, the position is at least a widely accepted one (Doty and Glick 1994; Miller 1996; Sanchez 1993).

The term typology is used to refer to a set of types developed on an *a priori* conceptual basis to operate as and serve the purposes of a theory. These constructs may be of an ideal nature or they may to varying degrees be intended to reflect the actual nature of the real world. These conceptual typologies are viewed as theories, and they may be good or not-so-good, just like any other theory. Taxonomies, on the other hand, are empirically derived clusterings developed through multivariate analysis of existing data. As such, they are data, not theories; description, not explanation. However, theoretical formulations may be developed inductively starting from taxonomies, thus folding a taxonomy into a more comprehensive theoretical system. Thus, a taxonomy alone does not constitute a theory, but each instance needs to be considered separately. For a more extended treatment of these matters, the reader is referred to Miner (1997).

Grounded Theory

Grounded theory focuses on qualitative data for the purpose of developing systematic, limited domain theories about observed phenomena. It derives its data from participant observation, direct observation, semistructured or even unstructured interviews, and case studies in essentially the same manner as an anthropologist studying a culture. Facets of these research data are sorted out of the mass of available qualitative information by means of consciously adopted strategies. These emerging concepts, grounded in the data, become the foundation of a growing theoretical understanding of the phenomena studied (Glaser and Strauss 1967; Turner 1983).

Such a theoretical approach is inductive, and the results are theoretical accounts of relatively small segments of reality. This process attempts to distill the essence of these segments, and in doing so creates a theory that is rich in terms of the depth of its content, but not broad. These grounded theory accounts may be used to develop more formal theory, however, by focusing on a domain of more general interest, generalizing from the specific. Within organizational behavior one will find little by way of grounded theorizing in the original sense. On the other hand, more formal theories having their origins in such grounded theorizing are in evidence. In any event it is important to keep in mind that the proper role of grounded theory is to generate theories, not to test them (Parry 1998). For a more detailed discussion of the use of grounded approaches in theory development, see Locke (2002), and for even more detail Locke (2001).

CONCLUSIONS

The philosophy of science as set forth here places considerable emphasis on the role of theory. The reason is that although quantum leaps in science are very rare in any event, they are only possible if theory provides the opportunity. Organizational behavior has had its share of theories, and enough of these have proven useful to move the field forward quite rapidly. However, it is important to understand that further progress requires more good theories, and these will be created only if the field fully recognizes what theory is and how it operates. Yet theory only becomes useful if it is validated by research. Managers should not accept theories and apply them to their work unless there is reason to believe that the theories are empirically valid. At the same time research results are the agents that determine whether theories are true or false. How good research is conducted is discussed in Chapter 2.

I noted in the preface that the theories of organizational process and structure presented and explored in this volume are those that meet one or more of the requirements for being labeled as *essential*—important, institutionalized, valid, and/or useful—as determined by scholars and intellectual leaders of the field. It is interesting to compare this listing with one published in the *Harvard Business Review* (Prusak and Davenport 2003), which appears to have been influenced much more, though certainly not exclusively, by the popular press.

The latter listing contains forty-eight "gurus," a number of whom in their writings deal with topics other than macro organizational behavior. There are only eight people whose names appear on both lists, however. Other listings contain even less overlap (see, for example, Greengard 2004). The heroes of science and academe are often distinct from those one is likely to run across in the world of practice and in the popular press. Accordingly, I think you will find some interesting, and very different, ideas in the chapters of this book that follow.

REFERENCES

Astley, W. Graham, and Zammuto, Raymond F. (1992). Organization Science, Managers, and Language Games. *Organization Science,* 3, 443–60.

Bacharach, Samuel B. (1989). Organizational Theories: Some Criteria for Evaluation. *Academy of Management Review,* 14, 496–515.

Berelson, Bernard, and Steiner, Gary (1964). *Human Behavior: An Inventory of Scientific Findings.* New York: Harcourt, Brace & World.

Beyer, Janice M. (1992). Metaphors, Misunderstandings, and Mischief: A Commentary. *Organization Science,* 3, 467–74.

Blood, Milton R. (1994). The Role of Organizational Behavior in the Business School Curriculum. In Jerald Greenberg (Ed.), *Organizational Behavior: The State of the Science.* Hillsdale, NJ: Lawrence Erlbaum Associates, 207–20.

Brooks, Margaret E., Grauer, Eyal, Thornbury, Erin E., and Highhouse, Scott (2003). Value Differences between Scientists and Practitioners: A Survey of SIOP Members. *The Industrial-Organizational Psychologist,* 40(4), 17–23.

Brown, Clarence W., and Ghiselli, Edwin E. (1955). *Scientific Method in Psychology.* New York: McGraw-Hill.

Campbell, John P. (1990). The Role of Theory in Industrial and Organizational Psychology. In Marvin D. Dunnette and Leatta M. Hough (Eds.), *Handbook of Industrial and Organizational Psychology,* Volume 1. Palo Alto, CA: Consulting Psychologists Press, 39–73.

Cheng, Tsz-kit, Sculli, Domenic, and Chan, Fiona S. (2001). Relationship Dominance: Rethinking Management Theories from the Perspective of Methodological Relationalism. *Journal of Managerial Psychology,* 16, 97–105.

Christensen, Clayton M., and Raynor, Michael E. (2003). Why Hard-Hosed Executives Should Care about Management Theory. *Harvard Business Review,* 81(9), 67–74.

Clegg, Stewart R., Hardy, Cynthia, and Nord, Walter R. (1996). *Handbook of Organization Studies.* London: Sage.

Cooper, Cary L., and Locke, Edwin A. (2000). *Industrial and Organizational Psychology: Linking Theory with Practice.* Oxford, UK: Blackwell.

Das, T. K. (2003). Managerial Perceptions and the Essence of the Managerial World: What Is an Interloper Business Executive to Make of the Academic-Researcher Perceptions of Managers? *British Journal of Management,* 14, 23–32.

Donaldson, Lex (1996). *For Positivist Organization Theory*. London: Sage.
————. (2002). Damned by Our Own Theories: Contradictions Between Theories and Management Education. *Academy of Management Learning and Education,* 1, 96–106.
Doty, D. Harold, and Glick, William H. (1994). Typologies as a Unique Form of Theory Building: Toward Improving Understanding and Modeling. *Academy of Management Review,* 19, 230–51.
Dubin, Robert (1976). Theory Building in Applied Areas. In Marvin D. Dunnette (Ed.), *Handbook of Industrial and Organizational Psychology*. Chicago, IL: Rand McNally, 17–39.
————. (1978). *Theory Building*. New York: Free Press.
Ford, Eric W., Duncan, W. Jack, Bedeian, Arthur G., Ginter, Peter M., Rousculp, Mathew D., and Adams, Alice M. (2003). Mitigating Risks, Visible Hands, Inevitable Disasters, and Soft Variables: Management Research That Matters to Managers. *Academy of Management Executive,* 17, 46–60.
George, Jennifer M., and Jones, Gareth R. (2000). The Role of Time in Theory and Theory Building. *Journal of Management,* 26, 657–84.
Glaser, Barney G., and Strauss, Anselm L. (1967). *The Discovery of Grounded Theory*. Chicago, IL: Aldine.
Gottfredson, Linda S. (1983). Creating and Criticizing Theory. *Journal of Vocational Behavior,* 23, 203–12.
Greengard, Samuel (2004). Guru Nation. *Workforce,* 83(4), 28–32.
Hartman, Edwin (1988). *Conceptual Foundations of Organization Theory*. Cambridge, MA: Ballinger.
House, Robert, Rousseau, Denise M., and Thomas-Hunt, Melissa (1995). The Meso Paradigm: A Framework for the Integration of Micro and Macro Organizational Behavior. *Research in Organizational Behavior,* 17, 71–114.
Kaplan, Abraham (1964). *The Conduct of Inquiry*. San Francisco, CA: Chandler.
Ketchen, David J., and Shook, Christopher, L. (1996). The Application of Cluster Analysis in Strategic Management Research: An Analysis and Critique. *Strategic Management Journal,* 17, 441–58.
Lammers, Cornelis (1988). Transience and Persistence of Ideal Types in Organizational Theory. *Research in the Sociology of Organizations,* 6, 203–24.
Lewin, Kurt (1945). The Research Center for Group Dynamics at Massachusetts Institute of Technology. *Sociometry,* 8, 126–35.
Locke, Edwin A. (2003). Good Definitions: The Epistemological Foundation of Scientific Progress. In Jerald Greenberg (Ed.), *Organizational Behavior: The State of the Science*. Mahwah, NJ: Lawrence Erlbaum, 415–44.
Locke, Karen (2001). *Grounded Theory in Management Research*. Thousand Oaks, CA: Sage.
————. (2002). The Grounded Theory Approach to Qualitative Research. In Fritz Drasgow and Neal Schmitt (Eds.), *Measuring and Analyzing Behavior in Organizations: Advances in Measurement and Data Analysis*. San Francisco, CA: Jossey-Bass, 17–43.
Mazza, Carmelo, and Alvarez, José L. (2000). Haute Couture and Prêt-à-Porter: The Popular Press and the Diffusion of Management Practices. *Organization Studies,* 21, 567–88.
McKelvey, Bill (1997). Quasi-natural Organization Science. *Organization Science,* 8, 352–80.
Meckler, Mark, and Baillie, James (2003). The Truth about Social Construction in Administrative Science. *Journal of Management Inquiry,* 12, 273–84.
Miller, Danny (1996). Configurations Revisited. *Strategic Management Journal,* 17, 505–12.
Miner, John B. (1984). The Validity and Usefulness of Theories in an Emerging Organizational Science. *Academy of Management Review,* 9, 297–306.
————. (1997). *A Psychological Typology of Successful Entrepreneurs*. Westport, CT: Quorum.
————. (2004). Congruence and the Significance of Careers in Testing Task Role Motivation Theory. Working Paper, Eugene, OR.
Mitchell, Terence R., and James, Lawrence R. (2001). Building Better Theory: Time and the Specification of When Things Happen. *Academy of Management Review,* 26, 530–47.
Mone, M.A., and McKinley, William (1993). The Uniqueness Value and Its Consequences for Organization Studies. *Journal of Management Inquiry,* 2, 284–96.
Parry, Ken W. (1998). Grounded Theory and Social Process: A New Direction for Leadership Research. *Leadership Quarterly,* 9, 85–105.
Pfeffer, Jeffrey (1991). Organization Theory and Structural Perspectives on Management. *Journal of Management,* 17, 789–803.
————. (1995). Mortality, Reproducibility, and the Persistence of Styles of Theory. *Organization Science,* 6, 681–86.
Priem, Richard L., and Rosenstein, J. (2000). Is Organization Theory Obvious to Practitioners? A Test of One Established Theory. *Organization Science,* 11, 509–24.

Prusak, Laurence, and Davenport, Thomas H. (2003). Who Are the Gurus' Gurus? *Harvard Business Review,* 81 (12), 14–16.

Rich, Philip (1992). The Organizational Taxonomy: Definition and Design. *Academy of Management Review,* 17, 758–81.

Roehling, Mark V., Cavanaugh, Marcie A., Moynihan, Lisa M., and Boswell, Wendy R. (2000). The Nature of the New Employment Relationship: A Content Analysis of the Practitioner and Academic Literatures. *Human Resource Management,* 39, 305–20.

Rynes, Sara L., Bartunek, Jean M., and Daft, Richard L. (2001). Across the Great Divide: Knowledge Creation and Transfer between Practitioners and Academics. *Academy of Management Journal,* 44, 340–55.

Rynes, Sara L., Brown, Kenneth G., and Colbert, Amy E. (2002). Seven Common Misconceptions about Human Resource Practices: Resource Findings versus Practitioner Beliefs. *Academy of Management Executive,* 16, 92–102.

Rynes, Sara L., Colbert, Amy E., and Brown, Kenneth G. (2002). HR Professionals' Beliefs about Effective Human Resource Practices: Correspondence between Research and Practice. *Human Resource Management,* 41, 149–74.

Rynes, Sara L., and McNatt, D. Brian (2001). Bringing the Organization into Organizational Research: An Examination of Academic Research inside Organizations. *Journal of Business and Psychology,* 16, 3–19.

Sanchez, Julio C. (1993). The Long and Thorny Way to an Organizational Taxonomy. *Organization Studies,* 14, 73–92.

Sandelands, Lloyd, and Drazin, Robert (1989). On the Language of Organization Theory. *Organization Studies,* 10, 457–78.

Schendel, Dan E., and Hofer, Charles W. (1979). *Strategic Management: A New View of Business Policy and Planning.* Boston, MA: Little, Brown.

Spell, Chester S. (2001). Management Fashions—Where Do They Come from and Are They Old Wine in New Bottles? *Journal of Management Inquiry,* 10, 358–73.

Staw, Barry M. (1991). Dressing Up Like an Organization: When Psychological Theories Can Explain Organizational Action. *Journal of Management,* 17, 805–19.

Steiner, George A., and Miner, John B. (1986). *Management Policy and Strategy.* New York: Macmillan.

Sutton, Robert I., and Staw, Barry M. (1995). What Theory Is Not. *Administrative Science Quarterly,* 40, 371–84.

Tosi, Henry L. (1992). *The Environment/Organization/Person Contingency Model: A Meso Approach to the Study of Organizations.* Greenwich, CT: JAI Press.

Turner, Barry A. (1983). The Use of Grounded Theory for the Qualitative Analysis of Organizational Behavior. *Journal of Management Studies,* 20, 333–48.

Van de Ven, Andrew H. (1989). Nothing Is Quite So Practical as a Good Theory. *Academy of Management Review,* 14, 486–89.

Webster, Jane, and Starbuck, William H. (1988). Theory Building in Industrial and Organizational Psychology. *International Review of Industrial and Organizational Psychology,* 3, 93–138.

Weiss, Richard M. (2000). Taking Science out of Organization Science: How Would Postmodernism Reconstruct the Analysis of Organizations? *Organization Science,* 11, 709–31.

Wright, Patrick M., and Boswell, Wendy R. (2002). Desegregating HRM: A Review and Synthesis of Micro and Macro Human Resource Management Research. *Journal of Management,* 28, 247–76.

CHAPTER 2

THE CONDUCT OF RESEARCH AND THE DEVELOPMENT OF KNOWLEDGE

To a substantial degree the value of a theory is demonstrated by the research it sparks and the extent to which it is confirmed by this research. Research is only possible, however, to the extent that measures of the variables of the theory are developed, that is, to the extent that the constructs are made operational. These twin topics of measurement and research concern us here, although we will not attempt to provide a detailed treatment. However, in later chapters we will be asking questions such as "Does this measure really effectively represent the constructs of the theory?" and "Does this research provide an appropriate test of the theory?" The answers to these questions will draw on some knowledge of both measurement procedures and research design, and the ensuing discussion is intended to provide a basis for understanding these areas.

MEASURING VARIABLES

Measures used in organizational research have often fallen short of what might be desired (Price and Mueller 1986). Many of organizational behavior's theories utilize constructs far removed from those previously measured in the social sciences. Thus it has been necessary in many cases to develop reliable and valid measures to represent new constructs, which is a time-consuming process. Many organizational measures are still at a primitive stage of development, and this situation can seriously hamper the interpretation of research results. This matter of effectively converting constructs into variables (see Figure 1.1 in Chapter 1) is what concerns us here.

Reliability

A major concern in research is the reliability of measurement. Measures that are sufficiently stable and unambiguous will not produce sizable differences in score values when applied to the same phenomenon on separate occasions. The reliability of a measure is usually established by a correlation coefficient. Different approaches are used to determine this reliability coefficient, but all approaches approximate the ideal procedure, which utilizes parallel forms of the same measure. Parallel forms exist when two indexes of the same construct contain the same number of items of each type, concentrate equally on the various aspects of the construct, and produce the same average scores and distributions of scores through the range of possible values. Once such parallel measures have been developed, reliability is determined by administering both measures in the same sample and correlating the scores on the two measures.

The value of a reliability coefficient fluctuates to some extent, depending on whether the parallel form or some other approach is used. However, if one wishes to use a measure in an individual situation—to measure the work motivation of a *particular* person, for instance, or to compute the average span of control in a *certain* company—reliability coefficients above .90 are required. If, on the other hand, one is dealing with group data such as mean work motivation scores in two units of a company or average span of control in relation to profitability in a number of companies, values down to about .70, and sometimes less, typically are acceptable. These standards represent what amount to "rules of thumb" or working conventions. Like many such conventions in science, they are enforced by gatekeepers such as journal editors and thesis or dissertation chairpersons.

The matter of reliability of measurement is important in research because it is impossible to interpret outcomes when unreliable measures are used and results are not statistically significant. The failure to obtain evidence of a relationship between two variables could be due to the fact that there is no relationship. But if one or both measures of the two variables are unreliable, a relationship may well exist that has not been discovered because of inadequate measures. The only satisfactory way to resolve this uncertainty is to develop and use measures of high reliability. Then if relationships are not found, they are very unlikely to exist in the world of reality. For an example of how reliability estimates may be used to differentiate measures, see Loo (2002).

Validity

The variables of a theory need to be made operational in the form of specific measures. Accordingly, the measures must truly reflect the underlying constructs; they must provide valid data regarding the phenomena that they are supposed to represent. If, in fact, they measure constructs other than the ones they are intended to measure, the theory may well be assumed to be disconfirmed when it is actually correct. Worse still, a theory may be accepted when in fact its variables have been incorrectly stated (Edwards 2003).

I once developed an index intended to measure conformity to organizational norms (Miner 1962). Subsequent research revealed that the index was almost completely unrelated to any other measure of conformity that could be identified in the literature. However, moderate relationships were found with measures of intelligence. Apparently, if the measure did tap some tendency to conform, it was not the same construct that other researchers had in mind when they used the term. A likely interpretation was that we had developed a measure that was in large part concerned with intelligence, although there was evidence of a relationship to a desire to escape into a crowd as well. This clearly was a much more complex construct than we had originally envisioned, one that our underlying theory was ill-equipped to handle.

This example demonstrates how one goes about determining the validity of a measure. If the measure is what it purports to be, there are certain phenomena to which it should be related and certain other phenomena to which it should not be related. In the case of conformity, there were other indexes of the construct available. Often, when a new and highly innovative theory is under test, other measures are not available. Nevertheless it should be possible to identify certain relationships that would be expected to appear with a high degree of likelihood. In this process, however, it is important not to rely on *face validity* alone. The measure that looks to be appropriate as an index of a given variable on further investigation may or may not prove to tap that construct.

As we shall see later, establishing the validity of a particular construct measure is not easy. To some degree the answer is always inferential (Cortina 2002). Yet there are organizational measures in which one can have considerable faith, while there are others that, even after long years of use, leave considerable doubt as to their construct validity. Certain statistical procedures have been developed to aid in construct validation (Bagozzi, Yi, and Phillips 1991), and these can be quite useful under appropriate circumstances. However, they do not circumvent the need for close reasoning and careful research design. In any event, in spite of occasional instances of confusion, reliability and validity need to be clearly differentiated (Schmidt, Viswesvaran, and Ones 2000). Validity coefficients tend to be much lower, with correlations of less than .20 being considered low, those in the .20 to .30 range being medium, and these above .30 being high; correlations of .50 or above are clearly large (Hemphill 2003).

A final point, however, should be noted with regard to the construct validity matter. There has been a tendency in recent years for reports of studies to neglect dealing with the validity of key measures (Scandura and Williams 2000). In fact there are those who argue that the term construct validity is an invalid concept, in need of elimination from the language of organizational behavior (Locke 2003). This is not the position taken here. Research aimed at validation, and construct validation in particular, can have important implications for the inductive reconstruction of a theory, or for its abandonment. We need more of this type of research, not less.

RESEARCH DESIGN

Research conducted to test theories characteristically investigates hypothesized relationships between variables. Such research is first concerned with whether a relationship exists at all and then with the causal nature of that relationship. Research focused on the existence of a relationship is relatively easy to conduct; however, research into the causal problem is clearly much less tractable.

The study of causation typically requires the collection of data over time, on the premise that the cause must be shown to precede the effect. There are now techniques, however, known collectively as causal modeling approaches, that under appropriate circumstances can be used with data collected at one time, as well as longitudinally. These techniques have expanded in number, in complexity, and in explanatory power over the past twenty years. Their use is increasing rapidly, and they appear to offer considerable promise in evaluating causal hypotheses (see Drasgow and Schmitt 2002 and Williams, Edwards, and Vandenberg 2003). In any event, the use of longitudinal designs should be employed if at all possible; longitudinal research involving data collection over time appears to be on the increase in organizational behavior (Hunt and Ropo 2003).

A second factor that makes identification of causal relationships difficult is the necessity for establishing adequate controls. Control may be accomplished statistically through the use of procedures that measure unwanted variables and then remove their effects from the relationship under study. However, these statistical techniques require that the data satisfy certain assumptions, and in many cases it is not at all clear that these assumptions can be met. The alternative is to control variables through the original design of the study. That is not always easy.

Laboratory Experiments

Much of the research on causal relationships has been done in the laboratory. An extreme instance of this laboratory research is computer simulation in which no real subjects are involved. More frequently, the experiment is of the small group or group dynamics type; experimental variables are introduced among subjects, often college sophomores, and the results are measured under highly controlled conditions. Because the study is conducted outside the real world of ongoing organizations, it is easier to use longitudinal measures and to control unwanted variables. Yet even here major difficulties in maintaining controls exist. Furthermore, the results are very much a function of the variables considered (this is particularly true of computer simulations). If the real world is not effectively modeled in the laboratory, or at least the key elements of that world, the results of laboratory experiments will not transfer.

This said, it appears that in many areas such transfers do occur (Locke 1986). Laboratory studies often appear to be well conducted, or conceivably field research is deficient in important areas, with the result that similar results are obtained. In any event, the evidence to date is that laboratory research, with its greater control, is much more valid than previously anticipated. There may be conditions under which this is not true. A degree of field research on laboratory findings still seems warranted. But, assuming initial confirmation, the need for extensive reiteration of these initial results does not seem as great as previously thought.

Field Experiments

The ideal situation is to take the techniques of sample selection, repetitive measurement, and variable control associated with laboratory research into the real world and conduct the same kind of research with ongoing organizations. In such a context the myriad variables that may be important do in fact operate, and any results obtained there can be expected to characterize the actual organizations to which any meaningful theory is addressed. The problem is that all the difficulties of designing and conducting good experiments that were so easily handled in the laboratory now become overwhelming. Real organizations have innumerable ways of resisting and undermining objective scientific research—not out of contrariness, but because the goals of the real world and the laboratory are different.

The difficulties of conducting causal research in organizations may be illustrated using a study by Belasco and Trice (1969) on the effects of a particular management development program. The study utilized 119 managers divided into four groups. Managers were assigned to each group on a random basis within sex, type of work supervised, and division groupings. In this manner as many factors as possible were held constant across the four groups to control for spurious factors that might contaminate the findings and make causal attribution difficult.

One group of managers was pretested, trained, and posttested on knowledge, attitudes, and behavior. The objective was to see if a change occurred on any of these factors.

A second group took the pretest, received no training, and then took the posttest. If this group changed as much as the first, clearly the training was not the cause of change. If this group did not change as much as the first, the training remained a strong contender as a cause.

A third group underwent no pretest, received training, and took the posttest. By comparing the posttest result for the third group with that for the first group, it was possible to identify any apparent change due to a sensitizing effect of the pretest (the groups were similar in all other respects). The problem addressed here is control for any effects the pretest may have had in alerting the managers to what they were supposed to learn later in training.

The fourth group received no pretest, no training, and only the posttest. This group, in comparison with the others, yields a measure of the effects of the passage of time only, and therefore isolates time from either repeated measurement or training as factors.

Clearly this kind of research requires a large number of subjects, the opportunity to assign them to groups as desired for research purposes, and extensive collaboration from the sponsoring organization throughout the study. And, as elaborate as the research plan is, it could be argued that a fifth group, undergoing some training of a relatively neutral nature, should have been included to create a placebo situation and cancel out any so-called Hawthorne effect (see Kahn 1975) produced by receiving special attention. Thus even this very complex experiment cannot be said to have achieved the ideal in terms of control. Such studies are very difficult to conduct, yet they continue to appear in the literature (see, for example, Probst 2003).

Quasi-Experimental Designs

Realistically elegant research designs with all possible controls are unlikely to be implemented in many organizations and if an organization does decide to go this route, it may well be an atypical organization. Accordingly certain variants have been proposed (Cook, Campbell, and Peracchio 1990; Evans 1999). These designs represent major advances over the noncausal, correlational analyses, but no one such study answers all questions. Basically these studies utilize as many components of the ideal experimental design as possible, while recognizing that it is better to conduct some kind of research related to causes than to do nothing. Hopefully, the larger number of research investigations carried out will compensate for the relative relaxation of control requirements. Accordingly, several interlocking investigations should develop the same level of knowledge as one very elegant study. On the other hand it is easy to relax scientific standards to the point where replication is not possible, and thus not obtain scientific knowledge that can be substantiated. Some trends in qualitative research on organizations show this tendency. It is important to maintain a clear distinction between scientific research and personal narrative in testing organizational behavior theories.

A number of examples of well-conducted quasi-experiments exist in the recent literature. The typical design calls for some combination of the elements considered in the previous section (see for example Markham, Scott, and McKee 2002). A particularly good discussion of the limitations that may be inherent in the quasi-experimental design is contained in Morgeson and Campion (2002). Descriptions of how quasi-experimental designs may be utilized in studying promotion effects are presented in a series of studies conducted within an international bank based in Hong Kong (see in particular Lam and Schaubroeck 2000).

Common Method Variance and Bias

Common method problems can arise from having a common rater provide the measures of variables, a common measurement context, a common item context, or from characteristics of the items in a measure. Of these, obtaining measures of both the predictor and criterion within the same study from the same person produces the most pronounced such results; these biases can be quite substantial (Podsakoff, MacKenzie, Lee, and Podsakoff 2003). Thus when the same person reports on the two types of variables, that person may change the correlations in an attempt to maintain logical consistency. The results are a function of the measurement method rather than of the underlying constructs.

Individuals' reports of their internal states (such as expectancies) may be obtained at the same time and from the same person as reports of past behavior related to these internal states. As a result of a desire to maintain cognitive consistency, these correlations can be inflated substantially (Lindell and Whitney 2001). This bias is introduced because of the measurement approach taken and the failure to use more appropriate designs.

Solutions to this type of problem, as is typical in organizational behavior research, focus on designing the problem away or controlling it with statistics. Unfortunately in the past, however, many studies have been conducted which did neither of these, thus simply ignoring the problem. What is needed is to separate the measures of the variables involved by using different sources, and thus different research designs. An alternative is to use measures of variables which are not self-evident (such as projective techniques), so that the individual cannot mobilize attempts to attain cognitive consistency. Attempts to solve common method problems through the use of statistical approaches have been numerous, but as yet no widely accepted solution has emerged.

Requirements for Conducting Experimental Research

Blackburn (1987) has set forth a list of what he labels the 10 commandments for conducting experimental research. These can serve as a guide in assessing research used to test theories in the organizational behavior field.

1. Thou shalt assess the extent to which the change actually took effect.
2. Whenever possible, thou shalt use multiple measures.
3. Whenever possible, thou shalt use unobtrusive measures.
4. Thou shalt seek to avoid changes in measurement procedures.

5. Thou shalt endeavor to use a randomized experimental design whenever possible.
6. In the absence of random assignment, thou shalt not select experimental or control groups on the basis of some characteristic that the group may possess to some unusual degree.
7. Thou shalt use appropriate statistical analyses to examine the differences between the experimental and control groups.
8. Whenever possible, thou shalt collect time-series data.
9. To the greatest extent possible, thou shalt protect the employee, the organization, and the experiment in that order.
10. Thou shalt report fully and honestly the procedures and results of the research.

Many of these points are illustrated in a book edited by Frost and Stablein (1992) which provides detailed descriptions of what actually happened in connection with seven research studies. This book is also a good source of information regarding ways in which qualitative research may be employed for purposes of inductive theory development.

THEORETICAL KNOWLEDGE OF ORGANIZATIONAL BEHAVIOR AND ITS OBJECTIONS

The high visibility of certain formulations that are clearly closer to philosophy than to scientific theory has lead some to question whether organizational behavior truly possesses any theories at all. This negative position has received additional support from some individuals, a number of them scientists who place very little stock in theory building in any event, preferring the slow but solid pace of unswerving empiricism. Yet there do appear to be a number of real scientific theories dealing with organizations, or at least explanations so advanced that not to call them theories is something of a quibble. This is not to say that these theories are necessarily and entirely valid; some of them have not been fully tested. But overall they have contributed substantially to our knowledge of organizations.

On the other hand there is a rather sizable body of literature which raises serious objections to the scientific concepts we have been considering. If one follows these views a quite different picture of our theoretical knowledge of organizational behavior emerges.

Objections to Scientific Dictates: Frontal Attacks

A common method of dealing with antithetical positions is to simply ignore them, thus avoiding the need to cite them or to consider the views at all (Martin and Frost 1996). I clearly could do this here. Yet the concept of science set forth in the preceding pages is what underlies the whole field of organizational behavior, and to simply ignore objections to it does not appear either to be intellectually honest or to truly reflect the reality of the times.

One "contra" position is that science as a whole, and certainly the organizational behavior part of it, has not proven convincing as a superior form of knowledge, that new narratives and new epistemologies are needed to supersede science, and that basically science has had its day and now has run out of steam (Burrell 1996). This is an across-the-board dismissal, and applies to all aspects of science. In my opinion this line of assault requires an equally direct response. Given the realities of the world around us, such arguments for the demise of science make no sense, and are best lumped with similar "end of the world" scenarios. Yet they persist (Alvesson 2003).

In addition to such blanket attacks a number of more specific objections have been raised which typically focus on some aspect of scientific theory and/or research. One such approach is to challenge the various assumptions of science (Kilduff and Mehra 1997). For instance the argument may be that natural groupings of organizations, groups, and individuals do not occur, that uniqueness is everywhere, and thus generalization from samples is not warranted. Another such argument is that things change so fast that the stability and constancy science requires is nonexistent; science gives way to journalism—the recording and explaining of fleeting phenomena. A third challenge asserts either that events are not determined, and thus cause-effect relationships do not exist, or that social science, as distinct from natural science, is concerned with meanings and significance, not causes. Finally, the trustworthiness of human processes of perception, memory, or reasoning may be questioned, thus introducing challenges to the observation and experience on which science is based. Advocates of these positions tend to give more credence to qualitative research than to quantitative (Kilduff and Kelemen 2003). Qualitative research is accordingly moved from its role as an adjunct to inductive theory building to a central role in theory testing.

Other objections are concerned with the objectivity and relevance of scientific research (see Ghate and Locke 2003). These views may emphasize the fact that people as the subjects of research react differently when they become aware of the researchers' hypotheses or experience a feeling of being controlled in the experimental situation; thus, the research process itself poses a threat to generalization. Alternatively, research studies, especially laboratory studies, may be viewed as lacking the realism required for generalization. Objections of these kinds seem to assert that all organizational behavior research is bad research and that researchers cannot overcome these threats to their findings through creative methodologies because objectivity is impossible to obtain. Data such as those summarized in Locke (1986) on the close proximity of laboratory and field research findings are totally ignored.

Postmodernism and Siblings

Some of the strongest attacks on social science, and inherently on organizational behavior, stem from a group of philosophies called critical theory, poststructuralism, and postmodernism (Agger 1991) or perhaps some combination of these terms (Voronov and Coleman 2003). These philosophies all had their origins outside the United States and it is there that they originally had the greatest impact. In certain respects they have been influenced by Marxist ideology (see Barrett 2003). These views differ in a number of their aspects (see Vibert 2004), but the opposition to social science is pervasive, as reflected in the positions noted in the previous section. Science is portrayed as a source of authority and a perpetuator of the status quo. As such it must be replaced. Objective analysis and a reliance on mathematics are rejected. In point of fact, this contra position operates to oppose anything that is institutionalized—that has achieved legitimacy and is taken for granted (Alvesson 2003; Clegg and Kornberger 2003). Thus, science, its theory and the like are merely part and parcel of a much wider enemy.

The preferred approach to gaining knowledge in these philosophies is one which focuses on obtaining detailed understandings of specific situations at a point in time. This approach has much in common with that of grounded theory, although references to that specific procedure by name appear to be rare since Silverman (1971). Studies in this vein collect a great deal of information, and often present much of the raw data to the reader in undigested form in lieu of statistical analyses. Typically the studies are used to both create theory and confirm it at one and the same time. Literary methods and storytelling may be used to present the results of data collection (Jermier 1985). Indeed the analysis of language and its usage has become pervasive within postmodernism (Alvesson and Kärreman 2000).

When grounded theory is used to create more formal theories, it parts company with postmodernism and its siblings to join company with science. This distinction is important. The qualitative approaches involved may serve to generate scientific theory, *or* they may yield the self-fulfilling prophesies of postmodernism.

Threats from Within the United States

Although critical theory, poststructuralism, and postmodernism have been slow in taking root in the United States, there have been manifestations of similar ways of thinking here for some time. This has been most characteristic of those in the organizational behavior field who espouse humanistic values with a substantial amount of passion (see Lawler, Mohrman, Mohrman, Ledford, and Cummings 1985; Tannenbaum, Margulies, and Massarik 1985). Argyris has attacked scientific research methodology on numerous occasions and proposes an anthropological approach, devoid of statistical analysis, to replace it (see, for instance, Argyris 1980). He continues to emphasize a similar position (Argyris 2004).

These attacks from within are described by Donaldson (1992), an Australian, as an outgrowth primarily of certain trends in organizational behavior in the United States. He summarizes this complex of ideas as follows—It:

1. stresses the empirical world as subjectively perceived and enacted rather than as brute fact,
2. asserts the superiority of qualitative over quantitative methods,
3. reveres paradox in both the content of theory and the formal expression of theory,
4. holds that scientific creativity is primarily linguistic inventiveness,
5. see itself as championing creativity,
6. is counter cultural in the sense of being ever-ready to cock a snook at the establishment and established ideas, and
7. would also claim that practicing managers would be better aided not by plodding positivism but by taking a mind-trip. (Donaldson 1992, 462)

This description is presented in connection with a rebuttal to an article by Astley and Zammuto (1992), to place that article in context.

Many other rebuttals to the various objections to scientific dictates exist in the literature. Among these Weiss (2000) is particularly impressive. Donaldson (2003) provides an analysis that points up the logical inconsistencies of postmodernism. McKelvey (2003) castigates postmodernism for ignoring research and the falsifiability of theories. Not infrequently the objections create a description of science that, although incorrect, makes it easy to mount an attack. In this process science may very well be redefined as art, with all the freedom to embody values and eliminate burdensome rules that art permits. Many of those who object to the standards and strictures of good theory and good research seem to be trying to remove what they perceive to be barriers that keep them from using the garb of science to advocate their values. Good science—whether in the form of theory construction or exemplary research—is very hard work. The rules of the game are onerous and they make good science difficult. But that is as it should be; they are there for a reason.

Furthermore, as Pescosolido and Rubin (2000) note, "The fault of postmodernism is that even in its radical insistence on diversity, it insists that its practitioners 'line up'" (p. 71). There is no freedom from rules of some kind, even in postmodernism.

VALUES AND KNOWLEDGE

Values are conceptions of good and bad that tend to carry with them a great deal of emotion. They attach to certain ideas and patterns of behavior and they provoke behavior consistent with the values as well. For an in-depth treatment of this values construct see Maierhofer, Kabanoff, and Griffin (2002).

Values in Organizational Behavior

Organizational behavior appears to have been influenced by two primary value dimensions throughout much of its history. One is the dimension extending from humanistic to scientific values. In recent years the humanistic pole increasingly has been joined by the often similar values of postmodernism and its siblings. The other dimension is essentially disciplinary in origin. At one end is psychology, while the other end is anchored primarily in sociology, joined on occasion by anthropology, political science, and economics. Basically these are values related to micro and macro levels of analysis.

This second, disciplinary dimension has undergone some transformation over the years. In an earlier period the dimension ranged from behavioral science (dominated in large part by psychology) to classical management theory. As classical theory has faded from the scene (see Miner 1995), the value differentiation involved has been replaced by one within the behavioral science designation itself. At present it appears to be particularly concerned with variations in the value placed on the study of individuals in organizations (see House, Shane, and Herold 1996 and Nord and Fox 1996).

Values of these kinds can play a useful role in theory construction, in part by focusing attention on specific areas of endeavor, and in part by motivating concerted efforts to construct theories that end by fostering understanding and prediction. However, values, other than those that foster objectivity, have no place in the conduct of research and thus in testing theory. To the extent they might intervene at this stage, replications of initial studies should serve to identify them. Finally, values can reappear in the evaluation segment of the overall theory process, the part that involves reaching a consensus among knowledgeable scholars regarding the goodness of a theory, and thus the contribution to knowledge involved (Miner 1990). The result is that those with different values may evaluate through different lenses, and as a consequence consensus may be hard to obtain. For a recent discussion of how values may play a role in science see Risman (2001).

Dispositions versus Situations: A Value-Laden Controversy

An example of the way in which values may produce different views and impede consensus is provided by the dispute over the study of individuals in organizations noted previously. This dispute simmered over a period of ten years or more before bursting into flame (Davis-Blake and Pfeffer 1989).

The latter paper contained an attack on the dispositional approach that underlies the concept of individual differences and the application of personality theory in organizational behavior. Dispositions are defined as unobservable mental states (constructs) such as needs, values, attitudes, and personalities that are relatively stable over time and that to varying degrees serve as determinants of attitudes and behavior in organizations. The argument is that dispositions are a mirage and that the only significant determinants of individual organizational behavior are situational in nature. Thus an antithesis is created pitting psychological constructs against sociological.

Later Nord and Fox (1996) authored a paper with the thesis that the individual (and individual personality) has disappeared from organizational behavior, being replaced by a contextual dimension consisting of attributes of the physical and social systems in which people exist (situations). The intent is to document the view that theories and research dealing with individual personality and dispositions have lost status to the point where organizational behavior is no longer interested in individual differences (and by implication *should* not be). There is reason to believe that this second attack from the sociological perspective may leave something to be desired in its coverage of the personality-related literature, but as an attack by fait accompli it clearly reveals the values of the authors.

These position statements from the situationalist perspective have not gone unanswered. In defense of the dispositional view George (1992) has offered a detailed consideration of much of the theory and research supporting an important role for personality in organizational behavior. House, Shane, and Herold (1996) also make a strong case for the retention of personality-based perspectives. The quote which follows appears to present a more balanced view of the issues and leaves the door open to both types of theory and research. It provides an instance of how extreme values may be reconciled and consensus thereby achieved.

> . . . personality is important for understanding at least certain classes of organizational phenomena. Obviously, this does not imply that situational factors are unimportant. Rather, it suggests that organizations do not stamp out all individual differences; being a member of an organization does not neutralize or negate one's own enduring predispositions to think, feel, and act in certain ways. An extreme situationalist perspective denies organizational participants their individuality and exaggerates organizations' abilities to manipulate and control their members. Likewise, an extreme dispositional position credits too much power to the individual and ignores important situational influences on feelings, thoughts, and behaviors. Hence, personality and situational factors are needed to understand much of organizational life. (George 1992, 205–6)

Positive Organizational Scholarship

Positive organizational scholarship is a value orientation of very recent vintage—too recent to be able to say where it is going as far as organizational behavior is concerned (Bernstein 2003; Cameron, Dutton, and Quinn 2003). It had its origins in psychology where it was in many respects a reaction to clinical psychology with its emphasis on illness, disorder, and thus the negative aspects of the human condition. Basically it is a movement, unrelated to any specific theory, which values excellence, thriving, flourishing, abundance, resilience, and virtuousness—anything associated with positive human potential.

Because scholarship here means science and scientific research, this is not another name for postmodernism. Certain ties to an earlier humanism and to the values of organization development are evident, but the coverage is broader than that. As noted, psychology is the discipline of origin, but the movement is interested in influencing any field that finds its values attractive. In short, it is a community of scholars, currently based in the school of business at the University of Michigan, devoted to learning about positive aspects of the human condition, particularly as reflected in organizational functioning. The scope of the movement is as yet unclear; it may ultimately come to represent a reemergence of humanism in organizational behavior, or something else. But the appeal to strong values and the attempt to mobilize them in support of its aims is clear.

THE ROLE OF CONSENSUS

Threats to a unified science of organizational behavior take two major forms—those that relate specifically to science, including its theory and method, and those that impair unity by jeopardizing the creation of a stable and widely recognized body of knowledge that might be presented to practitioners as a basis for their actions. The latter is the concern of this discussion.

The Consensus Problem

A lack of consensus appears to exist in the field of organizational behavior, and as a result the field's limited amount of hard knowledge is often bemoaned. The evidence is there, but the consensus of knowledgeable scholars that makes it knowledge often is out of reach because conflicting values block the way. Testimony to this effect is not hard to find.

In the introduction to his volume dealing with organizational behavior's conceptual base Hartman (1988) discusses this fragmentation using terms such as "disarray," "no consensus," "conflict," "disunity," "disagreements." The authors of a more recent handbook of the field (Clegg, Hardy, and Nord 1996) use their introduction to paint a picture which presents organizational behavior as infused with controversy and partisan politics; this latter volume appears in its own way to contribute to the fragmentation as well, even to extol it.

A well-argued treatment of the consensus problem is that of Pfeffer (1993), which subsequently has sparked a great deal of debate pro and con. The thesis of this paper is that when sciences have developed shared theoretical structures and methodological approaches about which there is substantial consensus, these sciences and their members have experienced a number of positive consequences, including increased allocations of monetary and other resources. Organizational behavior, being fragmented as it is, holds a position low in the pecking order when rewards and resources are distributed among the sciences. In short we are not viewed as doing a very good job, and this is true because of our lack of consensus. Pfeffer argues that consensus can be attained through the efforts of an elite network of individuals who utilize political positions and processes to impose a uniformity of view on a discipline. He seems to say that this should happen in organizational behavior. This appeal for consensus is reiterated in a later paper (Pfeffer 1995), but it is apparent that he prefers consensus around certain theoretical positions over others.

Not surprisingly a number of organizational behaviorists jumped up to dispute Pfeffer on a variety of grounds. In general the thrust of these views is that consensus is not really a desirable goal after all, and that enforced consensus is particularly undesirable. Tolerance for diverse approaches, theories, and methods should not be suppressed, and in any event there is no one best way that clearly deserves a dominant position. On occasion this rebuttal is mixed with a substantial dose of anti-science rhetoric (Van Maanen 1995).

All this having been said, it remains true that science relies on some degree of consensus among knowledgeable scholars, and that science has proved over and over again that its methods can advance understanding, prediction, and control to the benefit of human society. Certainly some degree of disconsensus can be absorbed and innovative, creative contributions should not only be tolerated, but supported. The questions are how much consensus is needed and in what areas; these are empirical questions as Pfeffer (1995) notes. It is amazing, once the emotions that values arouse are activated, how difficult it is to see the balanced, middle ground. For a balanced discussion of these issues from a perspective tempered by the passage of time see Fabian (2000).

The Inability to Compare Competing Theories

One outgrowth of the consensus problem is a view that one cannot decide objectively between competing theories which use different languages, hold different assumptions, and utilize different constructs, thus reflecting totally disparate value systems. Under these circumstances comparisons are impossible in the same sense that "comparing apples and oranges" is impossible. Science is said to be at a loss in such instances, and amongst the theory pluralism that we face at present science becomes essentially useless (Scherer and Dowling 1995). Note that this argument requires a large number of very different theories coming together from different directions to offer contradictory solutions to common problems. This must be so if science is to be effectively neutralized. Thus, "create as many new and unique theories as you possibly can" becomes the rallying cry of proponents of this view; they are out to sink consensus (Clegg and Ross-Smith 2003). Practitioners in particular are left helpless to make decisions in the face of this barrage of competing theories and may be expected to eschew organizational behavior altogether.

The response to this line of reasoning is that it creates a pseudo-problem, a mirage, that is readily soluble in that science serves to test theories through research which is just as applicable to competing theories as to any others (McKinley 1995). Although valid, this position needs some amplification, however.

First, the theory pluralism that exists at present is not made up exclusively of scientific theories. There are a number of philosophic statements in existence which do not generate testable hypotheses and thus are not falsifiable. Subtracting this philosophic content reduces the degree of theory pluralism substantially. For example, many of the phenomena that exist in this world have multiple religious explanations, and scientific explanations (confirmed by research) as well. To include the religious "theories," which are untestable, as part of the total count of scientific theories is unwarranted.

Second, a close study of existing organizational behavior theories reveals that the most frequent situation is one where the theories occupy different, nonoverlapping domains. There are instances of overlap and even some cases of competing positions, but this is not the norm by any means. Those who argue that an inability to compare competing theories is a major barrier to attaining consensus are simply wrong, at least insofar as organizational behavior is concerned; there are not that many competing theories, once theoretical domains are clearly drawn.

Third, competing theories can be compared using appropriate research designs. Differential experimentation which serves to determine the relative effectiveness of various approaches or hypotheses is commonly conducted. Any good theory contains clear specifications for operationalizing its variables and these may be used in comparative research. For a good example of how research to deal with competing theoretical positions may be conducted see Latham, Erez, and Locke (1988) and the more extended treatment of this research contained in Frost and Stablein (1992). What is clearly evident here is that with sufficient creative input into the research process science can handle competing theoretical positions (see also McKinley 1995 on this point). Thus a basis for achieving consensus, where it might otherwise appear to be lacking, does exist within science.

Fourth, a consensus of knowledgeable scholars can develop in the absence of full agreement among protagonists. Rensis Likert's theory of systems 1–4 and 4T (see Miner 2002) was found to be deficient in certain respects, based on extensive research conducted to test aspects of the theory. Yet to my knowledge Likert never repudiated his theory, and continued'to hold out against the growing consensus until his death. This is not unusual and it does not matter. A few voices in opposition does not vitiate consensus.

Fifth, it is not correct to say consensus is totally lacking in organizational behavior; agreement among knowledgeable scholars in support of a theory occurs quite often. But the qualifier *among knowledgeable scholars* is important here. Organizational behavior has developed a breadth and depth of information that defies comprehension by a single person. There are specialties and subspecialties, and it is these that furnish the knowledgeable scholars whose judgment is at issue. To add in the many who know little or nothing about a particular theory and its research is bound to create an appearance of disconsensus as competing values become involved against an ambiguous (uncertain) background, but that is not the kind of consensus science seeks.

Sixth, practitioners (such as managers) do not require a consensus on the part of organizational behavior to utilize the tools, technology, and theories of that discipline. It would certainly be helpful if such a consensus existed, but managers in a particular area of a business are not necessarily uninformed consumers; they can make judgments as to the validity and usefulness of what comes to them from organizational behavior, and they do so all the time. Many of these inputs from organizational behavior prove useful and help to solve important practical problems. As a former practitioner of organizational behavior in the personnel research unit of a large corporation and a consultant in that area throughout my professional career, I can attest to the practical value of these inputs. In actuality the freedom from political wars that the practitioner has may compensate for any lack of knowledge. Certainly errors are made, but low levels of consensus do not prevent practitioners from making choices among the potpourri of organizational behavior tools, technologies, and theories. And again, as Donaldson (1992) contends, the degree of consensus available to practitioners is probably greater than the critics have maintained.

The Road to Consensus

It becomes apparent from the above discussion that it would be very useful to have an operational measure of consensus on various matters, within organizational behavior. With hard data on what knowledgeable scholars think it would be possible to avoid much of the ambiguity that surrounds this treatment.

Actually during the1980s a certain amount of data on the extent of consensus around first generation organizational behavior theories which had achieved considerable visibility did become available (Miner 1990). The correlations among data from different sources ranking these theories as to their validity ranged from .74 to .94. This is indicative of a considerable amount of consensus. More recent research of this nature provides evidence of increasing consensus around a number of theories in organizational behavior (Miner 2003). The field is still very young and it is too early to expect high levels of agreement, but we are moving in that direction.

One might think that consensus could be obtained by noting the most frequently cited publications in the field, and then building a picture of organizational behavior's knowledge base from the content of these publications. Unfortunately, however, evidence indicates that those publications that do particularly well in citation counts do so not because of the perceived quality of the publication or its usefulness to practitioners, but because of the usefulness to scholars of the field in carrying out their professional tasks (Shadish 1989). This is not the stuff out of which a picture of our knowledge base can be created. Furthermore, the use of citation counts in this manner has been a source of considerable controversy on many grounds (see Hébert 2004).

Yet there are multiple signs pointing to improving consensus as organizational behavior matures. One such sign is the increasing degree to which citations to other disciplines are appearing in the journals (Blackburn 1990). Discourse across disciplines is on the upswing; talking only with those people within the field who represent a reflection of one's own image is decreasing. When communication opens up in this way, at least the potential for consensus opens up as well.

A second encouraging sign is the relatively recent emergence not of meso theories per se, since such theories have in fact been in existence for some time, but of an explicit concern with the identification and creation of such theories, which bridge a major value-gap in the field. To the extent they prove valid, meso theories can represent a major integrating force within organizational behavior. We will see a number of instances of meso theorizing in what follows, and discuss other cases where a theory could be extended advantageously in a meso direction.

In writing meso theory one is forced to deal both with psychological and sociological variables as well as with the literatures that surround those variables. The result should be an integrated theory that not only ties together the two levels of analysis, but commits the author to some type of synthesis of the two value positions. Accordingly a strong commitment to a meso approach to theorizing could go a long way toward fostering consensus, and firming up a stable knowledge base for organizational behavior.

In short, although it does seem that consensus is at a rather low level overall within organizational behavior, there are subfields and sectors where this is not the case. Thus a body of accepted knowledge does exist within the field, and is available to practitioners—a smaller body than many would desire, but still important. Furthermore, there are certain trends in evidence that seem to argue for improved consensus in the future.

CONCLUSIONS

This chapter has delved into the characteristics of research that can be used to test scientific theories. In all of this it should be understood that organizational behavior research may serve additional functions beyond merely testing theory. Hypotheses derived from practice may be evaluated through research to determine whether what has been assumed to be true is really true. Areas that present particular problems may be studied to obtain a clearer picture of the landscape. The point is that scientific research in organizational behavior is not simply a matter of theory testing. Yet theory testing is the most important function of organizational behavior research, because a well-validated theory can establish a wide range of knowledge.

In the preceding discussion, certain terms that are to be found in the references, and which are often used in the literature, have been deliberately avoided. This is in part because these terms have taken on a variety of value-laden excess meanings that tend to stereotype the user. In some instances the terms are too ambiguous for most scientific purposes as well. Kuhn (1970) in introducing the term "paradigm" intentionally used it with a wide range of meanings (Astley and Zammuto 1992), and it continues to possess this same ambiguity today. In addition to paradigm I have avoided such terms as normal science, positivist theory, and incommensurability for the same reasons.

This is not to say that most of the concepts that appear to be covered by these terms are not treated—to the contrary they are treated in detail, but using other words. Nor am I trying to avoid labeling my own position. The discussion here clearly identifies my commitment to science and spells out at considerable length the concept of science I have in mind. Terms such as paradigm, normal science, positivist theory, and incommensurability come to organizational behavior from philosophy, however. As a result there is no commitment to make them precise and specific, in the mode of science. At the same time there is no necessary commitment on the part of organizational behavior to make them part of our vocabulary—and we should not.

REFERENCES

Agger, Ben (1991). Critical Theory, Poststructuralism, Postmodernism: Their Sociological Relevance. *Annual Review of Sociology,* 17, 105–31.

Alvesson, Mats (2003). Interpretive Unpacking: Moderately Destabilizing Identities and Images in Organization Studies. In Edwin A. Locke (Ed.), *Postmodernism and Management: Pros, Cons, and the Alternative.* Oxford, UK: Elsevier Science, pp. 3–27.

Alvesson, Mats, and Kärreman, Dan (2000). Taking the Linguistic Turn in Organizational Research—Challenges, Responses, Consequences. *Journal of Applied Behavioral Science,* 36, 136–58.

Argyris, Chris (1980). *Inner Contradictions of Rigorous Research.* New York: Academic Press.

Argyris, Chris (2004). *Reasons and Rationalizations: The Case of Organization Studies.* New York: Oxford University Press.

Astley, W. Graham, and Zammuto, Raymond F. (1992). Organization Science, Managers, and Language Games. *Organization Science,* 3, 443–60.

Bagozzi, Richard P., Yi, Youjae, and Phillips, Lynn W. (1991). Assessing Construct Validity in Organizational Research. *Administrative Science Quarterly,* 36, 421–58.

Barrett, Edward (2003). Foucault, HRM and the Ethos of the Critical Management Scholar. *Journal of Management Studies,* 40, 1069–87.

Belasco, James A., and Trice, Harrison M. (1969). *The Assessment of Change in Training and Therapy.* New York: McGraw-Hill.

Bernstein, Susan D. (2003). Positive Organizational Scholarship: Meet the Movement—An Interview with Kim Cameron, Jane Dutton, and Robert Quinn. *Journal of Management Inquiry,* 12, 266–71.

Blackburn, Richard S. (1987). Experimental Design in Organizational Settings. In Jay W. Lorsch (Ed.), *Handbook of Organizational Behavior.* Englewood Cliffs, NJ: Prentice Hall, pp. 126–39.

Blackburn, Richard S. (1990). Organizational Behavior: Whom Do We Talk to and Who Talks to Us? *Journal of Management,* 16, 279–305.

Burrell, Gibson (1996). Normal Science, Paradigms, Metaphors, Discourses, and Genealogies of Analysis. In Stewart R. Clegg, Cynthia Hardy, and Walter R. Nord (Eds.), *Handbook of Organization Studies.* London: Sage, pp. 642–58.

Cameron, Kim S., Dutton, Jane E., and Quinn, Robert F. (2003). *Positive Organizational Scholarship: Foundations of a New Discipline.* San Francisco, CA: Berrett-Koehler.

Clegg, Stewart R., Hardy, Cynthia, and Nord, Walter R. (1996). *Handbook of Organization Studies.* London: Sage.

Clegg, Stewart R., and Kornberger, Martin (2003). Modernism, Postmodernism, Management and Organization

Theory. In Edwin A. Locke (Ed.), *Postmodernism and Management: Pros, Cons, and the Alternative.* Oxford, UK: Elsevier Science, pp. 57–88.

Clegg, Stewart R., and Ross-Smith, Anne (2003). Revising the Boundaries: Management Education and Learning in a Postpositivist World. *Academy of Management Learning and Education,* 2, 85–98.

Cook, Thomas D., Campbell, Donald T., and Peracchio, Laura (1990). Quasi Experimentation. In Marvin D. Dunnette and Leaetta M. Hough (Eds.), *Handbook of Industrial and Organizational Psychology,* Volume 1. Palo Alto, CA: Consulting Psychologists Press, pp. 491–576.

Cortina, Jose M. (2002). Big Things Have Small Beginnings: An Assortment of "Minor" Methodological Misunderstandings. *Journal of Management,* 28, 339–62.

Davis-Blake, Alison, and Pfeffer, Jeffrey (1989). Just a Mirage: The Search for Dispositional Effects in Organizational Research. *Academy of Management Review,* 14, 385–400.

Donaldson, Lex (1992). The Weick Stuff: Managing Beyond Games. *Organization Science,* 3, 461–66.

Donaldson, Lex (2003). A Critique of Post-modernism in Organizational Studies. In Edwin A. Locke (Ed.), *Postmodernism and Management: Pros, Cons, and the Alternative.* Oxford, UK: Elsevier Science, pp. 169–202.

Drasgow, Fritz, and Schmitt, Neal (2002). *Measuring and Analyzing Behavior in Organizations: Advances in Measurement and Data Analysis.* San Francisco, CA: Jossey-Bass.

Edwards, Jeffrey R. (2003). Construct Validation in Organizational Behavior Research. In Jerald Greenberg (Ed.), *Organizational Behavior: The State of the Science.* Mahwah, NJ: Lawrence Erlbaum, pp. 327–71.

Evans, Martin G. (1999). Donald T. Campbell's Methodological Contributions to Organization Science. In Joel A. C. Baum and Bill McKelvey (Eds.), *Variations in Organization Science: In Honor of Donald T. Campbell.* Thousand Oaks, CA: Sage, pp. 311–38.

Fabian, Frances H. (2000). Keeping the Tension: Pressures to Keep the Controversy in the Management Discipline. *Academy of Management Review,* 25, 350–71.

Frost, Peter J., and Stablein, Ralph E. (1992). *Doing Exemplary Research.* Newbury Park, CA: Sage.

George, Jennifer M. (1992). The Role of Personality in Organizational Life: Issues and Evidence. *Journal of Management,* 18, 185–213.

Ghate, Onkar, and Locke, Edwin A. (2003). Objectivism: The Proper Alternative to Postmodernism. In Edwin A. Locke (Ed.), *Postmodernism and Management: Pros, Cons, and the Alternative.* Oxford, UK: Elsevier Science, pp. 249–78.

Hartman, Edwin (1988). *Conceptual Foundations of Organization Theory.* Cambridge, MA: Ballinger.

Hébert, Richard (2004). "Highly Citied, Highly Controversial." *American Psychological Society Observer,* 17(3), 1, 35–40.

Hemphill, James F. (2003). Interpreting the Magnitudes of Correlation Coefficients. *American Psychologist,* 58, 78–79.

House, Robert J., Shane, Scott A., and Herold, David M. (1996). Rumors of the Death of Dispositional Research Are Vastly Exaggerated. *Academy of Management Review,* 21, 203–24.

Hunt, James G., and Ropo, Arja (2003). Longitudinal Organizational Research and the Third Scientific Discipline. *Group and Organization Management,* 28, 315–40.

Jermier, John M. (1985). "When the Sleeper Walks": A Short Story Extending Themes in Radical Organization Theory. *Journal of Management,* 11(2), 67–80.

Kahn, Robert L. (1975). In Search of the Hawthorne Effect. In Eugene L. Cass and Frederick G. Zimmer (Eds.), *Man and Work in Society.* New York: Van Nostrand Reinhold, pp. 49–63.

Kilduff, Martin, and Kelemen, Michaela (2003). Bringing Ideas Back in: Eclecticism and Discovery in Organizational Studies. In Edwin A. Locke (Ed.), *Postmodernism and Management: Pros, Cons, and the Alternative.* Oxford, UK: Elsevier Science, pp. 89–109.

Kilduff, Martin, and Mehra, Ajay (1997). Postmodernism and Organizational Research. *Academy of Management Review,* 22, 453–81.

Kuhn, Thomas (1970). *The Structure of Scientific Revolutions.* Chicago, IL: University of Chicago Press.

Lam, Simon S. K., and Schaubroeck, John (2000). The Role of Locus of Control in Reactions to Being Promoted and to Being Passed Over: A Quasi Experiment. *Academy of Management Journal,* 43, 66–78.

Latham, Gary P., Erez, Miriam, and Locke, Edwin A. (1988). Resolving Scientific Disputes by the Joint Design of Crucial Experiments by the Antagonists: Application to the Erez-Latham Dispute Regarding Participating in Goal Setting. *Journal of Applied Psychology,* 73, 753–72.

Lawler, Edward E., Mohrman, Alan M., Mohrman, Susan A., Ledford, Gerald E., and Cummings, Thomas G. (1985). *Doing Research That Is Useful for Theory and Practice.* San Francisco, CA: Jossey-Bass.

Lindell, Michael K., and Whitney, David J. (2001). Accounting for Common Method Variance in Cross-sectional Research Designs. *Journal of Applied Psychology,* 86, 114–21.

Locke, Edwin A. (1986). *Generalizing from Laboratory to Field Settings.* Lexington, MA: Lexington Books.

Locke, Edwin A. (2003). Good Definitions: The Epistemological Foundation of Scientific Progress. In Jerald Greenberg (Ed.), *Organizational Behavior: The State of the Science.* Mahwah, NJ: Lawrence Erlbaum, pp. 415–44.

Loo, Robert (2002). A Caveat on Using Single-Item versus Multiple-Item Scales. *Journal of Managerial Psychology,* 17, 68–75.

Maierhofer, Naomi I., Kabanoff, Boris, and Griffin, Mark A. (2002). The Influence of Values in Organizations: Linking Values and Outcomes at Multiple Levels of Analysis. *International Review of Industrial and Organizational Psychology,* 17, 217–63.

Markham, Steven E., Scott, K. Dow, and McKee, Gail H. (2002). Recognizing Good Attendance: A Longitudinal, Quasi-experimental Field Study. *Personnel Psychology,* 55, 639–60.

Martin, Joanne, and Frost, Peter (1996). The Organizational Culture War Games: A Struggle for Intellectual Dominance. In Stewart R. Clegg, Cynthia Hardy, and Walter R. Nord (Eds.), *Handbook of Organization Studies.* London: Sage, pp. 599–621.

McKelvey, Bill (2003). Postmodernism versus Truth in Management Theory. In Edwin A. Locke (Ed.), *Postmodernism and Management: Pros, Cons, and the Alternative.* Oxford, UK: Elsevier Science, pp. 113–68.

McKinley, William (1995). Commentary on Scherer and Dowling. *Advances in Strategic Management,* 12A, 249–60.

Miner, John B. (1962). Conformity Among University Professors and Business Executives. *Administrative Science Quarterly,* 7, 96–109.

———. (1990). The Role of Values in Defining the 'Goodness' of Theories in Organizational Science. *Organization Studies,* 11, 161–78.

———. (1995). *Administrative and Management Theory.* Aldershot, UK: Dartmouth.

———. (2002). *Organizational Behavior: Foundations, Theories, and Analyses.* New York: Oxford University Press.

———. (2003). The Rated Importance, Scientific Validity, and Practical Usefulness of Organizational Behavior Theories: A Quantitative Review. *Academy of Management Learning and Education,* 2, 250–68.

Morgeson, Frederick P., and Campion, Michael A. (2002). Minimizing Tradeoffs When Redesigning Work: Evidence from a Longitudinal Quasi-experiment. *Personnel Psychology,* 55, 589–612.

Nord, Walter R., and Fox, Suzy (1996). The Individual in Organizational Studies: The Great Disappearing Act? In Stuart R. Clegg, Cynthia Hardy, and Walter R. Nord (Eds.), *Handbook of Organization Studies.* London: Sage, pp. 148–74.

Pescosolido, Bernice A., and Rubin, Beth A. (2000). The Web of Group Affiliations Revisited: Social Life, Postmodernism, and Sociology. *American Sociological Review,* 65, 52–76.

Pfeffer, Jeffrey (1993). Barriers to the Advance of Organizational Science: Paradigm Development as a Dependent Variable. *Academy of Management Review,* 18, 599–620.

Pfeffer, Jeffrey (1995). Mortality, Reproducibility, and the Persistence of Styles of Theory. *Organization Science,* 6, 681–86.

Podsakoff, Philip M., MacKenzie, Scott B., Lee, Jeong-Yeon, and Podsakoff, Nathan P. (2003). Common Method Biases in Behavioral Research: A Critical Review of the Literature and Recommended Remedies. *Journal of Applied Psychology,* 88, 879–903.

Price, James L., and Mueller, Charles W. (1986). *Handbook of Organizational Measurement.* Marshfield, MA: Pitman.

Probst, Tahira M. (2003). Exploring Employee Outcomes of Organizational Restructuring: A Solomon Four-group Study. *Group and Organizational Mangement,* 28, 416–39.

Risman, Barbara J. (2001). Calling the Bluff of Value-free Science. *American Sociological Review,* 66, 605–11.

Scandura, Terri A., and Williams, Ethlyn A. (2000). Research Methodology in Management: Current Practices, Trends, and Implications for Future Research. *Academy of Management Journal,* 43, 1248–64.

Scherer, Andreas G., and Dowling, Michael J. (1995). Towards a Reconciliation of the Theory-Pluralism in Strategic Management—Incommensurability and the Constructivist Approach of the Erlangen School. *Advances in Strategic Management,* 12A, 195–247.

Schmidt, Frank L., Viswesvaran, Chockalingam, and Ones, Deniz S. (2000). Reliability Is Not Validity and Validity Is Not Reliability. *Personnel Psychology,* 53, 901–24.

Shadish, William R. (1989). The Perception and Evaluation of Quality in Science. In Barry Gholson, William R. Shadish, Robert A. Neimeyer, and Arthur C. Houts (Eds.), *Psychology of Science: Contributions to Metascience.* Cambridge, UK: Cambridge University Press, pp. 383–426.

Silverman, David (1971). *The Theory of Organizations.* New York: Basic Books.

Tannenbaum, Robert, Margulies, Newton, and Massarik, Fred (1985). *Human Systems Development.* San Francisco, CA: Jossey-Bass.

Van Maanen, John (1995). Style as Theory. *Organization Science,* 6, 133–43.

Vibert, Conor (2004). *Theories of Macro Organizational Behavior: A Handbook of Ideas and Explanations.* Armonk, NY: M. E. Sharpe.

Voronov, Maxim, and Coleman, Peter T. (2003). Beyond the Ivory Towers: Organizational Power Practices and a "Practical" Critical Postmodernism. *Journal of Applied Behavioral Science,* 39, 169–85.

Weiss, Richard M. (2000). Taking Science out of Organization Science: How Would Postmodernism Reconstruct the Analysis of Organizations? *Organization Science,* 11, 709–31.

Williams, Larry J., Edwards, Jeffrey R., and Vandenberg, Robert J. (2003). Recent Advances in Causal Modeling Methods for Organizational and Management Research. *Journal of Management,* 29, 903–36.

PART II

ORGANIZATIONAL DECISION MAKING

CHAPTER 3

ADMINISTRATIVE BEHAVIOR AND ORGANIZATIONS

HERBERT SIMON
JAMES MARCH AND HERBERT SIMON

<table>
<tr><td>Background</td><td></td></tr>
</table>

Importance rating	★ ★ ★ ★ ★
	Institutionalized
Estimated validity	★ ★ ★ ★ ★
Estimated usefulness	★ ★
Decade of origin	1940s

Organizational decision making is a topic that has been part of organizational behavior since the beginning. Theories of this kind have played an important role in the field, not only in their own right, but also in their implications for other topic areas. The particular theories to be considered include some of the most influential in organizational behavior. Although the theories treated tend to focus on decision making, they cover a number of conventional components of organizational functioning that characteristically relate to the decision process. In this chapter we take up Simon's theoretical work and his joint efforts with March; here the emphasis on rational decision making within the bounds of possibility is pronounced. In particular the discussion focuses on two books that in many ways established the foundations for the field of organizational behavior—Simon's *Administrative Behavior* and March and Simon's *Organizations*.

BACKGROUND

Herbert Simon was born in 1916 and received his doctorate in 1942 from the University of Chicago in political science, the same school and discipline that awarded his undergraduate degree as well (in 1936). For the three years before obtaining the Ph.D. he worked on public administration research at the University of California at Berkeley. His first regular faculty appointment was back in Chicago at Illinois Institute of Technology (IIT), again in political science, but with a developing interest in economics. After seven years at IIT, Simon moved to the School of Industrial Administration, then in the process of being founded, at Carnegie Institute of Technology (now Carnegie Mellon University). The move was precipitated by his interest in economics, the publication of *Administrative Behavior* in 1947, and his continuing mathematical orientation to social science. At this point, any formal identification with political science ended, but by his own admission, Simon has always been something of a politician within the intellectual community, and his original choice of a field of study reflects this (Simon 1991a).

The years at Carnegie, at least the early ones, were marked by considerable controversy and ultimately by his movement from the developing field of organizational behavior to psychology, a move that was formally consummated in 1970. This was both a departmental transfer and a shift in primary field, but both had been in process for a number of years. Much of Simon's research and publication from the early 1960s on was in cognitive processes, artificial intelligence, and computer modeling. His appointment in psychology became joined with another in computer science. He became emeritus from Carnegie Mellon in 1993. He died in 2001 (for more information, see Anderson 2001).

Chester Barnard's writings had a strong influence on Simon and his formulations regarding decision-making processes. Simon repeatedly acknowledges this influence in his *Administrative Behavior* (1974). In fact, Barnard critically reviewed the original manuscript for that book and wrote a foreword for the first edition. Simon's views on the decision to participate in an organization and on organizational authority derive from Barnard. In many respects Simon took the abstract philosophizing of Barnard, the scholarly business manager, and converted it into testable propositions subject to scientific research (see Miner 2002).

James March was born in 1928. He did his undergraduate work at the University of Wisconsin. Serving at Stanford University since 1970, he has had an equally diverse array of discipline associations, including appointments in political science, education, sociology, and business administration. He, too, started in the field of political science with a Ph.D. from Yale in 1953. From 1953 to 1964 he was with Simon at Carnegie before taking an administrative position at the University of California (Irvine) for six years. He has been emeritus from Stanford since 1995. Unlike Simon, March has remained largely within the field of organizational behavior, insofar as his intellectual contributions are concerned, throughout his career, although his approach to the field has drawn on many different literatures (see Augier and Kreiner 2000).

THE THEORY OF ADMINISTRATIVE BEHAVIOR

Simon's *Administrative Behavior* (1947), which was developed from his dissertation, is unusual in a number of respects. For one thing it contributed substantially to his winning the Nobel prize in economics (see Leahey 2003). Like so many others, Simon also attempted to demolish classical management theory, but instead of arguing primarily on grounds of humanism or adaptive inflexibility, he attacked it for logical inconsistency, pervasive ambiguity of statement, and failure to measure up to the demands of scientific theorizing. While rejecting the normative principles of classical theory, Simon (1946) did not then advocate a new normative theory to replace them. Instead, he took only a first step toward reconstruction—the setting forth of a vocabulary and conceptual framework. His clear intent was to focus primarily on decision-making processes, which indeed has been the primary thrust of his entire professional career (see Augier 2001).

Limits to Rationality

A central thesis in Simon's thinking was that rational decision making is limited or bounded by (1) a person's skills, habits, and reflexes; (2) the values and concepts of purpose that influence the decision; and (3) the person's knowledge, particularly of the consequences of alternatives. Inherent in this view is the idea that decisions involve not only factual judgments, but also ethical or value judgments that relate to the goals and purposes to be served. In a very rough sense *administration* relates to factual judgments and *policy* to value judgments. In the same sense, facts more often tend to be related to means and values to ends.

Simon's views in this area must be set against the prevailing concept of a highly rational, maximizing decision maker, as epitomized by *economic man:*

> It is impossible for the behavior of a single, isolated individual to reach any high degree of rationality. The number of alternatives he must explore is so great, the information he would need to evaluate them so vast that even an approximation to objective rationality is hard to conceive. Individual choice takes place in an environment of "givens"—premises that are accepted by the subject as bases for his choice; and behavior is adaptive only within the limits set by these "givens." (Simon 1947, 79)

Behavior thus fails of objective rationality in several respects:

1. Rationality requires a complete knowledge and anticipation of the consequences that will follow on each choice. In fact, knowledge of consequences is always fragmentary.
2. Since these consequences lie in the future, imagination must supply the lack of experienced feeling in attaching value to them. But values can be only imperfectly anticipated.
3. Rationality requires a choice among all possible alternative behaviors. In actual behavior, only a very few of all these possible alternatives ever come to mind. (Simon 1947, 81)

Within an organization, the decision process begins with *substantive planning*—the broad decisions affecting values; methods of attaining those values; and needed knowledge, skills, and information. Second, there is *procedural planning,* involving decisions about mechanisms to direct attention and channel information in accordance with the substantive plan. Finally, there is *execution* based on day-to-day decisions. The hierarchy of steps increasingly restricts alternatives and limits the decision process. Consistent with this objective, work is divided among members, standard practices are introduced, decisions are transmitted through the organization, and members are trained in matters related to their decisions. Thus, much of organizational structure and process is explained in relation to making decisions manageable.

Simon (1947) devoted considerable attention to the criterion of efficiency, which requires that the alternative selected be the one that will yield the greatest net return. If costs are fixed, the decision should maximize income, and if income is fixed, it should minimize costs. When efficiency is the accepted criterion, rationality governs decision making, much as it does in economic theory when an attempt is made to maximize utility. Given the limits to rationality, Simon did not assert that managerial decisions are characteristically dominated by the criterion of efficiency. Yet, Simon seemed to favor that end highly and to argue for maximization of efficiency and rational decisions to the extent that available data permitted. On occasion he even seemed to imply that rationality often is attainable. In subsequent treatments, however, he was less optimistic (Simon 1957a; Simon, Smithburg, and Thompson 1950).

Inducements-Contributions Equilibrium

Business organizations have at least three kinds of participants—entrepreneurs, employees, and customers. Entrepreneurs enter into contracts with employees to obtain their time and effort and with customers to obtain their money to pay wages and thus maintain the employment contract. Though in businesses the inducement—money—is indirect, in some organizations, such as churches, the inducement for members may be some direct personal value. In any event, a necessary condition for gaining and continuing to belong to an organization is some form of inducements-contributions agreement.

When the contributions are adequate to attract what is needed to provide the appropriate kinds and amounts of inducements, the organization prospers. One kind of contribution in such situations is a willingness to accept authority. This willingness extends over a zone of acceptance the width of which is determined by the nature and extent of inducements. If the employment contract terms, implicit or explicit, are favorable, an employee can be expected to contribute willingly over a broad range of activities. But if the inducements provide little satisfaction of personal goals, contributions and the zone of acceptance shrink.

In these relationships, authority is defined as "the power to make decisions which guide the actions of another" (Simon 1947, 125). Authority is only one form of influence, which also includes persuasion and suggestion. Authority exists only as long as it is accepted, and thus only as long as what is required falls within the zone of acceptance.

Models of Man and Other Extensions

In the period following the first publication of *Administrative Behavior* Simon developed his concepts more fully in a number of articles. These articles, as well as others unrelated to organizational structure and process, were brought together in a single volume entitled *Models of Man* (Simon 1957b). In the same year, *Administrative Behavior* (1957a) was republished with a lengthy introduction qualifying and extending Simon's earlier views. In both publications the term *satisficing* began to be used to refer to the behavior of those who "have not the wits to maximize."

In elaborating on the idea that administrative theory is, in fact, synonymous with the theory of intended and bounded rationality, Simon amended his prior views to include the satisficing concept:

1. While economic man maximizes—selects the best alternative from among all those available to him, his cousin, whom we shall call administrative man—satisfices—looks for a course of action that is satisfactory or "good enough."

2. Economic man deals with the "real world" in all its complexity. Administrative man recognizes that the world he perceives is a drastically simplified model of the buzzing, blooming confusion that constitutes the real world. He is content with this gross simplification because he believes that the real world is mostly empty—that most of the facts of the real world have no great relevance to any particular situation he is facing. He makes his choices using a simple picture of the situation that takes into account just a few of the factors that he regards as most relevant and crucial. . . . Administrative man is able to make his decisions with relatively simple rules of thumb that do not make impossible demands upon his capacity for thought (Simon 1957a, xxv–xxvi).

In publication after publication Simon attacks the economic theory that assumes perfect knowledge and ignores the reality of bounded rationality. Under bounded rationality, the decision maker, instead of maximizing, searches only until he finds an alternative where the payoff is good enough. There is no need to look beyond this point for an alternative that will yield an even higher payoff. In formulating the satisficing concept, Simon assumes a sequential pattern of choice:

The aspiration level, which defines a satisfactory alternative, may change from point to point in this sequence of trials. A vague principle would be that as the individual, in his exploration of alternatives, finds it easy to discover satisfactory alternatives, his aspiration level rises; as he finds it difficult to discover satisfactory alternatives, his aspiration level falls. . . . Such changes in aspiration level would tend to bring about a "near-uniqueness" of the satisfactory solutions, and would also tend to guarantee the existence of satisfactory solutions. For the failure to discover a solution would depress the aspiration level and bring satisfactory solutions into existence. (Simon 1957b, 253)

Elaborating further on the inducements-contributions equilibrium, Simon notes that employment contracts and sales contracts differ in that the former specify only a zone of acceptance of authority (and perhaps areas of nonacceptance), rather than specific terms and actions for each party. Yet, as Simon himself recognizes, his theory tends somewhat inconsistently to assume rational, utility-maximizing behavior in the employment relationship:

Each participant will remain in the organization if the satisfaction (or utility) he derives from the net balance of inducements over contributions (measured in terms of their utility to him) is greater than the satisfaction he could obtain if he withdrew. The zero point in such a "satisfaction function" is defined, therefore, in terms of the opportunity cost of participation. (Simon 1957b, 173)

THE THEORY OF ORGANIZATIONS

The book *Organizations* (March and Simon 1958) has much in common with Thompson's *Organizations in Action* (1967) (see Chapter 11 of this volume). However, March and Simon's inventory of propositions is largely induced from empirical research, while Thompson's derives from conceptual premises. Many March and Simon hypotheses deal with such variables as motivation, group behavior, and leadership that fall entirely within the confines of organizational behavior at the micro level. At the micro level March and Simon's theory is now primarily of historical interest, having been superseded by other, more sophisticated formulations. The following discussion will focus on the theory's more comprehensive concepts and propositions relating to the organization as a whole, including its processes of decision making.

Satisficing and Bounded Rationality

The March and Simon (1958) discussion of decision making followed already familiar lines. However, some new concepts were added and old ones developed more fully. The concept of performance program, which appeared to be roughly analogous to role prescription, was invoked in the discussion of control and coordination systems. Performance programs, though intended to make behavior within an organization more predictable, are themselves selected on a satisficing basis, thus making it difficult to predict which performance programs will be chosen. Programs differ in their degree of stress on means and ends, and thus in the amount of discretion they permit.

Division of work is viewed as a means of simplifying the decision process. Units are established on the basis of purpose, and subgoals are introduced so that decision makers may face problems with which they can cope. Once units are created, the problem of interdependence arises. In stable, predictable environments there is considerable tolerance for interdependence, and process specialization can be carried quite far. In more rapidly changing environments specialization carries much higher risks. Thus organizations attempt to stabilize their environments by homogenizing materials, using interchangeable parts, holding buffer inventories, and the like to maintain specialization. Yet coordination problems remain:

> We may label coordination based on pre-established schedules *coordination by plan,* and coordination that involves transmission of new information *coordination by feedback.* The more stable and predictable the situation, the greater the reliance on coordination by plan; the more variable and unpredictable the situation, the greater the reliance on coordination by feedback. (March and Simon 1958, 160)

In general, highly programmed tasks drive out unprogrammed tasks. Organizations that do not give special consideration to this fact will fail to plan and innovate. To obtain unprogrammed action, organizations must establish specially budgeted planning units with their own specific goals or introduce hard-and-fast deadlines for the completion of unprogrammed tasks. Whether innovation occurs at the top levels of an organization depends on the type of coordination used. Feedback coordination facilitates, and coordination by plan limits, innovative decision making at the top.

The concept of bounded rationality provides a rationale not only for the division of work, but also for the decentralization of decision making. Given existing limits on human capacity, decentralized systems in which decisions are moved down and out to larger numbers of individuals are preferred over centralized systems.

The Decision to Participate

A stable inducements-contributions equilibrium is posited as a necessary condition for organizational survival. Increases in inducements decrease the tendency for an individual to leave the organization. The inducements-contributions balance is influenced by both perceived

Figure 3.1 **Major Factors Influencing Perceived Desirability and Ease of Movement from an Organization**

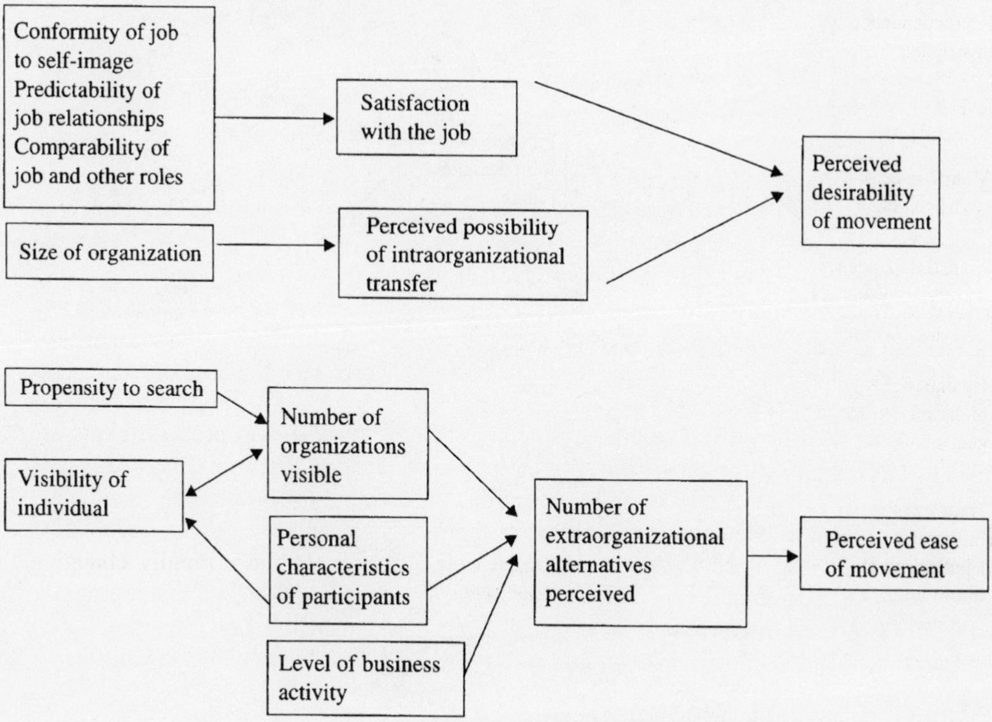

Source: Adapted from March and Simon (1958, 99, 106).

desirability and perceived ease of leaving. Propositions relating various factors to both perceived desirability of movement and perceived ease of movement are shown in Figure 3.1.

Conflict

Conflict in organizations may be within the individual, in that known, acceptable decision alternatives are not available, or between individuals (or groups), in that different individuals make different choices. Conflict of the latter type is of prime concern here. Conflict within the individual is important too, in that it retards choice, and choice is a necessary condition for intergroup conflict.

Figure 3.2 outlines the major propositions involving intergroup conflict. The formulations relating to joint decision making are of particular interest. Sharing a common service unit and being adjacent to another unit in a flow-chart sense are given as examples of situations calling for joint decision making. Conflict is expected to be high in these instances. Conflict is most likely to be related to budgeting and monetary allocations and will tend to increase when overall resources are reduced.

Reactions to conflict include (1) problem solving, often with a search for new alternatives; (2) persuasion, often with a search for previously unconsidered superordinate objectives;

Figure 3.2   **Major Factors Influencing Intergroup Conflict**

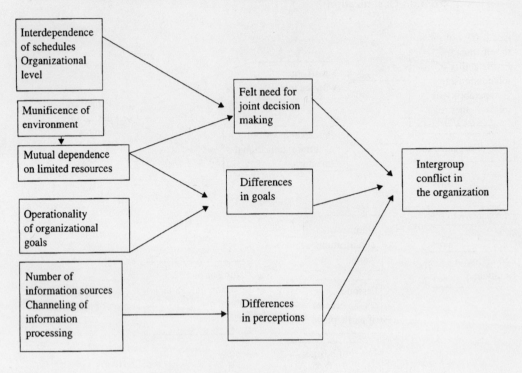

Source: Adapted from March and Simon (1958, 128).

(3) bargaining, where goal disagreements are taken as inevitable; and (4) politics, where the conflict arena is expanded to include other groups and constituencies. Typically, managerial hierarchies prefer problem solving and persuasion to bargaining and politics and will prefer to use them in conflict resolution. Problem solving and persuasion put less strain on the status and power systems.

Theoretical Extensions

Simon continued to build on this theory in varied ways and in a somewhat intermittent manner. Much of his effort was devoted to extending the concepts of bounded rationality in areas of human problem solving and computer science. In some cases these activities are clearly within the confines of organizational behavior, sometimes they are of only tangential relevance, and more often they are not of the field at all. The present discussion focuses on the organizational behavior end of this continuum.

Organizational Goals

In 1964 Simon published an article dealing with goals that he subsequently included in the third edition of *Administrative Behavior.* His discussion was described as "generally compatible with, but not identical to, that of my colleagues, R.M. Cyert and J.G. March" (Simon

1976, 257). In fact it was the beginning of a separation in viewpoints that took Simon and March in different directions after their collaboration on *Organizations* in 1958.

For Simon, goals were value premises for decisions and must be clearly distinguished from individual motives. In his view goals became synonymous with constraints:

> A course of action, to be acceptable, must satisfy a whole set of requirements, or constraints. Sometimes one of these requirements is singled out and referred to as the goal of the action. But the choice of one of the constraints, from many, is to a large extent arbitrary. For many purposes it is more meaningful to refer to the whole set of requirements as the (complex) goal of the action. This conclusion applies both to individual and organizational decision-making. (Simon 1976, 262)

These goals/constraints can serve to generate alternatives or, in the more traditional role of goals, to test alternatives. Used in the former sense, there appears to be little goal congruence among the subunits of an organization, and goal conflict seems rampant. Used in the latter, traditional sense, the sharing of constraint sets becomes much more widespread.

Simon (1976) gave less emphasis to bargaining and loosely bound coalitions than Cyert and March (1963) did. The goals/constraints emerge out of the inducements-contributions equilibrium, but they are also strongly influenced by the system of organizational roles in which decisions made in one unit serve as constraints for other parts of the organization. The coupling here is loose, but the decisions that produce the role structure can be measured against various organizational goals (other constraints) and corrected accordingly. Personal motives become much less important in organizational decisions than programmed organizational roles. Furthermore, given a hierarchical system, it is logical to use the term *organizational goal* to refer to "the constraint sets and criteria of search that define roles at the upper levels" (Simon 1976, 277) and "to describe most business firms as directed toward profit making—subject to a number of side constraints" (278).

Computers, Decisions, and Structures

From an early period Simon was concerned with the influence of computers on organizational decision making and, because decisions are the raison d'être for structure, on organizational design as well. His views appeared in what is essentially the third edition of a book first published in 1960 titled *The New Science of Management Decision* (Simon 1977). In this book Simon described programmed and nonprogrammed decisions and the techniques applicable to each. Simon's views in this regard are contained in Table 3.1.

Basically, Simon (1977) viewed hierarchy as an essential feature of large, complex systems of any kind. Applying this concept to organizations, nonprogrammed decision making is characteristic at the top levels, programmed decision making at the middle level, and the basic work processes, the actual doing, at the bottom level. The same hierarchical structure and subdivision into units is ascribed to computer systems, a natural outgrowth of the decision-making focus involved. "Hierarchy is the adaptive form for finite intelligence to assume in the face of complexity" (Simon 1977, 114). Thus, adding computers to the decision process should not change the essentially hierarchical nature of organizations.

Earlier, Simon (March and Simon 1958) had espoused decentralization to facilitate coping with complex decisions. At this point he said:

Table 3.1

Techniques of Decision Making Utilized in Programmed and Nonprogrammed Approaches

Types of Decisions	Techniques Applicable

Programmed
  Repetitive and routine
  A definite procedure has been worked out
    so that decisions do not have to be handled
    de novo each time they occur
	Traditional
	  1. Habit
	  2. Standard operating procedures
	  3. Organizational structure
	Modern
	  1. Operations research
	  2. Electronic data processing

Nonprogrammed
  Novel, unstructured, and unusually consequential
  No cut-and-dried method for handling the problem
    because it has not arisen before, or because its
    precise nature and structure are elusive and
    complex, or because it is so important that it
    deserves a custom-tailored treatment
	Traditional
	  1. Judgment, intuition, and creativity
	  2. Selection and training of executives
	Modern
	  1. Heuristic problem solving applied to
	    training humans
	  2. Constructing heuristic computer
	    programs

Source: Adapted from Simon (1977, 46 and 48).

In the first twenty years after the Second World War there was a movement toward decentralization in large American business firms. This movement was probably a sound development, but it did not signify that more decentralization at all times and under all circumstances is a good thing. It signified that at a particular time in history, many American firms, which had experienced almost continuous long-term growth and diversification, discovered that they could operate more effectively if they brought together all the activities relating to individual products or groups of similar products and decentralized a great deal of decision making to the departments handling these products or product groups. . . . In the past ten years we have heard less about decentralization. . . . Some of this reversal of trend was produced by second thoughts after the earlier enthusiasm for product-group divisionalization. . . . A second force working toward recentralization of decisions has been the introduction of computers and automation. (Simon 1977, 116)

In short, computers now make it unnecessary to decentralize to handle complex decisions and, combined with operations research techniques, computers tend to foster coordination and planning at superordinate levels—thus centralization. The result is a greater rationalization of the system, perhaps with fewer levels of hierarchy, but with a greater broadening through the addition of staff positions. "For some managers, important satisfactions derived in the past from certain kinds of interpersonal relations with others will be lost. For other managers, important satisfactions from a feeling of the adequacy of their professional skills will be gained" (Simon 1977, 133).

The Role of Expertise and Intuition

More recently Simon's contributions to organizational behavior focused on expert decision making—expert systems, intuitive competence, organizational learning, and the like (Simon 1987, 1991b; Prietula and Simon 1989). These are ideas that came out of his work in cognitive science, artificial intelligence, and computer systems. The goal of much of this work was to create computer systems that can perform expert professional tasks competently.

Simon's thesis was that intuition is really not much different from other problem solving, but it is problem solving embedded in years of experience so that it has become automatic and not easily accessible to consciousness.

> . . . [T]he intuitive skills of managers depend on the same kinds of mechanisms as the intuitive skills of chessmasters or physicians. . . . The experienced manager, too, has in his or her memory a large amount of knowledge, gained from training and experience and organized in terms of recognizable chunks and associated information. (Simon 1987, 61)

This kind of intuition yields competent decisions because of its origins in lengthy learning. It should be contrasted with intuition embedded in stress and emotion, which is much more likely to yield irrationality. Failure of expert intuition may also result from insufficient attention, so that the necessary chunks of knowledge are not built up in memory.

Organizational learning occurs either as a consequence of the learning of existing members or by bringing in new members with new knowledge to contribute. The experts that possess this essential learning include top management, but they may be found anywhere in the organization. Organizational memories are built up out of such learning. To understand organizations it is important to

> . . . explore the contents of important organizational memories, the way in which these contents are accessed (or ignored) in the decision making process, and the ways in which they are acquired by organizations and transmitted from one part of an organization to another. Among the contents of organizational memories perhaps the most important ones are the representations of the organization itself and its goals, for it is this representation (or representations, if it is not uniform throughout the organization) that provides the basis for defining the roles of organization members. (Simon 1991b, 133)

Here it sounds very much like Simon was describing the deciphering of culture.

A further point in this connection is that organizational learning may be lost if key experts leave the organization. One way of protecting against this is the creation of computerized expert systems that contain the problem-solving capabilities of the experts.

The Commentaries

In 1957 Simon updated *Administrative Behavior* via a lengthy introduction; in 1976 he utilized the same approach, but added a set of articles reprinted from his past publications. The approach taken in 1997, however, was to append commentaries, some quite extensive, to the original eleven chapters. Although containing a substantial number of references, the commentaries did not focus on the current status of the field; rather, the references were spread about equally over the five decades of the past fifty years and the discussion was similarly dispersed in time. Thus, much of what was said there has already been considered here. Yet there are some significant additions to theory.

One such addition has to do with the role of authority and structuring—

> . . . people are more creative, and most capable of self-actualizing, when their environment provides them with an appropriate amount of structure, not too much and not too little—

another with the consequences of participation—

> . . . at least two crucial conditions must be satisfied in order for participation to increase production: (1) the basic attitude of the employees to the organization must be sufficiently positive . . . (2) the employees must, through observation or otherwise, have access to information about the manufacturing process. (Simon 1997, 203, 205)

Unless the above conditions are met, employees are unlikely to be either willing or able to increase output.

Simon also devoted considerable discussion to organizational structuring viewed as a decision-making and information-processing system. He suggested dividing an organization not on the basis of the usual departmentation, but according to the principal components into which the decision-making process divides (elsewhere these are said to be setting the agenda, representing the problem, finding alternatives, and selecting alternatives). This is consistent with the constraints of bounded rationality. Beyond this, decision problems should be factored so as to minimize interdependence among components and to conserve attention. It is not division of labor that is important in the modern organization, but factorization of decision making. Thus, one should start by examining the information system and the decisions it supports, quite independent of the existing department structure. Unfortunately, Simon did not move beyond this to give specific normative guidelines for organizational design.

Decision makers acquire a representation of their situation that selects from operative goals that part that reflects the information to which they typically attend. Thus decision makers in one unit, focused on a particular type of information, come to identify with a set of goals and world view that differ sharply from those held by decision makers in other units. Similarly, chief executives from different functional backgrounds may see different things as they face the same problem, and derive different solutions; this is a process of selective perception.

EVALUATION AND IMPACT

For a number of years Simon's research was conducted outside the field of organizational behavior. However, he did engage in organizational behavior research in the early years. As to applications, there has been little explicit emphasis of this kind, consistent with the basically descriptive nature of his theories. Occasionally normative statements did appear in Simon's writings, but rarely to the point of positing a technology for practice. However, the Simon, Smithburg, and Thompson (1950) text in public administration was strongly influenced by Simon's theoretical views regarding the process and role of decision making. *Organizations,* on which Simon and March collaborated, was largely devoid of suggestions for application, consistent with March's (2003) explicit dedication to scholarship for its own sake, independent of its consequences.

Simon's Early Studies

Initially, Simon conducted studies in the field of governmental administration that, though applied in nature, had little relationship to his theories. There were, for instance, analyses of optimal case loads for welfare workers (Simon and Devine 1941) and of the fiscal factors associated with consolidating local governments (Simon 1943). A later study dealt with the organization of the accounting function in seven companies (Simon, Guetzkow, Kozmetsky, and Tyndall 1954). Though the research provides some qualified support for segmentation and decentralization, it does not relate these factors to the need to simplify decision making. In fact, the research appears to have been conducted without reference to theoretical concepts of any kind.

Subsequent studies were more closely related to the theory. A laboratory investigation of behavior in varied communication nets demonstrated the impact of programming differences on problem solving (Guetzkow and Simon 1955). A detailed analysis of the decision processes employed by a company investigating the feasibility of utilizing electronic data processing equipment demonstrated both a tendency to break down the decision into more manageable units and the use of extensive search procedures, which were treated in accordance with the theory of satisficing (Cyert, Simon, and Trow 1956). A study of executives working in different functional areas of a business indicated, as expected, that the executives' departmental identifications exerted considerable influence on the ways they perceived problems (Dearborn and Simon 1958). Though limited by small sample sizes and other considerations, and thus far from conclusive in and of themselves, these studies began to build a structure of support for the theory.

Bounded Rationality and Satisficing

Writing in the third edition of *Administrative Behavior,* Simon (1976) notes:

> In view of the substantial body of evidence now available in support of the concept of bounded rationality, of satisficing, and of the limited rationality of administrative man, I do not regard the description of human rationality . . . as hypothetical but as now having been verified in its main features. (xxxi)

In this connection he mentions a study by Clarkson (1962) described in Cyert and March (1963) and another by Soelberg (1966), as well as research conducted by the theorists themselves. The Clarkson study compared predictions made from a model developed from the Cyert and March (1963) theory with actual portfolio decisions made by a bank trust officer. Insofar as quasi resolution of conflict and uncertainty avoidance are concerned, the model agrees almost perfectly with the theory. Problemistic search and organizational learning are less clearly represented. Yet the decision-making process modeled is, in a sense, simpleminded, constrained in its computations, and adaptively rational. Such a theory-based model comes close to depicting reality.

The Soelberg (1966) study confirms the theory only in part. What emerges from this and other studies is a frequent tendency to search beyond the point of choice, but not with a view to maximizing; rather, the objective is to validate or confirm the choice. Furthermore, there are sizable differences between individuals in the degree to which their decisions approach the maximizing, validating or confirming, and satisficing modes. To the extent evidence is available, goals other than profit appear to influence top-level decisions, and firms in which the rationality is less bounded are more likely to be profitable, in spite of the frequent use of satisficing. Managers are more likely to approximate rationality in their decision making than unskilled and semiskilled workers (Arroba 1978). It seems apparent that bounded rationality and satisficing in one form or another are indeed important aspects of the decision-making process, but that more complex, specific, and probably more normative formulations are needed to improve understanding, prediction, and practice (Bowen and Qiu 1992).

In this vein, Whyte (2000) sets forth a decision-making process in seven steps designed to approximate maximum rationality:

1. Identifying objectives to be achieved by the decision.
2. Generating a comprehensive list of well-developed alternatives.
3. Searching widely for information with which to determine the quality of the alternatives.
4. Engaging in unbiased and accurate processing of all information relevant to the assessment of the alternatives.
5. Reconsidering and reexamining all the pros and cons of the alternatives.
6. Examining the costs, benefits, and risks of the preferred choice.
7. Developing plans to implement the decision, monitor the results, and react in the event that known risks become a reality. (316–17)

Whyte notes a number of conditions that may lead to deviations from such an effective decision-making strategy and thus to a closer approach to satisficing.

Indeed, the tendency for satisficing to arise in a number of different forms has become apparent as bounded rationality has been considered further. Schramm-Nielsen (2001) finds that the preferred approach to decision making among Danish managers is close to the original satisficing concept of administrative man, but that French managers seem to be analytically rational in their search for alternatives while at the same time exhibiting creative irrationality with more use of emotion and impulse at other stages of the decision-making process. Thus there is a clear difference in the time spent at different points in Whyte's (2000) process model.

Sanders and Carpenter (2003) find that, owing partly to cognitive limitations of the kind that typically operate to produce satisficing, managers tend to permit factors to enter into the calculus that otherwise perfectly rational managers would ignore or significantly discount. They document this conclusion with regard to the adoption of stock repurchase plans by companies. Depending on what factors thus enter, however, this process can produce quite variant versions of satisficing. In particular it appears that overconfidence may enter as a substitute for an adequate search for alternatives, with the result that overly risky decisions may be made in certain instances where they are not really warranted (see Lovallo and Kahneman 2003). This process has been found to operate in making decisions with regard to the introduction of new products, for instance (Simon and Houghton 2003).

Inducements and Contributions

The inducements-contributions component of the theory can be derived from a number of theories of organizational behavior, at least as it relates to individual satisfaction, turnover, and performance. There are no comparative studies available that would indicate that the theory, as stated here, is superior. Nevertheless, there are studies that establish some validity for the inducements-contributions formulations (see Staw 1974). Changes, and particularly reductions, in inducements tend to increase turnover and reduce overall contributions.

Research relating this factor to organizational survival is limited. Furthermore, there have been few attempts to identify the confines of the zone of acceptance under specific circumstances. How do variations in inducements actually influence contributions? For whom? When? What kinds of inducements and contributions? The theory as stated is difficult to test because of its broad nature. Specific hypotheses are needed that go beyond the general framework that the theory provides.

Selective Perception

Several studies have been conducted bearing on the Dearborn and Simon (1958) study and the theoretical view that experience in a functional area influences aspects of problem solving. None of these studies completely replicates the Dearborn and Simon research, and, in fact, questions have been raised regarding the interpretation of that particular study as well. The best conclusion available at present, based on studies that seem to deal most effectively with confounding factors, is that functional background does exert an influence on perceptual processes and approaches in problem solving (Beyer, Chattopadhyay, George, Glick, ogilvie, and Pugliese 1997; Waller, Huber, and Glick 1995). However, this influence does not always take the exact form that Simon's theory would anticipate. It does, however, result in a narrowing effect on managerial cognitive processing (Geletkanycz and Black 2001) and it appears to make for an emphasis on division of labor, including specialization, at the expense of interunit coordination, integration, and communication (Heath and Staudenmayer 2000).

Other Research Issues

Figures 3.1 and 3.2 present flow charts depicting relationships among theoretical variables related to turnover and intergroup conflict. These subjects have been and are being researched consistently. The March and Simon formulations have provided a framework for developments in these fields, and much of the work being done builds on this beginning. Theory and research in these areas have now moved well beyond the March and Simon theory, but the influence of that theory is still manifest.

Turning now to the more recent theoretical extensions, the theory as it relates to expertise and intuition has been given a certain amount of research attention. Simon (1987) notes a doctoral dissertation at Carnegie Mellon by Bouwman in which the decision processes of expert financial analysts were computer modeled as the analysts attempted to detect company problems from examination of financial statements. The model was then compared to behavioral results—"a close match is usually found." A second dissertation at Carnegie Mellon by Bhaskar computer modeled the thinking of business students and experienced business managers as they considered a business case. The two groups solved the case about equally well, but the business managers accomplished this result much more rapidly; they identified the key features quickly with the appearance of intuition, while the students engaged in more conscious, explicit analysis.

These results appear to confirm Simon's theory in many of its aspects. However, research carried out by Lomi, Larsen, and Ginsberg (1997), also using computer modeling, raises questions regarding the efficacy of experience in moving toward an optimal solution. Experts may learn from experience, but that does not ensure that the experience will be interpreted correctly. The theory clearly needs to be more explicit as to who will benefit from experience sufficiently to reach expert status and achieve valid intuition; many people apparently do not. Analyses that expand upon the Simon framework in such ways indeed do appear to be underway (Gavetti and Levinthal 2000).

Controversies

In the 1990s certain attacks upon the theory appeared under what might broadly be construed as the postmodernist banner. The first of these (Mumby and Putnam 1992) reinterprets *Administrative Behavior* and the concept of bounded rationality in ways that I am sure Simon would not recognize. In several respects this interpretation is incorrect, and in placing the label of sexism on the author it appears to do an injustice. The presentation is an instance of philosophy with an unabashedly political agenda, not of science or testable theory. A similar article by Kilduff (1993) makes an attack on *Organizations* in much the same vein. The intellectual vendetta is somewhat more muted here than in the previous article, and the claim that the March and Simon theory suffers from some logical inconsistency does have a certain justification, although the issues involved are not central to the theory. Both articles are presented as intended to open debate and raise new considerations and in that spirit it seems important to mention them. However, their contribution to science and to theoretical evaluation is minimal at best.

Against this backdrop I feel it is only just to mention that many others have found the theories involved to be valid and useful—both the satisficing concept (see Koopman and Pool 1990, Winter 2000) and aspects of the *Organizations* theory (see Bowen and Siehl 1997). It is not clear to me why certain people feel compelled to attack this particular theoretical approach on nonscientific grounds. Perhaps this type of attack is an inevitable consequence of developing a widely known and influential theory.

Argyris (1973, 1976) has been a consistent critic of the Carnegie theorizing as a whole for some time. His initial concern, consistent with his own theoretical position (see Chapter 17 in this volume), was that these theorists espoused a traditional, pyramidal organization that did not adequately consider man's self-actualizing and often nonrational nature. He argued that theories of this type, though said to be descriptive, inevitably become normative and incorrectly perpetuate the status quo.

In reply to this attack Simon (1973) cited a number of instances in which Argyris (1973) misrepresented or misinterpreted his views. More important, however, Simon seriously questioned Argyris's essential assumption:

> The charge is not that the theories are wrong, but that, right or wrong, they are anti-revolutionary and reactionary. We are not to describe social phenomena as they are, because describing them legitimizes them, and makes them harder to change. . . . Argyris' argument that we must not describe the world as it is lest we prevent its reform is of a piece with the general antirationalism of the contemporary counter culture. . . . [K]nowledge about the world and about ourselves is better than ignorance. Nothing in human history refutes that belief, or suggests that we can save mankind by halting descriptive research on the rational aspects of human behavior. (Simon 1973, 351)

A balanced view of the theories proposed by Simon and March would be to recognize the fact that considerable research support exists for many of the theoretical propositions, but that certain limitations exist as well. Simon first set out to establish a descriptive framework and a vocabulary for dealing with organizations. He, and March, were highly successful in this endeavor. But the framework is still only a framework; the theory's authors provide few details between the supporting timbers, either through their research or by further theorizing. Descriptive theory can give rise to normative theory, but except for a certain implicit, normative flavor that Argyris detected, this has not happened. The framework appears solid, however, and can serve as a basis for further construction.

CONCLUSIONS

I return to the box at the beginning of this chapter to get an overall assessment of administrative behavior and organizations theory. The importance rating of 5.81 is the second highest of any of the theories included in this book. The theory has been institutionalized, thus reflecting its longstanding legitimacy in providing a framework for organizational behavior thinking and research. The estimated validity of five stars is consistent with these judgments. There are points at which the theory lacks the specificity that in hindsight might appear desirable, but this was a theory that came into being at the same time as organizational behavior was emerging. Clearly it has provided the grounding needed to conduct research as more precise propositions have evolved. No field could have asked for a more valuable send-off than organizational behavior received from the theorizing of Simon and March. This type of accolade applies, however, only to the validity issue; the theory did much less for the development of practice. The two stars given in this latter regard reflect the lack of guidelines for applications and the generally descriptive, rather than normative, nature of the theorizing.

In the following chapters I follow the contributions of March as he developed the ideas found within the *Organizations* book further. March has been one of the truly great theorists of the organizational behavior discipline, and it is fruitful to follow the course of his thinking as it evolved.

REFERENCES

Anderson, John R. (2001). Herbert A. Simon (1916–2001). *American Psychologist,* 56, 516–18.
Argyris, Chris (1973). Some Limits of Rational Man Organizational Theory. *Public Administration Review,* 33, 253–67.
———. (1976). Single-Loop and Double-Loop Models in Research on Decision Making. *Administrative Science Quarterly,* 21, 363–75.
Arroba, Tanya Y. (1978). Decision-Making Style as a Function of Occupational Group, Decision Content and Perceived Importance. *Journal of Occupational Psychology,* 51, 219–26.
Augier, Mie (2001). Simon Says: Bounded Rationality Matters—Introduction and Interview. *Journal of Management Inquiry,* 10, 268–75.
Augier, Mie, and Kreiner, Kristian (2000). An Interview with James G. March. *Journal of Management Inquiry,* 9, 284–97.
Beyer, Janice M., Chattopadhyay, Prithviraj, George, Elizabeth, Glick, William H., ogilvie, dt, and Pugliese, Dulce (1997). The Selective Perception of Managers Revisited. *Academy of Management Journal,* 40, 716–37.
Bowen, David E., and Siehl, Caren (1997). The Future of Human Resource Management: March and Simon (1958) Revisited. *Human Resource Management,* 36(1), 57–63.
Bowen, James, and Qiu, Zi-lei (1992). Satisficing When Buying Information. *Organizational Behavior and Human Decision Processes,* 51, 471–81.
Clarkson, G.P.E. (1962). *Portfolio Selection: A Simulation of Trust Investment.* Englewood Cliffs, NJ: Prentice Hall.
Cyert, Richard M., and March, James G. (1963). *A Behavioral Theory of the Firm.* Englewood Cliffs, NJ: Prentice Hall (1992 reprint, Oxford, UK: Blackwell).
Cyert, Richard M., Simon, Herbert A., and Trow, Donald B. (1956). Observations of a Business Decision. *Journal of Business,* 29, 237–48.
Dearborn, DeWitt C., and Simon, Herbert A. (1958). Selective Perception: A Note on the Departmental Identifications of Executives. *Sociometry,* 21, 140–44.

Gavetti, Giovanni, and Levinthal, Daniel (2000). Looking Forward and Looking Backward: Cognitive and Experiential Search. *Administrative Science Quarterly,* 45, 113–37.

Geletkanycz, Marta A., and Black, Sylvia S. (2001). Bound by the Past? Experience-Based Effects on Commitment to the Status Quo. *Journal of Management,* 27, 3–21.

Guetzkow, Harold, and Simon, Herbert A. (1955). The Impact of Certain Communication Nets upon Organization and Performance in Task-Oriented Groups. *Management Science,* 1, 233–50.

Heath, Chip, and Staudenmayer, Nancy (2000). Coordination Neglect: How Lay Theories of Organizing Complicate Coordination in Organizations. *Research in Organizational Behavior,* 22, 153–91.

Kilduff, Martin (1993). Deconstructing *Organizations. Academy of Management Review,* 18, 13–31.

Koopman, Paul L., and Pool, Jeroen (1990). Decision Making in Organizations. *International Review of Industrial and Organizational Psychology,* 5, 101–48.

Leahey, Thomas H. (2003). Herbert A. Simon—Nobel Prize in Economic Sciences, 1978. *American Psychologist,* 58, 753–55.

Lomi, Alessandro, Larsen, Erik R., and Ginsberg, Ari (1997). Adaptive Learning in Organizations: A System Dynamics-Based Exploration. *Journal of Management,* 23, 561–82.

Lovallo, Don, and Kahneman, Daniel (2003). Delusions of Success—How Optimism Undermines Executives' Decisions. *Harvard Business Review,* 81(7), 57–63.

March, James G. (2003). A Scholar's Quest. *Journal of Management Inquiry,* 12, 205–7.

March, James G., and Simon, Herbert A. (1958). *Organizations.* New York: Wiley (1992 reprint, Oxford, UK: Blackwell).

Miner, John B. (2002). *Organizational Behavior: Foundations, Theories, and Analyses.* New York: Oxford University Press.

Mumby, Dennis K., and Putnam, Linda L. (1992). The Politics of Emotion: A Feminist Reading of Bounded Rationality. *Academy of Management Review,* 17, 465–86.

Prietula, Michael J., and Simon, Herbert A. (1989). The Experts in Your Midst. *Harvard Business Review,* 67(1), 120–24.

Sanders, William G., and Carpenter, Mason A. (2003). Strategic Satisficing? A Behavioral-Agency Theory Perspective on Stock Repurchase Program Announcements. *Academy of Management Journal,* 46, 160–78.

Schramm-Nielsen, Jette (2001). Cultural Dimensions of Decision Making: Denmark and France Compared. *Journal of Managerial Psychology,* 16, 404–23.

Simon, Herbert A. (1943). *Fiscal Aspects of Metropolitan Consolidation.* Berkeley, CA: Bureau of Public Administration, University of California.

———. (1946). The Proverbs of Administration. *Public Administration Review,* 6, 53–57.

———. (1947, 1957a, 1976, 1997). *Administrative Behavior: A Study of Decision-Making Processes in Administrative Organizations.* 1st, 2nd, 3rd, and 4th ed. New York: Free Press.

———. (1957b). *Models of Man: Social and Rational.* New York: Wiley.

———. (1964). On the Concept of Organizational Goals. *Administrative Science Quarterly,* 9, 1–22.

———. (1973). Organization Man: Rational or Self-Actualizing? *Public Administration Review,* 33, 346–53.

———. (1977). *The New Science of Management Decision.* Englewood Cliffs, NJ: Prentice Hall.

———. (1987). Making Management Decisions: The Role of Intuition and Emotion. *Academy of Management Executive,* 1, 57–64.

———. (1991a). *Models of My Life.* New York: Basic Books.

———. (1991b). Bounded Rationality and Organizational Learning. *Organization Science,* 2, 125–34.

Simon, Herbert A., and Devine, William R. (1941). Controlling Human Factors in an Administrative Experiment. *Public Administration Review,* 1, 485–92.

Simon, Herbert A., Guetzkow, Harold, Kozmetsky, George, and Tyndall, Gordon (1954). *Centralization vs. Decentralization in Organizing the Controller's Department.* New York: Controllership Foundation.

Simon, Herbert A., Smithburg, Donald W., and Thompson, Victor A. (1950). *Public Administration.* New York: Knopf.

Simon, Mark, and Houghton, Susan M. (2003). The Relationship Between Overconfidence and the Introduction of Risky Products: Evidence from a Field Study. *Academy of Management Journal,* 46, 139–49.

Soelberg, Peer (1966). Unprogrammed Decision Making. *Academy of Management Proceedings,* 26, 3–16.

Staw, Barry M. (1974). Attitudinal and Behavioral Consequences of Changing a Major Organizational Reward: A Natural Field Experiment. *Journal of Personality and Social Psychology,* 29, 742–51.

Thompson, James D. (1967). *Organizations in Action.* New York: McGraw-Hill.

Waller, Mary J., Huber, George P., and Glick, William H. (1995). Functional Background as a Determinant of Executives' Selective Perception. *Academy of Management Journal,* 38, 943–74.

Whyte, Glen (2000). Make Good Decisions by Effectively Managing the Decision-Making Process. In Edwin A. Locke (Ed.), *Handbook of Principles of Organizational Behavior.* Oxford, UK: Blackwell, 316–30.

Winter, Sidney G. (2000). The Satisficing Principle in Capability Learning. *Strategic Management Journal,* 21, 981–96.

CHAPTER 4

BEHAVIORAL THEORY OF THE FIRM

RICHARD CYERT
JAMES MARCH

Importance rating	★ ★ ★ ★ ★
	Institutionalized
Estimated validity	★ ★ ★ ★
Estimated usefulness	★ ★ ★
Decade of origin	1960s

Simon and March began to go their separate ways in the early 1960s; their views diverged initially on the commitment to rationality and regarding the nature of organizational goals. However, the major disparity was that Simon in large part left organizational behavior for cognitive psychology and computer science, while March remained within the field, although with some return to political science as well, as reflected in two books (March and Olsen 1989, 1995) that contain only limited discussion of aspects of organizational behavior theory.

BACKGROUND

The major features of James March's background have been described previously (see Chapter 3 in this volume). He was hired by Simon at Carnegie right out of his Yale doctorate in political science. But he remained at Carnegie only until 1964, right after the publication of *A Behavioral Theory of the Firm* with Richard Cyert.

In contrast to Simon and March, Cyert remained much more closely associated with Carnegie and with the discipline of economics. After obtaining his doctorate from Columbia, Cyert served both as dean of the graduate school of industrial administration and as president of Carnegie Mellon University. Subsequent to the publication of his book with March, Cyert worked on relating the basic formulations to economic theory per se (Cyert and Hedrick 1972), on using those formulations as a framework for looking at organizational theory (Cyert and MacCrimmon 1968), and on commenting on the field of university administration (Cyert 1975). The result was not so much a further extension of the theory as a placing of its major concepts in perspective. His major focus throughout most of his career was on performing as a university administrator. He died in 1998, eight years after retiring as president of Carnegie Mellon.

March has also collaborated extensively with Johan Olsen, initially professor of political science at the University of Bergen in Norway and more recently research director at Advanced Research on the Europeanization of the Nation-State in Norway as well as professor of political science at the University of Oslo. He obtained his doctorate from the University of Bergen in 1971. As a result of this association and others, March has spent considerable time in scholarly circles in Scandinavia.

THEORETICAL FORMULATIONS

Building on a collaboration begun a number of years before, Cyert and March (1955, 1956) extended their early ideas in various papers and ultimately published the most fully developed version of their theory in *A Behavioral Theory of the Firm* (1963). The theory takes the firm as its basic unit; attempts to predict firm behavior with regard to pricing, output, resource allocation, and the like; and focuses on the actual processes of organizational decision making.

Goal Formation

The firm is viewed as a coalition of managers, workers, stockholders, customers, and others, each with their own goals. The objectives that emerge out of this coalition are determined by bargaining, stabilized by various internal control processes, and adjusted over time in response to environmental change. Within the coalition some members exert greater influence and make greater demands for policy commitments than others. Such commitments, once made, become stabilized in the form of budget allocations, particular divisions of labor, and the like. At the same time, clear, logical conflicts between the demands of different coalition members often remain unresolved in the goal structure. Conflicts may remain unresolved because attention tends to focus sequentially on first one goal and then another, thus skirting the need to deal with incompatibilities.

A coalition is viable, and thus an organization exists, if the payments (inducements), including influence over goals, are adequate to keep coalition members in the organization. These demands of members tend to be roughly correlated with the resources available to the organization, but the correlation is indeed rough:

> Because of these frictions in the mutual adjustment of payments and demands, there is ordinarily a disparity between the resources available to the organization and the payments required to maintain the coalition. This difference between total resources and total necessary

payments is what we have called *organizational slack*. Slack consists in payments to members of the coalition in excess of what is required to maintain the organization. (Cyert and March 1963, 36)

Examples cited are excessively high dividends or wages, unnecessary public services, overstaffing, and the like. Such slack tends to absorb variability in the firm's environment; it increases when the environment is munificent and decreases as the cycle shifts toward barrenness.

Though the goals that emerge out of bargaining within the coalition may vary widely, a limited set is considered sufficient to account for most of the variance. These are classifiable as production goals (with regard to both the smoothing and the level of production), inventory goals, sales goals, market share goals, and profit goals. Goal conflict in these areas is rarely fully resolved. Rather it tends to be suffered through mechanisms such as decentralization of goal attention, sequential attention to various goals, and adjustments in slack.

Expectations and Choice

The concepts of organizational expectations and choice set forth by Cyert and March (1963) closely follow those considered previously. However, the authors provide certain more specific formulations. They develop an executive decision tree model as follows:

1. Forecast competitors' behavior
2. Forecast demand
3. Estimate costs
4. Specify objectives

These four steps are taken in no particular order. When all four are completed, the organization moves to:

5. *Evaluate plan* by examining the results of steps 1–3 to see if at least one alternative meets the objectives of step 4. If one does, the organization immediately moves to step 9.
6. *Reexamine costs* if step 5 does not yield a satisfactory alternative. After reexamination, return to step 5.
7. *Reexamine demand* if step 5 still fails to yield a satisfactory alternative. Again, return to step 5 after the reexamination.
8. *Reexamine objectives,* following the same pattern as that followed in steps 6 and 7. There is a tendency to revise objectives downward as necessary.
9. *Select alternative.*

Such a decision system is viewed as adaptive in the following sense:

1. There exist a number of states of the system. At any point in time the system in some sense "prefers" some of these states to others.
2. There exists an external source of disturbance or shock to the system. These shocks cannot be controlled.
3. There exist a number of decision variables internal to the system. These variables are manipulated according to some decision rules.

4. Each combination of external shocks and decision variables in the system changes the state of the system. Thus, given an existing state, an external shock, and a decision, the next state is determined.
5. Any decision rule that leads to a preferred state at one point in time is more likely to be used in the future than it was in the past. (Cyert and March 1963, 99)

The decision rules or standard operating procedures are both general and specific. Three basic principles appear to govern at the general level—avoid uncertainty, maintain the rules, and use simple rules. At the specific level there are four major types of procedures—task performance rules, continuing records and reports, information-handling rules, and plans. Plans are defined at one and the same time as goals, schedules, theories, and precedents.

These standard operating procedures exert a major impact on decision-making behavior within the firm as follows:

1. *Effects on individual goals within the organization.* The specification of a plan or other rule has a direct effect on the desires and expectations of organizational members.
2. *Effects on individual perceptions of the state of the environment.* Different parts of the organization see different environments, and the environments they see depend on the rules for recording and processing information.
3. *Effects on the range of alternatives considered* by organization members in arriving at operating decisions. The way in which the organization searches for alternatives is substantially a function of the operating rule it has.
4. *Effects on the managerial decision rules used* in the organization. In fact, these rules frequently are specified explicitly. (Cyert and March 1963, 112)

What these theorists have done is develop more fully the idea that various "rules of thumb" are used in reaching decisions when satisficing occurs.

Relational Concepts

Underlying the formulations on organizational goals, expectations, and choice are four major relational concepts: (1) *quasi resolution of conflict,* which involves goals that operate as aspiration-level constraints imposed by the demands of coalition members; (2) *uncertainty avoidance,* which is accomplished by focusing on more predictable short-term environments and short-run feedback or by arranging a negotiated environment; (3) *problemistic search,* which is concerned with engineering a solution to a specific problem—a solution that is motivated, simple-minded to the degree possible, and biased by the prior training, hopes, and conflicting goals of those involved; and (4) *organizational learning,* which results in changes and adaptations in goals, in attention rules, and in search rules. The way these concepts enter into the organizational decision process is outlined in the decision tree of Figure 4.1.

As developed, the theory is essentially descriptive in nature. It attempts to understand and predict what executives do and will do, rather than to state what they should do. To the extent there are normative implications, these appear to have emerged as an afterthought; they have clearly not been the central focus of the theorists' efforts. This is consistent with March's longstanding dedication to knowledge for its own sake as opposed to relevance and solving immediate managerial problems (see Huff 2000, March 2003).

Figure 4.1   **Organizational Decision Process at an Abstract Level**
(Start is at the point of receiving feedback from past decisions)

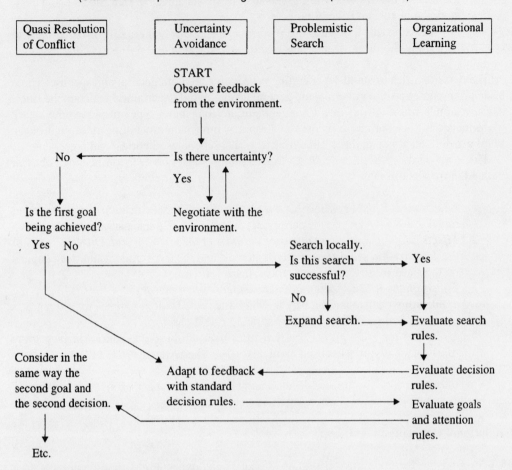

Source: Adapted from Cyert and March (1963, 126).

The Second Edition (1992)

The 1992 edition does not change the main body of the presentation. It does, however, eliminate several chapters dealing with model building and also the appendixes, which are most
immediately relevant for economics. Most importantly, it contains an epilogue devoted to
placing the book in the context of developments since 1963.

In the latter connection, the core ideas of the behavioral theory of the firm are said to be
(1) *bounded rationality* (see Chapter 3 of this volume for details); (2) *imperfect environmental matching,* so that it is important to specify the processes of organizational adaptation; and
(3) *unresolved conflict,* such that the interests of individuals and subgroups are constantly
being renegotiated. How these ideas have infiltrated economic theory and behavioral studies
of organizational decision making are then considered. This treatment, although helpful,
particularly in providing an understanding of how economic theory has developed in the
interim, does not represent an original contribution to theory formulation.

THEORETICAL EXTRAPOLATIONS INTO THE GARBAGE CAN MODEL

March's theorizing has been a continuing process, and although not strictly speaking a part of the behavioral theory of the firm, a number of extrapolations from aspects of that theory have appeared over the years. One such is the garbage can model.

Throughout Simon's writings there runs an implicit normative underpinning that says some type of rationality, to the extent it is possible, is always to be desired (see Chapter 3). In contrast, March has increasingly moved away from such a position. The following statement appears to epitomize his views:

> Interesting people and interesting organizations construct complicated theories of themselves. In order to do this, they need to supplement the technology of reason with a technology of foolishness. Individuals and organizations need ways of doing things for which they have no good reason. Not always. Not usually. But sometimes. They need to act before they think. (March 1973, 423)

From this orientation, the so-called garbage can model of organizational choice emerged (Cohen, March, and Olsen 1972; Cohen and March 1974; March and Olsen 1976).

Organized Anarchies

The garbage can model applies in situations where organized anarchies exist, and the university setting is cited as a prime example of such a context. The characteristics of an organized anarchy are:

1. *Problematic goals*—preferences are ill-defined and inconsistent, and are discovered most frequently through action rather than serving as a basis for action.
2. *Unclear technology*—the organization does not understand its own processes and thus operates from trial and error, learning from accidents of the past, imitation, and the power of necessity.
3. *Fluid participation*—participants change frequently and the amount of attention given to the organization by any one participant can vary significantly.

In such an organization issues tend to have low salience for most participants, being important primarily for symbolic reasons; there is a great deal of inertia; the occasion of a decision provides a garbage can into which all types of problems of current concern may be thrown; choice processes are easily overloaded; and the information base available for search and learning tends to be very limited. Ambiguity permeates not only the goal structure and the understanding of technologies and environments, but also the interpretation of past events, the organization's history, and even the concept of organizational membership.

Organizational Choice

The concept of organizational choice is described as follows:

> Although organizations can often be viewed as vehicles for solving well-defined problems and as structures within which conflict is resolved through bargaining, there are also sets of

procedures through which organizational participants arrive at an interpretation of what they are doing and what they have done while doing it. From this point of view, an organization is a collection of choices looking for problems, issues and feelings looking for decision situations in which they might be aired, solutions looking for issues to which they might be the answer, and decision makers looking for work. . . . A key to understanding the processes within organizations is to view a choice opportunity as a garbage can into which various problems and solutions are dumped by participants. (Cohen and March 1974, 81)

Among the hypotheses proposed are:

1. As the load on the decision system increases, so too does the number of decisions made by flight (problems leaving choices thus making a choice that solves nothing possible) and oversight (choices being activated without being attached to problems, with the result that there is speedy acceptance).
2. Which problems and solutions are attended to in the context of which choices depends on the timing of appearance and who is available at the time to participate.
3. Problems, solutions, and attitudes that are persistently present are attended to more consistently than those that are sporadic.
4. Rules limiting the flow of problems to choices and the flow of participants to choice (controlling who may participate in the decision) change the process and the outcomes.
5. Given the widespread use of flight and oversight, the movement of certain problems to certain choices affects not only the choices to which the problems move, but the choices left alone as well.
6. Problems and solutions are debated to a degree because of the positive rewards associated with participation in the process of debate, rather than with decision outcomes. (See March and Olsen 1976, 174)

The elements of the theory are best understood in the context of a computer simulation (Cohen, March, and Olsen 1972). In this simulation certain factors are fixed—the number of time periods considered, the number of choice opportunities, the number of decision makers involved, the number of problems, and the solution coefficient for each time period. Entry times for choices and problems were varied across time periods using randomly generated sequences. Net energy load on the organization, which was defined as the difference between the participant energy required to solve all problems and the total amount of such energy available to the organization, varied from light to moderate to heavy. The relation between problems and choices (access structure) was established in three ways—(1) any active problem has access to any active choice; (2) important problems have access to many choices, and important choices are accessible to important problems only; (3) access between problems and choices is highly constrained and specialized. A similar structuring process was used to establish the relation between decision makers and choices (the decision structure), and the categories were again unsegmented, hierarchical, and specialized. The distribution of energy among decision makers, reflecting the amount of time spent by each on organizational problems, varied from important people with low energy, through equal energy for all decision makers, to important people with high energy.

When such a simulation is run, certain consistencies appear that might best be considered specific hypotheses for subsequent empirical investigation:

1. Resolution of problems as a style for making decisions is not the most common style, except under conditions where flight is severely restricted (for instance, specialized access) or a few conditions under light load. Decision making by flight and oversight is a major feature of the process in general.
2. The process is quite thoroughly and quite generally sensitive to variations in load. . . . an increase in the net energy load on the system generally increases problem activity, decision-maker activity, decision difficulty, and the uses of flight and oversight.
3. A typical feature of the model is the tendency of decision makers and problems to track each other through choices. . . . Both decision makers and problems tend to move together from choice to choice.
4. There are some important interconnections among three key aspects of the efficiency of the decision processes specified. The first is problem activity . . . a rough measure of the potential for decision conflict. . . . The second aspect is problem latency, the amount of time problems spend activated but not linked to choices. The third aspect is decision time, the persistence of choices. Presumably a good organizational structure would keep both problem activity and problem latency low through rapid problem solution in its choices. In the garbage can process such a result was never observed.
5. The process is frequently sharply interactive. . . . Phenomena are . . . dependent on the particular combination of structures involved. . . . High segmentation of access structure generally produces slow decision time. . . . A specialized access structure, in combination with an unsegmented decision structure, produces quick decisions.
6. Important problems are more likely to be solved than unimportant ones. Problems which appear early are more likely to be resolved than later ones.
7. Important choices are less likely to resolve problems than unimportant choices. Important choices are made-by oversight and flight. Unimportant choices are made by resolution.
8. Although a large proportion of the choices are made, the choice failures that do occur are concentrated among the most important and least important choices. Choices of intermediate importance are virtually always made. (Cohen, March, and Olsen 1972, 9–11)

Organizational Attention

Such concepts as net energy load refer to the matter of participant attention. What happens in a decision situation is strongly dependent on who pays attention to what, and when (March and Olsen 1976). Organizational structures, rules, and role expectations have a lot to do with this process; they serve as constraints on attention, while normally specifying only upper and lower limits for involvement. As with access and decision structures, attention may be organized so that all are affected equally by constraints, on a specialized basis, or on a hierarchical basis. Which attention structure will predominate is a function of the interdependencies of individual and group actions and the distribution of competencies, values, and resources.

Attention is often a consequence of competing demands on an individual's time, and as a result those who end up making a decision tend to be those who have nothing better to do. This is particularly true in unsegmented, permissive attention structures. Since status tends to attach more to the right to attend to a particular decision than to actual participation in it, individuals often compete for the right and then fail to attend. Nevertheless, more than any other factor, attention is predictable from knowledge of standard operating procedures and administrative roles.

Learning Under Ambiguity

The preceding theory of organizational attention contains a number of concepts and variables, but the theoretical relationships are not fully developed. The same may be said of formulations relating to organizational learning (March and Olsen 1976). The major focus of organizational learning is on the individual, and thus all but a few of the formulations are of more relevance for the study of micro organizational behavior than of organizational structure and process.

A primary point is that organizational learning is not necessarily adaptive or a source of wisdom and improved performance under conditions of ambiguity. Learning may well yield myths, fictions, folklore, and illusions rather than improvement. This is because it is not always obvious what happened, or why it happened, or whether what happened is a good thing. Given this ambiguity, learning can get far removed from what rationality would indicate.

Under such circumstances a theory of organizational learning would need to include:

1. Ideas about the ways in which information exposure, organizational memory, and the retrieval of history vary across individuals and subunits.
2. Ideas about how incentives and motivation for various forms of learning operate.
3. Ideas about how preexisting understandings, beliefs, and attitudes may condition learning.
4. Ideas about how the timing, order, and context of information influence the development of beliefs. (March and Olsen 1976, 59–60)

Specific hypotheses at the organizational level regarding such variables are not presented.

Domain Considerations

As originally formulated, the garbage can model applied to decision making in universities, and that was its domain. Gradually this domain expanded, especially into public bureaucracies, although there never has been any claim that all decision making is of this type. There do appear to be many situations outside universities in which garbage can processes exist while still being constrained in some manner by social norms, organizational structures, and networks of connections that restrict the entry of decision makers, problems, choices, and solutions (March 1994). In a hierarchic system, for instance, important decision makers have access to many choices that are not available to less important decision makers. Similar types of access structures can be specified for solutions and problems. After all, the garbage can model is not a system of total disorder; it may only seem so when considered from a standard means-ends perspective (March 1988).

Out of extended exposure to naval operations and personnel, certain limiting propositions bearing on the garbage can model as applied to this context were developed. Similar propositions might be set forth for other domain extensions:

> Proposition 1: In order to accommodate important features of military organizations and situations, garbage can models need to include significant elements of structure that are absent from most discussions of the model in the theoretical literature.

Proposition 2: Although military decision making is rarely, if ever, a pure case of unsegmented garbage can decision making, there are significant garbage can elements even in the most operational decisions.

Proposition 3: Although military decision making cannot be managed effectively by assuming a pure garbage can, significant insights into managerial problems and possibilities can be obtained by combining a more traditional view with some elements of garbage can thinking. (March and Weissinger-Baylon 1986, 4–5)

Another possible extension of the garbage can approach involves participative decision making in groups, which is not a large extension but an important one. March (1994, 166–68) concludes in this regard:

... [P]articipation is very likely to be frustrating ... a natural sequence to be expected is one in which participation first increases the attraction to decision making and then gradually decreases it. ... One person's effects on a decision are lost in the effects of others, and one decision's effects are lost in the general confusions of history. ... [E]xperience is likely to teach that participation is a fraud and a waste.

These hypotheses take a more negative tone than those Simon proposed for participation, but both envisage the real possibility of nil effects.

In concluding his primer on decision making, March (1994) argues for the need to suspend, temporarily at least, the operation of the system of reasoned consistency in an organization. He suggests such things as treating the self as a hypothesis, treating intuition as real, treating hypocrisy as a transition, treating memory as an enemy, and treating experience as a theory. Organizations need both playfulness and consistency and they tend to come down hard on the side of consistency. To get more organizational play, periods of temporary relief from control, coordination, and communication should be introduced.

EVALUATION AND IMPACT

Simon, March, and Cyert all carried out studies related to their theories in the early years, sometimes in collaboration with each other. March continued doing research in organizational behavior long after the others had ceased to do so, but even he moved away from empirical analyses roughly at the point when he became engaged primarily with problems related to organizational learning (see Chapter 5 in this volume).

Research on the Behavioral Theory of the Firm

These studies involving March appear to have contributed primarily to the development of the behavioral theory, rather than to testing it. Throughout the middle and late 1950s March conducted a number of investigations related to group processes and the dynamics of influence (for example, see March 1956), but it was only toward the very end of the decade that he and Cyert began to collaborate on the research that provided an underpinning for their theory.

In one instance, a series of decisions dealing with renovating old equipment, finding new working quarters, selecting a consulting firm, and choosing a data processing system were studied in much the same manner as Cyert, Simon, and Trow (1956) had done. It was found that marginal advantages of alternatives were considered only in the grossest sense, search was carried out in a bargaining context, computations were simple and focused on feasibility considerations, and individual and unit biases permeated the decisions (Cyert, Dill, and March 1958). A subsequent laboratory study substantiated the existence of bias in sales and cost estimates, but found in addition that those obtaining the false information tended to apply a suitable bias discount (Cyert, March, and Starbuck 1961). This finding, that bias may not be a significant factor in overall organizational decisions, as opposed to individual decisions, is not fully congruent with the theory, and the authors noted the need for further study on this point.

Cyert and March (1963) reported on several studies in which their formulations regarding expectation and choice processes were used to develop computer models. The results obtained were then compared with actual empirical data. A duopoly model was used to generate profit figures, which were then compared with longitudinal results reported for American Can Company and Continental Can Company. The fit, though by no means perfect, was reasonably good. This was also true of a model constructed to predict price and output decisions in a department store. Actual decisions were predicted accurately in 88 to 96 percent of the cases, depending on the particular output or price index used. Though the behavioral theory of the firm was not compared with alternative theories in these studies, its predictive power appeared to be considerable.

Working from several case studies, Feldman and March (1981) presented evidence that organizations systematically collect more information than they use in the decision process; they act first and receive requested information later, they solicit reports and do not read them. The authors interpreted this phenomenon as reflecting the symbolic value that information has in portraying a commitment to rational choice.

Research more recently continues to provide support for the Cyert and March theory. A series of studies by Prietula and Watson (2000) on the duopoly model extended the prior research by varying certain factors that had previously been standardized. The results were generally, although not always, consistent with the theory. A problem remains, however, in that once again the "studies" were all simulations. There are empirical tests using organizational data that derive in part from the behavioral theory of the firm formulations (see Greve 2003; Miller and Chen 2004). However, these studies apply to extensions of theory in areas such as innovations and risk taking, which were not central to the Cyert and March (1963) formulations. Considerable room still exists for empirical research focused specifically on the central tenets of the behavioral theory of the firm.

Research in the Garbage Can

March originally viewed educational institutions as the prime examples of organized anarchies, and he has conducted considerable research on educational organizations. Much of this research is tangential to the garbage can model, however, and some is totally unrelated. The original presentation of the model discussed extensively the expected consequences of reduced slack for universities that were rich and poor, small and large (Cohen, March, and Olsen 1972). Specific predictions were made in a computer model for universities in the various categories. The results are interesting and provocative, but they say little about the validity of the theory. In the words of the authors:

The application of the model to this particular situation among American colleges and universities clearly depends upon a large number of assumptions. Other assumptions would lead to other interpretations of the impact of adversity within a garbage can decision process. Nevertheless, the derivations from the model have some face validity as a description of some aspects of recent life in American higher education. (Cohen, March, and Olsen 1972, 15)

Unfortunately, hard data were not available to the authors.

Similarly, March's basic studies of college administrators, though intended to illustrate the garbage can model, fail to prove its validity (Cohen and March 1974; March and Olsen 1976). They simply were not designed for this purpose. On the other hand, certain case studies described by March and Romelaer in the March and Olsen volume deal with decisions such as eliminating a program in speech, transferring a program in architecture, changing a grading system, and introducing a new doctoral field in economics that are clearly understandable within the garbage can framework.

Several investigations by March also touch on the garbage can model without really testing it. Thus a study extending over more than thirty years of the positions held by school superintendents indicates an almost random pattern, with the performance of individuals having practically no significance. This finding is at least consistent with the concept of the nonheroic, somewhat powerless top administrator in organized anarchies (March and March 1977), but it does not deal with why the results occur. In another study, university departments were found to attempt to change their curricula to make them more attractive to students when the university was experiencing financial difficulty, but this effect was less pronounced in departments with greater research reputations (Manns and March 1978). These results say something about coalitions, bargaining power, and the like, but they do not provide direct support for the garbage can model.

Thus, research evidence in support of the theory remains inadequate, awaiting studies by individuals other than March. The following prescription for action in university settings also must be held in abeyance for lack of evidence:

> One of the complications in accomplishing something in a garbage can decision-making process is the tendency for any particular project to become entwined with a variety of other issues simply because those issues exist at the time the project is before the organization. A proposal for curricular reform becomes an arena for a concern for social justice. . . . A proposal for bicycle paths becomes an arena for discussion of sexual inequality. It is pointless to try to react to such problems by attempting to enforce rules of relevance. . . . The appropriate tactical response is to provide garbage cans into which wide varieties of problems can be dumped. The more conspicuous the can, the more garbage it will attract away from other projects. . . . On a grand scale, discussions of overall organizational objectives or overall organizational long-term plans are classic first-quality cans. . . . On a smaller scale, the first item on a meeting agenda is an obvious garbage can. (Cohen and March 1974, 211)

Decisions in Coalitions

The concept of an organization as a coalition in which goals and decision outcomes are determined by bargaining, and slack plays an important role, has been studied primarily through analyses of actual decisions in organizations. One area of study has been budget decisions in universities. Budget allocations to departments have been found to be closely related to power position within the coalition, irrespective of actual departmental needs as reflected in work load, number of faculty, and the like (Pfeffer and Moore 1980). The power of a department was particularly manifest under conditions of scarcity.

Other research indicates that repetitive, programmable decisions in business firms tend to coincide closely with expectations from the Cyert and March (1963) theory. Factors such as multiple goals, constraints, satisficing, uncertainty avoidance, bargaining, standard operating procedures, and rules of thumb were all in evidence in the weekly advertising decisions of a supermarket chain, and these factors tended to operate as the theory would predict (Rados 1972).

On the other hand, to predict top-level strategy decisions that are one of a kind, the Cyert and March (1963) theory, though still applicable, needs considerable elaboration. In a field study of decisions related to investments and acquisitions by a rapidly growing computer firm it was found that sequential bargaining across hierarchical levels played an important role, that uncertainty of outcome tends to elicit a greater number of criteria or goals, and that search may be elicited by factors other than problems, and by opportunities in particular (Carter 1971). The original theory seems to need a greater degree of specification if it is to be applied to strategic decisions.

The important role that slack plays in maintaining coalitions has been documented. Both too much slack and too little can prove detrimental to innovation, however (Nohria and Gulati 1996). Slack does serve to foster more experimentation and thus innovative breakthrough, but it can also produce a lack of discipline over innovative projects to the point where they become nonproductive and fail to be implemented.

Organized Anarchies

Previously in this chapter we have noted case studies of decisions in which observation, interviews, and occasionally records were used to obtain data. In these instances the data collection is characteristically unstandardized, and replication of the research would be difficult, even if exactly the same decision situation could be identified. Such analyses of small numbers of cases are very useful for constructing descriptive theories, but much less useful for testing them. Unfortunately, the research on organized anarchies and the garbage can model tends to be of this kind.

The March and Olsen (1976) volume contains descriptions of a university dean selection decision (by Olsen), a medical school location decision (by Kare Rommetveit), decision making in an experimental free school (by Kristian Kreiner and Soren Christensen), a racial desegregation decision in a school district (by Stephen Weiner), and a university reorganization decision (by Olsen). These decisions are said to be consistent with the garbage can model, and they appear to have much in common with that model, as does the R & D department decision making described by McCaskey (1979). The model unquestionably "rings a bell" when held up against the realities of these decision situations. On the other hand, none of these studies explicitly tests hypotheses derived from the theory.

One study in the March and Olsen volume tests hypotheses based on the theory in a context that could well qualify as organized anarchy. This research (by Per Stava) deals with certain college location decisions in Norway that were inherently political in nature. Various demographic indexes were used to predict where the colleges would be located, and these predictions were then compared with the actual decisions made by the Norwegian parliament. The results are rather surprising:

Our analysis supports legal-bureaucratic theories of political choice. . . . Not power, not interest groups, not voters, but some simple, even sensible, rules come to dominate—without explicit computation. . . . [T]he system pursues a political solution within highly restrictive normative rules of equity. Although, as far as we know, no one in the system calculated anything approximating our weighted distance criterion, the process constrained itself to solutions consistent with such a conception of fairness and need. . . . [O]ur analysis indicates a case for treating decisions as explainable in terms of stable, structural elements in the situation. (Stava, in March and Olsen 1976, 217)

If the context was that of organized anarchy, then the findings do not fit the hypothesized garbage can model.

Since the 1970s there has been considerable study and use of the garbage can concepts, although attention tended to drop off from the 1990s on. There have been several reviews, of which March and Weissinger-Baylon (1986) and Magjuka (1988) are typical. It now seems apparent that the garbage can as originally proposed is atypical in bureaucratic organizations. It tends to be constrained and channeled by structure in numerous respects, including the degree to which participation is fluid; hierarchic positions tend to force participation in certain decisions. There clearly are elements of the garbage can in these contexts as reflected in the three propositions set forth by March and Weissinger-Baylon (1986) for the military, but even these theoretical modifications may overstate the case for deviations from rationality. Heller, Drenth, Koopman, and Rus (1988), for instance, found no support for the garbage can model in their multinational study of decision making in bureaucracies, and they cite additional research to this same effect.

The initial computer simulations advanced when the garbage can idea was proposed left out people in structures and thus were incomplete. Several attempts to remedy this situation have been published, and progress is evident (Masuch and LaPotin 1989). Yet as a method of testing the theory for validity, this approach appears to be inadequate at the present stage of our knowledge; the model has become hugely complex and external validation very difficult.

Evidence from a study of college textbook publishing decisions (Levitt and Nass 1989) indicates also that this complexity may well have been understated. In this study the environment beyond the publishing company, not just company structure, was found to exert an influence on decision processes that were inherently of a garbage can nature. Orderliness was introduced as a function of the actions of competitors, professional characteristics, and customer (university) arrangements.

What emerges from the research is that situations that give every indication of being examples of garbage can decision making often turn out to be much more ordered and rational than they first appeared. The basis for the rationality is by no means self-evident, but with sufficient study it tends to reveal itself. This does not mean necessarily that the garbage can elements are entirely eliminated, but they are reduced. Given this situation it may be best to consider garbage can decision making as an ideal or pure case, appropriate for theoretical analysis, but not often adequate to the task of understanding and predicting the actual outcomes of a decision process without considerable supplementing and restructuring. This is not to say that viewing decisions from a garbage can perspective may not provide useful information. What is needed are data on where, when, how often, and to what extent the garbage can model fits.

Overview

March's emphasis on the value of foolishness in organizational decision making is distinctly at variance with Simon's stress on the intendedly rational (see Chapter 3 in this volume). In fact, foolishness appears to be strongly aligned with Barnard's (see Miner 2002) appeal to intuition, which Simon rejected. Similarly, the organized anarchy view of universities that March propounds does not fit well with the much more rational view that Cyert (1975) came to espouse as a university president. Cyert himself explains the difference in viewpoint as largely temporal, with the organized anarchy concepts applying in times of high slack and his own current views being more descriptive of what happens under low-slack conditions. However, March himself does not propose that slack be used as a contingency variable here and the research on university budgeting only partially supports Cyert's suggestion.

Thus, there is some disparity among the Carnegie theorists. However, Argyris (1976) is consistently critical. He accuses Cohen and March (1974) of Machiavellian tactics, such as the suggestion that garbage cans be created to attract problems away from other projects, and of sanctioning deceit. The charge is that the theory fosters the status quo, though now the status quo is organized anarchy. But to this is added a charge of thwarting openness and trust. To know how the organizational world is and to develop tactics for coping with reality hardly seem to be undesirable scientific goals. In fact we often must understand reality before we can decide whether it should be and can be changed. One must question whether Argyris's criticisms here are consistent with the goals of science as considered in Chapter 1.

Yet, Argyris has continued his attacks more recently. He is concerned about a blindness to double-loop learning (see Chapter 17 in this volume) and a tendency to place core concepts beyond the requirements of empirical falsifiability, as well as a resort to defensive reasoning (Argyris 1996). These concerns are developed at some length; a rebuttal is contained in Miner and Mezias (1996). It appears that March's sin is that he failed to utilize Argyris's variables and terminology, even though he began developing his ideas well before Argyris published on the subject.

Cohen and March (1974) provide a set of rules for operating in a garbage can context. Briefly these rules are: spend time, persist, exchange status for substance, facilitate opposition participation, overload the system, provide garbage cans, manage unobtrusively, and interpret history—guidelines that Argyris considered Machiavellian. These guidelines appear to make sense, given a controlled anarchy. But such face validity, rather than true empirical evidence, suggests caution. No studies have been done where interventions of these kinds have been introduced and the consequences measured. In fact, although it appears that garbage can decision situations do exist, we have no way of measuring the extent of their presence and knowing when these types of interventions might be appropriate.

Argyris's views should be contrasted with a more balanced position, as set forth by Vibert (2004). Here, the behavioral theory of the firm is said to provide "intriguing insight" that has proved helpful in many respects and has exerted influence on subsequent theorizing with regard to firm functioning. Nevertheless, Vibert refers to certain limitations of the theory that have been noted by others. Thus, the effects of the environment external to the firm are largely ignored, the rooting of the model in individual decision processes may fail to reflect the realities of organizational decision making, the role of emotions in reaching decisions is inadequately depicted, and the theory does not address the fact that decisions may not precede all organizational actions (Chakravarthy and White 2001). Others have noted that the theory is also of limited value in predicting the kinds of strategies that firms adopt at certain points in time (Bromiley, Miller, and Rau 2001).

Vibert (2004) himself is critical of the garbage can theory on the grounds that it derives from a computer simulation, it has a limited domain with uncertain boundaries, and it is far from parsimonious. Yet the latter consideration may be justified in view of the complexity that theory attempts to model. Overall, Vibert seems more favorably disposed toward the behavioral theory of the firm than toward its garbage can extrapolation.

CONCLUSIONS

The ratings noted initially for the behavioral theory of the firm are not as high as some might have anticipated. The importance rating, reflecting peer perceptions, at 5.43 is well up on the scale and the data are consistent with the fact that the theory is institutionalized. However, I have similar and separate ratings for the garbage can model and in that instance this figure falls to 4.38 (see Miner 2003). Although clearly respectable, this evaluation of the garbage can work, which is not institutionalized, reflects some concern relative to the behavioral theory and what was evident in Chapter 3.

The estimated validity, at three stars, is lower than might be expected from an institutionalized theory. The problem is that much of the "research" involves case studies of decisions and computer simulations. This needs to be supported by more substantial research on samples of real organizations. There has been some empirical work of this kind, but not enough and not sufficiently focused on key theoretical propositions. In part this appears to be a function of March's exit from the research stage some years ago. The usefulness rating of two stars reflects the lack of normative theorizing, consistent with March's antipathy toward things practical. He has done something on this score with regard to the garbage can model, but with no research to substantiate his recommendations. All in all, the theorizing says little that we can be sure of with regard to how applications might be instituted.

REFERENCES

Argyris, Chris (1976). Single-Loop and Double-Loop Models in Research on Decision Making. *Administrative Science Quarterly,* 21, 363–75.
———. (1996). Unrecognized Defenses of Scholars: Impact on Theory and Research. *Organization Science,* 7, 79–87.
Bromiley, P., Miller, K.D., and Rau, D. (2001). Risk in Strategic Management Research. In Michael A. Hitt, R. Edward Freeman, and J.S. Harrison (Eds.), *The Blackwell Handbook of Strategic Management.* Oxford, UK: Blackwell, 259–88.
Carter, E. Eugene (1971). The Behavioral Theory of the Firm and Top-Level Corporate Decisions. *Administrative Science Quarterly,* 16, 413–28.
Chakravarthy, B.S., and White, R.E. (2001). Strategy Process: Forming, Implementing, and Changing Strategies. In Andrew Pettigrew, Howard Thomas, and R. Whittington (Eds.), *Handbook of Strategy and Management.* London, UK: Sage, 182–205.
Cohen, Michael D., and March, James G. (1974). *Leadership and Ambiguity: The American College President.* New York: McGraw-Hill.
Cohen, Michael D., March, James G., and Olsen, Johan P. (1972). A Garbage Can Model of Organizational Choice. *Administrative Science Quarterly,* 17, 1–25.
Cyert, Richard M. (1975). *The Management of Nonprofit Organizations.* Lexington, MA: D.C. Heath.
Cyert, Richard M., Dill, William R., and March, James G. (1958). The Role of Expectations in Business Decision Making. *Administrative Science Quarterly,* 3, 307–40.

Cyert, Richard M., and Hedrick, Charles L. (1972). Theory of the Firm: Past, Present, and Future: An Interpretation. *Journal of Economic Literature,* 10, 398–412.

Cyert, Richard M., and MacCrimmon, Kenneth R. (1968). Organizations. In Gardner Lindzey and Elliot Aronson (Eds.), *Handbook of Social Psychology.* Reading, MA: Addison-Wesley, 568–611.

Cyert, Richard M., and March, James G. (1955). Organizational Structure and Pricing Behavior in an Oligopolistic Market. *American Economic Review,* 45, 129–39.

———. (1956). Organizational Factors in the Theory of Oligopoly. *Quarterly Journal of Economics,* 70, 44–64.

———. (1963). *A Behavioral Theory of the Firm.* Englewood Cliffs, NJ: Prentice Hall (1992 reprint, Oxford, UK: Blackwell).

Cyert, Richard M., March, James G., and Starbuck, William H. (1961). Two Experiments on Bias and Conflict in Organizational Estimation. *Management Science,* 7, 254–64.

Cyert, Richard M., Simon, Herbert A., and Trow, Donald B. (1956). Observations of a Business Decision. *Journal of Business,* 29, 237–48.

Feldman, Martha S., and March, James G. (1981). Information in Organizations as Signal and Symbol. *Administrative Science Quarterly,* 26, 171–86.

Greve, Henrich R. (2003). A Behavioral Theory of R&D Expenditures and Innovations: Evidence from Shipbuilding. *Academy of Management Journal,* 46, 685–702.

Heller, Frank, Drenth, Pieter, Koopman, Paul, and Rus, Veljko (1988). *Decisions in Organizations: A Three-Country Comparative Study.* London: Sage.

Huff, Anne S. (2000). Citigroup's John Reed and Stanford's James March on Management Research and Practice. *Academy of Management Executive,* 14, 52–64.

Levitt, Barbara, and Nass, Clifford (1989). The Lid on the Garbage Can: Institutional Constraints on Decision Making in the Technical Core of College-Text Publishers. *Administrative Science Quarterly,* 34, 190–207.

Magjuka, Richard (1988). Garbage Can Theory of Organizational Decision Making: A Review. *Research in the Sociology of Organizations,* 6, 225–59.

Manns, Curtis L., and March, James G. (1978). Financial Adversity, Internal Competition, and Curriculum Change in a University. *Administrative Science Quarterly,* 23, 541–52.

March, James C., and March, James G. (1977). Almost Random Careers: The Wisconsin School Superintendency, 1940–72. *Administrative Science Quarterly,* 22, 377–409.

March, James G. (1956). Influence Measurement in Experimental and Semi-Experimental Groups. *Sociometry,* 19, 260–71.

———. (1973). Model Bias in Social Action. *Review of Educational Research,* 42, 413–29.

———. (1988). *Decisions and Organizations.* Oxford, UK: Blackwell.

———. (1994). *A Primer on Decision Making: How Decisions Happen.* New York: Free Press.

———. (2003). A Scholar's Quest. *Journal of Management Inquiry,* 12, 205–7.

March, James G., and Olsen, Johan P. (1976). *Ambiguity and Choice in Organizations.* Bergen, Norway: Universitetsforlaget.

———. (1989). *Rediscovering Institutions: The Organizational Basis of Politics.* New York: Free Press.

———. (1995). *Democratic Governance.* New York: Free Press.

March, James G., and Weissinger-Baylon, Roger (1986). *Ambiguity and Command: Organizational Perspectives on Military Decision Making.* Marshfield, MA: Pitman.

Masuch, Michael, and LaPotin, Perry (1989). Beyond Garbage Cans: An AI Model of Organizational Choice. *Administrative Science Quarterly,* 34, 38–67.

McCaskey, Michael B. (1979). The Management of Ambiguity. *Organizational Dynamics,* 7(4), 31–48.

Miller, Kent, and Chen, Wei-Ru (2004). Variable Organizational Risk Preferences: Tests of the March-Shapira Model. *Academy of Management Journal,* 47, 105–15.

Miner, Anne S., and Mezias, Stephen J. (1996). Ugly Duckling No More: Pasts and Futures of Organizational Learning Research. *Organization Science,* 7, 88–99.

Miner, John B. (2002). *Organizational Behavior: Foundations, Theories, and Analyses.* New York: Oxford University Press.

———. (2003). The Rated Importance, Scientific Validity, and Practical Usefulness of Organizational Behavior Theories: A Quantitative Review. *Academy of Management Learning and Education,* 2, 250–68.

Nohria, Nitin, and Gulati, Ranjay (1996). Is Slack Good or Bad for Innovation? *Academy of Management Journal,* 39, 1245–64.

Pfeffer, Jeffrey, and Moore, William L. (1980). Power in University Budgeting: A Replication and Extension. *Administrative Science Quarterly,* 25, 637–53.

Prietula, Michael J., and Watson, Harry S. (2000). Extending the Cyert-March Duopoly Model: Organizational and Economic Insights. *Organizational Science,* 11, 565–85.

Rados, David L. (1972). Selection and Evaluation of Alternatives in Repetitive Decision Making. *Administrative Science Quarterly,* 17, 196–206.

Vibert, Conor (2004). *Theories of Macro Organizational Behavior: A Handbook of Ideas and Explanations.* Armonk, NY: M.E. Sharpe.

CHAPTER 5

ORGANIZATIONAL LEARNING CONCEPTS

JAMES MARCH

Importance rating	★ ★ ★ ★ ★
Estimated validity	★ ★ (★)
Estimated usefulness	★ (★)
Decade of origin	1980s

Organizational learning is a topic to which March has devoted much of his attention in recent years, primarily in articles scattered throughout the literature, but also in a book (March 1999), which brings together a number of these articles in one place. This pursuit of organizational learning is in fact another extrapolation from his behavioral theory of the firm theorizing (see Chapter 4). However, March's ideas have developed gradually from that early beginning, with a particular acceleration occurring in the late 1980s and thereafter.

BACKGROUND

James March is a familiar figure in these pages by now (see Chapters 3 and 4). In writing on organizational learning he has collaborated with a number of individuals; yet, he has not really joined forces with specific others as he did at an earlier point with Herbert Simon, Richard Cyert, and Johan Olsen. For a timely statement of March's activities and thinking see Augier (2004).

DEVELOPMENT OF THE CONCEPTS OF ORGANIZATIONAL LEARNING

March's previous forays into organizational learning provided little by way of concrete concepts that could provide a basis for research (see Cyert and March 1963). Now, however, his thinking has evolved much more fully.

The Roles of History, Experience, and Memory

Learning occurs in organizations by encoding inferences derived from history into a variety of routines that guide behavior (Levitt and March 1988). These routines can persist even though considerable turnover in personnel occurs; thus, they are organizational, not individual in nature. They can change as a result of further experience, which is viewed as successful. There is a potential problem, however, in that favorable performance with an inferior procedure leads the organization to accumulate even more experience with that procedure while minimizing the amount of experience with a superior procedure, which because of this lack of experience is not learned and used. This is termed a competency trap. In all of this it is important to recognize that history is not guaranteed to have any optimal result or certain destiny (March 1994).

Actually what is learned is determined less by history than by the way history is interpreted, and this can vary in different parts of an organization. These interpretations of history are stored in organizational memory, or at least some of them are. Memory tends to be orderly, but it can be inconsistent and ambiguous too. Furthermore, errors may arise out of the ways in which memory is maintained and accessed. In many respects organizational memory appears to have much the character of organizational culture.

Some organizations, in some manner, learn to learn and some do not. They learn from experience, but this process is confounded by such problems as paucity, redundancy, and complexity inherent in this experience base. Learning does not by any means assure intelligent behavior. Yet history and its lessons as encoded in routines do lead to useful learning of some kinds. Furthermore, as compared with alternatives such as bargaining, learning may do quite well; organizations make mistakes with the alternatives also.

When Experience Is Limited

The preceding discussion deals with generalities. There are not a great many testable hypotheses, although a framework for generating hypotheses is provided. However, there are instances in which March becomes more specific; although again hypotheses may not follow. The case where organizations attempt to learn from history, even though the amount of experience available is quite limited, is one such instance (March, Sproull, and Tamuz 1991).

An approach in these situations is to experience the history available more richly—to look at more aspects of the experience, consider more observations or interpretations, and experience more preferences. A second approach is to expand the experience base by considering near-histories (events that almost happened) and hypothetical histories (events that might have happened given certain reasonable conditions). Both of these approaches are suspect, however, in terms of their reliability and validity. These two criteria can conflict in that the stable, shared knowledge required for reliability can restrict discovering contrary experience of a kind that permits valid learning.

Certainly, many of the ways organizations handle small histories are hard to justify, even though they appear to consistently believe they can do so. In the end we are left with four basic questions that need to be resolved before this belief can be supported:

1. What is the evidential standing of imagination (near and hypothetical histories)?
2. What is the proper process for combining expectations and interrelated, cumulated aspects of rich description into an interpretation of history?

3. What is the proper trade-off between reliability and validity in historical interpretation?
4. What are the relative values of multiple observations of events and multiple interpretations of them? (March, Sproull, and Tamuz 1991, 10–11)

Exploration and Exploitation

Exploration involves learning through experimentation with new approaches—the returns are uncertain, distant, and likely to be negative. Exploitation involves learning through a process of refining and extending existing competencies—the returns are predictable, proximate, and positive. Yet an emphasis on exploitation can compromise competitive position in such a way that finishing near the top is precluded (March 1991a).

Organizations that resort to exploration almost exclusively create the risk that they will run up major costs and gain few benefits; there may be too many undeveloped, unimplemented ideas. But an exclusive reliance on exploitation can lead to being trapped in a status quo that is suboptimal. Clearly, maintaining some type of balance between the two is to be desired, since they compete for scarce resources, and few organizations will be able to afford heavy investments in both directions. Thus, the need for a trade-off that is somehow balanced is hypothesized, although the exact point of balance is not stated, nor is a method for determining it. March (1999) continues to leave these problems unresolved; he says that balance here is a nice word, but a cruel concept, difficult, if not impossible, to define.

Simplification and Specialization

Many of the cognitive limits that restrict rationality also restrict learning. These individual limitations are also joined by those of an organizational nature. Two mechanisms are specified to facilitate learning under such circumstances. One is *simplification,* whereby experience is restricted to the environment in which action occurs. Isolated subunits can be the site of learning, which is impossible when there are several simultaneously interacting units. Thus, buffers around units are created, environments are enacted, and departmental boundaries are created, in order to facilitate learning.

Specialization seeks the same result. Learning tends to focus attention and to narrow down the scope of competence. Thus several different, small learning locales often become substitutes for one another.

These two mechanisms can improve organizational performance, but they can limit performance as well because they tend to mean that both the long run and the larger picture are ignored. They also create a tendency to overlook failures because successes are magnified, thus driving out understanding of the risks of failure.

> As learners settle into these domains in which they have competence and accumulate experience in them, they experience fewer and fewer failures. Insofar, as they generalize that experience to other domains, they are likely to exaggerate considerably the likelihood of success . . . confidence finds confirmation in its own imagination . . . learning is less self-correcting than might be expected. (Levinthal and March 1993, 104)

Learning-Linked Concepts

March has developed a treatment of several other factors in relation to his learning formulations. One of these is risk taking (March 1996, Denrell and March 2001). Here what is important for present purposes is the link to organizational learning, not the more extensive development of risk taking and risk avoidance. Experimental learning is said to favor less risky alternatives, and thus the status quo, when outcomes are positive; this learning disadvantage for risky alternatives is characterized as being substantial. When learning to choose among alternatives with outcomes in the negative zone, risky choices are much more frequent, especially in the short run. Thus risk taking is seen as a function of simple trial-and-error learning, rather than of trait-based preferences, and this may be confirmed by running computer simulations; risk preferences can be interpreted as learned responses that affect risk taking in a systematic way. The basic result, that experiential learning is linked to greater risk avoidance for gains than for losses, emerges as fairly robust in the computer simulations. "When adaptation is slowed, made imprecise, or recalled less reliably, the propensity to engage in risky and new activities is increased" (Denrell and March 2001, 523).

These systematic consequences of learning in the simulations follow from certain assumptions built into the computerized logic. There are sets of assumptions that do not produce these results, and other assumptions have not been applied. We do not know what range of assumptions actually hold in the real world. Thus, March's formulations linking learning to risk must be treated as hypotheses awaiting substantiation from empirical research.

Anther learning-linked concept, and an unlikely one, given March's proclivity for contributing to knowledge for its own sake rather than to practical usefulness (see Huff 2000), is management consulting. Here the idea is that consultants help organizations by pooling the experience that facilitates learning using many organizations (March 1991b). Experiential learning tends to be deficient in that it exaggerates the importance of actual perceived events, relative to what might have happened, and to close the door on experimentation. The role of consultants is to avoid these problems by drawing upon a wider pool of organizational experience, thus permitting the copying of another firm's successful solution.

Also, consultants may contribute by providing new interpretations of experience, thus overcoming some of the deficiencies of firm-specific experiential learning. They provide new interpretive schemas, and new ways of looking at histories and possibilities. "Good consulting . . . becomes useful less by being precisely correct than by being interesting in a way that is not redundant with ordinary knowledge" (March 1991b, 20).

The Dynamics of Rules

Together with two of his doctoral students March has written a small book dealing with how organizations develop rules to enable them to codify learning from experiences of the past so as to deal with similar problems in the future (March, Schulz, and Zhou 2000). Data are presented bearing on the birth, revision, and suspension of rules at Stanford University over a period of almost 100 years. The speculations developed from these data are intended to contribute to both a theory of rules and a theory of organizational change via learning. Thus, the contribution of the book "is primarily hypothesis generation, not hypothesis testing . . . the generalizability of specific results to other organizations is presently unknown" (Pinfield 2002, 229). In many respects the data contribute to a grounded theory centered upon the written rules developed at one university (see Chapter 1).

Rules are defined as explicit or implicit norms, regulations, and expectations that regulate the behavior of individuals and their interactions. Organizational rules are seen as reacting to internal and environmental pressures through learning and problem solving, accumulating the residues from these processes in the form of collections of rules. The higher the density of rules in an area, the lower the birthrate of new rules. The higher the suspension of old rules, the higher the birthrate of new ones. Rule histories exert a strong influence. Thus, the longer a rule regime endures and the later in that regime a particular rule has been revised, the less the chances of rule change. The more a rule has been revised previously, the greater the probability that that rule will be revised again. Changes in organizational size and in specific programs appear to have few effects on either rule births or changes. Although the number of rules increases over time, this increase occurs at a decreasing rate. As attention focuses on a particular area, the rate of rule birth and revision increases.

Many of these processes mirror what happens when organizational learning occurs:

> Organizational learning processes mediate impulses from the environment in various ways. Impulses can be deflected and relayed to other parts of the system (via attention diffusion). They can be absorbed (by existing rules). They can be selected, filtered, or amplified by the structure of attention. They can be integrated with other elements adopted in the past (rule resilience). They encounter more susceptibility when rule regimes are young and less when regimes are mature. External environments are important, but our empirical findings show that the effects of external environments are complicated by the way organizational learning shapes the connection between technical problems and environmental demands, on the one hand, and organizational rule production and change, on the other. (March, Schulz, and Zhou 2000, 195–96)

The primary message emerging from this analysis is one of:

> . . . organizational rules and routines as vital parts of organizational learning. . . . [R]ules play an important role in organizational learning processes because they retain organizational lessons learned in the past. . . . [O]rganizational rules track environmental changes and pressures, but the tracking is imprecise. . . . [T]he major results of the present study are amenable to learning interpretations. (March, Schulz, and Zhou 2000, 198–99)

EVALUATION AND IMPACT

The theory of learning as set forth by March is more extensive than what is covered here, but it is set forth in chunks in different locations at different points in time and often with considerable overlap; I have endeavored to cover the essential elements. March is much more adept at framing problems and unearthing competing tendencies than at establishing hypotheses for experimental test, although he hopes that research will occur. The failure to create hypotheses impacts upon the ease with which research is generated and thus upon the way in which the theory may be evaluated.

The Situation Prior to the Turn of the Century

Organizational learning is defined differently by different authors and occurs in a variety of types (Miller 1996). One result is that the limited research on the topic is spread over a wide range of areas. Argyris's approach is considered in Chapter 17 in this volume, but it has not evoked much research; the same can be said of March's approach. As Miner and Mezias (1996) note "Historically, learning articles have consisted primarily of—

1. general schematic models of organizational learning,

2. field-based qualitative insights, and
3. simulation studies. (95)

There is a "dramatic need for more systematic empirical learning research with special emphasis on longitudinal studies" (94). Expressions of need such as this are to be found throughout the organizational learning literature.

Yet there is good reason to believe that organizational learning has been a "hot topic" for some time, not only among scholars, but for practitioners as well, in spite of the limited empirical base. There has in fact been research on why this has occurred. The antecedents appear to be:

1. the shift in the relative importance of factors of production away from capital toward labor, particularly intellectual labor;
2. the ever more rapid pace of change in the business environment;
3. widespread acceptance of knowledge as a prime source of competitive advantage;
4. the greater demands being placed on all businesses by customers;
5. increasing dissatisfaction, among managers and employees, with the traditional, command-and-control, management paradigm; and
6. the intensely competitive nature of global businesses. (Harvey and Denton 1999, 897)

These forces should eventually lead to research on March's theory, which is arguably the most promising theory of organizational learning currently available. Yet it is sobering that a search of the literature has turned up only one study prior to 2000 focused directly on that theory with acceptable sample size and design—a study primarily in the strategic management domain, dealing with the fate of expansion efforts. The finding with regard to the theory was that "learning is not confined to identifiable points of feedback such as net present value or actual dissolution, but in fact is far more continuous, haphazard, and idiosyncratic" (Pennings, Barkema, and Douma 1994, 635). This relates to the idea that learning can occur even from near decisions and failures.

Research in the 2000s

Things have improved somewhat in the 2000s, although the amount of research focused specifically on March's theorizing remains rather sparse. A major problem is that because March did not present propositions and hypotheses, and did not conduct his own research in the learning area, clear guidelines as to what to test do not exist in the literature. Thus, researchers usually do not indicate that their studies represent a test of the March position, presumably because they are not sure whether this is the case or not.

An example of an instance where this did not occur is McGrath's (2001) study of exploratory learning. She says that her research "offers empirical evidence supportive of March's (1991a) argument. When higher variety is needed, less oversight is valuable. When less variety is needed, more oversight is appropriate. . . . the degree of exploration does indeed, as March (1991a) suggested, matter" (128). These results emerged from an analysis of fifty-six new business development projects.

Yet other research on exploration and exploitation is not as explicit as to its theoretical source, while at the same time giving some general support to the March formulations. Hayward (2002) found evidence that exploration in making acquisitions was associated with the success of the acquisition, but not to the point of extreme exploration (the inverted U hypothesis); exploitation of past approaches did not work as well. Other research on acquisitions (Baum, Li, and Usher 2000), however, concluded that exploitative approaches were more successful. And, under certain circumstances, it appears that exploitation can operate to crowd out exploration (Benner and Tushman 2002). Miller and Shamsie (2001) report a tendency for exploration to predominate in the early years of a Hollywood studio head's tenure (resulting eventually in financial success), followed by a resort to exploitation (resulting eventually in financial decline). These findings clearly add up to considerable support for the exploration-exploitation formulations, but not necessarily for any particular view of the processes involved. There appears to be more complexity here than even March envisioned.

Other pockets of research activity exist. Chuang and Baum (2003) found clear evidence of experimental learning in the naming strategies of nursing home chains. They also found that this learning is often filled with error, but that it is still reactive to failure-induced learning processes. As March indicated, learning is not always a positive factor. Bunderson and Sutcliffe (2003) conducted research on management team learning and determined that teams that place a great deal of emphasis on learning tend to perform less well, at least in the short run; they appear to compromise performance by overemphasizing learning considerations.

Research of a Tangential Nature

Another thrust in recent research has been to test theories that relate to March's concepts of learning, but that are not identical with them. These tests, tangential as they are, still have implications for what March said. A good example is Greve's (2003) book on performance feedback theory, which derives its basic ideas from Cyert and March (1963) and what is said there about organizational learning, but actually gives little attention to learning phenomena per se. Four propositions are set forth, but none of these actually mentions learning. Yet evidence is adduced to support two of these that do bear on March's theorizing:

2. Problemistic search is increased when the organization performs below the aspiration level and decreased when the organization performs above the aspiration level.
3. Managerial preference for financially risky actions is increased when the organization performs below the aspiration level and decreased when the organization performs [above] the aspiration level. (Greve 2003, 58–59)

This, of course, has implications for the learning-linked risk taking that March proposes.

A study of alliances in biotechnology extends the exploration-exploitation formulations as follows:

Hypothesis 1: There exists a system of new product development linking exploration alliances to products on the market with exploration alliances predicting products in development, products in development predicting exploitation alliances, and exploitation alliances predicting products on the market.

Hypothesis 2: The product development path leading from exploration alliances to products on the market is moderated negatively by firm size. (Rothaermel and Deeds 2004, 206, 208)

These hypotheses are confirmed, extending March's theorizing into product development alliances. A similar extension of March's concepts of learning involves an analysis of knowledge flows within an organization, both vertically and horizontally. "[L]earning processes do affect outflows, but . . . some learning processes (those related to collecting new knowledge) mainly affect vertical outflows, while others (those related to combining old knowledge) mainly affect horizontal outflows" (Schulz 2001, 676). Clearly the widespread focus on research in the exploration-exploitation tradition has sparked a considerable expansion of theorizing in that area, provoking research on new topics.

In another study focused on communicating learning results across units and levels, Bontis, Crossan, and Hulland (2002) found that:

1. there is a positive relationship between the stocks of learning at all levels in an organization and its business performance, and
2. the misalignment of stocks and flows in an overall learning system is negatively associated with business performance. (459)

Thus, their results indicate that organizational learning across levels is more relevant for organizational performance than either individual or group learning, but this learning must be fully coordinated.

Research has also been conducted on how and when people learn from imagination and thinking about what might have been—thus, learning from near-histories and hypothetical histories (Morris and Moore 2000). Unfortunately, however, the hypotheses involved and the findings deal with individual learning, not organizational. The results seem to have implications for what March talked about, but they need to be extended to the organizational level.

To test the dynamics of rules, a case analysis of rules imposed over an almost twenty-year period in a German bank considered a set of hypotheses, some of which were derived from the March, Schulz, and Zhou (2000) analysis, using procedures that often differed from those used previously. The six hypotheses specified that *the rate of rule change:*

1. Decreases as rule volume increases.
2. In a specific area will decrease as the area's rule volume increases.
3. Decreases with the age of the rule system.
4. Decreases as the number of previous changes in a rule increases.
5. Decreases as the age of the rule at the beginning of a new version of that same rule increases.
6. Increases as rule size increases. (Beck and Keiser 2003)

Hypotheses 1, 2, and 3 were rejected, hypothesis 4 was sustained, hypothesis 5 had extensive support, and hypothesis 6 was supported. Seemingly, rule histories in different organizations take different paths and reflect different learning histories.

Theories Built on the March Learning Framework

The preceding section considered a number of theories that arose out of the March learning framework, proposed propositions or hypotheses, and were subjected to research tests. The most extensive such treatment is the Greve (2003) theory. However, there are other theories that derive from the March concepts, although the research on them to date is more theory-generating than theory-confirming. The existence of these theories provides testimony as to the current impact of March's theorizing.

One such example is the theory proposing that organizational learning be reformulated as a series of cascading team learning opportunities, thus connecting individual and organizational formulations (Edmondson 2002). This theory arose out of an exploratory analysis of twelve work teams and their learning experiences.

A second example is a theory setting forth "an integrated framework that conceptualizes how exploitation is interlaced with exploration within and between organizations" (Holmqvist 2004, 80), including the key organizational mechanisms involved. The theory derives from a case study of product development projects initiated by a Scandinavian software producer over several years that admittedly has only limited generalizability.

My third example presents the view that improvisation is a special type of learning that represents a form of real time, short-term learning and that has the potential to either enhance or detract from other learning processes (Miner, Bassoff, and Moorman 2001). Organizations are said to be able to develop competencies in generating and deploying improvisational learning. This theory was a product of field observations dealing with new product development activities in two firms and extended prior thinking on organizational improvisation and learning. The authors feel that they have been able to attain some generality, but that further studies of improvisation in a range of firms is needed. I would concur that further theory-conforming work is called for.

Overview

I have held previously, with regard to what is presented in Chapters 3 and 4, that March's theorizing is helpful to scholars, in many instances has empirical support, and provides a solid foundation for the study of organizational decision making, but that a need exists for more extensive research to fill holes in the support and to answer important questions. To a large extent I feel the same about the organizational learning concepts, especially in view of what has happened in the past few years. Prior to the turn of the century, I was much less sanguine and felt that the theory had gravitated to a locale on the theoretical terrain map situated close to organizational culture (Miner 2002). Much that could be said about one approach seemed to apply to the other, and the problems seemed to be similar. Now, with the added research developments, I feel more optimistic, but still have certain concerns related to the culture analogy. There is a tendency to amorphousness about March's theorizing in the learning area that is not helped by the repeated failure to offer propositions, measures, hypotheses, and ground-breaking research.

The emphasis on descriptive theory, rather than normative, continues with the learning concepts, and the state of the available research knowledge, being of such recent origin, is insufficient to justify applications to practice. At best, March's concepts of learning provide practitioners with a way of considering and talking about aspects of their organizational world, especially with regard to new product development.

A review of March's 1999 book, *The Pursuit of Organizational Intelligence,* by Anne Miner (2002) presents an assessment of his learning concepts that is perhaps more favorable than mine, because it emphasizes theory formulation more and research evidence less, but it is a very articulate statement:

March has assembled a coherent volume of prior work that explicates key issues in organizational learning and adaptation, provides insights about theorizing itself, and demonstrates directly what lively theory development looks like. . . . [T]he book offers an opportunity to dip into an ongoing conversation that will almost certainly yield unexpected insights and stimulate important ideas. . . . [S]ome readers see a trace of contrarian spirit in March's work. . . . This volume does include careful explications of the details in the lack of clothes on a variety of emperors. Characteristically, however, these commentaries avoid cynicism and encourages a heroic combination of remaining aware[ness] of our limitations while sustaining passion for our scholarly missions. . . . [T]he papers here do not include theory-testing empirical papers. . . . Even readers who don't agree with March's perspective will find the papers worth revisiting. (174–75)

Later Miner (2002) adds:

The book is one of those slender classics in which a particularly gifted member of our community has stepped back to offer his map of the journey that our field has taken and peers into the future to illuminate where and how we may continue the journey. It is an exceptional read, a stellar reference, and a one-of-a-kind conversation partner for the trip. (178)

Although I would fully support this last quote, I would also note that the first quote recognizes disbelievers and the scarcity of theory-testing research.

CONCLUSIONS

This is one of the few instances in which ratings developed at the end of the prior century need to be updated and changed based on what has happened (namely, the research) more recently. The effects on the importance ratings yield no basis for change, since these are already at the five-star level, with a mean value of 5.20. However, the outburst of research in the period from 2000 on, as against a barren research landscape in the preceding years, appears to justify a rise in the estimated validity rating from two stars to three. This research explosion is still small by most standards, and much of the research is somewhat off target insofar as providing direct tests of the theory per se. Furthermore, it does not always appear to have confirmed March's theorizing completely; in fact, in a number of instances just the opposite appears to be true. Thus, only the three-star rating now seems justified.

With regard to the estimated usefulness criterion, I have also moved the rating up (from one star to two stars) based on the treatment of consulting activities, which, however, is not supported by research, and the research related to product development. I still feel that there is little here for the practitioner due to the lack of normative statements, the theorist's disenchantment with practical applications, and the void in research devoted specifically to matters of usefulness, as well as the uncertain research support for some of the learning concepts.

As we shift next to the theory developed by Karl Weick, we move into what looks to be another world. In fact, decision making is not even the explicit matter of concern. Yet the theory deals with the same domain covered by decision-making theorists and is concerned with many of the same issues.

REFERENCES

Augier, Mie (2004). James March on Education, Leadership, and Don Quixote: Introduction and Interview. *Academy of Management Learning & Education,* 3, 169–77.

Baum, Joel A.C., Li, Stan X., and Usher, John M. (2000). Making the Next Move: How Experiential and Vicarious Learning Shape the Locations of Chain Acquisitions. *Administrative Science Quarterly,* 45, 766–801.

Beck, Nikolaus, and Kieser, Alfred (2003). The Complexity of Rule Systems, Experience and Organizational Learning. *Organization Studies,* 24, 793–814.

Benner, Mary J., and Tushman, Michael (2002). Process Management and Technological Innovation: A Longitudinal Study of the Photography and Paint Industries. *Administrative Science Quarterly,* 47, 676–706.

Bontis, Nick, Crossan, Mary M., and Hulland, John (2002). Managing an Organizational Learning System by Aligning Stocks and Flows. *Journal of Management Studies,* 39, 437–69.

Bunderson, J. Stuart, and Sutcliffe, Kathleen M. (2003). Management Team Learning Orientation and Business Unit Performance. *Journal of Applied Psychology,* 88, 552–60.

Chuang, You-Ta, and Baum, Joel A.C. (2003). It's All in the Name: Failure-Induced Learning by Multiunit Chains. *Administrative Science Quarterly,* 48, 33–59.

Cyert, Richard M., and March, James G. (1963). *A Behavioral Theory of the Firm.* Englewood Cliffs, NJ: Prentice Hall (1992 reprint, Oxford, UK: Blackwell).

Denrell, Jerker, and March, James G. (2001). Adaptation as Information Restriction: The Hot Stove Effect. *Organization Science,* 12, 523–38.

Edmondson, Amy C. (2002). The Local and Variegated Nature of Learning in Organizations: A Group-Level Perspective. *Organization Science,* 13, 128–46.

Greve, Henrich R. (2003). *Organizational Learning from Performance Feedback: A Behavioral Perspective on Innovation and Change.* Cambridge, UK: Cambridge University Press.

Harvey, Charles, and Denton, John (1999). To Come of Age: The Antecedents of Organizational Learning. *Journal of Management Studies,* 36, 897–918.

Hayward, Mathew L. A. (2002). When do Firms Learn from Their Acquisition Experience? Evidence from 1990–1995. *Strategic Management Journal,* 23, 21–39.

Holmqvist, Mikael (2004). Experiential Learning Processes of Exploitation and Exploration Within and Between Organizations: An Empirical Study of Product Development. *Organization Science,* 15, 70–81.

Huff, Anne S. (2000). Citigroup's John Reed and Stanford's James March on Management Research and Practice. *Academy of Management Executive,* 14, 52–64.

Levinthal, Daniel A., and March, James G. (1993). The Myopia of Learning. *Strategic Management Journal,* 14, 95–112.

Levitt, Barbara, and March, James G. (1988). Organizational Learning. *Annual Review of Sociology,* 14, 319–40.

March, James G. (1991a). Exploration and Exploitation in Organizational Learning. *Organization Science,* 2, 71–87.

———. (1991b). Organizational Consultants and Organizational Research. *Journal of Applied Communication Research,* 19, 20–31.

———. (1994). The Evolution of Evolution. In Joel A.C. Baum and Jitendra V. Singh (Eds.), *Evolutionary Dynamics of Organizations.* New York: Oxford University Press, 39–49.

———. (1996). Learning to Be Risk Averse. *Psychological Review,* 103, 309–19.

———. (1999). *The Pursuit of Organizational Intelligence.* Oxford, UK: Blackwell.

March, James G., Schulz, Martin, and Zhou, Xueguang (2000). *The Dynamics of Rules: Change in Written Organizational Codes.* Stanford, CA: Stanford University Press.

March, James G., Sproull, Lee S., and Tamuz, Michal (1991). Learning from Samples of One or Fewer. *Organization Science,* 2, 1–13.

McGrath, Rita G. (2001). Exploratory Learning, Innovative Capacity, and Managerial Oversight. *Academy of Management Journal,* 44, 118–31.

Miller, Danny (1996). A Preliminary Typology of Organizational Learning: Synthesizing the Literature. *Journal of Management,* 22, 485–505.

Miller, Danny, and Shamsie, Jamal (2001). Learning Across the Life Cycle: Experimentation and Performance among the Hollywood Studio Heads. *Strategic Management Journal,* 22, 725–45.

Miner, Anne S. (2002). Review of James G. March's *The Pursuit of Organizational Intelligence*. *Administrative Science Quarterly*, 47, 174–78.

Miner, Anne S., Bassoff, Paula, and Moorman, Christine (2001). Organizational Improvisation and Learning: A Field Study. *Administrative Science Quarterly*, 46, 304–37.

Miner, Anne S., and Mezias, Stephen J. (1996). Ugly Duckling No More: Pasts and Futures of Organizational Learning Research. *Organization Science*, 7, 88–99.

Miner, John B. (2002). *Organizational Behavior: Foundations, Theories, and Analyses*. New York: Oxford University Press.

Morris, Michael W., and Moore, Paul C. (2000). The Lessons We (Don't) Learn: Counterfactual Thinking and Organizational Accountability after a Close Call. *Administrative Science Quarterly*, 45, 737–65.

Pennings, Johannes M., Barkema, Harry, and Douma, Sytse (1994). Organizational Learning and Diversification. *Academy of Management Journal*, 37, 608–40.

Pinfield, Larry (2002). Review of March, Schulz, and Zhou's *The Dynamics of Rules*. *Personnel Psychology*, 55, 227–30.

Rothaermel, Frank T., and Deeds, David L. (2004). Exploration and Exploitation Alliances in Biotechnology: A System of New Product Development. *Strategic Management Journal*, 25, 201–21.

Schulz, Martin (2001). The Uncertain Relevance of Newness: Organizational Learning and Knowledge Flows. *Academy of Management Journal*, 44, 661–81.

ORGANIZING AND SENSEMAKING

KARL WEICK

Importance rating	★ ★ ★ ★ ★
Estimated validity	★ ★
Estimated usefulness	★ (★)
Decade of origin	1960s

Weick's original theorizing appears primarily in three books, although there are important theoretical contributions contained in some of the essays that he has so frequently sprinkled across the journal and book chapter literature of organizational behavior. Many of these essays are reproduced in Weick (2001). The books, however, form the framework through which the theory is presented here. These are the first (Weick 1969) and second (Weick 1979) editions of the *Social Psychology of Organizing* and *Sensemaking in Organizations* (Weick 1995).

BACKGROUND

Born in 1936, Weick did his undergraduate work at Wittenberg College and went on to Ohio State University, where he was strongly influenced by Harold Pepinsky, a counseling psychologist with diverse interests. Although he originally enrolled in the industrial psychology program at Ohio State, he earned a Ph.D. in 1962 in organizational psychology. His early writing out of the doctorate was often concerned with issues related to cognitive dissonance and involved considerable reporting of empirical research.

From Ohio State, Weick went on to Purdue, where he taught industrial psychology. He then moved to the University of Minnesota, where his work turned increasingly toward social psychology, and then finally he obtained his first business school appointment at Cornell in 1972. There he edited *Administrative Science Quarterly* and stayed for the longest stint to that point in his career. In 1984 Weick moved again, to the business school at the University of Texas, and then in 1988 he returned to the Midwest at the University of Michigan, where he has remained since. Increasingly his writing has taken the form of books and essays rather than empirical research. He says he studies "interpretation, sensemaking, equivocality, stress, dissonance, and crises behavior" (Weick 1993a, 312).

These are not subjects that one often finds listed together, and the subject matter is presented in ways that are often difficult to understand. Van Maanen (1995, 135), who admires this work immensely, says "Weick . . . has produced a substantial body of work. It is a body of work I have tried to enter and understand (not always successfully)." Pugh (in Greenwood and Devine 1997), who is much less of an admirer, says—

> In the early 70s there was a conference, and we had Karl Weick over because he was a big name in process in those days. Somehow or other I can't relate to what he has to say. At that time, I said "I don't understand what the second half of the book is about." And he said, "Well I don't think I understand what the second half of the book is about." . . . Karl Weick's paradigm doesn't relate to me, and I don't understand it. It think it's interesting, but the things he talks about are not things that interest me. I'm working in a different paradigm. (207)

Not surprisingly, Weick's name is not to be found in Pugh and Hickson's (1993) *Great Writers on Organizations*. Weick's writing tends to elicit a bimodal distribution on the favorability-unfavorability dimension, and he recognizes that fact. But on any scale rating ease to difficulty of understanding, the opinion is almost unanimous—this is not an easy read. Previously I took an approach similar to Pugh's and did not include Weick's work in my discussions of major theories, in large part because I was not sure I could reflect his ideas correctly. Now, I feel compelled to tackle them, but I do so with some sense of uncertainty. In any event, the reader should be assured that the complexity of Weick's writings is indeed recognized by their author; he merely feels that complexity is required to reflect the realities of organizational life (Coutu 2003).

ORGANIZING THEORY

Weick's *The Social Psychology of Organizing* (1969) seems to have been titled to reflect both its similarity to and differences from a very influential book with much the same name published three years earlier (Katz and Kahn's *The Social Psychology of Organizations*) (see Chapter 9). The disparity in title serves to point up the fact that Weick's focus is indeed on the *process* of organizing. Furthermore, his book is introduced as directed to the student with no prior background in social psychology; this would seem to place an undue burden on the introductory student.

Concepts of Organization

Weick does not place strong emphasis on organizational goals. In fact, according to Weick, organizational actions may well precede goals, and accordingly the goal statements of organizations are essentially retrospective. Weick attributes rationality primarily to small groups, with the result that he finds organizations to be characterized by multiple, often contradictory, rationalities. Groups are the key to understanding organizations. Organizations are to be understood in terms of processes underway, and thus organizing activities; there are regularities in such activities, but structure at a point in time is unimportant.

Organizing involves adapting to an environment that is in fact enacted by interdependent human actors within the organization. This environment is closely tied to whatever enjoys the organizational actor's attention. Organizing focuses on removing uncertainty so that equivocality is reduced and information obtained. Actions come first and provide the content for cognition; thus planning does not control actions, but actions control plans. This type of formulation leaves planning with a very limited role in organizational functioning (and strategy too).

These and other concepts of organization may be summarized as follows:

1. Processes involved in organizing must continually be reaccomplished.
2. Control is a prominent process within organizations, but it is accomplished by relationships, not by people.
3. Goal consensus is not a precondition of order and regularity.
4. Triads are the basic unit of analysis in organization theory.
5. Attentional processes are a crucial determinant of human organizing.
6. Organizations continue to exist only to the degree that they are able to maintain a balance between flexibility and stability (attainment of one is at the expense of the other).
7. Organizing is directed toward removing equivocality from the information environment (the equivocality of processes must match the equivocality of their informational inputs). (Weick 1969, 36–41)

According to Weick, processes are individual behaviors interlocked among people; thus the behaviors of one person become contingent upon those of another. These interlocked behaviors stabilize and are repeated. This regularity is what is called organizational structure, and people try to preserve it as long as it remains rewarding. These interlocked behaviors are the basic elements of organizing; each process within organizing contains sets of interlocked behaviors that can serve to remove a certain amount of equivocality from the information fed to the process.

Processes of Organizing

Weick's organizing processes are derived from theories of sociocultural evolution. These processes are related using the model of Figure 6.1. I will attempt to explain that model. The basic processes are enactment, selection, and retention.

Assuming that actors can modify the ways in which the model unfolds, and thus exert control over at least some aspects, it is not unreasonable to expect that these choice points occur at the output side of the retention process; thus the feedback loops in Figure 6.1. The basic questions are "Knowing what I know now, should I (1) Notice something new? and (2) Act differently?" Nevertheless, rules determine the course of these evolutionary processes; organizing is in fact the set of rules governing the ways in which elements interact to produce predictable outcomes.

Figure 6.1   **Weick's Original Model of Organizing**

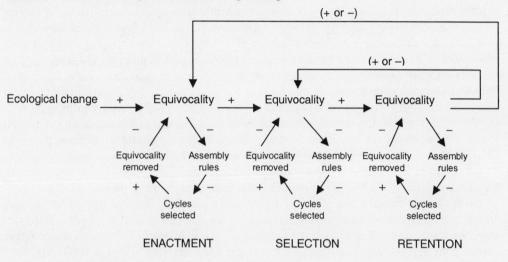

Source: Weick (1969, 93).

With regard to the enacted environment:

1. The creation of meaning is an attentional process, but it is attention to that which has already occurred.
2. Since the attention is directed backward from a specific point in time, . . . whatever is occurring at the moment will influence what the person discovers when he glances backward.
3. Memory processes . . . influence meaning.
4. Only when a response occurs does the stimulus become defined.
   It is these primitive meanings, these bits of enacted information, that constitute the informational input for subsequent processes of selection and retention. (Weick 1969, 65, 69)

These informational inputs derive from collective, not individual, actions. Ecological change sparks collective actions, and ecological change gains its control over organizations in this manner. These actions are the raw material from which the primitive meanings are derived. The selection process then sorts these equivocal outputs from enactment to make them less equivocal. Equivocality is constantly removed as we progress through the model.

The three processes all contain both assembly rules and interlocked behavior cycles. The assembly rules deal with such matters as effort (select cycles that require the least effort), frequency (select cycles that have occurred most often previously), success (select cycles that have worked to remove equivocality), permanence (select cycles that will yield the most stable change), and so on. Ten are listed—these four, plus duration, availability, personnel, relevance, reward, and disturbance. The greater the equivocality operationalized, the fewer the rules activated to compose the process. This is so because when the input is less equivocal more certainty exists and therefore more rules can be activated in assembling a process to deal with this input. The interlocked behavior cycles consist of an action by one person (assembles a set of criteria for application to the input), a response by another person (accepts or rejects assemblage), and a double interact (abandons, revises, or maintains assemblage). When behaviors are thus selected for a process, interpersonal networks are in fact selected and stable interaction patterns activated.

In Figure 6.1, since the equivocality-to-assembly-rules path is inverse, it is given the sign –. The path from assembly rules to behavior cycles is similar, and thus also is designated with a –. The path from the behavior cycles selected to equivocality removal is direct, and thus given the sign + (the more the cycles the more the removal). The equivocality-removed-to-equivocality-remaining path is of course inverse (–). Remaining equivocality is passed along to the next process. The three processes function similarly, but they differ in the kinds of assembly rules operating, and the amount of equivocality in the typical inputs involved.

Returning to the feedback loops, choices may be made that hold largely equivocal or largely unequivocal content in the retention process. "Unless the actor treats retained content as both equivocal and unequivocal, the system in which he is involved will not survive. In order to maintain the balance between stability and flexibility necessary for system survival, he must treat retained content as equivocal in one of his two decisions about future acts or choices, and treat it as unequivocal in the other decision" (Weick 1969, 80). Thus both deviation-amplifying and deviation-counteracting loops are necessary. A system will survive only if an odd number of negative cycles exist.

Based on these statements and the model of Figure 6.1, Weick (1969, 91) sets forth a definition as follows: "Organizing consists of the resolving of equivocality in an enacted environment by means of interlocked behaviors embedded in conditionally related processes." Organizing is thus a matter of information processing. Equivocality must be registered prior to its removal. For registry to occur, the order inherent in the input must match that of the process to which the information is an input. For equivocality to be removed, the order must be greater than that inherent in the input to the process. All this is accomplished within a process by the number of behavior cycles applied, thus removing equivocality, and the number of assembly rules used, thus registering equivocality. In enactment, the interstructured behavior cycles are concerned with doing, acting, and performing. In selection, these cycles are concerned with choosing which among the previous actions should be "repeated, acknowledged, and given the status of beneficial experience" (Weick 1969, 95).

Consequences

In concluding his statement of the theory, Weick (1969) says:

> . . . [T]he basic point here is that once the particular pattern of relationships is specified, predictable consequences should be observed. . . . [O]nce the observer specifies the elements and relationships, he can test, refine, and even refute the ideas mentioned here. Even though the model is general it is still refutable. If a system with an odd number of negative cycles disintegrates, or if a system with an even number of negative cycles survives, then we are wrong. If the relationships not under the control of human actors (i.e., enactment $\xrightarrow{+}$ selection $\xrightarrow{+}$ retention) do not exhibit direct causal ties, then we are wrong. And if any of the other assumed causal relationships are nonexistent, then we are wrong. (96)

Thus the theory is said to be empirically testable. So too are certain hypotheses derived from the theory, such as:

. . . [I]f the actor's performance of an assigned task removes equivocality in the informational inputs he attends to, then productivity and satisfaction should become more closely tied together, and both should be high. (99)

For decision making, the theory implies that past experience and satisficing are much less important than the state of the informational input (its equivocality). For planning, the important factor is the form of reflection produced by the plan, not the form of anticipation.

. . . [A] dyad in which members cooperate should be *less* satisfying than a dyad in which they alternate between cooperation (socialized action) and competition (individual action). (105)

Guidelines for action are also set forth, predicated on some degree of validation of the theory.

1. Don't panic in the face of disorder—disorder is needed to handle equivocality of input.
2. You never do one thing all at once—it takes time for the self-correcting nature of the system to unfold.
3. Chaotic action is preferable to orderly inaction—only action can provide a basis for learning.
4. The most important decisions are often the least apparent—the key decisions are those influencing the feedback loops from retention.
5. You should coordinate processes rather than groups—locate the three organizing processes, determine the direction of their causal ties, and then adjust the linkages to assure an odd number of negative cycles. (Weick 1969, 106–8)

Ten Years Later

The second edition of *The Social Psychology of Organizing* is a much expanded (from 121 pages to 294), grossly reordered version, with many more examples and quotes, and some new content. Things are often worded differently. Organizing, for instance, is now defined as "a consensually validated grammar for reducing equivocality by means of sensible interlocked behaviors" (Weick 1979, 3).

The concept of *cause map* is introduced to describe what goes on in a group discussion. It indicates which events affected which others and the direction of this affect (+ or –). Such a map facilitates determining the number of negative signs involved in interactions and thus whether the odd number required for stability and deviation counteraction is present. The list of possible assembly rules is expanded from the ten noted previously to sixteen (adding uncertainty, obligations, precedent, absorption, enhancement, and mutilation). The sequence within a process set forth in the lower part of Figure 6.1 is changed as follows (Weick 1979, 117):

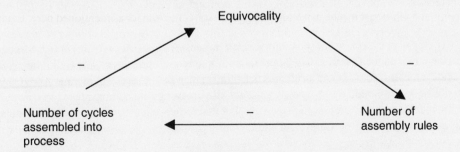

The raw material moving from enactment to selection as its input consists of equivocal enactments and also cause maps of varying equivocality.

Although Weick continues to emphasize process, he does feel it is possible to state where the organization resides.

> The organization consists of plans, recipes, rules, instructions and programs for generating, interpreting, and governing behavior that are jointly managed by two or more people. . . . you look at the contents of the retention process, you identify the dominant assembly rules, you pinpoint the interpersonal cycles that tend to be most salient and incorporated into the largest number of processes, and you try to articulate the cause maps that recur. . . . These several properties constitute the stability, continuity, and repetition that produces the impression of similarity across time in the processes that occur. (Weick 1979, 235)

Yet elsewhere there is a statement to the effect that the complexity of organization can be described only by sets of differential equations, which in turn require measures of the variable elements. Constructing such measures is said to be "next to impossible and probably not worth doing any way" (212). In the second edition, references to testability, refutability, and hypotheses of the kind noted in the first edition (dealing with satisfaction and productivity) have completely disappeared.

Nevertheless, the guidelines for actions are retained and expanded. The first four of these remain the same, but the fifth is replaced by six new guidelines:

5. There is no solution—origins are typically impossible to discover because they are often remote from the symptom.
6. Stamp out utility—when people adapt to one situation they lose resources needed to adapt to other situations in the future.
7. The map is the territory—the cause maps produced do in fact create the territory the organization inhabits.
8. Rechart the organizational chart—do this by replacing people with variables (assertiveness, compliance, delegation, demand for control, rigidity of behavior, and the like).
9. Visualize organizations as evolutionary systems—this has much the quality of the previous fifth guideline.
10. Complicate yourself—for instance, for a period of time discredit all that has been known previously by resort to some procedure such as randomization; thus introducing new equivocality. (Weick 1979, 246–63)

Finally, as part of a much-expanded vocabulary introduced into the theory, Wieck invokes the concept of loose coupling (among enactment, selection, and retention processes for instance). Weick initially introduced this concept several years earlier to describe the operation of educational organizations. There he made the following points:

> . . . [C]oncepts such as loose coupling serve as sensitizing devices. . . . to notice and question things that had previously been taken for granted . . . preoccupation with rationalized, tidy, efficient, coordinated structures has blinded many . . . to some of the attractive properties of less rationalized . . . events. . . . By loose coupling, the author intends to convey the image that coupled events are responsive, but that each event also preserves its own identity and some evidence of its physical and logical separateness. . . . Loose coupling also carries connotations of impermanence, dissolvability, and tacitness. (Weick 1976, 2–3)

For a number of reasons, Weick clearly favors loose coupling of organizational elements and processes; innovation tends to be fostered.

SENSEMAKING THEORY

Weick did not present a third version of his organizing theory, but in several essays during the 1980s and early 1990s he elucidates on earlier statements. One such essay is a discussion of enactment as it occurs under crisis conditions (ecological change) (Weick 1988). Here enactment is described as a process in which "First, portions of the field of experience are bracketed and singled out for closer attention on the basis of preconceptions. Second, people act within the context of these bracketed elements, under the guidance of preconceptions, and often shape these elements in the direction of preconceptions" (307). Because actions tend to be somewhat further along than understanding of these actions, crises may be intensified before a person knows what they are doing. Loose coupling can help here. So too can improvisation, which can correct blind spots inherent in an existing design (Weick 1993b).

One of these interim essays seems to question previously stated theory (Daft and Weick 1984) and consequently introduces certain logical inconsistencies. The model proposed sets forth enacting, discovering, undirected viewing, and conditioned viewing as top management interpretation modes. Thus, enactment is downplayed at the expense of three other processes given equal billing. Furthermore, strategy formulation and decision making, formerly relegated to subsidiary status, are now placed center stage. It is not clear whether this formulation represents a new theory intended to replace parts of organizing theory, or an aberration occasioned by the particular joint authorship involved. In any event, the next book (Weick 1995) does not restate organizing theory, but rather sets forth a new but related perspective.

Properties of Sensemaking

The book *Sensemaking in Organizations* may be viewed as one long (200 page) response to the sentence-completion stem "Sensemaking is . . ." The process is first described in terms of seven characteristics:

1. Grounded in identity construction—and thus in the creation of individual and organizational identity.
2. Retrospective—in the same manner as enactment.
3. Enactive of sensible environments—as with enactment.
4. Social—basically a social, not individual, process embedded in conversation, group discussions, and the like.
5. Ongoing—based on continued bracketing and segmenting of moments in the flow of life.
6. Focused on and by extracted cues—these cues from the environment are both the targets and the grist of the process.
7. Driven by plausibility rather than accuracy—based on reasonable explanations of what might be happening. (Weick 1995, 18–61)

Three quotes from Weick (1995) may help to set the scene:

> The dominance of retrospect in sensemaking is a major reason why students of sensemaking find forecasting, contingency planning, strategic planning, and other magical probes into the future wasteful and misleading if they are decoupled from reflective action and history. (30)

Once people begin to act (enactment), they generate outcomes (cues) in some context (social), and this helps them discover (retrospect) what is occurring (ongoing), what needs to be explained (plausibility), and what should be done next (identity enhancement). (55)

If accuracy is nice but not necessary in sensemaking, then what is necessary? The answer is, something that preserves plausibility and coherence, something that is reasonable and memorable, something that embodies past experience and expectations, something that resonates with other people, something that can be constructed retrospectively but also can be used prospectively, something that captures both feeling and thought, something that allows for embellishment to fit current oddities, something that is fun to construct. In short . . . a good story. . . . sensemaking is about plausibility, coherence, and reasonableness. (60–61)

Sensemaking in Organizations

Much of Weick's discussion of sensemaking is generic in that it applies well beyond the bounds of organizational behavior. However, he does speak at times to organizational issues specifically. In this connection he marshals support from some fifty-five sources in the literature of organizations extending back to Roethlisberger and Dickson, Barnard, and Weber, as well as March and Simon.

Both organizing and sensemaking are of the same nature in that they are concerned with imposing order, counteracting deviations, simplifying, and connecting. Organizational forms represent bridging operations between "the intersubjective and the generically intersubjective" (Weick 1995, 73). These bridging operations form a common ground between organizing and sensemaking. Furthermore, organizations must retain certain common meanings and joint understandings as people come and go. If this capability for mutually reinforcing interpretation disappears as people are replaced, then neither organization nor sensemaking can be maintained.

Using concepts such as these, Weick (1995) develops "a common core that enables us to represent the setting in which organizational sensemaking occurs" (75). Steps toward a picture of the common core would include the following:

1. A basic focus of organizing is the question, how does action become coordinated in the world of multiple realities?
2. One answer to this question lies in a social form that generates vivid, unique, intersubjective understandings that can be picked up and enlarged by people who did not participate in the original construction.
3. There is always some loss of understanding when the intersubjective is translated into the generic. The function of organizational forms is to manage this loss by keeping it small and allowing it to be renegotiated.
4. To manage a transition is to manage the tension that often results when people try to reconcile the innovation inherent in intersubjectivity with the control inherent in generic subjectivity. Organizational forms represent bridging operations that attempt this reconciliation on an ongoing basis.
5. Reconciliation is accomplished by such things as interlocking routines and habituated action patterns, both of which have their origin in dyadic interaction.
6. And finally, the social forms of organization consist basically of patterned activity developed and maintained through continuous communication activity, during which participants evolve equivalent understandings around issues of common interest. (75)

What Weick is doing here is providing a bridge that was previously lacking between the small-group level and the organization. Yet there is no restatement of organizing theory to make this contribution clear.

With regard to organizational forms, Weick posits that they tend to be devised starting at the bottom of the hierarchy and working upward. The result is a potentially incoherent assortment of issues that is supposed to be managed at the top because of the great diversity that exists at the bottom. Making sense of this ambiguity may well be beyond human capability. Accordingly "the best organizational design is to do away with the top-management team. Because the organization makes sense, literally and figuratively, at the bottom, that is all the design that is necessary" (117). This would appear to represent a degree of loose coupling well beyond anything envisaged previously; it also puts an end to hierarchy. Toward the end of his 1995 book Weick comes out strongly for movement away from hierarchy to horizontal structuring; generic subjectivity becomes meaningless in a system of unit change and flux, and intersubjective sensemaking becomes the defining property of organizations. Thus, Weick both specifies the procedures for generic subjectivity (as reflected in processes of arguing, expecting, committing, and manipulating that define roles and produce premises for action) and questions the need for generic subjectivity in organizations of the future.

Guidelines for practice emerging out of the extended definition of sensemaking are as follows:

1. Talk the walk—walking (action) sets the means for finding things worth talking about.
2. Every manager an author—the words that are chosen make a big difference.
3. Every manager a historian—any decision maker is only as good as the memory that can be brought to bear and the history that can be constructed retrospectively.
4. Meetings make sense—they are the main place where sensemaking occurs.
5. Stamp in verbs—verbs, not nouns, capture action and thus establish the path for sensemaking.
6. Encourage shared experience—stories about shared experience engage culture.
7. Expectations are real—expectations provide filters and guidance for the actions that permit sensemaking. (Weick 1995, 182–91)

Research on Sensemaking?

A reviewer who read an early draft of the 1995 book is quoted by Weick as being surprised by the lack of empirical, quantitative research invoked in support of the theory. The clear implication is that such research is needed to test these ideas. Weick's reply is typically equivocal, but he does note that "close to 50% of the items in the reference list are qualitative empirical studies" (169). He argues that sensemaking is best understood using methodologies such as naturalistic inquiry, grounded theory, critical incidents, case scenarios, dialectical analysis, field observations, laboratory study, and participative observation. An example of a study of this kind described as using iterative grounded theory as its research method is presented in Orton (2000).

The emphasis in these approaches is on the qualitative, although certain of these methodologies may be cast to provide quantitative tests of theory as well. Weick emphasizes characteristics such as preserving action that is situated in context, de-emphasizing researcher-specified measures, observing close in and not from the armchair, participants defining the work environment, de-emphasizing hypotheses, testing against common sense rather than a priori theories, subordinating precision and replicability to vividness of meaning, examining a small number of cases in detail, choosing settings less for representativeness than for access to phenomena, and dealing with meanings rather than frequency counts. These are the mind-sets for methodology associated with the study of sensemaking. There is no definite specification as to whether they are intended to generate theory or to test it, but the implication is that both are being invoked. If so, this is distinctly at variance with the position set forth in Chapter 1 of this book.

The Theory Post-1995

Weick has continued to produce essays since the sensemaking book, but with no specific pattern of focus. In Weick and Westley (1996) the fact that organizing creates opportunities for learning is stressed. What is learned are intersubjective meanings embedded in a culture. Thus learning and organizations conceptualized as cultures are closely related.

In Weick (1998) there is a further development of prior statements on the value of organizational improvisation, as modeled after jazz improvisation. Improvisation is a response to an inability to plan, and can be a major source of innovation. Yet it produces surprises and that can represent a problem. Thus improvisation can be both a benefit and a liability for organizations. It does appear, however, to be close to the root process in organizing. This particular essay seems to be more a matter of thinking out loud than of true theory formulation. It is best understood as pretheory in nature, what is often referred to by a title containing "Toward a Theory of . . ."

In Weick, Sutcliffe, and Obstfeld (1999) an argument is set forth to the effect that high-reliability organizations, which must constantly cope with the potential for devastating error, can provide a model for mainstream organizations, especially those emphasizing quality, or resorting to major decentralizations, or engaged in considerable outsourcing, or participating in interorganizational networks, or driven to minimize slack in their operations—in short a very large number of organizations. A model for such high-reliability organization is (see Weick, Sutcliffe, and Obstfeld 1999, 91).

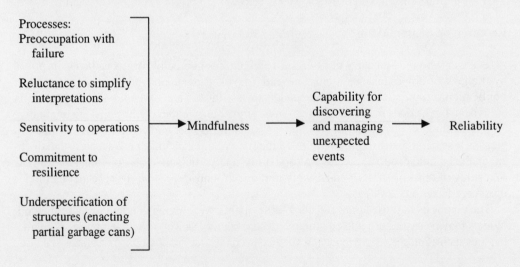

People invoke structures to justify prior commitments; they then use these structures to produce some order out of what was previously very similar to a decision garbage can (see Chapter 4) (see Weick 1993d).

The key concept here is *mindfulness,* which is "as much about the quality of attention as it is about the conservation of attention. It is as much about what people do with what they notice as it is about the activity of noticing itself. Mindfulness involves interpretive work directed at weak signals, differentiation of received wisdom, and reframing, all of which can enlarge what is known about what was noticed" (Weick, Sutcliffe, and Obstfeld 1999, 89–90).

Notice that all of these essays in the latter 1990s are related primarily to aspects of organizing, not sensemaking per se, although aspects of the sensemaking vocabulary may be introduced. This thrust continues to the present, with a piece on how architecture infuses organizational design practices (Weick 2003a).

A book by Weick and Sutcliffe (2001) presents the high-reliability organization arguments in expanded form. Among the five processes of mindfulness one change is introduced, however—deference to expertise is substituted for underspecification of structures. A number of cases are presented to exemplify managing the unexpected following Weick's usual practice.

Application

This same book (Weick and Sutcliffe 2001) contains recommendations and guidelines for using the theory to achieve mindfulness and high reliability in ongoing organizations. This concern with application is not entirely new in Weick's writings, but phenomena of this kind are not often discussed. For an example of the application to practice of sensemaking theory, see the nineteen implications for administration given in Weick (1985). These latter are typically imprecise, however, and take such forms as "be patient," "anticipations matter," and "be willing to leap before you look."

In contrast, the Weick and Sutcliffe (2001) normative theorizing is much more specific. An audit for determining how mindful an organization is contains questionnaire items dealing with the following:

1. A starting point for your firm's mindfulness (eight items).
2. Assessing your firm's vulnerability to mindfulness (twelve items).
3. Assessing your firm's tendency toward doubt, inquiry, and updating (nine items).
4. Assessing where mindfulness is most required (nine items).
5. Assessing your firm's preoccupation with failure (nine items).
6. Assessing your firm's reluctance to simplify (twelve items).
7. Assessing your firm's sensitivity to operations (eight items).
8. Assessing your firm's commitment to resilience (ten items).
9. Assessing the deference to expertise in your firm (eight items). (90, 95–96, 100, 102, 104, 106, 108, 110)

Responses to these items may be scored and guidelines for interpreting these scores are provided. Unfortunately, however, no data are given, and no evidence as to the validity of such an audit is addressed.

The concept of safety culture is then invoked with the objective of creating organizational mindfulness. Guidelines for achieving a safety culture are noted—fifteen in all—yet once again these tend to be imprecise: "stalk the anomalous," "don't underestimate the power of social influence," "act your way into new values," "crystallize the culture in symbols," "think safety first," and "arm yourself for guerilla warfare" (139–46). Certainly what is involved here is an attempt to make the theory useful. Yet the only data actually brought to bear to establish that the guidelines do in fact accomplish what they are intended to accomplish derive from the descriptions and plausible interpretations of a number of cases. We do not know how selective the case descriptions are and how valid the interpretations are. No basis for generalization is provided. This is much more journalism than science.

A subsequent argument for mindfulness, presented from a quite different perspective, does nothing to overcome this problem (Weick 2003c).

EVALUATION AND IMPACT

It should be evident that Weick's commitment to the testing of his theories via the usual scientific approaches has waned over the years, to the point where a legitimate question can be raised as to whether he is writing untestable philosophy or testable scientific theory. He himself would probably opt for the latter, but with the proviso that something other than the usual scientific approaches should be applied. In actual fact he has moved increasingly closer to the philosophy of postmodernism and its methods of confirmation. All this is something at which we need to take a close look. The journey from solid scientific research on cognitive dissonance to postmodernistic philosophy is not easily explained (see Weick 2004).

Weick's Own Evidence

Bougon, Weick, and Binkhorst (1977) report on a quantitative study of cause maps generated by the nineteen members of the Utrecht Jazz Orchestra. This study involves measurement and ranking of variables, cross-validation of results in a holdout sample, regression analysis, and significance tests. The findings are consistent with certain statements from organizing theory to the effect that the structure of causality among variables (the pattern of relations), rather than variable content, determines the fate of the system and that what ties thought together among members ties the organization together. Cause maps generated by members are useful means of studying these phenomena, and rankings of variables provided by these maps explain a sizable amount of participants' perceived influence over the variables. This is a solid and ingenious beginning toward the unraveling of the empirical basis for organizing theory. Measures of theoretical variables are in fact constructed from the cause maps. A subsequent article puts more flesh on these bones, and develops the idea of cause maps further (Weick and Bougon 1986). Cognitive mapping along these lines can be a highly useful technique (see Clarke and Mackaness 2001).

Yet this is where, for all practical purposes, the research program ended. Subsequently Weick moved to qualitative case data, consistent with his prescriptions in Weick (1995), which were often data provided by other authors and sources of a kind that may be suspect (see Brown 2004). One instance is an analysis of the airplane collision that occurred on the runway at Tenerife airport. In this paper Weick (1990) appears to be not so much testing theory as groping toward the creation of theory. Another instance involves an analysis of the process of operating nuclear-powered Navy aircraft carriers (Weick and Roberts 1993). Here the data are used to provide examples for the development of theoretical constructs such as collective mind and heedful interrelating. In Weick (1993c) the case of a group of firefighters who parachuted into a remote area in an attempt to control a forest fire, and in a number of instances died as a result, is interpreted according to organizing theory. Yet this interpretation is no more compelling than those that might have been derived from other, competing theories. There is no actual test of Weick's theory involved. This whole process is relived in a recent case history of the Bristol Royal Infirmary pediatric cardiac surgery program in England, a program that suffered from an excessive death rate (Weick 2003b).

In essays of these kinds Weick presents a story interwoven with theory that is driven by plausibility, but not necessarily by accuracy. On the latter score we simply do not have the data to reach a determination. Weick wants us to accept his explanations, and what he says makes sense, but that is the end of it. Other possible explanations are not considered, and certainly none is ruled out. A common practice is to actually use the case information to move on to further theory development, leaving the matter of testing the prior theory completely up in the air. Weick emerges as an inveterate theorizer who cannot resist a theorizing opportunity; constructing theory is what he finds interesting, and he is creative in what he does. The cases provide an ideal incubator for his skill, and this is an entirely appropriate use of this material. However, the Weick of the past twenty-five years or so appears very unlikely to return to the mundane matter of empirical testing that characterized his earlier years. He is now hooked on theorizing, if not on philosophizing.

Some idea of how he goes about this process is provided by an analysis of Weick's work carried out by Lundberg (1999). This analysis is titled to indicate how Weick approaches the selection of *research* topics, but in actual fact, since there has been no real research recently, it deals with setting agendas for theorizing. What Weick appears to do is utilize one or more of six approaches:

1. Notice an anomaly, and try to explain it.
2. Notice the level of analysis that dominates the explanation of something, and try an explanation at another level.
3. Notice (or create) language that may enrich explanation and explore it.
4. Notice common or simple activities or things and exploit them as metaphors.
5. Notice the context of an explanation, and apply the explanation to another context.
6. Notice commonly accepted knowledge or practices, and pursue possible counterintuitive explanations. (34–37)

This is how Weick engages his very considerable creative capabilities.

Evidence Adduced by Others

Weick's writings contain frequent citations to a wide range of literatures, but these sources do not necessarily contain research evidence in direct support of the point being made. In fact an extensive search reveals no studies conducted by others that indicate that a direct test of hypotheses derived from Weick's theories has been carried out, and the theory confirmed, in whole or in part. This is presumably because of difficulties in understanding and interpreting what Weick has written, and in measuring his variables. Ambiguity, whatever its other benefits may be, does not attract scientific research.

However, Weick's theories are frequently cited by others, and it may prove useful to understand how this occurs. One type of instance involves a research study that deals with a related topic (such as relationships between cognition and action), but does not directly test

Weick in this regard. At the same time Weick's concepts are invoked, and research focused on them is urged (see, for example, Thomas, Clark, and Gioia 1993). This approach, which makes use of Weick's ideas not to generate research hypotheses but to aid in the interpretation of results, is found not only prior to the sensemaking volume but afterwards as well (Gioia and Thomas 1996). Tangential research of this kind related to Weick's constructs deals with such matters as loose coupling (Beekun and Glick 2001), cause mapping of planned organizational change (Weber and Manning 2001), and decision making in complex organizations (Sutcliffe and McNamara 2001). Findings from these studies sometimes are, and sometimes are *not,* consistent with Weick's theorizing. On occasion this research is somewhat flawed as well.

Another approach is to publish a review or analysis that attests to the tenability of some position Weick has taken, even though no clear empirical evidence or compelling argument is provided. Thus a construct may be promoted, or a way of approaching a problem. An example is the Sandelands and Stablein (1987) piece, which argues for the potential value of the concept of organizational mind (mindfulness), an essay that Weick then used subsequently to support his development of related theory.

Theorizing Built on Weick's Constructs

Some theorists have utilized Weick's constructs as a major input to the expounding of some new theory that goes well beyond what Weick said, and often takes a completely new direction as well. Such approaches include a view of entrepreneurship that builds upon organizing theory (Hill and Levenhagen 1995), a theory of creativity in organizations that draws from both the organizing and the sensemaking theories (Drazin, Glynn, and Kazanjian 1999), and a theory of organizational technology implementation that takes its lead primarily from sensemaking theory (Griffith 1999).

In recent years this approach has accelerated. Weick's constructs may not operate to provoke research, but they certainly have contributed to a great deal of theory development. The sensemaking formulations appear to have been particularly attractive in this regard. The mindfulness construct is used to explain decisions by managers in the face of bandwagons (Fiol and O'Connor 2003). Weick's view of disaster dynamics is treated and expanded upon in Rudolph and Repenning (2002). Carroll, Rudolph, and Hatakenaka (2002) deal with learning processes in high-hazard organizations, and reach some conclusions that differ from Weick's. Departures are also evident in a theory put forth by one of Weick's former co-authors (Roberts and Bea 2001) in the high-hazard organization context. Other such embellishments on Weick's sensemaking constructs could be noted, but these should be sufficient.

Utilization of the organizing constructs is less extensive, but it does exist. Thus, Kamoche, Cunha, and Cunha (2003) develop an extrapolation from Weick's jazz metaphor for improvisation, and Tsoukas and Chia (2002) extend his views on organizational change. All in all, Weick's writings extending over many years have continually stimulated theorists to think further; one could only hope that they might have had the same impact on researchers.

Overview

Weick's writings have been described as insightful, innovative, artsy, having the character of montage, lacking sharp definition, possessing an unsettling order, devoid of descriptive certainty, and failing to provide detachable conclusions (Van Maanen 1995). The "unusual phrases, labels, titles, reversals, sweeps and swoops of wordplay [suggest] something of a protest and an example of how to break from the frozen technical writing codes" (139). Certainly Weick does not make it easy for the researcher to formulate a study to determine the validity of what he is saying. At times there appears to be a deliberate effort to thwart research on the ideas presented. For some, all this is frustrating and thoughtless; for others it reflects genius at work. I have tried to provide sufficient quotes from Weick's books and essays so that readers may make their own determination in this regard. A quote from an outside observer may also help:

> . . . [W]hat counts as data in Weick's world . . . is quite different from what we find almost anywhere else in the literature. Moreover, the constructs he provides us with for making sense of these data . . . seem to enjoy a different epistemological status than the independent and dependent variables we are so accustomed to coming across in the organizational sciences. They're harder to grasp, lend themselves less readily to compact summary in the standard tables that adorn our journals, and seem to have no p values attached to them, yet, ironically—or perhaps revealingly—there is never a feeling of insignificance surrounding them. (Kramer 2002, 749)

Another question that has been posed is whether Weick really believes and intends that sensemaking is an entirely retrospective process. His failure to make room for prospective sensemaking seems to fly in the face of everyday experience (Gioia and Mehra 1996). Does Weick's position on enactment reflect the totality of his views or is he merely trying to make a point? Is strategic planning pointless, as Weick most typically implies? Is meaning always a retrospective attribution, and decision making and intention unimportant? What about the evidence for goal-setting theory, which Weick does not consider? (see Miner 2005). I must admit that Weick seems to be wrong in his rejection of intention, prospective goals, and such matters as vision and planning, but then it is possible that he is a bit tongue-in-cheek on this score. I wish I felt more certainty regarding what he really thinks.

A final point relates to the extent to which Weick has come to embrace the philosophy of postmodernism. Certainly he has moved in that direction over the years, and postmodernists often welcome him as one of their own. Yet Weick has not repudiated his ties to science, even though these ties often seem to have more of a dotted line quality than one could hope for, and in some instances he appears to retreat from postmodernist positions that he cannot condone (see, for example, Weick 2002). There are those who clearly want more postmodernity from Weick than he appears willing to give (see Magala 1997). Disagreements with Weick's theorizing may be found among those of a postmodernist persuasion, as well as those who do not fit that description (see Wright, Manning, Farmer, and Gilbreath 2000; Vibert 2004). Once again we are left with a high degree of ambiguity. Presumably Weick would not have it any other way.

CONCLUSIONS

The ratings for organizing and sensemaking indicate considerable disparity. The importance rating is high at 5.41. Thus it is at essentially the same level as that noted in Chapter 4 for Cyert and March's behavioral theory, although in this instance the data do not indicate that the theory is institutionalized. In contrast, the estimated validity of two stars is decidedly low for theories included in this volume. Weick's theorizing has not sparked research either by himself or by others; it has not been tested, and in many respects it appears to be untestable. This is the basis for my validity evaluation, and I believe I am on solid ground in reaching this conclusion. However, the disparity from the importance rating is strange. Clearly Weick writes about important topics. Many people appear to view his arguments favorably; they may consider his "data" sufficient to establish plausibility, and perhaps even significance (for purposes of generalization). Nevertheless, the fact of the matter is that I do not have the information needed to explain the importance–validity disparity.

As to usefulness, this is a case where my original evaluation requires some change. Weick and Sutcliffe (2001) was published after the initial rating was made, and it contains a substantial contribution to practice that could be a basis for research on its usefulness, although it has not been; the authors do not present such data. In view of this situation I have raised the usefulness evaluation from 1 to 2 in the box at the beginning of this chapter.

The presentation of image theory in Chapter 7 takes us into the area of behavioral decision making in much greater depth than has been the case with the other chapters of this part. In this sense Beach's theory complements the theories that have been considered to date, rather than reworking the same ground.

REFERENCES

Beekun, Rafik I., and Glick, William H. (2001). Development and Test of a Contingency Framework of Coupling: Assessing the Covariation Between Structure and Culture. *Journal of Applied Behavioral Science*, 37, 385–407.

Bougon, Michel, Weick, Karl, and Binkhorst, Din (1977). Cognition in Organizations: An Analysis of the Utrecht Jazz Orchestra. *Administrative Science Quarterly*, 22, 606–39.

Brown, Andrew D. (2004). Authoritative Sensemaking in a Public Inquiry Report. *Organization Studies*, 25, 95–112.

Carroll, John S., Rudolph, Jenny W., and Hatakenaka, Sachi (2002). Learning from Experience in High-Hazard Organizations. *Research in Organizational Behavior*, 24, 87–137.

Clarke, Ian, and Mackaness, William (2001). Management 'Intuition': An Interpretative Account of Structure and Content of Decision Schemas Using Cognitive Maps. *Journal of Management Studies*, 38, 147–72.

Coutu, Diane L. (2003). Sense and Reliability: A Conversation with Celebrated Psychologist Karl E. Weick. *Harvard Business Review*, 81(4), 84–90.

Daft, Richard L., and Weick, Karl E. (1984). Toward a Model of Organizations as Interpretation Systems. *Academy of Management Review*, 9, 284–95.

Drazin, Robert, Glynn, Mary Ann, and Kazanjian, Robert K. (1999). Multilevel Theorizing About Creativity in Organizations: A Sensemaking Perspective. *Academy of Management Review*, 24, 286–307.

Fiol, C. Marlene, and O'Connor, Edward J. (2003). Waking Up! Mindfulness in the Face of Bandwagons. *Academy of Management Review*, 28, 54–70.

Gioia, Dennis A., and Mehra, Ajay (1996). Review of Karl Weick's *Sensemaking in Organizations*. *Academy of Management Review*, 21, 1226–30.

Gioia, Dennis A., and Thomas, James B. (1996). Identity, Image, and Issue Interpretation: Sensemaking During Strategic Change in Academia. *Administrative Science Quarterly*, 41, 370–403.

Greenwood, Royston, and Devine, Kay (1997). Inside Aston—A Conversation with Derek Pugh. *Journal of Management Inquiry*, 6, 200–8.

Griffith, Terri L. (1999). Technology Features as Triggers for Sensemaking. *Academy of Management Review*, 24, 472–88.

Hill, Robert C., and Levenhagen, Michael (1995). Metaphors and Mental Models: Sensemaking and Sensegiving in Innovative and Entrepreneurial Activities. *Journal of Management*, 21, 1057–74.

Kamoche, Ken, Cunha, Miguel P., and Cunha, João V. (2003). Toward a Theory of Organizational Improvisation: Looking Beyond the Jazz Metaphor. *Journal of Management Studies*, 40, 2023–51.

Kramer, Roderick M. (2002). Review of Karl Weick's *Making Sense of the Organization*. *Administrative Science Quarterly*, 47, 748–52.

Lundberg, Craig C. (1999). Finding Research Agendas: Getting Started Weick-Like. *The Industrial-Organizational Psychologist,* 37(2), 32–39.

Magala, Slawomir J. (1997). The Making and Unmaking of Sense (Book Review Essay—*Sensemaking in Organizations). Organization Studies,* 18, 317–38.

Miner, John B. (2005). *Organizational Behavior 1: Essential Theories of Motivation and Leadership.* Armonk, NY: M.E. Sharpe.

Orton, James D. (2000). Enactment, Sensemaking and Decision Making: Redesign Processes in the 1976 Reorganization of US Intelligence. *Journal of Management Studies,* 37, 213–34.

Pugh, Derek S., and Hickson, David J. (1993). *Great Writers on Organizations: The Omnibus Edition.* Aldershot, UK: Dartmouth.

Roberts, Karlene H., and Bea, Robert G. (2001). When Systems Fail. *Organizational Dynamics,* 29, 179–91.

Rudolph, Jenny W., and Repenning, Nelson P. (2002). Disaster Dynamics: Understanding the Role of Quantity in Organizational Collapse. *Administrative Science Quarterly,* 47, 1–30.

Sandelands, Lloyd E., and Stablein, Ralph E. (1987). The Concept of Organization Mind. *Research in the Sociology of Organizations,* 5, 135–61.

Sutcliffe, Kathleen M., and McNamara, Gerry (2001). Controlling Decision-Making Practice in Organizations. *Organization Science,* 12, 484–501.

Thomas, James B., Clark, Shawn M., and Gioia, Dennis A. (1993). Strategic Sensemaking and Organizational Performance: Linkages among Scanning, Interpretation, Action, and Outcomes. *Academy of Management Journal,* 36, 239–70.

Tsoukas, Haridimos, and Chia, Robert (2002). On Organizational Becoming: Rethinking Organizational Change. *Organization Science,* 13, 567–82.

Van Maanen, John (1995). Style as Theory. *Organization Science,* 6, 133–43.

Vibert, Conor (2004). *Theories of Macro Organizational Behavior: A Handbook of Ideas and Explanations.* Armonk, NY: M.E. Sharpe.

Weber, Paula S., and Manning, Michael R. (2001). Cause Maps, Sensemaking, and Planned Organizational Change. *Journal of Applied Behavioral Science,* 37, 227–51.

Weick, Karl E. (1969, 1979). *The Social Psychology of Organizing.* 1st ed., 2nd ed. Reading, MA: Addison-Wesley.

———. (1976). Educational Organizations as Loosely Coupled Systems. *Administrative Science Quarterly,* 21, 1–19.

———. (1985). Sources of Order in Underorganized Systems: Themes in Recent Organizational Theory. In Y. Lincoln (Ed.), *Organizational Theory and Inquiry: The Paradigm Revolution.* Beverly Hills, CA: Sage, 106–36.

———. (1988). Enacted Sensemaking in Crisis Situations. *Journal of Management Studies,* 25, 305–17.

———. (1990). The Vulnerable System: An Analysis of the Tenerife Air Disaster. *Journal of Management,* 16, 571–93.

———. (1993a). Turning Context into Text: An Academic Life as Data. In Arthur G. Bedeian (Ed.), *Management Laureates: A Collection of Autobiographical Essays,* Vol. III. Greenwich, CT: JAI Press, 285–323.

———. (1993b). Organizational Redesign As Improvisation. In George P. Huber and William H. Glick (Eds.), *Organizational Change and Redesign: Ideas and Insights for Improving Performance.* New York: Oxford University Press, 346–79.

———. (1993c). The Collapse of Sensemaking in Organizations: The Mann Gulch Disaster. *Administrative Science Quarterly,* 38, 628–52.

———. (1993d). Sensemaking in Organizations: Small Structures with Large Consequences. In J. Keith Murnigham (Ed.), *Social Psychology in Organizations: Advances in Theory and Research.* Englewood Cliffs, NJ: Prentice Hall, 10–37.

———. (1995). *Sensemaking in Organizations.* Thousand Oaks, CA: Sage.

———. (1998). Introductory Essay: Improvisation as a Mindset for Organizational Analysis. *Organization Science,* 9, 543–55.

———. (2001). *Making Sense of the Organization.* Oxford, UK: Blackwell.

———. (2002). Essai: Real-Time Reflexivity: Prods to Reflection. *Organization Studies,* 23, 893–98.

———. (2003a). Organizational Design and the Gehry Experience. *Journal of Management Inquiry,* 12, 93–97.

————. (2003b). Hospitals as Cultures of Entrapment: A Re-Analysis of the Bristol Royal Infirmary. *California Management Review,* 45(2), 73–84.

————. (2003c). Positive Organizing and Organizational Tragedy. In Kim S. Cameron, Jane E. Dutton, and Robert E. Quinn (Eds.), *Positive Organizational Scholarship: Foundations of a New Discipline.* San Francisco, CA: Berrett-Koehler, 66–80.

————. (2004). Mundane Poetics: Searching for Wisdom in Organization Studies. *Organization Studies,* 25, 653–68.

Weick, Karl E., and Bougon, Michel G. (1986). Organizations as Cause Maps. In Henry P. Sims and Dennis A. Gioia (Eds.), *Social Cognition in Organizations.* San Francisco, CA: Jossey-Bass.

Weick, Karl E., and Roberts, Karlene H. (1993). Collective Mind in Organizations: Heedful Interrelating on Flight Decks. *Administrative Science Quarterly,* 38, 357–81.

Weick, Karl E., and Sutcliffe, Kathleen M. (2001). *Managing the Unexpected: Assuring High Performance in an Age of Complexity.* San Francisco, CA: Jossey-Bass.

Weick, Karl E., Sutcliffe, Kathleen M., and Obstfeld, David (1999). Organizing for High Reliability: Processes of Collective Mindfulness. *Research in Organizational Behavior,* 21, 81–123.

Weick, Karl E., and Westley, Frances (1996). Organizational Learning: Affirming an Oxymoron. In Stewart R. Clegg, Cynthia Hardy, and Walter R. Nord (Eds.), *Handbook of Organization Studies.* London: Sage, 440–58.

Wright, Charles R., Manning, Michael R., Farmer, Bruce, and Gilbreath, Brad (2000). Resourceful Sensemaking in Product Development Teams. *Organization Studies,* 21, 807–29.

CHAPTER 7

IMAGE THEORY

LEE ROY BEACH

Importance rating	★ ★ ★
Estimated validity	★ ★ ★ ★
Estimated usefulness	★ ★ ★
Decade of origin	1980s

Image theory emerged initially as an attempt to develop further the ideas of Miller, Galanter, and Pribram (1960). It is directly in the tradition of behavioral decision theory, and represents an approach to applying this type of theory first to individual decision processes and then to decisions at the organizational level. In doing this it moves to quite advanced conceptualizations in this area, of a kind that break considerably with the classical versions of decision theory and with those most frequently associated with economics.

BACKGROUND

Image theory was created at the University of Washington by Lee Roy Beach in conjunction with a number of students and colleagues, including initially and most notably Terence Mitchell (see Miner 2005). Beach, however, has been by far the most consistent contributor to the theory's development, and is an author of many articles on the topic, as well as of five books that he either wrote himself or edited.

He was born in 1936, did his undergraduate work at the University of Indiana and obtained his doctorate from the psychology department at the University of Colorado in 1961. Thus, he is another who turned to major theorizing only later in his career and in fact only shortly before accepting a business school appointment. After obtaining his degree Beach served in research positions of various kinds—as an aviation psychologist and a human factors scientist— and in a postdoctoral appointment in psychology at the University of Michigan. He joined the psychology faculty at the University of Washington in 1966 and ultimately became department chair. In 1989 he moved to the University of Arizona for a position in the business school and it is there that the majority of his work on image theory occurred. He retired from Arizona in 2001 and at that point, for all practical purposes, his contributions to the field ceased.

Beach has been publishing research on decision processes since 1961. However, it was only in the latter 1980s that he began publishing on what he named image theory. The theory was in fact developed in response to a felt need to correct earlier work on what was called the strategy selection model (Beach and Mitchell 1978). The result was a rather large number of journal articles and essays setting forth the theory in various forms (Beach and Frederickson 1989; Beach and Mitchell 1987; Beach, Smith, Lundell, and Mitchell 1988; Beach and Strom 1989; Mitchell, Rediker, and Beach 1986). By the time he reached Arizona, however, Beach was ready to publish a comprehensive theory of individual decision making (1990), and thus formulated the major statement of image theory as it applies to the individual level. This book is the primary source for the discussion that follows, although a parallel journal publication is utilized as well (Mitchell and Beach 1990).

THE INDIVIDUAL THEORY

The first book on image theory was originally intended to be a joint product with Terence Mitchell, but Mitchell had to withdraw because of time demands (Beach 1990).

The Essential Framework

According to Beach, *images* represent the cognitive structures that summarize a decision maker's knowledge of what is to be accomplished, why, how, and the results of action. The *value image* (elsewhere called the self image) represents the decision maker's values, standards, ideals, precepts, beliefs, morals, and ethics (taken together these are called *principles*). These principles serve to establish whether a decision is right or wrong. The *trajectory image* represents an agenda for the future, consisting of *goals*. Concrete surrogate events serve as *markers* to indicate goal achievement. The *strategic image* contains the *plans* to achieve goals, the behavioral *tactics* to implement plans, and *forecasts* of the future anticipated if a plan is adopted and/or implemented. On occasion strategic images are broken down into action images (plans and tactics) and projected images (forecasts).

These images, along with other elements of the theory, are set forth in Figure 7.1. This figure, in somewhat varied forms, is contained in a large number of Beach's publications of the early period.

Two kinds of decisions are noted. *Adoption decisions* are concerned with the adoption or rejection of candidates for inclusion in the images noted above. *Progress decisions* are concerned with whether a given plan on the strategic image is working to produce progress to the goal.

Figure 7.1   **The Elements and Diagrams of Image Theory**

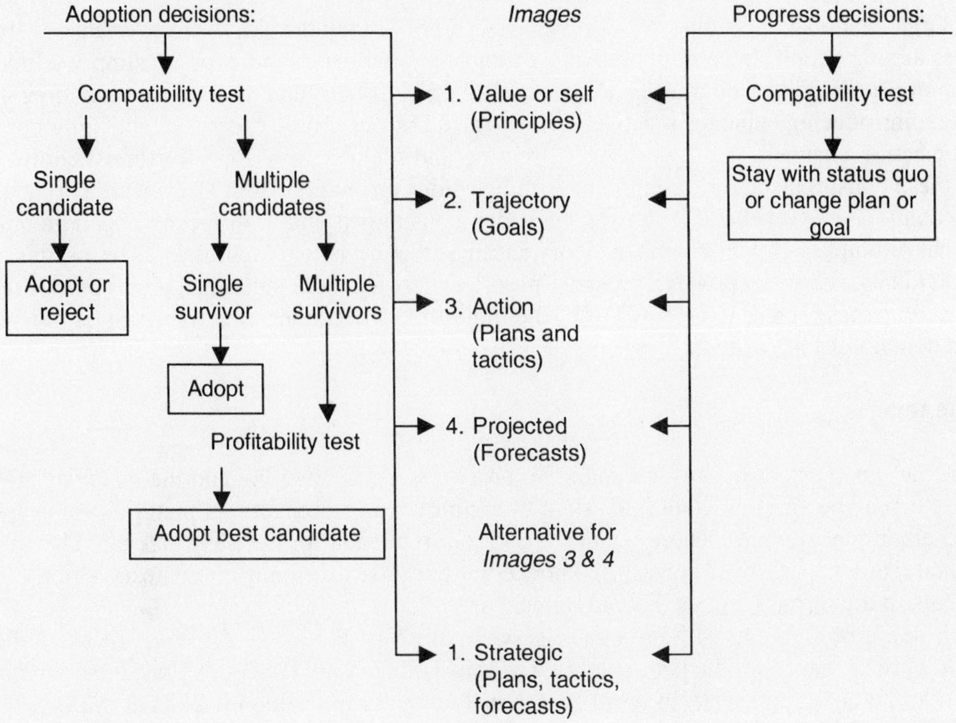

Adoption decisions:	Images	Progress decisions:
Compatibility test	1. Value or self (Principles)	Compatibility test
Single candidate / Multiple candidates	2. Trajectory (Goals)	Stay with status quo or change plan or goal
Adopt or reject		
Single survivor / Multiple survivors	3. Action (Plans and tactics)	
Adopt	4. Projected (Forecasts)	
Profitability test		
Adopt best candidate	Alternative for *Images 3 & 4*	
	1. Strategic (Plans, tactics, forecasts)	

Source: Adapted from Mitchell and Beach (1990, 11); Beach and Mitchell (1990, 13).

Framing occurs as the decision maker utilizes recognition or identification of the current context to define a subset of the constituents of images as having particular relevance for a decision to be made. Meaning comes from the image constituents so activated. Either some successful action from the past is mobilized in the form of a *policy* or appropriate goals and plans are created.

Two tests are applied in the process of making adoption and progress decisions:

> The *compatibility test* assesses whether the features of a candidate for adoption "violate" (are incompatible with) the relevant (framed) constituents of the various images, and whether the forecasts based upon the constituents of the strategic image "violate" the relevant constituents of the trajectory image. The *profitability test,* which applies only to adoption decisions, assesses the relative ability of competing candidates to further the implementation of ongoing plans, attain existing goals, and comply with the decision maker's principles. The object of the compatibility test is to screen out the unacceptable. The object of the profitability test is to seek the best. (Beach 1990, 9)

Candidates that pass the compatibility test are adopted if there is only one such candidate. In the case of progress decisions there must be compatibility between the trajectory image (goals) and strategic image (forecasts). These processes are diagrammed in Figure 7.1. The compatibility test is a screening process, while the profitability test is used to choose the best among multiple alternative candidates.

Organizational decisions are addressed only briefly; they develop from overlapping images among people, become shared as a result of similar experiences, or are simply a function of organizationwide images. Organizations exert influence on decisions by dividing up tasks, introducing standard practices, communicating objectives widely, establishing communication channels, and by extensive training and socialization. Decisions must conform to these constraints and be congruent with decisions emanating from elsewhere. Top management, like everyone else, has its decisions constrained and is influenced by organizational principles. However, image theory assumes that decisions occur only as properties of individuals, and social processes merely inform, or restrict, these individual processes. Group decisions thus represent a transform of the individual's decisions; that transform is outside the domain of image theory.

The Images

The various types of images are cognitive processes, as are framing and the two tests. The images may be visual, mental (pictorial), or cognitive (a combination of pictorial, semantic, and emotional content). These images are in fact schemata for decision making. They are called frames when they consist of knowledge that gives meaning to contexts; often this occurs in the form of stories that are domain specific.

Value images, along with principles, serve to motivate the whole decision process. Principles are primarily products of culture. Trajectory images are the set of goals a person has decided to adopt and seek. In terms of a goal hierarchy, the value image is at the top, the trajectory image is intermediate, and the strategic image is at the lowest level of the list, corresponding to alternative courses of action.

The plans in the strategic image are for the purpose of achieving goals derived from the trajectory image. Planning is not necessarily all good, however. One can plan too much when forecasting is not feasible. Policies represent preformulated plans that can be activated when the framed context is seen to be one that has arisen previously. Forecasting involves the ability to devise possible futures, to establish the outcome of implementing a plan. Goals are a function of imperatives generated by principles, or of the need to introduce some type of goal to complement already existing goals; they may also stem from perceived external necessity or suggestion. Goals may be packaged alone without an accompanying plan, unstated but inherent in a plan, or explicitly stated with a goal and its plan operating together.

Framing and Deliberation

Framing acts to establish what a decision is about and defines the issues that may prove relevant. The context provides certain cues that the decision maker uses for purposes of framing. A frame is the portion of a person's knowledge base that is brought to bear on a particular context to endow it with meaning. As contexts evolve, frames must be changed. Failure of action can signal the need for such a change—the old frame is no longer effective. This kind of reframing is one way to deal with context-frame incongruity; another way is to act upon the context to force it back into line with the frame. Different people, of course, may have quite different frames for the same context.

Decision deliberation is what happens as the decision maker thinks about making the decision and implementing it. The decision maker uses the compatibility and profitability tests, but mostly identifies and clarifies issues, which happens during framing. Also deliberation serves to generate new candidate principles, goals, and plans and allows the decision maker to use the experiences considered to make forecasts, build confidence, assess risks, and deliberate over how the adopted candidate might be presented to others.

The Compatibility Test

The function of the compatibility test is that it serves "to screen out adoption candidates that do not conform to the principles, or that adversely affect the goals and plans that make up the frame of the context within which adoption is being considered. . . . It also serves to detect the possible failure of ongoing plans when the forecasted results of their implementation do not include their goals" (Beach 1990, 71). This test involves as its major variables violations, a rejection threshold, and the decision rule. The decision rule is that if the negative weighted sum of violations exceeds the negative rejection threshold, the candidate decision is rejected; if not, it is accepted.

Expressed in mathematical terms this may be summarized as follows:

$$C = \sum_{t=1}^{n} \sum_{c=1}^{m} W_c V_{tc}; V_{tc} = -1 \text{ or } 0, 0.00 \leq W \leq 1.00$$

where the compatibility, C, is zero when a candidate has no violations and decreases (i.e., is more and more negative) as the number of violations increases; t is a relevant attribute of the candidate; c is a relevant image constituent; V is a violation of image constituent c by attribute t of the candidate; and W is the importance weight for each of the relevant image constituents—W is between and including 0.00 and 1.00 (Beach 1990, 73).

Thus, violations of image constituents may be weighted differently (W).

Information about nonviolations is used in part to help define what a candidate is, and in part to establish a stopping rule to limit search and deliberation. The profitability test is invoked in addition only when there are multiple surviving candidates (see Figure 7.1).

The compatibility test operates as a means to make intuitive decisions, and as such it may well not be part of conscious experience. Since image theory is not a normative theory, but rather entirely descriptive, the author notes that generally when intuition conflicts with rational analysis, intuition tends to win out.

The Profitability Test

The profitability test involves a number of different strategies. The strategy selection process is influenced by aspects of the decision problem, the environment, and the decision maker. Depending on these factors, the person attempts to select the strategy that involves the least investment for a correct decision. The task is to balance perceived utilities against both probabilities and costs for each available strategy and thus to select a strategy that seems to offer the best hope of success with the least resource investment.

Most important decisions turn out to be compatibility ones, involving a single alternative weighed against the status quo. Thus, the much more complex profitability process is not required very often. As evidence of the potential for applied usefulness of image theory, Beach (1990) presents descriptions of its use in auditing, in making decisions about child-bearing, and as applied to governmental decision making (specifically with regard to the Cuban missile crisis).

Subsequent Theorizing

Subsequent to 1990 there have been a number of statements of the individual theory in some form. A chapter by Beach, Mitchell, Paluchowski, and van Zee (1992) explores extensions in decision framing and deliberation, but the material is essentially the same as that presented previously. Beach (1993a) presents a historical analysis of the development of behavioral decision theory, contending that at each stage there has been a shift away from economic formulations and toward the psychological. The major theoretical contribution here is an emphasis on the role played by preformulated policies. Most behavior is in fact guided by past experience in this way. Only rarely does choice come into the picture with multiple surviving candidates and the invoking of a profitability test. Beach (1996) is basically devoted to applications and contains little by way of new individual theory by the author. We will return to these applications later. Beach (1997) is an overview of the psychology of decision making in general, which includes a limited statement of the individual theory. Beach (1998) is intended to draw together image theory research and extensions to theory. The latter, however, are not basic in nature and in fact are rarely a product of the theory's author at all (this is an edited volume with a third of the chapters written by other authors than Beach).

The point is that individual image theory has been quite stable. It is not a theory that has continually evolved over the years like many other theories considered elsewhere in this book and generally in the field of micro organizational behavior (see Miner 2005).

THE ORGANIZATIONAL THEORY

The organizational theory is closely tied to the individual version. It, too, had its early origins in the 1980s (Mitchell, Rediker, and Beach 1986). However, I will focus on the more fully developed statements published in the 1990s.

Decision Making in Organizations

Beach and Mitchell (1990) updated image theory as applicable to organizations by positing that there are four images. The *organizational self-image* consists of the organizational decision makers' perceptions of the beliefs, values, morals, ethics, and norms that combine to form its principles and serve as imperatives for the organization. This self-image is analogous to the organization's culture, gives rise to the organization as a collective, and transcends the characteristics of individual members. The *organizational trajectory image* is the organization's agenda for the future and may be articulated only in the minds of top managers or diffused more widely in the organization. The *organizational action image* consists of plans and tactics that in turn guide subunits. The *organizational projected image* refers to anticipated events and states that are forecasted if a plan were to be adopted or is in process (6–7).

From there the organizational theory moves to much the same ground as the individual theory (see Figure 7.1). Choices are made between retaining the status quo or introducing

Figure 7.2 **Elements of the Framing Process**

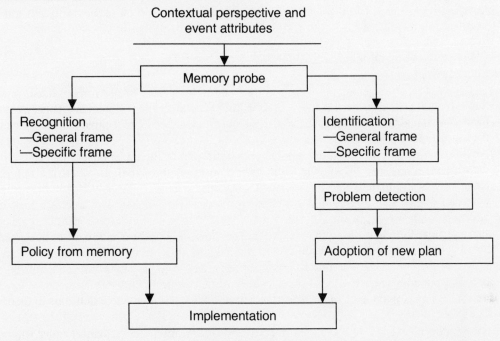

Source: Beach and Mitchell (1990, 14). Copyright © 1990 by The Academy of Management Review. Reprinted with permission from Elsevier Science.

change. Change is resisted by organizations because it violates images by expending energy that could be devoted to existing goal attainment. Yet, nonoptional changes may emerge from the environment and then top management's function is to provide for smooth transitions.

With regard to frames and policies, decisions are said to follow the processes depicted in Figure 7.2. Policies are goals and their associated plans tied to a particular specific frame. The process set forth here remains more individual than organizational; there is no organizational memory, or learning, construct. However, group decision making is considered.

Joint decisions of this kind are fostered when a decision extends beyond the authority of a single person. With regard to a theory for such a situation, the authors say:

> This is not the place to elaborate on small group interaction, the vagaries of intra-organizational communication, or the complexities of organizational politics, coalitions, bargaining, power-plays, etc. Instead, to avoid straying from the central issue of Image Theory, we will take an idyllic, if unrealistic, view of how groups work. (Beach and Mitchell 1990, 18)

In the process they assume away most differences in images and frames. Only very specific frames are expected to differ to some extent and thus can serve as a source of conflict.

In such an idyllic social setting discussion and persuasion are used to influence the decision process toward consensus. If this fails to produce image similarity, stalemates and postponement are likely, or perhaps voting. Thus individuals remain individuals. "The group's decision is not the result of it acting as some sort of single decision making organism that has a single will" (19). One comes away at this point with the feeling that moving beyond the individual level leaves the authors somewhat uncomfortable and takes them into territory that is not of great interest.

Further to Organizational Culture Factors

Yet Beach (1993b) develops the organizational culture construct in much more detail in a book intended primarily for business students, not as a theoretical statement. Theory certainly is embedded here, but it is handled tangentially, and references to image theory per se are minimized for some reason.

According to Beach, decision responsibility rests within organizations. Understanding these organizations requires knowledge of their culture (the basic beliefs), their vision (the agenda of goals), and their activities (what is being done to achieve these goals and the plans that guide them). These three understandings provide mental images to a decision maker (the value, trajectory, and action images of Figure 7.1). The images in turn provide guidelines that enter into the making of right decisions—those that are compatible with, promote, and enhance the organization's culture, vision, and activities. In this context *leadership* is defined as the art of understanding an organization so well that one can help it accomplish its goals without compromising its identity (culture is the core of that identity).

Culture serves in the role of principles where it:

- Specifies what is of primary importance to the organization, the standards against which its successes and failures should be measured.
- Dictates how the organization's resources are to be used, and to what ends.
- Establishes what the organization and its members can expect from each other.
- Makes some methods of controlling behavior within the organization legitimate and others illegitimate—that is, it defines where power lies within the organization and how it is to be used.
- Selects the behaviors in which members should or should not engage and prescribes how these are to be rewarded and punished.
- Sets the tone for how members should treat each other and how they should treat non-members: competitively, collaboratively, honestly, distantly, or hostilely.
- Instructs members about how to deal with the external environment: aggressively, exploitatively, responsibly, or proactively. (Beach 1993b, 12)

Changing organizational culture requires changing activities initially and then permitting culture to adapt. The shift in activities may be imposed, or members may be convinced on the basis of crisis, or, ideally, a gradual evolution may be instituted. Beach here presents and develops his Organizational Culture Inventory to measure beliefs about how employees should be treated and what opportunities should be afforded them, about professionalism and support of efforts to do a good job, and about how the organization interfaces with the environment and strives to accomplish its mission.

The organizational vision provides direction, the agenda the organization perceives itself to be pursuing; it is rather imprecise, and establishes the general shape of plans. It is important that it be characterized by thrust and scope, as well as serving to build consensus within the organization. Culture and vision interact to influence decision making, which in turn leads to activities. Decision making is defined as the mechanism by which the need to abandon the status quo is evaluated and, if change is needed, the means by which a new direction is selected.

Organizational Decision Making

At this point Beach moves to a discussion of decision making, which is handled much as it was previously in theoretical discussions, but with some different terminology. The results are given in Figure 7.3. The previous terminology is given at the end of arrows around the outside of the diagrams. There does not appear to be a great deal that is new here. Goals are tactical, operational, and strategic. Tests are carried out to determine if a forecast fits with the vision. Beach gives the following requirements for testing for quality (the compatibility test) to screen candidates for adoption:

- Only consider one candidate at a time.
- Do not make comparisons between candidates.
- Only take the candidate's violations into account.
- Do not attempt to balance nonviolations against violations; meeting some standards does not compensate for failing to meet other standards.
- Weight the seriousness of each violation by the importance of the violated standard.
- Reject the candidate if its violations are too important or too many for you to feel comfortable with.
- Assign all survivors to a choice set, and;
- If, after all candidates have been screened, the choice set contains only one survivor, adopt it;
- If the choice set ends up containing two or more survivors, choose the best of them based upon relative qualities of potential outcomes. (Beach 1993b, 102)

Group decisions continue to be derived from the private decisions of group members. The decision that emerges from a group is negotiated based on these individual decisions. Negotiation strategies are yielding, compromise, contending, and problem solving.

Elsewhere Beach sets forth the essence of organizational decision making as follows:

> The theoretical mechanism of primary interest involves assessment of the compatibility of a decision option with the organization's culture—where an option is defined as a possible course of action in the case of a member who is making a decision, or a proposed course of action in the case of a decision that has been made by leaders. Image theory predicts that when compatibility is low, the option will be rejected. This means that when an acculturated member is making decisions for the organization, he or she will tend not to make decisions that are incompatible with its culture; when leaders make culturally incompatible decisions, the organization's members will tend not to endorse the decision. (Weatherly and Beach in Beach 1998, 212)

From this, the following hypotheses may be derived:

1. Different groups will have different degrees of cultural fragmentation, and this can be measured.
2. The more compatible a decision option is with the culture, the more likely it will be chosen.

Figure 7.3   **Organizational Framework for Understanding Decision Making**

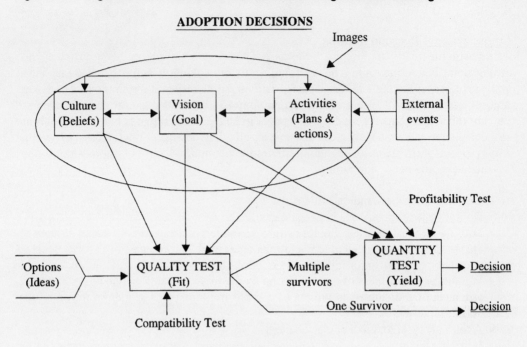

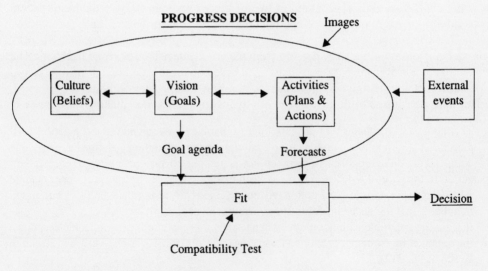

Source: Adapted from Beach (1993, 94).

3. Members will be more likely to accept the decision of leaders if the goal or plan fits the culture.
4. When a culture differs from what members think it should be, these members will be less committed, less satisfied, and more inclined to turnover.

EVALUATION AND IMPACT

In a presentation of image theory research Beach (1998) notes that the coverage is concerned with studies of the compatibility test and of the profitability test. Oddly missing is research dealing with the images themselves, an omission that Beach himself notes. He attributes this to difficulties in determining how to study images in a scientifically satisfying way. The problem is, however, that almost all of the studies are of a laboratory nature using student subjects, and a very high proportion of this extant research has involved Beach's participation. For this reason I do not report on findings dealing with the images of the theory—there are none—and also deal with all of the research at once. So much involves Beach that it would be pointless to separate his work out. In fact almost all of it involves the author and/or his students.

Research on the Compatibility Test: Adoption

Compatibility decisions are the aspect of the theory that has attracted the greatest amount of research. Adoption decisions have been studied the most. A common concern has been to determine whether violation decisions dominate the decision process and, if so, what kind of a threshold emerges. One such study utilized a student looking for a job as the standardized role, with a set of preestablished jobs to be considered. The use of violations to reject jobs was in fact characteristic, with nonviolations playing practically no role (Beach and Strom in Beach 1998). After four violations the candidate tended to be rejected, reflecting a reasonably stable threshold. All this is quite consistent with theory.

The next step in validating research was to determine whether differential weighting of violations during screening, as reflected in the equation for the compatibility test, does occur. A study to determine this involved a decision to purchase a toaster, with various descriptors entered into the process on a standardized basis (Beach, Puto, Heckler, Naylor, and Marble in Beach 1998). The data clearly supported the hypothesis that weighting of violations is evident. Under time constraints it was found that the compatibility test is retained, and no change in threshold appears either. The subjects simply speed up, or depending on the conditions, perform more poorly. This research also utilized a job search scenario (Benson and Beach in Beach 1998). The point is that time pressure does not result in a change in decision strategy.

A different research thrust looked into the question of whether screening (the compatibility test) and choice (the profitability test) do in fact use different processes and information sources. The problem faced by the students was to choose a room to rent for a friend from out of town. Screening was done first to establish a short list, and then additional information was provided, followed by a specific choice (van Zee, Paluchowski, and Beach in Beach 1998). Information used to carry out screening was not used in the subsequent choice process, only the additional information exerted an influence at that point. It appeared that screening and choice were viewed as completely different tasks with quite varied information requirements. A subsequent study confirmed this interpretation with a somewhat different decision task and also showed that, while screening for violations did not utilize probability information, choice decisions clearly did incorporate probability considerations (Potter and Beach in Beach 1998). These results provide strong support for the compatibility–profitability differentiation, while at the same time demonstrating that the compatibility test is essentially conservative in nature.

The implication of these findings is that screening plays a very important role in decision making and that the two-step process hypothesized by image theory is entirely defensible. There are other data that lead to similar conclusions. Asare and Knechel (1995), for example, used auditors as subjects in decisions with regard to audit clients. Decision making based on violations and the existence of thresholds were clearly apparent. Seidl and Traub (1998) in Germany found substantial support for the compatibility test using a laboratory approach with students, a decision on screening candidates for a position, and a revised approach to analysis. Ordóñez, Benson, and Beach (1999) studied the effects of a manipulation that made the student subjects more accountable for the results of their decisions. This increased realism had no effect on the tendency to follow image theory by screening out bad options rather than screening in good ones, but it did serve to create greater stringency in screening by lowering threshold values.

An early study of adoption decisions deserves particular attention because it was not of a laboratory nature (Beach, Smith, Lundell, and Mitchell 1988). It was conducted using managers from three firms who were interviewed regarding firm principles and decision-making processes. The degree of agreement on principles was found to be closely associated with firm turnover. It was also related to agreement in evaluations of alternative plans considered to achieve a specific goal. Evaluated compatibility of any one of these alternative plans was a function of the extent to which company principles were violated by that plan. Thus both principles and violations operated in the manner image theory would anticipate. The compatibility equation received support as well.

Research on the Compatibility Test: Progress

A major contributor to the research on progress decisions has been Kenneth Dunegon. In one such research program he carried out various laboratory studies in which students made decisions in the context of project team scenarios. The data indicated that when goals and forecasts were compatible, subjects were more likely to continue a project and to commit additional resources to it (Dunegon in Beach 1998). In further extensions of this program it became apparent that when progress toward goals is satisfactory, subjects devote little deep thinking to the project and invest more resources almost automatically. Only when progress is unacceptable does real deliberation occur (Dunegon, Duchon, and Ashmos in Beach 1998).

Dunegon (1993) also conducted studies on the framing of decisions that in one instance involved engineering team personnel in a field setting. When the same information is framed both positively and negatively the decision-making processes invoked tend to differ. Again, positive framing produces more automatic processes, while negative framing brings more controlled and thorough processes into play. Thus, although compatibility remains in evidence, negative framing acts to reduce the fit between current and trajectory images. Accordingly, organizations may be best served by framing information negatively in order to induce deliberation; it pays to depict the glass as half empty rather than as half full.

Schepers and Beach (in Beach 1998) followed up on Dunegon's work, studying the amount of overtime subjects were willing to work depending on the way a decision is framed. When the framing serves to produce low compatibility, motivation to improve progress toward the goal, and thus work more overtime, is increased. Apparently, in the case of progress decisions violations and unsatisfactory progress do not necessarily mean that the person stops implementing the plan and looks for another plan. Rather the incompatibility acts as feedback to elicit attempts to improve upon the plan and to work harder. This distinction between adoption and progress compatibility was not inherent in the original theory, and appears to suggest much more complex processes in the latter instance than had been envisioned previously.

Research conducted in two government departments utilized questionnaire data to determine compatibility between perceived supervisory behavior and the ideal image for a supervisor. This discrepancy measure was related to measured satisfaction with supervision. As compatibility decreased and violations increased, satisfaction levels decreased slowly up to ten or twelve violations, and then dropped sharply. The rejection threshold appeared to be roughly ten violations (Bissell and Beach in Beach 1996). This finding was replicated in another study of fast food restaurant employees. In this latter research, hope for improvement in the situation was also determined and proved effective in adding to satisfaction levels above and beyond the effects of compatibility levels alone (Richmond, Bissell, and Beach 1998). These studies represent the major efforts to study progress decisions outside the laboratory.

Research on the Profitability Test

Studies of the profitability test, and how decisions to select a strategy for making that test are made, are generally of a 1970s vintage and thus antedate image theory. The key studies were carried out in a laboratory setting and indicated that the costs and benefits of alternative strategies are taken into account, utilizing a mechanism that is congruent with that of the subjective expected utility (SEU) model. Yet strategy selection and then a decision utilizing the strategy that appears most attractive does occur. All this does not prove that the SEU model is actually used, but the results match up with such an approach (Christensen-Szalanski in Beach 1998).

With regard to this situation, and presumably at the same time providing an explanation of why profitability research has not progressed further, Beach (1998, 140) has the following to say:

> . . . [N]either Mitchell nor I have ever been completely comfortable with the SEU mechanism. On the other hand, the data seem to support the model, and we have not had a better idea about how to formulate the selection mechanism, so we are stuck with the SEU formulation until something better comes along.

In the late 1970s also, McCallister, Mitchell, and Beach (in Beach 1998) did a study in the laboratory in which significance, irreversibility, and accountability were varied. When all three were high, the strategy for choice selected was the most highly analytic available; when all three were low, the least analytic strategy was utilized. Again, it is important to note that this research preceded image theory, and influenced it as well. It appears that people do carry out the profitability test using a wide repertoire of approaches, but it is not entirely clear how this fact interfaces with and integrates into image theory.

Research on the Organizational Theory

Research on the organizational theory, as opposed to the individual, is hard to find. There is one research effort, however, that builds upon the idea that an organization's culture provides a value image for its members. The central concept is that, in view of their shared understandings of a common culture, vision, and set of plans, managers will tend to favor certain decision options and avoid others. The Organizational Culture Survey was used to test the hypothesis that different organizations are characterized by varying degrees of cultural fragmentation (Weatherly and Beach in Beach 1996; 1998).

The initial study compared a financial services organization (successful) with a utility (on the verge of bankruptcy) on some fifteen different cultural values. The profiles of different levels within the financial services firm were remarkably similar, suggesting a unified culture. In the utility, two different views of the culture appeared—one at the top and one at the lower levels. Score variances were consistently greater in the utility.

Additional studies moved to more specific image theory hypotheses. A group of utility managers was studied to determine whether a decision option that is more compatible with an organization's culture would be chosen or endorsed more by members; this proved to be the case. Subjects from both companies were studied to establish whether members are more likely to support a top management decision when the features of this option are compatible with the features of their organization's culture; this proved to be the case. Utility employees were involved in a study designed to test the hypothesis that the greater the difference between member perceptions of the existing culture and how they feel that culture should be (ideal), the less committed they would be, the less satisfied, and the more inclined to turnover; all three of these expectations proved to be correct.

These findings have much in common with those of Bissell and Beach (in Beach 1998). More data on the degree of fragmentation issue are presented elsewhere as well (Beach 1993b), adding information on several government agencies (unified cultures) and on various professional school groups (fragmented cultures). Clearly, variations in fragmentation levels do occur. It would appear that they have consequences for organizational decision making as well.

The lack of research on image theory's organizational aspects, nevertheless, represents a problem. Certainly what research there is is supportive in the sense that the hypotheses tested were developed from image theory, and they were confirmed. Yet other theories may be supported by these same results. The findings would appear to be quite consistent with most theorizing in the area of organizational culture; they are not specific to image theory.

Normative Applications of a Descriptive Theory

Image theory is descriptive in nature, aimed at achieving understanding, not at providing guidelines for practice. Thus Beach (1998, 131) says, "Image theory is not sufficiently well-developed to justify giving managers advice about how to go about their work." Yet after this disclaimer, he does move a few tentative steps in the direction of application, and this happens rather often throughout his writings. The edited volume *Decision Making in the Workplace* (Beach 1996) contains a number of essays by Beach, his students, and others that touch upon various applications of image theory. Some examples follow.

In that book Cynthia Stevens's work, for example, carries implications for job and career decision making and for management's role as a source of information on positions. Byron Bissell's research on supervision is interpreted in terms of its implications for management. Thomas Lee provides what he calls an unfolding model of voluntary turnover in organizations and discusses possible applications. Both James Frederickson and Stephen Asare treat aspects of the auditing process and consider how image theory might be used in this context. The research by Kristopher Weatherly discussed previously contains some quite specific recommendations for the management of culture, as does an essay by Kenneth Walsh.

There are a number of pieces in this book that carry implications for planning processes. Helmut Jungermann and Eric DeBruyn are concerned with the pluses and minuses of forecasting and policy use in planning under varied circumstances. Christopher Puto and Susan Heckler focus on the consumer's decision processes in developing ideas for designing marketing plans and communication strategies. This same consumer emphasis is evident in Kim Nelson's discussion of social responsibility dimensions, which deals with image theory's use in this context. We have already considered Kenneth Dunegon's research on framing and its implications for managerial decision making and planning.

All of these applications are presented more in the nature of suggestions for use than as specific guidelines. There is little by way of testing of fully developed application programs to see if they work in the real world of organizations. Yet a concern with normative applications is clearly evident, to a rather surprising degree for a descriptive theory. Furthermore, these suggestions for practice range over a wide panorama of topic areas. Also, image theory's decision framing construct has been viewed as having normative implications (Carlson and Connerley 2003).

Looking to the Future

Image theory represents a major departure from traditional decision theory (see Connolly in Beach 1996). It has amassed a significant amount of research in support of several of its central constructs. For a quite recent theory its accomplishments are indeed impressive, and as Connolly notes there are numerous avenues for research waiting to be opened (see also Connolly and Beach in Beach 1998).

In some ways it is surprising that image theory has provoked so little research outside the boundaries of the Universities of Washington and Arizona, where it has had its homes. Mention should be made of a study on decision risk conducted at Michigan State University, which, although somewhat tangential, does provide some support for image theory's views on choice (Hollenbeck, Ilgen, Phillips, and Hedlund 1994). Also, the work on formulating the unfolding model of employee turnover mentioned previously has undergone considerable development on both theoretical (Lee and Mitchell 1994) and empirical (Lee, Mitchell, Wise, and Fireman 1996) fronts. This model draws on contributions from image theory and demonstrates some of the more comprehensive uses to which the theory may be put; yet it remains a product of the University of Washington (see also Mitchell and Lee 2001). Perhaps it is too early in image theory's trajectory to anticipate a major outpouring of interest and research beyond its home grounds, although relatively little has occurred since Beach's retirement.

In any event, for lack of such an outpouring, we are largely left with Beach's own earlier views regarding the future of his theory. He lists a number of major tasks:

1. Images—research is lacking; the greatest need is for a measurement method so that the research can be conducted; perhaps a cognitive psychologist will take up this problem and develop a solution.
2. Compatibility and screening—the laboratory research remains somewhat stilted and artificial; in particular an approach that deals effectively with continuous variables is needed.

3. Compatibility and progress—there has been some movement to casting the theory in mathematical terms, but not enough; theory development that would result in mathematical formalization is needed.

4. Profitability and choice—this is the biggest flaw in image theory; the reliance on subjective expected utility theory is unacceptable; a whole new theory appears needed here, one that would not require the notion of different strategies or the idea of a repertoire of strategies.

5. Extensions—the most important idea here, as part of the organization theory, is that culture provides the value image that decision makers for organizations use; thus individuals have their own value image and one for the organization as well, but these two need not be very different; all this has profound implications for leadership and for dealing with organizational change. (Beach 1998, 263–68)

Beach (1998, 268) ends with, "the image theory description of organizational decisions affords the opportunity to conduct theory-driven applied research." Thus, at this point, normative applications of the descriptive theory are specifically envisaged. For this goal to be achieved a great deal more research on and in the organizational context will be required, and I suspect some more fully developed theorizing as well.

CONCLUSIONS

Image theory is in the tradition of behavioral decision theory, as is the theory of behavior in organizations (see Miner 2002), but it takes a very different slant on the nature of decision-making processes, accepting the view that human beings will rarely if ever go through the lengthy weighting of alternatives that traditional theory requires. Thus, image theory comes out much closer to the view of bounded rationality discussed by Simon and March (see Chapter 3). It also seems to have the potential for integration with approaches such as Lord's ideas regarding implicit leadership theories (see Miner 2005) and Weick's cognitive mapping (see Chapter 6). However, the constructs of these theories differ, and it will take considerable research to bring them together.

The ratings of image theory present something of an enigma. With an importance rating of 3.65, the theory is distinctly on the low side in part at least because it is not widely known outside of decision-making circles. Yet, based on the extensive research by Beach and his students, the theory's estimated validity has to be rated at four stars. As Beach himself notes in his own evaluation, sizable gaps in both theorizing and research coverage exist, but that does not detract from the substantial body of research confirming many of the theoretical formulations, especially those related to the compatibility test.

As to estimated usefulness, I rate image theory at three stars. A number of applications have been proposed, and some have been shown to actually work in practice. More detailed technologies would be helpful and certainly more applied research is to be desired. Yet among theories in the decision-making area, all of which are essentially descriptive in nature, image theory stands out by moving further into the normative domain than any of the others.

This ends our consideration of theories of organizational decision making. The remainder of this volume is concerned with more explicit theorizing focused directly on organizational processes and structures. In this regard I begin with a group of theories that utilize systems concepts in one way or another.

REFERENCES

Asare, Stephen K., and Knechel, W.R. (1995). Termination of Information Evaluation in Auditing. *Journal of Behavioral Decision Making,* 8, 21–31.

Beach, Lee Roy (1990). *Image Theory: Decision Making in Personal and Organizational Contexts.* Chichester, UK: John Wiley.

———. (1993a). Four Revolutions in Behavioral Decision Theory. In Martin M. Chemers and Roya Ayman (Eds.), *Leadership Theory and Research: Perspectives and Directions.* San Diego, CA: Academic Press, 271–92.

———. (1993b). *Making the Right Decision: Organizational Culture, Vision, and Planning.* Englewood Cliffs, NJ: Prentice Hall.

———, (Ed.). (1996). *Decision Making in the Workplace: A Unified Perspective.* Mahwah, NJ: Lawrence Erlbaum.

———. (1997). *The Psychology of Decision Making: People in Organizations.* Thousand Oaks, CA: Sage.

———, (Ed.). (1998). *Image Theory: Theoretical and Empirical Foundations.* Mahwah, NJ: Lawrence Erlbaum.

Beach, Lee Roy, and Frederickson, James R. (1989). Image Theory: An Alternative Description of Audit Decisions. *Accounting, Organizations and Society,* 14, 101–12.

Beach, Lee Roy, and Mitchell, Terence R. (1978). A Contingency Model for the Selection of Decision Strategies. *Academy of Management Review,* 3, 439–49.

———. (1987). Image Theory: Principles, Goals, and Plans in Decision Making. *Acta Psychologica,* 66, 201–20.

———. (1990). Image Theory: A Behavioral Theory of Decision Making in Organizations. *Research in Organizational Behavior,* 12, 1–41.

Beach, Lee Roy, Mitchell, Terence R., Paluchowski, Thaddeus F., and van Zee, Emily H. (1992). Image Theory: Decision Framing and Decision Deliberation. In Frank Heller (Ed.), *Decision-Making and Leadership.* Cambridge, UK: Cambridge University Press, 172–88.

Beach, Lee Roy, Smith, B., Lundell, J., and Mitchell, Terence R. (1988). Image Theory: Descriptive Sufficiency of a Simple Rule for the Compatibility Test. *Journal of Behavioral Decision Making,* 1, 17–28.

Beach, Lee Roy, and Strom, Eric (1989). A Toadstool Among the Mushrooms: Screening Decisions and Image Theory's Compatibility Test. *Acta Psychologica,* 72, 1–12.

Carlson, Kevin D., and Connerley, Mary L. (2003). The Staffing Cycles Framework: Viewing Staffing as a Series of Decision Events. *Journal of Management,* 29, 51–78.

Dunegon, Kenneth J. (1993). Framing, Cognitive Modes, and Image Theory: Toward an Understanding of a Glass Half Full. *Journal of Applied Psychology,* 78, 491–503.

Hollenbeck, John R., Ilgen, Daniel R., Phillips, Jean M., and Hedlund, Jennifer (1994). Decision Risk in Dynamic Two Stage Contexts: Beyond the Status Quo. *Journal of Applied Psychology,* 79, 592–98.

Lee, Thomas W., and Mitchell, Terence R. (1994). An Alternative Approach: The Unfolding Model of Employee Turnover. *Academy of Management Review,* 19, 51–89.

Lee, Thomas W., Mitchell, Terence R., Wise, Lowell, and Fireman, Steven (1996). An Unfolding Model of Voluntary Employee Turnover. *Academy of Management Journal,* 39, 5–36.

Miller, George A., Galanter, E., and Pribram, K.H. (1960). *Plans and the Structure of Behavior.* New York: Holt, Rinehart, and Winston.

Miner, John B. (2002). *Organizational Behavior: Foundations, Theories, and Analyses.* New York: Oxford University Press.

———. (2005). *Organizational Behavior 1: Essential Theories of Motivation and Leadership.* Armonk, NY: M.E. Sharpe.

Mitchell, Terence R., and Beach, Lee Roy (1990). ". . . Do I Love Thee? Let Me Count . . ." Toward an Understanding of Intuitive and Automatic Decision Making. *Organizational Behavior and Human Decision Processes,* 47, 1–20.

Mitchell, Terence R., and Lee, Thomas W. (2001). The Unfolding Model of Voluntary Turnover and Job Embeddedness: Foundations for a Comprehensive Theory of Attachment. *Research in Organizational Behavior,* 23, 189–246.

Mitchell, Terence R., Rediker, Kenneth J., and Beach, Lee Roy (1986). Image Theory and Its Implications for Organizational Decision Making. In Henry P. Sims and Dennis A. Gioia (Eds.), *The Thinking Organization.* San Francisco, CA: Jossey-Bass, 293–316.

Ordóñez, Lisa D., Benson, Lehman, and Beach, Lee Roy (1999). Testing the Compatibility Test: How Instructions, Accountability, and Anticipated Regret Affect Prechoice Screening of Options. *Organizational Behavior and Human Decision Processes,* 78, 63–80.

Richmond, Sandra M., Bissell, Byron L., and Beach, Lee Roy (1998). Image Theory's Compatibility Test and Evaluations of the Status Quo. *Organizational Behavior and Human Decision Processes,* 73, 39–53.

Seidl, Christian, and Traub, Stefan (1998). A New Test of Image Theory. *Organizational Behavior and Human Decision Processes,* 75, 93–116.

PART III

SYSTEMS CONCEPTS OF ORGANIZATIONS

CHAPTER 8

CONTROL THEORY
(USING THE CONTROL GRAPH)

ARNOLD TANNENBAUM

Importance rating	★ ★ ★
Estimated validity	★ ★ ★ ★
Estimated usefulness	★ ★
Decade of origin	1950s

The label *control theory* emerges often in organizational behavior, typically with very different meanings and with reference to theories that have little in common. The theory referred to here is the product of Arnold Tannenbaum, came out of the University of Michigan, and has been operationalized using the control graph method. In particular, this theory should not be confused with a "control theory" based on the tenets of cybernetics that carries the same name but has little to do with Tannenbaum's views (Vancouver and Putka 2000).

BACKGROUND

Arnold Tannenbaum received his first degree in electrical engineering from Purdue University in 1945. He became associated with the Center for Group Dynamics when it moved from MIT to Syracuse University after Kurt Lewin's death (see Miner 2005). After completing his doctorate in social psychology with Floyd Allport at Syracuse University in 1954, Tannenbaum moved with the Center for Group Dynamics to the Institute for Social Research at the University of Michigan, where he remained as program director and professor in the psychology department.

In Tannenbaum's (1956) own view, his theory emerged out of the early Michigan studies contrasting leadership behaviors in high- and low-producing work groups, out of research by Morse and Reimer in which he played an active role (Morse, Reimer, and Tannenbaum 1951), and out of the early work on hierarchical influence and linking pin relationships done by Pelz. Tannenbaum interprets all these studies as analyses of the effects of variations in the amount and distribution of control. They are limited in scope, however, to the work group and to supervisory practices. Tannenbaum extended the framework of control to the total organization.

Much of Tannenbaum's thinking about the role of control in organizations was influenced by Allport's views on interpersonal control and dominance relationships. However, Tannenbaum was interested in theory at the organizational level from an early time (Morse, Reimer, and Tannenbaum 1951). As a formal entity, control theory was created as a framework for a study of four local unions.

Since Tannenbaum's control theory was closely intertwined with other work at the Institute for Social Research at the University of Michigan, where Rensis Likert's theory of systems 1–4 and 4T was the dominant position during the 1960s and 1970s, I need to provide some background on Likert's views as context for Tannenbaum. This is particularly important because Tannenbaum's theory arose out of a desire to deal with certain topics that he felt were not handled adequately by the early Michigan work. Elsewhere, I have dealt with Likert's theory in considerable detail (Miner 2002); that theory is not discussed in this volume in that same detail because it fails to meet any of the criteria established for an "essential" theory. However, I should note that Likert's ideas have provided some of the impetus to positive organizational scholarship as described in Chapter 2 (Cameron, Dutton, and Quinn 2003).

LIKERT'S THEORY OF THE PARTICIPATIVE ORGANIZATION

Likert set forth his theory in three books, published in 1961, 1967, and (coauthored with his wife, Jane Likert) 1976.

New Patterns of Management

The first comprehensive statements of Likert's views (Likert 1961) contained extensive discussions of research conducted by the staff of the Institute for Social Research during the late 1940s and the 1950s. Such sequencing might give the impression that the 1961 theory was an outgrowth of prior research and that this research cannot legitimately be viewed as a test of the theory. Yet Likert's earlier writings, extending back to the 1940s, contain many statements that are analogous to those set forth more formally in the 1961 volume. Thus, key concepts such as the principle of supportive relationships and the value of participative management appear to have guided the research of the University of Michigan group from the beginning.

The principle of supportive relationships is stated in somewhat varied forms in Likert's writings, but the meaning changes very little:

The leadership and other processes of the organization must be such as to ensure a maximum probability that in all interactions and all relationships with the organization each member will, in the light of his background, values, and expectations, view the experience as supportive and one which builds and maintains his sense of personal worth and importance. (Likert 1961, 103)

As a theoretical hypothesis, this statement should be prefaced with "If a high-producing organization is desired . . ."

This basic principle assumes an extremely important and influential role for leadership in the organization. Effective leaders are those who are employee-centered, in that they behave in ways that create a perception of supportiveness. At the same time, they transmit high-performance goals through a kind of "contagious enthusiasm" and possess the needed technical competence.

The major source of supportive relationships lies in the work group. Thus a derivation from the basic principle states:

Management will make full use of the potential capacities of its human resources only when each person in an organization is a member of one or more effectively functioning work groups that have a high degree of group loyalty, effective skills of interaction, and high performance goals. . . . An organization will function best when its personnel function not as individuals but as members of highly effective work groups with high performance goals. Consequently, management should deliberately endeavor to build these effective groups, linking them into an overall organization by means of people who hold overlapping group membership. The superior in one group is a subordinate in the next group and so on through the organization. (Likert 1961, 104–5)

Individuals who are in these positions of dual group membership ideally should exert influence in both groups—both upward and downward, as members and as leaders. In doing so they perform the linking pin function and open up channels of communication through the organization. Failure to perform the linking pin function effectively results in work group failure at the subordinate level. To the extent that there are many such failed groups and to the extent that groups of this kind exist toward the top of the hierarchy, the organization as a whole will function less effectively. Thus, open, two-way communication and influence are essential to organizational effectiveness. Group and intergroup meetings facilitate two-way communication and influence. Lateral or horizontal groupings and committees act as buffers against failures in the vertical linking pin system and are therefore recommended. The overall, overlapping group structure tends to bind group goals into those of the organization and creates unity of effort and a capacity to deal with conflict.

The key to an effective organization is an integrated system of overlapping groups. Therefore it becomes crucial to establish the conditions that make for effective group functioning. Likert (1961) notes twenty-four such characteristics, virtually all of which involve some application of the principle of supportive relationships.

Likert distinguishes three sets of variables that have major significance for organizational functioning. Figure 8.1 presents these variables and their relationships. Likert particularly emphasizes the intervening variables and their measurement. He comes to this position via the following logic. There is often a sizable lag between a change in the causal variables and any resultant change in end-result variables. This lag, like that associated with technological

Figure 8.1   **Relationships Between Causal, Intervening, and End-Result Variables Showing Measurements Yielding Prompt and Delayed Information**

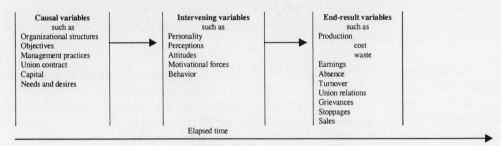

Source: Adapted from Likert (1961, 201).

innovation, may well be measured in years. Accordingly, to determine within a reasonable period of time what effects have been set in motion by a change and thus to establish a short feedback cycle, one must obtain measures of intervening variables. Effects may not show at the end-result point for years.

An important example of the need for a focus on intervening variables is provided by autocratic, production-oriented supervision. Such supervision can obtain results, but at the expense of squandering human assets, a process similar to liquidating physical assets. If the accounting system measures end-result variables only, these may be unaffected for some time, and the manager involved may be promoted to repeat the process before the consequences emerge. On the other hand, an accounting system that deals with intervening variables will identify the nature and extent of the decline in human assets, and thus in the quality of the human organization, and will deduct these changes against the productivity figures, making them look much less impressive. Consequently the manager who violates the principle of supportive relationships is less likely to be promoted, and the organization will benefit as a result.

Though the principle of participation is emphasized as the best guide for managerial action throughout the 1961 book, Likert does not explicitly relate it to other alternative management systems until the next to the last chapter. Here he describes what he calls exploitive authoritative, benevolent authoritative, and consultative systems and sets them against the participative group system that embodies the principle of participation. The four systems are differentiated with regard to motivational forces, communication, interaction-influence, decision making, goal setting, control, and performance. The participative group system is said to operate toward the end of a single continuum on which the other systems also fall. Under the participative group system greater total influence is exerted in the organization as a whole, and consequently performance is more effective overall. However, "the amount and character of participation need to be geared to the values, skills, and expectations of the people involved if productive results are to be obtained. . . . Participation should not be thought of as a single process or activity, but rather as a whole range of processes and activities" (Likert 1961, 242).

The Human Organization

The second of Likert's books (1967) covers much the same ground as the first, but a number of concepts are elaborated more fully, and there is a more pronounced emphasis on certain facets, such as establishing high goals, organization structuring, and accounting for human assets.

Exploitive authoritative, benevolent authoritative, consultative, and participative group systems are now labeled systems 1, 2, 3, and 4 for the first time, and the list of characteristics of these systems is extended in the areas of leadership, communication, decision making, control, goal setting, and training. Furthermore, the total list, minus the performance items, is converted into a questionnaire that may be used to obtain reports on the current organization, past states of the organization, ideal circumstances, and so on. This Profile of Organizational Characteristics provides an index of how closely an organization approximates the theoretically superior system 4. Shifts toward that system are expected to result in long-range improvements in productivity, labor relations, costs, and earnings.

On the other hand, shifts away from system 4, as occur in most cost-reduction efforts, will set in motion strong negative influences on intervening variables, even though the immediate results may be favorable. These negative influences are related to a definite sequence of events that does not manifest itself fully in end-result variables for three or four years, or even longer. The human relations approach to management often is introduced at this point as a salve for the existing system 2 organization. Because it does not actually shift the organization toward system 4, however, it does not work. A shift can be achieved by teaching managers system 4 principles.

Changes in an organization toward a new system should be internally consistent. One cannot achieve the desired results by changing only certain aspects of the system: the whole system needs to be shifted over a wide range of causal variables. The list of such variables in Likert's 1967 book is expanded considerably beyond those noted in the 1961 volume, as is the list of intervening variables. Likert indicates that such variables should be measured periodically to monitor the progress and comprehensiveness of change.

Likert (1967) rejects the classical management (see Miner 2002) view that an individual should have only one boss. He advocates horizontally overlapping groups with linking pins for many purposes and comprehensive group decision making for resolving any conflicts that may develop. Cross-function work groups that are product related should be introduced at both higher and lower levels in the organization. Geographic cross-function groups also may be introduced.

For effective coordination, the whole organization must consist of multiple, overlapping groups that are skillful in group decision making. Such a structure is not consonant with systems such as 2, but is compatible with system 4. Product management and similar work forms can be introduced successfully by extremely able managers in systems other than 4, but these forms will produce much better results in their natural environment.

New Ways of Managing Conflict

Likert's third book dealing with system 4 theory (Likert and Likert 1976) contains considerably less organization theory that is original than its predecessors. However, the systems 1 through 4 continuum is extended to cover a larger number of organizational forms.

System 0 covers permissive, laissez-faire organizations with little functional differentiation, large spans of control, and considerable confusion regarding roles. As might be expected from its position on the continuum, an organization of this kind is not hypothesized to be effective. On the other hand, the system 5 organization of the future is hypothesized to be extremely effective. The authority of hierarchy will disappear, and authority will accrue entirely from group relationships and linking pin roles. Whereas system 4 organizations operate from an interplay of group and hierarchical forces, system 5 organizations will function almost entirely as overlapping groups.

The central thesis of the Likert and Likert (1976) book is that system 4 is the best method currently available for dealing with conflict, not only in the organizational context, but in other contexts as well. The essential propositions are that:

1. Conflict involves interactions among people or social units and occurs in a social system.
2. Conflict resolution depends on the effectiveness of the social system used.
3. The closer the social system is to system 4, the greater the probability of constructive conflict resolution.
4. System 4 can be used in every conflict situation by those who wish to achieve resolution. Applying system 4 to conflict situations requires an understanding of system 4 principles, skill in their use, and the passage of time.

Thus, one would anticipate that a move to system 4 in an organization ultimately would not only improve productivity and profits (Likert says by 20 to 40 percent), but also cause a marked reduction in conflict.

Likert and Likert also introduce here the concept of system 4T. In system 4T, the designation T refers to *total*. System 4T theory states that there are additional factors beyond position on the system 1 through 4 continuum that contribute to organizational effectiveness. Likert had previously mentioned a number of these factors without specifically incorporating them into his theory. He now included these aspects of the human organization above and beyond the system continuum:

1. The levels of performance goals held by the leader and transmitted to subordinates.
2. The levels of knowledge and skill of the leader with regard to the technical field, administration, interaction processes, and problem solving.
3. The capacity and motivation of the leader to provide planning, resources, equipment, training, and help to subordinates.
4. The degree to which the structure provides for optimum differentiation and for sufficient linkages.
5. The extent to which stable working relationships exist within units.

The theory as it was now stated is clearly much more than a theory of the effects of participation. In fact, system 4 loses its preeminent role. Likert and Likert note that "If an organization, or a department, scores high on the system 1 to 4 scale and low on one or more of the other dimensions, such as technical competence or level of performance goals, the probabilities are great that it will not be highly effective in conflict management or performance" (1976, 50).

System 4T also introduces the concept of peer leadership and organizational climate. Peer leadership occurs when subordinate group members engage in leadership behavior. Such behavior tends to reflect the style of the leader. Under system 4T, peer leadership tends to strengthen the organization and has positive effects. In systems 1 or 2 it may well restrict output.

Organizational climate is defined as a composite state influenced by group member perceptions of the situation in the department, or some larger organizational entity, in which their group resides. It is influenced most by behavior toward the top of the organization and can severely constrain the type of management possible at lower levels. In system 4T, organizational climate is hypothesized to be a positive force.

In essence, Likert believed that there are general principles applicable to all managerial situations, though actual applications may vary with the particular culture involved. Likert does not spell out in any specific detail what cultural variations would be expected to have what effects under what circumstances. As a result, findings that fail to support Likert may be attributed to cultural variations on an ad hoc basis.

THE EVOLUTION OF CONTROL THEORY

With this background on the predominant theory at the University of Michigan, I turn now to the development of control theory as set forth in a series of articles and then bound together after original publication and republished as a book. This edited volume (Tannenbaum 1968) contains material extending back to 1956.

The Theory as Articulated for the Union Research

Tannenbaum's first theoretical statement sets forth his basic conceptual framework (see Tannenbaum and Kahn 1957, Tannenbaum 1968). He defines control in a number of publications as "the capacity to manipulate available means for the satisfaction of needs." Control is concerned with the allocation of rewards and punishments in an organization, and for this reason differences in control systems strongly influence the way organizations function. Within the more recent literature, Tannenbaum's control would seem to be reflected in such concepts as agency and stewardship controls (Tosi, Brownlee, Silva, and Katz 2003), in various forms of accountability controls as well as aspects of the span of control (Gittell 2000), and in normative control (Robertson and Swan 2003).

Control may vary both in total amount within the organization, from whatever source, and in distribution. Characteristically, distribution is considered in terms of groups at different levels in the organizational hierarchy. Within the union context, high control at the rank-and-file level and low control at the officer level is associated with *democracy*. In contrast, high officer and low membership control reflects an *autocratic* or oligarchic system. In the *laissez-faire* or anarchic model, the amount of control in the organization is low at all levels; no one exercises much control. Where the amount of control in the organization is high for both officers and rank-and-file members, the system is *polyarchic*.

Tannenbaum describes the way control works using several postulates:

1. There must be both a subject and an object, in that someone must control something. Controlling is the active aspect; being controlled, the passive.
2. Controlling must be motivated to occur. Thus there must be a perception of worthwhile rewards associated with the behavior.
3. Internal control within an organization and external control of the environment are closely related.
4. Control involves several phases of activity: the *legislative,* in which policies and courses of action are decided; the *administrative,* in which policies and courses of action are interpreted and implemented; the *sanctions,* in which rewards and punishments are given or withheld. (Tannenbaum and Kahn 1958, 154–55)

Tannenbaum does not offer clear-cut statements of his hypotheses. Nevertheless, they can be gleaned from a close reading of his articles and books. In the union research, member control was hypothesized to be positively related to member participation, as reflected in such activities as attendance at meetings, for instance. A similar relationship was expected to exist for total amount of control.

The amount of control in the organization consistently plays a more important role in the theory than does the distribution of control. Thus, the amount of control is hypothesized to relate positively to organizational power over the environment, competition and intraorganizational conflict, member loyalty, interorganizational conflict (with management, for instance), militancy, member conformity, and receipt of sanctions. Though total control is expected to exert a causal influence on these variables, reciprocal relationships are anticipated as well. A factor such as organizational power can contribute to total control, in addition to being caused by it.

Tannenbaum refers to the set of variables considered in this section as the *organizational power syndrome*. These variables are expected to yield increased order and uniformity in an organization. However, within this syndrome it is the total amount of control that matters. High total control is associated with a strong organization that is effective in the pursuit of its goals. However, a variety of distribution patterns can yield this same result. Even in discussing employee-centered leadership in this early period, Tannenbaum only goes so far as to state that this style fosters membership control and member participation; he does not extend the hypothesis to organizational effectiveness, as Likert did.

> In the typical evaluation of democracy in organizations and communities, great emphasis is put upon the distribution of control and all too little on the total amount of control exercised. . . . We should think less in terms of the autocratic-democratic dichotomy and more in terms of the basic dimensions of control, within which an infinite number of patterns can be found. (Tannenbaum and Kahn 1958, 237)

Tannenbaum's specific hypotheses about elevated member control and a democratic model involve member participation in union activities and a greater member interest in broad social goals, as opposed to bread-and-butter issues. In addition, Tannenbaum attributes the widely observed tendency for unions to become less democratic over time primarily to a relative decrease in member control in the later, more stable period.

Extensions During the 1960s

During the 1960s, Tannebaum increasingly extended control theory from its original focus on local unions into the domain of organizations in general. These developments are documented in an early review article (Tannenbaum 1962) and in *Control in Organizations* (Tannenbaum 1968).

One major change introduced early in the decade was to relate increases in relative amounts of control at lower levels, and thus a particular control distribution, to organizational effectiveness. This was a step that Tannenbaum had not taken when the theoretical focus was on unions only. It puts him much more in line with Likert's views on the superiority of democratic (system 4) forms over more autocratic forms, and Tannenbaum (1968, 57) acknowledges his debt to Likert in this regard.

At the same time, the theory continued to stress the importance of the total amount of control. The relationship with effectiveness is reciprocal: greater control yields greater organizational effectiveness, and effectiveness contributes to greater control. Tannenbaum qualified the hypothesis as follows, however:

> ... [T]oo much control may be as dysfunctional as too little, and a hypothesis more general than that offered above would specify an optimum level of control above or below which the organization would function below its potential. We are not yet in a position to specify the optimum for specific organizations. We can safely assume, however, that many ... organizations are operating at a level considerably below it. (Tannenbaum 1968, 58)

In another new hypothesis, Tannenbaum states that "across areas of experience, satisfaction will be a positive function of control" (Tannenbaum 1968, 241). On the average, people who have greater control over an aspect of their work will be more satisfied in that regard, though for some few individuals, control may not have this significance.

Tannenbaum elaborates on the view that the total amount of control in an organization is not a fixed sum at some length, particularly with reference to how expansion may occur.

1. There may be an expansion into the organization's external environment, such that greater influence over competitors, governments, and the like occurs.
2. There may be certain kinds of internal changes—either in the structural factors that determine member interactions and influence, or in the motivational factors that cause members to exercise control and to become amenable to control.

Control may expand as a function of increased interpersonal exchange, greater personal inclusion in the organization, co-optation of new members, and the like. Participative approaches of the kind represented by system 4 are particularly likely to increase the amount of control in this manner. The "influence pie" is expanded from within, as more organizational members exert influence on each other.

Participation and Control

Over the years, control theory became increasingly concerned with the nature of various types of participative systems and their relationships to the total influence pie.

> Participation is often thought to imply taking power from managers and giving it to subordinates, but in fact managers need not exercise less control where there is participation. A reduction in managerial power *may* occur, but it need not. ... [T]he participative organization may be one in which the *total amount of control* is higher than in the nonparticipative organization. ... [T]he success of participative approaches hinges not on reducing control, but on achieving a system of control that is more effective than that of other systems. In fact, many participative schemes are really designed implicitly, if not explicitly, to legitimize, if not enhance, the control exercised by managers. (Tannenbaum 1974, 78–79)

As an outgrowth of this view, specific hypotheses were formulated (Rosner, Kavcic, Tannenbaum, Vianello, and Wieser 1973):

1. The degree of workers' participation in decision making is related positively to the amount of total control in the organization, and more specifically to the amount of control by the workers as a whole and by management.
2. The relationship between workers' participation in decision making and the amount of management control is mediated both by the frequency of communication between subordinates and superiors and by the amount of the workers' control.
3. A rise in the amount of workers' control increases trust in management, which in turn increases management control.
4. A rise in the amount of workers' control contributes to a sense of worker responsibility, which in turn increases management control.

According to these formulations, shifts in the direction of participative management would not be expected to eradicate hierarchy. Control would increase in the ranks of management also, though probably the *relative* amount there would be somewhat less than under a less participative system. For control theory, participation effects of this kind are not restricted to approaches such as system 4; they may occur under the impact of a socialist economy as well (Tannenbaum, Kavcic, Rosner, Vianello, and Wieser 1974). Thus, the general hypothesis is that people at the upper level in organizations will have consistently greater control than those below, but that in organizations designed on the basis of socialist ideological principles this hierarchic differential will be smaller than elsewhere (Tannenbaum and Rozgonyi 1986).

THE CONTROL GRAPH METHOD

Most research bearing on control theory has utilized a measurement procedure developed at the inception of the theory. The existence of the control graph method has been a boon to researchers. On the other hand, such extensive reliance on a single procedure for operationalizing theoretical variables raises questions about construct validity and the specificity of results to the particular measure used.

The Nature of the Method

The control graph method uses survey methodology. Through a questionnaire, members of the organization are asked to indicate how much control they believe individuals at various levels exert. Thus, in the union research, questions cast in the format "In general, how much do you think _____ has to say about how things are decided in this local?" were asked for the president, the executive board, the plant bargaining committee, and the membership (Tannenbaum and Kahn 1958). Responses were given on a five-point scale, ranging from "a great deal of say" to "no say at all."

These scale values are averaged for all respondents to obtain scores reflecting control exercised at each organizational level. A graph is then constructed on which the amount of control reported for each level is plotted against the hierarchical level involved. Figure 8.2 illustrates various possible results. Line 1 is positively sloped and reflects a democratic control structure. Line 4 is negatively sloped and reflects an autocratic or centralized structure. Both lines indicate the same amount of control, but the control distributions vary dramatically.

Figure 8.2 **Hypothetical Control Lines**

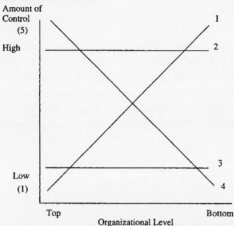

Line 3 reflects an essentially laissez-faire structure with very little control at any level. Line 2 reflects a polyarchic system. A comparison of these two lines reveals sizable differences in the amount of control exercised in the organizations, even though the distributions are identical. The lines of Figure 8.2 have been selected to portray hypothetically pure cases. In actual practice the lines drawn to connect the various points on the hierarchical scale may yield a great variety of curves. Straight-line relationships occur only rarely.

Although control graphs typically are constructed to reflect control actually exerted (or active control), there are several alternative measures in the literature. One alternative is an index of passive control, which indicates the extent of control over each hierarchical level (Tannenbaum 1968). The basic data derive from essentially the same questions used to measure active control. However, in this instance respondents rate on a five-point scale the amount of influence exerted by each level on all levels, including the level in question, as in Figure 8.3. The scores for the levels are then averaged in terms of influence perceived from all sources, and the points plotted just as with active control. In general, these passive control curves tend to be flatter than active control curves: being controlled is more equally distributed across hierarchical levels. The data of Figure 8.3 also permit the construction of separate curves showing the amount of control exerted by each level on the various levels (top management, management below the top level, rank-and-file), though such a detailed approach is not commonly used.

Another measure deals with ideal or desired control (Tannenbaum 1968). In this variant the word *should* is substituted for *does* in the questions (see Figure 8.3). Comparisons characteristically are made between actual and ideal curves. The ideal values tend to be higher than the actual, with the discrepancy being greatest at the lower levels.

On occasion, specific questions are asked about control in various areas (wages and salaries, hiring, pricing, investments, and so on) as a supplement to or replacement for the more global questions (Tannenbaum 1968). The responses to a number of specific questions may be summed to obtain a total measure. In this approach, as with the other measures discussed, question wording has not been completely standardized. There are variations from study to study, and it is not entirely clear what effects these variations may have on results. Also, the verbal descriptors applied to the five points on the scale have not always been the same.

Figure 8.3   **Typical Set of Questions for Constructing Active and Passive Control Curves**

1.   In general, how much say or influence does top management have on what the following groups do in the company?

	Little or no influence	Some influence	Quite a bit of influence	A great deal of influence	A very great deal of influence
Top management	_____	_____	_____	_____	_____
Management below the top level	_____	_____	_____	_____	_____
The rank-and-file workers	_____	_____	_____	_____	_____

2.   In general, how much say or influence does management below the top level have on what the following groups do in the company?

	Little or no influence	Some influence	Quite a bit of influence	A great deal of influence	A very great deal of influence
Top management	_____	_____	_____	_____	_____
Management below the top level	_____	_____	_____	_____	_____
The rank-and-file workers	_____	_____	_____	_____	_____

3.   In general, how much say or influence do the rank-and-file workers have on what the following groups do in the company?

	Little or no influence	Some influence	Quite a bit of influence	A great deal of influence	A very great deal of influence
Top management	_____	_____	_____	_____	_____
Management below the top level	_____	_____	_____	_____	_____
The rank-and-file workers	_____	_____	_____	_____	_____

Difficulties with the Control Graph Method

The reliability of the control graph has received only limited attention. The use of large numbers of raters whose reports are averaged should provide a reliable result, however, the use of a very limited number of questions to fix points on a curve suggests that reliability may not be as great as desired. Tannenbaum and Cooke (1979) note a lack of predicted correlations between the perceptions of various groups concerning the influence exerted by these groups. The problem is great enough to suggest low reliability in a measure that combines responses. In one study, judgments by the rank and file and by board members regarding the control of the president correlated 0.50, but the correlations for the control of the rank and file itself and of the board were 0.25 and 0.18, respectively (Tannenbaum 1968). Findings of this kind suggest that the composition of the sample used to determine control values may exert considerable influence on the results obtained.

Tannenbaum (1968) also contains data on the split-half reliabilities (corrected for group size) of various control indexes. These range from 0.53 to 0.84, with a median of 0.67. Here, as elsewhere, the argument for reliability is predicated on the use of large numbers of respondents whose ratings are averaged. Ideally, however, data from repeat administrations would be used to determine reliabilities. Such data do not exist in the published literature. Furthermore, other investigators have reported split-half reliabilities well below 0.67 (Pennings 1976).

To this problem with reliability may be added certain other difficulties that the authors themselves raised at an early point (Tannenbaum and Kahn 1957):

1. There is no provision for scaling the hierarchical level and amount of control dimensions to achieve equal units of measurement. As a result, unknown biases may be introduced into the findings.
2. The theory assumes a measure of actual control in organizations, while the measure is a perceptual one. The measures may not be analogous with the theory's constructs.
3. The control graph does not deal with the means through which control is exercised and thus may be insufficient.
4. It may be more appropriate to deal with specific areas in which control is exercised, rather than to use a global index.
5. The roles of passive and ideal control curves need to be explored further.

Among these points, matters of construct validity and difficulties in global measurement have received the most attention. In addition, certain aspects of the reliability problem, which Tannenbaum tends to de-emphasize, have been given consideration.

On Construct Validity

The question of whether actual control, as opposed to mere perception of control, is represented in the control graph has been the subject of considerable research. Tannenbaum (1968) presents evidence that, though individual perceptions influence the results obtained, group or structural factors also tend to operate. The latter are interpreted as specific structural effects of actual control, with the qualification:

It must be noted, however, that this particular interpretation does not follow necessarily from the logic of our analysis. It is possible, for example, that our measures have tapped some cultural stereotype common to the office as a whole, rather than the actual behaviors assumed to be associated with control and bases of power. (Tannenbaum 1968, 222)

Overall, the results from this line of research are consistent with the idea that a sizable amount of variance in control graph measures is attributable to actual control, but they do not extend to the point of certain proof.

One problem with the control graph method is that respondents are free to interpret "say or influence" in their own way. Thus, what is said to be influence at one level may not be the same thing as influence at another. There is evidence that this is the case:

> . . . [I]nfluence is specific as to hierarchic level. This indicates that the levels not only are perceived to have a different degree of influence, but that there is also a qualitative difference. . . . [T]he questions measure influence in three dimensions, one for each hierarchical level. This means that it is not possible to draw a control curve as this requires unidimensional variables. (Gundelach and Tetzschner 1976, 59–60)

Conclusions such as these appear somewhat extreme, based on the data; at the very least, one can utilize measures of slope and total control to test the theory, whether or not a graph actually is constructed. Yet questions as to what the control graph measures mean are raised by this type of analysis—questions that are given further credence by the fact that, in the measurement of control, different hierarchical groups often yield different outcomes. It appears that control under one circumstance is not the same as control under another, and that the control graph method lacks the capacity to differentiate.

Evidence indicates that a majority of individuals respond to the questionnaire in a theoretically appropriate manner, although this is certainly not true of all. Attempts to correlate control graph measures with other measures that appear to tap the same constructs have produced favorable results. Thus the distribution measures do correlate (averaging in the 0.50s) with other indexes of centralization (Tannenbaum 1968) and both slope and total control show the expected relationships with independent measures of participation (Tannenbaum, Kavcic, Rosner, Vianello, and Wieser 1974). All in all, it appears that the global questions yield only very rough measures of actual control, and do so with considerable "noise," and that the underlying constructs tapped by given measures may vary considerably, depending on the specific question, the respondent sample, the organization, and other circumstances.

Many problems associated with the control graph method might be solved by substituting a series of questions about influence in specific decision areas for the global questions. This approach should establish constructs with greater precision and at the same time increase reliability, because scores are based on a greater number of items. Yet, when one gets down to the matter of predicting criteria, there appears to be no difference between the standard global measure and an index based on eight specific items. The latter is more reliable, and results are not significant on all criteria for either measure, but the data do not support an outright rejection of the global measure for the more specific index (Patchen 1963). Also, the subjective nature of the control graph data should not be viewed as a deficiency. In addition to what has been noted previously regarding the convergence of subjective and objective control data, recent research on the comparability of subjective and objective performance measures contributes to a conclusion that the two typically yield essentially the same results (Wall, Michie, Patterson, Wood, Sheehen, Clegg, and West 2004).

EVALUATION AND IMPACT

Much of the research on control theory has been conducted by Tannenbaum and his associates. This research often has been international in character, with particular focus on socialist economic systems. However, a number of studies, both domestic and international, have been conducted without any involvement of the author of the theory.

Union Research

Questionnaire data to include control graph measures were obtained from rank-and-file members of four union locals in Michigan. The number of respondents per local varied from 163 to 223 (Tannenbaum and Kahn 1958). In general the control curves sloped positively toward greater control in the membership and bargaining committee than in the president and executive board, though there were sizable variations from local to local. The more democratic the local (the greater the member control), the more member participation, as reflected in attendance at meetings. As hypothesized, a similar relationship held for total control. The greater the positive slope of the control curve for the local, the more likely members were to endorse broad social goals. However, this finding did not apply to political action and appeared to reflect primarily a desire for expanded organizing activity.

Analyses dealing with the organizational power syndrome produced consistently supportive results. Total control proved to be related to union power, union–management conflict, intralocal conflict, loyalty, conformity, and participation in union affairs. High total control was associated with uniformity in a wide range of areas.

Overall, these results support control theory, but in several respects the union research must be viewed as a pilot study. The findings are presented as comparisons between ranks for four organizations, too few for appropriate statistical testing. Furthermore, the data are concurrent and do not yield evidence to support the causal hypotheses of the theory. Though the authors advance suggestions as to the relative effectiveness of the locals, they report no direct tests of hypotheses related to effectiveness and control in the original study.

Predicting Organizational Effectiveness

Among the theory's hypotheses, those dealing with the prediction of organizational effectiveness have received the greatest research attention subsequent to the union studies. Researchers have focused on the view that the total amount of control in an organization contributes in an important way to an effective organization. However, a number of studies also have dealt with the hypothesis that a more positive, or at least a less negative, control curve and thus a more democratic system is a source of success.

Total amount of control has been found to correlate positively with independent measures of organizational effectiveness in a wide range of situations. A review and reanalysis of early University of Michigan studies reported a significant relationship for five out of six studies (Smith 1966). Similarly, a report on early research conducted in Yugoslavia indicated consistently positive results with the total control index, though measures of control distribution did not produce the hypothesized relationship in any instance (Rus 1970).

A review by Tannenbaum and Cooke (1979) of many more studies yielded essentially the same conclusions. Over twenty studies were considered, many of them unpublished. Only a small fraction of the studies failed to yield some evidence of a significant positive relationship between total control and organizational effectiveness.

Research dealing with the distribution of control, or slope of the control curve, has not produced the same consistent results as total amount of control. Often the correlations do not attain statistical significance. When they do, it may be that the more democratic systems are more effective but this is by no means always true. Based on the evidence, Tannenbaum's early hesitation in endorsing democratic control structures seems justified. He would have done well to hold to this position after the union research. (For a review of research on this issue see chapter 12 in Miner 2005.) The research is entirely consistent with the control theory findings.

Tannenbaum summarized the findings in *Control in Organizations* as follows:

1. Organizations with influential rank-and-file members *can be* as effective as organizations with relatively uninfluential members (contrary to the traditional view).
2. Organizations with powerful officers can be as effective as organizations in which the officers are less influential (contrary to most participative views).
3. Organizations with influential rank-and-file memberships are likely to be more effective than those with uninfluential memberships *provided* the officers are not less influential (contrary to the traditional views).
4. Organizations with powerful officers are likely to be more effective than those with less powerful officers *provided* the memberships are not less influential (contrary to most participative views).
5. Organizations with influential leaders *and* members are likely to be more effective than organizations with less influential members and/or leaders (contrary to both traditional and participative views).
6. Differences in power between persons of different rank are *not* likely to be associated with criteria of performance. This statement sharply contradicts some arguments for participative organization to the extent that these arguments identify participation with "power equalization." (Tannenbaum 1968, 309–10)

Control theory hypothesizes not only a relationship between amount of control and effectiveness but also a causal relationship. Increased control should produce greater effectiveness; yet, at the same time, greater effectiveness should increase control. Studies dealing with causation are few in number, but they do exist. In one instance, measures of the amount of control taken in one year correlated significantly with a number of performance criteria obtained a year later (predictive). Criteria obtained at the same time as the control data (concurrent) yielded much lower and generally nonsignificant results (Tannenbaum 1968, 125–28). In this particular study significant predictions from performance to control level were not obtained.

A longitudinal study conducted by Farris (1969), on the other hand, yields evidence of a stronger effect of performance on control than of control on performance. The generally low correlations in this instance, however, make interpretation difficult.

One of the few laboratory studies dealing with control theory further supports the view that greater control can contribute to greater effectiveness (Levine 1973). The control levels in three-person problem-solving groups were experimentally manipulated. Groups with a high total amount of control performed consistently better and were more satisfied. Accordingly, it seems appropriate to conclude that high levels of control can be a source of effectiveness.

Control and Satisfaction

There are a number of studies in which total amount of control is positively related to measures of satisfaction, loyalty, morale, and the like. Positive slope, or its approximation, also tends to be related to variables of this kind, but not to the degree that amount of control is. Unlike the analyses involving organizational effectiveness criteria, however, those utilizing satisfaction criteria typically risk contamination due to common method variance, since the same questionnaire was used to measure both the control variables and the criteria. Correlations as high as .90 between total amount of control and satisfaction suggest that common method variance may well be a problem, given the relatively low reliability of control measures.

In any event, though control theory anticipates a positive overall relationship between amount of control and satisfaction, it further hypothesizes that individuals will experience greater satisfaction in areas where their control is greater. In general this appears to be true (Tannenbaum 1968). Workers tend to report greater satisfaction in areas in which, on independent evidence, they would be expected to exert greater control. In one instance where control was expanded in certain areas and not others, the changes in control correlated .46 with increases in satisfaction.

Participation and the Expandable Influence Pie

Control theory posits that increases in control at lower levels through the introduction of participative procedures can, and frequently do, result in increases in control at upper levels also, thus expanding the total amount of control in the organization considerably. As a consequence, a resort to participative management would not be expected to eliminate hierarchy, though the degree of negative slope in the control curve might be reduced somewhat.

An early study cited by Likert (1961) compared control curves for departments that varied in the extent to which participative procedures were applied. Differences in control at the worker level reflected the participation differences. Furthermore, the same rank ordering was maintained at the higher management level. Participative approaches were correlated with a greater amount of control in general, as the theory would anticipate, and with greater productivity as well. All of the control curves exhibited a negative slope, irrespective of the level of participation.

This and other concurrent evidence tends to substantiate the expandable pie concept (Tannenbaum and Cooke 1974). Studies of industrial firms consistently indicate that hierarchical control systems predominate even in socialized societies (Tannenbaum, Kavcic, Rosner, Vianello, and Wieser 1974; Tannenbaum and Rozgonyi 1986). Exceptions involving positive slopes appear to occur in voluntary organizations and local unions, where the departure from bureaucratic organization is sizable. There is also some basis for anticipating a less hierarchical curve in professional organizations (Farris and Butterfield 1972).

Measures of participation tend to correlate positively with the total amount of control in the organization (Tannenbaum, Kavcic, Rosner, Vianello, and Wieser 1974). Yet the reverse also may be true in some cases:

Data from the international study also show that coercion as a "basis of power" for the supervisor tends to be negatively correlated with the total amount of control in organizations. However, these correlations are not always large, and an exception occurs in 10 Yugoslav plants where, for reasons that we do not understand, a high level of control is associated with coercive leadership practices. (Tannenbaum and Cooke 1974, 40)

Furthermore, the international research finds that the greater total control in participative systems is primarily a function of differences at lower levels, not all levels:

The major contribution to the enhanced influence in the participative, compared to the nonparticipative, plants appears to result from the greater influence of workers. . . . This power equalization, however, does not mean a reduction in the control exercised by managers—managers, on the average, hold their own. (Rosner, Kavcic, Tannenbaum, Vianello, and Wieser 1973, 207)

Though this outcome is not entirely consistent with theoretical predictions and the earlier Likert (1961) data, other hypotheses regarding participation are supported in this study. Frequency of superior–subordinate communication and amount of worker control tend to mediate the relationship between worker participation and management influence in a positive manner. Similarly, trust in management and a sense of worker responsibility (and thus presumably a lack of worker–management conflict) mediate the relationship between worker and manager control.

The studies considered to this point do not indicate that increasing participation at lower levels will *cause* an expansion of total control, though the results generally are consistent with such an interpretation. To answer the causal questions, longitudinal research to observe the effects of expanded participation over time is needed.

An effort to obtain longitudinal data of this kind was incorporated in research conducted at the textile firms—Harwood and Weldon (see Miner 2005). Control graphs, obtained at Weldon in 1962, 1963, and 1964, during the period of a concentrated effort to increase participation, indicate that very little change in actual control occurred. If anything, there was a diminution of control at higher levels and an increase at lower levels; no expansion of the influence pie occurred. Data from Harwood over the same period indicated that an increase in total control did occur there, which was in evidence at all levels (Marrow, Bowers, and Seashore 1967). However, Harwood had already shifted to a participative system by 1962, and the Harwood measures taken from 1962 to 1964 were intended as controls for those at Weldon.

This suggests that delayed response may be characteristic of increases in control, and indeed the data collected at Weldon in 1969 indicate an increase in total control over the earlier period (Seashore and Bowers 1970). The change was most pronounced at the highest level and quite minimal at the employee level. Thus the role played by participation in the 1969 results becomes problematic. The findings from the Weldon research as a whole are subject to multiple interpretations; this appears to be no less true of the control graph findings.

Other attempts at longitudinal analyses carried out in conjunction with early University of Michigan studies also fail to yield the anticipated results. In one instance comparisons of data collected in 1958 and in 1961 during a period of intensive efforts to introduce participative procedures in experimental groups within a plastic containers manufacturer produced only very weak evidence of an increase in total control. The increases that were found occurred entirely at the upper levels; actual employee control did not increase, though the results for desired control were consistent with expectations for a program to increase employee participation (Tannenbaum 1968, 165–84).

Control graphs in Yugoslavia were compared over a five-year period. Since the laws in that country had been moving progressively to define enterprises as essentially participative in nature, sizable increases in control were anticipated over the period of the study. Once again the changes in actual total control were minimal, though positive, and primarily attributable to increases in control at the top of the organizations. At the same time, desired control increased more substantially, especially at the worker level. In this case, the time spans involved appear broad enough to have captured any lag effects that might have been present (Tannenbaum 168, 91–109).

In another study, control graphs were constructed from the responses of all personnel in branch offices of an insurance company to questionnaires administered before and three months after a management development program for branch managers was carried out (Baum, Sorensen, and Place 1970). The program was human relations oriented and stressed power equalization. This emphasis was clearly evident in the scores on desired control, which shifted sharply in a power-equalized direction in the experimental branches where the managers received the training and failed to shift in the control branches where managers did not receive the training.

Nonetheless, total actual control did not increase after training, and though control at lower levels shifted upward, the control exercised by the branch managers decreased. These effects were still in evidence after the control group data were used to correct for apparent regressions toward the mean. In this instance no expansion in the influence pie occurred—what the workers won, the managers lost.

The pattern of a high positive correlation between participative approaches and total control in concurrent studies, combined with little evidence that participation *causes* increased control, suggests that high levels of control may contribute to a resort to participation on the part of managers. This would seem particularly feasible if control contributes to organizational effectiveness (as it apparently does) and in organizations where there is considerable control at high levels. High-level managers who exert a sizable influence on their organizations and who are well entrenched by virtue of managing an effective organization may simply be in the best position to risk introducing participative procedures.

It has been suggested also that the expandable influence pie concept will hold only where intraorganizational conflict (as, for instance, between management and workers) is at a minimum. In the presence of conflict, what one level wins, the other loses, as in the insurance firm (Gundelach and Tetzschner 1976). In the absence of conflict, trust, responsibility, two-way communication, and the like can operate to permit greater control at all levels. Data presented by Smith (1966) indicate that in bureaucratic systems such as industrial organizations, high levels of conflict are likely to be associated with low levels of overall control, with the result that laissez-faire (or anarchy) is approached. In contrast, less conflict is associated with greater overall control. Here, also, we cannot identify cause-and-effect relationships, but since the expandable pie hypothesis is not always valid, it seems reasonable to posit internal conflict as a moderator.

In describing such a conflict-laden situation, where the results do not fit the theory, Tannenbaum notes:

. . . [D]emocratic control (i.e., positive slope) does not have the predicted effect. . . . While the pattern of control may lead to high rank-and-file morale, it does not appear to promote basic identification with organizational objectives and practices or motivated action leading to high performance. It appears that in this organization, high rank-and-file control relative to the leaders may have the effect of members acting simply in terms of their own self-interests and not accepting the contributions of leaders. . . . In the absence of shared organizational norms and a system of high mutual influence (i.e., high total control) to regulate and coordinate member action with respect to these norms, it is not surprising that democratic control is not conducive to high organizational performance. (1968, 163)

The Role of Hierarchy in System 4 and Control Theory

System 4 theory has not been found successful in developing a conceptually sound method of dealing with hierarchy. Because the roots of the theory are in group dynamics, the whole matter of hierarchical relationships has not been well integrated with other constructs. In many respects, control theory may be viewed as an attempt to fill this gap in the system 4 theory. Control theory focuses primarily on hierarchy and attempts to integrate it with participative management.

Control theory has been only partially successful in integrating hierarchy with participative management. The difficulties have been in handling participation. The simplest hypothesis is that the concept of slope can be used to represent participation and that the more positive or less negative the slope, the more democratic and effective the organization. Support for this hypothesis has been obtained only rarely, and then typically not in business firms.

The more complex hypothesis dealing with participation left hierarchy intact (and the negative slope that goes with it), while tying participation into the finding that total control consistently was related to effectiveness. Here, too, however, the participation part of the hypothesis runs into difficulty. Attempts to introduce participative approaches have the expected impact on levels of desired control, but not on other aspects of the control graph. If anything, the data appear to be explained best by the following hypothesis: Where considerable control in an absolute sense exists above the worker level, there is a greater willingness to expand worker control, and the total amount of organizational control is likely to expand only in those instances where conflict between workers and management is at a minimum.

In spite of its failures (or very limited success) in dealing with the concept of participation, control theory has made a sizable contribution to the understanding of organizational functioning. The finding that satisfaction tends to be greater in areas where the individual experiences greater control provides new insights into job enrichment research (see Miner 2005). Knowing that organizations can vary in total amount of control—that control is not a fixed sum and that therefore control gained by some members need not be control lost by others—is valuable in understanding both organization–member and organization–environment relationships.

However, the most important contribution of control theory is the hypothesis (now soundly grounded in research) that a greater amount of control overall contributes to a more effective organization. This finding has emerged from study after study in spite of major imperfections in the questionnaire used. Because most imperfections, such as unreliability of measurement, would tend to void the finding of any significant results, the underlying phenomenon in this case must be very powerful indeed. Furthermore, the parallel between the findings on the amount of control and those on the stocks of learning across levels of an organization (Bontis, Crossan, and Hulland 2002) may well be of theoretical significance. Expanding the theory to incorporate not just control, but knowledge supplies and perhaps communication patterns, would seem to be not only feasible, but quite fruitful.

Control theory thus provides a basis for understanding how organizational effectiveness is obtained. Effectiveness appears to be a product of control processes that produce uniformity and coordinate effort behind goals; the result is a type of conformity. However, the pressures toward conformity need not come only from the top for the organization to be effective; ideally, control comes from all directions. It is important to recognize in this connection that control at any level includes control from within one's own group. Thus, rank-and-file groups can exert very strong influence on their members, resulting in a greater amount of control than bureaucracy can produce (Barker 1993).

Tannenbaum has indicated that the relationship between control and effectiveness might be curvilinear. Yet tests of the theory have continued to treat the hypothesis as linear, and that is the hypothesis the research supports. It seems reasonable that an organization might experience too much control, but the theory lacks specificity in this area and relevant research is nonexistent.

Application

Control theory has not generated any applications that are uniquely its own. However, the theory clearly implies that anything that can be done to increase the amount of organizational control and/or the perception of it will contribute to a more effective organization. Though guidelines for accomplishing this have not been developed and the introduction of participative management seems insufficient, several recommendations can be made.

For one thing, control in the sense that Tannenbaum uses the term is not the same as managerial control in the traditional literature. There, managerial control is defined as the steps a manager takes to assure that actual performance conforms as nearly as practical to plan. Control of this kind invariably involves evaluation and feedback. In contrast, Tannenbaum is concerned with a much broader concept, which encompasses managerial control, as well as other types of influence. Accordingly, increasing the total amount of control should not be equated with introducing an expanded array of managerial control systems. This may be part of the process, but it is certainly not all that Tannenbaum intended or that the research supports.

Furthermore, expanding control may well require increasing control at the lower levels— that is, not only the receipt of control, but also its exercise. As Tannenbaum (1966) notes, managers may resist this on the strength of a fixed-pie assumption. If conflict is rampant in the organization, the managers' assumption that their own control will suffer may be correct. Accordingly, it may be essential to develop mutual trust and a sense of responsibility before expanding control levels.

Control theory does not concern itself with how to increase organizational control, and this is one of its major deficiencies from the viewpoint of the practitioner. On the other hand, the theory has produced one conclusion that has tremendous practical significance: Organizations do need to be well controlled, and this does not have to be accomplished through centralization and a steep slope of hierarchy.

CONCLUSIONS

I have classified Tannenbaum's control theory as a systems theory for several reasons. One reason for this classification is the overlap with Likert's system 4, and the fact that certain aspects of control theory were in fact incorporated in system 4 by Likert. Another consideration is that systems theorizing tends to be wide ranging in its constructs, with variables so interrelated that everything seems to be related to everything else. This can be both a strength and a weakness; within control theory both the positive and negative consequences are evident. Clearly control theory extends across the organizational boundary into an open systems environment. The theory that concerns us in the next chapter is more explicit in its focus on open systems theorizing, but control theory is not devoid in this regard.

The ratings for control theory are much like those for Likert's theory, with one important exception—the much greater validity of control theory. The importance rating is at 3.58 (not particularly high), but estimated validity is at four stars, largely because of the consistent and important research support for the findings regarding total organizational control. This is a finding unique to Tannenbaum's control theory and it has very significant implications for organizational functioning. Yet, it has not been extended into the world of practice to the extent that might be desired; the estimated usefulness of control theory is only at the two-star level.

REFERENCES

Barker, James R. (1993). Tightening the Iron Cage: Concertive Control in Self-Managing Teams. *Administrative Science Quarterly,* 38, 408–37.

Baum, Bernard H., Sorensen, Peter F., and Place, William S. (1970). The Effect of Managerial Training on Organizational Control: An Experimental Study. *Organizational Behavior and Human Performance,* 5, 170–82.

Bontis, Nick, Crossan, Mary M., and Hulland, John (2002). Managing an Organizational Learning System by Aligning Stocks and Flows. *Journal of Management Studies,* 39, 437–69.

Cameron, Kim S., Dutton, Jane E., and Quinn, Robert F. (2003). *Positive Organizational Scholarship: Foundations of a New Discipline.* San Francisco, CA: Berrett-Koehler.

Farris, George F. (1969). Organizational Factors and Individual Performance: A Longitudinal Study. *Journal of Applied Psychology,* 53, 87–92.

Farris, George F., and Butterfield, D. Anthony (1972). Control Theory in Brazilian Organizations. *Administrative Science Quarterly,* 17, 574–85.

Gittell, Jody H. (2000). Paradox of Coordination and Control. *California Management Review,* 42 (3), 101–17.

Gundelach, Peter, and Tetzschner, Helge (1976). Measurement of Influence in Organizations—Critique of the Control-Graph Method. *Acta Sociologica,* 19, 49–63.

Levine, Edwin L. (1973). Problems of Organizational Control in Microcosm: Group Performance and Group Member Satisfaction as a Function of Differences in Control Structure. *Journal of Applied Psychology,* 58, 186–96.

Likert, Rensis (1961). *New Patterns of Management.* New York: McGraw-Hill.

———. (1967). *The Human Organization: Its Management and Value.* New York: McGraw-Hill.

Likert, Rensis, and Likert, Jane G. (1976). *New Ways of Managing Conflict.* New York: McGraw-Hill.

Marrow, Alfred J., Bowers, David G., and Seashore, Stanley E. (1967). *Management by Participation.* New York: Harper and Row.

Miner, John B. (2002). *Organizational Behavior: Foundations, Theories, and Analyses.* New York: Oxford University Press.

———. (2005). *Organizational Behavior 1: Essential Theories of Motivation and Leadership.* Armonk, NY: M.E. Sharpe.

Morse, Nancy C., Reimer, Everett, and Tannenbaum, Arnold S. (1951). Regulation and Control in Hierarchic Organizations. *Journal of Social Issues,* 7(3), 41–48.

Patchen, Martin (1963). Alternative Questionnaire Approaches to the Measurement of Influence in Organizations. *American Journal of Sociology,* 69, 41–52.

Pennings, Johannes M. (1976). Dimensions of Organizational Influence and Their Effectiveness Correlates. *Administrative Science Quarterly,* 21, 688–99.

Robertson, Maxine, and Swan, Jacky (2003). "Control—What Control?" Culture and Ambiguity Within a Knowledge Intensive Firm. *Journal of Management Studies,* 40, 831–58.

Rosner, Menachem, Kavcic, Bogdan, Tannenbaum, Arnold S., Vianello, Mino, and Wieser, Georg (1973). Worker Participation and Influence in Five Countries. *Industrial Relations,* 12, 200–12.

Rus, Veljko (1970). Influence Structure in Yugoslav Enterprise. *Industrial Relations,* 9, 148–60.

Seashore, Stanley E., and Bowers, David G. (1970). Durability of Organizational Change. *American Psychologist,* 25, 227–33.

Smith, Clagett G. (1966). A Comparative Analysis of Some Conditions and Consequences of Intra-Organizational Conflict. *Administrative Science Quarterly,* 10, 504–29.

Tannenbaum, Arnold S. (1956). The Concept of Organizational Control. *Journal of Social Issues,* 12(2), 50–60.

———. (1962). Control in Organizations: Individual Adjustments and Organizational Performance. *Administrative Science Quarterly,* 7, 236–57.

———. (1966). *Social Psychology of Work Organization.* Belmont, CA: Wadsworth.

———, (Ed.). (1968). *Control in Organizations.* New York: McGraw-Hill.

———. (1974). Systems of Formal Participation. In George Strauss et al. (Eds.), *Organizational Behavior: Research and Issues.* Madison, WI: Industrial Relations Research Association, 77–105.

Tannenbaum, Arnold S., and Cooke, Robert A. (1974). Control and Participation. *Journal of Contemporary Business,* 3(4), 35–46.

Tannenbaum, Arnold S., and Cooke, Robert A. (1979). Organizational Control: A Review of Studies Employing the Control Graph Method. In Cornelis J. Lammers and David Hickson (Eds.), *Organizations Alike and Unlike.* London: Routledge and Kegan Paul, 183–210.

Tannenbaum, Arnold S., and Kahn, Robert L. (1957). Organizational Control Structures: A General Descriptive Technique as Applied to Four Local Unions. *Human Relations,* 10, 127–39.

———. (1958). *Participation in Union Locals.* Evanston, IL: Row, Peterson.

Tannenbaum, Arnold S., Kavcic, Bogdon, Rosner, Menachem, Vianello, Mino, and Wieser, Georg (1974). *Hierarchy in Organizations: An International Comparison.* San Francisco, CA: Jossey-Bass.

Tannenbaum, Arnold S., and Rozgonyi, Tomás (1986). *Authority and Reward in Organizations: An International Research.* Ann Arbor, MI: Survey Research Center, Institute for Social Research, University of Michigan.

Tosi, Henry L., Brownlee, Amy L., Silva, Paula, and Katz, Jeffrey P. (2003). An Empirical Exploration of Decision-Making Under Agency Controls and Stewardship Structure. *Journal of Management* Studies, 40, 2053–71.

Vancouver, Jeffrey B., and Putka, Dan J. (2000). Analyzing Goal-Striving Processes and a Test of the Generalizability of Perceptual Control Theory. *Organizational Behavior and Human Decision Processes,* 82, 334–62.

Wall, Toby D., Michie, Jonathan, Patterson, Malcolm, Wood, Stephen J., Sheehan, Maura, Clegg, Chris W., and West, Michael (2004). On the Validity of Subjective Measures of Company Performance. *Personnel Psychology,* 57, 95–118.

CHAPTER 9

THE SOCIAL PSYCHOLOGY
OF ORGANIZATIONS

DANIEL KATZ
ROBERT KAHN

Importance rating	★ ★ ★ ★ ★
Estimated validity	★ ★ ★
Estimated usefulness	★ ★
Decade of origin	1960s

The theory considered in this chapter makes comprehensive use of the systems concept, eventually incorporating major formulations regarding the environment and its interactions with organizations. Thus this is truly an open systems theory in a sense that the system 4 and control formulations are not. The distinction here is between using systems concepts and developing a full-blown systems theory.

Daniel Katz and Robert Kahn propose a social psychology of organizations that has the same origins as the theories Likert and Tannenbaum developed at the University of Michigan. Katz and Kahn both were involved in the early research on participative management conducted by the Institute for Social Research. Both acknowledge a clear debt to Rensis

Likert. Yet their theory represents in many respects an alternative to system 4 theory, while maintaining the same behavioral humanist value orientation.

The Katz and Kahn theory is set forth primarily in two editions of a book titled *The Social Psychology of Organizations,* which were published in 1966 and 1978. These books enjoyed considerable popularity during the 1970s and the 1980s as the most sophisticated statements of the Michigan way of thinking.

BACKGROUND

Daniel Katz was born in 1903. His undergraduate degree was from the University of Buffalo and his doctorate in social psychology was obtained from another upstate New York school, Syracuse University. That was in 1928, and his mentor was Floyd Allport. He spent the next fifteen years in the psychology department at Princeton University. During World War II he was a member of the federal government group with Likert, working on survey research studies. After the war ended Katz took a position as chairman of the psychology department at Brooklyn College, but by 1947 he had followed the other members of the Likert group to the newly founded Institute for Social Research at the University of Michigan. He remained there for the rest of his career, holding an appointment in the psychology department as well. Katz did not have an appointment in the business school at Michigan and in fact was well into his career as a social psychologist and in his fifties when organizational behavior was born. He died at age ninety-five in 1998.

Robert Kahn was born in 1918 and received his education from the University of Michigan, culminating in a doctorate in social psychology in 1952. He remained at Michigan throughout his career, with appointments at the Institute for Social Research's Survey Research Center as well as the departments of psychology and public health. His position in the public health department was an outgrowth of his work on role conflict, stress, and related health matters. He is currently an emeritus professor at Michigan.

The Michigan theorists appear to have found in the Institute for Social Research the same type of multidisciplinary melting pot function that business schools provided for many other organizational behavior theorists. Both Likert and Katz had well-established careers in other areas when organizational behavior came into being, and thus the business schools offered them little by way of unique opportunity. Tannenbaum and Kahn were of a somewhat younger age cohort, but followed the role models provided for them, in large part because the Institute for Social Research served many of the functions a business school might have offered.

INITIAL SYSTEMS THEORY

The book that first presents the social psychology of organizations is in part a theoretical statement and in part a review of organizational literature in certain areas (Katz and Kahn 1966). The theory is covered largely in the first seven chapters and reviewed in the last, though several important theoretical statements occur in the intervening chapters on power and authority and on leadership.

The Systems Concept

The basic model involves energic inputs, the transformation of these inputs within the system, and an output that recycles or returns as energic input to keep the system going. In many cases, outcomes are converted to money, which in turn provides the needed input. The defining characteristics of such open systems are:

1. The importation of *energic inputs* from the social environment.
2. Transformation of available energy as *throughput,* so that work is done within the system.
3. The exportation of a product or *output* into the environment.
4. A *cycle of events* in which the product exported to the environment provides the energy for repetition of the cycle.
5. The development of *negative entropy,* whereby more energy is imported from the environment than is expended in work, thus counteracting the entropic imperative, which inevitably tends toward disorganization and death.
6. The existence of *information inputs* or signals about how the environment and the system are functioning; *negative feedback* from internal functioning, which provides information to correct deviations from course; and a *coding* process that simplifies energic and information inputs and permits their selective reception.
7. A *steady state* that preserves the character of the system and is marked by a stable ratio of energy exchanges and relations between the parts.
8. Movement in the direction of increasing *differentiation,* elaboration, or specialization.
9. The operation of the principle of *equifinality,* under which a system can achieve the same final state from different initial conditions and by various paths. (Katz and Kahn 1966, 19–26)

Defining Characteristics and Structures

Energic inputs are differentiated as *maintenance* inputs that sustain the system and *production* inputs that are processed and yield productive outputs. System integration is achieved through the operation of *roles,* or standardized patterns of behavior required of all who perform a function or set of tasks; *norms,* or expectations of role incumbents that serve to verbalize and sanction role requirements; and *values,* which are even more general ideological justifications and aspirations.

The theory posits five basic types of subsystems:

1. *Production* or technical—concerned with the throughput and the work done.
2. *Supportive*—concerned with procurement of inputs, disposal of outputs, and institutional functions related to the environment.
3. *Maintenance*—concerned with tying people to their roles, either through selection of personnel or through rewards and sanctions, thus preserving the system.
4. *Adaptive*—concerned with adaptive change to environmental variations.
5. *Managerial*—concerned with direction, coordination, and control of other subsystems and activities. This system operates through the use of regulatory mechanisms that utilize feedback about output as related to input, and through authority structures that legitimize directives in some manner. (Katz and Kahn 1966, 39–43)

A number of other constructs and processes are proposed, the most theoretically relevant of which are system *boundaries*—those barriers between system and environment that determine degrees of openness for the system—and *leading* systems—those that exert greater influence over the inputs of other component systems, and thus control interactions.

The authors describe the developmental process in organizations as follows:

Table 9.1

The Dynamics and Mechanisms of Subsystem Structures

Subsystem structure	Dynamic (common motivation)	Mechanisms
Production	Technical proficiency	Division of labor Job specifications and standards
Supportive (Boundary) 　Procurement and disposal	Focused manipulation of environment	Control of sources of supply Creation of image
Institutional	Social manipulation and integration	Contributing to community Influencing social structure
Maintenance	Maintaining steady state; predictability	Standard legitimized procedures System rewards Socialization
Adaptive	Pressing for change	Recommending changes to management
Managerial 　Conflict resolution within hierarchy	Control	Sanctions of authority
Coordinating functional structures	Compromise vs. integration	Alternative concessions Adjudication machinery
Coordinating external requirements with resources and needs	Long-term survival Optimization Improving resource use Increasing capabilities	Increasing business volume Adding functions Controlling environment Organization planning

Source: Adapted from Katz and Kahn (1966, 86).

At Stage 1 certain characteristics of a human population and some common environmental problem interact to generate task demands and a primitive production structure to fulfill them. At Stage 2 devices for formulating and enforcing rules appear. An authority structure emerges and becomes the basis for managerial and maintenance subsystems. Stage 3 sees the further elaboration of supportive structures at the organizational boundaries—structures for procurement, disposal, and institutional relations. (Katz and Kahn 1966, 109)

As set forth in Table 9.1, the consequence of this evolution is a set of structures, each with its own dynamic, or common motivation for the group, and mechanisms for achieving this dynamic. Within the managerial structure a maximization principle is hypothesized, which as a dynamic often tends to override the maintenance of a steady state. This is so because:

1. The proficiency dynamic leads to an increase in organizational capabilities.
2. Expansion is the simplest method of dealing with problems of internal strain.
3. Expansion is also the most direct solution in coping with problems of a changing social environment.
4. Bureaucratic role systems in their nature permit of ready elaboration.
5. Organizational ideology encourages growth aspirations. (Katz and Kahn 1966, 99–100)

Organizational Typology and Effectiveness

Organizations fall into four major types, based on the functions they perform for society. Productive (economic) organizations create wealth, manufacture goods, and provide services.

Maintenance organizations socialize people for their roles in society, including other organizations. Adaptive organizations create knowledge and often apply it as well. Managerial (political) organizations adjudicate, coordinate, and control resources and people.

In addition, organizations may be classified in terms of many secondary characteristics. Among these are throughput as it relates to products or people; maintenance through intrinsic or extrinsic rewards; degree of permeability of organizational boundaries; extent of structural elaboration; and steady state or maximization as the dominant dynamic.

A condition for organizational survival is negative entropy, whereby more energy is brought into the organization than emerges as output. Some energy is consumed by the organization in creating and maintaining itself. If this amount is large, the organization is inefficient; thus, efficiency is defined in terms of the ratio of energic output to energic input.

Organizational effectiveness, on the other hand, is defined as the maximization of energic return to the organization by all means. To the extent economic and technical means are employed for energic return, efficiency is affected as well. But maximization by political means is also possible and often is of considerable significance. Here the maximization typically occurs at some cost to the environment, either in the form of other organizations (such as competitors) or individuals. However, the authors also define as political certain processes carried out within the organization's boundaries, such as paying lower wages than other firms. As they themselves indicate, their distinction between efficiency and political effectiveness as components of organizational effectiveness is somewhat arbitrary (Katz and Kahn 1966, 165–70).

Organizational Roles

Katz and Kahn (1966) define an organization as an open system of roles, thus emphasizing a view of organizations as contrived in nature and consisting of a structure of acts or events. This role-related component of the theory was first proposed and defined at an earlier date (Kahn, Wolfe, Quinn, Snoek, and Rosenthal 1964), as were other concepts and constructs.

Roles are made up of certain recurrent activities within the total, interrelated pattern that yields the organizational output. Specifically, roles are those activities existing within a single subsystem and a single office. An *office* is a point within organizational space consisting of one or more roles to be performed by individuals. Individuals are surrounded by others, including superiors and subordinates, who operate as role senders to them. This process of role sending and receiving is described in Figure 9.1. *Role conflict* occurs when compliance with role sendings of one type would make it difficult or impossible to comply with role sendings of another type. *Role ambiguity* arises from a lack of role-related information or inadequacies in the communication of such information. In an ongoing organization, the simplicity of Figure 9.1 is often disturbed when one role involves many activities, when multiple roles exist in a single office, or when one person occupies several offices.

Though Katz and Kahn tend to de-emphasize hypothesis formulation, they offer four statements that they call interesting speculations or predictions about organizational roles:

1. The more activities contained within a role, the more likely it is to be varied and satisfying, the more likely it is to involve coordination among the activities it comprises, and the less immediate will be the necessity for coordination with other roles and offices.
2. The more interrole coordination an organization requires, the more the achievement of coordination is assigned to offices high in the organizational structure.

Figure 9.1   **Model of the Role Episode**

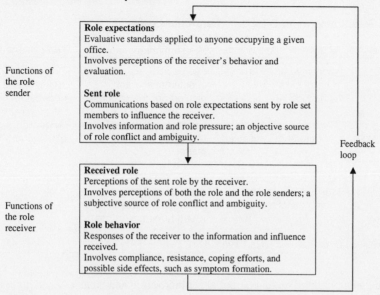

Functions of
the role
sender

Role expectations
Evaluative standards applied to anyone occupying a given
office.
Involves perceptions of the receiver's behavior and
evaluation.

Sent role
Communications based on role expectations sent by role set
members to influence the receiver.
Involves information and role pressure; an objective source
of role conflict and ambiguity.

Feedback
loop

Functions of
the role
receiver

Received role
Perceptions of the sent role by the receiver.
Involves perceptions of both the role and the role senders; a
subjective source of role conflict and ambiguity.

Role behavior
Responses of the receiver to the information and influence
received.
Involves compliance, resistance, coping efforts, and
possible side effects, such as symptom formation.

Source: Adapted from Kahn, Wolfe, Quinn, Snoek, and Rosenthal (1964, 26) and Katz and Kahn (1966, 182).

3. The more coordinative demands concentrated in a given office, the more the incumbent seeks a generalized, programmed solution. . . . Such a programmed solution is sought because it can be set up to hold for a considerable period of time, thus relieving the incumbent of the continuing press of certain types of decisions.
4. The greater the programming of interjob coordination, the greater will be the use of organizational authority and sanctions. (Katz and Kahn 1966, 181–82)

Hierarchic and Democratic Systems

One other area in which Katz and Kahn formulate specific hypotheses with regard to organizational process and structure is that of hierarchic versus democratic organization. They argue that hierarchic systems survive longer and are more efficient:

1. When the tasks do not require creativity and when identification with organizational goals is not essential.
2. When environmental demands are clear and obvious so that information about them is redundant and multiple processors of this information are not needed.
3. When rapid decision making is necessary.
4. When the environment is such that it requires little adaptive change, thus approximating the conditions of a closed system. (Katz and Kahn 1966, 214)

Essentially the opposite set of conditions argue for a democratic organizational structure. With regard to formal, hierarchic structure the authors conclude:

It is an instrument of great effectiveness; it offers great economies over unorganized effort; it achieves great unity and compliance. We must face up to its deficiencies, however. These

Table 9.2

Leadership Requirements at Different Hierarchic Levels

Hierarchical level	First-level supervision	Middle management	Top management
Nature of leadership required	Administration—the use of existing structure	Interpolation—supplementing and piecing out the structure	Origination—change, creation, and elimination of structure
Required cognitive abilities and skills	Technical knowledge; Understanding of rules	Subsystem perspective—two-way orientation of leader	Systemic perspective—external and internal
Required emotional abilities and skills	Equity and fairness in applying rules and using sanctions	Integration of the immediate work group with the larger system (good human relations)	Charisma

Source: Adapted from Katz and Kahn (1966, 312).

include great waste of human potential for innovation and creativity and great psychological cost to the members. . . . The modification of hierarchical organization to meet these criticisms is one of the great needs of human life. (Katz and Kahn 1966, 222)

Hierarchic Position and Leadership

Leadership theory in the 1960s, and for a considerable period of time thereafter, rarely gave much attention to position in the hierarchic organization as a variable of importance; the focus was on leadership of a group. The work of Katz and Kahn (1966) is one exception. Effective leaders are differentiated by position level and by the types of relationships and role expectations associated with that level. These leadership requirements are outlined in Table 9.2. Presumably an organization staffed to meet these requirements at each level would be more effective than one not so staffed.

OPENING THE THEORY UP

The theory set forth in the 1978 edition of the Katz and Kahn book is largely unchanged, although there are some important additions as well as many embellishments and expanded examples. The book grew by over 60 percent, but many of the additions were nontheoretical in nature.

The Principle of Integration

One change in 1978 is the explicit inclusion of integration as a characteristic of open systems. Thus the list of nine defining characteristics of open systems is extended to include *integration* and *coordination*. These characteristics counter differentiation and unify the system. Integration may be achieved through shared norms and values. Unification through coordination involves fixed control arrangements such as setting the speed of an assembly line.

As organizational structures grow, there is a tendency toward increased differentiation or specialization, followed by a complementary tendency toward increased integration or coordination. As the structure divides, integration is increasingly needed. Both differentiation and integration can be pushed beyond the point of maximum system return, however. An optimum point, and thus a curvilinear relation to efficiency, is posited. In particular, the use of fixed coordination devices is questioned when they are applied at high levels across many units of the system. Making decisions at lower levels, where they can apply to a smaller slice of the organization, is considered preferable.

The Environment

Katz and Kahn's 1978 treatment devotes considerably more attention to the environment and to organizational methods of coping with it than did their 1966 version, thus countering a potential source of criticism for an open systems theory. Though much of the discussion draws heavily on the theory and research of others, some original theory is included.

Five environmental sectors within which organizations function are identified:

1. The value patterns of the cultural environment.
2. The political structure or pattern of legal norms and statutes.
3. The economic environment of competitive markets and inputs.
4. The informational and technological environment.
5. The natural or physical or ecological environment, including geography, natural resources, and climate. (Katz and Kahn 1978, 124)

Each of these sectors may vary along four dimensions drawn largely from sociotechnical systems theory (see Chapter 10 in this volume): stable to turbulent, homogeneous to diverse, random to clustered, and scarce to munificent. Thus an organization may have a stable natural environment and a turbulent economic one, and so on. Generally, Katz and Kahn do not hypothesize about relationships among dimensions across sectors, but instead stress the need for measurement and empirical study. However, the sectors are thought to reflect a hierarchy of complexity, especially with regard to turbulence. As a lower-level sector, such as the natural environment, fails to provide stability, each higher-level sector is mobilized for that purpose. If all else fails, including political stabilization, turbulence may be reduced by a resort to common cultural values in the manner advocated by sociotechnical systems theory.

Katz and Kahn summarize organizational response in coping with environments as follows:

> The lack of assurance of sustained inputs and continuing markets for outputs leads to various forms of organizational response to reduce uncertainty. The first attempt is to control the environment directly and to incorporate it within the system. Then come efforts at indirect control through influencing other systems by means of political manipulation or economic bargaining. Or the organization may move to change its own structure to accord with environmental change. The concept of the temporary society can be considered in this context for it calls for adaptive, problem solving task forces. (Katz and Kahn 1978, 141)

AFTER *THE SOCIAL PSYCHOLOGY OF ORGANIZATIONS*

After they published the second edition of their major statement on organization theory, it seemed likely that Katz and Kahn would follow up with more theorizing of an open systems,

Figure 9.2   **Theoretical Framework for the Study of Stress in Organizations**

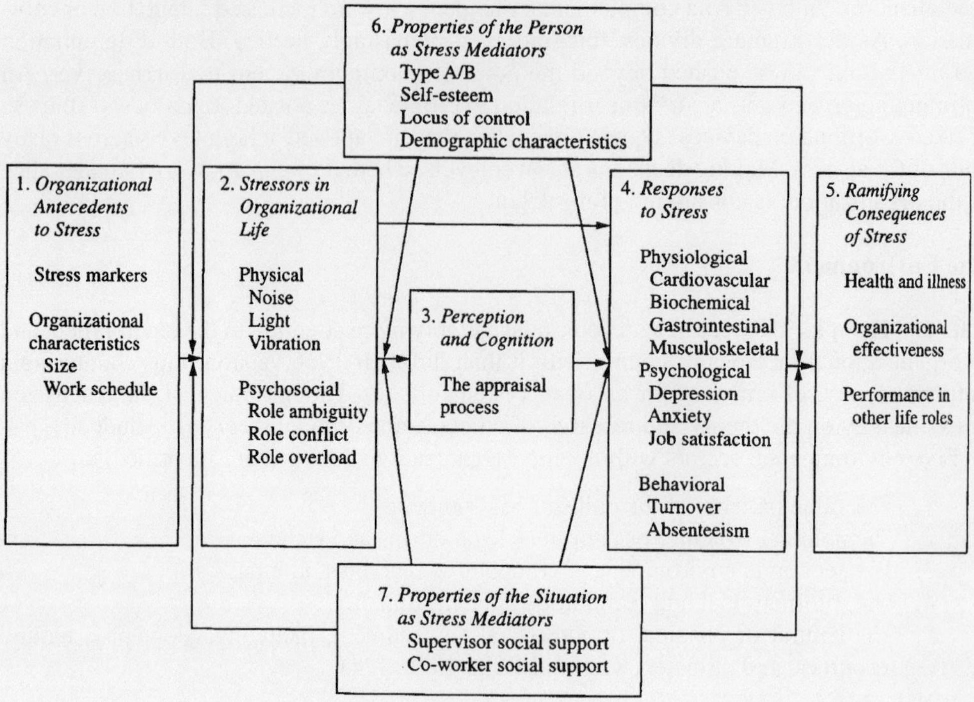

Source: Kahn and Byosiere (1992, 592). Copyright © 1992 by Consulting Psychologists Press. Reprinted with permission.

environment-related nature, given the trend from the first to the second volumes. However, this did not happen. They published an edited book of readings with Stacy Adams (see Miner 2005), which organized its subject matter in a manner roughly parallel to that used in *The Social Psychology of Organizations,* and operated as a supplement to that book (Katz, Kahn, and Adams 1980), but no new theory was introduced. At this point Katz was nearing the end of his professional career and Kahn's interests shifted almost entirely to matters of stress and health.

Essentially Kahn followed the lead, emanating from his early work on role phenomena, to difficulties associated with role processes that produced stress and subsequently health problems. His publications on the topic of stress included, in particular, Kahn (1981), Sutton and Kahn (1987), and Kahn and Byosiere (1992). This latter work contains the most specific statements of how role difficulties fit into the process of stress development in organizations. Figure 9.2 outlines this process; see particularly 2. Stressors in organizational life.

EVALUATION AND IMPACT

Except in the area of role processes, the authors of the social psychology of organizations theory have not conducted research testing their ideas. That has been left to others.

The Status of Research

The consequence of the authors' failure to conduct research on their own theory, as is so often the case, has been that only limited research is available. A number of studies, such as

Pfeffer's (1972) investigation of mergers, take their lead from open systems concepts. But such studies typically cite several related theoretical positions at once. The most that can be said about the theory from this type of research is that environmental factors are important for organizations and that organizations attempt to cope with these factors. There is nothing, other than general support for an open systems concept, that bears specifically on the constructs and hypotheses of the Katz and Kahn (1966 1978) theory as distinct from similar theories, some of which precede by a number of years the first Katz and Kahn statement. The problem appears to be that psychological open systems theory is stated abstractly without any indication of how to measure the variables operationally. Such circumstances almost invariably stifle research on a theory, because researchers cannot be sure they are really testing the theory.

A rare instance of research that appears to relate specifically to the theory is a study by Staw and Szwajkowski (1975). This study tests the general proposition that organizations must import resources from the environment to survive and that, in less munificent environments, organizations will exert greater effort to obtain these resources. The specific hypothesis tested was that in scarce environments companies will be more likely to engage in unfair market practices or restraint of trade to procure added resources. This hypothesis represented an extrapolation from the Katz and Kahn (1966) statements. The research was subsequently used in Katz and Kahn (1978) in the formulation of more specific statements on the effects of environmental scarcity or munificence.

Staw and Szwajkowski (1975) found that companies involved in litigation over practices such as price fixing, illegal merger, refusal to deal, and the like had not only been less profitable over the preceding five years, but also came from industries that were equally low in profitability. The data do not unequivocally support a causal interpretation from environmental scarcity to increased effort to secure inputs, but they are entirely consistent with such a hypothesis.

Hierarchic Concepts

A striking aspect of the Katz and Kahn theory is its segmented nature. With many theories, verification of one hypothesis leads to the assumption of truth for other logically related hypotheses. This often cannot be done with Katz and Kahn's formulations. The role-related concepts have no necessary relationships to open systems concepts; they could be embedded in a quite different theoretical milieu and still operate in the same manner. Similarly, the theoretical statements regarding hierarchic versus democratic systems and the hierarchic concept of leadership have no necessary relationships to the rest of the theory. Accordingly, the research evidence that follows must be considered applicable only within very narrow limits.

Hierarchic systems are expected to function best when creativity is not required, environments are obvious, rapid decisions are needed, and closed system conditions apply. Baum (1978) tested the effects of a strongly rules-oriented procedure for handling absenteeisms under circumstances he interpreted as hierarchically ideal. The objective was to compare the effects on chronic absentees of hierarchically controlled procedures and preestablished punishments with decentralized, flexible control conditions. The results clearly support the hierarchic approach under the circumstances specified. Absenteeism was reduced substantially more under experimental conditions than under control conditions.

The above findings support the Katz and Kahn theory as long as one assumes that conditions appropriate for a hierarchic approach existed. In a previous study that compared the effects of a similar legalistic approach on classroom attendance with a laissez-faire approach, the results were similar. Both attendance and performance improved under the standardized attendance rules (Baum and Youngblood 1975). The two studies combined suggest that preestablished, hierarchic approaches with high legitimacy may be effective, irrespective of circumstances. It is not at all certain that a classroom environment meets the theoretical requirements for a hierarchic system, though some might contend that an intermediate accounting class of the kind used in this research does.

Another of the generally rare tests of the hierarchic formulations is the study contrasting various leadership theories by Mott (1972). Measures of the required cognitive and emotional abilities and skills were developed specifically for this study (following the lead of Table 9.2). These were related to effectiveness measures obtained at the branch and division levels of an organization.

None of the measures was related to branch effectiveness, so the theory fails to gain support there. Furthermore, technical skill and fairness were significantly related to division effectiveness, which they should not have been according to the theory. Significant relationships were also obtained at the division level for subsystem perspective and integration. These correlations were in accord with the theory and were the highest obtained in the study. Systemic perspective did not achieve a satisfactory level of significance. Overall, the data indicate that the variables of the Katz and Kahn theory are related to organizational effectiveness, but not necessarily in the manner specified by the theory.

The Kahn Studies of Role Stress

Given the segmented nature of the Katz and Kahn theory, it is possible to test parts of the theory without saying much about the remainder. This is particularly true of the formulations about organizational roles that antedated the major theoretical statement by two years. Actually, the role-related concepts have been the subject of considerable research, which often has supported the theory.

Kahn, Wolfe, Quinn, Snoek, and Rosenthal (1964) studied role processes associated with various offices in the managerial subsystems of seven firms. They conducted standardized interviews with role receivers to get at role perceptions and responses and with role senders for each receiver to get at role expectations and pressures. In addition, a nationwide survey dealing with role conflict and ambiguity was used to determine the generalizability of the intensive study results. This survey involved 725 employed individuals.

The findings indicate widespread role conflict and ambiguity. Both phenomena have negative consequences for the individual, including reduced job satisfaction, low confidence, and tension, as well as a tendency to withdraw from the sources of tension. Role conflict tends to be high in boundary-spanning positions, those extending both outside the company and outside the department, in innovative problem-solving positions, and in management positions. Individuals differ not only in the degree of objective role conflict they elicit from senders, but also in the degree of role stress they actually experience.

Though organizational performance was not measured in this research, the authors argue strongly for the desirability of reducing role stress. This need appears to increase as organizations grow in size up to about 5,000 persons; beyond that point the stress curve levels off. The increase with size is attributed to burgeoning coordination devices, which in turn increase the potential for role conflict. The solution recommended is giving each work group as much autonomy as possible. When the principle of coordinative economy is followed, the organization is "decentralized, flat, and lean, a federated rather than a lofty structure" (Kahn, Wolfe, Quinn, Snoek, and Rosenthal 1964, 395). Whether such organizations are more effective is, of course, an empirical question, extending well beyond the bounds of the research into roles actually conducted.

Role-Related Research

The finding that negative consequences for both the individual and the organization are associated with role conflict and ambiguity is one of the best substantiated in the organizational behavior literature (see, for example, King and King 1990, Grover 1993, Smith and Tisak 1993). King and King say that reviews and meta-analyses "all concur that role conflict and role ambiguity are associated with dissatisfaction, tension and anxiety, lack of commitment and involvement, propensity to leave the organization, and to a lesser extent performance" (58). In this respect, then, the Katz and Kahn theory receives strong support. There is sufficient recent evidence on this point to allay possible concerns about post hoc theorizing (see, for example, Siegall 2000). Yet the effects on job performance overall are much more evident for role ambiguity than for role conflict (Tubre and Collins 2000).

There are studies that do not support the theory, but the negative results usually can be accounted for by special features of the particular investigation, including measurement considerations. Measurement concerns have abounded in this area, with much of the controversy involving arguments for and against specific instruments (see, for example, Netemeyer, Johnston, and Burton 1990; Harris and Bladen 1994). Yet the research utilizes a variety of instruments while reaching much the same conclusions. At times the arguments over measurement methodology seem overly esoteric and to have lost their ties to the original theory. Nevertheless, it has been possible to establish relationships with indexes of organizational effectiveness, thus extending the scope of the findings even beyond that of the original research. In one study, for example, a significant correlation of 0.37 was obtained between a role clarity measure and the effectiveness of twenty regional offices of an insurance company (Posner and Butterfield 1978).

Of the various aspects of the Katz and Kahn theory, those regarding role relationships have had the greatest continuing impact over the years on the conduct of research. A number of examples of such research can be noted from the recent period. Thus, interrole conflict among accountants, where firm requirements were in opposition to professional norms, displayed the anticipated negative consequences in one study (Lui, Ngo, and Tsang 2001). Also, consistent with theoretical expectations, role senders (managers and spouses) in a work–family conflict situation tended to prevail dependent on the relative strength of the pressure from each source (Greenhaus and Powell 2003).

A study of student-athletes found that under conditions of resultant conflict the anticipated negative consequences did emerge. However, if a subject was able to separate the two roles, this negative outcome was no longer in evidence (Settles, Sellers, and Damas 2002). In a study of international joint ventures, signing a more complete contract served to reduce role conflict and ambiguity involving relationships between the two partners (Gong, Shenkar, Luo, and Nyaw 2001). Furthermore, greater political skill has been found to reduce the negative effects of role conflict (Perrewé, Zellars, Ferris, Rossi, Kacmar, and Ralston 2004). Clearly role theory has now built upon the role conflict and ambiguity constructs to add in methods of ameliorating their effects.

Reformulations at the Subsystem Level

A series of publications (Doll and Melcher 1976; Doll 1977a 1977b) report on attempts to operationalize certain constructs of the Katz and Kahn theory and relate the constructs to behavior. In this research the independent variables are role expectations, norms, and values as measured by questionnaire items. The dependent variables are commitment to membership, dependability of role performance, and the degree of extrarole performance that spontaneously supports organizational goals; these three contribute to an overall index of individual behavior. Independent and dependent variables seem to have been measured within the same questionnaire. Reliabilities are said to be satisfactory, but are not reported.

In operationalizing variables, this research often moves beyond the Katz and Kahn (1966) statements. In addition, new hypotheses are occasionally derived from the theory. These procedures are justified on the grounds that the original theory is too loosely stated to be tested. However, one wonders if the Katz and Kahn theory or some other explanation was in fact tested. On the other hand, this research indicates how useful the theoretical constructs and variables may be as building blocks in the development of more precise and sophisticated theories.

Table 9.3 shows the correlations between certain aspects of production and maintenance subsystems and overall individual behavior. Subjects were 226 individuals occupying various roles in twenty-five organizations. As hypothesized, the increasing complexity of the production subsystem that accompanies increasing size is associated with less efficient behavior. The only departure from this pattern is the lack of a significant relationship between unpredictable role behavior and overall behavior. Within the maintenance subsystem the hypothesized relationships consistently occurred, but role expectations regarding intrinsic satisfactions in the work appear to be most important. Overall, the data clearly support the reformulated theory. Similar results were obtained when communication processes were studied (Doll 1977b).

Applications

The Katz and Kahn approach has not been a major source of applications for practice. However, applications are discussed, and certain possible potential uses are inherent in the authors' other work.

In their writing about open systems theory the authors endorse several applications, particularly certain change procedures (Katz and Georgopoulos 1971; Katz and Kahn 1966 1978). They note the general need for an enlargement of adaptive subsystems to cope with changing environments and new social inputs.

In this connection Katz and Kahn advocate a much greater application of democratic principles. They recommend the use of project teams that combine service and production functions, sensitivity training, and organization development programs of various kinds. The objective is to move toward a system with broader, more flexible roles and more open subsystem boundaries—in short, debureaucratization. At the same time, value changes are needed:

> The task for the adaptive processes of an organization is one of the creative adaptation of central values to changing inputs.
> . . . Adaptation through genuine participation and active involvement based upon democratic principles and processes can still be successful. The great need of our time is a reformulation

Table 9.3

**Correlations Between Aspects of Production and Maintenance
Subsystems and Overall Behavior**

Independent variables	Dependent variable: Overall behavior
Production subsystem	
Complexity of the role set	−0.35*
Degree to which functional specialization is extensive (many role restrictions)	−0.41*
Unpredictability of role behavior	0.09
Degree to which role expectations regarding task demands are high	−0.32*
Maintenance subsystem	
Degree to which role expectations relate extrinsic rewards to performance and seniority	0.23*
Degree to which role expectations associating intrinsic satisfactions with role performance are extensive	0.51*
Degree to which role expectations associate undesirable behavior with institutionalized rather than capricious punishments	0.28*
Degree to which values and norms are explicit	0.36*

Source: Adapted from Doll and Melcher (1976, 292) and Doll (1977a, 340).
*Correlations statistically significant.

of social values that would make possible a higher level of integration for all social systems. (Katz and Georgopoulos 1971, 365–66)

With regard to legislated placement of worker representatives on corporate boards as a step toward representative democracy along lines that have become commonplace in Europe, the authors have this to say:

The movement toward legislated worker representation in the conduct of enterprise is both a significant force for future organizational change and a reflection of changes that have already occurred at the organizational level. An employing organization is a system that exists in a larger social context, and that context includes both labor unions and legislative bodies. Organizational change can be extended or contained, accelerated or retarded, demanded or denied by these contextual agencies. (Katz and Kahn 1978, 746)

These endorsements of democratization within organizations do not represent a necessary logical outgrowth of open systems theory, even though they are stated in the terminology of the theory. In fact, the attendance control system developed by Baum (1978), which appears to be a logical development from the theory, clearly moves in the direction of hierarchic rather than democratic processes. Other theories considered in this volume contain inherent rationales for the generally democratizing change procedures they have either generated or embraced. The theories may be wrong, but if they are right, the applications proposed follow logically. This is much less true of psychological open systems theories that are inherently neutral in the hierarchy–democracy debate. Given this situation, it is difficult to understand why Katz and Kahn recommend democratization, except as a value as opposed to a scientific conclusion.

Since the social psychology of organizations formulations were first published, its constructs often have been used to interpret organizational phenomena and the results of research studies. In these instances the theory has not been tested, but rather used as a framework for explaining organizational processes.

Thus, Katz and Golomb (1974–75) used the concepts of integration (role expectations, norms, and values), effectiveness, and adaptive value modification at the individual, systemic, and societal levels to analyze the kibbutzim communities in Israel. The authors also used their constructs of boundary transactions and environmental feedback systems as a framework for a study of the reactions of recipients of government services to their "bureaucratic encounters" (Katz, Gutek, Kahn, and Barton 1975; Kahn, Katz, and Gutek 1976) and for an analysis of feedback as it operates in social systems in general and in governmental program evaluation in particular (Katz 1975). Similarly, Smith and King (1975) utilized open systems concepts in their study of the effectiveness of different mental hospitals. Rosen (1970) did not originally formulate his study of the effects of rotating foremen across work groups in open systems theory terms, but he found the theory useful in developing an ad hoc interpretation of the results.

These examples suggest that the theory, or at least certain constructs of the theory, might be useful to practitioners in developing working theories to cope with day-to-day decisions in ongoing organizations. Managers in particular need such working theories to filter and organize the information that comes to them. Inevitably they will develop some theories, and the Katz and Kahn framework offers some promise for this purpose. However, if the theory is to be widely applied in this way, it must be restated and transmitted with this purpose in mind, either in published form or through management development programs.

Contributions from the Systems Approach

The systems approach to theorizing tends to be static rather than dynamic, to thwart hypothesis formation, and thus to limit rather than accelerate research on a theory. The Katz and Kahn theory does nothing to rebut these conclusions. Clearly the authors are well aware of the problem:

> In some respects open-system theory is not a theory at all; it does not pretend to the specific sequences of cause and effect, the specific hypotheses and tests of hypotheses which are the basic elements of theory. Open-system theory is rather a framework, a meta-theory, a model in the broadest sense of that overused term. Open-system theory is an approach and a conceptual language for understanding and describing many kinds and levels of phenomena. (Katz and Kahn 1966, 452; 1978, 752)

An article by Ashmos and Huber (1987) provides a good discussion of the limitations and potential of the systems approach.

The strength of systems thinking, and this is apparent in the social psychology of organizations formulations, is that it provides a classification system and framework for organizing important variables. In the literature one encounters frequent references to the Katz and Kahn formulations, but they are more often cited for conceptual clarification than for research hypotheses. When the theory is considered in formulating hypotheses, it tends to be used at such a high level of abstraction that it cannot be differentiated from a number of similar theories. Often the concepts are stated so broadly they contribute very little to prediction and understanding. Yet the organizing properties of the systems approach should not be underestimated.

CONCLUSIONS

With an importance rating of 5.33, the social psychology of organizations demonstrates substantial support from the field of organizational behavior. The theory's validity, however, is somewhat suspect, not so much because the theory has been shown to be wrong as because hypotheses derived from it have not been tested with sufficient frequency; thus the three stars. The problem appears to be inherent in the reliance on systems theorizing, which, by its very nature, tends to thwart hypothesis formulation and thus the research that would provide for validation. Because the Katz and Kahn theory is so segmented, it requires considerable research to provide support within each sector. Some supportive research has emerged, especially in the area of role relationships, but not enough to meet the requirements of such a multifaceted theory.

I have given the theory's estimated usefulness two stars, largely because of the failure to formulate specific applications and thus applied research. Clearly the emphasis on participative management has been the subject of considerable research; yet this emphasis does not derive from the theory's systems model and its legitimate ties to the theory seem fragile at best. The Katz and Kahn formulations have provided a framework from which certain practical applications have been developed, but specific guidelines for practice are lacking.

REFERENCES

Ashmos, Donde P., and Huber, George P. (1987). The Systems Paradigm in Organization Theory: Correcting the Record and Suggesting the Future. *Academy of Management Review,* 12, 607–21.

Baum, John F. (1978). Effectiveness of an Attendance Control Policy in Reducing Chronic Absenteeism. *Personnel Psychology,* 31, 71–81.

Baum, John F., and Youngblood, Stuart A. (1975). Impact of an Organizational Control Policy on Absenteeism, Performance, and Satisfaction. *Journal of Applied Psychology,* 60, 688–94.

Doll, William J. (1977a). The Maintenance Subsystem of the Katz and Kahn Framework. *Midwest Division of the Academy of Management Proceedings,* 334–45.

———. (1977b). The Regulatory Mechanisms of the Katz and Kahn Framework. *Academy of Management Proceedings,* 37, 188–97.

Doll, William J., and Melcher, Arlyn S. (1976). The Production Subsystem of the Katz and Kahn Framework—A Reformulation and Empirical Evaluation. *Midwest Division of the Academy of Management Proceedings,* 285–96.

Gong, Yaping, Shenkar, Oded, Luo, Yadong, and Nyaw, Mee-Kau (2001). Role Conflict and Ambiguity of CEO's in International Joint Ventures: A Transaction Cost Perspective. *Journal of Applied Psychology,* 86, 764–73.

Greenhaus, Jeffrey H., and Powell, Gary N. (2003). When Work and Family Collide: Deciding Between Competing Role Demands. *Organizational Behavior and Human Decision Processes,* 90, 291–303.

Grover, Steven L. (1993). Why Professionals Lie: The Impact of Professional Role Conflict on Reporting Accuracy. *Organizational Behavior and Human Decision Processes,* 55, 251–72.

Harris, Michael M., and Bladen, Amy (1994). Wording Effects in the Measurement of Role Conflict and Role Ambiguity: A Multitrait-Multimethod Analysis. *Journal of Management,* 20, 887–901.

Kahn, Robert L. (1981). *Work and Health.* New York: Wiley.

Kahn, Robert L., and Byosiere, Philippe (1992). Stress in Organizations. In Marvin D. Dunnette and Leaetta M. Hough (Eds.), *Handbook of Industrial and Organizational Psychology,* Vol. 3. Palo Alto, CA: Consulting Psychologists Press, 571–650.

Kahn, Robert L., Katz, Daniel, and Gutek, Barbara (1976). Bureaucratic Encounters—An Evaluation of Government Services. *Journal of Applied Behavioral Science,* 12, 178–98.

Kahn, Robert L., Wolfe, Donald M., Quinn, Robert P., Snoek, J. Diedrick, and Rosenthal, Robert A. (1964). *Organizational Stress: Studies in Role Conflict and Ambiguity*. New York: Wiley.

Katz, Daniel (1975). Feedback in Social Systems: Operational and Systemic Research on Production, Maintenance, Control, and Adaptive Functions. In C.A. Bennett and A.A. Lumsdaine (Eds.), *Evaluation and Experiment: Some Critical Issues in Assessing Social Programs*. New York: Academic Press, 465–523.

Katz, Daniel, and Georgopoulos, Basil S. (1971). Organizations in a Changing World. *Journal of Applied Behavioral Science,* 7, 342–70.

Katz, Daniel, and Golomb, Naphtali (1974–75). Integration, Effectiveness and Adaptation in Social Systems: A Comparative Analysis of Kibbutzim Communities. *Administrative Science Quarterly,* 6, 283–315, 389–421.

Katz, Daniel, Gutek, Barbara A., Kahn, Robert L., and Barton, Eugenia (1975). *Bureaucratic Encounters: A Pilot Study in the Evaluation of Government Services*. Ann Arbor, MI: Institute for Social Research, University of Michigan.

Katz, Daniel, and Kahn, Robert L. (1966, 1978). *The Social Psychology of Organizations*. New York: Wiley.

Katz, Daniel, Kahn, Robert L., and Adams, J. Stacy (1980). *The Study of Organizations*. San Francisco, CA: Jossey-Bass.

King, Lynda A., and King, Daniel W. (1990). Role Conflict and Role Ambiguity: A Critical Assessment of Construct Validity. *Psychological Bulletin,* 107, 48–64.

Lui, Steven S., Ngo, Hang-Yue, and Tsang, Anita W. (2001). Interrole Conflict as a Predictor of Job Satisfaction and Propensity to Leave: A Study of Professional Accountants. *Journal of Managerial Psychology,* 16, 469–84.

Miner, John B. (2005). *Organizational Behavior 1: Essential Theories of Motivation and Leadership*. Armonk, NY: M.E. Sharpe.

Mott, Paul E. (1972). *The Characteristics of Effective Organization*. New York: Harper and Row.

Netemeyer, Richard G., Johnston, Mark W., and Burton, Scot (1990). Analysis of Role Conflict and Role Ambiguity in a Structural Equations Framework. *Journal of Applied Psychology,* 75, 148–57.

Perrewé, Pamela L., Zellars, Kelly L., Ferris, Gerald R., Rossi, Ana Maria, Kacmar, Charles J., and Ralston, David A. (2004). Neutralizing Job Stressors: Political Skill as an Antidote to the Dysfunctional Consequences of Role Conflict. *Academy of Management Journal,* 47, 141–52.

Pfeffer, Jeffrey (1972). Merger as a Response to Organizational Interdependence. *Administrative Science Quarterly,* 17, 382–94.

Posner, Barry Z., and Butterfield, D. Anthony (1978). Role Clarity and Organizational Level. *Journal of Management,* 4(2), 81–90.

Rosen, Ned A. (1970). Open Systems Theory in an Organizational Sub-System: A Field Experiment. *Organizational Behavior and Human Performance,* 5, 245–65.

Settles, Isis H., Sellers, Robert M., and Damas, Alphonse (2002). One Role or Two: The Function of Psychological Separation in Role Conflict. *Journal of Applied Psychology,* 87, 574–82.

Siegall, Marc (2000). Putting the Stress Back into Role Stress: Improving the Measurement of Role Conflict and Role Ambiguity. *Journal of Managerial Psychology,* 15, 427–39.

Smith, Carlla S., and Tisak, John (1993). Discrepancy Measures of Role Stress Revisited: New Perspectives on Old Issues. *Organizational Behavior and Human Decision Processes,* 56, 285–307.

Smith, Clagett, G., and King, James A. (1975). *Mental Hospitals: A Study in Organizational Effectiveness*. Lexington, MA: Heath.

Staw, Barry M., and Szwajkowski, Eugene (1975). The Scarcity-Munificence Component of Organizational Environments and the Commission of Illegal Acts. *Administrative Science Quarterly,* 20, 345–54.

Sutton, Robert I., and Kahn, Robert L. (1987). Prediction, Understanding, and Control as Antidotes to Organizational Stress. In Jay W. Lorsch (Ed.), *Handbook of Organizational Behavior*. Englewood Cliffs, NJ: Prentice Hall, 272–85.

Tubre, Travis C., and Collins, Judith M. (2000). Jackson and Schuler (1985) Revisited: A Meta-Analysis of the Relationship Between Role Ambiguity, Role Conflict, and Job Performance. *Journal of Management,* 26, 155–69.

CHAPTER 10

SOCIOTECHNICAL SYSTEMS THEORY

ERIC TRIST
FRED EMERY

Importance rating	★ ★ ★ ★ ★
Estimated validity	★ ★ ★
Estimated usefulness	★ ★ ★ ★
Decade of origin	1960s

In many respects sociotechnical systems theory is the European counterpart of system 4 theory (see Chapter 8). It has been associated closely from its beginnings with the Tavistock Institute of Human Relations in London, just as system 4 theory has been associated with the Institute for Social Research at the University of Michigan. Collaboration between these two organizations has been considerable over the years, including joint editorial responsibility for the journal *Human Relations*.

The Tavistock Institute was an outgrowth of the Tavistock Clinic formed in 1920 to provide psychotherapy to those who could not otherwise afford it. The institute emerged as a separate, incorporated entity when the clinic entered the British national health service after

World War II (Dicks 1970). One major figure in the institute and its chairman for many years was Eric Trist, who is the primary author of sociotechnical systems theory. Trist was joined in his theoretical efforts and in his research by others who were either employed by the institute or strongly influenced by it. Thus, in many respects, sociotechnical systems theory is a product of the same kind of group interaction on which the theory itself often focuses.

BACKGROUND

Eric Trist was born in 1909. He attended Cambridge University, where he obtained his first degree in English literature and, in 1933, a second degree in psychology. His emphasis was on a mix of social psychology and psychoanalysis (Trist 1993). He spent the next two years in the United States at Yale studying social anthropology. On returning to England, Trist worked primarily as a researcher at the University of St. Andrews, investigating unemployment problems. When World War II broke out, he joined the army and became a clinical psychologist at the Tavistock Clinic, an association that lasted for many years in one form or another. His interest in groups was kindled by this early exposure to group psychotherapy from a psychoanalytic perspective (Fox 1990).

Trist himself noted four phases in his career in England. First he was a social psychologist, then a specialist in group dynamics with a psychoanalytic orientation, then a specialist in sociotechnical systems, and finally a specialist in socio-organizational ecology (Trist 1993). His major theorizing arose from the last two phases. His theories were influenced by psychoanalysis, Kurt Lewin, the personality-culture approach, and open systems theory (Trist and Murray 1990). He was also influenced by a strong set of values that included responsible self-regulation, freedom from oppression, democracy, self-determination of work activities, fair treatment, and workplace dignity for all (Pasmore and Khalsa 1993). He was a humanist, and his approach to research was essentially that of ethnography, a combination that allowed him to focus his research efforts where his values could be engaged.

In 1966 Trist left Tavistock for the business school at UCLA. Then, three years later, he moved to the Wharton School at the University of Pennsylvania. On retiring from Wharton in 1978 he went to York University in Canada from which he retired in 1985. He died in 1993.

Sociotechnical theory was a group product, consistent with its authors' commitment, and the commitment of the Tavistock organization, to democracy and participative principles. Trist noted ten other contributors, but among these, Fred Emery, an Australian, stands out (Fox 1995). Especially in the later years, when Trist devoted much of his energy to applied action research projects, Emery became the major theoretical contributor. He was born in Australia in 1925 and entered into the sociotechnical work when he joined Tavistock as a UNESCO fellow in 1951. He remained at Tavistock until 1969, when he returned to Australia to join the faculty of the Australian National University in Canberra. He died in 1997.

STATEMENTS OF THE THEORY

Sociotechnical systems theory dates from the description of the change from a system of coal mining that emphasized autonomous work groups to a more mechanized system extrapolated from factory procedures (Trist and Bamforth 1951). It was the thesis of Trist and of Bamforth, who had been a miner himself, that the introduction of the new longwall methods broke up the existing sociotechnical whole and created an imbalance:

... [A] qualitative change will have to be effected in the general character of the method so that a social as well as a technological whole can come into existence. Only if this is achieved can the relationships of the cycle work-group be successfully integrated and a new social balance be created. . . . [I]t is difficult to see how these problems can be solved effectively without restoring responsible autonomy to primary groups throughout the system and ensuring that each of these groups has a satisfying sub-whole as its work task, and some scope for flexibility in work-pace. . . . [I]t is likely that any attempts in this direction would require to take advantage of the recent trend of training face-workers for more than one role, so that interchangeability of tasks would be possible within work teams. (Trist and Bamforth 1951, 38)

Open Systems and the Causal Textures of Environments

Sociotechnical theory began with the idea that there must be a best match, or joint optimization, between the task or technical environment and the social system. The theory at this stage operated at the work-group level primarily and gave little attention to the functioning of the organization as a whole. However, at least as early as 1959, the theory was extended through the introduction of open systems concepts (Trist 1969).

An enterprise is an open system that engages in continuing exchanges with other enterprises, institutions, and individuals in its external environment. Its sociotechnical system must permit it to maintain a steady state in which work can be done in the face of changing environmental circumstances. This open systems approach contrasts with that of closed systems, which regard the enterprise as "sufficiently independent to allow most of its problems to be analyzed with reference to its internal structure and without reference to its external environment" (Trist 1969, 270).

With the introduction of open systems concepts, sociotechnical theory became concerned with the total organization, including top management. Its authors also began creating a typology of environments that organizations (or segments of organizations) might face. The typology focuses on the different causal textures of environments—"the extent and manner in which the variables relevant to the constituent systems and their inter-relations are, independently of any particular system, causally related or interwoven with each other" (Emery and Trist 1973, 41). Four ideal types of environments are described in various publications (Emery and Trist 1965, 1973; Emery 1967; Trist 1976a, 1977).

In the *placid random* environment the interconnectedness of elements is at a minimum, and change is slow, if it occurs at all. Factors that may help or hinder goal achievement are randomly distributed, so that the optimal strategy is simply trying to do the best one can on a local basis; planning in any real sense is not possible. Learning occurs, but only at the level of simple conditioning. Placid random environments are said to typify preagricultural, primitive societies and to occur only in certain specialized subsystems of modern societies—certain types of small job shops, surviving general stores, typing pools, and assembly lines.

Although *placid clustered* environments, too, change slowly, the grouping of factors within them follows some logic. Organizations in such environments can develop environmental knowledge and use that knowledge to position themselves effectively. Traditional agricultural and business societies were of this type. Firms of limited size that possess a distinctive competence and fill a stable market demand have placid clustered environments in the present business structure.

With the advent of industrialism, environmental change accelerated and large-scale bureau-cracies emerged to cope with this change. The *disturbed reactive* context is characterized by competitive challenge, and organizations in such environments must develop strategies to deal with other organizations of the same kind having the same goals. As a result, organizations in such an environment are continually engaged in a complex set of reactions to each other.

Disturbed reactive environments are said to have reached their peak after World War II. The predominant form since then increasingly has been the *turbulent field*. From a theoreti-cal perspective only the turbulent environment is of central significance to the theory. Change is rampant in turbulent fields. But this change arises "not simply from the interaction of the component organizations, but also from the field . . . The 'ground' is in motion" (Emery and Trist 1965, 26).

Turbulent fields have emerged as a consequence of the development of huge organiza-tions that exert effects beyond their industries, the increasing significance of public and governmental actions for economic organizations, the rapid change occasioned by increased research and development, and the expanded scope and speed of communication. Such fields introduce so much greater uncertainty than their predecessors that individual organizations can no longer cope with it through their own independent efforts. Strategic planning, as it was utilized in other environments, is inadequate when change is rampant.

Just as system 4 theory (Chapter 8 in this volume) introduced a possible fifth system without elaborating on it, so sociotechnical theory merely touches on a fifth type of environ-ment in a footnote:

> Any attempt to conceptualize a higher order of environmental complexity would probably involve us in notions similar to vortical processes. We have not pursued this because we cannot conceive of adaptation occurring in such fields. In case there may be something to the hunch that a type V environment has the dynamics of a vortex, it is worthwhile noting that vortices develop at system boundaries when one system is moving or evolving very fast relative to the other. (Emery and Trist 1973, 41)

Postindustrial Society

Emery and Trist contend that society is still utilizing an organizational structure appropriate to disturbed reactive environments in trying to cope with the more complex turbulent envi-ronments of the present. This cannot possibly work, because turbulent environments are too fast-changing, complex, interdependent, and uncertain for the essentially rigid and uncre-ative bureaucratic form. This theme is elaborated in a variety of viewpoints (Emery 1967, 1974; Emery and Trist 1965, 1973; Trist 1973, 1975a, 1976a, 1976b, 1977, 1985; Trist, Emery, and Murray 1997). A key concept of bureaucracy is redundancy of parts, whereby the work is broken down to the simplest and least costly elements possible. Individuals who perform such work are easily trained and replaced, but reliable control systems (requiring additional redundancy) are needed to make the system operate effectively. Such systems are so cumbersome that they are unresponsive to turbulent environments.

Organizations by their nature require redundancy to minimize error in the face of environ-mental change. However, an alternative design to redundancy of parts is redundancy of func-tions among individuals and units that have wide repertoires of activities and are self-regulating. "Only organizations based on the redundancy of functions have the flexibility and innovative potential to give the possibility of adaptation to turbulent conditions" (Trist 1977, 273).

Table 10.1

Changes Associated with the Move to a Postindustrial Society

Cultural Value Changes
1. From achievement to self-actualization
2. From self-control to self-expression
3. From independence to interdependence
4. From endurance of distress to capacity for joy

Changing Organizational Philosophies
1. From mechanistic to organic forms
2. From competitive to collaborative relations
3. From separate to linked objectives
4. From a view of one's resources as owned absolutely to a view of one's resources as shared with society

Changing Ecological Strategies
1. From responsive to crisis to crisis-anticipation strategies
2. From specific to comprehensive measures
3. From requiring consent to requiring participation
4. From damping conflict to confronting conflict
5. From short to long planning horizons
6. From detailed central control to generalized control
7. From small local government to large area government
8. From standardized to innovative administration
9. From separate to coordinated services

Source: Adapted from Emery and Trist (1973, 174, 182, and 186).

In addition, turbulent environments require a set of simplifying values, much like systems of professional ethics, to foster intraorganizational and interorganizational collaboration rather than competition. Organizations, accordingly, become institutionalized and act in accord with the needs of the larger society. Hierarchy is reduced, if not eliminated, and alternatives such as composite, autonomous groups, matrices, and networks are fostered (Herbst 1976). Because organizational design principles imply certain values, the movement toward these nonhierarchical forms and toward redundancy of functions can only occur within a value system that stresses the worth of individuals and of democratic processes.

Moving toward a postindustrial society capable of coping with a turbulent world requires active intervention:

1. The *object of intervention* is to increase the probability of the advent of one of the more rather than one of the less desirable of the "alternative futures" which seem to be open.
2. The *instrument of intervention* is "adaptive planning"—the working out with all concerned of plans subject to continuous and progressive modification which are what have to be made when what has to be done cannot be decided on the basis of previous experience.
3. The *agency of intervention* is government—but in collaboration with other key institutional groups—for adaptive planning will require the active participation as well as the free consent of the governed. (Emery and Trist 1973, 124)

As a result of this planned intervention, the changes noted in Table 10.1 will occur. A new set of values, congruent with postindustrialism, will replace the Protestant Ethic values of industrialism. "The core relevant values involved are those associated with organizational democracy" (Trist 1976a, 18).

Autonomous Work Groups

Much of this argument for organizational democracy must be considered social philosophy rather than testable scientific theory, but at the level of organizational design, sociotechnical theory contends that a turbulent world has already arrived and that democratic alternatives to hierarchy will be more effective than bureaucracy. Here, hypotheses of a scientific nature are indeed advanced, and they indicate a very specific type of democratic organization.

In writing about sociotechnical systems theory as applied to work groups, Trist typically credits certain hypotheses developed by Emery (Trist 1973, 1975a). Though formulated much earlier, these hypotheses were first published in Emery and Thorsrud (1976). They state how a sociotechnical system should be organized and operated to produce positive outcomes in the modern world.

In this context the primary task of management is to cope with the environment across the boundary of the organization. To the extent management must "coordinate internal variances in the organization" it will be less effective (Emery and Thorsrud 1976, 5). Organization members must be given considerable autonomy and selective independence if the enterprise is to achieve the steady state it needs for effectiveness in its environment.

This inevitable theoretical commitment to autonomous work groups appears inconsistent with the contingency concepts of sociotechnical theory. The explanation given is as follows:

> It seemed that there was "The Myth of the Machine." The organization theory opposing ours was not "a machine theory of organization" but a general theory of bureaucracy. . . . In the first and older perspective our task was to prove for each technology that organizational choice was possible; as each new technology emerged our task was on again. In the second perspective, the relevance of our approach could be established by asking a single question: Is management necessary to the organization? If the answer is yes, then, regardless of technology, some degree of self-management of groups of members is possible. Sociotechnical theory does not thereby go out of the door. To go from what is organizationally possible to what is viable one must answer such critical questions as "what groups should be formed around what tasks"; "how semi-autonomous"; "what degree of multiskilling is necessary." These questions can be answered only by some form of socio-technical analysis in each practical instance. (Emery and Thorsrud 1976, 7)

At best this view assigns the theory's sociotechnical aspects a role secondary to environmental determinism and antibureaucracy.

Much of the theory deals with job enrichment—challenging job content, opportunity to learn, individual decision making, recognition in the workplace, the opportunity to relate work to social life, and a sense that the job leads to a desirable future. In a more specific sense this means task variety, tasks forming meaningful wholes, optimum length of work cycle, individual goal setting coupled with feedback, inclusion of auxiliary and preparatory tasks, inclusion of tasks worthy of community respect, and the perception of a contribution to product utility. These hypotheses for positive outcomes are not unlike those of other job enrichment views (see Miner 2005).

But "the redesigning of jobs leads beyond the individual job to the organization of groups of workers and beyond into the revision of our notions about supervision and the organization of support services. . . . the implications were even wider . . . a challenge to traditional management style and philosophy" (Emery and Thorsrud 1976, 17). At the group level this calls for interlocking tasks, job rotation, or physical proximity where there is task interdependence or stress, or where individual jobs do not create a perception of contribution to product utility. Multiskilling of operators, according to the principle of redundancy of functions, is necessary for job rotation and a key concept of the theory. Information for self-control should be made immediately available to the operators themselves. Meetings and contacts that foster group formation should be institutionalized. Foremen should be trained to deal with groups rather than individuals. Incentives should be of a group nature. The group must monitor and control individual contributions and assign tasks. In essence the system is one of group rather than hierarchical control, and effort is induced by group processes rather than superior managers. Thus group productivity is fostered by:

1. Communicating quickly, directly, and openly the needs for coordination arising from task or individual variability.
2. Allocating tasks and other rewards and punishments to control what they consider to be a fair contribution by members. (Emery and Thorsrud 1976, 163)

Though the term *autonomous work group* is typically used to describe this type of organization, the groups are in fact only semi-autonomous, since they are dependent on the company for resources, and the company remains responsible for compliance with legal constraints. The degree of autonomy will vary with the circumstances. At a minimum, the group will decide on working methods and work allocation. Beyond this the members may control changes in the composition of the group, the equipment and tools used, maintenance, planning, quality standards, and, at the highest level, the defining of work goals. Thus much of the traditional supervisory task is taken over by the group. What remains to supervision is not the exercise of power over individuals, but the coordination of the group with the resources and objectives of the larger organization.

Herbst (1976) extended the theoretical treatment of nonbureaucratic structures designed to cope with turbulent environments. His *composite autonomous group* comes closest to what has been discussed previously. In such a context all members can perform all tasks. Consequently there is no special leadership function, and members can adopt whatever work structures and procedures seem desirable. Because of complete multiskilling, group size must remain small, though sets of autonomous groups linked by rotation of membership are possible.

The *matrix group* contains members who have a primary specialist function, but some overlapping competencies with other members. The lack of complete multiskilling introduces some structural constraints, but permits much larger group sizes. Such groups may produce a variety of products and may choose their own procedures and even input needs. Generally, members work in small subsets, with those subsets *directively correlated* toward specified goals.

A *network group* tends to be widely dispersed. Long-term, directive correlations that are accepted by members focus their efforts on particular aims; correlations of this kind exist in the professions. Network groups typically find ways to go beyond what is already established. Members are maximally autonomous, but build on and extend each other's work. In principle, such groups are temporary systems set up to achieve particular goals; competencies are overlapping, and size is limited.

To deal with larger organizational structures, the theory posits linked, composite, autonomous groups; networks of networks; and matrices of organizational units. All these nonbureaucratic structures are hypothesized to be superior to the bureaucratic hierarchy.

However, Herbst makes the following statement:

> ... [T]here are conditions, especially in the field of public administration, where bureaucratic organizations function well. . . . [R]elevant conditions for this are:
>
> 1. That the task be decomposed into independent parts.
> 2. Both the nature and requirements for task performance are stable over fairly long periods of time.
> 3. Sufficient areas of discretion and responsible autonomy with respect to task performance exist at all levels so that even the lowest level provides the opportunity for the performance of a relatively autonomous professional role.
>
> At the present time these conditions are decreasingly met. (1976, 19)

Such a theoretical statement appears consistent with the contingency aspects of sociotechnical theory, but inconsistent with the Emery and Thorsrud (1976) statements of the inevitable superiority of autonomous work groups over bureaucracy. One could avoid the contradiction by reference to alternative types of environments, but Herbst does not do this. Indeed, if government is to be the key source of interventions for adaptive planning and changes to cope with turbulent environments, it would be hard to argue that government itself does not face such an environment.

Alternative and Elaborated Positions

The scientists concerned with sociotechnical systems theory constitute a network group, as described by Herbst. Trist and Murray (1990) note seventeen organizational members of this network in eight countries, primarily in Europe but also in the United States, Canada, Australia, and India. The individuals whose ideas have been considered to this point constitute the core of the group, but there are others whose contributions either extend the theory or, in a few instances, provide alternative explanations. The status of these contributions relative to the basic theory is not clear. In some cases the core group seems to have granted its stamp of approval, as when Trist endorses a book in its foreword (Kingdon 1973, Susman 1976), but even then agreement on all points is not certain. In some areas even Trist and Emery appear to have disagreed with each other (Trist, Emery, and Murray 1997).

Alternative and elaborated positions have developed and extended sociotechnical theory as it relates to the causal textures of environments and to the turbulent field in particular (see, for example, Terreberry 1968). Other contributions deal with autonomous work groups (see Susman 1976, Cummings and Srivastva 1977). Kingdon (1973) devotes particular attention to the matrix group, and to organizations that incorporate this structure. Miller and Rice (1967) extend the theory to ways in which commitment can be achieved in sociotechnical systems and to the importance of group and organizational boundary definitions.

The subject of commitment has been picked up at various points by both Emery and Trist and elaborated most fully in Ketchum and Trist (1992). This discussion is closely allied to the job enrichment literature considered in Miner (2005) and extends the previous discussions in this regard. Employee commitment is a goal of sociotechnical systems and it is achieved by satisfying the following intrinsic needs:

1. The need for the job to be reasonably demanding in terms other than sheer endurance and to provide a minimum of variety (not necessarily novelty, which is too much for some people though the spice of life for others). This is to recognize enfranchisement in problem solving as a human right.
2. The need to be able to learn on the job on a continuing basis. Again, this is a question of neither too much nor too little, but of matching solutions to personal requirements. This is to recognize personal growth as a human right.
3. The need for some area of decision making that the individual can call his own. This recognizes the opportunity to use one's own judgment as a human right.
4. The need for some degree of social support and recognition in the workplace, from both fellow workers and bosses. This recognizes "group belongingness" as a human right.
5. The need to be able to relate what one does and what one produces to one's social life. That is, to have a meaningful occupational identity that gives a man or woman dignity. This recognizes the opportunity to contribute to society as a human right.
6. The need to feel that the job leads to some sort of desirable future (not necessarily promotion). It may involve training or redeployment—a career at shop floor level leading to the development of greater skill. It includes being able to participate in choosing that future. This recognizes hope as a human right. (Ketchum and Trist 1992, 10–11)

Beyond these intrinsic motivations it is important to provide for certain extrinsic satisfactions. Thus sociotechnical system design should include steps to assure fair and adequate pay, job security, appropriate benefits, safety in the work environment, good health, and due process to protect rights. To this list Trist added that *gainsharing* should eventually be provided, so that employees may share in the added material fruits made possible by the developing partnership between workers and managers, and thus to prevent perceptions of inequity by workers (see Fox 1995).

SOCIOTECHNICAL RESEARCH

The research generated by sociotechnical systems theory has involved, almost without exception, either the introduction of autonomous work groups in situations where they did not previously exist or the study of such groups after they emerged spontaneously. Unfortunately, many of these investigations are better classified as case studies or demonstration projects than as scientific research studies, since systematic measurement and controls are lacking. (These studies are considered as examples of applications in the next section.) The following discussion focuses on research that can be considered legitimate tests of the theory.

Coal Mining Studies

Although the original work on the mining of coal in England was ethnographic and involved merely describing what happened (Trist and Bamforth 1951), subsequent investigations in the same context have taken a more scientific form.

Table 10.2

Comparisons of Results of Conventional and Composite Autonomous Group Systems of Coal Mining

	Conventional longwall system	Composite, autonomous group system
Productivity as a percent of estimated face potential	78	95
Percent of shifts lagging behind established production cycle	69	5
Absenteeism without reason as a percent of possible shifts	4.3	0.4
Absenteeism because of sickness or other reasons as a percent of possible shifts	8.9	4.6
Absenteeism because of accidents as a percent of possible shifts	6.8	3.2

Source: Adapted from Trist, Higgin, Murray, and Pollack (1963, 123 and 125).

In one instance comparisons were made between two groups of approximately forty workers. One group utilized the then conventional longwall method of mining that was technology-dominated, highly specialized, and segmented. The other group—a more sociotechnically balanced, composite, autonomous group—used the same technology (Trist, Higgin, Murray, and Pollock 1963; Trist 1969). The composite, autonomous group was characterized by (1) multiskilling so that task continuity could be maintained from shift to shift; (2) self-selected teams that allocated tasks among themselves; (3) payment based on a bonus allocated by the group in equal shares; and (4) a generally high degree of group autonomy and self-regulation. None of these factors was present in the conventional group. An attempt was made to match the coal panels mined by the two groups so that only differences in work organization would be reflected in the results. Though the findings as given in Table 10.2 were not subjected to statistical test, the pattern for the sociotechnical system was clearly superior.

A second study compared two groups, organized to varying degrees according to composite autonomous principles (Trist, Higgin, Murray, and Pollock 1963). Here, the differentiation was less pronounced than in the previous study, but the matching of coal panels to eliminate differences attributable to the difficulty of the work was good. The more autonomous group was found to be more productive, even though the comparison group exercised a degree of autonomy. A factor in this result appears to be the greater creativity in dealing with work problems exhibited by the more autonomous group.

In interpreting the results of this and the preceding research it is important to recognize that an autonomous group approach had been characteristic in the industry prior to the introduction of the longwall technology. In fact, the early sociotechnical systems theory hypotheses derived from study of these early autonomous groups. Many miners had long experience with this approach and tended to revert to it in some situations, even after the longwall technology was introduced. Accordingly, the experimental groups were more emergent than contrived and appear to be particularly congruent with sociotechnical concepts. The authors note: "In pits where there is no composite tradition resistance to the introduction of composite working is likely to be considerable" (Trist, Higgin, Murray, and Pollock 1963, 292–93). Given this situation, the extent to which the early coal mining findings can be generalized is left in doubt.

More recent research with the Rushton Mining Company in Pennsylvania deals directly with this problem (Goodman 1979). Autonomous group procedures were introduced in some sections and not in others. Furthermore, the procedures were introduced in the various sections with a time lag to further facilitate control comparisons. There was no previous history of autonomous group functioning in this situation. The experimental procedures were introduced by a research team headed by Eric Trist and were generally comparable to those of the early British studies (Susman 1976; Trist, Susman, and Brown 1977).

The initial reports appear to have been favorable (Mills 1976). However, comprehensive comparisons of experimental and control sections prior to and during the first seventeen months of the study were mixed:

1. *Productivity.* The experiment did not significantly increase productivity.
2. *Safety.* The experiment did not significantly affect accident rates. There were significant reductions in the number of violations of . . . mining regulations. Safety practices and attitudes toward better safety practices improved. . . .
3. *Job Skills.* Miners in the experimental section reported that the programme had substantially increased their job skills.
4. *Job Attitudes.* Greater feelings of responsibility, more interest in work, more positive feelings about one's work group seem to be attributable to the experiment.
5. *Communication.* There was much more communication both vertically and horizontally, whereas previously communication had been primarily from top to bottom.
6. *Managerial Stress.* The programme increased stress for the supervisors of the experimental crew and some middle managers.
7. *Labour-Management Relations.* There were no changes in traditional indicators of labour-management relations such as the number or content of grievances. (Goodman and Lawler 1979, 152)

Two additional points are important. The top wage was introduced in experimental sections for all members, consistent with the concept of multiskilling. Because of a variable wage scale, significant earnings differences existed in the control sections. This fact appears to have been a source of some conflict within the mine, but also may have fostered more positive attitudes in the autonomous groups. In addition, it is apparent that without a historical background favorable to the approach, sociotechnical systems procedures may be resisted. There were several votes against installing autonomous groups and other evidence of resistance from certain quarters, including some members of management (Trist, Susman, and Brown 1977).

Eventually, after several years, the experimental interventions disappeared from Rushton. A major factor was a strike by the union, but multiple sources of resistance actually combined gradually to thwart the program.

Indian Textile Mill Studies

In addition to the British coal mining studies, probably the best known investigation emanating from the Tavistock group is an analysis of the introduction of autonomous work groups into two textile mills in India. After the beginning of the research in 1953, the Ahmedabad Manufacturing and Calico Printing Company was involved in several studies, and data are available for a seventeen-year period (Rice 1958, 1963; Miller 1975). Because production figures were obtained for a period prior to the creation of the experimental groups and because certain comparisons are made both between autonomous and nonautonomous groups within the company and between the company and the industry as a whole, this research seems to qualify as an experiment.

In the two years after the autonomous groups were formed there was an increase in productivity from approximately 80 percent to 95 percent of potential, a change that is attributed to the sociotechnical procedures on the basis of control comparisons. At the same time, the quality of work improved significantly, by a factor of 59 percent. Follow-up data through 1960 indicate that the company assumed a position of considerable competitive advantage over other leading mills after the introduction of the autonomous groups.

Ten years later one group formed on an autonomous basis was still functioning in that manner and maintaining its high performance (Miller 1975). However, other autonomous groups were not doing as well. Furthermore, these groups appear to have backed away from the sociotechnical procedures over the years under the pressures of environmental change (a result not predicted by the theory because autonomous groups should be ideally suited to cope with change and uncertainty). In one group it now seemed that the experimental induction never really took at all, except briefly to impress the researchers. Unfortunately, there were no measures to determine exactly how autonomous various groups were at different times; data on this point are essentially impressionistic.

Interpretations of this research tend to vary widely. Katz and Kahn (1978, 709) indicate that, "By and large the history of the effects of the experimental plan is an amazing success story." Many others have taken a similar position, though characteristically without considering Miller's (1975) follow-up data. Of particular interest are Miller's comments on the use of experimental and control comparisons within the company:

> Comparisons of performance data need to be treated with a good deal of caution. It is virtually impossible to make precise comparisons between different types of looms weaving different types of cloth. Before and after comparisons on the same looms weaving a similar type of cloth are more reliable. (Miller 1975, 356)

Yet, even in this instance, variations in the quality of yarn and supplies and in the criteria of measurement cloud the attribution of change over time to worker performance.

This matter of what caused the changes has been a major source of concern. Roy (1969) argues that a key factor may well have been the sizable pay increases instituted with the introduction of the sociotechnical system. He presents evidence from his own research supporting this interpretation. Certainly a confounding of experimental changes and pay increases has characterized sociotechnical research. However, it is not possible to account for the *continued* high performance of the one autonomous group on this basis, given changes in the payment system that occurred over the years (Miller 1975).

Research in Norway and Sweden

Sociotechnical theory was next extended to studies in Norway and subsequently in Sweden. Here, the applications were widespread, facilitated by positive government interventions and a friendly social climate. Yet the emphasis was on demonstration projects and case applications, rather than on scientific studies. There was a tendency to assume that industrial democracy was good and then move on to problems of dissemination, rather than to question basic theoretical hypotheses.

Figure 10.1 **Gulowsen's Group Autonomy Scale**

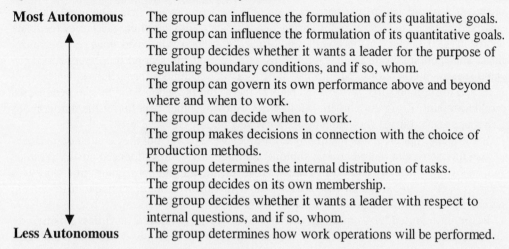

Most Autonomous   The group can influence the formulation of its qualitative goals.
The group can influence the formulation of its quantitative goals.
The group decides whether it wants a leader for the purpose of regulating boundary conditions, and if so, whom.
The group can govern its own performance above and beyond where and when to work.
The group can decide when to work.
The group makes decisions in connection with the choice of production methods.
The group determines the internal distribution of tasks.
The group decides on its own membership.
The group decides whether it wants a leader with respect to internal questions, and if so, whom.
Less Autonomous   The group determines how work operations will be performed.

Source: Adapted from Gulowsen (1972, 376–78).

One exception to this generalization involved a study conducted in a Swedish tobacco company (Agervold 1975). Comparisons of an autonomous group with a similar nonautonomous group in another factory tended to support the hypothesis of more positive attitudes in the sociotechnical context. However, it is apparent that plant differences per se account for part of the differential, and the experimental effects must be discounted proportionately. Because the results of statistical tests are not provided, it is difficult to evaluate these attitudinal findings but it would appear that the impact of introducing autonomous work groups was not pronounced. Data on productivity changes indicate a 14 percent increase at the very least in the experimental group, but it is difficult to evaluate this because control figures are not given.

In studies such as this the question of the extent to which the dictates of sociotechnical systems theory really were followed is important. If the experimental interventions did not take or were somewhat less than what the theory would anticipate, any failure to achieve hypothesized results would be expected. A first attempt at dealing with this measurement problem was proposed by Gulowsen (1972).

Figure 10.1 shows a scale of items indicating the degree to which a group is autonomous. The scale has been applied to eight different work groups, and based on these data, it appears to be unidimensional or cumulative in that a positive response to a higher-level item implies a positive response to all lower-level items. Unfortunately, scales such as this have not been used widely in research on sociotechnical systems theory. As a result, unfavorable findings often are explained post hoc as incomplete experimental induction, and no solid evidence is offered of the degree to which an autonomous system was in fact created.

Additional Research

A number of studies have been conducted in various locations around the world that speak to the validity of sociotechnical theory. There are not a great many such studies, but several bear noting; they are spread over a considerable time span. Pasmore (see Pasmore and

Sherwood 1978) carried out one of the few studies comparing alternative approaches to organizational change in two parallel units of a food processing firm. One unit was first surveyed, then fed the results of the survey in accordance with the Michigan survey feedback approach (see Chapter 8 in this volume and Miner 2002), then redesigned along sociotechnical lines, and then surveyed again. During this same period the second unit experienced the same survey interventions, but did not shift to a sociotechnical form. Subsequently, both units had the second survey results fed back to them, and the second unit then experienced a sizable amount of job enrichment, though not enjoying other benefits of the autonomous group approach. Finally, both units were surveyed again.

Significant improvements in employee attitudes were found, but they could not be attributed to any particular intervention technique; all three procedures produced positive results. In terms of productivity and cost savings, however, the autonomous group procedure was clearly superior. In particular there was a sizable savings in labor costs due to a 19 percent reduction in personnel required to operate the unit.

Research reported by Cummings and Srivastva (1977) produced much less positive results. In one instance sociotechnical procedures were introduced into the estimating and die engineering components of an aluminum forging plant. Control comparisons were made with data obtained from the personnel, engineering, and information systems groups in the same plant. The overall effects of the autonomous group procedure appear to have been a significant negative shift in attitudes, a decrease in productivity, at least as experienced by those involved, and a generally more negative evaluation of the experimental groups by outside departments using their services. The experiment was terminated by management after six months.

A second study in the same company compared a wheel line production unit organized on a sociotechnical basis with another unit not so organized (Cummings and Srivastva 1977). There was little attitudinal change, other than a greater amount of insecurity in the experimental group. Absenteeism was higher in the autonomous groups, and the members of these groups perceived their performance as poorer. Their supervisors rated their performance higher than did the supervisors of the control subjects, but these measures appear to have a potential for bias.

Though the overall results of the second study were perceived more positively by the company's management, neither set of findings supports sociotechnical theory. Cummings and Srivastva (1977) attribute the results to the failure of sociotechnical interventions to take fully under the impact of individual resistance and the economic crisis position of the company at the time of the study. Though the authors used no comprehensive measure of experimental take such as Gulowsen's (1972), there is some evidence to support their contentions. On the other hand, the theory would not have predicted the results obtained. If anything, sociotechnically organized groups should ultimately emerge as more effective, not less effective, in coping with turbulent environmental circumstances.

In any event, other research conducted in a more favorable economic milieu did yield more positive outcomes. The initial results, obtained when autonomous groups were introduced in one of the Mead Corporation's plants, appeared to be very favorable, though control data were not available (Bramlette, Jewell, and Mescon 1977). Subsequently, two sociotechnically organized plants in this company were compared with plants of a more traditional nature (Beldt 1978). The data indicate that the experimental plants were distinctly superior in terms of absenteeism, production volume per worker hour, labor costs per unit of output, and employee satisfaction.

On the other hand, it is not entirely clear what caused these outcome differences. The sociotechnical plants had younger workers who were somewhat better educated, and one plant utilized an exceptionally advanced technology. Furthermore, the workers in the experimental plants did not exhibit the value structures one might anticipate. Such factors as trust, cooperation, autonomy, creativity, and equality were not more highly valued in the autonomous groups; compassion, tolerance, individuality, and risk actually were valued less. But skill and success were valued highly, and the few managers required in these plants were strongly managerially motivated individuals. It may be that for some reason the experimental plants attracted people more motivated toward, and more capable of, outstanding productivity.

Research since has been able to utilize better controls and longitudinal analyses to achieve more definitive results. A study conducted in a confectionery company in England utilizing a consultant from Tavistock was particularly well designed (Wall, Kemp, Jackson, and Clegg 1986). It extended well beyond the initial period during which positive results were most likely to be obtained. There is no question that stable and lasting changes occurred—perceived work autonomy and intrinsic job satisfaction both shifted in a positive direction. But job motivation, commitment, mental health, and job performance did not improve. Turnover increased, although external labor force factors may have been involved. Although productivity levels appear to have been unchanged, certain cost savings were realized because the need for managers was less and indirect labor costs decreased. All in all, the changes were viewed as less than anticipated.

A comparable study conducted in a minerals processing company in Australia provides further evidence (Cordery, Mueller, and Smith 1991). Once again job satisfaction appears to have been increased, and more broadly now to include commitment, but trust in management showed no differences. Both turnover and absenteeism were higher under autonomous conditions. Productivity differences could not be determined with certainty, but appear not to have been present. There clearly was a reduction in managerial and support personnel, with a resulting decline in labor costs. Contiguous units not provided an opportunity to participate in the sociotechnical program were clearly adversely affected by it (high turnover, work stoppages, etc.). The results overall are mixed; there were clear changes, but they were both positive and negative in their effects.

DEMONSTRATIONS AND APPLICATIONS

Interpreting the results of research conducted to test sociotechnical theory is not easy, even when the researcher makes a serious effort to utilize adequate scientific controls. In the projects considered in this section, however, interpretation is practically impossible. The projects are important because they demonstrate the nature of and sometimes the pitfalls associated with sociotechnical systems design, and not because they contribute to evaluation of the underlying theory. In this respect the term *experiment* as applied to these projects is often inappropriate and misleading.

Principles of Sociotechnical Systems Design

Among individuals presenting guidelines or principles for undertaking sociotechnical interventions are some of the original theorists, for example Trist (1975b), Herbst (1976), Emery and Trist (1978), and Ketchum and Trist (1992). Cummings and Srivastva (1977) describe a systematic procedure for implementing sociotechnical systems. The principles presented by Cherns (1977, 55–63) are comprehensive:

1. *Comparability.* The means to design must be consistent with the end to be achieved. If people in the organization are to share in decision making, they must share in the design.

2. *Minimal Critical Specification.* At each stage of the design what is critical should be identified and only that should be specified. . . . Precision about what has to be done may be necessary, but rarely precision about how it is to be done. . . . If you specify more than you need, you foreclose options that should be kept open.

3. *Variance Control.* If variances cannot be eliminated, they should be dealt with as near to their point of origin as possible. A variance is an unprogrammed event. . . . Applying the principle of variance control would lead us to incorporate inspection with production, allowing people whenever possible to inspect their own work.

4. *Multifunction.* Design the organization so that it can achieve its objectives in more than one way. Allow each unit a repertoire of performance . . . redundancy of functions.

5. *Boundary Location.* Roles that require shared access to knowledge or experience should be within the same departmental boundaries.

6. *Information Flow.* Information systems should be designed to provide information to the organizational unit that will take action on the basis of the information. . . . sophisticated information systems can supply a work team with exactly the right kind and amount of feedback, thus enabling the team to learn to control the variances that occur in its spheres of responsibility.

7. *Support Congruence.* The system of social support should be designed to reinforce the behaviors that the organization structure is designed to elicit. If an organization is designed on the basis of group or team operations with team responsibility, a payment system based on individual performance would be incongruent.

8. *Design and Human Values.* A prime objective of organizational design should be to provide a high quality of working life to its members.

9. *Transitional Organization.* There is a changeover period from old to new that requires a transitional organization. . . . What is required is a careful rehearsal of the roles that have to be performed during the changeover, especially the continuing training role of the supervisor.

10. *Completion.* Design is an iterative process. The closure of options opens new ones . . . the multifunctional, multilevel, multidisciplinary team required for the original design is also needed for its evaluation and review.

An application concern that has arisen out of experience with the history of actual interventions is that the program may dissipate over time, often after a promising early period. This was the experience at Rushton. Or diffusion to other locations may be stifled so that the intervention site becomes a walled enclave. Failures of these kinds may be associated with the flow of business cycles, and formulations to that effect have been offered (DeGreene 1988). However, sociotechnical systems theory's authors have tended to emphasize the peripheral nature of most interventions. The projects are carried out in new plants or other locations that are far removed from headquarters and they tend to receive little or no attention from top management.

To counteract this Ketchum and Trist (1992) have proposed that a center-out, rather than a periphery-in, strategy be utilized when projects are first introduced in a firm. In reality this is a top-down strategy; support for change is obtained from top management first and this group then goes public, establishing beach heads for sociotechnical innovations at strategic points in the company. This center-out principle clearly calls for use of the hierarchy and in doing so assumes that hierarchy exists—somewhat strange for a theory that elsewhere has placed strong emphasis on utilizing substitutes for hierarchy. There is a logical inconsistency here.

Another point that bears mention involves an area in which one might think principles might operate but none are stated. Experience appears to indicate that certain types of people perform better under sociotechnical conditions than others, and in fact there is evidence to this effect (Neuman 1991). Given the clinical background of the theory's authors, principles specifying how individual differences should operate in the staffing of sociotechnical interventions would be expected. Yet such principles do not exist, thus implying that the theory works with everyone. The frequent finding of high turnover belies that conclusion. This appears to be an instance in which theoretical opportunity has been foregone.

A wide range of applications based on the existing principles are reported in the literature (see in particular Trist and Dwyer 1982; Trist 1985; Trist and Murray 1993). Fox (1995) notes some thirty organizations so involved. The examples that follow are among the most widely discussed.

The Norwegian Industrial Democracy Program

The Norwegian projects are unusual in that they represent a concerted effort on the part of industry, unions, and eventually government to change a whole society. The first four projects considered here were undertaken in the early 1960s with active assistance from the Tavistock group (Emery and Thorsrud 1976). Subsequent diffusion has been slow within Norway, and the massive social change originally envisaged has not occurred (Thorsrud, Sorensen, and Gustavsen 1976). Yet there have been other applications, some of the most interesting being in the shipping industry (Herbst 1974).

The first project, undertaken in the wire drawing department of a steel mill (Christiana Spigerverk), met with considerable resistance at the shop floor level initially and had continuing problems with union manning requirements throughout. Except for two weeks in the middle of the project when conditions were optimal, little success was in evidence. A major problem was that multiskilling and the introduction of a group bonus system brought earnings of the autonomous groups to a level that disrupted the overall factory pay structure. As a result, strong pressures against "rate busting" were exerted on the groups, pressures to which they responded. In this first effort the groups seemed unable to cope with strong environmental forces.

Autonomous groups were introduced among operators in the chemical pulp department and considerably later in a paper machines department (Hunsfos Pulp and Paper). Overall this project appears to have been a qualified success. Major improvements occurred in the initial period, but there was a subsequent loss of momentum. "Considerable resistance occurred among foremen and production management and among some operators who previously held protected, high status jobs" (Thorsrud, Sorensen, and Gustavsen 1976, 434). However, a degree of management acceptance did develop, and efforts to expand the project into other areas were undertaken. It is not entirely clear from the published report what the long-term consequences for the Hunsfos firm were.

Initial changes were introduced in a small plant in a rural location (NOBO Factories), and within that plant in a new department producing electric panel heaters. The project was apparently a major success:

> The company management were well experienced in making these sorts of measures of worker productivity and well aware of the sorts of allowances that have to be made, often intuitively, for the effects of equipment change. They believed the observed changes were real and were significant. Their calculations also led them to believe that quality standards had improved and maintenance costs dropped. (Emery and Thorsrud 1976, 96)

When the production process was transferred to a new location and expanded, the autonomous group procedures went with it and have continued in use. Diffusion to the main company did not occur, however.

Another project initially involved the introduction of sociotechnical approaches throughout a new fertilizer plant (Norsk Hydro). The plant was manned at a level sharply below comparable plants without autonomous work groups, at sizable cost savings.

. These savings existed even though compensation levels rose with multiskilling and bonus payments. Yet, in spite of the generally favorable evaluation of the fertilizer plant results, diffusions to other existing plants did not progress on schedule. Management resistance to revised roles was considerable. In one instance a plant that had initiated autonomous groups was shut down because of market factors. There were union sources of resistance as well. All in all, the results, though favorable, did not achieve the breadth of application originally envisaged. A much more recent attempt to institute participative management in Norway did not draw upon the sociotechnical experience at all (see Hennestad 2000).

Swedish Extensions

Diffusion in Norway was slow; in Sweden, on the other hand, diffusion was rapid (Peterson 1976). Apparently the idea of industrial democracy on the shop floor is particularly consonant with Swedish culture. Furthermore, it is in Sweden that some of the most dramatic shifts away from assembly line technology have occurred.

The initial pilot project (Saab-Scania) was undertaken in 1969 in units of a truck plant. The results of this effort were then utilized in 1972 to start up an engine manufacturing plant organized on a sociotechnical basis. In this latter instance there was no assembly line in the conventional sense; the plant was designed to permit parallel groups to assemble complete engines at their own pace. The results of the pilot project were generally favorable. It is difficult to evaluate the total plant project and difficult as well to turn back from the sociotechnical commitment embodied in the design of the plant itself.

> By the conventional criteria of management, the system is a success. Quantity of production is within the expectation (worker minutes per engine) of conventional assembly methods. Absence and turnover, which were special problems in the assembly operation, are now no higher than in other worker categories. . . . Changes of this kind require investment, in many senses of that word. The system of parallel workshops requires more space than the conventional assembly line. The method of conveying engines and materials was more costly to install. To these costs must be added the time of the committees that labored to invent and create the system. (Katz and Kahn 1978, 726, 728)

A project very similar to Saab-Scania occurred at the Volvo plant at Kalmar, except that the scale was larger. Again a new factory was involved, but in this case a total automobile was the product. The assembly process was broken down into a series of group operations, with inspections built into each group (Gyllenhammar 1977). The Kalmar plant appeared to have been somewhat more expensive to build than conventional plants and about as efficient. However, a major objective was to deal with the company's labor supply problems and that was accomplished. Also fewer supervisors were needed, and the technology permited greater flexibility in introducing new models. The company clearly was satisfied with the results, and the sociotechnical approach was diffused to other operations.

General Foods at Topeka

The Topeka project was carried out in a new plant of small size. It was generally considered to be a success from the beginning (Walton 1972). As in many such projects, staffing could be maintained at a low level due to multiskilling. Costs were consistently low, though the extent to which this was a function of the new equipment is unknown.

Subsequent events at the Topeka plant did not follow as positive a course (Walton 1977). Commitment to the sociotechnical approach within the work force was cyclical, but some erosion was in evidence overall. Problems with the payment system continued, particularly problems with the group-based allocations of rewards. Plantwide issues were not dealt with as effectively as they could be. Though opposition from within grew, the autonomous groups remained solidly in place. Furthermore, production costs continued to be low, absenteeism and turnover rates acceptable, and overall job satisfaction high.

The Topeka project received considerable coverage in the business press. Nevertheless, diffusion within General Foods did not occur, and it remains unclear what caused the success obtained. There have been arguments that the interpretations developed from the available evidence extend well beyond what the data justify, to the point that they represent advocacy much more than science (Yorks and Whitsett 1985). Reports on other sociotechnical projects, such as the one at Shell Oil, have also been criticized as not fully and truly presenting the facts, with the result that an overly rosy picture emerged (see Blackler and Brown 1980).

EVALUATION AND IMPACT

Much of what has been said about systems 4 and 4T and the Michigan theorizing in general (Chapters 8 and 9) is equally applicable to sociotechnical systems theory. Both originated at the work group level and seem to work best there. In larger organizational and environmental contexts they tend to run into difficulties.

The Theory as Related to Environments and Management

As it deals with causal textures of environments, sociotechnical theory has been the subject of considerable criticism. Rhenman (1973) takes issue with several of the theory's basic propositions in the environmental area:

1. All environments contain some random elements, some clustering, some risk of reaction, and a certain amount of structural change.

2. The four classes of environment suggested by Emery and Trist leave no room for distinguishing between different types of value environments.
3. Structural change in the environment need not always be a disadvantage. For organizations that can dominate their environment in particular, such changes can be of positive value. In this context I question Emery and Trist's claim that some sort of matrix organization is needed to deal with the turbulent environment. (190)

Others, as well, have raised serious questions regarding the type of environment-organization fit proposed by sociotechnical theory (Nickerson and Zenger 2002). There is in fact little evidence that bureaucratic organizations are inherently incapable of coping with turbulent environments and that sociotechnical organizations are particularly adept in this regard. The position that bureaucracies are inevitably too rigid and bound by tradition to cope with rapid change through innovation is not supported by the evidence. Furthermore, there is no logical reason why the processes and procedures generated by autonomous groups cannot become equally entrenched over time; in fact, there is reason to believe that they do (Barker 1993). Nor is there any basis for concluding that autonomous groups are necessarily inherently creative. In line with this position is the finding that autonomous work groups often are vulnerable to turbulent forces and changing conditions in their environments, not only in the start-up phase but also after they are established. Evidence to this effect comes from Miller (1975), Cummings and Srivastva (1977), and Walton (1977).

The role of management in a sociotechnical system presents certain problems. There appears to be no place in the theory for the manager who coordinates internal variances in the organization. Theoretically this should be done closer to the variances themselves, by the workers. Seemingly this argues for a positively sloped control curve and flies directly in the face of much evidence generated by control theory, as discussed in Chapter 8. The theory's hypotheses about management have never been tested adequately. Rice (1963) devotes considerable attention to changes at this level but does not make them a subject of research investigation.

The introduction of autonomous groups tends to generate considerable managerial stress, presumably as a result of the role ambiguity that results. In one apparently successful application, plant managers were found to be of a type who usually perform very well in bureaucratic settings (Beldt 1978). Though government is considered to be the intervention agent of choice, top management has in fact filled that role much more frequently and apparently with greater success. These and other considerations related to the role of management are not handled in a logically consistent manner by sociotechnical systems theory, if they are handled at all.

The original emphasis on organizational designs that are contingent on an optimal social-technical fit seems inconsistent with the subsequent advocacy of autonomous work groups as the one best (and bureaucracy as the one worst) design. As Herbst (1976) suggests, there must be situations where bureaucracy is appropriate, given the technological context. Working up from a kind of technological determinism does not necessarily produce the same result as working down from a corresponding kind of environmental determinism. The inconsistencies that may result are, at least in part, a function of the theory's network form of authorship, but they are real, nevertheless.

The Theory as Related to Work Groups

The foregoing discussion yields a rather dismal picture for sociotechnical systems theory. However, when one moves to the work group level where the theory began, the picture brightens. This is the level at which the research has been done, and the results often are positive. It is hard to predict whether the outcome will be greater output, better quality, less absenteeism, reduced turnover, fewer accidents, greater job satisfaction, or what, but the introduction of autonomous work groups is often associated with improvements.

It is difficult to understand why a particular outcome such as increased productivity occurs in one study and not another, and why on some occasions nothing improves. Sociotechnical systems theory is of little help in explaining these variations. Furthermore, what actually causes the changes when they do occur is not known. It is tempting to assert that change is caused by industrial democracy per se, but the sociotechnical approach calls for making so many changes at once that it is almost impossible to judge the value of the individual variables, including those of industrial democracy. Increased pay; self-selection of work situation; multiskilling, with its resultant job enrichment; and decreased contact with authority almost invariably occur in autonomous work group studies. The compounding of experimental variables makes interpretation very hazardous.

Even among work groups, sociotechnical theory has faced its share of criticism, primarily on grounds of incompleteness. Thus, Hackman (1978) contends:

1. The theory does not specify the attributes of group tasks that are required for creation of effective autonomous work groups . . . because key task attributes are not specified, it is not possible to devise measures of those attributes for use in theory guided diagnoses of work systems prior to change, in evaluations of the effects of changes on the work, or in tests of the conceptual adequacy of the theory itself.
2. Individual differences among people are not explicitly dealt with in the sociotechnical approach. . . . The theory does not deal with the fact that social needs vary in strength among people. Such differences may affect whether individuals seek to participate in an autonomous group.
3. The theory does not address the internal dynamics that occur among members of work groups. . . . The assumption apparently is that members of autonomous work groups will develop on their own satisfactory ways of working together. . . . Given the substantial evidence about ways that groups can go "sour," the validity of that assumption must be considered questionable. (64)

Certainly sociotechnical theory has suffered as a consequence of inattention to measurement; little has been done to follow up on Gulowsen's (1972) initial work. Accordingly, it is often impossible to determine whether an appropriate test of the theory has actually been carried out.

Hackman's point about individual differences is equally well taken. Apparently, autonomous work groups are not for all. Many may view the forced social interaction with distaste and rebel against the tyranny of group decision. Theoretical extension and research into individual differences seem curiously lacking, given the clinical background of the original Tavistock unit.

Pros and Cons of Application

The basic question insofar as application is concerned is whether autonomous groups should be introduced. That the theory itself has run into difficulties is of little managerial significance. The theory has spawned an approach that may well be justified in its own right. If anything, the techniques of sociotechnical application appear to have outdistanced the theory.

It seems apparent that sociotechnical approaches are more likely to work in certain contexts than others. Small town environments, small work forces, new locations (start-up situations, greenfield sites), geographic separation from the rest of the company, and extensive planning horizons seem to help, although they do not guarantee diffusion to other locations. The absence of a union, or at least of a militant union, represents a favorable situation as well. Converting an existing workforce to sociotechnical approaches and dealing with more authoritarian cultures can introduce problems (Fairhurst, Green, and Courtright 1995). Organizational and national cultures that are favorable to job autonomy and participative process provide fertile ground for sociotechnical approaches. Evidence indicates that the Nordic countries, such as Norway and Sweden, as opposed to the United States, Canada, and Australia, provide a favorable climate for interventions of this type (Dobbin and Boychuk 1999). In addition certain technologies seem to foster sociotechnical approaches and others to thwart them (Sorensen 1985).

Sociotechnical interventions certainly can produce resistance, either in the short run or over long periods, and this resistance can escalate. The approach is best recommended where there is a reasonable chance of success and where the company faces a basic problem that sociotechnical concepts can reasonably be calculated to solve, as in the instance of Volvo's labor force difficulties. Success has occurred consistently where the scale is small and the context is isolated enough to permit social pressures to operate uncontested, or where social pressures are supported by external forces.

The sociotechnical approach appears to reduce manpower needs. Because of multi-skilling, more flexible work organization, and the assumption of managerial tasks by the work group, fewer people are needed. Thus, even though each person is typically paid more, total costs tend to be reduced. This is a major managerial advantage, but for unions it means fewer potential dues-paying members and for the society as a whole it may mean increased unemployment.

I end with a generally favorable vote for the sociotechnical approach, given the right circumstances and the right people, though it is not necessarily a favorable vote for sociotechnical theory and the reasons it espouses for introducing autonomous work groups. Even more, the apparent success of applications of the sociotechnical approach calls for expanded research.

Recent Developments

The sociotechnical approach and organization development have tended to merge in recent years so that autonomous work groups are now often introduced as organization development interventions. In fact this kind of merging has become so prevalent that it is very difficult to determine what approach in practice is an application of what theory. One thing is certain—teams in some form under some name have been widely adopted (Varma, Beatty, Schneier, and Ulrich 1999), and they travel under a great many different names; examples are autonomous work groups and sociotechnical systems, but also self-managing work teams, self-organizing teams, empowered groups, self-regulating work groups, self-directed teams, high performance work systems, and bossless teams. A designation involving the term empowerment seems to be gaining considerable currency with a wide variety of meanings attached to the term (Wall, Wood, and Leach 2004).

The expansion of these approaches appears to reflect competitive pressures and the need to reduce costs much more than the compelling logic of theoretical statements, but nevertheless there are theoretical factors at work. In fact sociotechnical systems theory is often credited with providing the underpinnings for the current burst of activity on the team front (see, for example, Moorhead, Neck, and West 1998). Yet roots of the current developments extend back into social learning theory and organizational behavior modification (see Miner 2005), and in many other directions. Empowerment in some form seems to have taken over and consolidated applications derived from a wide range of theoretical perspectives, often leaving the theoretical underpinnings behind. This emphasis on empowerment is clearly evident in recent research (Labianca, Gray, and Brass 2000; Leach, Wall, and Jackson 2003) and in the conceptual literature (Kirkman and Rosen 2000, Prasad and Eylon 2001).

CONCLUSIONS

The parallels between the theoretical developments initiated from the Institute for Social Research at the University of Michigan and those coming out of the Tavistock Institute are many. However, the differences point up the relative strengths of the two organizations. These differences became manifest at an early meeting between the two groups (Trist, Emery, and Murray 1997). There was some tension generated because the Tavistock people "wanted to get on with things which were of practical interest" while perceiving the Michigan group as having "gone into methodology and concept development." As Trist notes, "We were moving into the society and they were moving away from it" (677). The Michigan approach was too academic for the action-oriented Tavistock consultants. This difference persevered for many years; it is clearly manifest in the different types of significant contributions that the two organizations have made.

Sociotechnical theory's importance rating is 5.09, down somewhat from the theories we have been considering, but still quite high. The estimated validity is at three stars, reflecting the strength of the theory at the group level and its failures in dealing with environmental considerations and management. Certain logical inconsistencies are present as well. The greatest strength of sociotechnical theory is its usefulness, rated at four stars. The concern of the Tavistock people for practical matters paid off in the development of an applied technology that has been shown to have many positive features. Hopefully, these will not be lost as they merge into the empowerment movement.

In Chapter 11 the discussion turns to a systems theory of a sociological nature that starts at the organizational level without ties to group dynamics. The question to be considered is whether under these circumstances the systems approach fares better as a basis for theory construction.

REFERENCES

Agervold, Mogens (1975). Swedish Experiments in Industrial Democracy. In Louis E. Davis and Albert B. Cherns (Eds.), *Cases and Commentary, Vol. 2, The Quality of Working Life.* New York: Free Press, 46–65.

Barker, James R. (1993). Tightening the Iron Cage: Concertive Control in Self-Managing Teams. *Administrative Science Quarterly*, 38, 408–37.

Beldt, Sandra F. (1978). An Analysis of Values in Traditional Organizations and Nontraditional Organizations Structured Using Socio-Technical Systems Design. Ph.D. Dissertation. Atlanta, GA: Georgia State University.

Blackler, Frank H.M., and Brown, Colin A. (1980). *Whatever Happened to Shell's New Philosophy of Management? Lessons for the 1980s from a Major Socio-Technical Intervention of the 1960s.* Westmead, UK: Teakfield.

Bramlette, Carl A., Jewell, Donald O., and Mescon, Michael H. (1977). Designing for Organizational Effectiveness: A Better Way; How It Works. *Atlanta Economic Review,* 27(5–6), 10–15, 35–41.

Cherns, Albert R. (1977). Can Behavioral Science Help Design Organizations? *Organizational Dynamics,* 5(4), 44–64.

Cordery, John L., Mueller, Walter S., and Smith, Leigh M. (1991). Attitudinal and Behavioral Effects of Autonomous Group Working: A Longitudinal Field Study. *Academy of Management Journal,* 34, 464–76.

Cummings, Thomas G., and Srivastva, Suresh (1977). *Management of Work: A Socio-Technical Systems Approach.* Kent, OH: Kent State University Press.

DeGreene, Kenyon B. (1988). Long Wave Cycles of Sociotechnical Change and Innovation: A Macropsychological Perspective. *Journal of Occupational Psychology,* 61, 7–23.

Dicks, Henry V. (1970). *Fifty Years of the Tavistock Clinic.* London: Routledge and Kegan Paul.

Dobbin, Frank, and Boychuk, Terry (1999). National Employment Systems and Job Autonomy: Why Job Autonomy is High in the Nordic Countries and Low in the United States, Canada, and Australia. *Organization Studies,* 20, 257–91.

Emery, Fred E. (1967). The Next Thirty Years: Concepts, Methods and Anticipations. *Human Relations,* 20, 199–237.

———. (1974). Bureaucracy and Beyond. *Organizational Dynamics,* 2(3), 3–13.

Emery, Fred E., and Thorsrud, Einar (1976). *Democracy at Work.* Leiden, the Netherlands: Martinus Nijhoff.

Emery, Fred E., and Trist, Eric L. (1965). The Causal Texture of Organizational Environments. *Human Relations,* 18, 21–32.

———. (1973). *Toward a Social Ecology.* London: Plenum.

———. (1978). Analytical Model for Sociotechnical Systems. In William A. Pasmore and John J. Sherwood (Eds.), *Sociotechnical Systems: A Sourcebook.* LaJolla, CA: University Associates, 120–31.

Fairhurst, Gail T., Green, Stephen, and Courtright, John (1995). Inertial Forces and the Implementation of a Socio-Technical Systems Approach: A Communication Study. *Organization Science,* 6, 168–85.

Fox, William M. (1990). An Interview with Eric Trist, Father of the Sociotechnical Systems Approach. *Journal of Applied Behavioral Science,* 26, 259–79.

———. (1995). Sociotechnical System Principles and Guidelines: Past and Present. *Journal of Applied Behavioral Science,* 31, 91–105.

Goodman, Paul S. (1979). *Assessing Organizational Change: The Rushton Quality of Work Experiment.* New York: Wiley.

Goodman, Paul S., and Lawler, Edward E. (1979). United States. In *New Forms of Work Organization,* 1. Geneva, Switzerland: International Labour Office, 141–73.

Gulowsen, Jon (1972). A Measure of Work Group Autonomy. In Louis E. Davis and James C. Taylor (Eds.), *Design of Jobs.* Baltimore, MD: Penguin, 374–90.

Gyllenhammar, Pehr G. (1977). How Volvo Adapts Work to People. *Harvard Business Review,* 55(4), 102–13.

Hackman, J. Richard (1978). The Design of Self-Managing Work Groups. In Bert King, Siegfried Streufert, and Fred E. Fiedler (Eds.), *Managerial Control and Organizational Democracy.* New York: Wiley, 61–91.

Hennestad, Bjørn W. (2000). Implementing Participative Management: Transition Issues from the Field. *Journal of Applied Behavioral Science,* 36, 314–35.

Herbst, P.G. (1974). *Sociotechnical Design: Strategies in Multidisciplinary Research.* London: Tavistock.

———. (1976). *Alternatives to Hierarchies.* Leiden, the Netherlands: Martinus Nijhoff.

Katz, Daniel, and Kahn, Robert L. (1978). *The Social Psychology of Organizations.* New York: Wiley.

Ketchum, Lyman D., and Trist, Eric L. (1992). *All Teams Are Not Created Equal: How Employee Empowerment Really Works.* Newbury Park, CA: Sage.

Kingdon, Donald R. (1973). *Matrix Organization: Managing Information Technology.* London: Tavistock.

Kirkman, Bradley L., and Rosen, Benson (2000). Powering Up Teams. *Organizational Dynamics,* 28(3), 48–66.

Labianca, Giuseppe, Gray, Barbara, and Brass, Daniel J. (2000). A Grounded Model of Organizational Schema Change During Empowerment. *Organization Science,* 11, 235–57.

Leach, Desmond J., Wall, Toby D., and Jackson, Paul R. (2003). The Effect of Empowerment on Job Knowledge: An Empirical Test Involving Operators of Complex Technology. *Journal of Occupational and Organizational Psychology*, 76, 27–52.

Miller, Eric J. (1975). Socio-Technical Systems in Weaving, 1953–1970: A Follow-Up Study. *Human Relations*, 28, 349–86.

Miller, Eric J., and Rice, A.K. (1967). *Systems of Organization: The Control of Task and Sentient Boundaries*. London: Tavistock.

Mills, Ted (1976). Altering the Social Structure in Coal Mining: A Case Study. *Monthly Labor Review*, 99(10), 3–10.

Miner, John B. (2002). *Organizational Behavior: Foundations, Theories, and Analyses*. New York: Oxford University Press.

———. (2005). *Organizational Behavior 1: Essential Theories of Motivation and Leadership*. Armonk, NY: M.E. Sharpe.

Moorhead, Gregory, Neck, Christopher P., and West, Mindy S. (1998). The Tendency Toward Defective Decision Making Within Self-Managing Teams: The Relevance of Groupthink for the 21st Century. *Organizational Behavior and Human Decision-Processes*, 73, 327–51.

Neuman, George A. (1991). Autonomous Work Group Selection. *Journal of Business and Psychology*, 6, 283–91.

Nickerson, Jack A., and Zenger, Todd R. (2002). Being Efficiently Fickle: A Dynamic Theory of Organizational Choice. *Organization Science*, 13, 547–66.

Pasmore, William A., and Khalsa, Gurudev S. (1993). The Contributions of Eric Trist to the Social Engagement of Social Science. *Academy of Management Review*, 18, 546–69.

Pasmore, William A., and Sherwood, John J. (1978). *Sociotechnical Systems: A Sourcebook*. LaJolla, CA: University Associates, 291–301.

Peterson, Richard B. (1976). Swedish Experiments in Job Reform. *Business Horizons*, 19(3), 13–22.

Prasad, Pushkala, and Eylon, Dafna (2001). Narrating Past Traditions of Participation and Inclusion: Historical Perspectives on Workplace Environment. *Journal of Applied Behavioral Science*, 37, 5–14.

Rhenman, Eric (1973). *Organization Theory for Long-Range Planning*. London: Wiley.

Rice, A.K. (1958). *Productivity and Social Organization: The Ahmedabad Experiment*. London: Tavistock.

———. (1963). *The Enterprise and Its Environment*. London: Tavistock.

Roy, S K. (1969). A Re-Examination of the Methodology of A.K. Rice's Indian Textile Mill Work Reorganization. *Indian Journal of Industrial Relations*, 5(2), 170–91.

Sorensen, Knut H. (1985). Technology and Industrial Democracy: An Inquiry into Some Theoretical Issues and Their Social Basis. *Organization Studies*, 6, 139–60.

Susman, Gerald I. (1976). *Autonomy at Work: A Sociotechnical Analysis of Participative Management*. New York: Praeger.

Sutton, Robert I., and Kahn, Robert L. (1987). Prediction, Understanding, and Control as Antidotes to Organizational Stress. In Jay W. Lorsch (Ed.), *Handbook of Organizational Behavior*. Englewood Cliffs, NJ: Prentice Hall, 272–85.

Terreberry, Shirley (1968). The Evolution of Organizational Environments. *Administrative Science Quarterly*, 12, 590–613.

Thorsrud, Einar, Sorensen, Bjorg A., and Gustavsen, Bjorn (1976). Sociotechnical Approach to Industrial Democracy in Norway. In Robert Dubin (Ed.), *Handbook of Work, Organization, and Society*. Chicago, IL: Rand McNally, 421–64.

Trist, Eric L. (1969). On Socio-Technical Systems. In Warren G. Bennis, Kenneth D. Benne, and Robert Chin (Eds.), *The Planning of Change*. New York: Holt, Rinehart and Winston, 269–82.

———. (1973). A Socio-Technical Critique of Scientific Management. In D.O. Edge and J.W. Wolfe (Eds.), *Meaning and Control*. London: Tavistock, 95–119.

———. (1975a). The New Work Ethic in Europe and America. In Carl A. Bramlette and Michael H. Mescon (Eds.), *Man and the Future of Organizations*, Vol. 4. Atlanta, GA: Department of Management, Georgia State University, 45–64.

———. (1975b). Planning the First Steps Toward Quality of Working Life in a Developing Country. In Louis E. Davis and Albert B. Cherns (Eds.), *Problems, Prospects, and the State of the Art, Vol. 1, The Quality of Working Life*. New York: Free Press, 78–85.

———. (1976a). *A Concept of Organizational Ecology*. Philadelphia, PA: Management and Behavioral Science Center, University of Pennsylvania.

————. (1976b). Action Research and Adaptive Planning. In A.W. Clark (Ed.), *Experimenting with Organizational Life.* London: Plenum, 223–36.

————. (1977). Collaboration in Work Settings: A Personal Perspective. *Journal of Applied Behavioral Science,* 13, 268–78.

————. (1985). Intervention Strategies for Interorganizational Domains. In Robert Tannenbaum, Newton Margulies, and Fred Massarik (Eds.), *Human Systems Development: New Perspectives on People and Organizations.* San Francisco, CA: Jossey-Bass, 167–97.

————. (1993). Guilty of Enthusiasm. In Arthur G. Bedeian (Ed.), *Management Laureates: A Collection of Autobiographical Essays.* Vol. III. Greenwich, CT: JAI Press, 193–221.

Trist, Eric L., and Bamforth, K.W. (1951). Some Social and Psychological Consequences of the Longwall Method of Coal-Getting. *Human Relations,* 4, 3–38.

Trist, Eric L., and Dwyer, Charles (1982). The Limits of Laissez-Faire as a Sociotechnical Change Strategy. In Robert Zager and Michael P. Rosow (Eds.), *The Innovative Organization: Productivity Programs in Action.* New York: Pergamon, 149–83.

Trist, Eric L., Emery, Fred, and Murray, Hugh (1997). *The Social Engagement of Social Science: A Tavistock Anthology, Vol. III: The Socio-Ecological Perspective.* Philadelphia, PA: University of Pennsylvania Press.

Trist, Eric L., Higgin, G.W., Murray, Hugh, and Pollock, A.B. (1963). *Organizational Choice: Capabilities of Groups at the Coal Face Under Changing Technologies.* London: Tavistock.

Trist, Eric L., and Murray, Hugh (1990). *The Social Engagement of Social Science: A Tavistock Anthology, Vol. I: The Socio-Psychological Perspective.* Philadelphia, PA: University of Pennsylvania Press.

————. (1993). *The Social Engagement of Social Science: A Tavistock Anthology, Vol. II: The Socio-Technical Perspective.* Philadelphia, PA: University of Pennsylvania Press.

Trist, Eric L., Susman, Gerald I., and Brown, Grant R. (1977). An Experiment in Autonomous Working in an American Underground Coal Mine. *Human Relations,* 30, 201–36.

Varma, Arup, Beatty, Richard W., Schneier, Craig E., and Ulrich, David O. (1999). High Performance Work Systems: Exciting Discovery or Passing Fad? *Human Resource Planning,* 22(1), 26–37.

Wall, Toby D., Kemp, Nigel J., Jackson, Paul R., and Clegg, Chris W. (1986). Outcomes of Autonomous Work Groups: A Long-Term Field Experiment. *Academy of Management Journal,* 29, 280–304.

Wall, Toby D., Wood, Stephen J., and Leach, Desmond J. (2004). Empowerment and Performance. *International Review of Industrial and Organizational Psychology,* 19, 1–46.

Walton, Richard E. (1972). How to Counter Alienation in the Plant. *Harvard Business Review,* 50(6), 70–81.

————. (1977). Work Innovation at Topeka: After Six Years. *Journal of Applied Behavioral Science,* 13, 422–33.

Yorks, Lyle, and Whitsett, David A. (1985). Hawthorne, Topeka, and the Issue of Science versus Advocacy in Organizational Behavior. *Academy of Management Review,* 10, 21–30.

CHAPTER 11

SOCIOLOGICAL OPEN SYSTEMS THEORY

JAMES THOMPSON

Importance rating	★ ★ ★ ★ ★
	Institutionalized
Estimated validity	★ ★ ★
Estimated usefulness	★
Decade of origin	1960s

Although the field of sociology has spawned more than one theory of organizational functioning and structure that utilizes systems concepts, the work of Thompson is more centrally focused on the open systems approach than any other. In its concern with technological variables (usually manufacturing technology) it is related to those theories that emphasize the technological imperative and thus the causal impact of technology on process and structure (see Miner 2002). In its concern with decision making it has much in common with the theories treated in Part II of this volume. Above all, however, Thompson's is an open systems theory dealing with organization–environment relationships and their effects.

BACKGROUND

James D. Thompson was one of a group of behavioral scientists brought together on the faculty of Cornell University's business school as organizational behavior was beginning to emerge as a distinct field. The prime mover in this development was Edward Litchfield, dean of the school. Thompson, after military service during World War II and an aborted and brief career in journalism, entered the doctoral program in sociology at the University of North Carolina in 1949. There he worked on an Air Force research project, obtained his degree, and remained in a research capacity with funding from the Ford Foundation.

His first regular faculty appointment was the one at Cornell. While there he became the founding editor of *Administrative Science Quarterly,* which began publication in 1956. When Litchfield moved on to the University of Pittsburgh as its president, Thompson went with him, again with an appointment in the business school. This association proved to be rather short-lived, and from there Thompson went to Indiana University for a six-year stint. As his interest in the study of organizations began to wane, he moved to the sociology department at Vanderbilt in 1968. Thompson died in 1973 at the age of fifty-three.

Throughout most of his career, Thompson was a conceptualizer and theorist rather than a researcher, though he did conduct some original organizational research at an early point (Thompson 1956). His later research derived from secondary sources and was not focused on the major hypotheses of his theory (McNeil and Thompson 1971). He wrote sparingly and succinctly. Two books contain practically all his theoretical writings, and those who read these books typically find themselves going back over sentences again and again to glean their full meaning. Strong humanist values did not play a role in these formulations.

THEORETICAL PROPOSITIONS

Thompson presented many of his ideas initially in various essay-type articles. These ideas subsequently were polished and extensively supplemented in his major work, *Organizations in Action* (Thompson 1967). He published a textbook dealing with the behavioral sciences in general (Thompson and Van Houten 1970) and, after his death, editors prepared a volume containing the papers that led up to *Organizations in Action,* selections from that book, and certain subsequent contributions, not all of which are focused on organizational issues (Rushing and Zald 1976).

Thompson's primary approach to theory construction was the conceptual inventory—a series of parallel propositions, usually stated in somewhat abstract terms, conceptually derived rather than drawn from an extensive perusal of existing research. This conceptual emphasis distinguishes Thompson from March and Simon (see Chapter 3 in this volume), whose approach to proposition formulation involved much greater empirical generalization. The theoretical variables are not tightly interrelated logically, however; the propositions do not derive from a common set of postulates and assumptions, as is the case with the most rigorous deductive theories. Rather, sets of propositions are developed to deal with various areas of major concern in the study of organizations.

Early Writings

Although we will rely on Thompson (1967) for a formal statement of the theory, knowledge of the variables he considered in prior publications should facilitate understanding. Early on,

Thompson established propositions based on such variables as the abstractness of the organization's goal as reflected in its product, the ease of utilizing the technology for new purposes, and the degree of mechanization as opposed to professionalization of the technology (Thompson and Bates 1957).

Subsequently, Thompson and McEwen (1958) analyzed organizational decision making in the goal-setting context. Organizations must gain support from their environments in setting goals, and this is accomplished by using the strategies of *competition* (rivalry between two or more organizations for the exchange of goods and services), *co-optation* (absorbing outsiders into the policy-making structure of the organization to avert threat), and *coalition* (combining organizations for a common purpose). As one moves up the scale from competition to coalition, environmental conditioning becomes increasingly costly, with coalition being the most extreme strategy.

Thompson and Tuden (1959) look at the internal processes of organizational decision, utilizing the proposition that the role of administration is often to manage the decision process as well as make the decisions. The key variables are the degree of agreement or disagreement among decision makers in their beliefs about the causation of alternative actions and in their preferences for possible outcomes. When agreement is high on both dimensions, decisions are made by specialists' *computations* and the appropriate structure is *bureaucracy*. When agreement about causation is lacking, decisions are made by majority *judgment* (voting) and the appropriate structure is a *collegium*. When agreement about outcomes is lacking, decisions are made by bargaining and *compromise* within a *representative body*. When disagreement rules on both dimensions, an *inspirational* decision, perhaps made by a charismatic leader, is needed, and the ideal structure involves the randomness and disorganization of *anomie*. Again, organizational costs associated with decision making increase as one moves from computation, through judgment and compromise, to inspiration.

Conflict in organizations is in part a function of the differentiations and interactions required by their technologies, but organizations also can exercise some control over these processes and thus have a degree of discretion in handling conflict (Thompson 1960). In addition to technology, the labor force and the heterogeneity of the task environment (the part of the environment that is not indifferent to the organization) can be sources of conflict. Technology produces conflict based on administrative allocations, and defense against conflict is achieved through varying organizational structures. The labor force produces conflict because employees bring latent roles to the job, as with nepotism and patronage; defense is achieved by limiting diversity through recruitment and selection. The task environment yields conflict as a result of competing pressures, and the defense against this is manipulating the exposure of members to these pressures.

Introduction of Systems Concepts

The preceding statements do not utilize systems concepts explicitly, though they do imply them. However, in 1962 Thompson wrote an article in which he focused on output roles and the nature of boundary-spanning transactions. The major variables he considered were the degree to which the output role incumbent was armed with set routines for dealing with individuals in the environment, such as customers, and the degree to which these nonmembers were compelled to participate in a relationship with the output role occupant. Thompson and Hawkes (1962) also utilize the *open system* concept explicitly in discussing reactions to community disaster.

By 1964 Thompson had begun to incorporate these systems formulations into his propositions on organizational functioning:

1. Variations in environmental conditions will bring about changes in decision strategies for input and output components of the firm.
2. Variations in environmental conditions can penetrate the input and output "buffers" and cause changes in the technical core of the organization (thus violating the ideal isolation of the technical core in its mediating role).
3. Variations in environmental conditions will alter the dependence of input, technical core, and output components relative to one another.
4. When input or output components transfer uncertainty rather than absorb it, there will be conflict among input, technical core, and output components. (Thompson 1964, 341–42)

At this point what had been a series of segmented theories of decision making, conflict, boundary roles, and the like was beginning to fuse into a more comprehensive statement under the open systems rubric.

The theory that resulted is presented in *Organizations in Action* (Thompson 1967). It spans a wide domain, but does not include voluntary organizations. The organizations covered operate as open systems facing uncertainty, but at the same time they need certainty; it is in this latter sense that they are said to be subject to criteria of rationality. Both the environment and technology are sources of uncertainty.

Rationality

Organizations engage in input activities. To be rational they strive to make their core technologies function as well as possible, and to accomplish this they seek to seal off these technologies from environmental influences—thus approximating closed system conditions.

Buffering on both the input and output sides is one way to stabilize the environment of the technical core. Examples of input buffering are stockpiling of raw materials and preventive maintenance; an example of output buffering would be using warehoused product inventories to deal with market fluctuations.

To the extent buffering is insufficient, *smoothing* or leveling activities are invoked to reduce environmental fluctuations. Reduced late-night airline fares and the scheduling of nonemergency operations for low-use periods by hospitals represent attempts to smooth input and output transactions.

When smoothing activities are inadequate, organizations resort to *forecasting* to anticipate fluctuations and adapt the technical core to them. Peak load periods are thus known in advance and may be treated as constraints. Staffing or other input levels can be increased to anticipate needs and an essentially closed-system logic can be maintained.

Finally, should all else fail, organizations must resort to *rationing*, whereby services or products are provided on some preestablished basis. Major environmental fluctuations, as for instance a community disaster facing a hospital or a sudden fad facing a manufacturer, can necessitate rationing. This strategy is less than ideal because the organization must forego opportunities (Thompson 1967, 19–23).

Domains of Organized Action

Organizations typically stake out a domain within which certain goods and/or services are provided. When this domain is recognized by those in the task environment who can provide needed support for the organization, a degree of domain consensus exists. Thus organizations develop dependencies on components of their environment, which vary with the degree of need (for a raw material, for instance) and the number of alternative sources of supply. For the organization, dependence and power relative to various environmental components are inversely related.

Under a competitive strategy, organizations seek to establish and hold power through maintaining multiple alternatives, prestige, and focusing their efforts on those components of the task environment that otherwise are most likely to place them in a dependent position. As noted previously, support from the environment, or power over it, may also be obtained by bargaining, co-optation, and coalition.

To the extent an organization is constrained from action in the various sectors of its environment, it will seek increasing degrees of power over those sectors in which it remains free to act. Thus a firm operating in an impoverished market will seek to exercise power over sources of raw materials and labor to adjust them to market demand for the product. To the extent such efforts fail, there is likely to be an attempt to enlarge the task environment, for instance, by involving previously uninvolved governmental units or by resorting to the courts (Thompson 1967, 32–37).

Design

Organizations may deal with environmental problems by placing their boundaries around activities that could be performed by other task environment components. In organizations where the technology is *long linked,* as with an assembly line, domains tend to expand through vertical integration, perhaps expanding backward into raw material production or forward into direct marketing. Organizations in which the technology is *mediating,* as with commercial banks that mediate between depositors and borrowers, expand their domains by increasing the populations served. *Intensive* technologies that draw on a variety of techniques to achieve a change in a person (as in a general hospital) or an object (as in the construction industry) require that the domain be expanded by incorporating the person or object involved. Intensive technology yields a custom-made output, and problems are reduced to the extent the client can be controlled.

These types of growth often yield a lack of balance in that capacities vary considerably from one component to another. To deal with such situations:

1. Multicomponent organizations subject to rationality norms will seek to grow until the least reducible component is approximately fully occupied.
2. Organizations with capacity in excess of what the task environment supports will seek to enlarge their domains (Thompson 1967, 39–48).

Technology and Structure

Components within an organization may be interdependent in various ways. Under *pooled* interdependence, each part makes a separate contribution to the whole and is in turn supported by the whole, as with branch sales offices. Under *sequential* interdependence, one part must act before another can, as in the relationship of production to marketing. Under *reciprocal* interdependence, the interdependence is two way and thus symmetrical. Operations and maintenance units are reciprocally interdependent in that maintaining equipment in good repair is an input to operations, while equipment needing repair is an input to maintenance. As one moves from pooled to sequential to reciprocal interdependence, coordination becomes more difficult and costly. The appropriate approach for pooled interdependence is *standardization;* for sequential interdependence, *planning* and scheduling; and for reciprocal interdependence, coordination by *mutual adjustment.*

Because coordination is costly, the ideal is to use standardization if possible, then planning, and finally mutual adjustment only if absolutely necessary. Components also are grouped to minimize coordination costs. Thus reciprocally interdependent units are placed together in small, relatively autonomous, local groups. If only sequential interdependence is involved, then these units are so grouped. With only pooled interdependence, positions are grouped homogeneously to facilitate the use of standardization.

Problems of reciprocal interdependence, if present, are dealt with at the lowest organizational levels possible. Groups higher up are developed to deal with sequential interdependence, and finally, toward the top, homogeneous units are created to facilitate standardization among components having pooled interdependence, as in a divisionalized structure. As a result of these priorities, similar positions may not be grouped together, and standardized rules must be used to blanket homogeneous positions across divisions. Liaison positions with staff designations are created to link the rule-making agency with these positions. When departments cannot handle all sequential interdependence, committees tend to be invoked to deal with the remaining coordination, and when departments cannot encompass all reciprocal interdependence, project teams are created (Thompson 1967, 54–61).

Rationality and Structure

The logic of organizational design based on technology must be supplemented by a concern with environmental characteristics. To the extent that the task environment is heterogeneous, an attempt will be made to identify homogeneous segments and create boundary-spanning units to deal with each. These units are further subdivided if the amount of interaction across the boundary requires it.

Organizations will rely heavily on standardized rules in coping with stable environments and with environments in which the range of variation is known. If the range of variation is very large or unknown, localized boundary-spanning units are needed to monitor and plan effectively.

Thompson specifies environments in terms of their homogeneity–heterogeneity and stability–variability, and he indicates organizational forms for boundary-spanning units to match these different environments:

Homogeneous-stable:	A few functional divisions utilizing standardized rules or adaptation.
Heterogeneous-stable:	A variety of functional divisions matched to homogeneous segments of the task environment and utilizing rules extensively.
Homogeneous-variable:	Geographically decentralized divisions concerned with planning responses to change.
Heterogeneous-variable:	Divisions functionally differentiated to match segments of the task environment and decentralized to monitor and plan. (Thompson 1967, 72–73)

What has been said about the effects of technology and environment on structure requires some integration. Thompson's propositions dealing with the joint effects of the two forces are as follows:

1. When technical-core and boundary-spanning activities can be isolated from one another except for scheduling, organizations under norms of rationality will be centralized with an overarching layer composed of functional divisions.
2. Under conditions of complexity, when the major components of an organization are reciprocally interdependent, these components will be segmented and arranged in self-sufficient clusters, each cluster having its own domain (. . . a product division or a profit center, or it may in general usage be known as a decentralized division). (Thompson 1967, 75–76)

Assessment

Sociological systems theory is more concerned than most theories with how organizations assess themselves and are assessed by others. One proposition states that assessments based on *efficiency* tests involving input-output calculations are most preferred, followed by *instrumental* tests (whether a desired state of affairs is achieved), and finally *social* tests, involving the judgments of reference groups. Often efficiency tests cannot be applied due to insufficient knowledge and ambiguous standards.

Other hypotheses about the assessment process include the following statements. Given stable task environments, organizations seek to demonstrate historical improvement; in dynamic environments they seek to demonstrate success relative to comparable organizations. Generally the demonstration of improvement along dimensions of particular concern to sectors of the environment on which the organization is most dependent is considered to be of greatest value.

In evaluating internal units, organizations are guided by the unit's method of coordinating interdependence. Accordingly, those units using standardized rules are assessed in terms of degree of adherence to those rules; those units following plans and schedules are assessed in terms of filling the previously established quotas; and units relying on mutual adjustment are assessed in terms of the expressed confidence of reciprocally dependent units (Thompson 1967, 87–95).

The Variable Human

Thompson (1967) devotes considerable attention to the inducement-contribution bargain, whereby organizational members either explicitly or implicitly agree to contribute effort in various forms and amounts in return for inducements such as pay. This bargain is determined through power processes. Where the technology is routine, collective bargaining is the method of choice. In intensive technologies, whether one achieves the occupational ceiling early or late is important. Those in early-ceiling occupations seek leverage to upgrade the occupation through collective action. Under late-ceiling conditions, such as those obtaining in the professions, the key element in bargaining is the person's visibility among occupational colleagues. Within management the bargain is strongly influenced by the individual's reputation for having scarce abilities to solve organizational problems. In roles that are boundary-spanning, the bargain is determined by the power of the environmental segment on which the organization depends and by the person's ability to handle this dependence effectively (Thompson 1967, 106–15).

Discretion

The exercise of discretion in organizations is not always viewed as attractive. Discretion tends to be avoided when uncertainty seems to outweigh the organization's predictive capacity and when the consequences of error appear to be great. Organizations themselves foster avoidance of discretion by using inappropriate structures and assessment criteria, and by assessing performance on various incompatible criteria. Several of Thompson's propositions deal with multiple consequences of discretion:

1. Organizations seek to guard against deviant discretion by policing methods.
2. Where workloads exceed capacity and the individual has options, he is tempted to select tasks that promise to enhance his scores on assessment criteria.
3. Where workloads or resource supplies fluctuate, the individual is tempted to stockpile (empire build).
4. Where alternatives are present, the individual is tempted to report successes and suppress evidence of failure. (Thompson 1967, 122–24)

Individuals in highly discretionary positions such as top management characteristically seek to maintain power that exceeds their dependence on others in the organization. When this is not possible, the individual will seek a coalition that may include essential segments of the task environment. Certainly changes in environmental dependencies can serve to restructure coalitions.

The number of political positions or power bases in an organization increases with the number of sources of uncertainty and with the degree of decentralization. However, power bases and organizational goals can change rapidly under conditions of a dynamic task environment or technology. Generally such changes are functional for the organization, and for that reason commitments to entrenched power, as in the case of a founding entrepreneur, should be avoided.

Control

The propositions dealing with control draw heavily on the concept of coalition—primarily the dominant coalition—and on Thompson and Tuden's (1959) typology of decision making. The dominant coalition increases in size with increases in the number of areas in the organization where it is necessary to rely on a judgmental decision; thus a shift in one area from the predominance of computational to judgmental decisions can be expected to place a representative of that area in the dominant coalition. Similarly, imperfections in the core technology and heterogeneity in the task environment foster coalition membership for task-environmental and technological specialists.

Conflict within the dominant coalition can be expected to increase (1) as interdependence increases, (2) as environmental forces require compromises on outcome preferences, and (3) as the variety of professions represented increases. When power is widely distributed within the dominant coalition, an inner circle emerges, without which the coalition would be immobilized. Under such circumstances the dominant coalition as a whole becomes a ratifying body. To the extent there is a central power figure, this individual is the one who can manage the dominant coalition.

At the conclusion of his book Thompson (1967) reemphasizes the importance of the open systems approach and of the dimension of certainty–uncertainty. Uncertainties come from inside and outside the organization. There are three major sources:

1. *Generalized uncertainty,* or lack of cause-effect understanding in the culture at large.
2. *Contingency,* in which the outcomes of organizational action are in part determined by the actions of environmental elements.
3. *Internal interdependence* of components. (Thompson 1967, 159)

As utilized by Thompson, the uncertainty concept is highly congruent with an open systems approach that emphasizes exchanges across organizational boundaries.

Later Writings

Thompson's writings after 1967 focus on two major themes. One involves extrapolating some of his ideas about organizations to other social units and in particular to society at large. The other involves speculations about social and organizational forms of the future. There is some minor reworking or reformulating of earlier views, but by and large the *Organizations in Action* propositions stand as the statements of the theory.

Thompson (1974a) extends his concept of technological determinism in organizations to society at large. In this view technology determines the type of interdependence, which in turn is a major factor in political orientations and societal identification. In considering interdependence, however, Thompson (1974a, b) now utilizes a somewhat different set of categories. Pooled and sequential interdependence remain essentially unchanged, but the concept of *intensive* interdependence is drawn from the prior categorization of technologies and substituted for reciprocal interdependence. Intensive interdependence is concerned with knowledge generation and application, and a major characteristic is its lack of permanence. As with reciprocal interdependence, units need to adjust to feedback from others, and indeed mutual adjustment remains the essential method of coordination.

Thompson (1974b) believes the future will see much greater use of intensive interdependence and of temporary systems, often involving the actions of sets of organizations, not merely sets of individuals. In many respects his views parallel those of certain organization development theorists. Of the organizational world of the year 2000, a time that is now a reality, he says:

> Many of us, or our successors, will hold regular jobs in formal organizations with geographic identities and regularities, with recognized clienteles and functions. . . . But I believe such things will be routine, taken for granted, unproblematic. Our preoccupations as a society, I believe, will not be in this arena, but rather with what I have tried to designate as *complex organizations* of a much more fluid, *ad hoc*, flexible form. Perhaps these should not be designed organizations at all, and the emphasis should instead be placed on the administration of temporarily organized activities . . . with the development of administration teams or cadres to specialize in a continuous process of synthesizing. Perhaps complex organizations of the future will be known not for their components but by their cadres, with each cadre devoted to mobilizing and deploying resources in shifting configurations, to employ changing technologies to meet changing demands. (Thompson 1973, in Rushing and Zald 1976, 245)

EVALUATION AND IMPACT

Obviously Thompson intended to state his propositions so that they might be tested. On the other hand, he is aware that he has not provided operational definitions of his variables, and he seems to have anticipated what has since turned out to be true—research tests have been few and far between:

> The propositions . . . have been stated in the form which allows them to be negated if incorrect. . . . Testable form is not enough, however. We must have operations which will enable us to say the specific conditions do or do not exist. Hopefully our propositions seem plausible and important, but it is unlikely that many will be treated as hypotheses for extensive testing, for in the process of the necessary conceptual refinement, more specific and subtle hypotheses will be generated. (Thompson 1967, 163)

Though there are some direct tests of one or more of Thompson's propositions, these are few. More commonly, certain theory concepts have been used in testing hypotheses that differ from, but are entirely consistent with, the hypotheses Thompson formulated. On occasion it seems that Thompson's propositions have been stretched to the breaking point to achieve consonance between them and the design or results of a particular study.

Co-optation and Coalition

The theory posits a hierarchy of procedures for dealing with environmental uncertainty running from the least costly, which is competition, through bargaining or contracting and co-optation, to the most costly, which is coalition or coalescing (Thompson and McEwen 1958, Thompson 1967). Though the preference hierarchy as such has not been studied, there is research evidence to support the hypothesis that co-optation and coalition are methods of dealing with uncertainty and interdependence.

Thus, for example, Pfeffer (1972a) studied corporate board memberships, relating board composition to such factors as need for access to capital markets and the extent of governmental regulation. The expectation was that representatives of financial institutions, attorneys, and other outsiders would be co-opted onto boards to deal with these external dependencies. Data are presented that are consistent with this expectation. Furthermore, companies that deviated from an optimum board structure commensurate with the dependency requirements existing in their particular industries were less profitable.

In another study Pfeffer (1972b) looked at the use of merger as a method of coping with uncertainty and interdependence. He found that merger behavior was better explained as an attempt to deal with input and output dependencies than it was by any competing hypotheses. Evidence is also presented to show that mergers are often used to reduce the impact of competition within an industry, and to achieve diversification that will reduce the company's dependence on a limited set of other organizations.

Analyses such as these, dealing with co-optation, coalescing, and related concepts are probably best viewed as supporting the open systems approach generally, rather than Thompson's theory specifically. The findings fit well with Thompson's views, but they can be explained equally effectively by other theories of a similar nature.

Protecting the Technical Core

An example of research that attempts to study the use of buffering and forecasting to protect the technical core is the work of Williams (1977), who hypothesized that investment in these mechanisms will be greater when they are particularly needed, because of a high degree of mechanization of the technical core. Hypotheses of this kind are more specific than the Thompson propositions, but are entirely consonant with them.

Consistent with the hypotheses, it was found that the use of buffering systems represented by disproportionately larger employment in the areas of facility maintenance, employee acquisition, and supervision was associated with various measures of throughput mechanization; the relationships are particularly strong for the extent of supervisory employment, with correlations in the 0.60s and 0.70s. Also, employment of individuals to deal with output transactions and to survey and forecast the environment was associated with greater throughput mechanization, but only under conditions of high environmental competition. Where competition was minimal, heavy investment in boundary personnel of this kind apparently was not needed to protect the technical core.

There is also evidence that the degree of smoothing in input and output transactions, such as sales, capital expenditures, and dividend payments, is associated with uncertainty reduction, as reflected in the lower volatility of various common stock return measures (Lev 1975). To the extent a company can achieve smooth flow across its boundaries from year to year, objective indexes of risk appear to be relatively low also.

Research of this kind dealing with methods of protecting the technical core tends to substantiate Thompson's hypotheses regarding specific mechanisms. However, nothing has been done to investigate priorities of usage hypothesized by the theory. Also, the advent of lean production has brought evidence that buffering is not always a desirable approach in dealing with technical core issues (Hargadon 2003).

Varieties of Technology

Numerous studies draw upon Thompson's typology of technologies to test various hypotheses about organizations and their members. These hypotheses often extend well beyond what Thompson actually said, and while they are typically confirmed by the research, the findings support his theoretical propositions only in a very general sense. Thus, Mahoney and Frost (1974) found differences in criteria of effectiveness associated with the dominant technology of a unit. Scheduling and coordination were important in achieving productivity in long-linked technology, and effectiveness was assessed without reference to interactions with other units. Interactions with other units became increasingly significant in assessing effectiveness as the technology changed to mediating and then to intensive. The quality of staff also became increasingly significant.

Clearly the various technologies have differential effects on numerous aspects of an organization and its employees. This way of considering technologies can prove useful (Mackenzie 1986). Technology, as Thompson conceived it, can make a difference in organizations; whether it makes a difference in exactly the way Thompson proposed is another question. On that point the evidence is extremely sparse. A major problem inhibiting research in this area, is that "Thompson's concepts are quite abstract, thus making them difficult to apply unambiguously even in a classification of organizations where one is provided with a great deal of information" (Morrissey and Gillespie 1975, 331).

Interdependence and Coordination

Evidence exists supporting Thompson's propositions regarding coordination. Thus, Reeves and Turner (1972) report that mutual adjustment appears to be the appropriate method of coordination under conditions of reciprocal interdependence. They base this conclusion on intensive case studies of batch production factories. However, they also report that high levels of uncertainty and complexity require the use of mutual adjustment as well, and that mutual adjustment may well be appropriate under uncertain conditions, irrespective of the nature of the interdependence. If anything, they believe that the uncertainty effects are greater than the interdependence effects. Other evidence as well gives credence to the important role played by uncertainty in determining modes of coordination (Argote 1982). Mutual adjustment appears to be more important than Thompson recognized (Heath and Staudenmayer 2000).

Baumler (1971) found in a simulation study that a coordination approach that approximated standardization yielded very positive results when interdependence was low, as in the pooled situation, but actually had a negative effect when interdependence was greater. On the other hand, a more informal approach approximating mutual adjustment worked well under conditions approaching reciprocal interdependence.

All in all, Thompson appears to have been right more often than not. Yet there is more to coordination than the interdependence relationships the theory proposes.

Environmental Stability and Homogeneity

Research such as that reported by Duncan (1972) offers considerable support for the homogeneity-heterogeneity and stability-variability dimensions of the environment formulated by Thompson. These dimensions appear to be important in managers' perceptions of environmental uncertainty. Thus, in homogeneous-stable contexts, little uncertainty is experienced, while in heterogeneous-variable situations it is considerable. Of the two dimensions, stability-variability seems to contribute more to uncertainty perceptions.

When one moves to the theory's more specific statements relating environmental characteristics to organizational structure, there is less support, however. For instance, a study conducted by Schmidt and Cummings (1976) failed to establish any relationship between environmental variability and structural differentiation. Initial analyses did suggest a relationship between environmental heterogeneity and differentiation. However, the size of the organization was found to mediate this relationship, and when these size effects were removed, heterogeneity and differentiation proved to be unrelated.

The general problem of how uncertainty about the environment affects organizational structure is a matter of concern for theories considered in subsequent chapters. However, Thompson's propositions in this area are relatively specific. There is little research bearing on them, and what does exist is nonconfirming.

Assessment

Although research on Thompson's propositions regarding assessment of organizational effectiveness is minimal, some findings support the differentiation among efficiency, instrumental, and social tests and the relationship of the use of these tests to such matters as decision certainty, change, and technology (Mahoney and Weitzel 1969).

A study by Schramm (1975) deals with the ways organizations such as universities seek to compete when they are forced to utilize social tests in comparisons with reference groups. From faculty salary information reported to the American Association of University Professors over a ten-year period it was apparent that reporting universities attempted to improve their relative positions along this dimension over time. Since salary levels have much to do with recruiting quality faculty (an area of much environmental dependence), competition on this variable is highly consistent with Thompson's hypotheses.

In addition, universities paying higher salaries and having other, higher-quality standards as well tended to join in the salary survey process at an earlier date, thus attempting to make their favorable assessment position visible. Universities that were not able to demonstrate a favorable rate of improvement in compensation tended to drop out of the survey process, presumably with a view to emphasizing other dimensions on which they could compete more effectively. Though not uniquely derivable from Thompson's propositions regarding assessment, Schramm's findings do support them in a number of respects.

A recent study by Nutt (2002) found that following Thompson's framework for matching assessment tests with the requirements of the situation produced better results as determined by uninvolved observers. Misusing or ignoring information that would have permitted more appropriate classification of the decision situation made for less successful decisions. These were managerial decisions of a strategic nature made in actual organizations. However, only 40 percent of the decisions studied were executed in accordance with Thompson's prescriptions; if the managers had followed theory more, they would have achieved greater success.

Discretion and Control

The theory posits that changes at the top levels of the hierarchy should reflect a responsiveness to organizational demands. In this view one would expect organizations facing unstable and hostile environments to experience greater turnover at the top simply to adjust to new contingencies. Furthermore, these personnel changes should be consonant with the problems faced. Data on turnover for hospital administrators support this. Although the relationships are not strong, they do reflect a consistent tendency for problem environments to be associated with low tenure (Pfeffer and Salancik 1977). Also, when the operating budget is obtained primarily from payments by private insurers, chief administrators with training in hospital administration tend to be brought in. There is a similar tendency to call in accountants. However, when private donations or government funds are critical to hospital operation, other personnel with more appropriate backgrounds are called in. Clearly organizational contingencies do relate to top-level staffing, as Thompson hypothesized.

There is other evidence that supports Thompson's propositions regarding discretion and control. Inner, elite circles are a reality in many organizations and serve as a major source of organizational innovation. The case analyses of batch production firms yield results that are consistent with the hypothesis that less perfect technologies are likely to be represented in the dominant coalition (Reeves and Turner 1972). However, the authors believe that the power of production management is as much a consequence of the critical role played in meeting market demand contingencies as it is a consequence of imperfections in the technology. All the evidence does not appear to be in on this proposition.

Application

Clearly Thompson's theory is an applied theory of organizational structuring and operation; it deals with practical problems ranging from strategy formulation to unit staffing. To the extent organizations wish to be rational (under norms of rationality), Thompson's theory is normative and explains what to do in a wide range of areas to make an organization more effective. But that is where it ends.

James Thompson was not a consultant to organizations (Perrow 1976), and he did not implement his ideas to determine how they worked. Except for a few laboratory studies, the research into Thompson's theory has not been experimental. It looks at what is, rather than at what happens when experimental changes are introduced. Causation is therefore difficult to establish. It should be possible to develop a technology of organizational intervention that matches the theory, but Thompson did not do it, and as is typically the case under such circumstances, others have not moved his theory across the application gap.

Schultheiss, a Westinghouse Electric manager, provides a ray of hope in her review of *Organizations in Action*:

> Over the past decade I have often been called upon to help other managers who have organizational problems or who desire to make some change or improvement in their organizations. Over and over again I have found myself relying on the meat of Thompson's theory in these situations. Thompson laid the groundwork for understanding the basics of organizational behavior and for helping managers detect when the components of their organization are out of alignment. (1991, 498)

There is a suggestion here that the theory could provide a working theory for managerial decision making, perhaps to supplant classical management theory, which has lingered on too long in serving that purpose. Yet Thompson's writings are too spare to do this for most managers. Someone needs to elaborate on them, if their practical utility is to be fully engaged. We have seen in the case of the Nutt (2002) study discussed previously, dealing with assessment tests, what could be accomplished were this done.

Critiques

Due to its high level of abstraction and the lack of operationalized constructs, Thompson's theory has inspired little research, and in those studies that have been done it is difficult to determine whether they are true tests of the theory or not. Furthermore, because the theory lacks logical interconnectedness, the verification of one theoretical proposition often does not increase confidence in the truth of other propositions not yet tested. As Astley (1991) notes in a companion review to that of Schultheiss, scholars have tended to use Thompson's work as a conceptual starting point and as a vehicle for interpreting theoretical inquiry rather than as a basis for empirical testing. For many it has provided a whole host of valuable concepts and a framework for the rational understanding of organizations and their actions, even if the hypothesized relationships remain untested or in some cases appear untenable.

There can be no question that Thompson's theoretical work is widely respected. Conceptually, it represented a major leap forward. Thompson used the deductive approach far more than any previous theorist to develop new constructs and new relationships. His work was, and remains, a tremendous creative accomplishment.

Against this background it is appropriate to consider not only the research evidence, but also the logical or conceptual criticisms that have been lodged against the theory. One such view is that Thompson is too uncritically accepting of current organizations and current organizational forms. He fails to deal with such problems as socially irresponsible behavior and illegal acts, the frustration of needs of lower-level employees by management, and the quality of work life (Perrow 1976). Perrow contends that Thompson was wrong in being so uncritical and that his contribution would have been much richer had he been less detached (rational?). Perrow's criticism is in many ways more philosophical than scientific; in his writings Thompson was not the humanist others might have wished him to be. From a scientific viewpoint a theorist has a right to define his domain, and as long as the domain is not trivial (and Thompson's clearly was not), he cannot be faulted on that score. Thompson chose to ignore voluntary organizations and to emphasize management and top-level strategy formulation over individual employee concerns. Such domain limitations are often good theoretical strategy; some would even argue that Thompson attempted to cover too large a theoretical domain.

Argyris (1972) has lodged a similar set of criticisms. He maintains that one must deal with the irrational as well as the rational, the informal as well as the formal, the psychological as well as the sociological, if one is to understand organizations. Furthermore, Argyris (1972, 26) views sociological open systems theory as "an explication of scientific management and engineering economics."

He continues:

> Although Thompson aspires to present a more realistic integration of the formal and natural system, the integration actually made favors the closed system, traditional management, economically oriented model which he rejects as incomplete. The "variable human" seems to be minimally variable and minimally human. . . . [M]an turns out to be the closed system Thompson so cogently describes as ineffective for existing living systems. Group dynamics and interpersonal relations are not included. (Argyris 1972, 33–34)

In line with his own theoretical formulations, Argyris maintains that all organizations utilize reciprocal interdependence and coordinate by mutual adjustment and those that do not cannot cope with a dynamic environment. On this latter point Thompson would argue that "under norms of rationality" change should occur as environmental concerns and internal interdependencies require and that to use a more costly level of coordination than the current situation requires is not rational. In view of the fact that mutual adjustment can on occasion actually increase interdependence, excessive use of the kind of approach Argyris suggests can escalate interdependence to a point where most organizations cannot cope, producing a state of near-anarchy.

Wanting a sociological open systems theory to be and to do things that it cannot be and do is a pervasive problem. A paper by Pondy and Mitroff (1979) takes the theory to task for not being open enough. In fact, the authors view the theory as essentially closed and controlled because it utilizes such concepts as standardization, buffering, and smoothing, which are attempts to introduce high degrees of certainty and stability into the organization. Pondy and Mitroff maintain that organizations need variety in their environments and without it they experience the equivalent of sensory deprivation; thus organizations should not strive for certainty, but rather should seek uncertainty and even evoke it in their environments. Under some circumstances this is probably correct, but the level of uncertainty can be so high that it threatens to overwhelm both organizations and individual human beings, and it was to such situations that Thompson addressed his theory.

At the level of what Thompson's theory is, rather than what it might be, there remain some definite problems. Perrow (1976) has raised questions about mediating technology and how it differs from long-linked technology. The two are actually much the same, with the major difference being that one deals with service industries and the other with production industries. With regard to Thompson's proposed differences, Perrow advances some very cogent arguments:

> Both have standardization and repetition as their basic characteristics. The only difference is that mediating technologies operate extensively with "multiple clients or customers distributed in time and space." But that is also true of firms with long-linked technologies, such as General Motors. And doesn't A. T. and T. or the post office (mediating technologies) use a highly standardized and repetitive technology, characteristic of the long-linked form? He says the organization with a mediating technology will handle uncertainty by increasing the populations served, while those with long-linked technologies integrate vertically. But Alcoa and G. M. certainly seek to increase the population served, and A. T. and T. has a significant degree of vertical integration. (Perrow 1976, 719)

Apparently those who have attempted to classify technologies according to Thompson's system also have had difficulties. The system is very abstract and should have been elaborated on with many more specific examples. Because the varieties of interdependence and of technology are so closely related, this matter of ambiguity and insufficient differentiation spills over into the interdependence formulations. Are intensive and reciprocal interdependence the same thing? What does pooled interdependence really mean? Users need a detailed guide for classifying organizations (or their units) by these typologies. Had Thompson applied his system he might have found that differences that appeared clear to him at a high level of abstraction were not nearly so clear at an operational level.

Many of Thompson's propositions have not as yet been adequately tested; we simply do not know if they are true or not. Yet other propositions have been supported, and even more *seem* to have been supported, though the hypotheses actually tested often are not the same as those proposed by Thompson. Only in the area of environmental effects on structure are there data that definitely question Thompson's propositions. The relationships with differentiation do not support his theory of environmental determinism. Many other studies raise serious questions about the validity of so-called structural contingency models of the kind discussed in this chapter and those that follow (Pennings 1992).

Yet in spite of the problems associated with obtaining research support for this approach to theorizing, it should be recognized that there are strong proponents as well (see Donaldson 2000, 2001) who believe the research support is there. Furthermore, as reflected in a recent book review symposium in the *Administrative Science Quarterly* published on the occasion of a reprinting of *Organizations in Action* (Thompson 2003), broad respect exists for this type of sociological open systems theory (Davis 2003; Weick 2003).

Without much more research into the propositions of Thompson's theory extending across the whole span of its domain, one cannot be sure where its most pronounced weak spots lie. Such research has been distinctly on the wane in recent years, to the point where our questions may never be answered. Thompson's creative genius deserves a better empirical response than it is now receiving. At the same time, the abstract, unrelated hypotheses generated by systems theories appear to be self-defeating insofar as research confirmation is concerned.

CONCLUSIONS

Thompson's theorizing has reaped an importance rating of 5.60, one of the very highest such evaluations by scholars of organizational behavior. Furthermore, sociological open systems theory is designated as institutionalized, consistent with the fact that the reissue of *Organizations in Action* was honored with a book review symposium in *Administrative Science Quarterly*. Much of the terminology of the theory, if not its actual propositions, has become embedded in the language of organizational behavior.

Yet sadly, the estimated validity of the theory achieves only a three-star status due to the limited research on many of the fifty-nine numbered and thirty-four subsidiary propositions spread across nine topic areas. What research has been done suggests that a four-star rating on validity would be more appropriate, but too much of the theory's subject matter has been left under- or unresearched. A broad and multifaceted theory such as this requires much more investigation. The estimated usefulness is even more deficient; I have given it only one star, simply because Thompson was not interested in such matters, and did not incorporate them in his theorizing. Potentially the propositions could be converted into guidelines for practice, but Thompson did not do that and the abstractness of the presentation in most cases would make it very difficult for someone else to do so.

In Chapter 12 we take up another systems theory of sociological origin that takes us once again back across the Atlantic to England.

REFERENCES

Argote, Linda (1982). Input Uncertainty and Organizational Coordination in Hospital Emergency Units. *Administrative Science Quarterly,* 27, 420–34.

Argyris, Chris (1972). *The Applicability of Organizational Sociology.* London: Cambridge University Press.

Astley, W. Graham (1991). Review of James Thompson's *Organizations in Action. Journal of Management,* 17, 499–500.

Baumler, John V. (1971). Defined Criteria of Performance in Organizational Control. *Administrative Science Quarterly,* 16, 340–49.

Davis, Gerald (2003). Review of James Thompson's *Organizations in Action. Administrative Science Quarterly,* 48, 502–5.

Donaldson, Lex (2000). Design Structure to Fit Strategy. In Edwin A. Locke (Ed.), *The Blackwell Handbook of Principles of Organizational Behavior.* Oxford, UK; Blackwell, 291–303.

———. (2001). *The Contingency Theory of Organizations.* Thousand Oaks, CA: Sage.

Duncan, Robert B. (1972). Characteristics of Organizational Environments and Perceived Environmental Uncertainty. *Administrative Science Quarterly,* 17, 313–27.

Hargadon, Andrew B. (2003). Review of James Thompson's *Organizations in Action. Administrative Science Quarterly,* 48, 498–501.

Heath, Chip, and Staudenmayer, Nancy (2000). Coordination Neglect: How Lay Theories of Organizing Complicate Coordination in Organizations. *Research in Organizational Behavior,* 22, 153–91.

Lev, Baruch (1975). Environmental Uncertainty Reduction by Smoothing and Buffering: An Empirical Verification. *Academy of Management Journal,* 18, 864–71.

Mackenzie, Kenneth D. (1986). *Organizational Design: The Organizational Audit and Analysis Technology.* Norwood, NJ: Ablex.

Mahoney, Thomas A., and Frost, Peter J. (1974). The Role of Technology in Models of Organizational Effectiveness. *Organizational Behavior and Human Performance,* 11, 122–38.

Mahoney, Thomas A., and Weitzel, William (1969). Managerial Models of Organizational Effectiveness. *Administrative Science Quarterly,* 14, 357–65.

McNeil, Kenneth, and Thompson, James D. (1971). The Regeneration of Social Organizations. *American Sociological Review,* 36, 624–37.

Miner, John B. (2002). *Organizational Behavior: Foundations, Theories, and Analyses.* New York: Oxford University Press.

———. (2005). *Organizational Behavior 1: Essential Theories of Motivation and Leadership.* Armonk, NY: M.E. Sharpe.

Morrissey, Elizabeth and Gillespie, David F. (1975). Technology and the Conflict of Professionals in Bureaucratic Organizations. *Sociological Quarterly,* 16, 319–32.

Nutt, Paul C. (2002). Selecting Decision Rules for Crucial Choices: An Investigation of the Thompson Framework. *Journal of Applied Behavioral Science,* 38, 99–131.

Pennings, Johannes M. (1992). Structural Contingency Theory: A Reappraisal. *Research in Organizational Behavior,* 14, 267–309.

Perrow, Charles (1976). Review of Rushing and Zald's *Organizations and Beyond. Administrative Science Quarterly,* 21, 718–21.

Pfeffer, Jeffrey (1972a). Size and Composition of Corporate Boards of Directors: The Organization and Its Environment. *Administrative Science Quarterly,* 17, 218–28.

———. (1972b). Merger as a Response to Organizational Interdependence. *Administrative Science Quarterly,* 17, 382–94.

Pfeffer, Jeffrey, and Salancik, Gerald R. (1977). Organizational Contexts and the Characteristics and Tenure of Hospital Administrators. *Academy of Management Journal,* 20, 74–88.

Pondy, Louis R., and Mitroff, Ian I. (1979). Beyond Open Systems Models of Organization. *Research in Organizational Behavior,* 1, 3–39.

Reeves, Tom K., and Turner, Barry A. (1972). A Theory of Organization and Behavior in Batch Production Factories. *Administrative Science Quarterly,* 17, 81–98.

Rushing, William A., and Zald, Mayer N. (1976). *Organizations and Beyond: Selected Essays of James D. Thompson.* Lexington, MA: D.C. Heath.

Schmidt, Stuart M., and Cummings, Larry L. (1976). Organizational Environment, Differentiation, and Perceived Environmental Uncertainty. *Decision Sciences,* 7, 447–67.

Schramm, Carl J. (1975). Thompson's Assessment of Organizations: Universities and the AAUP Salary Grades. *Administrative Science Quarterly,* 20, 87–96.

Schultheiss, Emily E. (1991). Review of James Thompson's *Organizations in Action. Journal of Management,* 17, 497–98.

Thompson, James D. (1956). Authority and Power in Identical Organizations. *American Journal of Sociology,* 62, 290–98.

———. (1960). Organizational Management of Conflict. *Administrative Science Quarterly,* 4, 389–409.

———. (1962). Organizations and Output Transactions. *American Journal of Sociology,* 67, 309–24.

———. (1964). Decision-Making, the Firm, and the Market. In William W. Cooper, Harold J. Leavitt, and Maynard W. Shelley (Eds.), *New Perspectives in Organization Research.* New York: Wiley, 334–48.

———. (1967). *Organizations in Action: Social Science Bases of Administrative Theory.* New York: McGraw-Hill.

———. (1973). Society's Frontiers for Organizing Activities. *Public Administration Review,* 33, 327–35.

———. (1974a). Technology, Polity and Societal Development. *Administrative Science Quarterly,* 19, 6–21.

———. (1974b). Social Interdependence, the Polity, and Public Administration. *Administration and Society,* 6, 3–21.

———. (2003). *Organizations in Action: Social Science Bases of Administrative Theory.* (Reprint Ed.). New Brunswick, NJ: Transaction Books.

Thompson, James D., and Bates, Frederick L. (1957). Technology, Organization, and Administration. *Administrative Science Quarterly,* 2, 325–43.

Thompson, James D., and Hawkes, Robert W. (1962). Disaster, Community Organization, and Administrative Process. In George W. Baker and Dwight W. Chapman (Eds.), *Man and Society in Disaster.* New York: Basic Books, 268–300.

Thompson, James D., and McEwen, William J. (1958). Organizational Goals and Environment: Goal-Setting as an Interaction Process. *American Sociological Review,* 23, 23–31.

Thompson, James D., and Tuden, Arthur (1959). Strategies, Structures, and Processes of Organizational Decision. In James D. Thompson, P.B. Hammond, Robert W. Hawkes, and B.H. Junker (Eds.), *Comparative Studies in Administration.* Pittsburgh, PA: University of Pittsburgh Press, 195–216.

Thompson, James D., and Van Houten, Donald R. (1970). *The Behavioral Sciences: An Interpretation.* Reading, MA: Addison-Wesley.

Weick, Karl E. (2003). Review of James Thompson's *Organizations in Action. Administrative Science Quarterly,* 48, 505–9.

Williams, William W. (1977). Organizational Size, Technology, and Employment Investments in Ancillary Specialisms. *Academy of Management Proceedings,* 37, 224–28.

CHAPTER 12

MECHANISTIC AND ORGANIC SYSTEMS

TOM BURNS
G.M. STALKER

Importance rating	★ ★ ★ ★ ★
	Institutionalized
Estimated validity	★ ★
Estimated usefulness	★
Decade of origin	1960s

Mechanistic and organic systems theory has much in common with Likert's differentiation of systems 1 to 3 as opposed to system 4 (see Chapter 8). Since the theory's original publication in 1961 by Tavistock, Tom Burns (in Burns and Stalker 1994) has credited his theory with close parallels to the theoretical positions developed by Woodward (see Miner 2002a) regarding various technologies, to Crozier's (1964) analyses of political processes in bureaucracies, and to March and Simon's (see Chapter 3 in this volume) treatment of programmed and nonprogrammed decision making. Yet Burns indicated that at the time of its formulation the theory was uninformed from any of these sources. It does, however, appear to be a product of many forces that were "in the air" during the 1950s and early 1960s when the theory was developed, particularly forces of this kind that existed in the social science intellectual community of Europe.

BACKGROUND

The field of organizational behavior in Europe during the early period did not involve business schools much, because few existed. The field focused on macro structural issues and was largely dominated by sociologists working either in sociology departments or independent research units, or both. Most of their research involved comparative case analysis, and direct ties to practice were limited.

Tom Burns was typical of this group. He spent more than thirty years at the University of Edinburgh in Scotland, from which he retired in 1981. His base was in what became the Department of Sociology, although he was also associated with the Social Science Research Center of the university. Prior to joining the Edinburgh faculty he worked during the postwar years in the area of urban sociology with the West Midland Group on Post-War Reconstruction and Planning in the United Kingdom.

Although the major statement of mechanistic and organic systems theory is to be found in one book, *The Management of Innovation* (Burns and Stalker 1961, 1994), Burns made other contributions to both sociology and organizational behavior. Noteworthy in the latter regard is his work on communication patterns in organizations (see Burns 1954) and on clique formation in organizations (see Burns 1955). Subsequent to the publication of his major theoretical work in 1961, Burns (1977) undertook a lengthy study of the BBC. This book expands on the earlier one, providing more detail on the idea that organizations possess formal authority and task systems, career systems that are laced with considerable competitive striving, and political systems focused on power relationships. It did not, however, change the theoretical position stated previously.

G.M. Stalker, a psychologist, worked with Burns in conducting interviews and carrying out observations for the Scottish phase of the research reported in *The Management of Innovation.* Subsequently he left the academic world and became a consultant. He has not contributed to the professional literature since.

DEVELOPMENT OF THE THEORY OF TWO SYSTEMS

Burns's theory was derived inductively from a series of case studies of firms operating primarily in the electronics industry in Great Britain. Thus to understand the theory it is necessary to start with this qualitative research and the circumstances surrounding it.

The Qualitative Research

The research was initiated as part of a project to monitor the progress of Scottish engineering firms as efforts were made to facilitate their entry into the new field of electronically controlled machinery and equipment. This project was carried out under the aegis of a voluntary association supported financially by industrial firms, local governments, and the unions, which in turn worked closely with the government of Scotland. Ultimately this effort was extended to England and included a number of firms more fully committed to electronics development than had been the case in Scotland.

The final sample of twenty firms (or segments of firms) included primarily these electronics firms faced with a changing technology, but also several companies from other industries, most of which had research and development interests in other fields. In addition to the changing technology of electronics engineering, many of these firms in the 1950s were forced to face the prospect of changing markets as a result of the government's decreased defense contracting after the war. This defense market was variable over a number of years, but eventually it became evident that, to survive, most firms would have to develop the unfamiliar commercial market existing beyond government. At the time of the study they were attempting to do this.

The sample thus accumulated was entirely opportunistic in nature—firms were gradually found over a period of several years that were willing to participate in the study. Each was studied separately using the case method. Outside observers came in and conducted unstructured interviews, attended meetings, and listened to conversations. Notes were made on the spot. The methodology was essentially that of the field sociology or social anthropology of the day. As the data were being collected the observers tried to construct a systematic explanatory description of the company situation, a description that was not only internally consistent but congruent with explanatory descriptions derived from other social systems as set forth in the literature.

This approach yielded no quantitative data; it was entirely qualitative. As the authors themselves state, "All this is very far removed from any method of investigation which could possibly be called scientific" (Burns and Stalker 1994, 13). Thus the only value of the studies themselves is in the theory they generated; they *prove* nothing. With regard to the method employed, the authors state further, "It does not share the principal advantage of the anthropological field method, which lies in a lengthy period of residence in the community being studied" (13). In fact, the authors provide no information on how much time they actually spent within each company.

Contingency Factors

The theory of mechanistic and organic (or sometimes organismic) systems uses change rather than the nature of the technology itself as a contingency variable (Burns 1963, Burns and Stalker 1994). Though the major emphasis is on technological change, market change is also a consideration. Both exert certain pressures on the organization that make particular organizational forms desirable:

> As the rate of change increases in the technical field, so does the number of occasions which demand quick and effective interpretation between people working in different parts of the system. As the rate of change increases in the market field, so does the need to multiply the points of contact between the concern and the markets it wishes to explore and develop. (Burns and Stalker 1994, 231)

This position emerges from the situation in which the authors found the firms they studied. The technological changes were inherent in the accelerating developments that were occurring in the knowledge base of the electronics field external to the firms, and thus in their environments. But these external changes were reflected in technological changes occurring within the firms as well, although to varying degrees. The market changes were not consequences of strategic choices made within the firms so much as forced responses to external factors associated with governmental actions. It is important to understand that the theory really dealt with these two specific and rather limited contingency variables, which in this instance happened to be highly correlated.

The impact of other states of technological and market change, such as those induced entirely by internal initiatives, is not clarified. Furthermore, technology and market are assumed to move as one, even though it is apparent that, in many other cases, this is not what happens. The theory is mute, for instance, regarding the situation where markets change and technology remains stable, or vice versa.

It is important to reemphasize that the contingency variables of the theory are indeed change factors—both technological and market—since confusion has occurred on this score. Donaldson (2001, 55) says: "There is, however, a commonality between Thompson and these other authors. For all of them the contingency factor is the task: task uncertainty for Burns and Stalker. . . ."

Yet change and uncertainty are not the same thing. They may often be correlated, but each can lead to a different outcome, and be precipitated by different antecedents. Furthermore, each is typically operationalized in a very distinctive manner. Donaldson does not make this differentiation, and as a result his formulations may be misleading. The contingency factor that Burns and Stalker emphasize again and again is change.

Ideal Types of Organization

Mechanistic systems, which are suited to stable conditions, and organic systems, which are appropriate to changing conditions that introduce new problems and unforeseen requirements for action, are posited as polarities, not as a dichotomy. Thus, intermediate stages may occur between the extremes, as described in Table 12.1, and firms may operate within both systems at the same time.

Organic organizations are stratified primarily in terms of expertise, and leadership accrues to those who are the best informed and capable. There is much more commitment to the organization, with the result that formal and informal systems become indistinguishable. A framework of values and beliefs, much like those characterizing a profession, develops that becomes an effective substitute for formal hierarchy. Yet the ambiguity and lack of structure can become a source of anxiety for many. Even when the organic system arises as a planned response to a rapidly changing technology that is little understood, managers often yearn for a greater degree of structure.

Burns and Stalker also note that members of organic systems frequently act in such a way as to openly or tacitly reject attempts to exercise authority over them (see also Burns 1957). This almost never happens in mechanistic systems. It appears to reflect the authority of expertise and knowledge that prevails in organic systems irrespective of designated rank.

In many respects organic systems have the characteristics of professional systems that operate to serve a client, which in this instance is the larger organization. And from the descriptions in the Burns and Stalker book it appears that the organic systems are primarily staffed with professionals; they may, however, exist in a larger organizational context that has few professionals and more real managers, and that represents a more mechanistic system. This is why some concerns are said to operate with a management system that includes both the mechanistic and organic forms.

Pathological Forms of the Mechanistic System

The need for structure, combined with certain political and personal career factors, can block change from mechanistic to organic forms, when such a change would be appropriate; the result is often some pathological form of the mechanistic system and less effective organizational performance (Burns 1963). Individuals in mechanistic systems may fail to adapt because they are committed to sectional groups or departments, and internal politics may serve to perpetuate existing forms. Similarly, it may be in the interests of individuals and their long-term career plans to maintain the status quo.

Three possible pathological responses to change and the consequent uncertainty are noted. First is the *ambiguous figure* system, wherein increasing numbers of exceptions to policy are referred to top-level managers, and lower-level managers start to bypass those above them to

Table 12.1

Characteristics of Mechanistic and Organic Systems

Mechanistic system (appropriate to stable conditions)	Organic system (appropriate to changing conditions)
1. The *specialized differentiation* of functional tasks into which the problems and tasks facing the concern as a whole are broken down	1. The *contributive nature* of special knowledge and experience to the common task of the concern
2. The *abstract nature* of each individual task, which is pursued with techniques and purposes distinct from those of the concern as a whole	2. The *realistic nature* of the individual task, which is seen as set by the total situation of the concern
3. The reconciliation, for each level in the hierarchy, of these distinct performances by the *immediate superiors*	3. The adjustment and *continual redefinition* of individual tasks through interaction with others
4. The *precise definition* of rights and technical methods attached to each functional role	4. The *shedding of responsibility* as a limited field of rights, obligations, and methods. Thus problems may not be avoided as someone else's responsibility
5. The *translation of rights* and obligations and methods into the responsibilities of a functional position	5. The *spread of commitment* to the concern beyond any technical definition
6. A *hierarchic structure* of control, authority, and communication	6. A *network structure* of control, authority, and communication. Sanctions derive from presumed community of interest with the rest of the organization
7. A reinforcement of the hierarchic structure by the location of *knowledge* of actualities exclusively *at the top* of the hierarchy	7. *Knowledge* about the technical or commercial nature of the task may be located *anywhere*. This location becomes the ad hoc center of authority and communication
8. A tendency for *interaction* between members of the concern to be *vertical*	8. A *lateral* direction of *communication* through the organization, resembling consultation rather than command
9. A tendency for operations and working behavior to be governed by the instructions and decisions issued by *superiors*	9. A content of communication that consists of *information and advice* rather than instructions and decisions
10. *Insistence on loyalty* to the concern and obedience to superiors as a condition of membership	10. *Commitment* to the concern's tasks and to the technological ethos of material progress and expansion is more highly valued than loyalty and obedience
11. A greater importance and prestige attaching to *local* than to cosmopolitan knowledge, experience, and skill	11. Importance and prestige attach to *affiliations and expertise* valid in the industrial and technical and commercial milieu external to the firm

Source: Adapted from Burns and Stalker (1994, 120–22).

get decisions made. The result is an overloaded chief executive, considerable conflict, and a highly politicized organization. A second response is the *mechanistic jungle,* in which more and more branches are added to the bureaucratic tree and increasing numbers of specialized positions are created to deal with new problems. Since the problems are often related to communication, the new positions tend to be of a liaison type, and the communication system becomes too complex to function. Finally, there is the *super-personal* or committee system response to change and uncertainty, which temporarily grafts committees onto the mechanistic structure to deal with special problems rather than making the needed change to an organic system.

The theory does not indicate when each of these responses might be anticipated, but all are considered nonfunctional under conditions of change (Burns 1963).

EVALUATION AND IMPACT

As indicated previously, the case studies that underlie the development of mechanistic and organic systems theory do not constitute scientific evidence in favor of the theory. The authors do not claim this, but later interpretations have on occasion taken such a position. In this connection it should be noted that most of the firms (or parts of firms) studied were in the rapidly changing electronics industry and thus, according to theory, should at least have tried to become organic in nature. However, a few firms were in other industries and these appeared to provide examples of companies operating in stable environments for whom their mechanistic systems were entirely appropriate (and yielded profitable operations). Thus, in the research, the theoretical continuum from mechanistic to organic seems to be fully confounded with the type of industry represented (rather than resulting from a comparison of certain electronics firms with other electronics firms). Similar research design problems are manifest often. It seems likely, given the inductive nature of the theory, that these problems have carried over from research to theory.

Research Tests

Given that the authors do not present theory testing research in *The Management of Innovation,* and have conducted no such research since, it becomes necessary to look elsewhere for evidence as to the validity of mechanistic and organic systems theory. There is not a great deal of this kind of research, but some does exist.

Ideally the hypothesis on technological change would be tested longitudinally. One such investigation compares increases in the scope of the technology in social service organizations with various structural changes (Dewar and Hage 1978). The data are consistent with the view that technological change produces more diversified and specialized occupational structures, but the anticipated effects of technological change on levels of hierarchy and factors associated with spans of control were minimal at best.

In another series of studies, various indexes of technological change taking place over considerable periods of time prior to the study were related to measures of centralization, specialization, formalization, spans of control, levels of hierarchy, and various staff personnel indexes (Reimann 1975, 1980). Though not specifically formulated in terms of the mechanistic-organic concept, many of the structural indexes clearly relate to it. Yet no significant relationships were found, nor were the variables of the study related to measures of organizational effectiveness. Keller, Slocum, and Susman (1974), utilizing a measure of the

Table 12.2

Relationships Between Frequency of Product Changes and Aspects of Structure in Manufacturing Firms

	Frequency of product changes		
Structural variable	Few (%)	Intermediate (%)	Many (%)
Number of subunits (division of labor)			
Few	0	13	64
Intermediate	31	56	36
Many	69	31	0
Levels of hierarchy			
Few	0	19	64
Intermediate	38	44	36
Many	62	37	0
Number of managers per employee			
Few	0	6	79
Intermediate	31	63	21
Many	69	31	0
Extent of programming of roles, output, and communications			
Low (organic)	0	6	72
Intermediate	23	81	21
High (mechanistic)	77	13	7

Source: Adapted from Harvey (1968, 255).

number of product changes in continuous process manufacturing organizations, also failed to find support for the Burns and Stalker theory, even though they made the mechanistic-organic differentiation explicit. Organic firms did prove to be more successful in process industries, but this was totally unrelated to the amount of technological change.

An earlier study by Harvey (1968) had utilized the product change measure and obtained more favorable results, though it did not include data on organizational effectiveness. The findings, given in Table 12.2 , clearly indicate that greater technological change is associated with a more organic organizational form. These results cannot be attributed to size effects.

On balance, this evidence is not strongly supportive of the Burns and Stalker hypotheses regarding technology. The Harvey (1968) study provides the most positive evidence, but since it does not test the hypotheses regarding success, even this support is only partial. Studies dealing with market change are nonexistent.

Bringing the Research Up to Date

In more recent years there have been many studies of the relations between technology and structural variables (see Goodman and Sproull 1990; Miller, Glick, Wang, and Huber 1991), but a dearth of research on technological change, as would be needed to test the Burns and Stalker theory in its comprehensive form. As others have noted, developments around the theory are essentially stagnant (Pennings and Harianto 1992). This state of affairs continues to the present. Yet the Burns and Stalker volume is one of the most widely cited in organizational behavior (Pennings 1992). It appears that the field has accorded the theory a degree of uncritical acceptance that the research evidence would not justify. The following quote offers a possible reason for this reaction:

So Burns' work is very appealing to me and also, because of its complexity and subtlety, is of lasting value. *Management of Innovation* pulls off the difficult trick of offering a simple message, suitable for summarizing in overhead transparencies or examination questions, while at the same time qualifying and complicating this message in an enormous variety of ways, many of which are both provisional *and* dependent upon the concerns and the point of view of the observer. (Turner 1995, 283)

What research has been conducted on mechanistic and organic systems concepts in the past couple of decades has dealt with the theory in a piecemeal fashion. Thus, a study by Russell and Russell (1992) has looked at the relation between innovation and organic structure—considered to be represented by decentralization, informality, and complexity of work. What it found, however, was that innovation (as represented by two separate measures) was related only to decentralization, not at all to informality or complexity. This suggests that the total organic system may not be required for innovation to occur, a result that is not what one would have expected from a reading of mechanistic and organic systems theory. In view of the fact that mechanistic systems are clearly capable of certain types of innovation on occasion (Daft 1982), the conceptual foundation of the organic type system as a distinct purveyor of innovation is brought into doubt.

A second relevant piece of research looked at communication patterns in two plants of the same company, one said to be mechanistic and the other organic (Courtright, Fairhurst, and Rogers 1989). In this instance the mechanistic plant was without question operating with a bureaucratic, hierarchic structure. The organic plant utilized self-managed teams and participatory decision making extensively. The focus on communication patterns seems entirely appropriate given Burns's prior interest in this matter and the attention given to it in the Burns and Stalker book. There organic communications are said to be horizontal or lateral, consultative, focused on information and advice, and to be rejecting of the exercise of authority over the individual.

In the study competitiveness and evidence of manager dominance were less pronounced in the organic context, as were disagreements, conflict, order giving, and attempts at control. The interactions appear to have been more frequently consultative in the organic plant. Overall, these findings seem to have much in common with what Burns and Stalker (1994) describe. However, conflict over the exercise of authority seems to be less, rather than more, prevalent in the organic plant. There is just enough disagreement inherent in the findings from the two sources to suggest that the two were not defining organic in quite the same way. The fact that teams and group decision making, as well as participation, were not part of the Burns and Stalker description of organic systems reinforces this conclusion. Yet, in other studies, the mechanistic-organic distinction has been found to differentiate distinct relationships that exist with regard to factors such as perceived justice (Ambrose and Schminke 2003). The two systems do appear to represent meaningful structural entities.

Organic Systems as Professional Forms

There has been a tendency to view organic systems as encompassing anything that is not bureaucratic, and to differentiate mechanistic from organic systems on the basis of the degree of social formality versus informality present (Morand 1995). Yet it is apparent that nonbureaucratic forms include at least three other types—the group system that the Michigan and sociotechnical theorists envisaged, professional systems, and at least some varieties of entrepreneurial systems (see Miner 1993). Lumping all three of these under the organic umbrella does not seem justified, and from the descriptions in *The Management of Innovation* it does not appear to be what Burns and Stalker intended either.

As indicated previously, group systems differ considerably from what Burns and Stalker described. Entrepreneurial or task systems tend to be smaller than many of the firms they studied, and these systems can well incorporate more structuring. From the descriptions provided it appears that the organic systems of Burns and Stalker were in fact professional in nature. The people described in the organic organizations were typically research scientists and engineers engaged in a process of innovation whereby the boundaries of firm knowledge were to be extended into new areas. The managers in such contexts were often professional leaders (Miner 2002b), and such people have been found to interpret issues differently from hierarchic managers (Golden, Dukerich, and Fabian 2000). Although the studies of these firms usually extended beyond the research or professional component into top management, the organic system concept appears to have had its home among the professionals where the actual innovations occurred (see Miner, Crane, and Vandenberg 1994). That the theory's authors focused on this particular context and described it with considerable flare is not surprising given their university (professional) backgrounds.

While the organic structure described appears to be primarily professional in form and staffed with professionals, the mechanistic firms came from outside the electronics industry, thus were not experiencing major technological and market changes, and, more importantly, did not appear to be of a kind where many professionals would be employed. That the mechanistic firms with capable managers and few professionals, and thus no meaningful professional components to deal with, tended to do well is not surprising—the manager-mechanistic fit is strong. Similarly, the organic systems (professional forms) with many competent professionals appear to have done well—the professional-organic fit is strong. The firms that did not do well were those with a mechanistic, hierarchic system, but many professionals, in the electronics industry—the mechanistic-professional fit involved was an inherently poor one and firm success should have suffered, which it did, as a result.

What this analysis suggests is that in fact technological and market changes were not the determining factors that the theory takes them to be. It is possible to explain the Burns and Stalker results in a more parsimonious fashion, without resort to environmental variables. The data provided by the theory's authors are inadequate to fully test this hypothesis, but they appear consistent with it, and the research results obtained from tests of the environmental change component of the theory do little to support that component's viability. There is a very good chance that mechanistic and organic systems theory made the mistake of interpreting concomitant events as causal agents. At the very least there is evidence of confounding on this score.

The Value of Conceptual Typologies

In Chapter 1 conceptual typologies were discussed as a particular kind of approach to theorizing. In the field of macro organizational behavior there appears to be considerable commonality in the types of organizations described by these typologies, although certain differences exist as well. Thus Lammers (1988) finds that some variant of the organic type can be traced back through various writers in Germany to as early as 1921. He also notes certain similarities to other types of more recent origin.

Typologies such as that of Burns and Stalker have been a subject of some controversy in organizational behavior. There are those who argue against the typological approach both as to its value and its characterization as theory (see, for example, Donaldson 1996). In doing so, they attempt to demolish the general case that underlies the mechanistic-organic typology, and thus, indirectly, and sometimes not so indirectly, that typology itself. I have stated my position on this matter in Chapter 1. An article by Meyer, Tsui, and Hinings (1993) discusses the issues involved at some length and comes to the conclusion that typologies are theories and have the potential to make valuable contributions to our knowledge of organizational behavior, a view that I strongly endorse. However, the reader should be aware that the literature contains criticisms of mechanistic and organic systems theory based on the fact that a conceptual typology is utilized. This is one type of criticism that in my opinion is unwarranted.

Application

The Burns and Stalker theory would seem to provide useful guidelines for organizational structuring. It has the advantage of considerable parsimony, although the professional organization interpretation suggests even more is possible. Yet it falls short of this goal in a number of respects. It fails to specify when the various pathological forms will emerge and to that extent is incomplete. The mechanistic-organic differentiation appears to be useful conceptually, but research evidence that this variable operates as hypothesized (at least in response to technological change) is sparse indeed. The kind of specifics required to generate mechanistic and particularly organic structures are lacking. There are no demonstration projects that the authors can point to as examples of what the theory espouses in a normative sense. The contrast with sociotechnical theory in this regard is striking. Furthermore, no recommendations are provided as to what should be done when technology and market considerations move in different directions.

Mechanistic and organic systems theory has not provided a basis for practice in any specific sense, and there is a real question as to whether it could or should do so in its present form. In fact, the theory's authors give little attention to the matter of application and merely describe what they found in the organizations they studied.

CONCLUSIONS

At the end of Chapter 10 I posed the question of whether sociological open systems theories, free of the ties to group dynamics so evident in their psychological counterparts, can be more useful or valid as systems approaches. On the evidence from the two theories considered in this and the previous chapters one would have to say that any improvement is minimal. Although more potentially researchable hypotheses do appear, they operate at such an abstract level and with an abundance of vagueness that serves to mystify the construction of operational measures; thus, very little relevant research has been conducted. In recent years this drought has reduced the research stream to little more than a few puddles.

Not only have the sociological versions of open systems theory lacked research, but the common problem of an application void continues. And there has been a special problem in that the literature on these theories has tended to generate a complex web of esoteric arguments, apparently as a substitute for doing the kind of research that would provide factual evidence on the issues. In fact, such research results as there are often tend to be lost in the heat of partisan debate.

This has been a particular problem with regard to contingency approaches of the kind utilized by Thompson and Burns and Stalker (see Fry and Smith 1987). The abstractions and ambiguity of the theorists seem to escalate in the hands of the critics, rather than producing attempts to overcome problems and yield acceptable measures that can be used in research. It should be emphasized that, in addition to their systems qualities, these are theories of a contingency nature that have much in common with Fiedler's contingency theory of leadership (see Miner 2005). That theory too has had more than its share of controversy, but in that instance the major questions have had to do with the legitimacy and interpretation of research results. Empirical matters of this latter kind come to the fore in the next chapter, as we look at an additional contingency theory of a sociological and systems nature.

The ratings of mechanistic and organic systems theory bring out an unusual problem. The importance figure is 5.42 and the theory is institutionalized. So far, so good; we have a theory that elicits very positive reactions from organizational behavior scholars. Yet, at least insofar as validity considerations are involved, I have to take issue with this evaluation. The theory evolved from qualitative research that had major deficiencies. That would not have been a problem had the theory corrected for these design problems, but instead it perpetuated the problems into the theory. Since the authors never conducted any theory-testing research, the difficulties continued. And, given the uncritical acceptance of the underlying theory development process, that is where we stand today, with very little confirming research still in the bank. As a result of this situation, I must bestow only two stars for validity. To the extent the importance ratings involved validity considerations, I find myself opposed to their conclusions; this is not a particularly valid theory. Nor, for the same reasons as often operate with systems theories, can I consider more than one star for estimated usefulness. All in all, were it not for the overwhelming support from others, I would not have considered the mechanistic and organic formulations an appropriate candidate for inclusion in a book on essential theories.

REFERENCES

Ambrose, Maureen L., and Schminke, Marshall (2003). Organizational Structure as a Moderator of the Relationship Between Procedural Justice, Interactional Justice, Perceived Organizational Support, and Supervisory Trust. *Journal of Applied Psychology,* 88, 295–305.

Burns, Tom (1954). The Directions of Activity and Communication in a Departmental Executive Group. *Human Relations,* 7, 73–97.

———. (1955). The Reference of Conduct in Small Groups: Cliques and Cabals in Occupational Milieux. *Human Relations,* 8, 467–86.

———. (1957). Management in Action. *Operational Research Quarterly,* 8, 45–60.

———. (1963). Industry in a New Age. *New Society,* 31 January, 17–20.

———. (1977). *The BBC: Public Institution and Private World.* London: Macmillan.

Burns, Tom, and Stalker, G.M. (1961). *The Management of Innovation.* London: Tavistock.

———. (1994). *The Management of Innovation.* Oxford, UK: Oxford University Press.

Courtright, John A., Fairhurst, Gail T., and Rogers, L. Edna (1989). Interaction Patterns in Organic and Mechanistic Systems. *Academy of Management Journal,* 32, 773–802.

Crozier, Michel (1964). *The Bureaucratic Phenomenon.* Chicago, IL: University of Chicago Press.

Daft, Richard L. (1982). Bureaucratic versus Nonbureaucratic Structure and the Process of Innovation and Change. *Research in the Sociology of Organizations,* 1, 129–66.

Dewar, Robert D., and Hage, Jerald (1978). Size, Technology, Complexity, and Structural Differentiation: Toward a Theoretical Synthesis. *Administrative Science Quarterly,* 23, 111–36.

Donaldson, Lex (1996). *For Positivist Organization Theory.* London: Sage.

———. (2001). *The Contingency Theory of Organizations.* Thousand Oaks, CA: Sage.

Fry, Louis W., and Smith, Deborah A. (1987). Congruence, Contingency, and Theory Building. *Academy of Management Review,* 12, 117–32.

Golden, Brian R., Dukerich, Janet M., and Fabian, Frances H. (2000). The Interpretation and Resolution of Resource Allocation Issues in Professional Organizations: A Critical Examination of the Professional-Manager Dichotomy. *Journal of Management Studies,* 37, 1157–87.

Goodman, Paul S., and Sproull, Lee S. (1990). *Technology and Organizations.* San Francisco, CA: Jossey-Bass.

Harvey, Edward (1968). Technology and the Structure of Organizations. *American Sociological Review,* 33, 247–59.

Keller, Robert T., Slocum, John W., and Susman, Gerald I. (1974). Uncertainty and Type of Management System in Continuous Process Organizations. *Academy of Management Journal,* 17, 56–68.

Lammers, Cornelis J. (1988). Transience and Persistence of Ideal Types in Organization Theory. *Research in the Sociology of Organizations,* 6, 203–24.

Meyer, Alan D., Tsui, Anne S., and Hinings, C.R. (1993). Configurational Approaches to Organizational Analysis. *Academy of Management Journal,* 36, 1175–95.

Miller, C. Chet, Glick, William H., Wang, Yau-de, and Huber, George P. (1991). Understanding Technology-Structure Relationships: Theory Development and Meta-Analytic Theory Testing. *Academy of Management Journal,* 34, 370–99.

Miner, John B. (1993). *Role Motivation Theories.* London: Routledge.

———. (2002a). *Organizational Behavior: Foundations, Theories, and Analyses.* New York: Oxford University Press.

———. (2002b). The Role Motivation Theories of Organizational Leadership. In Bruce J. Avolio and Francis J. Yammarino (Eds.), *Transformational and Charismatic Leadership: The Road Ahead.* Oxford, UK: Elsevier Science, 309–38.

———. (2005). *Organizational Behavior: Essential Theories of Motivation and Leadership.* Armonk, NY: M.E. Sharpe.

Miner, John B., Crane, Donald P., and Vandenberg, Robert J. (1994). Congruence and Fit in Professional Role Motivation Theory. *Organization Science 1,* 5, 86–97.

Morand, David A. (1995). The Role of Formality and Informality in the Enactment of Bureaucratic versus Organic Organizations. *Academy of Management Review,* 20, 831–72.

Pennings, Johannes M. (1992). Structural Contingency Theory: A Reappraisal. *Research in Organizational Behavior,* 14, 267–309.

Pennings, Johannes M., and Harianto, Farid (1992). Technological Networking and Innovation Implementation. *Organization Science,* 3, 356–82.

Reimann, Bernard C. (1975). Organizational Effectiveness and Management's Public Values: A Canonical Analysis. *Academy of Management Journal,* 18, 224–41.

———. (1980). Organizational Structure and Technology in Manufacturing: System versus Work Flow Level Perspectives. *Academy of Management Journal,* 23, 61–77.

Russell, Robert D., and Russell, Craig J. (1992). An Examination of the Effects of Organizational Norms, Organizational Structure, and Environmental Uncertainty on Entrepreneurial Strategy. *Journal of Management,* 18, 639–56.

Turner, Barry A. (1995). A Personal Trajectory Through Organization Studies. *Research in the Sociology of Organizations,* 13, 275–301.

Chapter 13

CONTINGENCY THEORY OF ORGANIZATIONS— DIFFERENTIATION AND INTEGRATION

PAUL LAWRENCE
JAY LORSCH

Importance rating	★ ★ ★ ★ ★
	Institutionalized
Estimated validity	★ ★ ★
Estimated usefulness	★ ★ ★ ★
Decade of origin	1960s

Although other theories of this type exist, the term *contingency theory* as used in the field of macro organizational behavior has become associated primarily with the formulations of

226

Paul Lawrence and Jay Lorsch. The basic statements of the theory appear in an article (Lawrence and Lorsch 1967a) and in a book (Lawrence and Lorsch 1967b), though reports on pilot studies and preliminary hypotheses that exerted considerable influence on these formulations were published earlier (Lorsch 1965, Lorsch and Lawrence 1965).

BACKGROUND

Paul Lawrence was born in 1922 and graduated from Albion College. A lifelong association with the Harvard Business School began in 1942, interrupted only by military service during World War II. Lawrence was at Harvard during some of Elton Mayo's tenure there and was strongly influenced in the early years by Fritz Roethlisberger (see Miner 2002). He was educated in the post-Hawthorne studies period, when the case tradition was developing there. His primary disciplinary identification, prior to the emergence of organizational behavior, was with applied sociology, although anthropology, especially in its methods, exerted a strong influence. He received his doctorate from the Harvard Business School in 1950.

Throughout his career Lawrence followed various emergent social problems, did field research on them typically in collaboration with others, and then wrote books on what was found (Lawrence and Lawrence 1993). The work on contingency theory of organization represented one such instance of delving into a specific problem area, and arose out of prior field work and analyses in the area of job enrichment (Turner and Lawrence 1965). Lawrence describes himself as a political liberal, and his humanism is reflected both in his selection of problems for study and in his approach to them. He retired from Harvard Business School in 1991.

Jay Lorsch was a doctoral student at Harvard when the contingency theory research was beginning and joined in the project as a research assistant to Lawrence. The collaboration has been a fruitful one, and Lorsch has remained at Harvard on the business school faculty throughout his career.

STATEMENTS OF CONTINGENCY THEORY

Although the contingency theorists acknowledge a number of debts in presenting their views, their most influential sources, other than the prior field research in the job enrichment area, appear to be Joan Woodward (see Miner 2002) and Burns and Stalker (see Chapter 12).

The Initial Hypotheses

The first formal statement of contingency theory defined an organization as "A system of interrelated behaviors of people who are performing a task that has been differentiated into several distinct subsystems, each subsystem performing a portion of the task, and the efforts of each being integrated to achieve effective performance of the system" (Lawrence and Lorsch 1967a, 3).

The task was to account for a whole input-transformation-output cycle, and the early formulations were focused on research, production, and sales subsystems. Unique to the definition, however, is the inclusion of differentiation and integration, which are defined as follows:

> *Differentiation* . . . the state of segmentation of the organizational system into subsystems, each of which tends to develop particular attributes in relation to the requirements posed by its relevant external environment.

> *Integration* . . . the process of achieving unity of effort among the various subsystems in the accomplishment of the organization's task. (Lawrence and Lorsch 1967a, 3–4)

Differentiation of subsystems was viewed in terms of four factors. In addition to the frequently cited *formalization of structure,* these were *orientation of members toward others, time orientation* of members, and *goal orientation* of the subsystem members. The three orientation factors are behavioral attributes. Hypotheses stating the relationships of these factors to the environment are as follows:

1. The greater the certainty of the relevant subenvironment, the more formalized the structure of the subsystem.
2. Subsystems dealing with environments of moderate certainty will have members with more social interpersonal orientations, whereas subsystems coping with either very certain environments or very uncertain environments will have members with more task-oriented interpersonal orientations.
3. The time orientations of subsystem members will vary directly with the modal time required to get definitive feedback from the relevant subenvironment.
4. The members of a subsystem will develop a primary concern with the goals of coping with their particular subenvironment. (Lawrence and Lorsch 1967a, 6–8)

Three additional hypotheses include the concept of integration and relate it to the environment and to differentiation:

1. Within any organizational system, given a similar degree of requisite integration, the greater the degree of differentiation in subsystem attributes between pairs of subsystems, the less effective will be the integration achieved between them.
2. Overall performance in coping with the external environment will be related to there being a degree of differentiation among subsystems consistent with the requirements of their relevant subenvironments and a degree of integration consistent with requirements of the total environment.
3. When the environment requires both a high degree of system differentiation and a high degree of integration, integrative devices will tend to emerge. (Lawrence and Lorsch 1967a, 10–12)

In these formulations no distinction was made between the actual environment and the environment as perceived by management.

Early Elaboration

The more extensive publication of the theory in book form (Lawrence and Lorsch 1967b) does not formally restate the seven hypotheses, though it does not clearly depart from them. However, differentiation and integration are defined somewhat differently:

> *Differentiation* . . . the difference in cognitive and emotions orientation among managers in different functional departments. [This was later amended to include "and the differences in formal structure among these departments." (Dalton, Lawrence and Lorsch 1970, 5)]

Integration . . . the quality of the state of collaboration that exists among departments that are required to achieve unity of effort by the demands of the environment. (Lawrence and Lorsch 1967b, 11)

Differentiation among functional specialists almost invariably creates a potential for conflict. Integration is the means by which conflicts are resolved. At the very simplest level, integration is achieved through adjudication within the management hierarchy. However, sizable demands created by the environment, which are typically mediated through the degree of differentiation, require the use of more extensive integration devices at lower levels. Among these integrative positions are product manager, program coordinator, project leader, planning director, and systems designer, which cut across and link major subsystems (Lawrence and Lorsch 1967c).

The environment includes not only forces external to the organization, but also "the physical machinery, the nonhuman aspect of production" (Lawrence and Lorsch 1967b, 27). The authors maintain that uncertainty may reside in equipment performance, as well as factors outside the firm's boundaries. Uncertainty is a product of unclear information, uncertain causal relationships, and long feedback spans from the environment. Accordingly, uncertainty would be greater for the research components of an organization than for the production subsystem. Highly uncertain environments require high degrees of differentiation and integration for effective performance (a state of unstable equilibrium). More certain environments typically require neither.

Integration is most appropriately achieved through confrontation or negotiated problem solving, rather than through the smoothing over of differences or the forcing of resolutions through the use of power or authority. Thus, in uncertain environments, where the demand for integration is high, effective organizations will use confrontation. In addition, influence should be based on competence and expertise, and insofar as special integrator positions have emerged, incumbents in those positions should maintain a balanced orientation toward the separate subsystems and convey a feeling that conflict resolution will be rewarded.

The Lorsch and Allen Extensions

Although the original theory dealt with differentiation among departmental subsystems organized on a functional basis, Lorsch and Allen (1973) subsequently extended it to cover corporate divisional and interdivisional relationships in firms organized into multiple product divisions. This extension provided hypotheses for the authors' own research. After carrying out this research, they formulated a set of hypotheses based on their findings and on the earlier hypotheses of Lawrence and Lorsch (1967b).

In all, Lorsch and Allen stated thirty-nine hypotheses. Many of these represent extensions of the earlier concepts to the more complex relationships of product division organization. Thus the environment for a division comes to include the corporate headquarters, and the complexity of the interdependence between headquarters and the division becomes a consideration in integration.

Lorsch and Allen add some new concepts to the theory. One factor influencing the extent of differentiation is the *cognitive limitation* imposed by individual information processing capabilities. Also, *economic risk* influences integration in that "Within a firm the greater the differentiation between any division and the corporate headquarters and the greater the

Figure 13.1 **Lorsch and Morse Statement of the Original Environment-Organization Fit**

Environment	Organization
Certainty of information	Formality of structure
	Interpersonal orientation
Time span of feedback	Time orientation
Dominant strategic variable	Goal orientation

Source: Adapted from Lorsch and Morse (1974, 9).

economic risk posed by that division, the greater the difficulties of achieving integration between these two units" (Lorsch and Allen 1973, 179).

The concept of *integrative effort* is introduced with the hypothesis that "Either an excess or a deficit of integrative effort relative to the degree of interdependence and of differentiation required at the corporate-divisional interface will tend to lead to less effective relationships among these units" (Lorsch and Allen 1973, 182).

Certain hypotheses are stated in such general terms it would be difficult to test them. An example is that "Corporations will tend to develop divisional performance evaluation systems which are broadly consistent with the overall uncertainty and the patterns of diversity and interdependence which characterize their total environments" (Lorsch and Allen 1973, 187).

The Lorsch and Allen (1973) volume, as in more recent writings (Lorsch 1976), gives somewhat less emphasis to environmental uncertainty as a contingency variable, while extending the contingency concept to other aspects of the environment; in particular, the homogeneity versus heterogeneity or diversity aspect of the environment. Heterogeneity may be correlated with uncertainty, but it is not the same thing.

The Lorsch and Morse Extensions

The formulations and extensions of contingency theory considered to this point deal with organization and environment and with the fit between the two. The work of Lorsch and Morse (1974) extends this theory to individual members of organizations. Previously people's predispositions were considered only as one among several environmental factors. Now the domain of the theory is extended to include micro organizational behavior. Lorsch and Morse view organizational and unit effectiveness as dependent on a total fit among environment, organization, and the individual. The original pattern is depicted as shown in Figure 13.1.

To this framework, Lorsch and Morse add as organizational factors the amount of *control* or *influence* members are expected to have over their own and others' activities and the degree to which members are expected to *coordinate* their activities. Table 13.1 gives the essence of the resulting theory. Manufacturing plants operating in environments with high certainty should exhibit the pattern shown on the left in the table. To the extent they depart from that pattern, they should be less effective. Similarly the pattern on the right fits uncertain environments of the kind research units often face. If the organization and its members do not operate as indicated, effectiveness should be low.

When organizational subsystems are structured and staffed in a manner appropriate to their environments, differentiation will result, given that the environments differ insofar as the hypothesized contingency variables are concerned. Thus, if the manufacturing plant and the research laboratory of Table 13.1 were in the same company, the differentiation would be appropriate because the company environment contains uncertainty as well as diversity

Table 13.1

Examples of High Environment-Organization-Individual Fit in Production and Research and Development Units

	Manufacturing plant	Research laboratory
Nature of environment	Certain	Uncertain
Organizational structures and processes	Short time orientation	Long time orientation
	Strong techno-economic goals	Strong scientific goals
	High formality of structure	Low formality of structure
	Influence concentrated at the top—directive	Influence diffused through many levels—participative
	High coordination	Low coordination
	Confrontation to resolve conflicts	Confrontation to resolve conflicts
Individual characteristics	Low cognitive complexity	High cognitive complexity
	Low tolerance for ambiguity	High tolerance for ambiguity
	Dependency in authority relationships	Independence in authority relationships
	Preference for group interaction	Preference for working alone
	High feeling of competence	High feeling of competence
Performance outcome	Effective	Effective

Source: Adapted from Lorsch and Morse (1974, 52, 112).

(certainty and uncertainty) (Lorsch 1977). On the other hand, in a highly uncertain environment the uncertainty might be diffused through all subsystems (at least in this sense, diversity would be minimal). Under these circumstances, all subsystems would tend to approximate the right side of Table 13.1 and differentiation would be low. Yet the theory argues for differentiation in the face of uncertainty. There appears to be a logical problem here. Under conditions of high uncertainty in all subsystems of the organization, should one differentiate the subsystems in terms other than goals, and if so, how?

In any event, Lawrence (1975) has subsequently endorsed the Lorsch and Morse extensions and formulated that theory in terms of competence motivation. The level of competence motivation is said to be a function of the fit or lack of fit between the certainty of the task, the personal characteristics of employees, and the organizational structure. In connection with this formulation Lawrence postulates that the level of uncertainty faced has escalated sharply over the past fifty years but that the human capacity to cope with uncertainty has expanded as well.

The Lawrence and Dyer Extensions

In their book titled *Renewing American Industry* Lawrence and Dyer (1983) present a new theory that nevertheless incorporates the differentiation and integration concepts. Key ideas related to the original theory are the following:

- The difficulty organizations experience in coping with their *resource domain* and with their *information domain* depends on the degree of uncertainty in these areas.
- The number of variations in an organization's immediate environment that directly influence its choice of which goods and services to supply is called its *information complexity.*
- The degree of difficulty an organization experiences in securing the resources it needs to survive and grow is called its *resource scarcity.*
- An organization is defined as being in a state of *readaptation* when its performance is simultaneously efficient and innovative.
- As information complexity increases, organizations must, within the limits of their resources, employ new kinds of specialists if they are to learn and innovate in regard to the new, incoming information. This is the process of *organizational differentiation* (D).
- As resource scarcity increases, organizations must increase the number of mechanisms available for coordinating their activities if they are to be efficient—up to the point, that is, that the scarcity of resources itself acts as a constraint. This is the process of *organizational integration* (I).
- Within a given firm, readaptation will be most likely when both organizational differentiation and organizational integration are high. (Lawrence and Dyer 1983, 5–12)

The book contains numerous concepts in addition to these, many of which extend into the domain of management strategy. Beyond differentiation and integration, various human resource practices and a balance of power similar to that suggested by Tannenbaum (see Chapter 8 in this volume) are proposed as means to the essential readaptive form.

Organizational adaptation and the more theoretically important *readaptation* are distinguished as follows:

> *Adaptation* . . . the process by which an organization and its environment reach and maintain an equilibrium ensuring the survival of the system as a whole.

> *Readaptation* . . . . a form of organizational adaptation in which the organization and its relevant environment interact and evolve toward exchanges that are more acceptable to the internal and external stakeholders as evidenced by high levels of innovation, efficiency, and member involvement. (Lawrence and Dyer 1983, 295)

These definitions clearly evidence the open systems nature of the contingency theory formulations. Further detail on this theory is given in Miner (2002).

HARVARD-BASED RESEARCH

The unfolding of contingency theory has coincided with major research studies conducted by the theorists. The usual pattern has been to undertake an exploratory study on a very limited sample, firm up the hypotheses on the basis of that work, and then extend the research to a larger sample as a full test of the theory. To the extent that the hypotheses tested in the final study are influenced by the pilot study findings and the organizations involved in the pilot study also are used in the final study, there is potential contamination in this strategy. This appears to have been the case in the Harvard studies, and so they cannot be considered full tests of the theory. Yet the studies constitute an important and widely cited body of research.

Table 13.2

Data on Environmental Uncertainty, Effectiveness, Differentiation, and Integration in Three Industries

Environment	Financial effectiveness rank of firms	Extent of differentiation		Effectiveness of integration	
		Rank	Score	Rank	Score
Plastics industry	1	4	8.7	2	5.6
(Relatively uncertain;	2	1	9.4	1	5.7
considerable diversity	3	5	7.5	3	5.3
of uncertainty)	4	2.5	9.0	4	5.1
	5	6	6.3	6	4.7
	6	2.5	9.0	5	4.9
Foods industry	1	1	8.0	1	5.3
(Relatively uncertain;	2	2	6.5	2	5.0
considerable diversity					
of uncertainty)					
Containers industry	1	1.5	5.7	1	5.7
(Low to medium	2	1.5	5.7	2	4.8
uncertainty; less					
diversity of uncertainty)					

Source: Adapted from Lawrence and Lorsch (1967b, 50, 103).

Studies in the Plastics, Foods, and Containers Industries

The pilot work for the research done in the plastics, foods, and containers industries made use of two firms in the plastics industry (Lorsch 1965; Lorsch and Lawrence 1965). The final study involved six firms in the plastics industry (Lawrence and Lorsch 1967a, 1967b) and two firms each in the foods and containers industries (Lawrence and Lorsch 1967b). Data were gathered on theoretically relevant variables using questionnaires and interviews with thirty to fifty managers in each company.

Within the plastics industry uncertainty was found to be at medium levels for the techno-economic (manufacturing) and market environments, but very high for the scientific environment. For the foods companies, techno-economic uncertainty was also medium, but market and scientific uncertainty were both considerably higher. As a result, the total environmental uncertainty for the foods companies was only slightly below that for plastics. On the other hand, the containers firms were found to operate in a more homogeneous environment of medium to low uncertainty throughout.

Table 13.2 contains the results of the research insofar as differentiation and integration are concerned. In the plastics industry, differentiation should be highly correlated with financial effectiveness; it is not. However, the relationship between differentiation and effectiveness in the foods industry is as hypothesized, though a somewhat higher differentiation score might have been expected in the more successful firm. In the containers industry differentiation is low, but the anticipated difference in financial effectiveness does not emerge; the more successful company does not fit its environment any better than the less successful. These data do not strongly support the differentiation hypotheses, though the authors cite more impressionistic findings that do.

The results involving integration are different. The findings are in accord with the theory for the plastics industry, and to a somewhat lesser degree for the foods industry. But in the more certain containers industry the original theory would have predicted that success would be associated with low integration. This is clearly not the case. The data from all three industries are consistent with the view that integration helps performance, and this appears to be true irrespective of any possible contingencies introduced by environmental uncertainty.

The major role of integrating units and individuals is hypothesized to be resolving conflicts among functional departments. These conflicts were expected to be greatest in more effective firms in highly uncertain environments; thus, the influence of integrators should be greater there. The data indicate, however, that integrator influence was high in all six plastics firms, irrespective of performance level. This appears consistent with the similarity of differentiation scores among these firms.

The findings do suggest that integrators in the more successful plastics firms tend to be intermediate with regard to goal, time, and interpersonal orientations, as well as formality of structure between the functional departments they integrate. They are also more likely to feel rewarded for resolving conflicts. There was a highly significant tendency for more effective plastics companies to use confrontation to resolve conflicts. On the other hand, the smoothing over of differences was used less in these more effective firms. However, in the foods industry, confrontation was most pronounced in the low-performance company and differences in smoothing scores were nonexistent. In the containers industry the successful firm used both confrontation and smoothing more, and forcing less. These results only partially support the theory.

Studies in Conglomerates and the Paper Industry

The pilot study for research done among six multidivisional firms made use of two conglomerates (Lorsch 1968). The research was then extended to include two more conglomerates and two paper companies. The divisions in all six firms handled different product lines (Lorsch and Allen 1973). Data were collected through interviews and questionnaires.

Findings on the major theoretical variables are given in Table 13.3. The first two firms listed are conglomerates, the second two are paper companies, and the third two are conglomerates. The data on integrative effort indicate that this variable cannot be substituted for integration in the theory; in fact, it is difficult to interpret these data in any manner. In a division-by-division analysis, integrative effort was correlated –0.70 with differentiation, the reverse of what might have been expected.

Among the three effective firms the first appears to fit the theory, the second is generally satisfactory, though it lacks integration, and the third is too integrated and probably too differentiated to be as effective as it is in its homogeneous and clearly very certain environment. The fourth firm also requires low differentiation and integration, but its moderate success level would lead one to expect somewhat higher differentiation scores. The fifth firm has a performance pattern consistent with its uncertainty scores, but totally inconsistent with the degree of environmental diversity. The final firm exhibits the reverse pattern—the performance results fit well for diversity, but one would expect a higher level of performance, given the uncertainty level.

Overall, the data do not provide any greater support for environmental diversity as a contingency variable than for uncertainty. Any way one computes it, the theory fails in two instances, succeeds in two, and yields somewhat equivocal results in the other two. Generally

Table 13.3

Data on Environments, Effectiveness, Differentiation, and Integration Based on Rankings for Six Firms

Environments		Financial effectiveness	Differentiation		Integration		
			Corporate-divisional	Total firm	Corporate-divisional		Interdivisional effort
Diversity	Uncertainty		divisional	firm	Actual	Effort	effort
1	1	1 (High)	3	1	1	6	5
3	3	2 (High)	1	2	4	5	6
4	5	3 (High)	2	4	2	2	1
5	6	4 (Moderate)	4	5	3	3	4
6	2	5 (Low)	6	6	6	1	3
2	4	6 (Low)	5	3	5	4	2

Source: Adapted from Lorsch and Allen (1973, 143, 153).

the straight, noncontingent relationships between differentiation and integration scores and effectiveness appear considerably more promising than the contingency hypotheses. However, division-by-division analyses within the conglomerates yield a significant relationship for integration only (0.62), not for differentiation. Across the two industrial environments it is clearly integration and not differentiation that is associated with success (Miner 1979).

One problem with the Lorsch and Allen (1973) report is that a great volume of data is presented, but not necessarily in a manner that makes it easy to relate the findings to the theoretical hypotheses. However, confrontation of conflict is associated with effective integration as expected, and confrontation also is related positively to firm effectiveness. Smoothing had no relationship to effectiveness, and forcing predominated in the less effective firms. In general this indicates the value of rationality in decision making. High performance in both the conglomerates and paper firms was reported to be associated with:

1. Intermediate orientation toward time, goals, and interpersonal relations, and high influence of linking functions.
2. Corporate-divisional influence balance.
3. Modes of resolving conflicts—the degree to which confrontation or problem solving was used.
4. Overall quality of upward and downward information flows. (Lorsch and Allen 1973, 158–59)

These findings support the idea that integration is a source of effectiveness, but since the variables involved are not related to environmental characteristics, it is impossible to consider them in the context of contingency theory itself.

Studies in Manufacturing and Research and Development

The pilot research for the Harvard study of manufacturing and R&D divisions in five companies was conducted in two containers plants of a single company and in two communications research laboratories of another company (Morse and Lorsch 1970). Subsequently the sample was extended to include a pair of plants manufacturing household appliances, two research laboratories working with proprietary drugs, and two medical technology laboratories (Lorsch and Morse 1974). In each company pair, one installation was considered to be effective and the other less so. Certain early analyses dealing with the relationship between uncertainty and personality considered only the four manufacturing plants and four of the research laboratories (Morse and Young 1973). In addition to interviews and questionnaires, psychological tests were administered to a cross section of managers in the plants, and managers and professionals in the laboratories.

The manufacturing plants were originally selected to represent an environment of some certainty, and their mean score of 6.3 on the uncertainty measure supports this conclusion. In contrast, the research laboratories had a mean uncertainty score of 15.4. The two groups were sharply distinguished on this index.

If one contrasts the data of Table 13.4 with the hypotheses embodied in Table 13.1, some striking disparities appear. Effective plants do not have lower scores than the ineffective plants on the personality variables, and the effective laboratories do not have higher scores than the ineffective laboratories. The only differences associated with organizational effectiveness are the scores on the feeling of competence measures, and these are as hypothesized. Since those who work in the more effective systems presumably are more competent, a finding that they feel so is not unexpected.

On the other hand, what emerges from the data is a clear indication that those individuals who work in research laboratories are more cognitively complex, more tolerant of ambiguity, more independent of authority, and more individualistic. Presumably that is a function of some combination of self-selection, professional selection, and acculturation.

In the manufacturing plants, time orientation did not differentiate the effective and ineffective organizations—in both, the time orientation was short. But all other structure and process variables in Table 13.1 did differentiate effective and ineffective organizations, and in the predicted direction. The more effective plants had stronger techno-economic goals, more formality of structure, greater influence at the top exercised in a more directive manner, a higher degree of coordination, and a greater use of confrontation to resolve conflicts.

In the research laboratories the pattern is almost completely reversed, as suggested by the hypotheses of Table 13.1. The more effective laboratories exhibit a longer time orientation, a greater commitment to scientific goals, less formality of structure, more influence at lower organizational levels, a more participative style, less coordination, and a greater use of confrontation. Clearly success is associated with very different organizational characteristics in the research and manufacturing contexts.

These results say nothing about the original *organizational* theory of differentiation and integration. The data are for single subsystems only. Furthermore, being concurrent, they are subject to multiple explanations. Though the authors emphasize the role of the fit between environment and organization, the findings may be explained without recourse to the environmental level and thus to the dimension of certainty-uncertainty:

1. The effective research units appear to have relied strongly on professional norms to induce and control individual efforts toward goal achievement. The less effective research units appear to have confounded the already existing professional system of norms by adding in a sizable amount of hierarchic pressures as well. That this should create role conflict and lower performance levels is entirely consistent with research findings.

2. The effective manufacturing plants clearly place strong reliance on hierarchic authority to induce goal contributions. . . . [T]he low performing manufacturing plants

Table 13.4

Individual Characteristics in Effective and Ineffective Organizations in Certain and Uncertain Environments

Individual characteristic	Certain (plants)		Uncertain (laboratories)		Certain total	Uncertain total
	Effective	Ineffective	Effective	Ineffective		
Cognitive complexity	4.2	4.2	5.2	5.2	(4.2	5.2)
Tolerance for ambiguity	2.6	2.5	2.9	2.9	(2.6	2.9)
Independence in authority relationships	2.2	2.1	2.8	2.9	(2.2	2.8)
Preference for working alone	2.4	2.4	3.0	3.0	(2.4	3.0)
Feeling of competence						
Measure 1	(1.2	0.5)	(1.2	0.2)	0.8	0.7
Measure 2	(2.4	1.2)	(2.3	1.0)	1.8	1.7

Source: Adapted from Lorsch and Morse (1974, 40–41, 43–44, 53–55).
( ) Difference statistically significant.

are often characterized by a basically laissez-faire approach, where strong inducements of any kind are lacking. Extrapolation from research on leadership would indicate that just such performance problems should occur in a laissez-faire context.
3. On occasion low performance in the manufacturing context was associated with a confounding of a hierarchic authority system with an inducement system that made use of group norms and pressures (participative decision making of a kind) to induce contributions. Again, the potential for role conflict was sizable, and the likelihood that this contributed to the performance deficiencies considerable. (Miner 1979, 290–91)

Case Studies

In addition to the full-scale studies noted previously, Lorsch and Lawrence (1970) edited a volume of studies, primarily doctoral dissertations, dealing with contingency theory. Included are the pilot studies for the Lorsch and Allen (1973) and Lorsch and Morse (1974) investigations.

The remaining papers, to the extent they report research at all, are case studies dealing with one or, at most, two organizations. There is, however, one exception among the Harvard studies of that period that did report new and relevant quantitative results. Neilsen (1974) studied two rather small firms utilizing the Lawrence and Lorsch measures and reported his findings in quantitative terms. Both firms were highly effective, but one faced an environment that was both more uncertain and contained a greater diversity of uncertainty levels. This greater uncertainty and diversity would have been expected to elicit more differentiation and integration to achieve such high effectiveness, but it did not. Overall, the two firms were equally differentiated. On the integration measures the firm facing the somewhat more certain and less diverse environment scored the highest. Since actual effectiveness data are not given, one cannot say whether this greater integration was related to better financial results. In any event, the pattern of the findings does not fit theoretical expectations.

Industry Studies

The Lawrence and Dyer (1983) book is devoted in large part to a set of historical studies dealing with the development of various industries in the United States. Davis Dyer is a historian and the analyses are well done. But they are not scientific research. The objective is theory generation, not theory testing. Such constructs as information complexity and resource scarcity remain unmeasured. Operationalizing the variables of the extended theory is admitted to be a difficult task and it is left to others. Thus, in the end, the theory simply is not tested by its authors.

Lawrence and Dyer recognize the problem here. In fact they do report on an attempt to develop systematic ratings of the components of information complexity and resource scarcity on a scale of 0 to 2. Of this effort at a more systematized approach the authors say:

> The mental gymnastics we went through in assigning these scores were complex, and in the last analysis they represent a series of judgments. It is interesting, however, to compare ratings made in this manner with the broader judgments we had earlier made for each industry. . . . The correspondence . . . is fairly close and the deviations are interesting. . . . [T]he correspondence is strong enough to suggest that further measurement work in this direction is warranted. (Lawrence and Dyer 1983, 333–34)

The authors have not undertaken this type of empirical exploration. In fact, Lawrence's (Lawrence and Nohria 2002) most recent book moves in the opposite direction, proposing a theory of human nature that is much more philosophy than science.

APPLICATIONS OF THE THEORY

From its beginnings contingency theory of organization has been closely tied to application. The original studies were part of organizational change programs that were first described in a paper written in 1965, though not published until later (Lorsch and Lawrence 1969). The theory rapidly became associated with the organization development movement (Lawrence and Lorsch 1969). In general Lorsch remained involved in the development of such applications (Lorsch 1977). Lawrence increasingly focused on the development of matrix organization structures, which, though they are not a derivative of contingency theory, fit well with the differentiation and integration concepts (Davis and Lawrence 1977).

The Contingency Approach to Organization Development

The approach taken in the initial change programs is described as follows:

> Our general approach, then, has been to spend considerable time and effort through the use of questionnaires, and a systematic interviewing program in gathering data to be analyzed in terms of a conceptual framework developed in our research efforts [contingency theory]. Having collected and analyzed these data we have then educated management to our conceptual scheme and have fed the data back to them, working through with them the meanings and the limitations of the data. The managers themselves have worked out whatever structural changes seemed required and have collaborated with us in the formulation of specific development programs to alleviate specific reorganizational problems. (Lorsch and Lawrence 1969, 471)

One type of specific development program frequently mentioned is a training effort in which members of differentiated departments are brought together for the purpose of gaining a better understanding of each other's roles. The objective is to confront sources of conflict and attempt to resolve them through mutual understanding (Lawrence and Lorsch

1967b; Lorsch and Lawrence 1969). In general these descriptions deal with the high differentiation and integration situation associated with high uncertainty. Though it is recognized that an environmental fit may require little differentiation or integration and that a change toward such a situation may also be facilitated through training, little attention is given to this type of contingency. It clearly is not what the authors are interested in.

Dealing with Interfaces

For purposes of organization development there are three important interfaces—organization–environment, group–group, and individual–organization (Lawrence and Lorsch 1969). First, sources of uncertainty in the environment and the needs of organization members are diagnosed and a picture of what the organization should be is drawn up. Then data are obtained on existing differentiation levels, integration methods, conflict resolution processes, and sources of dissatisfaction. By comparing what is with what should be, one can obtain a blueprint for change that is tailored to the specific organization.

In initiating change at the organization–environment interface many different approaches may be employed, ranging from training to internal realignments of departments to major structural reorganizations. At this interface the major goal is the appropriate type and degree of differentiation. As a result, a major structural intervention may be introduced at an early stage of the organization development program.

However, once appropriate differentiation is achieved, there arises a need to effect integration and collaboration among the diverse elements. The basic sequence of activities is diagnosis, design, action planning, implementation, and evaluation. Diagnostic data are fed back to organization members in a *differentiation laboratory* designed to provide understanding of the varying outlooks of different units. It is focused on the group–group interface and constitutes both action planning and implementation.

More Recent Practice

With greater experience in undertaking organization development applications Lorsch (1977) seems less inclined to rely on precise measurement instruments and is more favorably disposed toward diagnosis based on clinical insights derived from top-level interviews. He also emphasizes that organizational design changes must be congruent with the preferences of top management to be effectively implemented. Finally, changes must be consistent with each other so that they all move toward the same objective.

In recent years neither Lawrence nor Lorsch have been contributors to the organization development literature. The approaches they proposed are certainly part of many practitioners' armamentaria, but activities such as redesigning organization structures are not currently at the forefront of organization development practice. Furthermore, knowledge of contingency theory of organizations among managers overall does not appear to be at a high level at the present time (Priem and Rosenstein 2000). There appears to have been some falloff in its use as a source of undergirding for practice in the more recent period; in fact, systemwide theories in general have exhibited limited attractiveness.

Introducing Matrix Organization

In a sense contingency theory of organization has adopted matrix organization; certainly it did not create it. The matrix structure was noted in the early theoretical publications as congruent with the needs created by a highly uncertain environment, but later Lawrence focused major attention on the matrix form (Davis and Lawrence 1977, 1978; Lawrence, Kolodny, and Davis 1977). In these writings matrix is defined as "any organization that employs a *multiple command system* that includes not only a multiple command structure but also related support mechanisms and an associated organizational culture and behavior patterns" (Davis and Lawrence 1977, 3).

The value of the matrix form is inherent in its potential for greater flexibility in responding to environmental pressures. Since environments vary in the pressures they produce, there are conditions under which matrix organization may not be needed, or may even be dysfunctional. Accordingly, one would not expect to find this type of structure emerging in all organizations.

There are three conditions (all of which must be present) under which the matrix is the preferred mode. First, two or more critical sectors such as functions, products, services, markets, or geographic areas must be highly salient for goal accomplishment at the same time. Second, the need to perform uncertain, complex, and interdependent tasks must exist so that a sizable information-processing capacity is required. Third, there must be a need to realize economies of scale by utilizing scarce human resources effectively.

Though these conditions are not specified in terms of contingency theory, they clearly assume a complex, uncertain, and perhaps highly competitive environment. The theory would posit a need for differentiation to process various types of information and for integration to coordinate the differentiation. The matrix organization contains both. Such an organization is specified, as one would expect from contingency theory, in terms of not only its structure but also its systems, culture, and behaviors—just as differentiation is.

The matrix emerges from the classical pyramidal form in which all members have one boss. In the next phase a temporary overlay is added to the functional structure in the form of project management. Typically these projects do not contain their own resources and draw on a variety of outside sources for this purpose. The key aspects of organization are a project manager, decentralized resource support, and centralized planning and control. Clearly the project aspect is not yet the coequal of the functional.

In a third phase the overlay becomes permanent, with a product or brand manager whose task is to maintain product viability in the marketplace and stable membership. Yet the overlay is still complementary to functional organization. Finally, in the mature matrix, a dual authority relationship emerges in which the power is balanced. There are two bosses representing two bases of organization. Typically these are function and product, but other bases may be used, even to the point of extending the matrix beyond two dimensions. The key roles are top leadership, which actually is outside the matrix, matrix managers who share subordinates with other matrix managers, and subordinate managers, who have two bosses.

Matrix forms involve increased interdependencies and thus increased communication and opportunity for conflict. As in contingency theory, confrontation is proposed as the best method of dealing with this conflict. The matrix structure requires collaboration to function, and the key ingredient for collaboration is said to be trust.

All of this means that new patterns of behavior must be learned if people are to function effectively in the new structure. This is facilitated through a *team-banding* process that may utilize a staff professional or process consultant in the role of catalyst. Team-building meetings are held that appear to have much in common with the differentiation laboratories previously discussed. These are aimed at identifying expectations and dealing with such matters as objectives, frequency of meetings, leadership, roles and responsibilities, decision modes, communication and conflict resolution patterns, and interpersonal problems.

In addition to such group procedures there is a need for individual development to provide knowledge and skills relevant to the matrix form. A training program for matrix managers involving skill training, experiential learning, and team building is recommended.

Potential Problems with Matrix

Many things can go wrong in organizations moving to the matrix structure (Davis and Lawrence 1978). A state of confusion may develop where no clear lines of authority are recognized (anarchy). An excessive amount of conflict related to a state of free-floating power (power struggles) may emerge. Matrix management may become equated with group decision making to an inappropriate degree (severe "groupitis"). Under conditions of business decline the matrix may be blamed for what is in fact poor management and be eliminated (collapse during economic crunch). Failure to realize possible economies of scale may occur, with the result that costs become excessive (excessive overhead). The matrix structure may gravitate from the higher levels of the organization downward, so that it exists only at the group and division levels (sinking to lower levels). Matrices within matrices within matrices often develop out of power fights rather than the logic of design (uncontrolled layering). Internal preoccupations may become so compelling that contact with the realities of the market is lost (navel gazing). There may be so much democracy that action is not taken when needed (decision strangulation) (Davis and Lawrence 1978, 129–44).

These problems can be overcome if the organization is aware of them, but to some extent they are inherent in the form itself. To these must be added the very real possibility of major role conflicts (see Chapter 9 in this volume). Yet Donaldson (2000) recommends the matrix structure under appropriate circumstances.

Research Evidence on Matrix

With the exception of their own work in several medical centers, the authors cite practically no research dealing with the matrix form. Even the authors' medical center research does not actually test the matrix form (Charns, Lawrence, and Weisbord 1977; Weisbord, Lawrence, and Charns 1978).

Interviews and questionnaires explicitly based on contingency theory were administered in nine medical centers. Differentiation and integration were found to be inadequate to environmental demands. Differences associated with technical specialties (departments) and functions (M.D. education, Ph.D. education, internship and residency training, research, and patient care) were in evidence, but there was considerable blurring in perceptions of them. Confrontation was not widely used to resolve conflicts.

The three conditions for the use of matrix organization appeared to be present. Greater differentiation and integration were needed, and the matrix form seemed to be an ideal method of accomplishing this. However, the research did not relate differentiation and integration measures to the effectiveness of the centers. Nor is there a report on the consequences of introducing a matrix structure.

Although extensively used in organizations, matrix structures have not been extensively tested by anyone; the problem is not unique to those who approach the matter from a contingency theory perspective. What research has been done suggests that the contingency theorists were wrong in positing a developmental sequence as the matrix evolves. Rather the form appears to be structurally stable once introduced (Burns and Wholey 1993). However, consistent with the contingency view, the matrix structure does appear to be introduced to meet problems of increased diversity.

The problems inherent in the matrix form take on added concerns because the result appears to be that contingency theory is pitted against the Katz and Kahn theory of the social psychology of organizations, and its subcomponent dealing with role processes. It would appear that matrix organization can yield considerable role conflict and ambiguity, as might be expected, and that negative consequences such as increased anxiety levels can be anticipated. Whether other advantages such as increased flexibility outweigh these negative considerations and whether the role conflict can be neutralized under certain circumstances is not known. Matrix structures clearly can produce a substantial amount of political activity with a variety of negative effects (Witt, Hilton, and Hochwarter 2001). This escalation of organizational politics, in addition to the role conflict, needs to be considered in introducing matrices.

Finally, there is reason to believe that practitioners tend to give more attention to the differentiation construct than to integration—just the opposite of what the research would support. This cognitive bias, which has been labeled "coordination neglect" (Heath and Staudenmayer 2000), may interfere with any application of contingency theory, including the matrix.

EVALUATION AND IMPACT

The Harvard research suffers from a potential source of contamination in moving from pilot study to theory to a research test that included the pilot data. The research considered below does not suffer from this problem.

Early Research on Measurement and Construct Validity

The initial methodological analyses of the Lawrence and Lorsch (1967b) environmental uncertainty operationalization were carried out on a sample of managers at the middle and top levels (Tosi, Aldag, and Storey 1973). The overall reliability of the scale was found to be 0.51, and the subscale values were 0.11 for research, 0.38 for manufacturing, and 0.52 for marketing. These values are low, but not surprising, considering the shortness of the instrument.

To get at construct validity, measures of volatility in the external environment were established from the range of fluctuations over a ten-year period. Technological, income, and sales volatility measures were calculated for the industry as a whole and for the firm in which each manager-respondent worked. The correlations between the uncertainty scale and these measures of actual environmental variation were uniformly low and, to the extent they were statistically significant, negative. A reanalysis of specific functions and their relevant environments did little to improve the degree or direction of the correlations.

In reply, Lawrence and Lorsch (1973) argued that the volatility measures did not tap what they meant by uncertainty and that the Tosi, Aldag, and Storey (1973) findings did not adequately reflect construct validity. Furthermore, the theorists note that they confirmed the results from the uncertainty scale in other ways in their research and that the Tosi, Aldag, and Storey subjects were not the best qualified to complete the scale. Overall, the results of this first methodological investigation appear to be a standoff, but they raise serious questions about scale reliability and the degree of match between uncertainty as perceived by managers and as reflected in the actual environment.

Lawrence and Lorsch (1967b) clearly utilized a measure of uncertainty as perceived by organizational decision makers, but in this early period they viewed the measure as roughly equivalent to the external circumstances and thus as providing a proxy for some not-easily-obtained objective index. Others have tended to emphasize the perceptual aspects more and the realities of the environment somewhat less, while noting that individual characteristics may also play a role in uncertainty perception.

Downey, Hellriegel, and Slocum (1975) reported low reliabilities for the uncertainty scale as utilized by Lawrence and Lorsch among the division managers of a conglomerate. They also analyzed industry volatility data and the managers' perceptions of a number of variables, such as competition, that are related to uncertainty. Overall, the data provide no evidence of construct validity. Even an alternative measure of the Lawrence and Lorsch uncertainty construct proved to be unrelated to the original scale. Other data do indicate a more positive relationship between perceived uncertainty and environmental aspects. However, the possibility that common method variance may have confounded these results cannot be excluded.

Individual differences can influence perceptions of uncertainty. One laboratory study developed evidence that preexisting tolerance for ambiguity can be an important determinant of these perceptions (McCaskey 1976). The following quote raises important new questions regarding contingency theory relationships:

> A person high in tolerance for ambiguity may take the same situation and make it into something more complex and uncertain than a person low in tolerance for ambiguity does. . . . Organization members seem to adjust the level of environmental uncertainty they perceive to fit their own needs for stimulation and closure. People more tolerant of ambiguity seem to want the challenge of working with greater uncertainty, even to the point of creating it themselves. For some jobs, for some organizations, greater tolerance for ambiguity is desirable. In other cases, if high tolerance for ambiguity people see and maybe create uncertainty even in relatively well-defined situations, high tolerance for ambiguity can be dysfunctional. (McCaskey 1976, 75)

Processes such as these, if they operate among top-level executives, could create havoc for the hypotheses of the Lawrence and Lorsch theory simply because environmental uncertainty (as perceived) now becomes a function of what the individual desires.

Although the operationalization of environmental uncertainty has been the focus of most concerns about the Lawrence and Lorsch (1967b) measures, there have been other such measurement problems as well. Fry, Kidron, Osborn, and Trafton (1980), for example, conducted analyses of the scale used to differentiate conflict resolution methodologies into confrontation, smoothing, and forcing approaches. They were unable to replicate the Lawrence and Lorsch findings and concluded that the scale does not provide valid and reliable measures of conflict resolution modes.

Evolving Conceptualization of Environmental Uncertainty

Given the confusion surrounding the uncertainty construct in the 1970s, it would not have been surprising to find work on the subject subsequently virtually abandoned. Yet this has not happened. Various researchers, such as Sharfman and Dean (1991), have developed useful objective measures of various components of environmental uncertainty. Certain of these measures appear to tap variables very much like the information complexity and resource scarcity constructs posited by Lawrence and Dyer (1983). We need to hear from Lawrence and Lorsch regarding their reactions to these new measures; yet they have been silent on the subject.

The Lawrence and Lorsch measure has been identified with *effect uncertainty,* whereby difficulty is experienced in predicting what the impact of environmental events on the organization might be (Milliken 1987). However, others have seemed to view the same measure as more an index of *state uncertainty,* where one does not understand how components of the environment might be changing (Miller and Shamsie 1999). There seems to be a great deal of uncertainty about what the original Lawrence and Lorsch uncertainty construct is.

Construct validity has been a continuing problem. It appears that using a measure of perceived environmental uncertainty as a proxy for objective reality (as Lawrence and Lorsch did) is not warranted in most cases (Boyd and Fulk 1996). The correlations tend to be marginal at best, and sometimes nonexistent.

All in all, even though both the conceptualization and measurement of environmental uncertainty have seen sizable improvements, as reflected for instance in the development of a perceived environmental uncertainty scale for the natural environment (Lewis and Harvey 2001), this has done little to improve the situation insofar as contingency theory is concerned. We still have what appears to be a poor measure insofar as the Lawrence and Lorsch (1967b) index is concerned, and a construct that accounts for little of the variation in organizational structuring (Nickerson and Zenger 2002).

Research Yielding Partial Theoretical Support

There is little research that might be considered a true replication of the Harvard studies. One exception is a study conducted in three banks that follows the original Lawrence and Lorsch (1967b) design closely (Herbert and Matthews 1977). In general, data at the subunit level for operations, customer service, and marketing are compatible with expectations. As a group, the banks operate in a moderately uncertain environment, below the plastics industry, but by no means as certain as containers, and the marketing environment appears particularly uncertain. In this context one would expect a moderate degree of differentiation *and* integration to yield financial success.

In actuality the most successful bank was the least differentiated but the most integrated. The differentiation level of this high performer might well be theoretically appropriate, and the low performing bank's high differentiation excessive, as the authors suggest. Yet the uncertainty score for the low performer was right up with the plastics firms, suggesting a possible need for its high differentiation. Differentiation and integration ranks were perfectly negatively correlated across the three banks, and in this instance, as in prior studies, it was integration that was correlated positively with success. The parsimonious explanation is that effective integration contributes to success, that differentiation matters little, and that environmental uncertainty as measured is not relevant.

In a series of widely cited studies Robert Duncan attempted to add a greater degree of precision to the uncertainty construct and to investigate various methods of adaptation. In the process Duncan (1972) developed a new measure of uncertainty that differentiated simple–complex and static–dynamic dimensions of the environment. He found, as hypothesized, that perceived uncertainty was greatest where the environment was experienced as dynamic and complex. Of the two environmental components, the static–dynamic contributed more to the perception of uncertainty. However, the uncertainty measure used, though conceptually similar to the measure used by Lawrence and Lorsch, does not appear to be closely related empirically.

Duncan (1973) also studied structural differences at the subunit level (not the total organization) as related to environmental uncertainty. He found that when uncertainty was high the more effective units were more likely to utilize different structures to deal with routine and nonroutine decisions. Thus there was differentiation within the same department. Though consistent with the perspective of Lawrence and Lorsch, this finding clearly goes beyond their actual theoretical statements.

In another study, Negandhi and Reimann (1973) considered thirty diverse manufacturing firms operating under pervasive growth market conditions in India. Construing the environment as stable and relatively certain overall, and extrapolating from contingency theory of organization, the authors hypothesized that centralization of decision making would be associated with organizational effectiveness. However, the results showed just the reverse; there was a marked tendency for the decentralized firms to be more effective.

Though the above results provide little support for contingency theory, an analysis in terms of market competition yields somewhat more favorable results (Negandhi and Reimann 1972). Under competitive circumstances decentralization was strongly associated with effectiveness. However, a significant though smaller relationship of the same kind was found under conditions of little competition. The authors interpret this as a reflection of the cultural context in India, thus adding another contingency variable to the theory.

Research conducted in Mexico and Italy yields support for the original theory without the need for cultural modification (Simonetti and Boseman 1975). In Italy decentralization was related positively to economic effectiveness in competitive markets and negatively under conditions of minimal competition. No significant differences were found in Mexico under limited competition; only the positive relationship between decentralization and effectiveness with high competition was significant.

Working from an initial finding that companies operating under conditions of high environmental uncertainty tended to use uncertainty reduction mechanisms such as staff services and vertical integration extensively, Khandwalla (1973) correlated these uncertainty-related variables with various indexes of differentiation and integration for high- and low-profit firms. Though the measures of variables are different from those of Lawrence and Lorsch, enough conceptual similarity exists to view the research as relevant for contingency theory. Under that theory one would expect higher levels of uncertainty to be compensated with greater differentiation and integration in the more effective firms, but not in the less effective.

The data yield mixed support for that expectation. As in other studies, uncertainty relates to decentralization, but the additional relationship to profitability is minimal. Only in a case of a vertical integration index can structural differentiation be said to be functional in the face of uncertainty. With regard to integration, the use of team decision making at the top level, and not the use of sophisticated controls, follows the theory. In this sense, uncertainty, coupled with integration, is associated with profitability; a lack of association is not. The total theory, that uncertainty requires differentiation and then, in turn, integration to produce effectiveness appears to be supported in two of twelve variable sets. Neither differentiation nor integration appears to be related consistently in a noncontingent manner to effectiveness. However, such noncontingent relationships do appear to exist for the decentralization measure of differentiation and the controls measure of integration—two of the five indexes.

Research That Is Nonsupportive

I have presented the partially supportive research in some detail because the various studies are supportive in different ways, and understanding the research approach is a necessary precondition for understanding the findings. In the case of nonsupportive studies this more comprehensive approach is not needed, the tests of contingency theory simply do not yield support, and there are a goodly number of these studies.

Pennings (1975), for example, studied forty brokerage offices of a single firm and found no evidence of a tie between various uncertainty-related environmental variables, indexes of structure, and effectiveness. The various environmental measures exhibited no consistent relationship with structure, and with uncertainty no relationship at all, nor did these variables relate to effectiveness. On the other hand, structure alone was closely tied to effectiveness:

> If the employees of the organization were left on their own, did not share ideas, were not informationally integrated, did not participate in decisions, and did not receive support, the effectiveness on any criterion will be below average. This is probably the best single state-ment that could summarize the relationship between structural variables and effectiveness. . . . From the results obtained, one questions the usefulness of the structural-contingency model. (Pennings 1975, 405)

Keats and Hitt (1988) describe their results, in the one area where significance was ob-tained, from a comprehensive study of manufacturing firms as follows:

> . . . [F]irms in this study that had unstable, and thus uncertain, environments reacted by divesting businesses and developing a simpler structure . . . the decision focus among the firms was on the reduction of uncertainty by retreating to a better-understood environment and creating a simpler organization rather than on risk reduction through increasing diver-sification. (587)

Elsewhere these authors say:

> Although early theorists argued that firms' structures should become more complex in the face of volatile environments (e.g., Lawrence and Lorsch), the results of this study suggest that firms develop simpler, more centralized structures when facing unstable environments. However, the differences between this study and earlier work might relate to differences in construct definition and measurement. (590)

In this study neither complexity nor resource scarcity exhibited any relationships in sup-port of theory.

The Authors' Current Views

On several occasions Lawrence or both Lawrence and Lorsch together have offered com-ments on their previous contingency theory work. Lawrence (1987) notes that the early en-thusiasm evoked by the theory has waned. Further, he feels that the contingency approach overall can be extremely variable in its effectiveness. Attempts to specify every possible con-tingency serve only to trivialize and are not useful. However, broadly powerful uniformities of the kind that the Lawrence and Lorsch theory and its elaborations attempt may provide somewhat less universal propositions, but in the appropriate domains can be very useful for practice.

Later Lawrence and Lorsch (1991) reiterate that their theory's influence is waning, not because it has been refuted but because it is aging. In general they feel that contingency theory has been supported by the bulk of the research that followed it. They note that problems have been identified in their environmental uncertainty measure. However, this is not a crucial failure since other evidence supported their conclusion in this area; "we . . . hope that someone with a greater interest and aptitude for instrument development than ourselves will undertake the difficult task of developing a better instrument" (492).

Lawrence, in his autobiography (Lawrence and Lawrence 1993), continues to reiterate his belief in the basic validity of contingency theory. He feels that the new, extended version of contingency theory presented in the book with Dyer has been underappreciated.

Unfortunately, nowhere in these commentaries is there a detailed, systematic response to the developing literature related to contingency theory. Yet I must concur with the theory's authors in their belief that the theory represents a major contribution to the organizational behavior field. It introduces several advances over its sister theory, the technological imperative (see Miner 2002). For one thing it deals with organizational subunits and their environments separately, thus avoiding the pitfalls of organizational averaging and abstractions; differentiated subunits are in fact a major component of the theory. Second, it addresses the problem of achieving organized effort toward goals through the introduction of the integration concept. This concept in one form or another has shown much promise in organization theory. Finally, contingency theory has spawned and lent support to applications, which though insufficiently tested, have the merit of bridging the gap between theory and practice.

The Status of Environmental Uncertainty

In one respect, however, contingency theory exhibits considerable vulnerability. The overwhelming problem is that of construct validity, or the basic question: What is uncertainty? It is not environmental change, as the mechanistic-organic formulations might suggest, because with improvements in forecasting techniques, many changes have become highly predictable and thus no longer a source of uncertainty. Uncertainty is not environmental diversity either, as some extensions to contingency theory might suggest. On logical as well as empirical grounds this equation breaks down. Under conditions of high uncertainty across all organizational subunits, uncertainty is at a maximum, but diversity (at least on the uncertainty variable) is low.

Contingency theory has been criticized for confusing internal technological uncertainty with its external environmental counterpart and for inappropriately equating subjective and objective uncertainty. Though the scope of the uncertainty variable Lawrence and Lorsch envisaged may well have been so great as to make it unmanageable, the greatest difficulties seem to revolve around the perceived uncertainty concept. Empirically it has proved almost impossible to demonstrate construct validity, and unreliable measures have emerged often enough to suggest an underlying ambiguity in the basic construct.

Perceived uncertainty is part of the original Lawrence and Lorsch measurement process and it seems to have a place in their construct as well. Yet it is not a direct match with the objective environment. It is strongly influenced by characteristics of the perceiver. Clearly organizations can fail because key decision makers distort uncertainty levels both upward and downward to an excessive degree and adjust organization structures and functioning inappropriately to something that is not really there. It is particularly common to keep perceived uncertainty low by totally ignoring major threats in the environment until it is too late. Here subjective and objective uncertainty are far from being the same thing.

To the extent the same individuals in a firm report on certainty levels in the environment and actually determine internal structures, there is a good probability that environmental uncertainty will be matched with internal structural uncertainty (organic forms) and environmental certainty with structural certainty (mechanistic forms). This is simply because those who prefer one or the other are likely to prefer it everywhere and to create a world to match. There is no reason why all this should have much to do with organizational effectiveness, and it typically does not.

At present it would appear that environmental uncertainty, at least as Lawrence and Lorsch conceived it, is a construct that is no longer theoretically useful. Donaldson (2001), among others, would take issue with this conclusion while indicating that the research support for the uncertainty moderator is much greater than I have indicated. We will consider this position in Chapter 15. What really is needed now is the formulation of a new theory specifying precisely how the components of uncertainty relate to other variables, including aspects of structure and effectiveness.

One additional problem clouds the understanding of differentiation-integration-uncertainty relationships as set forth by contingency theory. Several writers have noted that in a mature context concurrent studies should yield high levels of differentiation and integration in an environment of *low* perceived uncertainty, because the organizational variables should have acted over time to tame the environment. Such effects, coupled with a sampling of organizations at different stages of adaptive change, could completely confound concurrent research results. The theory does not deal with such matters as time lags and reciprocal effects between organization and environment. Others, including Lawrence and Lorsch (1991), have noted that there is a need for longitudinal research that would deal with these issues, but there is also a need for theoretical extensions that indicate what to expect if such research were conducted.

CONCLUSIONS

The Lawrence and Lorsch theory has widespread support among scholars of organizational behavior, with an importance rating of 5.39 and a designation as institutionalized. This represents a high level of endorsement. Estimated validity is at three stars, reflecting the fact that the research has often been nonsupportive, but that the theory has still coined a number of valuable constructs, including the separate specification of organizational subunits and the positioning of integration as a key organizational variable. Estimated usefulness is set at four stars, to indicate that contingency theory has promoted, endorsed, and created a number of applications, primarily in the context of organization development and matrix structures. The authors fostered organization development practice at an early point and in that process set in motion an application that has come to enjoy considerable success (see Chapter 18 for more detail on organization development).

Contingency theory of organization, like other comprehensive systems theories and theories utilizing the contingency approach, has suffered from severe problems related to the measurement of its major constructs. These measurement problems are not fully divorced from difficulties inherent in the constructs themselves, and the way they are defined. Given this situation, the tendency has been to look beyond systems theory to other types of formulations. The primary alternative thus introduced has been some variant of Weber's concept of bureaucracy. Theories of this type start with the idea of bureaucracy and then seek to extend it in some way to deal with the issues that systems theories have considered. Thus, we introduce Part IV with a consideration of Weber in Chapter 14.

REFERENCES

Boyd, Brian K., and Fulk, Janet (1996). Executive Scanning and Perceived Uncertainty: A Multidimensional Model. *Journal of Management,* 22, 1–21.

Burns, Lawton R., and Wholey, Douglas R. (1993). Adoption and Abandonment of Matrix Management Programs: Effects of Organizational Characteristics and Interorganizational Networks. *Academy of Management Journal,* 36, 106–38.

Charns, Martin P., Lawrence, Paul R., and Weisbord, Marvin R. (1977). Organizing Multiple-Function Professionals in Academic Medical Centers. In Paul C. Nystrom and William H. Starbuck (Eds.), *Prescriptive Models of Organizations.* New York: North-Holland, 71–88.

Dalton, Gene W., Lawrence, Paul R., and Lorsch, Jay W. (1970). *Organizational Structure and Design.* Homewood, IL: Irwin-Dorsey.

Davis, Stanley M., and Lawrence, Paul R. (1977). *Matrix.* Reading, MA: Addison-Wesley.

———. (1978). Problems of Matrix Organizations. *Harvard Business Review,* 56(3), 131–42.

Donaldson, Lex (2000). Design Structure to Fit Strategy. In Edwin A. Locke (Ed.), *The Blackwell Handbook of Principles of Organizational Behavior.* Oxford, UK: Blackwell, 291–303.

———. (2001). *The Contingency Theory of Organizations.* Thousand Oaks, CA: Sage.

Downey, H. Kirk, Hellriegel, Don, and Slocum, John W. (1975). Environmental Uncertainty: The Construct and Its Application. *Administrative Science Quarterly,* 20, 613–29.

Duncan, Robert B. (1972). Characteristics of Organizational Environments and Perceived Environmental Uncertainty. *Administrative Science Quarterly,* 17, 313–27.

———. (1973). Multiple Decision-Making Structures in Adapting to Environmental Uncertainty: The Impact on Organizational Effectiveness. *Human Relations,* 26, 273–91.

Fry, Louis W., Kidron, Aryeh G., Osborn, Richard N., and Trafton, Richard S. (1980). A Constructive Replication of the Lawrence and Lorsch Conflict Resolution Methodology. *Journal of Management,* 6, 7–19.

Heath, Chip, and Staudenmayer, Nancy (2000). Coordination Neglect: How Lay Theories of Organizing Complicate Coordination in Organizations. *Research in Organizational Behavior,* 22, 153–91.

Herbert, Theodore T., and Matthews, Ronald D. (1977). Is the Contingency Theory of Organization a Technology-Bound Conceptualization? *Journal of Management,* 3, 1–10.

Keats, Barbara W., and Hitt, Michael A. (1988). A Causal Model of Linkages Among Environmental Dimensions, Macro Organizational Characteristics, and Performance. *Academy of Management Journal,* 31, 570–98.

Khandwalla, Pradip N. (1973). Viable and Effective Organizational Designs of Firms. *Academy of Management Journal,* 16, 481–95.

Lawrence, Paul R. (1975). Individual Differences in the World of Work. In Eugene L. Cass and Frederick G. Zimmer (Eds.), *Man and Work in Society.* New York: Van Nostrand, 19–29.

———. (1987). Historical Development of Organizational Behavior. In Jay W. Lorsch (Ed.), *Handbook of Organizational Behavior.* Englewood Cliffs, NJ: Prentice Hall, 1–9.

Lawrence, Paul R., and Dyer, Davis (1983). *Renewing American Industry: Organizing for Efficiency and Innovation.* New York: Free Press.

Lawrence, Paul R., Kolodny, Harvey F., and Davis, Stanley M. (1977). The Human Side of the Matrix. *Organizational Dynamics,* 6(1), 43–61.

Lawrence, Paul R., and Lawrence, Anne T. (1993). Doing Problem-Oriented Research: A Daughter's Interview. In Arthur G. Bedeian (Ed.), *Management Laureates: A Collection of Autobiographical Essays,* Volume II. Greenwich, CT: JAI Press, 111–48.

Lawrence, Paul R., and Lorsch, Jay W. (1967a). Differentiation and Integration in Complex Organizations. *Administrative Science Quarterly,* 12, 1–47.

———. (1967b). *Organization and Environment: Managing Differentiation and Integration.* Boston, MA: Graduate School of Business Administration, Harvard University.

————. (1967c). New Management Job: The Integrator. *Harvard Business Review,* 45(6), 142–51.

————. (1969). *Developing Organizations: Diagnosis and Action.* Reading, MA: Addison-Wesley.

————. (1973). A Reply to Tosi, Aldag, and Storey. *Administrative Science Quarterly,* 18, 397–98.

————. (1991). Review of *Organization and Environment. Journal of Management,* 17, 491–93.

Lawrence, Paul R., and Nohria, Nitin (2002). *Driven: How Human Nature Shapes Our Choices.* San Francisco, CA: Jossey-Bass.

Lewis, Gerard J., and Harvey, Brian (2001). Perceived Environmental Uncertainty: The Extension of Miller's Scale to the Natural Environment. *Journal of Management Studies,* 38, 201–33.

Lorsch, Jay W. (1965). *Product Innovation and Organization.* New York: Macmillan.

————. (1968). Organizing for Diversification. *Academy of Management Proceedings,* 28, 87–100.

————. (1976). Contingency Theory and Organization Design: A Personal Odyssey. In Ralph H. Kilman, Louis R. Pondy, and Dennis P. Slevin (Eds.), *The Management of Organization Design: Strategies and Implementation.* New York: North-Holland, 141–65.

————. (1977). Organizational Design: A Situational Perspective. *Organizational Dynamics,* 6(2), 2–14.

Lorsch, Jay W., and Allen, Stephen A. (1973). *Managing Diversity and Interdependence: An Organizational Study of Multidivisional Firms.* Boston, MA: Graduate School of Business Administration, Harvard University.

Lorsch, Jay W., and Lawrence, Paul R. (1965). Organizing for Product Innovation. *Harvard Business Review,* 43(1).

————. (1969). The Diagnosis of Organizational Problems. In Warren G. Bennis, Kenneth D. Benne, and Robert Chin (Eds.), *The Planning of Change.* New York: Holt, Rinehart, and Winston, 468–76.

————. (1970). *Studies in Organizational Design.* Homewood, IL: Irwin-Dorsey.

Lorsch, Jay W., and Morse, John J. (1974). *Organizations and Their Members: A Contingency Approach.* New York: Harper and Row.

McCaskey, Michael B. (1976). Tolerance for Ambiguity and the Perception of Uncertainty in Organization Design. In Ralph H. Kilman, Louis R. Pondy, and Dennis P. Slevin (Eds.), *The Management of Organization Design: Research and Methodology.* New York: North-Holland, 59–85.

Miller, Danny, and Shamsie, Jamal (1999). Strategic Responses to Three Kinds of Uncertainty: Product Line Simplicity at the Hollywood Film Studios. *Journal of Management,* 25, 97–116.

Milliken, Frances J. (1987). Three Types of Perceived Uncertainty About the Environment: State, Effect, and Response Uncertainty. *Academy of Management Review,* 12, 133–42.

Miner, John B. (1979). The Role of Organizational Structure and Process in Strategy Implementation: Commentary. In Dan E. Schendel and Charles W. Hofer (Eds.), *Strategic Management: A New View of Business Policy and Planning.* Boston, MA: Little, Brown, 289–302.

————. (2002). *Organizational Behavior: Foundations, Theories, and Analyses.* New York: Oxford University Press.

Morse, John J., and Lorsch, Jay W. (1970). Beyond Theory Y. *Harvard Business Review,* 48(3), 61–68.

Morse, John J., and Young, Darroch F. (1973). Personality Development and Task Choices: A Systems View. *Human Relations,* 26, 307–24.

Negandhi, Anant R., and Reimann, Bernard C. (1972). A Contingency Theory of Organization Re-Examined in the Context of a Developing Country. *Academy of Management Journal,* 15, 137–46.

————. (1973). Task Environment, Decentralization, and Organizational Effectiveness. *Human Relations,* 26, 203–14.

Neilsen, Eric H. (1974). Contingency Theory Applied to Small Business Organizations. *Human Relations,* 27, 357–79.

Nickerson, Jack A., and Zenger, Todd R. (2002). Being Efficiently Fickle: A Dynamic Theory of Organizational Choice. *Organization Science,* 13, 547–66.

Pennings, Johannes M. (1975). The Relevance of the Structural-Contingency Model for Organizational Effectiveness. *Administrative Science Quarterly,* 20, 393–410.

Priem, Richard L., and Rosenstein, J. (2000). Is Organization Theory Obvious to Practitioners? A Test of One Established Theory. *Organization Science,* 11, 509–24.

Sharfman, Mark P., and Dean, James W. (1991). Conceptualizing and Measuring the Organizational Environment: A Multidimensional Approach. *Journal of Management,* 17, 681–700.

Simonetti, Jack L., and Boseman, F. Glenn (1975). The Impact of Market Competition on Organizational Structure and Effectiveness: A Cross-Cultural Study. *Academy of Management Journal,* 18, 631–38.

Tosi, Henry, Aldag, Ramon, and Storey, Ronald (1973). On the Measurement of the Environment: An Assessment of the Lawrence and Lorsch Environmental Uncertainty Questionnaire. *Administrative Science Quarterly,* 18, 27–36.

Turner, Arthur N., and Lawrence, Paul R. (1965). *Industrial Jobs and the Worker: An Investigation of Response to Task Attributes.* Boston, MA: Harvard Graduate School of Business Administration.

Weisbord, Marvin R., Lawrence, Paul R., and Charns, Martin P. (1978). Three Dilemmas of Academic Medical Centers. *Journal of Applied Behavioral Science,* 14, 284–304.

Witt, L.A., Hilton, Thomas F., and Hochwarter, Wayne A. (2001). Addressing Politics in Matrix Teams. *Group and Organization Management,* 26, 230–47.

PART IV

BUREAUCRACY-RELATED CONCEPTS

CHAPTER 14

THE THEORY OF BUREAUCRACY

MAX WEBER

Importance rating	★ ★ ★ ★ ★
	Institutionalized
Estimated validity	★ ★ ★ ★
Estimated usefulness	★ ★ ★
Decade of origin	1900s (in German)

Max Weber has been adopted by the field of sociology at least in part because, although he wrote in German, much of his work was translated into English by sociologists. Before his works were available in translation, they were known in this country for many years, and indeed read in the German, but only by a very limited audience.

Weber's views were formally introduced in the United States through a variety of translations and compilations. The most comprehensive, though still incomplete, early statements of his theory of bureaucracy appeared in the translations by Gerth and Mills (Weber 1946) and by Parsons and Henderson (Weber 1947). The following discussion draws primarily on the comprehensive, three-volume *Economy and Society* translated by Roth and Wittich (Weber 1968), especially on the first and third volumes. Talcott Parsons at Harvard was particularly instrumental in bringing Weber's theories to the United States, and to the English-speaking world in general. Note, however, that this did not happen, insofar as his theory of bureaucracy is concerned, until a quarter century after Weber's death in 1920 at the age of 56.

BACKGROUND

Weber was originally educated in Germany as a lawyer. Much of his early writing dealt with legal history. In addition to law and history, Weber produced major contributions to the fields of economics, religion, and political science. However, he became best known in sociology, the field in which his theory of bureaucracy had the greatest influence. Though associated with several German and Austrian universities, Weber stayed longest at the University of Heidelberg. Due to a substantial inheritance and intermittent periods of debilitating depression, he did not teach regularly and in fact spent a number of years as a private scholar (Marianne Weber 1975). When he did teach, his subject was economics, and he presented himself as an economist throughout his life (Swedberg 2003).

Although not of major concern here, Weber was more widely known initially for his thesis that one consequence of the rise of Protestantism in previously Catholic Europe was the development of capitalism (Weber 1930). In this view, the Protestant ethic said that God intended profitability, and blessed it as well; that waste, and thus not devoting time to profitable labor, was contrary to God's will; that division of labor was to be desired, since it contributed to the quality and quantity of production; and that hard work was in the nature of a duty to God, which contributed to the accumulation of wealth that in turn should be put back into capitalistic endeavors. These views reflect the scope of Weber's intellect. In many ways he was rewriting history. There is some evidence of this tendency in his writings related to bureaucracy as well.

THE THEORY

Weber's approach to theory construction is scholarly, and his statements often are documented from a historical perspective. Though some people, particularly those of a human relations bent, typically view classical management theory (see Miner 2002) and bureaucratic theory as comparable, even to the point of not differentiating between them, a reading of the two indicates major differences. Weber is primarily interested in the role of bureaucracy in the historical development of society and its organizational forms. Classical theory focuses on problems of managerial practice. Both fail to operationalize variables and conduct relevant research, but Weber is much more concerned with clarity of definition.

There has been considerable controversy regarding certain aspects of the translation of Weber (Weiss 1983). In order to make as clear as possible the interpretation I place on his writings the following discussion utilizes direct quotes frequently. These quotes are consistently from the more comprehensive Roth and Wittich (1968) translation.

The Nature of Organization

Weber sees an organization as a particular type of social relationship that is either closed to outsiders or limits their admission and has its regulations enforced by a chief, usually with the assistance of an administrative staff. The key factor is some hierarchy of authority that serves to ensure that members will carry out the order governing the organization. This order may be self-enacted or imposed by an outside agency. Organizational structure refers to the specific manner in which the authority is distributed.

The concept of rules plays an important role in Weber's theory, especially rationally established rules. A *formal organization* is one with a continuously and rationally operating staff. Such a staff possesses power—a probability that its commands will be obeyed. It utilizes discipline—a probability that as a result of habit, commands will result in immediate and automatic obedience.

This staff, which is comparable to the managerial component of today's organizations, is a special group that can be trusted to execute existing policy and carry out commands. It may be tied to the chief in a number of ways, including custom, emotion, and material interest. A key factor in the continued domination of the organization by those at the top is the law of the small number:

> The ruling minority can quickly reach understanding among its members; it is thus able at any time quickly to initiate that rationally organized action which is necessary to preserve its position of power. Consequently it can easily squelch any action of the masses threatening its power. . . . Another benefit of the small number is the ease of secrecy as to the intentions and resolutions of the rulers and the state of their information. (Weber 1968, 952)

Pure Types of Authority: Rational-Legal

Weber's theory gives considerable attention to concepts such as authority, domination, command, power, and discipline; this focus appears to have alienated theorists of a human relations orientation. Yet these are important concepts for organizational theory.

Authority is said to be legitimized or validated by appeal to one or more of three possible grounds: rational-legal rules, personal authority invested with the force of tradition, and charisma. These are pure types that rarely occur alone in nature. In practice, systems of authority typically are mixtures or modifications of the three.

Rational-legal authority provides a basis for the organizational structure termed bureaucracy. It involves:

> . . . a system of consciously made *rational* rules (which may be agreed upon or imposed from above), which meet with obedience as generally binding norms whenever such obedience is claimed by him whom the rule designates. In that case every single bearer of powers of command is legitimated by the system of rational norms, and his power is legitimate insofar as it corresponds with the norm. Obedience is thus given to the norms rather than to the person. (Weber 1968, 954)

Norms are established because of expediency and/or value-rationality; they apply to the members of the organization, but may extend beyond that to the sphere of power of the organization. There is a consistent system of rules—stated in the abstract, but applied to particular cases. Even those in authority are thus subject to an impersonal order. An individual obeys only as an organization member and in response to the law or an impersonal order, not to an individual. Thus obedience is required only within a legitimate, rationally established jurisdiction.

The categories of rational-legal authority are described as follows:

1. A continuous rule-bound conduct of official business.
2. A specified sphere of competence (jurisdiction). This involves:
   a. A sphere of obligations to perform functions which have been marked off as part of a systematic division of labor.
   b. The provision of the incumbent with the necessary powers.
   c. That the necessary means of compulsion are clearly defined and their use is subject to definite conditions. . . .
3. The organization of offices follows the principle of hierarchy; that is each lower office is under the control and supervision of a higher one. . . .

4. The rules which regulate the conduct of an office may be technical rules or norms.
5. ... it is a matter of principle that the members of the administrative staff should be completely separated from ownership of the means of production. ... There exists, furthermore, in principle complete separation of the organization's property (respectively capital), and the personal property (household) of the official.
6. ... there is also a complete absence of appropriation of his official position by the incumbent. ...
7. Administrative acts, decisions, and rules are formulated and recorded in writing.
8. Legal authority can be exercised in a wide variety of different forms. (Weber 1968, 218–19)

Traditional and Charismatic Authority

Traditional authority derives from the personal loyalty associated with a common upbringing. It is based on the sanctity of longstanding rules and powers, tradition, and custom. To some extent these traditions specify the exact content of command, but they may also provide a wide range for individual discretion. Thus traditional authority attaches to the person, not to an impersonal position. It tends to be present where positions of power are filled on the basis of family membership, as in kingdoms and family-owned firms. Here, as in the traditional family, obedience is to the person.

Like traditional authority, charismatic authority is also personal. The leader's personality interacts with followers so that they attribute supernatural, superhuman, or at least exceptional powers to the leader. Charismatic authority rests on recognition by others and results in complete devotion to the leader. The hierarchical powers on which charisma is based must be frequently demonstrated and serve to benefit the followers, or authority will disappear. Typically, a charismatic community emerges over which the leader often exercises arbitrary control. Irrationality and emotional ties are characteristic. Economic considerations are downplayed. Free of ties to rules, whether rationally or traditionally derived, this kind of authority can be a major force for change and revolution.

Combined Authority

Authority and willingness to obey are based on beliefs. These beliefs, which bestow prestige, are typically complex, and accordingly few organizations operate from a single authority base. Rational-legal authority tends to become infused with tradition over time. Bureaucratic organizations tend to be headed at the very top by charismatic leaders, not bureaucratic officials, and they function more effectively if this is so.

Historically, many organizations have developed from a structure of charismatic authority, to rational-legal, to traditional, and then as traditional authority has failed, they have returned to the revolutionary charismatic form. Charismatic authority alone is highly unstable. The charismatic community that maintains itself over time must become rationalized or traditionalized to some degree. This routinization of charisma is particularly important to succession.

Weber views the emergence of an administrative staff as essential to stable organization. Continued obedience requires an effort to enforce the existing order, and this in turn is a consequence of a solidarity of interests, a consistent value system extending beyond the chief and the staff. At some points Weber appears to equate the very existence of an organization with some degree of rationalized bureaucracy, but he is not consistent in this regard (Weber 1968).

Though a generally authoritarian orientation is often attributed to bureaucratic theory, Weber is clearly positively disposed toward certain democratic and collegial forms. In establishing patterns of succession and routinizing charismatic systems, elections and other democratic procedures may emerge. Such procedures can be a major antiauthoritarian force and a force for rationality. As organizations become large, full collegiality is no longer possible, but other forms of democracy involving representation are still viable. In fact, Weber tends to associate the democratization of society with the growth of bureaucratic organizations. Under such conditions bureaucracy contributes to the leveling of social and economic differences. At the same time democracy may come into conflict with bureaucratic tendencies under certain conditions; for instance, a bureaucratic emphasis on career service may conflict with democratic endorsements of election for short terms and the possibility of recall from office.

Aspects of Bureaucracy

Many aspects of bureaucracy have been considered as a natural outgrowth of the discussion of different types of legitimate authority—especially the rational-legal type—but other factors are involved. Furthermore, Weber viewed bureaucracy as a modern organizational form, superior to other forms in a number of respects. He tended to associate it not only with societal, if not organizational, democracy, but also with the growth of a capitalistic economic system and with a certain disesteem for "irrational" religion.

Bureaucracy involves sets of jurisdictional areas ordered by rules. Needed activities are assigned to jurisdictions as duties, authority to elicit behavior to carry out these duties is strictly defined and delimited, and the filling of positions is based on preestablished qualifications. There is a clearly established hierarchy of subordination and appeal. Management positions presuppose thorough training in a specialized area. In addition, a comprehensive knowledge of the organization's rules is required. In a fully developed bureaucracy the needs for the various kinds of knowledge and expertise and for their application are sufficient to produce a full-time position.

Entry into bureaucratic management is based on a set course of training and usually on performance on prescribed examinations. Appointment tends to be by superior authority (election represents a departure from true bureaucracy). After appointment, the individual enters on a career in the organization and can expect to progress up the hierarchy. Compensation is a salary plus a pension in old age. Certain rights go with appointment to the office and protect an incumbent against arbitrary, personal action.

Bureaucratic systems dominate through knowledge, and this fact gives them their rationality. The result is a climate of formal impersonality, without hatred or passion, and hence without affection or enthusiasm. Movement toward such an organizational form is fostered by sheer growth of an organization, and consequently of the administrative task. Bureaucracy is also fostered by the qualitative expansion of administrative tasks—the knowledge explosion and the taking on of added activities by the organization (Weber 1968).

Normative Statements

Weber described bureaucracy at considerable length and placed it in historical perspective, but he also hypothesized that the kind of organization he described would be more effective than alternative forms on a number of counts:

The purely bureaucratic type of administrative organization—that is, the monocratic variety of bureaucracy—is, from a purely technical point of view, capable of attaining the highest degree of efficiency and is in this sense formally the most rational known means of exercising authority over human beings. It is superior to any other form in precision, in stability, in the stringency of its discipline, and in its reliability. It thus makes possible a particularly high degree of calculability of results for the heads of the organization and for those acting in relation to it. It is finally superior both in intensive efficiency and in the scope of its operations, and is formally capable of application to all kinds of administrative tasks. (Weber 1968, 223)

And again:

The fully developed bureaucratic apparatus compares with other organizations exactly as does the machine with the non-mechanical modes of production. Precision, speed, unambiguity, knowledge of the files, continuity, discretion, unity, strict subordination, reduction of friction and of material and personal costs—these are raised to the optimum point in the strictly bureaucratic administration. . . . As far as complicated tasks are concerned, paid bureaucratic work is not only more precise but, in the last analysis, it is often cheaper than even formally unremunerated honorific service. (Weber 1968, 973–74)

Nowhere does Weber contend that the members of such organizations will be happier or more satisfied, but he does contend that bureaucracy works, and to some degree it works for individual members also by freeing them from the inequities of arbitrary authority. Ultimately, bureaucracy works so well that it is practically indestructible. Once such a system is set in motion it is almost impossible to stop, except from the very top; the sum of the parts is an effective organization, but no one part, no single official, is powerful enough to disrupt the whole.

Contrasts with Other Forms

Weber contrasts bureaucracy with other types of organizations that rely more heavily on traditional and charismatic authority, what he calls prebureaucratic forms. Traditional authority is particularly manifest in patrimonial organizations, which lack the bureaucratic separation of private and official spheres. Under traditional conditions, decisions tend to be ad hoc rather than predetermined by rules, and loyalty is not to the duties of an impersonal office, but to a ruler as a person. Ineffectiveness becomes a matter of arousing the ruler's disfavor rather than failing to perform the duties of the position. Feudalism involves much that is patrimonial, but relationships are more fixed than in many other such forms. Elements of routinized charisma are in evidence as well.

In a sense, charismatic authority is antithetical to the idea of organization. Yet a personal staff of disciples characteristically arises to form a charismatic aristocracy. The basic system tends to be communal, with the leader issuing dispensations according to his personal desires. Under such conditions the leader can introduce changes rapidly—there are no rules or traditions to block them. Bureaucracy can produce change as well, but it does so by first changing the material and social order along rational lines, and then the individuals.

Discipline in a modern factory is much the same as in the military or on a plantation, but it is more rational:

With the help of suitable methods of measurement, the optimum profitability of the individual worker is calculated like that of any material means of production. On this basis, like the American system of scientific management, it triumphantly proceeds with its rational conditioning and training of work performances, thus drawing the ultimate conclusions from the mechanization and discipline of the plant. . . . This whole process of rationalization, in the factory as elsewhere, and especially in the bureaucratic state machine, parallels the centralization of the material implements of organization in the hands of the master. Thus, discipline inexorably takes over ever larger areas as the satisfaction of political and economic needs is increasingly rationalized. This universal phenomenon more and more restricts the importance of charisma and of individually differentiated conduct. (Weber 1968, 1156)

Weber does not say he likes all this; his writing is in fact quite objective and neutral. But he certainly respects it, and he appears to be to some degree afraid of it as well.

EVALUATION AND IMPACT

One reason for the extensive discussion of Weber's ideas that has occurred over the years is the uncertainty as to what he really said. These differences are based only in part on difficulties of translation. Weber often returned to the same subjects, approaching them from different angles and providing fuel for numerous interpretive debates (Turner 1983). Thus, Weber's statements are on occasion conflicting or ambiguous on the role of collegiality vis-à-vis bureaucracy; the extent to which bureaucracy may be defined as a self-contained and self-perpetuating entity as opposed to a tool of the user; the relationship of centralization to bureaucracy; the power of bureaucracy; the degree of voluntary versus imperative control inherent in rational-legal authority; and the distinction between the concept of organization as a whole and its bureaucratic subtype. Weber strove for clarity of definition but conveyed a message of considerable fuzziness on certain issues (Abrahamsson 1977). Scientifically, the theory is logically inconsistent to a degree.

Criticisms of Bureaucracy

Weber was not totally unaware that there are dysfunctions and unanticipated consequences of bureaucracy. Such matters were considered, though they were not his major concern. Thus, the existence and activities of the informal organization represent departures from the ideal type. That Weber did not deal with such matters at length reflects the nature of his domain choice. He wanted to establish how and why bureaucracy works under ideal conditions. This in itself is a massive undertaking, and one cannot legitimately fault Weber for not extending his theory with the same detail into new domains. Yet, others have done so since.

Much the same argument applies to the contention that Weber failed to consider organization–environment interactions and produced an overly limited, closed-system theory. As Aldrich and Pfeffer (1976) point out, Weber's historical and comparative analyses dealt at length with the impact of social structure on bureaucracy. And McNeil (1978) has drawn upon Weber's views as a frame of reference for describing how organizations gain power over their environments. Certainly, Weber's formulations regarding external forces are incomplete, relative to his theory of internal factors. Yet, significant theory construction invariably requires focusing on some one domain and not others.

As indicated in Chapter 10 in this volume, there has been considerable discussion of the decline of bureaucracy, as well as of approaches to replace it. Perhaps Weber was wrong in emphasizing bureaucracy's strength and resiliency. This has been the position of many organization development practitioners (see Chapters 17 and 18). As DiMaggio (2001) notes, in recent years bureaucratic structures have become flatter, headquarters staff size has become smaller, there is more reliance on teamwork and less on narrow job descriptions, and a variety of types of collaboration have emerged. All in all, the structures involved have become looser; however, they remain of a bureaucratic nature. These revised, flatter systems have been found to produce better performance, but beyond that no particular bureaucratic form of organization appears to make any difference (Nohria, Joyce, and Roberson 2003). From a legal perspective (Kraakman 2001), and in the view of a long-term advocate of the use of groups (Leavitt 2003), bureaucracy is here to stay; it has not been and will not be supplanted. For an example of how far the structure may be stretched and still remain bureaucracy, see Ashcraft (2001).

Questions have also arisen regarding the role of what has come to be called universalistic personnel practices that involve an emphasis on goal-oriented meritocracy, in bureaucracy. Research evidence indicates that where universalism prevails bureaucracy is more complete and effective, as compared with a resort to particularism, with its focus on individual characteristics and favoritism (Pearce, Branyiczki, and Bigley 2000). Thus, as Weber indicated, judgments based on merit do appear to be essential to a well-functioning bureaucracy.

Knowledge and Innovation

With regard to the role of rationality and knowledge in bureaucracy, Weber appears to have been both right and wrong. Knowledge related to strategic decision making and policy implementation for the specific organization does concentrate at the top of the hierarchy and greater rationality tends to accrue with it. However, knowledge that is less organization-specific does not relate to the bureaucratic hierarchy in the manner Weber proposed. This latter, professional knowledge is a source of power, and in a general sense Weber was correct in equating authority and knowledge. But he did not differentiate rational-legal authority from the value-rational type that underlies professional systems (Satow 1975). Not only does Weber's theory fail to comprehend professional organizations, which appear to fall outside its domain, but it also fails to deal with professional systems, knowledge, and authority lying predominantly within bureaucratic organizations. To this latter extent it is deficient within its own domain.

Such professional components within bureaucratic organizations do not appear to be mere deviant cases, but rather separate, distinct systems with their own characteristics and sources of authority. Accordingly, Weber's theory is often criticized as failing to provide for organizational innovation beyond what is achieved through professional activities. As indicated in Chapter 13, however, innovation is typically essential to organizational effectiveness. Yet bureaucracy is often said to stifle innovation and creativity.

The best evidence on these matters derives from a meta-analysis of a rather extensive literature dealing with the determinants of innovation rates in organizations. The results are given in Table 14.1. Included there are not only the average correlations, but the author's expected relationships derived from theory and in some instances prior research (Damanpour 1991). In large part these hypotheses posit a positive relationship between professional factors and innovation, but a negative relationship between bureaucratic factors and innovation.

Table 14.1

Findings from Meta-Analysis Regarding Determinants of Innovation Rate

	Meta-analytic finding	Fit
Characteristics hypothesized to have *positive* relationship with innovation rate		
Specialization	0.39	Yes
Functional differentiation	0.34	Yes
Professionalism	0.17	Yes
Managerial attitude toward change	0.27	Yes
Managerial tenure	Not significant	No
Technical knowledge resources	0.47	Yes
Administrative intensity	0.22	Yes
Slack resources	0.14	Yes
External communication	0.36	Yes
Internal communication	0.17	Yes
Characteristics hypothesized to have *negative* relationship with innovation rate		
Formalization	Not significant	No
Centralization	−0.16	Yes
Vertical differentiation	Not significant	No
Size	0.32	No

Source: Adapted from Damanpour (1991, 558–59, 568).

Where positive relationships are expected, they are in fact obtained with only one exception, and that involves a characteristic (managerial tenure) that does not concern professionals. Note, however, that significant positive results occur for managerial attitude toward change and administrative intensity, which also are not professional in nature. In any event, the truly professional factors all yield correlations that fit with the expected higher levels of innovation. The presence and effective utilization of professionals does make for a higher innovation rate.

As to the negative impact of bureaucracy, the data present a different picture. As noted, some factors associated with managers, and thus the bureaucratic component, yield *positive* correlations with innovation. Even more important, support for the bureaucratic hypotheses (at the bottom of Table 14.1) is minimal—only one fit out of four possible is obtained, and that, involving centralization, is far from strong. All in all, there is little here to confirm the idea of an inhibiting impact of bureaucracy on innovation.

One possible explanation of these types of findings is that professional systems generate technical innovations and bureaucratic systems generate administrative innovations (Daft 1982). Thus, each segment has its own special type of proclivity in this regard. Since administrative innovations have been studied less, they would weigh in less strongly in any composite analysis. This type of moderator effect is not supported, however, in the Damanpour (1991) meta-analysis; the two types of systems appear to be both capable of generating innovations of either kind. Truly innovative organizations apparently introduce a prevailing climate in all their components that fosters innovation of any kind (see also Damanpour and Gopalakrishnan 2001).

The literature on innovation has continued to produce mixed results and theoretical deadends over a considerable period of time (see Hage 1999). In this context the Damanpour

(1991) results, based as they are on quantitative findings and relatively free of theoretical preconceptions, stand out as providing the best indication of the state of current knowledge. This position is further supported by an updated meta-analysis focused on the organizational size relationship that reaches the same conclusion as Damanpour's prior work; size and innovation are positively related (Camisón-Zornoza, Lapiedra-Alcamí, Segarra-Ciprés, and Boronat-Navarro 2004).

Research on Aspects of Bureaucratic Theory

Research on the theory, to the extent it has been conducted with appropriate samples and measures, has in general supported the descriptive theory, though more as a composite of variables than as a single type. Formalization, standardization, and specialization tend to be highly correlated, and thus to vary together, as the theory would predict.

A considerable body of research relates large size in both composite units and total organizations to the bureaucratic nexus. There are studies that find only a weak relationship here, and there is reason to question whether size is necessarily a cause of the structure, but size typically has something to do with bureaucracy. Though small bureaucracies are possible, small organizations are more likely to take some other form. Furthermore, bureaucratization seems unlikely to continue unabated beyond some level of growth. Nevertheless, bureaucracy appears to be the preferred method of structuring large organizations of any type. Thus, the overall data support Weber on this point.

The centralization-decentralization variable and results related to it have been the subject of major controversy. Some view Weber's bureaucracy as incorporating centralization, while others think just the opposite. There is considerable confusion regarding how centralization should be operationalized and what the limits of the construct are. This is only part, but a very important part, of the construct validity problem that sometimes plagues the theory.

We know little about Weber's normative theory of bureaucratic superiority. Whether a bureaucratic system at its best is superior to a professional system at its best, for instance, is a completely unanswered question. Furthermore, the significance and role of charismatic leaders at the top of bureaucratic organizations remains highly uncertain. On the other hand, there is evidence that increases in various bureaucratic characteristics, as organizations approach the ideal type, are associated with more positive organizational outcomes. Many of these issues considered in this section are the subject of treatments later in Part IV; thus we should reserve final judgment on these matters.

The Influence Exerted

As Vibert (2004) notes, "the bureaucratic form remains the dominant description of large-scale organization for much of the work force" (88). Also, a whole set of theories arose out of Weber's formulations regarding bureaucracy, many of which attempt to move well beyond what has been considered here. Without question, Weber's insights have exerted substantial influence on subsequent research and theory, although there has been considerable fluctuation in the extent of that impact at different times over the past half century. Overall, however, our understanding of organizations took a quantum leap when Weber's theory finally became widely known. Those who desire more comprehensive knowledge of the consequences of that leap should consult Conger (1993) on charismatic leadership and Clegg (1995) on Weber's macro theory impact.

The influence of Weber's formulations regarding charisma on modern-day leadership theory is evident in the work of House and Bass (see Miner 2005, Chapters 18 and 19). Macro organizational behavior contributions that owe a primary debt to Weber include Selznick's (1949) analysis of the Tennessee Valley Authority and Gouldner's (1954) study of a gypsum plant. Other sociologists who have drawn heavily on Weber to develop their theories include Peter Blau (see Chapter 16 in this volume) and James D. Thompson (see Chapter 11 in this volume). In the present day, Weber's influence is particularly apparent in the new institutionalism of sociologists such as Powell and DiMaggio and Richard Scott (see Chapter 20 in this volume). Although sociology has perpetuated the Weberian tradition most, political science has done so as well (see, for instance, Victor Thompson 1961).

CONCLUSIONS

The theory of bureaucracy has an importance rating among those who are particularly knowledgeable in the field of organizational behavior of 5.90, the highest such rating attained by any theory contained in this book. Not surprisingly, the theory is institutionalized as well; its widespread influence almost guarantees that. Tests of the theory carried out up to the present are almost universally supportive (see Chapters 15 and 16 in this volume), and thus I rate the validity of the theory at four stars. There are some logical inconsistencies and ambiguities that detract from the validity simply because one does not know what to test. In some areas the theory strikes out, or fails to have attracted the needed research, but these defects are not the norm—far from it.

The rating with which I have the greatest difficulty has to do with estimated usefulness. Bureaucracy theory did not invent the bureaucratic form; it described it and attributed normative powers to it. Yet, because it was first written in German, and did not come to the English-speaking world for many years, the likelihood that Weber's writings had a substantial influence on bureaucracy's widespread adoption seems small. We would in all probability have had bureaucracy in our large organizations on much the same scale without them. Nevertheless, as the theory became more widely known, it no doubt contributed to the refinement of bureaucracies already in existence everywhere. I have responded to this situation with a three-star rating on estimated usefulness; this may be too conservative, but it is in line with what has been awarded to other theories.

Next, I take up a theory that guided the most comprehensive program of research on bureaucratic structures that has ever been undertaken. It refines Weber's theory somewhat to make it more suitable for research testing, and elaborates on it as well. But the essence of what follows is to cast the words of a man who was really a historian and a lawyer so as to make them subject to scientific test.

REFERENCES

Abrahamsson, Bengt (1977). *Bureaucracy or Participation: The Logic of Organization*. Beverly Hills, CA: Sage.

Aldrich, Howard E., and Pfeffer, Jeffrey (1976). Environments of Organizations. *Annual Review of Sociology*, 2, 79–105.

Ashcraft, Karen L. (2001). Organized Dissonance: Feminist Bureaucracy as Hybrid Form. *Academy of Management Journal*, 44, 1301–22.

Camisón-Zornoza, César, Lapiedra-Alcamí, Rafael, Segarra-Ciprés, Mercedes, and Boronat-Novarro, Montserrat (2004). A Meta-Analysis of Innovation and Organizational Size. *Organization Studies*, 25, 331–61.

Clegg, Stewart R. (1995). Of Values and Occasional Irony: Max Weber in the Context of the Sociology of Organizations. Research in the Sociology of Organizations, 13, 1–46.

Conger, Jay A. (1993). Max Weber's Conceptualization of Charismatic Authority: Its Influence on Organizational Research. *Leadership Quarterly*, 4, 277–88.

Daft, Richard L. (1982). Bureaucratic versus Nonbureaucratic Structure and the Process of Innovation and Change. *Research in the Sociology of Organizations*, 1, 129–66.

Damanpour, Fariborz (1991). Organizational Innovation: A Meta-Analysis of Effects of Determinants and Moderators. *Academy of Management Journal*, 34, 555–90.

Damanpour, Fariborz, and Gopalakrishnan, Shanthi (2001). The Dynamics of the Adoption of Product and Process Innovations in Organizations. *Journal of Management Studies*, 38, 45–65.

DiMaggio, Paul, (Ed.) (2001). *The Twenty-First-Century Firm: Changing Economic Organization in International Perspective*. Princeton, NJ: Princeton University Press.

Gouldner, Alvin (1954). *Patterns of Industrial Bureaucracy*. New York: Free Press.

Hage, Jerald T. (1999). Organizational Innovation and Organizational Change. *Annual Review of Sociology*, 25, 597–622.

Kraakman, Reinier (2001). The Durability of the Corporate Form. In Paul DiMaggio (Ed.), *The Twenty-First-Century Firm: Changing Economic Organization in International Perspective*. Princeton, NJ: Princeton University Press, 147–59.

Leavitt, Harold J. (2003). Why Hierarchies Thrive. *Harvard Business Review*, 81(3), 97–102.

McNeil, Kenneth (1978). Understanding Organizational Power: Building on the Weberian Legacy. *Administrative Science Quarterly*, 23, 65–90.

Miner, John B. (2002). *Organizational Behavior: Foundations, Theories, and Analyses*. New York: Oxford University Press.

———. (2005). *Organizational Behavior 1: Essential Theories of Motivation and Leadership*. Armonk, NY: M.E. Sharpe.

Nohria, Nitin, Joyce, William, and Roberson, Bruce (2003). What Really Works. *Harvard Business Review*, 81(7), 43–52.

Pearce, Jone L., Branyiczki, Imre, and Bigley, Gregory A. (2000). Insufficient Bureaucracy: Trust and Commitment in Particularistic Organizations. *Organization Science*, 11, 148–62.

Satow, Roberta L. (1975). Value-Rational Authority and Professional Organizations: Weber's Missing Type. *Administrative Science Quarterly*, 20, 526–31.

Selznick, Philip (1949). *TVA and the Grass Roots*. Berkeley, CA: University of California Press.

Swedberg, Richard (2003). The Changing Picture of Max Weber's Sociology. *Annual Review of Sociology*, 29, 283–306.

Thompson, Victor A. (1961). *Modern Organization*. New York: Knopf.

Turner, Stephen P. (1983). Weber on Action. *American Sociological Review*, 48, 506–19.

Vibert, Conor (2004). *Theories of Macro Organizational Behavior: A Handbook of Ideas and Explanations*. Armonk, NY: M.E. Sharpe.

Weber, Marianne (1975). *Max Weber: A Biography*. Trans. and ed. Harry Zohn. New York: Wiley.

Weber, Max (1930). *The Protestant Ethic and the Spirit of Capitalism*. Trans. Talcott Parsons. London: Allen and Unwin.

———. (1946). *From Max Weber: Essays in Sociology*. Trans. and ed. Hans H. Gerth and C. Wright Mills. New York: Oxford University Press.

———. (1947). *The Theory of Social and Economic Organization*. Trans. and ed. Talcott Parsons and A.M. Henderson. New York: Free Press.

———. (1968). *Economy and Society,* Volumes I–III. Trans. and ed. Guenther Roth and Claus Wittich. New York: Bedminster.

Weiss, Richard M. (1983). Weber on Bureaucracy: Management Consultant or Political Theorist? *Academy of Management Review*, 8, 242–48.

CHAPTER 15

THEORY UNDERGIRDING THE ASTON STUDIES

DEREK PUGH
DAVID HICKSON
C. ROBERT HININGS

Importance rating	★ ★ ★ ★
Estimated validity	★ ★ ★ ★
Estimated usefulness	★ ★ ★
Decade of origin	1960s

The theory considered in this chapter remains relatively close to Weber's formulations, while recognizing dysfunctions and elaborating in other ways as well. The theory developed by the Aston researchers is intertwined with a large body of research conducted by the theorists and those associated with them. Joan Woodward's theory of the technological imperative (see Miner 2002) stimulated the Aston work initially, but there is much more to the program than that.

The comprehensiveness of the Aston approach, in terms of both personnel and scope is reflected in the following:

> The first generation of Aston scholars included Derek Pugh (who went on to become professor at the London Business School and subsequently to the Open University), David Hickson (who became professor at the University of Bradford), and C.R. (Bob) Hinings (who became professor at the University of Birmingham and is now at the

University of Alberta). The focus of the first generation was upon the relationship between organization structure and contingency variables such as technology, size, and environment.

The second generation of Aston scholars included Diane Pheysey (who remained at Aston), Kerr Inkson (who moved to the University of Auckland), and Roy Payne (who became professor at the University of Sheffield). The second generation focused on the relationship between organizational structure and organizational climate.

The third generation of Aston scholars involved Lex Donaldson (now at the Australian Graduate School of Management), John Child (now at the University of Cambridge), and Charles McMillan (now at York University, Canada). This generation broadened the scope of the Aston Studies to include organizational performance and cross-cultural analysis. (Greenwood and Devine 1997, 201)

The genesis of all this was in the collaboration of Pugh, Hickson, and Hinings. Among these three Pugh is generally recognized as the senior member of the group at the time; he was also the intellectual leader and the most experienced researcher. Hickson (1996) says that his lead authorship of the initial articles was "well merited by intellectual contributions." Elsewhere (Hickson 1998) he refers to Pugh's "massive input" to the research.

BACKGROUND

Derek Pugh was born in 1930. He was educated at the University of Edinburgh while Tom Burns was on the faculty, and majored in psychology; he continued on at the university after receiving his master's degree, doing some teaching and conducting research on absenteeism. Subsequently he moved to Birmingham College of Technology in the Department of Industrial Administration, essentially a business school appointment. Several years later the college became the University of Aston in Birmingham. Pugh received his doctorate from that university. In 1968 he accepted an appointment at the London Business School at a time when the Aston research group was beginning to break up. He remained there for fifteen years and then shifted to the Open University, from which he retired in 1995 (Pugh 1996).

David Hickson also was born in England, in 1931. His highest earned degree is a master of science in technology from the University of Manchester, although his subsequent appointment at Aston was in sociology. After a rather brief stint at the University of Alberta in Canada, he returned to England and the University of Bradford in organizational analysis and management; that was in 1970 (Hickson 1998). He has remained at Bradford throughout the remainder of his career, although as of 2000 he has listed himself as semiretired.

Christopher Hinings, who prefers to be called "Bob," was born in England in 1937. His highest degree is a B.A. from the University of Leeds in sociology. Like Hickson he moved early in his career to Aston with a sociology appointment, then on to the University of Alberta, back to the University of Birmingham, and finally to Alberta again in 1983. There he has remained since.

The Aston studies, initiated in 1961, were carried out by a group that was transformed several times as generations came and went. The unit was formally terminated in 1973, but it had not been active for several years previous to that time. Actually, after 1968 the major work was conducted by a group that was reconstituted at the London Business School; this too ultimately lost out to turnover (see Child 2002).

FROM THE ASTON STUDIES TO ASTON THEORY

There is no one place where the Aston theory is formally stated. It is intertwined with the research and spread over a number of years and publications. As Warner (1981) says "there is a potentially brilliant empirical theory of organizations to be written by the Aston gurus" (450). This void remains unfilled.

However, the Aston researchers compiled their major publications extending from 1963 to 1981 in a series of four books. The first of these (Pugh and Hickson 1976) deals with the original studies on organizational structure and context conducted in the English Midlands; Pugh is author or co-author of all of the papers. The second volume (Pugh and Hinings 1976) includes papers dealing with extensions and replications of the original work; of the nine papers Pugh co-authored only one, but he does contribute to the introduction and the concluding remarks. Volume III (Pugh and Payne 1977) goes beyond the organizational level to consider research on roles and groups as they relate to organization; here Pugh co-authored two of the nine papers plus the introductory and concluding materials. The fourth volume (Hickson and McMillan 1981) presents a number of studies using the Aston methodology and conducted in various countries around the world; Pugh is not represented here at all.

These are the sources from which I have distilled the Aston theory. In the discussion that follows I use citations to this four-volume series often. However, the reader should be aware that a much-expanded version, that nevertheless has been described as containing "nothing very new" (Sorge 2001, 724) also exists (Pugh 1998).

The Constructs of the Theory

The Aston research began with a set of assumptions (Pugh and Hickson 1976, vi–vii; Pugh 1976, 63):

1. In order to find which organizational problems are specific to particular kinds of organizations, and which are common to all organizations, comparative studies are needed which include organizations of many types.
2. Meaningful comparisons can only be made when there is a common standard for comparison—preferably measurement.
3. The nature of an organization will be influenced by its objectives and environments, so these must be taken into account.
4. Study of the work behaviour of individuals or groups should be related to study of the characteristics of the organization in which the behaviour occurs.
5. Studies of organizational processes of stability and change should be undertaken in relation to a framework of significant variables and relationships established through comparative studies.

Thus comparative research using measures of pre-established variables was to be emphasized. This represented a reaction against the ambiguity of the case approach that had heretofore prevailed in the European study of organizations (see Chapter 12 in this volume on Burns and Stalker's mechanistic and organic systems). However, to conduct the research it was necessary to have measures, and these presupposed constructs. This part of the theory came from a reading of the existing management and social science literature and was thus a priori; a major influence within this literature was Max Weber (see Chapter 14 in this volume).

The major structural variables that emerged from this process were:

- *Specialization*—the degree to which activities are divided into specialized roles, the number of different specialist roles established.
- *Standardization of workflow activities*—the degree to which standard rules and procedures for processing and controlling work exist.
- *Standardization of employment practices*—the degree to which standardized employment practices in, for example, recruiting, promoting, and disciplining employees exist.
- *Formalization*—the degree to which instructions, procedures, and the like are written down and documented, then filed.
- *Centralization*—the degree to which authority to make decisions is located at the top of the management hierarchy.
- *Configuration*—a blanket concept used to cover factors derived from the organization chart: (1) the length of the chain of command, (2) the size of spans of control, (3) the percentage of specialized or support personnel. (Pugh 1976, 65)

In addition, dimensions were established for the context within which this structure operated:

- *Origin and history*—whether the organization was privately founded and changes in such factors as ownership and location.
- *Ownership and control*—type of ownership, whether private or public, and the degree of concentration of ownership.
- *Size*—the number of employees, net assets held, extent of market position, and the like.
- *Charter*—the nature and range of goods and services.
- *Technology*—the degree of integration in the organization's work process.
- *Location*—the number of geographically dispersed operating sites.
- *Dependence*—the extent of dependence on customers, suppliers, trade unions, owning groups, and the like. (Pugh 1976, 71)

These are the constructs entered into the macro analyses, which are the source of the most important contributions from the Aston research. There are additional micro variables; we will consider these shortly.

Based on factor analysis, groupings of the basic variables were established as follows:

- *Structuring of activities*—combining specialization, standardization, and formalization into one construct.
- *Centralization of decisions* (concentration of authority)—combining centralization with the existence of considerable decision-making power in a higher level chief executive, board, or council (in the case of a subsidiary). Standardization of employment activities loads on this factor.
- *Line control of workflow*—combining aspects of configuration (high percentage of line subordinates, low ratio of subordinates to superiors) with impersonal control through formalization of role performance (a component of formalization). Operational (but not personnel) control resides in the line hierarchy.

"These basic dimensions . . . are very much the stuff of which bureaucracy is made. Conceptually they stand in the Weberian tradition" (Pugh and Hickson 1976, 4). And again "we must first of all isolate the conceptually distinct elements that go into Weber's formulation of bureaucracy. . . . The insights of Weber can then be translated into a set of empirically testable hypotheses" (28). This is what the Aston researchers attempted to do.

Certain other constructs beyond those noted previously are utilized on occasion:

- *Flexibility*—a structural variable involving the determination of changes over a period of time—the amount, the speed, the acceleration, and so on.
- *Charter*—a contextual variable describing the purpose and ideology of the organization.
- *Resources*—a contextual variable dealing with the human, ideational, financial, and material resources at an organization's disposal.

Performance is considered to be represented by an organization's success in reaching its stated goals in various areas. Little use is in fact made of performance variables in the research, however. There is also some variation in the specific constructs designated and the nature of their operationalization.

Macro Relationships and Hypotheses

In contrast to the theoretical constructs, which were established in advance of the research, the theory's hypotheses have an empirical derivation; they arose out of the original Aston research and thus cannot be tested using it. The one exception to this statement occurs in the case of technology. There was a test of the technological imperative carried out using an operationalization of Woodward's technology construct (production continuity) and also a measure of integration in the work process (workflow integration) designed for use beyond the manufacturing context (see Miner 2002). This was in fact a test of a non-Aston theory, which specifies a direct causation from technology to structure (the technological imperative).

Figure 15.1 presents the framework for the Aston hypotheses. The findings from the initial Aston study can be summarized as follows:

1. The division of labor (specialization), the existence of procedures (standardization), and the use of written communication and role definition (formalization) are highly related and can be summarized by a single structural dimension called "structuring of activities." This dimension is primarily related to the size of the organization, and secondarily to its technology. Large organizations with automated and integrated technologies will have more specialists, more procedures, and will use written means of communication and role definition. Size is quite clearly the most important factor here.
2. The locus of authority (centralization) is negatively related to specialization, and a number of measures of centralization can be summarized by a single structural dimension called "concentration of authority." This is primarily related to the dependence of the organization on other organizations. Those organizations that are dependent on other organizations by virtue of ownership ties or economic integration will centralize many decisions.
3. Various aspects of role structure, such as the number of employees in the direct line hierarchy, the span of control of the first-line supervisor, and so on, are related and can be summarized by a single structural dimension called "line control of workflow."

Figure 15.1 **The Framework for the Aston Hypotheses**

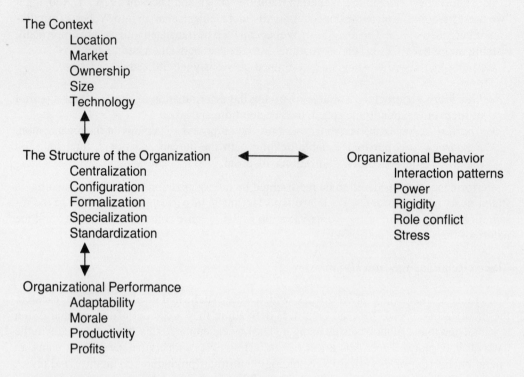

The Context
>   Location
>   Market
>   Ownership
>   Size
>   Technology

The Structure of the Organization ←——→ Organizational Behavior
>   Centralization   Interaction patterns
>   Configuration   Power
>   Formalization   Rigidity
>   Specialization   Role conflict
>   Standardization   Stress

Organizational Performance
>   Adaptability
>   Morale
>   Productivity
>   Profits

Source: Adapted from Pugh and Hickson (1976, 186).

Organizations with integrated and automated technologies will control work by means of procedures and specialists outside the line chain of command, and vice versa. (Pugh and Hinings 1976, ix–x)

These findings relate context variables to organization structure and provide "a set of hypotheses for testing in further studies" (ibid., x). Thus the theory's hypotheses are direct empirical generalizations.

These hypotheses may be outlined as follows:

- Size is related to structuring of activities, with larger organizations likely to be highly structured.
- Dependence is related to concentration of authority, with organizations that have greater dependence more likely to have a greater concentration of authority (centralization).
- Technology is related to some configurational features, with organizations having more integrated technologies likely to have less line control of the workflow. (Pugh and Hickson 1976, 10–13)

Causation and Determinism

Note that these hypotheses state context-structure relationships, but they do not specify causation. Yet causation is of concern to the researchers. "The Aston studies were designed . . . to bring us nearer to the study of generalizable causal relationships" (Pugh and Hickson 1976, 189).

At one point (Pugh and Hickson 1976, 13–14) the authors seem to be tendering causal hypotheses running from the contextual aspects of the hypotheses just stated to the structural, at least in the sense that decisions on contextual matters serve to constrain choices on structure. Later, however (Ibid., 107–108), they are much more tentative on this score. The discussion uses words such as *"tempting to* argue," *"can be* hypothesized," *"may be* hypothesized," *"can be* suggested." The discussion ends with the following statement:

> But a cross-sectional study such as this can only establish relationship. Causes should be inferred from a theory that generates a dynamic model about changes over time. The contribution of the present study is to establish a framework of operationally defined and empirically validated concepts. (Ibid., 108)

Furthermore, these relationships are viewed as potentially reciprocal in that causation can run from context to structure and/or structure to context. This is what the two-headed arrows in Figure 15.1 indicate. The exact nature of the causation is not specified there. Choice, as in the choice of a growth strategy, can clearly enter into the relationships. The idea of complete determination from context to structure is firmly rejected:

> If we could make perfect predictions in every case it would mean that context entirely determines the structure of the organizations, and that the views and strategic choices of top managers are irrelevant (Child 1972a). This is obviously not so. (Pugh and Hickson 1976, 187)

Without evidence from longitudinal studies as a basis, the authors are unwilling to theorize regarding causation, but they do posit that complete determinism, using such factors as size, dependence, and technology as contingency variables, is not their theory; there must be some room for choice. They end by saying, "Where causal imagery is used, it is put forward hypothetically to initiate further study" (ibid.). Yet the Pugh (1998) version introduces revived equivocality on this issue.

Taxonomy of Bureaucratic Structures

While Weber set forth a single concept of bureaucracy, the Aston authors propose a taxonomy that differentiates several forms within the overall bureaucratic concept. In this regard they break with Weber and enter into new territory.

In its simplest form, the taxonomy may be characterized by two dimensions: centralization of decisions (concentration of authority) and structuring of activities, to yield four basic forms (Pugh and Hickson 1993): personnel bureaucracy, full bureaucracy, nonbureaucracy, and workflow bureaucracy. The taxonomy is empirically based, derived from factor analysis using the data from the original study. In its more complete form (see Figure 15.2), three dimensions interact to produce seven different forms. Potentially there are twelve types, but empirically only seven cells are occupied by clusters of organizations. In Pugh and Hickson

Figure 15.2 **The Aston Bureaucratic Taxonomy**

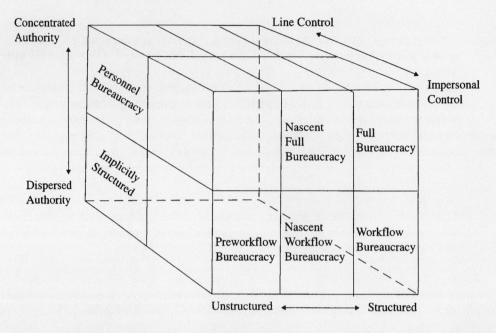

Source: Pugh, Hickson, and Hinings (1969, 123). Copyright © 1969 by Johnson Graduate School of Management, Cornell University. Reprinted with permission.

(1993) implicitly structured organizations are labeled nonbureaucracies. Nonbureaucracies are typically rather small firms, whereas workflow bureaucracies tend to be large. The authors recognize that the theory might be influenced by its empirical base; there was only one full bureaucracy, for instance, in the original sample and no autonomous professional organizations. Empirically derived theoretical statements of this kind definitely need to be cross-validated on a new sample.

In addition to the taxonomy, the terminology of Figure 15.2 implies certain hypotheses regarding the form of the developmental sequence. This sequencing is based on size and runs from "implicit" to "pre-" to "nascent," and then eventually to the complete bureaucratic type. Thus a movement toward more bureaucracy over time is hypothesized.

The Theory as Extended in a Micro Direction

It is interesting to note that, although Pugh was trained as a psychologist and identifies himself as such (Pugh 1996), the Aston studies, with only a few exceptions, were published in the literature of organizational behavior and of sociology. These few exceptions occur when the studies move in a micro direction.

Figure 15.1 includes a component labeled organizational behavior. This component considers relationships between context/structure and aspects of group and role structure, as well as individual attitudes and behavior. The major hypothesis of micro organizational behavior that the Aston studies advanced is the administrative reduction of variance thesis. This may be stated as follows:

... [T]he two main structural variables (structuring of activities and concentration of authority) increase the degree of specificity of role-prescriptions characteristic of the organization, and, in an environment thus formally defined in terms of highly prescribed roles, relatively cautious and conformist behaviour becomes most appropriate. Thus, in the role sending activities described by Kahn et al. (1964) [see Chapter 9 in this volume], where formal roles are mediated by interpersonal role-conceptions and expectations, conformity and stability become highly valued. In this relatively stable organizational and social environment interpersonal conflict is less likely. Thus a single explanatory causal chain is hypothesized, whereby administrative factors in structured and/or concentrated authority organizations reduce the amount of variance in roles, and thereby the amount of innovation and flexibility encouraged in interpersonal relations and conflict engendered by interpersonal behaviour. Organizational variables, role variables, and interpersonal variables are linked. (Pugh and Payne 1977, 15–16)

This is the idea that bureaucracy constrains innovation (see Chapter 14 in this volume).

A variation on this theme is subsequently posited as related to climate within an organization and to group structure, utilizing the Burns and Stalker terminology (see Chapter 12 in this volume):

A mechanistic structuring of activities, through division of labour, standardized procedures and written specification over-prescribes the tasks of managers and is, therefore, not likely to produce a developmental climate where people are stimulated to be innovative. Secondly, the centralization and the high ratio of superordinates characteristic of such organizations are likely to lead to an emphasis on control. At the group level, a mechanistic structure is likely to result in low task complexity, especially at lower levels, and in greater formality of relationships, with emphasis on memos, minutes, written instructions and agendas limiting the opportunity for spontaneous, informal communication. Lack of autonomy may accompany the formality, since authority in a mechanistic organization tends to be concentrated at the top of the hierarchy.

Many writers have argued that top executives are likely to have great influence on the climate of the organization, and, once the top policy makers have made decisions, they exert pressure on subordinates to execute them. Members under such pressure and control, who must execute decisions in which they have not participated, are not likely to have a high sense of involvement in the group's activities and goals, and therefore are not likely to take great satisfaction in their work. (Pugh and Payne 1977, 72–73)

Domain Extensions

A number of studies have been undertaken with the objective of extending the generalizability of the original Aston findings beyond the cross-sectional analysis of work organizations in the English Midlands from which they derived. These extensions do not have a broad theoretical underpinning, but there are some hypotheses to be considered.

One set of extensions involves the movement of the theoretical domain outward from work organizations of a business and governmental nature to include organizations that incorporate voluntary members. These would include occupational interest associations, local government departments, churches, and colleges, with their unpaid councilors, pupils, laity, and rank-and-file members. The implicit hypothesis is that the bureaucratic findings can be extended into this domain, and thus the theory would cover organizations with voluntary members as well as work organizations (Pugh and Hinings 1976). Remember that Thompson (see Chapter 11 in this volume) explicitly excluded voluntary organizations from the domain of his theory.

A second extension applies to the international arena and appears to have preceded the research that extends beyond England's borders. This is referred to as the bold culture-free hypothesis; it is in fact the widely held convergence hypothesis. In this view, relationships between the structural characteristics of work organizations and organizational context variables will be stable across societies throughout the world. Societies converge upon certain common features of their work organizations as related to structure and context.

· This formulation was subsequently modified to a degree and stated as "The traditionalism of industrialized societies is negatively related to the formalization of their work units, but not otherwise to the organizational structures of these units" (Hickson and McMillan 1981, 47).

The idea here is that a highly traditionalized society will not require the high degree of formalization in its organizations that a less traditionalized society does; the two factors serve in lieu of one another. It is not entirely clear whether this hypothesis was generated prior to the initial research related to it or afterwards. Insofar as cultural variations across societies enter into the macro level process of organizations, they are expected to do so through the medium of choice.

Finally, the theory's domain is extended to include change over time in one respect. Based on a small-scale pilot study, a ratchet mechanism is proposed whereby increases in the size of an organization over time would bring about increased structuring, but subsequent decreases in size would not result in decreased structuring. This hypothesis clearly seems to say something about the way that size *causes* structuring, and thus seems to be an exception to prior disclaimers.

EVALUATION AND IMPACT

The Aston theory is a refinement of Weber's theory of bureaucracy. In many respects research on one is research on the other. Yet, as we have seen, there are departures as well between the two theories. Given the preceding theoretical statements, the original Aston studies may be viewed as in large part theory testing for Weber's theory, but theory forming for the Aston theory. The research results are in fact incorporated in the latter theory, and in reviewing the theory we have reviewed the results as well. Nevertheless it may prove helpful to look at these findings more closely, in part to substantiate the support for Weber (see Chapter 14 in this volume); in part to indicate the size of the relationships.

Initial Aston Research on Macro Variables

The initial study was conducted in the English Midlands in the area around Birmingham. The measures were developed with considerable sophistication, using standardized interviews with knowledgeable personnel and corroboration from organizational documents. Specialization, standardization, and formalization are highly correlated with each other, though the particular measure dealing with standardization of selection procedures, advancement, and the like does not always follow the expected pattern (see Table 15.1). However, centralization is, if anything, negatively related to the other criteria, again with the exception of the index of standardization of personnel procedures. Size of organization tends to reinforce

Table 15.1

Correlations Among Structural Measures and Involving Contextual Variables from the Original Aston Study

Structural measures	Specialization		Standardization		Formalization	
	Functional	Overall	Personnel procedures	Overall	Performance recording	Overall
Specialization						
Functional						
Overall	0.87*					
Standardization						
Personnel procedures	−0.15	0.09				
Overall	0.76*	0.80*	0.23			
Formalization						
Performance recording	0.66*	0.54*	−0.12	0.72*		
Overall	0.57*	0.68*	0.38*	0.83*	0.75*	
Centralization	−0.64*	−0.53*	0.30*	−0.27	−0.27	−0.20

Contextual variables	Structuring of activities	Concentration of authority (centralization)	Line control of workflow
Size of organization (employees)	0.69*	−0.10	0.15
Workflow integration (technology)	0.34*	−0.30*	−0.46*
Dependence	−0.05	0.66*	0.13

Source: Adapted from Pugh and Hickson (1976, 57, 100, 103, 141).
*Correlations statistically significant.

these patterns. Larger size is associated with more specialization, standardization, and formalization, but less centralization. The magnitude of the correlations in this study is impressive, although there may be some overlap in the content of certain measures. Data bearing on hypotheses relating context to structure are given in the lower part of Table 15.1.

Aston Replications

Findings from two major British replication studies are summarized in Table 15.2. The variables considered are those hypothesized as characteristics of bureaucracy by Grinyer and Yasai-Ardekani (1980) in their study of forty-five companies located in southeast England. Data are also given in Table 15.2 for Child's (1972b) national study of eighty-two manufacturing concerns. With the exception of the proportion of managers, the variables are all consistently intercorrelated, but in contrast to the data of Table 15.1, the overall centralization results are not only all negative, but also all statistically significant. Further breakdown of the centralization variable indicates that this departure from theory occurs in production, personnel, buying, and organizing decisions. The departure is much less for marketing and financial decisions, though these correlations are not significantly positive either.

In the national study, the stability of the factor structure underlying the theory reflected in Figure 15.2 was analyzed. Primarily because of the centralization findings, the structure did not remain stable. The data bring the concentration of authority dimension into question and suggest that decentralization is a component of structuring. "The solution whereby structuring of activities and concentration of authority represent underlying dimensions of organization

Table 15.2

Significant Correlations Among Structural Variables: National and Southeast England Studies

	Functional specialization	Formalization	Proportion of managers	Levels of hierarchy
Formalization				
National	0.69			
Southeast	0.70			
Proportion of managers				
National	—	—		
Southeast	0.31	0.28		
Levels of hierarchy				
National	0.51	0.48		
Southeast	0.63	0.56	—	
Centralization—overall				
National	−0.28	−0.53		−0.41
Southeast	−0.63	−0.43	—	−0.46
By decision type (all southeast)				
Production	−0.63	−0.46	—	−0.52
Marketing	−0.30	—	—	—
Budget change	—	—	—	—
Personnel and buying	−0.58	−0.48	—	−0.63
Organizational change	−0.42	−0.34	—	—

Source: Adapted from Child (1972, 169) and Grinyer and Yasai-Ardekani (1980, 412–13).

structure requires further empirical examination . . . the taxonomy . . . should be utilized with caution" (Child 1972b, 174). Based on his analysis of the national study data, Mansfield (1973) goes so far as to suggest that the Weberian concept of a single bureaucratic type not be abandoned in favor of the empirical taxonomy.

Figure 15.3 presents the results of the national study in a form that amounts to a set of empirically derived hypotheses for further study. Note that the arrows are primarily unidirectional, reflecting "the likely directions of dominant influence," and thus a commitment as to causality. Also, decentralization is now bound directly into the bureaucratic concept, rather than separated out, as in the original Aston study.

The different results regarding centralization between the Aston and national studies—and also the southeast England study—have been the subject of considerable discussion (Donaldson, Child, and Aldrich 1975). Random fluctuations and differences in degree of organizational diversity likely have combined to produce the disparity.

Pugh and Hinings (1976), however, hold to the original view that centralization should be handled separately and not considered part of the structuring of activities factor. They add to this the following statement:

. . . [D]iscussion of centralization using the Aston schedule needs to be handled with care. The Aston measures had low reliability in the initial study. . . . [C]entralization is a more complex concept than standardization (and formalization). . . . [I]n the case of centralization, the original measure has clear weaknesses, and subsequent findings based on it are confusing. (172)

Figure 15.3 **Summary of Relationships Suggested by the National Study**

Context   Complexity   Bureaucratic control

                                    +   Decentralization

Size of   +   +
organization ─────────────────────┐   ┌──────────────────────────┐
                                   │   │ Specialization of roles │
Integration and automation   +   │   │   │
of technology ─────────────────────┤   │ Specialization of functions │   +   ┌──────────────────────┐
                            _   │   │   │──────────│ Formalization: │
Number of ──────────────────────────┤ │ Level of specialist   │   │ Standardization   │
operating sites   +   │ │ qualifications   │   │ of procedures   │
                                    └──┤   │   │   │
                                       └──────────────────────────┘   │ Documentation   │
                                                                             └──────────────────────┘
Environmental
context   +

Degree of contact across   Size of owning group
organizational boundaries:
(a) with other organizations, i.e.
    activities contracted out;
(b) with owning group

Source: Adapted from Child in Pugh and Hinings (1976, 63).

If reliability and construct validity problems are present, this would normally be expected to lower correlations. This, too, may account for the results obtained in the original study.

Several different indexes of company economic performance were considered in the national study, but no strong relationships were found. Thus, once again company performance could not be incorporated in the model.

Aston Research Extending in a Micro Direction

Very little research has been done at the micro level; most of the studies relate macro variables to group structure and aspects of climate (Pugh and Payne 1977). They do not support the administrative reduction of variance thesis. Innovative role-sending, while associated with structuring of activities, relates positively, not negatively as hypothesized (Pugh 1976).

The research on organizational climate and the climate of line subgroups is equally disappointing. Evidence for the idea that bureaucracies in their true form produce dysfunctions that limit innovation and development was nowhere to be found (see, in this connection, Chapter 14 in this volume). Climate appears to be independent of context and structure.

The authors conclude from this line of research that:

> The negative psychological consequences of bureaucracy predicted by many writers on organizations do not appear in any strong and consistent way. . . . the administrative reduction of variance thesis does not apply in any simple way at the lower levels of management and supervision. . . . bureaucratic structures can provide satisfying work environments. . . . the climate studies show no evidence that less attractive climates consistently occur in bureaucratic structures. (Pugh and Payne 1977, 160–62)

Table 15.3

Patterns of Relationships (Correlations) Between Contextual and Structural Variables in International Studies

| | Structural variables | | |
Contextual variables	Formalization	Specialization	Centralization
Size	Plus	Plus	Minus
Size of parent organization	Plus	Plus	(Not indicated)
Dependence	Usually plus	(Not indicated)	Plus

Source: Adapted from Hickson and McMillan (1981, 193).

Some of these findings might be accounted for on the basis of measurement unreliability, but there are significant findings in a direction opposite to those hypothesized and the results have been established in multiple studies. All in all, attempts to extend the Aston research in a micro direction have not been very successful. Perhaps this is why this research thrust remains so abbreviated.

Aston Research on Domain Extensions

First the Aston theory was extended to cover voluntary organizations and in some cases to professional units as well. Does the research support this kind of domain extension? This research looked at trade unions, professional associations, local government units, churches, colleges, and technological institutes (Pugh and Hinings 1976). Although there is evidence of bureaucracy in this type of situation, the patterns of variables do not always follow the Aston theory, and the extent of influences from voluntary and professional components appears to exert a strong effect on the amount and form of bureaucratization. Size continues to be an important factor. The findings appear to be not unlike those reported in a study of voluntary organizations by Wilderom and Miner (1991). In any event, one cannot assume that the Aston theory, to the extent it has been supported by research, is equally applicable to organizations beyond its original domain of bureaucratic work organizations; sometimes in certain respects it is, sometimes not.

The second extension was international in nature. These studies were conducted beyond England in Canada, the United States, Germany, Poland (under communism), Jordan, Egypt, India, Japan, and Sweden (Hickson and McMillan 1981). The results indicate that, although there are cultural variations in context and structure and their relationships, the differences between organizations within nations are greater than the differences between nations, thus supporting the convergence hypothesis. The prevailing pattern of relationships found in these international studies is indicated in Table 15.3. A meta-analysis of the relationships involving size supports these findings for specialization and formalization, but found no relationship for centralization (Miller 1987); the much larger number of studies included in the meta-analysis thus strengthens one's faith in the results.

Research on the interchangeability of societal traditionalism and organizational formalization is more limited than that on the convergence hypothesis. It is, in fact, restricted to the finding that in England, with its strong traditionalism, formalization scores tend to be low; in Canada formalization scores are intermediate; and in the United States, with relatively little

Table 15.4

Statistically Significant Correlations of Technology Measures and Size with Structural Variables

Structural variables	All organizations (N = 46)		Manufacturing organizations (N = 31)		
	Technology (Aston)	Size (employees)	Technology (Aston)	Technology (Woodward)	Size (employees)
Degree of structuring of activities	0.34	0.69	—	0.41 (0.07)[a]	0.78
Role specification	0.38	0.75	—	0.52 (0.26)[a]	0.83
Functional specialization	0.44	0.67	—	—	0.75
Standardization of procedures	0.46	0.56	—	—	0.65
Formalization of documentation	—	0.55	—	—	0.67
Degree of concentration of authority	−0.30	—	—	—	—
Standardization of selection/ promotion	−0.38	0.31	—	0.43 (0.29)[a]	0.42
Centralization of decisions	—	−0.39	—	—	−0.47
Organizational autonomy	—	—	—	—	—
Degree of control of workflow by line managers	−0.46	—	—	—	—
Formalization of role performance recording	0.41	0.42	—	—	0.45
First-line span of control	0.35	—	—	−(0.36)[b]	—
Percent workflow managers	−0.53	—	—	—	—
CEO span of control	—	0.32	—	—	—
Levels of management	—	0.67	—	0.51 (0.26)[a]	0.77
Percent direct workers	—	—	—	—	−0.46
Percent nonworkflow personnel	0.34	0.36	—	—	0.53
Size (number of employees)	—		—	0.47	
Woodward technology measure			0.46		

Source: Adapted from Hickson, Pugh, and Pheysey (1969, 386, 391).
[a]Figures in parentheses are partial correlations with size removed—none significant.
[b]Curvilinear correlation in parentheses—significant and in accord with Woodward theory.

societal traditionalism, organizational formalization has been found to be high. No actual measures of traditionalism were obtained. Clearly this hypothesis requires more research.

The third extension, longitudinally over time to create dynamic knowledge of organizations, as incorporated in the ratchet mechanism, has not been the subject of published research by the Aston group.

The Aston Studies as They Relate to Technology

Table 15.4 contains data for workflow integration, production continuity, and size as measured by number of employees, correlated with three composite measures of structure (structuring of activities, concentration of authority, control of workflow by line managers), their major component scales, and other indexes considered by Woodward (see Miner 2002). The findings do not provide strong support for the technological imperative. In manufacturing organizations, where one would expect the theory to apply, there are few significant correlations with any technology measure, and the significant correlations with technology that do emerge can be explained in terms of the larger and more frequently significant size correlations. Only a marginally significant curvilinear relationship to the first-line supervisor's span of control is as hypothesized.

Within the much more diverse total sample, technology does yield significant correlations, but those for size are usually larger. In general, technology tends to be the better predictor only when structural factors close to the workflow are considered. Given that most of their organizations were larger than Woodward's, the authors hypothesize:

> Structural variables will be associated with operations technology only where they are centered on the workflow. The smaller the organization, the more its structure will be pervaded by such technological effects: the larger the organization, the more these effects will be confined to variables such as job counts of employees on activities linked with the workflow itself, and will not be detectable in variables of the more remote administrative and hierarchical nature. (Hickson, Pugh, and Pheysey 1969, 394–95)

There have been several replication studies conducted on a more limited scale that support the original Aston finding that size-structure correlations typically exceed those for technology and structure. Data from two such studies are given in Table 15.5. Again, the correlations obtained with the Aston workflow integration measure of technology tend to shrink when the sample is limited to manufacturing firms only. Also, though size yields larger correlations, and more significant values as well, one cannot conclude that technology is unrelated to important structural dimensions.

Results from the national study relating to technology characteristically confirm the earlier Aston findings (see Child and Mansfield 1972). Size continues to yield high correlations with structural variables, but those for technology are not negligible. Though significant correlations with technology occur close to the technology in various staffing ratios, they also emerge in relation to structuring activities more generally.

In contrast to all preceding studies, the national research included measures of organizational performance bearing on Woodward's hypothesis that organizations in the middle range of structure for a technology group would be more successful. Donaldson (1976) indicates that analyses of the relationships involving organizational structure show little association with performance, and nothing to support Woodward.

Handling Professionalism

For Weber, knowledge was the key to power in bureaucracies and should be positively related to the other indexes. Those who question that conclusion have focused on professional knowledge, not the kind of knowledge that is indigenous to the organization itself. Within the professional domain, however, a good case can be made that knowledge does not follow the path Weber proposed. Not only are organizations in which professional components predominate structured differently than bureaucracies, but within bureaucracies themselves professionalization, like centralization, often does not exhibit the expected relationships.

The finding that variables do not relate in the same manner in professional and semiprofessional organizations as they do in bureaucracies appears characteristic (Hage and Aiken 1967). Within bureaucracies the evidence is that decentralization tends to occur in conjunction with bureaucratization; in professional systems this pattern does not emerge. Hall (2001) emphasizes the incompatibility of bureaucratic and professional systems. There clearly are

Table 15.5

Correlations of Technology and Size with Structural Variables in Two Studies

Structural variables	Forty organizations in the English Midlands		Twenty-five Midlands manufacturing firms		Twenty-one U.S. (Ohio) manufacturing firms	
	Technology (Aston measure)	Size (Employees)	Technology (Aston measure)	Size (Employees)	Technology (Aston measure)	Size (Employees)
Degree of structuring of activities	0.51*	0.61*	0.30	0.71*	0.59*	0.72*
Functional specialization			0.27	0.80*	0.64*	0.82*
Formalization of documentation			0.26	0.51*	0.45*	0.48*
Degree of concentration of authority	−0.39*	0.11	−0.25	0.00	0.30	0.35
Size	0.23		0.31		0.75*	

Source: Adapted from Inkson, Pugh, and Hickson (1970, 321) and Inkson, Schwitter, Pheysey, and Hickson (1970, 361).

*Correlations statistically significant.

instances in which bureaucracy incorporates professional components effectively, but that does not mean that the two are part of the same process. Professional indexes and the characteristics of bureaucracy are generally unrelated, but if significance is obtained, it is in a negative direction.

The Aston researchers and Aston theory do not clearly distinguish bureaucratic and professional systems. This would be expected to dilute the results and make the theory less powerful. It appears to have produced major problems for the taxonomy of bureaucratic subtypes.

In the area of bureaucratic subtypes it is important to distinguish between taxonomies of forms within the overall bureaucratic concept and taxonomies that extend beyond bureaucracy. The Aston formulations lack theoretical precision in this regard. Furthermore, like so many theories based on factor analysis, they do not hold up in subsequent investigations. Accepting the Aston theory as an alternative to Weberian bureaucracy does not seem warranted.

Yet approaches of more recent vintage that have much in common with the Aston taxonomy have not fared well at the hands of research either. A case in point is the Mintzberg (1983) typology, which clearly spreads beyond bureaucracy. It, like the Aston approach, has failed to achieve validation from research (Doty, Glick, and Huber 1993).

Normative Findings

Weber clearly did consider monocratic bureaucracy superior to other organizational forms. To test this position would require comparisons pitting bureaucracy against various other types of organizations. In such studies the influence of factors other than the organizational system, such as resource inputs and environmental forces, would have to be controlled. Thus, for example, the influences of human resource inputs such as intellectual abilities and appropriate personality characteristics would have to be removed. The difficulty of conducting such comparative research is obvious, and accordingly, data of this kind are lacking. On the other hand, there are studies in which variations along some dimension of bureaucracy are related to success. Research of this type does not really test Weber's superiority hypothesis, but it does provide insights into the effectiveness of bureaucracy in attaining desired goals.

Paulson (1974) studied a number of health-related organizations, many of which were clearly nonbureaucratic in nature. Though public agencies were analyzed separately from voluntary and professional organizations, it is still not clear that a purified bureaucratic sample was obtained. Nevertheless, high formalization and low centralization are most likely to relate to effectiveness, and structural factors in any event are generally rather weak predictors of organizational outcomes in this health-related context.

However, a study by Becker and Neuhauser (1975) of thirty community hospitals yields somewhat stronger conclusions. Standardization or formalization of procedures and a variable referred to as visibility of consequences, which appears to reflect organizational rationality, both showed substantial positive relationships to various effectiveness indexes in the administrative (bureaucratic) components of the hospitals. In the medical (professional) components, standardization related negatively to effectiveness, but the rationality variable remained positively correlated; once again the disparity between bureaucratic and professional systems is emphasized. In a subsequent study of insurance companies that focused only on the visibility of consequences concept, positive relationships with efficiency measures were obtained.

Reimann and Negandhi (1975) found in their study in India that formalized process (manufacturing) and particularly personnel controls, coupled with decentralization, promoted organizational effectiveness. The combination of high formalization in the form of controls and low centralization is associated with greater effectiveness than either alone. A study by Evans and Rauch (1999) found that resort to bureaucratic processes in state economic agencies was highly correlated with country economic growth in a sample of thirty-five developing nations.

Thus, there are data that support the view that aspects of bureaucracy are related to organizational success, or at least can be found so under appropriate circumstances. It would appear that aspects of other organizational forms, such as the professional, yield the same result. Thus, the superiority of the bureaucratic form has not been demonstrated; but the Aston theorists did not say this, only Weber did.

The Role of Size

Research on relationships involving organizational size has continued since the Aston studies and is supportive of the Aston theory. The ratchet mechanism has generally been found to operate as hypothesized, at least in the sense that decreases in organizational size do not produce declines in structural variables commensurate with the increases produced by growth (Meyer, Stevenson, and Webster 1985). It becomes increasingly apparent that to really understand size and its influence on structuring and other organizational variables it is important to conduct longitudinal studies. Size at a point in time is a product of cycles of growth and decline; growth in particular is important, since most organizations start small (Weinzimmer, Nystrom, and Freeman 1998). The Aston approach, with its emphasis on cross-sectional analyses, represents a good beginning, but it needs to be supplemented with longitudinal work, as Pugh recognized.

Application

What has Aston theory contributed to organizational planning and design? From the perspective of practice the greatest contribution appears to be inherent in the scales and measures of organizational characteristics. These have been published widely in appendices to articles and book chapters. They indicate exactly what to do if one wishes to achieve greater standardization, or formalization, and so forth. Thus, within the range of discretion available they say how choices may be carried out. There is no evidence that I am aware of as to how widely the measures are used in this manner, but they are available and can be used to help design organizations. A close reading of them will certainly contribute to a practitioner's understanding of design considerations. Perusal of Pugh's contributions clearly indicates that he was aware of the practical value inherent in producing measures of bureaucracy, although other scholars with a different orientation to the field have been critical on this score, considering the measures unexciting and really of little practical value (see Marsden and Townley 1996).

Recent developments, however, suggest that these measures can be useful in bringing about changes that serve to transform bureaucracies to make them more successful (DiMaggio 2001; Nohria, Joyce, and Roberson 2003). They can help in flattening companies, increasing spans of control and adding horizontally organized teams. They can also assist in *reducing* the amount of formalization (i.e., work rules and task specifications).

Thus, the number of managers needed declines and a looser, more effective form of bureaucracy is established.

An additional point on applications has to do with the findings with regard to the administrative reduction of variance thesis, and thus the frequently posited dysfunctions of bureaucracy. It appears that these dysfunctions do not emerge as nearly the problem some have contended. The Aston research in this micro area did not confirm theory, but it should not be ignored. It says that bureaucracy is not so bad, and that when appropriate in terms of the size of the organization and relationships to external entities, it should be implemented, not avoided.

CONCLUSIONS

The mean importance rating for the Aston theorizing is 4.28—not as high a level as many of the theories presented here, but still quite respectable. The estimated validity of the theory is four stars. This reflects the fact that by and large the relationships among variables are as hypothesized and seemingly in accordance with Weber's thinking. Size emerges as a dominant factor and it appears to surpass technology. The matter of causality is never handled consistently, centralization is somewhat of a problem, and professionalism exerts an uncertain influence on the bureaucratic subtypes, but these are small difficulties in the overall context of demonstrating the reality of bureaucracy.

The significant implication of the theory and the research for practice is inherent in the measures of bureaucratic variables. For those who would devise and plan organization structures, these measures are invaluable. They clearly warrant three stars in their own right. Unfortunately, the measures have not been cast in a form that makes them easy to apply, and other applications have not been developed. One could hope for demonstration projects where changes were introduced and effects measured over time. Unfortunately, there is little of this type of endeavor.

Blau's theory of differentiation that follows has much in common with the Aston theorizing and is similarly rooted in Weber. Both theories are given a dominant position in structural contingency theory (Donaldson 2001), which I will discuss after Blau in Chapter 16.

REFERENCES

Becker, Selwyn W., and Neuhauser, Duncan (1975). *The Efficient Organization*. New York: Elsevier.
Child, John (1972a). Organizational Structure, Environment and Performance—the Role of Strategic Choice. *Sociology*, 6, 1–22.
———. (1972b). Organization Structure and Strategies of Control: A Replication of the Aston Study. *Administrative Science Quarterly*, 17, 163–77.
———. (2002). Mix Context and Choice, and Add a Large Dose of Serendipity. In Arthur G. Bedeian (Ed.), *Management Laureates: A Collection of Autobiographical Essays*, Vol. 6. Oxford, UK: Elsevier Science, 3–52.
Child, John, and Mansfield, Roger (1972). Technology, Size, and Organizational Structure. *Sociology*, 6, 369–93.
DiMaggio, Paul (Ed.) (2001). *The Twenty-First-Century Firm: Changing Economic Organization in International Perspective*. Princeton, NJ: Princeton University Press.
Donaldson, Lex (1976). Woodward, Technology, Organizational Structure and Performance—A Critique of the Universal Generalization. *Journal of Management Studies*, 13, 255–73.
———. (2001). *The Contingency Theory of Organizations*. Thousand Oaks, CA: Sage.
Donaldson, Lex, Child, John, and Aldrich, Howard (1975). The Aston Findings on Centralization: Further Discussion. *Administrative Science Quarterly*, 20, 453–60.

Doty, D. Harold, Glick, William H., and Huber, George P. (1993). Fit, Equifinality, and Organizational Effectiveness: A Test of Two Configurational Theories. *Academy of Management Journal,* 36, 1196–1250.

Evans, Peter, and Rauch, James E. (1999). Bureaucracy and Growth: A Cross-National Analysis of the Effects of Weberian State Structures on Economic Growth. *American Sociological Review,* 64, 748–65.

Greenwood, Royston, and Devine, Kay (1997). Inside Aston: A Conversation with Derek Pugh. *Journal of Management Inquiry,* 6, 200–8.

Grinyer, Peter H., and Yasai-Ardekani, Masoud (1980). Dimensions of Organizational Structure: A Critical Replication. *Academy of Management Journal,* 23, 405–31.

Hage, Jerald, and Aiken, Michael (1967). Relationships of Centralization to Other Structural Properties. *Administrative Science Quarterly,* 12, 72–92.

Hall, Richard H. (2001). *Organizations: Structures, Processes, and Outcomes.* Englewood Cliffs, NJ: Prentice Hall.

Hickson, David J. (1996). The ASQ Years Then and Now Through the Eyes of a Euro-Brit. *Administrative Science Quarterly,* 41, 217–28.

———. (1998). A Surprised Academic: Learning from Others While Walking on Thin Ice. In Arthur G. Bedeian (Ed.), *Management Laureates: A Collection of Autobiographical Essays,* vol. 5. Greenwich, CT: JAI Press, 93–128.

———. (2000). Listing in Cary L. Cooper (Ed.), *Who's Who in the Management Sciences.* Cheltenham, UK: Edward Elgar, 207–9.

Hickson, David J., and McMillan, Charles J. (1981). *Organization and Nation: The Aston Programme IV.* Westmead, Farnborough, Hampshire, UK: Gower.

Hickson, David J., Pugh, Derek S., and Pheysey, Diana C. (1969). Operations Technology and Organization Structure: An Empirical Reappraisal. *Administrative Science Quarterly,* 14, 378–97.

Inkson, J.H.K., Pugh, Derek S., and Hickson, David J. (1970). Organization Context and Structure: An Abbreviated Replication. *Administrative Science Quarterly,* 15, 318–29.

Inkson, J.H.K., Schwitter, J.P., Pheysey, Diana C., and Hickson, David J. (1970). A Comparison of Organization Structure and Managerial Roles: Ohio, U.S.A. and the Midlands, England. *Journal of Management Studies,* 7, 347–63.

Mansfield, Roger (1973). Bureaucracy and Centralization: An Examination of Organizational Structure. *Administrative Science Quarterly,* 18, 477–88.

Marsden, Richard, and Townley, Barbara (1996). The Owl of Minerva: Reflections on Theory in Practice. In Stewart R. Clegg, Cynthia Hardy, and Walter R. Nord (Eds.), *Handbook of Organization Studies.* Thousand Oaks, CA: Sage, 659–75.

Meyer, Marshall W., Stevenson, William, and Webster, Stephen (1985). *Limits to Bureaucratic Growth.* New York: Walter de Gruyter.

Miller, George A. (1987). Meta-analysis and the Culture-Free Hypothesis. *Organization Studies,* 8, 309–26.

Miner, John B. (2002). *Organizational Behavior: Foundations, Theories, and Analyses.* New York: Oxford University Press.

Mintzberg, Henry T. (1983). *Structure in Fives: Designing Effective Organizations.* Englewood Cliffs, NJ: Prentice-Hall.

Nohria, Nitin, Joyce, William, and Roberson, Bruce (2003). What Really Works. *Harvard Business Review,* 8i(7), 43–52.

Paulson, Steven K. (1974). Causal Analysis of Interorganizational Relations: An Axiomatic Theory Revisited. *Administrative Science Quarterly,* 19, 319–37.

Pugh, Derek S. (1976). The Aston Approach to the Study of Organizations. In Geert Hofstede and M. Sami Kassem (Eds.), *European Contributions to Organization Theory.* Amsterdam, The Netherlands: Van Gorcum, Assen, 62–78.

———. (1996). A Taste for Innovation. In Arthur G. Bedeian (Ed.), *Management Laureates: A Collection of Autobiographical Essays,* Vol. IV. Greenwich, CT: JAI Press, 235–76.

———. (1998). *The Aston Programme, Vols. I–III: The Aston Study and Its Developments.* Aldershot, UK: Ashgate/Dartmouth.

Pugh, Derek S., and Hickson, David J. (1976). *Organizational Structure in Its Context: The Aston Programme I.* Westmead, Farnborough, Hants, UK: Saxon House.

———. (1993). *Great Writers on Organizations: The Omnibus Edition.* Aldershot, UK: Dartmouth, 12–18.

Pugh, Derek S., Hickson, David J., and Hinings, C. Robert (1969). An Empirical Taxonomy of Structures of Work Organizations. *Administrative Science Quarterly,* 14, 115–26.

Pugh, Derek S., and Hinings, C. Robert (1976). *Organizational Structure Extensions and Replications: The Aston Programme II.* Westmead, Farnborough, Hampshire, UK: Saxon House.

Pugh, Derek S., and Payne, Roy L. (1977). *Organizational Behavior in Its Context: The Aston Programme III.* Westmead, Farnborough, Hants, UK: Saxon House.

Reimann, Bernard C., and Negandhi, Anant R. (1975). Strategies of Administrative Control and Organizational Effectiveness. *Human Relations,* 28, 475–86.

Sorge, Arndt (2001). Review of Derek Pugh's *The Aston Programme, Vols. I–III. The Aston Study and Its Developments. Organization Studies,* 22, 717–24.

Warner, Malcolm (1981). Review of *Organization and Nation: The Aston Programme IV. Journal of Management Studies,* 18, 448–50.

Weinzìmmer, Laurence G., Nystrom, Paul C., and Freeman, Sarah J. (1998). Measuring Organizational Growth: Issues, Consequences, and Guidelines. *Journal of Management,* 24, 235–62.

Wilderom, Celeste P.M., and Miner, John B. (1991). Defining Voluntary Groups and Agencies within Organization Science. *Organization Science,* 2, 366–78.

THEORY OF DIFFERENTIATION

PETER BLAU

Importance rating	★ ★ ★ ★
Estimated validity	★ ★ ★ ★
Estimated usefulness	★ ★ ★
Decade of origin	1970s

Blau's theory was developed in parallel with the Aston theory, but on the other side of the Atlantic. Both theories represent attempts to formulate hypotheses based on Weber (see Chapter 14 in this volume) and, having converted Weber to more readily testable form, to actually carry out the necessary research to test these hypotheses. The two programs were initiated during the 1960s and reached the publication phase at much the same time. Each theory cites the other, but the two appear to have evolved independently.

In addition to Weber, Blau appears to have been influenced indirectly in his approach by other classical sociological theorists—Simmel, Durkheim, and to a degree Marx (Calhoun and Scott 1990). The most important direct influences seem to have come from Robert Merton and Paul Lazarsfed, the latter primarily in the area of research methodology, both of whom were Blau's mentors as a graduate student at Columbia University (Merton 1990).

BACKGROUND

Peter Blau was president of the American Sociological Association in 1974, and he has written on a variety of sociological topics throughout his career. Thus, his contributions are often identified more with sociology than with organizational behavior, and are indeed more central to sociology than those of the Aston theorists. Yet Blau's theorizing is of considerable importance for macro organizational behavior as well.

His sociological education began at Elmhurst College, near Chicago, which he entered upon coming to the United States in 1939 at the age of twenty-one from Vienna, Austria (Blau 1995). He was a Jew who escaped from the Nazis to emigrate to the United States. After college and several years in the army, he entered graduate study in sociology at Columbia University. He obtained his doctorate there in 1952 but wrote his dissertation during stints as a faculty member at Wayne State University and Cornell University. In 1953 he began his regular professorial career in the sociology department at the University of Chicago, where he remained for seventeen years. Then, in 1970, he returned to Columbia. After that he was on the sociology faculties at the State University of New York at Albany and at the University of North Carolina. He died in 2002.

Blau's contributions to the study of organizations were intermittent throughout his career. His graduate study did focus in that area and his dissertation, later published as a book (Blau 1955), utilized the Hawthorne studies as a model and considered interpersonal and group relationships in two government agencies. This, and most of Blau's work in the field of organizational science over the next few years, was primarily micro in nature. The initial signs of a more macro orientation began to appear in a text published with Richard Scott (Blau and Scott 1962). Later in the 1960s Blau began research (and formal theory construction) of a more basically structural type, building on the 1962 groundwork. Yet this did not come to fruition in the form of a fully developed theory for some time (Blau 1970a). Later in the 1970s Blau's interests shifted from differentiation within organizations to differentiation within societies, and to problems of inequality.

Thus, Blau's status as an organizational theorist did not become established until the middle of his career, and he did not produce his theory of organizational differentiation until he was over fifty. Prior to that time he was at least as well known for his other contributions to sociology—to social exchange theory and to the understanding of occupational mobility, for example. He was approaching forty as the field of organizational behavior came into being in the business schools. The fact that he had an interest in Marxian theory of class differences and a socialist background (Blau 1995) may well have contributed to his never having taken a business school position.

THEORETICAL POSITIONS

Many of Blau's writings on organizations originally appeared as articles in the sociological literature. These have been compiled in a volume titled *On the Nature of Organizations* (Blau 1974), and it is to this volume that primary reference will be made.

Blau on Weber

Blau accepts a number of the criticisms of Weber developed by others. He agrees that Weber failed to recognize certain dysfunctions created by bureaucracy such as the encouragement of less personally responsible behavior. Basically, Weber focused on the functions of bureaucratic institutions within the larger society and failed to deal effectively with many problems of their internal workings. In discussing promotion he emphasized the use of objective, rational procedures, but failed to deal with the relative worth of seniority and merit. In the same vein, while noting numerous departures from the bureaucratic ideal, Weber did not recognize the existence and role of informal organization as a social entity.

Blau notes certain difficulties inherent in Weber's concept of authority, in his utilization of the ideal type or pure case, and in his handling of the interface between bureaucracy and democracy. These difficulties are exacerbated by the fact that Weber was not entirely consistent in his treatment of these matters.

The theory recognizes both a voluntary element and imperative control in rational-legal authority, but it does not attempt to reconcile the two. Blau proposes that the key factor is the development of norms of compliance within the subordinate group. The individual complies in part because the power to orchestrate sanctions resides in the superior and creates subordinate dependence, but in the context of group norms subordinates may obey even when they would not otherwise voluntarily comply.

One difficulty with the use of ideal types such as bureaucracy is that they freeze relationships so that factors vary together, when in reality these factors may vary independently under certain conditions. As an approach to theory construction, the ideal type is at one and the same time a conceptual scheme and a set of hypotheses. It specifies aspects of a bureaucracy that are highly salient, and criteria for identifying bureaucracy in terms of these aspects. But it also states hypotheses about relationships among the aspects and their relation to efficiency that are empirically testable. If the empirical facts do not confirm the hypotheses in all respects, the ideal type becomes meaningless. Blau argues for abandoning ideal type constructs in bureaucratic theory in favor of a set of hypotheses relating key variables under specified circumstances.

Weber discussed democracy and collegiality on numerous occasions, but he never distinguished between them and bureaucracy in any systematic manner. It is almost as if Weber did not know quite what to do with democracy within his historical framework. He bordered on, but did not actually deal with, the distinction posed by sociotechnical theory (see Chapter 10 in this volume). Blau suggests that bureaucratic and democratic (group) systems are different and should be treated as such.

At various points in other writings Blau takes up dysfunctions of bureaucracy that Weber did not recognize. He notes the tendency for impersonal government agencies to provide inappropriate or insensitive treatment to clients (Blau 1955); the nonresponsiveness to membership interests characterizing certain oligarchies (Blau 1956); the ways in which corporate structures mobilize power in support of purposes that may be inimical to human welfare, as well as that threaten individual liberties and democratic institutions (Blau and Schoenherr 1971); and the fact that overly centralized bureaucracies may have deleterious consequences for the exercise of professional discretion (Blau 1973).

Clearly Blau departs from Weber in a number of respects, but he also recognizes that bureaucratic structures are indispensable to the utilization of complex technologies and to the support of arrangements involving advanced division of labor, both of which yield major social benefits. Of Weber himself he says: "Perhaps the most difficult task for a scholar is to develop a new approach to the study of reality. . . . It is no exaggeration to say that Weber was one of the rare men who has done just this" (Blau 1974, 57).

In addition, Blau has given particular attention to operationalizing the constructs of bureaucratic theory—size, complexity, specialization, expertness, administrative staff, hierarchy, rules, impersonality, and career stability. This is not done in the same manner as the Aston researchers, but it is done effectively nevertheless.

Professionalism, Expert Knowledge, and Bureaucracy

Weber held that the major source of rational-legal authority was expert knowledge that accrued to those at higher levels in the bureaucratic system in increasing proportions. In many respects Weber was right. Communication comes down through a bureaucracy, and thus each higher level can know more. Knowledge that is idiosyncratic to the particular organization—knowledge of rules and information related to strategic decision making—is clearly a function of hierarchical position. But Weber failed to reckon with the organizational value of professional knowledge (legal, scientific, medical, and the like), which enters the organization through professional components and often at relatively low levels. Under such circumstances a hierarchical superior may be expert on strictly organizational issues, but not on professional knowledge relevant to the concern.

Blau recognized this problem and viewed professional authority as a separate entity that need not vary with bureaucratic variables such as the specialized division of labor. Certainly, there are marked similarities between bureaucratic and professional systems—impersonality, rational decision making, and an emphasis on technical expertness. But there are many differences also. In stressing the differences and noting the potential sources of conflict between the two types of authority Blau departs significantly from Weber's theory.

At the same time Blau (1973) did use bureaucratic concepts in his analysis of colleges and universities, just as the Aston researchers did. Heydebrand (1990) contends that in so doing Blau introduced a number of inconsistencies and anomalies that are at variance with the very nature of bureaucracy. There is indeed reason to believe that Blau did not fully resolve the theoretical problems to be found at the interface between bureaucratic and professional systems.

Differentiation in Organizations

Building on the results of a study of governmental employment security units, Blau developed a largely deductive theory of differentiation in organizations that primarily extends Weber's position rather than opposes it. Differentiation occurs when the number of geographical branches, occupational positions, hierarchical levels, and divisions, or units within branches or divisions, increases. The hypotheses are:

1. Increasing size generates structural differentiation in organizations along various dimensions at decelerating rates.
   1A. Large size promotes structural differentiation.
   1B. Large size promotes differentiation along several different lines.
   1C. The rate of differentiation declines with expanding size.
      1.1. As the size of organizations increases, its marginal influence on differentiation decreases.
      1.2. The larger an organization is, the larger is the average size of its structural components of all kinds.
      1.3. The proportionate size of the average structural component, as distinguished from the absolute size, decreases with increases in organizational size.
      1.4. The larger the organization is, the wider the supervisory span of control.
      1.5. Organizations exhibit an economy of scale in management.
      1.6. The economy of scale in administrative overhead itself declines with increasing organizational size.

2. Structural differentiation in organizations enlarges the administrative component.

    2.1. The large size of an organization indirectly raises the ratio of administrative personnel through the structural differentiation it generates.

    2.2. The direct effects of large organizational size lowering the administrative ratio exceed its indirect effects raising it owing to the structural differentiation it generates.

    2.3 The differentiation of large organizations into subunits stems the decline in the economy of scale in management with increasing size. (Blau 1974, 302–17)

These propositions have been restated more recently as follows:

First, the large size of organizations increases their differentiation in various dimensions at decelerating rates. This is the case whether the division of labor, vertical levels, horizontal subdivisions, or other forms of differentiation are examined. For every form of differentiation, in other words, the size of an organization is positively related to the extent of differentiation, but all these correlations are most pronounced for smaller organizations and become increasingly attenuated for those in the larger size range. In mathematical terms, the influence of size on differentiation is indicated by a polynomial with a positive main and a negative squared term.

Second, large size reduces administrative overhead (the proportion of administrative personnel), which implies an administrative economy of scale. Third, degree of differentiation, which entails greater structural complexity, is positively related to administrative overhead. Finally, large size directly reduces yet indirectly (mediated by its influence on differentiation) increases administrative overhead; but the direct negative exceeds the indirect positive effect on administrative cost; this produces the net negative effect that finds expression in the administrative economy of scale.

The theory seeks to explain why the rate of differentiation with the increasing size of organizations declines for larger organizations. The inference made is that the feedback effect of the rising administrative cost of increasing organizational differentiation, and hence complexity, with growing size are responsible. To sustain the economy of scale in administrative cost from which large organizations benefit, they must not become so differentiated that the administrative cost of complexity absorbs this economy of scale; this is effected by dampening the influence of expanded size on enhancing differentiation and complexity. (Blau 1995, 12)

The theory as stated is deductively derived, but the deductive process starts with an induction from the Blau and Schoenherr (1971) research finding that organizational membership size is highly correlated with the extent of differentiation (Slater 1985).

Decentralization in Bureaucracies

Blau (1974) makes a distinction between managing through direct and indirect controls. Direct control involves close observation and corrective orders. Indirect control relies more on impersonal procedures that automatically limit behavior. Examples of indirect controls are automation and personnel merit standards. Clearly, indirect control has been expedited with the aid of computers. Direct control reflects centralization, while indirect control indicates standardization or formalization.

Weber may be interpreted to the effect that centralization and formalization both increase with greater bureaucratization; the two go together. Blau (1970b) proposes, however, that formalization through indirect controls actually restricts the manager and serves as a means of decentralization. In this view direct and indirect control are alternatives, and define two different types of bureaucracies. Modern bureaucracies stress the formalization of indirect control and are more decentralized.

Whether this is a true departure from Weber depends on whether one interprets the use of indirect controls as formalization or simply as another type of authority. Comments by discussants following the presentation of Blau's (1970b) paper reflect uncertainty on this point and raise questions of construct validity for the Weber theory. Note that this is an area in which the Aston theory ran into difficulty as well. In any event, Blau's theory of alternative control procedures can stand on its own merits.

EVALUATION AND IMPACT

Much of the research on Blau's theorizing was conducted by Blau himself in conjunction with others. These studies were all cross-sectional in nature. However, a body of research does exist that goes beyond this, in that others not directly involved with the theory have conducted the studies and changes over time have been considered.

Blau's Comparative Studies

Blau's (1955) early research focused on informal relationships within individual bureaucracies, such as consultations between federal enforcement agents on different problems, even when this practice was officially proscribed. However, his most important contributions to the theory of bureaucracy are comparative analyses across multiple organizations (Blau and Schoenherr 1971; Blau 1974; Blau, Falbe, McKinley, and Tracy 1976). Blau assumed that bureaucratic characteristics are actually variables and that therefore real-world (as contrasted with ideal type) bureaucracies are bureaucratic to varying degrees.

The theory of organizational differentiation evolved from a study of employment security units, so that study cannot be used to test the theory. However, subsequent research on samples drawn from government finance departments, department stores, universities and colleges, teaching hospitals (Blau 1974), and manufacturing plants (Blau, Falbe, McKinley, and Tracy 1976) consistently supports the theoretical hypotheses across all types of differentiation. The role of size in organizational structure appears to be important, and correlations with differentiation are substantial, rising as high as the 0.80s in certain instances. This is consistent with the Aston findings.

Clearly, Weber viewed size as a major correlate of bureaucracy, though he did not rule out bureaucratization of small organizations. Weber's predominant position on centralization appears to be that it occurs in conjunction with bureaucracy; yet, some of Weber's statements may be and have been interpreted differently on occasion. This makes the relationship between centralization and other indexes of bureaucratization, such as formalization and control, particularly important. Blau and Schoenherr's (1971) research has addressed this issue.

The data from state employment agencies shown in Table 16.1 indicate a generally negative relationship, in that increases in formalization are accompanied by *less* centralization. The only meaningful exceptions relate to hiring decisions, in which there is a tendency for more standardized performance ratings and more managers (more control) to be associated

Table 16.1

Correlations Between Various Indexes of Formalization or Control and Indexes of Centralization in State Employment Agencies

	Centralization			
Formalization or control	Of hiring decisions	Of budget proposals	Of organization change decisions	Of other decisions
Extent of personal rules and regulations	−0.18	−0.34*	−0.10	−0.19
Number of civil service appointments	−0.02	0.05	−0.18	−0.33*
Extent of computerization	−0.34*	−0.29*	−0.22	−0.12
Degree of standardization of performance ratings	0.27*	0.07	−0.09	−0.28*
Proportion of managers	0.29*	0.22	0.07	−0.29*

Source: Adapted from Blau and Schoenherr (1971, 416–17).
*Correlations statistically significant.

with more centralization. Blau and Schoenherr (1971) conclude that top management needs to decentralize decisions as the organization grows and the levels of hierarchy increase, but that top management actually does this only when the risks of decentralization can be minimized. The indirect control made possible by standardized procedures, rules, computerized systems, and the like becomes a necessary condition for moving decisions downward. These results certainly go beyond Weber.

Early External Research on Differentiation Theory

Blau (1995) concludes from his own research on organizations of varied types that, irrespective of type, (1) large organizations are more differentiated than small, (2) large organizations have less administrative overhead than small ones, and (3) more differentiation raises administrative overhead. These conclusions are consistent with theory, but they derive from cross-sectional studies only. They may be diagrammed as follows:

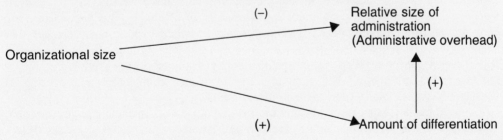

Blau (1995) recognizes, however, that evidence from other sources, using different approaches, does not always support these conclusions. It is to this evidence, particularly that accumulated up to the early 1980s, that we now turn.

It seems apparent that the strong positive correlation involving size and differentiation has been found often enough to be taken seriously. There have been exceptions, as Hall (2001) notes. However, these are most likely to occur when measures based on perceptual rather than objective data are used, and when the studies include organizations that have large nonbureaucratic components (professional, voluntary). There is a problem as to the direction of causation also. A number of investigators, among whom Meyer (1982) is typical, indicate that size increases may well result from a proliferation of hierarchic levels and specialized subunits, rather than the reverse.

As to the negative correlation between size and administrative overhead, the results of numerous studies are mixed. Travers (1978) reviewed twenty-seven such studies and could not identify any consistent pattern. There certainly are some substantial negative relationships that have been established in particular investigations, but these are matched by equally large positive correlations, and a number of nonsignificant findings as well. Travers believes the major factor contributing to this inconsistent pattern is the extreme variation of operationalizations of administrative overhead, and of size as well. In both instances, certain peripheral groups such as unpaid members, part-time employees, seasonal workers, and the like may or may not be included. The problem appears to be inherent in the lack of clearly defined theoretical constructs.

Furthermore, and perhaps even more important, is the fact that the studies reviewed contained extremely diverse types of organizations. Only half of the studies focused on distinctly bureaucratic samples of organizations in business and government. The others utilized schools, colleges and universities, and voluntary organizations that contained sizable components of a nonbureaucratic nature; these latter components were not excluded from the analyses. In spite of Blau's (1995) contention that his theory applies widely to organizations of any type, it seems quite possible that it is limited to the domain of bureaucratic systems. If so, this could well account for the inconsistent results.

Regarding the relationship between differentiation and administrative overhead, Blau's research clearly established a positive correlation. Subsequent studies have not typically dealt with this segment of the theory, perhaps because the results were viewed as self-evident. However, nothing that would challenge Blau's positions appeared in the early period.

Longitudinal Studies

Like the Aston researchers, Blau utilized cross-sectional studies in his own investigations. However, the two theories differ in that the Blau formulations have sparked longitudinal investigations by others. A certain amount of research of this nature was published in the early period. However, research designs have improved steadily, and some of the later contributions have been much more definitive in their findings. These studies do not directly test hypotheses advanced by Blau, since organizational growth and decline were not explicitly included in his formulations. Yet, implicitly, the theory does seem to apply to the processes of change that get organizations to their current status.

One significant finding from this longitudinal line of research is that not merely size, but organizational age and change in size affect organizational restructuring processes (Baker and Cullen 1993). Current size is the best predictor of restructuring, but it is joined in important ways by the period over which the organization has survived and by periods of growth and decline. These results were obtained in a study of colleges and universities.

Going beyond the prediction of restructuring, Cullen, Anderson, and Baker (1986) look at the relationships among the three theoretical variables of the differentiation theory under conditions of change in a sample of universities. The results for periods of decline in size were as follows:

1. Differentiation decreased in 60 percent of the universities, but sometimes proportionately slower than the decline, and subunits were added in some cases.
2. Administrative staff decreases occurred with either greater or less than proportional reductions in roughly 40 percent of the universities, but more typical was an actual increase in administrative overhead.
3. Decreasing differentiation did not lead to a decrease in administrative staff; on the contrary, over 50 percent of the universities added administrators with reduced differentiation. (222–24)

These results are interpreted as running contrary to Blau's theory in all three instances. The results for periods of growth were no more encouraging, although cross-sectional analyses did replicate Blau's findings, and the theory, in most respects. Accordingly, the theory is interpreted as a theory of scale, but not of change. Interestingly, it also appears to apply under conditions of very rapid organizational growth. The failure to support theory insofar as size–administrative relationships (#2 above) are concerned has also been found in school districts (Ford 1980). There is something of a ratchet mechanism involved here.

A study by McKinley (1987) looked into the differentiation–administrative overhead relationship specifically, and did so in a clearly bureaucratic context of manufacturing firms. Under conditions of decline in size the theory once again was not confirmed; the expected strong positive relationship was no longer in evidence when decline occurred.

Finally, there is compelling evidence that size can be a consequence of changes in organization resulting in differentiation (Meyer, Stevenson, and Webster 1985). Thus, the counter-theoretical position that had been advocated previously now appears to be correct. The evidence comes from a study of financial components in three city governments over many years. Apparently, adding components drives the size of the organization upward somewhat later. This does not always happen, but it is the more likely situation.

Critiques of Blau's Theory

In reviewing the evidence on differentiation theory, Bluedorn (1993) concludes that the major challenge to the theory comes from longitudinal studies such as those just considered. These studies raise questions that move well beyond the content of the original theory, and in fact indicate that a more comprehensive theory dealing with change as well as scale is now needed.

Donaldson (1996, 2001) interprets Blau's theory and research as consistent with structural contingency theory and accordingly endorses the theory of differentiation. In the process he reviews a number of countervailing studies and offers arguments to refute them. In addition, he presents the results of a meta-analysis covering some seventeen studies (eight of them the Blau studies) on the size–administrative overhead relationship. This meta-analysis yields an average correlation of –0.45, consistent with theory, but heavily weighted by the results from Blau's research on government organizations.

The review by Donaldson (1996) fails to treat a number of the longitudinal studies that I have included in the previous section primarily because they seem to me to have something new and important to say; he does consider other longitudinal studies, however. The meta-analysis of the relationship between size and administrative overhead is heavily weighted with Blau's own research and appears to incorporate at most three of the twenty-seven studies on the subject reviewed by Travers (1978). Of the nine studies included that do not derive from the Blau research program, four yield positive correlations and five negative.

Argyris (1972), in contrast to Donaldson, takes a negative position on Blau's theory and research. He emphasizes Blau's failure to consider the informal organization (although Blau [1955] had done this in his dissertation). He also takes issue with the way in which variables were operationalized in the research (using official descriptions of organization structures) on the grounds that these may well be invalid. To some extent Blau has answered Argyris's arguments with his research outside the civil service context. On one point, however, this is clearly not the case. Blau's theory of differentiation specifies causal influences from size to the structural variables. However, his tests of the theory are cross-sectional, rather than longitudinal, and thus do not bear directly on the causal hypotheses. Clearly, additional research is needed that considers what organizations do as they increase in size and what temporal relationships are involved. As we have seen, this early criticism has been answered by more recent longitudinal tests of the theory, but not entirely to the satisfaction of the theory's advocates.

Turner (1977) takes Blau to task on philosophical grounds, questioning the role of explanation and Blau's claim to deductive rigor. This critique is aimed as much at all the theoretical approaches of modern sociology as at Blau's theory specifically. It fails to deal with the argument that, irrespective of its construction or its level of explanation, a theory that generates empirical support and deals with important questions may be valuable as a source of understanding, prediction, and/or control.

Blau's views of professional knowledge and decentralization have received considerable support. There is also reason, based on the research, to favor his concept of bureaucratic theory as a set of interrelated hypotheses over the ideal type construction proposed by Weber. Blau raises certain questions regarding Weber's handling of democratic or collegial systems as opposed to bureaucracy. Such systems, like the professional, appear to be different, and there is substantial evidence to support this position. In view of this situation, the next step in research would seem to require disentangling bureaucratic systems from other types of systems to carry out tests of bureaucratic theories, such as Blau's and that of the Aston researchers, in organizations that are predominantly bureaucratic in nature, or in the bureaucratic components of mixed organizations.

A final point has been raised by Scott (1990). His view is that structures are often determined not by size, but by cultural forces such as belief systems, laws, and regulatory frameworks, as well as professional norms and pressures to conform to existing modal models. Thus size arguments must compete with a variety of alternative explanations. To evaluate these claims, comparative research beyond what has been considered here is needed.

Application

Almost everything that has been said with regard to the Aston theory is equally applicable to Blau's theory of differentiation and his related views. These are both theories for organization planning and for designing organization structures. They yield useful measures that can be used to diagnose current organization structures and to change them. To the extent the theories have been found valid, they should be followed in structuring and restructuring bureaucratic systems. Research on Blau's theory suggests that, in periods of organizational decline in particular, bureaucracies may remain overstructured in ways that are costly and may even threaten organizational survival. This is something that those who design organizations may find useful to keep in mind and consider as their organizations undergo change.

STRUCTURAL CONTINGENCY THEORY

Structural contingency theory draws heavily upon Blau's theory and in important respects is an outgrowth of the Aston theorizing. Although it is endorsed in varying degrees, from mildly to quite strongly, by a number of scholars (see, for example, Pennings 1992 and Vibert 2004), the major advocate who has done the most to systematize the approach is Lex Donaldson. It is not featured here as a distinct theory because it fails to meet the requirements for being established as "essential," but it does require some discussion because of its ties to the theory of differentiation.

Donaldson was mentioned previously as one of the third generation of Aston scholars. He worked with John Child and to a lesser extend Derek Pugh at Aston and at the London Business School, where he received his doctorate, but he never published with Pugh. He has been in Australia for many years at the University of New South Wales in the Australian Graduate School of Management. Although he has been primarily a theorist and critic, he has published several reports of his own research related to structural contingency theory (Donaldson 1982, 1987).

Scope and Coverage

Structural contingency theory is rooted in the contingency approach as treated in numerous previous chapters in this volume as well as in this chapter. Which specific theories are involved has not been consistently indicated, a situation that may be related to the fact that the theory has changed somewhat through a number of statements and restatements.

Initially Donaldson (1985) appears to have had the Aston theory in mind, when he discussed structural contingency theory, and thus the contingency variables of size, dependence, and technology. Beginning in 1995 he stressed a much wider range of contingency and systems theorists, although the listing continued to vary from statement to statement. The definitive position at present appears to be that of Donaldson (2001). There the contingencies marshaled are as follows (with their theories, as well as my estimated validity for each):

	Validity
Task uncertainty	
Burns and Stalker (Chapter 12)	2
Hage (Defined by Donaldson 2001 as similar to Burns and Stalker)	—
Lawrence and Lorsch (Chapter 13)	3
Technology	
Perrow (see Miner 2002)	2
Thompson (Chapter 11)	3
Woodward (see Miner 2002)	1
Size	
Aston group (Chapter 15)	4
Blau (this chapter)	4
Strategy	
Chandler (see Miner 1982)	—
Mean for seven theories rated	2.7

The validity data are considered later in discussing the evaluation of structural contingency theory.

In other contexts strategy is defined as the overarching contingency factor (Donaldson 2000) governing all others. Yet Chandler's theory of strategy and structure is much more a part of the strategic management field than of organizational behavior, and consequently is not considered in this volume. It is discussed at length in Miner (1982) in a manner commensurate with the approach used in this book and much of the research on it is considered there also. Donaldson's selection of strategy and structure theory seems somewhat strange in that the theory is not nearly as closely identified with organizational behavior as others that might have been chosen, and the introduction of strategy (read choice) as a contingency variable creates certain problems for the theory. A major consideration appears to have been the relevance of Donaldson's (1987) own research on the subject.

Donaldson (2001) takes all of these theories to be supported by the research evidence and thus to be valid theoretical positions. In his prior treatments of some of these theories, however, he has been less inclined to endorse them.

Statements of the Theory

The theory views the organization as adaptive in its structuring to the particular states of the contingency variables. Changes in structure occur incrementally to achieve this adaptation. The causal flow is clearly stated to be from contingency factor to structural factor; there is no equivocating in this regard. Furthermore, it takes a fit between contingency and structural variables to achieve positive outcomes. When the two are out of fit, organizational performance will suffer. A structural adaptation to regain fit occurs as follows:

1. There is . . . a fit between the organizational structure and the contingency which affects organizational performance.
2. There is the idea that a change by the organization in its contingency variables causes it to move from fit to misfit.
3. There is the idea that misfit causes structural change.
4. There is also the idea . . . that the organization by changing its organization structure moves from misfit into fit. (Donaldson 1995, 33)

At stage 2 the misfit eventually operates to degrade performance. This triggers an incremental process of structural change to adapt to the new contingency state. The structural changes are in degree of bureaucratization, divisionalization, organicness and the like, depending on the contingency variable involved. Yet whether this gradually evolving process truly describes the realities of structural change is subject to considerable question (Nickerson and Zenger 2002).

According to Donaldson (1995), structural contingency theory is the base onto which aspects of other theories may be added to fill in holes in the structural contingency formulations; thus a single theory of organization, at least at the macro level, is created. The result is an overarching theoretical integration, which the field needs at the present time. Newer theories would contribute only in limited and localized ways, building on the central core of structural contingency theory.

In discussing the theory thus created, Donaldson (1996) sets forth six characteristics:

1. It is *nomothetic,* meaning that the phenomena are analyzed using a general framework, with factors that apply to all organizations, both for the contingency factors (such as size and strategy) and for the organizational structure (like specialization and centralization). General causal relationships in the form of lawlike regularities are sought between contingency and structural factors.

2. The research associated with the theory is *methodologically positivist* in that there is much use of comparative empirical research, often with the measurement of variables and statistical analysis of data.
3. The theory explains organizational structure by *material factors* such as size, technology, and so on, rather than by ideationalist factors such as ideas, ideologies, perceptions, norms, and the like.
4. The theory is *deterministic* in that managers are seen as having to adopt the organizational structure that is required by the contingency factors in order to gain organizational effectiveness.
5. The theory is closely *informed by empirical research* rather than armchair speculation or extended theorizing prior to empirical data collection.
6. The theory is consciously scientific in style, with *the aim being to produce scientific knowledge of the type achieved in the natural sciences.* (3)

Structural contingency theory utilizes objective *determinism* to state the causal flow from contingency variables to structural. It utilizes *functionalism* and thus holds that structure is determined ultimately by functional necessity and the drive for organizational effectiveness. It utilizes *Cartesianism* in that organizations are seen as taking many different positions in multidimensional space; thus, it employs continuous variables rather than types of organizations. It assumes that *generalization* is possible, desirable, and can be demonstrated for organizational structures. In this regard Donaldson (2003) takes issue with the proponents of postmodernism.

The contingency variables emphasized by the theory have changed in different presentations. Another area of change is determinism and its alternative—human choice. At an early point Donaldson adopted a view much like that of Child (1972) that incorporated strategic choice in the contingency process. Over time this has changed to a strict determinism or imperative (comparable to the technological imperative view, but extrapolated to all contingency factors). It thus extends well beyond the original Aston view that contingency factors set constraints on managerial discretion. Causation from structure to contingency, and thus the idea of a proactive organization producing changes in its environment, is rejected.

This position, of course, creates problems vis-à-vis previous statements regarding the role of strategy as a contingency variable. His position now is to define Chandler's growth strategy as simply diversification (Donaldson 2001). This interpretation appears to depart from Chandler, from Child's (1997) position, and from established understandings in the field of strategic management.

Donaldson also recognizes a problem around the concept of fit when multiple contingency variables are involved; this is the matter of what he calls Cartesianism. In Donaldson (2001) he develops a complex argument conceptually linking the various types of contingencies espoused by the theories he endorses. However, he does not present empirical data, such as correlations, on the relationships involved. Apparently he assumes some degree of variation among the various contingency factors; accordingly, he recommends that all operative contingencies be combined additively. Yet in providing an example he indicates that one contingency should be utilized in part of the structure and another in a different part. It is not at all clear where the different contingencies should be applied to obtain optimum fit and why this represents an additive fit. This whole matter of multiple fits is crucial to the theory; it is badly in need of conceptual clarification and empirical verification. However, research in this vein to date often has presented daunting obstacles (see Harris 2004).

Evaluation and Impact

The deliberate narrowing of the field of study and approaches to it, as well as the simplification of theory that Donaldson advocates—in fact the whole idea of a core supertheory to which other theories become secondary—have not gone unchallenged. Critics have converged on this narrowing aspect of structural contingency theory from a variety of directions and philosophical perspectives (see, for example, Aldrich 1988; Clegg 1988; Child 1988). The consensus appears to be that we are not yet at a point in macro organizational behavior where we can afford to forego innovation, creativity, and the development of new ideas; perhaps we never will be. To put blinders on numerous theoretical positions and approaches to theory development before testing has occurred does not appear likely to yield benefits equal to the potential costs. Reducing the great variety of theoretical positions is laudable only after the theories have been created and found wanting in the crucible of research, not before the theories are born. If structural contingency theory is indeed the supertheory, then research will establish it as such, when studied in comparison to other positions.

This brings us to the validity of the theory. Since structural contingency theory is in large part a composite of contingency theories already considered, the evidence on these theories is relevant. Donaldson consistently claims substantial support for these theories, while admitting to several problem areas. The evidence presented in the last few chapters is not nearly as forgiving. The theories typically have research support in certain respects, but there are other areas of major failure and a goodly ground that has not been investigated.

A particularly weak feature in the research on contingency theories is the tie between structural fit and outcomes. Research support in this area has been far less frequent than might be desired, as Donaldson (1995) recognizes. Also, the very limited support for the Burns and Stalker formulations (Chapter 12) has been acknowledged by Donaldson (1995). The ratchet mechanism, which research appears to support, would seem to argue that when organizational size decreases, and a misfit with structure is created, the original high structuring is often maintained, not reduced to regain fit as the theory would predict. All in all one must question the overwhelming research validation of the theory that Donaldson claims; at no point does he work through the various contingency theories citing the evidence and weighing it, as has been done in the chapters of this book.

When this is done here, the results are as noted previously. The validity evaluations range from 1 to 4; only in the case of size (the Aston and the Blau theories) are they strongly supportive. The mean rating for the seven theories on which evaluations are available is 2.7—not a particularly strong showing for the contingency theories Donaldson (2001) has most recently marshaled to his cause.

As the same time, more positive statements should be acknowledged. A review of Donaldson's (2001) book, which appears to be the magnum opus on structural contingency theory, is quite laudatory (Meeus 2002), and indeed the arguments presented there are often complex and thought provoking. On the empirical side, a recent laboratory study using teams, not organizations, demonstrated that fit between the predictability of the environment and structure (divisional or functional) was a strong predictor of performance (Hollenbeck, Moon, Ellis, West, Ilgen, Sheppard, Porter, & Wagner 2002). Thus, the link between structural fit and the outcomes aspect of structural contingency theory is validated at least in this particular experimental setting.

CONCLUSIONS

Returning to the earlier part of this chapter, and the treatment of the theory of differentiation, Blau's theory receives an importance rating of 4.31. Organization behavior scholars appear to judge his theory, that from Aston, and structural contingency theory at essentially the same level. The validity rating, at four stars, has already been noted. This is commensurate with the same evaluation applied to the Aston theory and exists for much the same reason—research that is largely supportive conducted by the author(s) and by others. The estimated usefulness, at three stars, also follows Aston. Again it is the development and presentation of measuring instruments that can be used in designing organizations that accounts for this result. At the same time, one could wish that more had been done to facilitate the organizational planning process.

Now we turn to a group of theories that place their primary emphasis not on the positive features of bureaucracy but on the dysfunctions. These latter are viewed as so overriding that bureaucracy must be destroyed as an organizational form. In Chapter 17 I take up the theoretical perspectives endorsed by Chris Argyris, extending from the early 1950s to the present (Argyris 2004).

REFERENCES

Aldrich, Howard (1988). Paradigm Warriors: Donaldson versus the Critics of Organization Theory. *Organization Studies,* 9, 19–25.

Argyris, Chris (1972). *The Applicability of Organizational Sociology.* Cambridge, UK: Cambridge University Press.

———. (2004). *Reasons and Rationalizations: The Limits to Organizational Knowledge.* Oxford, UK: Oxford University Press.

Baker, Douglas D., and Cullen, John B. (1993). Administrative Reorganization and Configurational Context: The Contingent Effects of Age, Size, and Change in Size. *Academy of Management Journal,* 36, 1251–77.

Blau, Peter M. (1955). *The Dynamics of Bureaucracy: A Study of Interpersonal Relations in Two Government Agencies.* Chicago, IL: University of Chicago Press.

———. (1956). *Bureaucracy in Modern Society.* New York: Random House.

———. (1970a). A Formal Theory of Differentiation in Organizations. *American Sociological Review,* 35, 201–18.

———. (1970b). Decentralization in Bureaucracies. In Mayer N. Zald (Ed.), *Power in Organizations.* Nashville, TN: Vanderbilt University Press, 150–74.

———. (1973). *The Organization of Academic Work.* New York: Wiley.

———. (1974). *On the Nature of Organizations.* New York: Wiley.

———. (1995). A Circuitous Path to Macrostructural Theory. *Annual Review of Sociology,* 21, 1–19.

Blau, Peter M., Falbe, Cecilia M., McKinley, William, and Tracy, Phelps K. (1976). Technology and Organization in Manufacturing. *Administrative Science Quarterly,* 21, 20–40.

Blau, Peter M., and Schoenherr, Richard A. (1971). *The Structure of Organizations.* New York: Basic Books.

Blau, Peter M., and Scott, W. Richard (1962). *Formal Organizations: A Comparative Approach.* San Francisco, CA: Chandler.

Bluedorn, Allen C. (1993). Pilgrim's Progress: Trends and Convergence in Research on Organizational Size and Environments. *Journal of Management,* 19, 163–91.

Calhoun, Craig, and Scott, W. Richard (1990). Introduction: Peter Blau's Sociological Structuralism. In Craig Calhoun, Marshall W. Meyer, and W. Richard Scott (Eds.), *Structures of Power and Constraint: Papers in Honor of Peter M. Blau.* Cambridge, UK: Cambridge University Press, 1–36.

Child, John (1972). Organizational Structure, Environment and Performance—the Role of Strategic Choice. *Sociology,* 6, 1–22.

———. (1988). On Organizations in Their Sectors. *Organization Studies,* 9, 13–19.

———. (1997). Strategic Choice in the Analysis of Action, Structure, Organizations and Environment: Retrospect and Prospect. *Organization Studies,* 18, 43–76.

Clegg, Stewart R. (1988). The Good, The Bad, and The Ugly. *Organization Studies,* 9, 7–13.

Cullen, John B., Anderson, Kenneth S., and Baker, Douglas D. (1986). Blau's Theory of Structural Differentiation Revisited: A Theory of Structural Change or Scale? *Academy of Management Journal,* 29, 203–29.

Donaldson, Lex (1982). Divisionalization and Diversification: A Longitudinal Study. *Academy of Management Journal,* 25, 909–14.

———. (1985). *In Defense of Organization Theory: A Reply to the Critics.* Cambridge, UK: Cambridge University Press.

———. (1987). Strategy and Structural Adjustment to Regain Fit and Performance: In Defense of Contingency Theory. *Journal of Management Studies,* 24, 1–24.

———. (1995). *American Anti-Management Theories of Organization: A Critique of Paradigm Proliferation.* Cambridge, UK: Cambridge University Press.

———. (1996). *For Positivist Organization Theory: Proving the Hard Core.* London: Sage.

———. (2000). Design Structure to Fit Strategy. In Edwin A. Locke (Ed.), *The Blackwell Handbook of Principles of Organizational Behavior.* Oxford, UK: Blackwell, 291–303.

———. (2001). *The Contingency Theory of Organizations.* Thousand Oaks, CA: Sage.

———. (2003). A Critique of Postmodernism in Organizational Studies. In Edwin A. Locke (Ed.), *Postmodernism and Management: Pros, Cons, and the Alternative.* Oxford, UK: Elsevier Science, 169–202.

Ford, Jeffrey D. (1980). The Administrative Component in Growing and Declining Organizations: A Longitudinal Analysis. *Academy of Management Journal,* 23, 615–30.

Hall, Richard H. (2001). *Organizations: Structures, Processes, and Outcomes.* Englewood Cliffs, NJ: Prentice Hall.

Harris, Randall D. (2004). Organizational Task Environments: An Evaluation of Convergent and Discriminant Validity. *Journal of Management Studies,* 41, 857–82.

Heydebrand, Wolf (1990). The Technocratic Organization of Academic Work. In Craig Calhoun, Marshall W. Meyer, and W. Richard Scott (Eds.), *Structures of Power and Constraint: Papers in Honor of Peter M. Blau.* Cambridge, UK: Cambridge University Press, 271–320.

Hollenbeck, John R., Moon, Henry, Ellis, Aleksander P.J., West, Bradley, J., Ilgen, Daniel R., Sheppard, Lori, Porter, Christopher O.L.H., and Wagner, John A. (2002). Structural Contingency Theory and Individual Differences: Examination of External and Internal Person-Team Fit. *Journal of Applied Psychology,* 87, 599–606.

McKinley, William (1987). Complexity and Administrative Intensity: The Case of Declining Organizations. *Administrative Science Quarterly,* 32, 87–105.

Meeus, Marius T.H. (2002). Review of Lex Donaldson's *The Contingency Theory of Organizations. Organization Studies,* 23, 986.

Merton, Robert K. (1990). Epistolary Notes on the Making of a Sociological Dissertation Classic: *The Dynamics of Bureaucracy.* In Craig Calhoun, Marshall W. Meyer, and W. Richard Scott (Eds.), *Structures of Power and Constraint: Papers in Honor of Peter M. Blau* Cambridge, UK: Cambridge University Press, 37–66.

Meyer, Marshall W. (1982). Bureaucratic Versus Profit Organization. *Research in Organizational Behavior,* 4, 89–125.

Meyer, Marshall W., Stevenson, William, and Webster, Stephen (1985). *Limits to Bureaucratic Growth.* New York: Walter de Gruyter.

Miner, John B. (1982). *Theories of Organizational Structure and Process.* Hinsdale, IL: Dryden—Chapter 10, pp. 293–320.

———. (2002). *Organizational Behavior: Foundations, Theories, and Analyses.* New York: Oxford University Press.

Nickerson, Jack A., and Zenger, Todd R. (2002). Being Efficiently Fickle: A Dynamic Theory of Organizational Choice. *Organization Science,* 13, 547–66.

Pennings, Johannes M. (1992). Structural Contingency Theory: A Reappraisal. *Research in Organizational Behavior,* 14, 267–309.

Scott, W. Richard (1990). Introduction to Part II: Formal Organization. In Craig Calhoun, Marshall W. Meyer, and W. Richard Scott (Eds.), *Structures of Power and Constraint: Papers in Honor of Peter M. Blau.* Cambridge, UK: Cambridge University Press, 181–89.

Slater, Robert O. (1985). Organizational Size and Differentiation. *Research in the Sociology of Organizations,* 4, 127–80.

Travers, Henry J. (1978). *Organization: Size and Intensity.* Washington, DC: University Press of America.

Turner, Stephen P. (1977). Blau's Theory of Differentiation: Is It Explanatory? In J. Kenneth Benson (Ed.), *Organizational Analysis: Critique and Innovation.* Beverly Hills, CA: Sage, 19–34.

Vibert, Conor (2004). *Theories of Macro Organizational Behavior: A Handbook of Ideas and Explanations.* Armonk, NY: M.E. Sharpe.

CHAPTER 17

GOAL CONGRUENCE THEORY AND ORGANIZATION DEVELOPMENT

CHRIS ARGYRIS

Importance rating	★ ★ ★ ★
Estimated validity	★ ★ ★
Estimated usefulness	★ ★ ★
Decade of origin	1950s

Organization development is not new to the readers of this volume. Likert (Chapter 8), created an organization development application that derived from his theory of system 4. Trist and Emery and their sociotechnical systems theory (Chapter 10) produced applications that were rapidly absorbed by organization development. Lawrence and Lorsch and their contingency theory of organization (Chapter 13) spawned an organization development intervention approach that, as we have seen, had considerable impact. In this chapter, additional theories that are closely linked to organization development are discussed. These are the theories of Chris Argyris. In this instance, the theorist's ideas led him first to embrace laboratory or sensitivity training as a method of interpersonal skill development, and he subsequently expanded his theories to include the broader arena of organization development. He expresses a strong and continuing emphasis on humanist values, which has caused him to condemn Weber's bureaucracy and the classical management theories of Fayol and Taylor (see Miner 2002a). At least in the early period, Argyris viewed bureaucracy as unacceptable because it deprived participants of their dignity and their capacity for growth. He argued that an alternative organizational form was needed, and organization development was the means to transformation.

BACKGROUND

Born in 1923, Chris Argyris did his undergraduate work in psychology at Clark University, from which he graduated in 1947. After earning a master's degree in psychology and economics at Kansas University, he moved on to the School of Industrial and Labor Relations at Cornell University and obtained his Ph.D. from there in 1951. During this period he appears to have been initially influenced most by Roger Barker and Fritz Heider, and in particular by the action research perspective of Kurt Lewin; all of these people were psychologists. At Cornell, however, his mentor was William Foote Whyte, a sociologist and applied anthropologist (Argyris 1992a). From that time onward he has been something of an all-purpose social scientist with publications in varied fields, but organizational behavior has been a major part of his identity since the field emerged.

From Cornell, Argyris went to Yale University, initially in the Labor and Management Center but later in the administrative sciences department (Putnam 1995). Then in 1971 he moved to Harvard, with appointments in education and business. Throughout the Yale period he was actively involved in the laboratory education movement and in T-groups. He has now retired from Harvard, but continues to write and consult.

An idea of Argyris's somewhat iconoclastic approach to the field may be gained from his stated methodology for research, which is to engage in active intervention within organizations. This intervention approach is guided by three "realizations":

1. The application of knowledge is the most robust empirical test of validity.
2. The rule that scientific research is descriptive can be the basis for limiting its validity and actionability.
3. The methodology for conducting rigorous empirical research is a methodology for controlling ideas and people. (Argyris 1998a, 877)

Clearly this iconoclasm is not the concept of research endorsed in this volume, but it does help explain the case-oriented brand of ethnography, as opposed to more controlled experimental designs, that Argyris has pursued in much of his work.

THE STAGES OF GOAL CONGRUENCE THEORY DEVELOPMENT

During the 1950s, when his goal congruence theory was crystallizing, Argyris was influenced by the thinking of E. Wight Bakke (1950), with whom he worked at the Yale Labor and Management Center. As we will see this influence from Bakke was temporary, however,

Personality and Organization

Argyris's investigation of the effects of budgets on managers reveals the issues with which he was concerned in his early theorizing and the direction of his thinking. Argyris reached

Table 17.1

Developmental Trends to a Mature, Healthy, Self-Actualizing Personality

FROM (as infants)	TO (as adults)
1. A state of passivity	A state of increasing activity
2. A state of dependence on others	A state of relative independence
3. Being capable of behaving in only a few ways	Being capable of behaving in many ways
4. Having erratic, casual, shallow, quickly dropped interests	Having deeper interests
5. Having a short time perspective (primarily in the present)	Having a much larger time perspective (extending into the past and future)
6. A lack of awareness of self	An awareness and control over oneself

Source: Adapted from Argyris (1957, 50).

the following conclusions after extensive, unstructured interviews with financial and operating managers in four manufacturing plants:

1. Budget pressure tends to unite the employees against management, and tends to place the factory supervisor under tension. This tension may lead to inefficiency, aggression, and perhaps a complete breakdown on the part of the supervisor.
2. The finance staff can obtain feelings of success only by finding fault with factory people. The feelings of failure among factory supervisors lead to many human relations problems.
3. The use of budgets as "needlers" by top management tends to make the factory supervisors see only the problems of their own department. . . . They are not "plant-centered" in outlook. (Argyris 1952, 25)

In building a theory to deal with such problems, Argyris first followed Bakke (1950) very closely (Argyris 1954). Subsequently, however, though retaining many of his earlier concepts, he developed goal congruence theory as a distinct entity in its own right (Argyris 1957).

A basic concept of Argyris's theory is that of the healthy adult personality, as distinguished from the personality of an infant or small child. Table 17.1 shows the dimensions of personality that are relevant; the individual's plotted scores (or profile) along these dimensions are equated with self-actualization. Individuals develop or progress to varying degrees along these dimensions. Various forces within society, including organizations, and within the individuals themselves inhibit this process.

A second building block of the theory is the concept of organization as epitomized in classical management theory (and bureaucratic theory). The principles of that theory are accepted as given because "to date no one has defined a more useful set of formal organization principles" (Argyris 1957, 58). Included are the principles of task specialization, chain of command, unity of direction, and span of control.

Such a formal organization is viewed as incongruent with development to a healthy, mature state as set forth in Table 17.1; it operates to inhibit members, forcing them back toward an infantile state. The potential incongruency between the developmental needs of individuals and the requirements of formal organization is exaggerated to the extent that:

1. Employees are more mature than the organization assumes.
2. The organization structure follows classical principles closely.
3. One moves downward in the organization.
4. The jobs approach an assembly line character. (Argyris 1957)

As a result of the incongruency, healthy employees often become passive, dependent, and submissive over time. In the process they experience the kinds of problems Argyris noted in his analysis of the effects of budgets. Frustration, conflict, failure, and a short time perspective prevail. Among other reactions, the employee may leave the organization (only to face the same problems elsewhere), attempt to move to high levels in the organization (though there are few such positions), adapt by resorting to emotional defense mechanisms such as escape from reality and psychosomatic illness, or become apathetic and uninvolved. The employee may also express aggression in the context of the informal work group by restricting output.

In reaction to the high turnover and absenteeism, low productivity, and lack of organizational identification thus produced, management often introduces more controls and becomes more directive. As a result, the undesired behavior is increased.

These processes are summarized in a set of ten basic theoretical propositions:

1. There is a lack of congruency between the needs of healthy individuals and the demands of the formal organization. . . . An administrator, therefore, is always faced with an inherent tendency toward continual disturbance.
2. The resultants of this disturbance are frustration, failure, short-time perspective, and conflict.
3. Under certain conditions the degree of frustration, failure, short-time perspective and conflict will tend to increase (among these conditions are those previously noted—greater employee maturity, structure follows classical principles, etc.).
4. The nature of the formal principles of organization cause the subordinate, at any given level, to experience competition, rivalry, intersubordinate hostility, and to develop a focus toward the parts rather than the whole.
5. The employee adaptive behavior maintains self-integration and impedes integration with the formal organization.
6. The adaptive behavior of the employees has a cumulative effect, feedbacks into the organization, and reinforces itself.
7. Certain management reactions tend to increase the antagonisms underlying the adaptive behavior. . . . These actions tend to be: (1) Increasing the degree of directive leadership. (2) Increasing the degree of management controls. (3) Increasing the number of pseudo human relations programs.
8. Other management actions can decrease the degree of incongruency between the individual and formal organization. . . . One way is to use a new input of individuals who do not aspire to be healthy, mature adults. A second way is to change the nature of the formal organizational structure, directive leadership, and management controls.

... [J]ob and/or role enlargement is one effective method to change the organization structure. . . . [E]mployee-centered leadership is one possible way to modify the directive leadership.

9. Job or role enlargement and employee-centered leadership will not tend to work to the extent that the adaptive behavior has become embedded in the original culture and the self-concept of the individuals.

10. The difficulties involved in proposition 9 may be minimized by the use of reality-oriented leadership (i.e., the leader ought to first diagnose what is reality and then use the appropriate leadership pattern). (Argyris 1957, 233–37)

Integrating the Individual and the Organization

Following the publication of his 1957 volume, Argyris expanded and modified his theory. Though this process appears to have been gradual, the outcome was a new, comprehensive theoretical statement (Argyris 1964). In this book he replaces his maturity or infant–adult dimension with certain formulations regarding psychological energy. Argyris maintains that psychological energy exists in all people, cannot be blocked permanently, and varies with the state of mind of the individual. Furthermore:

> *The potential energy* an individual has available to him will be a function of the degree of self-esteem: the higher the self-esteem the greater the *potential energy*. The actual energy an individual has will be a function of the degree to which he can experience psychological success. Psychological success (and its derivatives of self-esteem, etc.) is therefore defined as the conditions for creating the proper state of mind. (Argyris 1964, 29)

Among other factors, a climate of trust serves to enhance opportunities for psychological success.

In restating his first theoretical proposition on the sources of incongruency, Argyris now substitutes "individuals aspiring for psychological success" for the former "healthy individuals." He no longer uses the specific statements given in Table 17.1. Not everyone desires psychological success, and it is the incongruency between individual needs and organizational form that causes disturbance and unintended consequences (such as passivity, aggression, etc.). This incongruency may result as much from placing a person who does not aspire to psychological success in a context where aspirations of this type are required, as from placing a person who does desire psychological success in the typical pyramidal organization. In any event, wherever such incongruencies exist, people will consume energy, producing unintended consequences of the organizational form, and thus divert energy from organizational goals.

Dropping the maturity dimension set forth in Table 17.1 creates a problem in defining self-actualization, which is retained in the theory. The solution is to view self-actualization as having no specific content. People have a need to actualize themselves that can be identified from their behavior. "The actualization can be in the direction of maturity. . . . However, in this scheme, the actualization could be toward apathy and alienation" (Argyris 1964, 142). This shift to a view of self-actualization as having no set content actually appeared several years earlier and was reflected in a procedure developed for scoring self-actualization as revealed in interviews (Argyris 1959, 1960a).

The next step was to set forth what Argyris (1964) calls the "mix model." Here he proposes that problems associated with incongruency are best overcome by modifying pyramidal organizations to provide more meaningful challenges and opportunities for psychological success. At the same time, individuals must be changed to make them less fearful of the opportunity for psychological success. These and other changes must be made to reduce disturbances and unintended consequences. The mix model presents a set of six hypotheses about how organizations should be changed to achieve these ends and make them "axiologically good," to use Argyris's term.

1. The direction of core activities such as achieving objectives, internal maintenance, and environmental adaptations should be spread in an interrelated manner throughout the organization, rather than concentrated in a single component such as top management.
2. The members of the organization should be aware of the organization as a totality in all its patterned interrelationships, rather than as a random set of parts.
3. The objectives that guide the organization should be those of the whole, rather than of individual components.
4. The organization should be able to influence goal attainment and internal maintenance in accordance with its own desires, rather than lacking influence in these respects.
5. The organization should be able to influence its externally oriented activities in its environment in accordance with its own desires, rather than lacking influence in this respect.
6. The nature of the organization's core activities should be influenced by considerations extending into both the past and the future, rather than being determined only by the present. (Argyris 1964, 151–54)

These hypotheses for integrating organizational and individual goals appear to have much in common with the hypotheses regarding individual development toward health and maturity set forth in Table 17.1 This relationship is in fact made explicit in an earlier statement:

> As long as complex organizations use people, it may be possible that they will tend to obtain greater commitment, flexibility, responsibility, and openness and thereby enhance their chances for survival and growth if they strive to create conditions wherein the individual is able to actualize his potential as much as possible. . . . [A] first step toward integrating the individual and the organization is for both to aspire toward the conditions represented by the axiologically good organization. (Argyris 1962a, 76)

The mix model is a statement of conditions for organizational effectiveness. However, the theory anticipates that the degree to which the organization's structure should fully match these conditions depends on the kinds of decisions to be made. Argyris's statements on organizational structures are given in Table 17.2. He indicates a clear need for varying structures in accordance with decision types. "If one asks the individual in the organization of the future to see the company organizational chart, he will be asked, 'For what type of decision?' In order to accomplish this, 'decision rules' will have to be defined to guide our choice of the proper structure." But the power to choose among structures remains democratic: ". . . the task of defining the decision rules to tell the participants which organization structure should be used under a given set of conditions will be assigned to as many partici-

Table 17.2

Conditions for the Use of Structures Having Varying Degrees of Axiological Goodness

Degree of axiological goodness	Type of organizational structure	Conditions for use
Low ↑	I. Pyramidal	1. When time is important and subordinate acceptance is assured
		2. When decisions are routine and the use of authority is legitimized
		3. When the decision does not affect the distribution of power, reward, controls, work specialization, or the centralization of information
		4. When a large number of people are involved and it is difficult to bring them together
		5. When the individuals do not desire psychological success
	II. Overlapping groups (Likert)	1. When the decision is not routine, but does not affect the distribution of power, control, information, and the specialization of work
		2. When time is important
		3. When the decision to make a change cannot be delegated to all
	III. Power according to functional contribution	Anywhere there are differences in competence. Individuals receive their power according to the perception that other members have of their potential contribution.
	IV. Power according to inevitable organizational responsibilities (each individual has equal power)	1. When decisions involve high responsibility and are basic to the organization
		2. When the decision affects the distribution of power, control, information, and the specialization of work
High		3. When the decision defines rules for the conditions under which a particular structure would be used

Source: Adapted from Argyris (1964, 198–210).

pants as possible. . . . If autocracy is to be used, the use of it will be defined under participative conditions (Structure IV)" (Argyris 1964, 211–12).

Table 17.2 represents Argyris's initial effort to provide guidelines for the participative selection of structures.

The Theory Revisited

In its earliest version, goal congruence theory carried a message that was distinctly anti formal organization. Subsequently, this message was muted somewhat, though it remained in evidence. In the third version (Argyris 1973, 1974a) there is some return to a more militant antiorganizational position.

Actually, by 1972 Argyris had revived the infant–adult dimensions of Table 17.1. While infant individuals in adult organizations and adult individuals in infant organizations both yield incongruence, the latter circumstances represent "the predominant conditions in 'real' life." Argyris presumed congruence between person and organization to be rare (Argyris 1972).

In his later, more formal restatement of the theory, the six infant–adult dimensions of Table 17.1 are reduced to four. These new dimensions are not entirely consistent with those stated previously, especially with regard to the development of abilities. Thus:

> Infants begin as—
> dependent and submissive
> having few abilities
> having shallow abilities
> having a short time perspective
> While adults strive toward—
> independence, autonomy, and control over the immediate world
> developing many abilities
> developing a few abilities in depth
> developing a longer time perspective.
> (Argyris 1973, 142)

Pyramidal organizations now are characterized by specialized and fractionalized work, established production rates and speed of work, order giving, performance evaluation, the use of rewards, and perpetuated membership. These are associated with bureaucracy and scientific management, rather than with classical management theory, as previously stated. The consequences of incongruence for organization members are fighting the organization, leaving it, apathy and indifference, or becoming market- (or pay-) oriented in dealing with the organization. References to upward mobility as a response have been consistently ignored after the first theoretical statements. In tone, the revisited theory is not a great deal different from the original version. However, there are specific variations that require somewhat different empirical tests. In particular, the future of formal organizations is viewed more negatively:

> . . . [N]one of the theories discussed (primarily those of bureaucracy and rational systems), with the exception of personality and organization theory and those similar . . . would predict the single most important trend about public and private organizations, namely, their increasing internal deterioration and lack of effectiveness in producing services or products. (Argyris 1973, 159)

ORGANIZATIONAL LEARNING AND DEFENSIVE ROUTINES

Starting in the mid-1970s, Argyris began to promulgate a view regarding organizational learning that has concerned him over the years since. This view appears to represent a whole new approach, with a new nomenclature, new constructs, and new collaborations. Yet the implicit humanism is still in evidence, and although antibureaucracy statements are less manifest, they are not gone. Furthermore, the goal congruence formulations have never been repudiated. In fact, they reemerge on several occasions. The characteristic infant–adult designation and the concept of psychological success are explicitly endorsed (Argyris 1990), and in several articles Argyris (1994, 1998b) invokes aspects of goal congruence theory to make a point. Thus, the two theories seem to stand side by side, not fully integrated, but still with the same humanistic values behind them and, as we will see, with a similar approach to application (see Argyris 2003).

From the mid-1970s onward Argyris has stated and restated his theory of organizational learning and defensive routines many times, often with the same examples and much the same wording, but with an orientation apparently intended to reach different audiences. Thus his books on the subject have typically been the products of different publishers and are presented with somewhat different thrusts. For example, Argyris (1980) seeks to engage organizational behavior and other social science researchers; Argyris (1982, 1993) speaks to organization development practitioners; Argyris (1985) packages the theory for those in the field of strategic management; Argyris (1990) focuses on managers and managers-to-be, thus coming closest to providing a textbook coverage of the theory; Argyris and Schön (1996) review an earlier statement, now with a strong emphasis on the organizational as opposed to individual nature of the theory; and Argyris (2000) talks to human resource managers who use advice from consultants and gurus. Another volume (Argyris 1992b) brings together a number of articles and book chapters related to the theory, most of them originally published in the period 1975 to 1991. I draw heavily on this source in presenting the theory. In his writings on learning Argyris often collaborated with Donald Schön, formerly a professor at MIT (see Lichtenstein 2000).

Learning and Its Types

Organizational learning is desirable. It is a means to detecting and correcting errors as well as a source of innovation. Important barriers to learning are some types of organizational defenses. These antilearning defenses are represented by policies, practices, or actions that prevent participants in the organization from experiencing embarrassment or threat, and also from discovering the causes of embarrassment or threat. Errors occur as plans and policies reach the implementation phase, and they are present by design rather than because of ignorance; they are designed to protect people from embarrassment and threat, and are thus part of the defensive routine. As Dachler (1994, 463) puts it:

> Argyris has repeatedly shown how hierarchical structures and their emphasis on control . . .
> bring about defensive reactions and therefore limit effective organizational learning. . . .
> [H]e seeks the solution in the "re-education" of (primarily powerful) individuals and in
> changes of structural and policy issues.

In the latter vein, Argyris (1992b, 4) says "social science should . . . pay attention to producing knowledge about virtual worlds that provide liberating alternatives . . . that endow human beings with competencies to reverse and undo the self-fueling, anti-learning, overprotective processes" (the organizational defenses).

An important distinction is made between espoused meaning, or theory, and people's views as reflected when they actually behave, their theories in use. Any real, meaningful behavior change requires changes in people's theories in use and in the learning system of the organization; espoused theories are merely window dressing.

Figure 17.1 sets forth two types of theories in use behind learning that are significant for the theory—single loop and double loop. Single loop learning may occur to a degree when

Figure 17.1 **The Distinction Between Single Loop and Double Loop Learning**

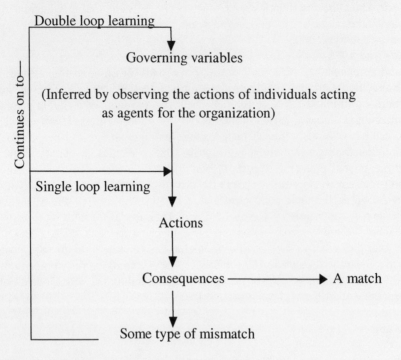

Source: Adapted from Argyris (1992, 8) and other sources by the same author.

matches are created so that the consequences of actions are what was intended. But, more frequently, learning is a result of a mismatch, where actions are corrected through feedback to align with consequences and then create a match; only the actions are changed, not the factors behind the actions. In double loop learning the change is deeper in that the governing variables are changed. The governing variables are those that can be inferred, by observing the actions of individuals acting as agents for the organization (top management), to drive and guide actions of others. Double loop learning is particularly relevant when an issue is complex and nonprogrammable and when the long-range effectiveness of the organization is involved.

When double loop learning is engaged by a mismatch or error, matters of trust and mistrust often arise that make correction difficult. Also, if the focus remains at the single loop level, people may "become servants of the status quo"—a phrase Argyris uses often. Unfreezing the models of organizational structures and processes now in good currency is essential to engage double loop learning. Inherent in the move to double loop learning are problems related to unawareness, suppression of feelings, and the need to alter reasoning processes. Achieving this type of learning is not easy.

Models I and II

According to Argyris, individuals design their actions, and in doing so they bring to bear theories in use that they mobilize for given situations. Under single loop learning conditions this theory in use has the characteristics of what Argyris defines as Model I, although in general people are not aware of this model in themselves. Table 17.3 sets forth Model I in a comprehensive form. Argyris presents this table on numerous occasions in somewhat different forms, although the basic format and message remain the same. Typically these versions represent abbreviations of what is contained in Table 17.3.

Model I tends to inhibit double loop learning, and organizations whose structure is congruent with that model are unlikely to be characterized by double loop learning. Such organizations have a pyramidal form, consisting of specialization of work, unity of command, and centralization of power. These conditions, which are essentially those of bureaucracy, are said to be congruent with the governing variables of Model I.

Model II is not the opposite of Model I, nor does it completely replace Model I. Model I theories in use continue to be appropriate when programmable, routine decisions are involved, and when a crisis must be handled. Furthermore, structural changes congruent with Model II do not actually work unless the individuals involved adopt Model II theories as their own.

Under Model II there is a continuous testing of the status quo. In this respect it has much in common with the basic tenets of postmodernism (Clegg and Kornberger 2003). The model represents an ideal state and involves sharing power with anyone who has relevant competence. People do not move to Model II without help. Argyris is much more tentative in depicting Model II than Model I, and the early publications did not provide a clear picture of it at all. However, Table 17.4 is based on recent statements plus several abbreviated versions proposed earlier. It provides a comprehensive coverage of Model II, comparable to that of Table 17.3 for Model I. Note that a major aspect of Model II is that power is dispersed. It requires unfreezing of a type that permits reexamining underlying values and assumptions at both the individual and organizational levels. For a discussion of Model I and Model II in action, see Roth and Kleiner (2000).

Originally in numerous publications Argyris took the position that only double loop learning and Model II could lead to "liberating alternatives and changing status quo." However, more recently he has come to question that conclusion based on field experience with certain methodologies in areas such as financial reporting:

> I began to observe examples where technical theories that were implemented correctly reduced the likelihood of embarrassment and threat in the first place. The routine single-loop features of technical theories also created liberating alternatives. Although they did not create double-loop learning, it appeared that they prevented the need for double-loop learning in the first place. (Argyris 1996, 80)

It is not clear how widespread Argyris found these exceptions to be.

Individual and Organizational Levels

At many points Argyris presents his ideas in such a way as to suggest he is writing personality theory, not organizational behavior theory. Yet this is not his intent (Crossan 2003). In a number of places he takes pains to differentiate organizational defensive routines from those of individuals. He notes that (1) people behave in a manner consistent with their organization's defensive routines, even though from personality research a much greater diversity of personalities would be expected; (2) although people move in and out of organizations, the

Table 17.3

Model I Theory in Use

Governing variables →	Action strategies →	Behavioral world consequences →	Learning consequences →	Consequences on effectiveness
1. Define goals; achieve them	1. Design and manage the environment unilaterally	1. Actor seen as defensive	1. Self-sealing processes	1. Decreased effectiveness over long term
2. Maximize winning; minimize losing	2. Own and control the task	2. Group and interpersonal relationships defensive	2. Single loop learning	
3. Suppress negative feelings in self and others	3. Protect self unilaterally	3. Defensive norms exist	3. Escalating error	
4. Be rational; minimize emotionality	4. Protect others unilaterally, so they are not hurt	4. Low freedom of choice; little risk taking or commitment	4. Little testing of theories publicly; much testing privately	

Table 17.4

Model II Theory in Use

Governing variables →	Action strategies →	Behavioral world consequences →	Learning consequences →	Consequences on effectiveness
1. Valid and confirmable information	1. Design situations and encounters such that participants can be origins and experience personal causation	1. Actor seen as minimally defensive	1. Reduction of self-fulfilling, self-sealing, error escalating processes	1. Increased effectiveness over long term
2. Free and informed choice	2. Task is jointly controlled	2. Group and interpersonal relationships minimally defensive	2. Double loop learning	
3. Commitment to a choice; monitoring of implementation	3. Protection of self is joint; oriented to growth	3. Learning-oriented norms	3. Frequent public testing of theories	
	4. Protection of others is bilateral	4. High freedom of choice; much risk taking and commitment	4. Effective problem solving	

Figure 17.2 **Organizational Defense Pattern**

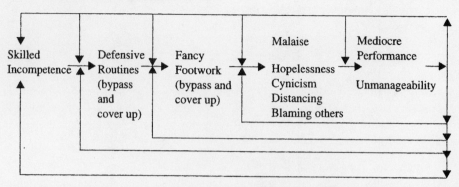

Source: Argyris (1990, 64). Copyright 1990. Reprinted by permission of Pearson Education, Inc.

defensive routines in place do not change over time; (3) the defensive routines appear to have the character of products of socialization; and (4) since the actions used to create or trigger the routines are used by most people, their source cannot be individual psychological anxiety (Argyris 1992b). Thus individuals act as agents for organizations as well as for themselves to produce defensive routines that prevent or distort valid information, are not discussible, and whose undiscussability is not discussible. All this is part of the organization's culture. Such a pattern is depicted in Figure 17.2.

The truly organizational nature of the theory is particularly manifest in Argyris and Schön (1996). There organizational learning is defined in terms that serve to emphasize the level at which the process occurs:

> Organizational learning occurs when individuals within an organization experience a problematic situation and inquire into it on the organization's behalf. They experience a surprising mismatch between expected and actual results of action and respond to that mismatch through a process of thought and further action that leads them to modify their images of organization or their understandings of organizational phenomena and to restructure their activities so as to bring outcomes and expectations into line, thereby changing organizational theory-in-use. In order to become organizational, the learning that results from organizational inquiry must become embedded in the images of organization held in its members' minds and/or in the epistemological artifacts (the maps, memories, and programs) embedded in the organizational environment. (16)
>
> Inquiry becomes organizational when individuals inquire on behalf of the organization, within a community of inquiry governed, formally or informally, by the roles and rules of the organization. (33)

ORGANIZATION DEVELOPMENT APPLICATIONS

Argyris's theoretical views call for a movement to organizational forms that are less formalized, pyramidal, and bureaucratic. He advocates various methods for achieving this objective, extending from laboratory (or T-group, or sensitivity, or human growth) training in the early period of his theory's development to learning seminars or workshops later, but these approaches are consistently part of an overall organization development effort, almost always starting at the top of the organization. For Argyris, organization development in some form became not only an application of his theories to practice, but a means to testing these theories against his experiences in the field, and thus refining the theories in various ways.

Laboratory Training

Argyris became involved with laboratory training at an early point in its history. In his early use of the approach he hypothesized that if executives could become more authentic, could increase their interpersonal competence, could change their values, and ultimately change their behavior, their organizations would shift to forms more appropriate than the pyramidal form. The objectives of training then are to increase:

1. Giving and receiving nonevaluative descriptive feedback.
2. Owning and helping others to own to their values, attitudes, ideas, and feelings.
3. Openness to new values, attitudes, and feelings as well as helping others to develop their degree of openness.
4. Experimenting (and helping others to do the same) with new values, attitudes, ideas, and feelings.
5. Taking risks with new values, attitudes, ideas, and feelings. (Argyris 1962b, 26)

Shifts in accordance with the objectives did occur among eleven top-level executives from the same division of a major company who trained together under Argyris. Changes in values and interpersonal competence were achieved. However, there also was evidence that the managers had considerable difficulty applying the new values and skills at work and that they experienced some fadeout in that the changes produced by training tended to disappear later. The impact at the organizational level appears not to have been great (Argyris 1962b). A second application study with members of a board of directors also suggests that individual changes occurred; these changes appear to have carried over from the laboratory sessions to the regular board meetings (Argyris 1965).

In spite of his initial enthusiasm for laboratory training in its various forms, Argyris (1992b) ultimately came to have serious doubts about it. The on-the-job effects anticipated were rarely in evidence. Furthermore, by the early 1970s, both the business world and the scientific community had become disenchanted with the approach. Opportunities to apply skills as a facilitator were drying up.

Organization Development

As Argyris presents it, organization development focuses more directly on organizational problems and change than does laboratory training, The basic cycle moves from the collection of information, to making an organizational decision, and finally to developing a commitment to that decision. The role of the interventionist is a relatively active one:

> The interventionist should attempt to create norms of individuality, concern, and trust. He should attempt to draw out conflict, threat, or confusion so that they may be dealt with openly. . . . [T]he interventionist should intervene so that the clients may experience psychological success. (Argyris 1970, 221)

Clearly, even where laboratory training is not used in the traditional manner, the commitment to its values and to goal congruence theory remains strong. In many cases Argyris

(1971) advocates the use of confrontation meetings in which important organizational problems of an interpersonal nature are faced openly. His reported examples deal almost exclusively with top-management groups. This pattern is particularly evident in a book dealing with an organization development project carried out with the staff of a major newspaper:

> The first step in the study was to conduct a diagnosis of the client system. This produced a map of the living system which identified some major internal factors causing organizational ineffectiveness. The factors were fed back to top management. . . . After obtaining valid information about the client system the next step was for the executives to decide if they wanted to take action to begin to correct the problems identified. . . . After the top executives chose to attempt to correct some of the problems, they faced the task of becoming internally committed to the actions implicit in the decision. The first step was to agree to attend a learning seminar. (Argyris 1974b, 276–77)

In this approach to organization development Argyris clearly views interpersonal change as a necessary prelude to organizational change. Furthermore, much of the original laboratory training is retained in the learning seminars. In the particular instance of the newspaper, this approach did not result in basic organizational changes, and, at least in a relative sense, the change program was a failure.

Learning Seminars as Organization Development

The learning seminars have evolved into an overall approach labeled action science (Argyris, Putnam, and Smith 1985). The activities in a seminar may be elucidated with reference to the learning paradox—the actions taken to promote productive organizational learning often actually inhibit deeper learning of the Model II type. To deal with this paradox, the facilitator is advised to:

1. Describe the defensive patterns that underlie the learning paradox.
2. Design, jointly with the participants, ways to interrupt the circular, self-reinforcing processes that inhibit double loop learning.
3. Help the participants assess the degree to which their action strategies are likely to limit the implementation of the solutions they have designed.
4. Help the participants realize how they have participated in creating and maintaining a behavioral world where the strategies they redesign to correct the situation are unlikely to be effective.
5. Involve the participants in sessions . . . where they can develop the concepts and skills they need in order to escape from this bind.
6. Reduce the use of defensive reasoning and increase the use of productive reason.
7. Reduce . . . organizational defensive routines, and replace them with high-quality inquiry, good dialectic, and double loop learning. (Argyris and Schön 1996, 282–84)

What is involved here is a process of using interpretations to help participants gain insight, thus following the model inherent in much psychotherapy. In the process participants will exhibit considerable emotionality beginning with bewilderment and frustration, but extending to anger and fear; the facilitator should respond with empathy while not allowing these emotions to become an excuse for backing off from the situation.

The steps in this organization development process go something like this (Argyris 1992b, Fulmer and Keys 1998):

1. Help participants (at the top level now) to become aware of their Model I theories in use and automatic counterproductive reasoning processes.
2. Help these participants to see how they create and maintain learning systems that feed back to sanction Model I.
3. Mix in the various organizational consequences, such as organizational defensive routines, so that participants come to see what is happening in their organization.
4. Help the top-level participants connect these kinds of knowledge with the actual business decisions they are making.
5. Help these participants learn the Model II theory in such a way as to be able to use it under low to moderate stress; thus, with practice, Model II becomes both an espoused theory and a theory in use.
6. Once the top people begin to behave consistently in a Model II mode, move the learning process down through lower management levels by conducting learning seminars there for those who want to participate (see, for example, Argyris 1992b, 34–35).

This process can be quite lengthy, but as Argyris notes, most people do not learn to play tennis over night either. As Model II is introduced, alternative governing values and behavioral strategies are given attention so that the status quo no longer exerts a binding influence; all this takes considerable time.

Put somewhat differently, these steps to overcoming organizational defenses run as follows: (1) make a diagnosis of the problem, (2) connect the diagnosis to the actual behavior of the participants, (3) show them how their behavior creates organizational defenses, (4) help them to change their behavior, (5) change the defensive routine that reinforced the old behavior, and (6) develop new organizational norms and culture that reinforce the new behavior (Argyris 1990, 155). This is a version of Lewin's unfreezing-moving-refreezing model (see Miner 2005).

Techniques of Action Science

One aspect of the action science organization development approach is the process of serial interpretation noted above, but there are other techniques as well, most of them founded in some variant of the case method (see Argyris 2002).

One such technique is for the facilitator to use preselected cases as a basis for group discussion, thus moving participants to particular issues considered important. Much more frequent, however, is the use of participant-written cases. These are presented to the group by one participant at a time; their form is as follows:

1. In one paragraph describe a key organizational problem as you see it.
2. Assume you could talk to whomever you wish to begin to solve the problem.
3. Next split your page into two columns. On the right-hand side write how you would begin the meeting; what you would actually say. Then write what you believe the other(s) would say. Then write your response to their response. Continue writing this scenario for two or so double-spaced written pages.

4. On the left-hand column write any idea or feeling that you would have that you would not communicate for whatever reason. (Argyris 1995, 23)

This case becomes a basis for lengthy discussion. Sometimes other participants are asked to provide a new version of the meeting in the case. Sometimes the participants role-play the meeting in various versions. The objective is to get the case writer to redesign his or her actions so as to move from the Model I that is invariably inherent in the original case to something closer to Model II. In this process, the top-management group comes to learn about its own group dynamics (Argyris 1991). This result is not unlike that obtained from laboratory training. Generally these sessions are tape recorded so that participants can listen to them later and continue their learning.

Another technique involves the construction of a diagram or action map by each participant. This map depicts the interdependence between governing conditions, action strategies, and several orders of counterproductive consequences, plus the feedback processes that maintain the pattern. It is intended to help participants determine the relevant variables, link them in a causal chain, and see the pattern established, thus making it easier to assess plausibility. The causal chain of such a map (with examples appended) might be as follows (Argyris and Schön 1996):

Governing conditions (low trust on interpersonal issues)
↓
Generic action strategies (craft attributions to be untestable)
↓
Consequences for group dynamics (become polarized)
↓
Consequences for group dynamics (exhibit low confidence in group effectiveness)
↓
Consequences for organization (exhibit bad-mouthing outside group)
↓
Consequences for problem solving (experience cynicism about effectiveness)
↓
Consequences for leadership (keep leadership style consistent with defenses)
↓
(earn criticism by acting out organizational defenses)
↓
(feel pulled apart)

There is a great deal here, in the learning seminars and action science as a whole, that harks back to laboratory training. Although the terminology is new, the basic concerns are similar—authenticity, openness, confrontation, and the like. Once again Argyris emphasizes questioning basic premises, cutting through defensiveness, and getting at the realities for the individual and the organization. In many respects the role of the facilitator or change agent has changed little over the years.

However, in one respect Argyris has introduced a major change—his concern for organizational effectiveness has now taken center stage. Perhaps as a result, his theoretical orientation has become one of the more popular underpinnings for organization development practice (Bazigos and Burke 1997).

This does not mean that organization development practitioners follow Argyris's approach explicitly, only that they draw upon it, and his theory, in concocting their own programs. Examples are the introduction of a gainsharing plan involving group incentives and a suggestion program in a manufacturing plant to foster learning and productivity (Arthur and Aiman-Smith 2001) and an attempt to introduce double loop learning in the Singapore national police force (Tan and Heracleous 2001). Other instances of efforts to employ Argyris's ideas through action research are Kowalski, Harmon, Yorks, and Kowalski's (2003) work with the U.S. Department of Veterans Affairs and Sugarman's (2001) report on various learning-based organization development projects.

EVALUATION AND IMPACT

In noting that Argyris's theories have exerted a strong influence on organization development practice I do not wish to imply that this is the only arena in which they have had an impact. Mainstream organizational behavior has on occasion found them quite appealing (see, for instance, Porter 1989), especially the treatment of goal congruence issues. And Argyris's organizational learning formulations have elicited positive reactions from a variety of sources, including scholars with a psychoanalytic orientation to the field (see, for example, Diamond 1986). Other theorists have often drawn heavily on Argyris in developing their own distinct views (see, for example, Lipshitz, Popper, and Friedman 2002).

To understand what has happened, we need to look at the historical development of research, and of ideas about research, much as we have considered the development of theory.

Argyris's Interview-Based Studies

In the 1950s and the early 1960s Argyris conducted several studies to test his views. In one such study, members of various departments of a bank were interviewed to determine the degree of fusion or goal congruence they experienced in their jobs and to relate this index to other factors in accordance with the theory (Argyris 1954). Though this study precedes Argyris's (1957) first formal statement of goal congruence theory, it tests certain hypotheses that are part of that theory.

Measures of the degree to which individual members actualize themselves in the organization and of the degree to which the organization appeared to express itself were obtained. When both indexes were high, as they were in three departments, the departments appeared to be effective; when the indexes were lower, as they were in one instance, the department exhibited more conflict and less organizational commitment. There was some evidence that low personal actualization scores were predictive of voluntary turnover. The reliability of the coding of interview data to obtain this personal actualization score was satisfactory, but the organizational measure yielded marginal reliability at best.

In subsequent research Argyris concerned himself less with the congruence of goals than with personal actualization. The emphases in the reports on these studies, which were carried out in two plants of a manufacturing firm, are somewhat different from one publication to another (Argyris 1958, 1959, 1960a, 1960b).

In this instance the coding reliability of the self-actualization index was rather low (roughly 70 percent agreement). Nevertheless, the scores did operate as hypothesized, with high scores characterizing the more effective plant. In addition, the self-actualization data support a number of theory-based predictions regarding differences between the two plants and between components within them.

In the less effective plant, employees reported more widespread pressure, and though the foremen did not exhibit the same pattern, those who experienced pressure, experienced it more intensely. The foremen also placed greater emphasis on promotion and pay, in accordance with the theory, but neither plant had much turnover at the foreman level. Among employees there was less concern with quality, less friendliness, and more pro-union sentiment in the less effective plant. These are, of course, concurrent findings; they do not establish cause and effect.

Early Research by Others

Argyris marshaled a considerable amount of research, the results of which could be predicted or explained by goal congruence theory (Argyris 1957, 1964, 1972, 1973). This was an impressive scholarly undertaking, as Porter (1989) has indicated; these findings appear convincing in that the studies consistently support the theory. Yet the use of ad hoc explanation, selective coverage of relevant research, and the fact that alternative theories might also predict and explain the same results raise a note of caution. In reality only research that is directly focused on theoretical hypotheses can establish the validity of the theory. In his reviews Argyris does note several studies that directly support the goal congruence hypotheses, though not with total consistency. In particular, positive consequences are likely to accrue from fusion or goal congruence. Unfortunately, most of these studies have not been published in the regular professional literature and cannot be evaluated adequately on the basis of Argyris's descriptions.

In reviewing related literatures, Argyris consistently comes to conclusions supportive of goal congruence theory. In many instances he reinterprets studies carried out without reference to his theories. Thus, it seems appropriate here to look at the conclusions reached by others who have reviewed the same literature.

James and Jones (1976) note a paucity of research dealing with relationships between organizational structure and the individual. However, they conclude that structural factors may influence attitudes and behavior as Argyris anticipates. Yet the evidence does not seem to support the view that formal organization has a direct linear impact on attitudes and behavior:

> . . . [A] high degree of formalization and standardization was found to be positively related to satisfaction and behavior because it reduced role ambiguity in one set of studies. However, formalization and specialization were described as deleterious to satisfaction and behavior when important task characteristics were deleted from jobs. . . . [N]onlinear relationships exist between formalization, specialization, standardization and behavior and attitudes where a certain level of structure is conducive to positive attitudes and behavior, but too much or too little structure has a negative connotation. (James and Jones 1976, 106)

Much the same conclusion emerged from a review by Bryman (1976). He points to considerable evidence that many people desire and prosper under a far greater degree of structure than Argyris would advocate. Structure provides stability and order, with the result that uncertainty and anxiety are reduced. There is no basis for concluding that individuals with needs of this kind are necessarily immature and emotionally unhealthy, nor that they constitute a small minority. All this fits with what was noted in Chapter 15 in this volume from the evidence developed by the Aston researchers. Evidence on this point is substantial, as is theory. Stinchcombe (1974) and others going back to Weber have maintained that an effective bureaucracy requires certain motivational patterns.

Baker, Etzioni, Hansen, and Sontag (1973) developed a measure of worker tolerance for bureaucratic structure based on attitudes toward rules and regulations, attitudes toward the legitimacy of authority, attitudes toward performing limited and structured tasks, and the capacity to delay gratification. This measure differentiates among organizational contexts in a manner that appears to be positively related to their degree of bureaucratization. It also predicts turnover within bureaucracies and performance ratings.

Gordon (1970) developed a similar instrument that tapped willingness to comply with a superior's wishes, confidence in expert judgment, preference for impersonal relationships, a desire for the security provided by rules and standard procedures, and a desire for the security of organizational identification. Correlations with other measures suggest considerable construct validity. This measure also differentiates among contexts with varying degrees of bureaucratization and predicts turnover in bureaucracies. I have developed a somewhat different approach of this nature in connection with the specification of managerial role motivation theory (see Miner 2005) that focuses on the personality characteristics required of managers in bureaucratic systems. Included are measures of characteristics related to functioning within the hierarchy—positive attitudes upward, competitiveness horizontally with peers, and the exercise of power downward; characteristics related to size of organization—assertiveness, and desire to stand out from the group, or be visible; and characteristics related to carrying out the functions of management. Research results indicate that these personality characteristics are a source of behavior and decisions appropriate to the bureaucratic managerial context (Miner 2002b). However, these results do not mesh nearly as well with nonmanagerial work and nonbureaucatic systems. Apparently there are people who cannot adapt to and experience considerable anxiety in bureaucratic managerial roles.

Inner Contradictions of Rigorous Research

By the mid-1960s at the latest Argyris had concluded that the research pattern emerging in organizational behavior was not of a kind that he wished to continue to endorse. As he indicated in Argyris (1968), he came to believe that scientific research has an authoritarian bias analogous to the effects of pyramidal organizations. Subjects react to experimental controls as they would to organizational controls, and the findings are distorted accordingly. His solution for this situation also derives from his theory: "reduce the researcher's control over the subject . . . to provide the subject with greater influence, with longer time perspective regarding, and greater internal involvement in, the research project . . . having worker representative groups (in organizations) and student representative groups (in universities) to help in the design and execution of research" (Argyris 1968, 193).

These ideas are intriguing. Yet certain assumptions are inherent in Argyris's position. First, he assumes the validity of goal congruence theory. If employees do not react to organizational controls as hypothesized, then the extension to experimental controls is not likely to be valid either, following Argyris's own logic. Second, he assumes that certain apparent similarities between the two situations make the theoretical extension from organization to research warranted. Both of these assumptions require evidence. On the latter there is almost no evidence. We do not know whether goal congruence theory works within the domain of scientific research because no one, including Argyris, has tested it there, with or without subject participation in the research design.

This issue has not gone away. It appears in a major statement by Argyris somewhat later (Argyris 1980), and he takes up aspects of the problem after that (see, for instance, Argyris 1982). Subsequently, Argyris seems somewhat ambivalent on the matter, frequently introducing statements such as "The systematic study of the program's effectiveness will have to wait for the results of the research" (Argyris 1989, 15). In no case are these references to research-in-progress followed later by reports of completed, systematic, scientific research studies. It appears that somewhere in the 1960s Argyris stopped any attempt at truly verifiable research of a scientific nature; it is not clear what he meant by his research-in-progress statements, but these appear to have been references to qualitative, ethnographic studies following upon various kinds of interventions. Even these have never been fully reported.

The consequence of all this has been that Argyris has not conducted, or reported, research on his theories after his initial studies. Furthermore, others have moved away from his theories out of a concern that their research might be viewed as inappropriate against the criteria for legitimate investigation Argyris had established. Let me elaborate.

Argyris's position is that:

1. The conditions of unilateral control embedded in rigorous research procedures create, for the subjects, conditions of dependence, submissiveness, and short time perspective.
2. The abstractions required for precision and quantification tend to lead to instruments whose meanings are not based on the action context experienced by subjects in their everyday life (hence the meanings may be confusing, unclear, and ambiguous).
3. The axiom that the purpose of science is to understand or explain while prediction and control are tests of our understanding and explanation leads to a social science of the status quo.

". . . The consequences previously described, coupled with their undiscussability, could lead people to misperceive the experimental manipulation and/or to unrealizingly distort what they report in instruments and during interviews as well as what they exhibit in their actual behavior" (Argyris 1980, 51–52). To avoid these consequences of the Model I situation that has been created, subjects must be involved in all phases of research design and planning so that they truly understand what is going on.

Argyris is clearly referring to the kinds of research utilizing self-report questionnaires and interviews that he himself has conducted. There are many other kinds of research. Furthermore, research can be devoted to normative ends, not just descriptions and understanding, and thus with a little ingenuity the researcher may produce findings that foster change, not just reinforcement of the status quo; much medical research on new treatments provides vivid examples.

In the process of arguing for this position Argyris attacks aspects of a number of theories considered in this book, such as James March's views related to organizational learning (see Argyris 1996). Yet it makes no sense to include research subjects in the test development and item selection phase of a study involving the use of an intelligence test, or to include subjects who have no knowledge of such matters in the planning of research that would ideally require a complex experimental design and sophisticated statistical analyses. It makes no sense that is, *unless* the objective is to undermine and block research of these kinds entirely. That may well be what Argyris is attempting to do. He argues for the use of qualitative case material (often derived from recorded transcripts), without either experimental or statistical controls, to test his theories. At one point (Argyris 1982), he dismisses the use of control groups in testing the effectiveness of his interventions as unwarranted; using participants as their own controls would be sufficient. He does not indicate a recognition of the fact that the results achieved by the two approaches are not the same, or note that some of his own early research did use a control group.

In this latter vein it is important to recognize that Argyris marshaled many studies in support of goal congruence theory, including some of his own, which, based on his subsequent position as to the conduct of valid research, would have to be brought into question. There is something of the "having your cake and eating it too" factor operating here. If Argyris changed his thinking as to the conduct of research at some point, he should say so, and explain how his prior interpretations are affected; this has not occurred.

The Future of Goal Congruence Formulations

Goal congruence theory faces many conceptual and empirical difficulties. A basic problem is the contention that bureaucracy *causes* emotional illness, infantile behavior, dependent personalities, and the like. The concept of human maturity set forth in Table 17.1 appears to be essentially valid. However, many personality theorists, including the writer, would add to the list a capacity to deal with authority relationships effectively, so that overreactions, either positive or negative, are minimized. In this view, then, learning to function in a bureaucratic system and to delay immediate gratification for future reward is a sign of maturity, not infantilism.

There is evidence that bureaucratic organizations tend to attract certain emotionally disturbed individuals at the lower levels, presumably because these people can function effectively in such positions. But this does not mean the organization *caused* the pathology. It seems probable that Argyris, observing organization members within a limited time span and noting the contiguity of pathology and formal structure, incorrectly attributed direct causation to the structure, when in fact it was often the ambiguity- and anxiety-reducing structure itself that permitted particular individuals to function in an organizational setting at all (Diamond 1986).

Actually, Argyris is not entirely consistent as to whether immature people (those lacking psychological success) are created by formal organizations, and thus can mature in an alternative structure, or whether they are of a personality type that functions well only in congruent systems (bureaucracies); he says both at different points. Obviously the implications for organizational design differ considerably in the two instances. Possibly both processes occur in different individuals, but then the theory should deal clearly with methods of identifying the two classes of people, which it does not.

A special problem arises with goal congruence theory in regard to the relationship between bureaucratic authority and dependency. The theory appears to confuse objective and subjective (personality-based) dependency. Hierarchical systems do create objective dependency relationships to varying degrees for most, if not all, members. But because one individual is dependent on another for rewards does not mean that that person constantly craves the support, help, approval, instruction, and domination of others, and becomes angry when they are not received, in the manner of the dependent personality. Certainly, bureaucratic systems do attract dependent personalities; they may well create some dependent personalities under certain circumstances; but they clearly attract a great many nondependent people, even though all work under a degree of objective dependency.

In his earliest theoretical statements Argyris did consider alternative responses to formal structure other than regression into passive dependency, including upward mobility in the organizational hierarchy. The theory did not specify how to identify such people, however, or mention alternative responses of this kind later.

Argyris has been criticized for neglecting individual differences and offering a "one best way" prescription analogous to scientific management. Argyris (1973) disputed this, and indeed such concepts as his reality-centered leadership and mix model do require contingent hypotheses. Furthermore, he now specifies (Argyris 2004, 19) that "some adults preferred infantile jobs." However, these ideas are given relatively little attention, have not been tested empirically, and at times are completely ignored. Often they are treated more as escape valves than as formal parts of the theory. To be useful, these hypotheses need to be much more clearly stated—where, when, and how various structures and leadership behaviors are to be used should be spelled out.

Individual personalities come in a great variety of forms. Some fit well and thrive in one type of organization, generating considerable energy for movement toward organizational goals, while others fit in another type. Some personalities may not fit any known organization. A society that is to use its human talent effectively must generate a variety of organizational forms. The mix model approaches this problem, but goal congruence theory as a whole tends to bypass it.

Lest I be considered as critical of Argyris as he has been of many other theorists, let me hasten to add an additional point, which I consider to be the saving grace of goal congruence theory. The essence of the theory is that when individual members and organizations fit each other—when their goals are congruent—organizational effectiveness will be fostered because members will devote their efforts to organizational goal achievement. This is an integration hypothesis, and it is consistently supported by the research of Argyris and of others cited in this chapter. Goal congruence theory emphasized, if it did not create, one of the most important concepts in organizational theory at an early time. For this Argyris deserves considerable credit.

The Future of Organizational Learning Formulations

As Argyris moved from goal congruence to a theory devoted to organizational learning and defensive routines, the ties to a single approach to organization development practice become much closer. There simply is no research on the theory itself, or marshaling of others' research that helps to validate the theory. Perhaps because of the strong practice emphasis early on, the learning theory often lacks precision. Exactly when Model I should be invoked and when Model II should be brought to bear is never clearly stated; all we know for sure is that one is mostly bad and one is good. In fact there is a certain amorphous quality to Model II that is never fully overcome, even with later efforts to achieve more precision. This ambiguity of formulation regarding Model II has been noted by many reviewers of Argyris's numerous books. As Lipshitz (2000, 471) notes, "it is difficult to understand in depth and extremely difficult to implement."

However, an even greater problem is the total reliance on not-fully-reported qualitative research evidence. I believe there is something to be said for involving subjects more directly in the whole research process on occasion, but not always, and not with a rigidity that severely limits the domain of scientific research. Argyris's theory can be, and should be, tested using rigorous research techniques—pre- and post-tests, control groups, reliable measures, and direct ties to effectiveness criteria. Without this we will never know whether the interventions work or whether the theory has validity.

This whole problem involving research validation of Model II and of interventions intended to enhance it within organizations is addressed often in Argyris (2004). He argues for empirical research in this regard repeatedly. Nevertheless, he continues to define acceptable research in such a manner that the conduct of this needed research does not appear possible. Certainly over the years neither Argyris nor anyone else has risen to the task. And sufficient questioning of Argyris's approach has occurred to warrant the conduct of research (see Seo 2003).

CONCLUSIONS

The box on goal congruence theory reflects an importance rating of 4.38, a validity rating of three stars, and a usefulness rating of three stars. None of these evaluations reach a level to justify inclusion in this book on essential theories. What is distinctive about goal congruence theory, and what justifies its inclusion here, is that all three ratings are respectable; they add up to a positive assessment and thus a designation as an essential theory, although no one value would warrant that status.

The estimated validity of goal congruence theory is hampered by its claim that bureaucracy often *causes* its various debilitating effects. Yet, on the plus side, the theory's argument that when individuals and organization form mesh (or fit), organizational effectiveness will benefit, appears to be correct. The minuses and pluses cancel one another out and thus the three stars appear appropriate. However, the theory of organizational learning and defensive routines does not rate as high, for lack of adequate validation research.

The estimated usefulness rating is based on the fact that the different organization development approaches proposed by Argyris are almost impossible to disentangle. In many respects his approach has moved away from the mainstream, and in doing so has become separated from the main body of validation research on organization development. It needs its own research stream, and in actual fact it has very little such research to support it. In the next chapter we consider an approach to organization development that has moved more to the center of the field.

REFERENCES

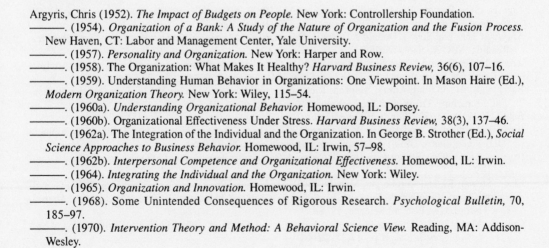

Argyris, Chris (1952). *The Impact of Budgets on People.* New York: Controllership Foundation.
———. (1954). *Organization of a Bank: A Study of the Nature of Organization and the Fusion Process.* New Haven, CT: Labor and Management Center, Yale University.
———. (1957). *Personality and Organization.* New York: Harper and Row.
———. (1958). The Organization: What Makes It Healthy? *Harvard Business Review,* 36(6), 107–16.
———. (1959). Understanding Human Behavior in Organizations: One Viewpoint. In Mason Haire (Ed.), *Modern Organization Theory.* New York: Wiley, 115–54.
———. (1960a). *Understanding Organizational Behavior.* Homewood, IL: Dorsey.
———. (1960b). Organizational Effectiveness Under Stress. *Harvard Business Review,* 38(3), 137–46.
———. (1962a). The Integration of the Individual and the Organization. In George B. Strother (Ed.), *Social Science Approaches to Business Behavior.* Homewood, IL: Irwin, 57–98.
———. (1962b). *Interpersonal Competence and Organizational Effectiveness.* Homewood, IL: Irwin.
———. (1964). *Integrating the Individual and the Organization.* New York: Wiley.
———. (1965). *Organization and Innovation.* Homewood, IL: Irwin.
———. (1968). Some Unintended Consequences of Rigorous Research. *Psychological Bulletin,* 70, 185–97.
———. (1970). *Intervention Theory and Method: A Behavioral Science View.* Reading, MA: Addison-Wesley.

————. (1971). *Management and Organizational Development: The Path from XA to YB.* New York: McGraw-Hill.

————. (1972). *The Applicability of Organizational Sociology.* Cambridge, UK: Cambridge University Press.

————. (1973). Personality and Organization Theory Revisited. *Administrative Science Quarterly,* 18, 141–67.

————. (1974a). Personality vs. Organization. *Organizational Dynamics,* 3(2), 3–17.

————. (1974b). *Behind the Front Page: Organizational Self-Renewal in a Metropolitan Newspaper.* San Francisco, CA: Jossey-Bass.

————. (1980). *The Inner Contradictions of Rigorous Research.* New York: Academic Press.

————. (1982). *Reasoning, Learning, Action: Individual and Organizational.* San Francisco, CA: Jossey-Bass.

————. (1985). *Strategy, Change, and Defensive Routines.* Boston, MA: Pitman.

————. (1989). Strategy Implementation: An Experience in Learning. *Organizational Dynamics,* 18(2), 5–15.

————. (1990). *Overcoming Organizational Defenses: Facilitating Organizational Learning.* Boston, MA: Allyn and Bacon.

————. (1991). Teaching Smart People How to Learn. *Harvard Business Review,* 69(3), 99–109.

————. (1992a). Looking Backward and Inward in Order to Contribute to the Future. In Arthur G. Bedeian (Ed.), *Management Laureates: A Collection of Autobiographical Essays,* Vol. 1. Greenwich, CT: JAI Press, 41–64.

————. (1992b). *On Organizational Learning.* Cambridge, MA: Blackwell.

————. (1993). *Knowledge for Action: A Guide to Overcoming Barriers to Organizational Change.* San Francisco, CA: Jossey-Bass.

————. (1994). Litigation Mentality and Organizational Learning. In Sim B. Sitkin and Robert J. Bies (Eds.), *The Legalistic Organization.* Thousand Oaks, CA: Sage, 347–58.

————. (1995). Action Science and Organizational Learning. *Journal of Managerial Psychology,* 10(6), 20–26.

————. (1996). Unrecognized Defenses of Scholars: Impact on Theory and Research. *Organization Science,* 7, 79–87.

————. (1998a). Award for Life Achievement in the Application of Psychology. *American Psychologist,* 53, 877–78.

————. (1998b). Empowerment: The Emperor's New Clothes. *Harvard Business Review,* 76(3), 98–105.

————. (2000). *Flawed Advice and the Management Trap.* New York: Oxford University Press.

————. (2002). Double-Loop Learning, Teaching, and Research. *Academy of Management Learning and Education,* 1, 206–18.

————. (2003). A Life Full of Learning. *Organization Studies,* 24, 1178–92.

————. (2004). *Reasons and Rationalizations: The Limits to Organizational Knowledge.* Oxford, UK: Oxford University Press.

Argyris, Chris, Putnam, Robert, and Smith, Diane M. (1985). *Action Science: Concepts, Methods, and Skills for Research and Intervention.* San Francisco, CA: Jossey-Bass.

Argyris, Chris, and Schön, Donald A. (1996). *Organizational Learning II: Theory, Method, and Practice.* Reading, MA: Addison-Wesley.

Arthur, Jeffrey B., and Aiman-Smith, Lynda (2001). Gainsharing and Organizational Learning: An Analysis of Employee Suggestions over Time. *Academy of Management Journal,* 44, 737–54.

Baker, Sally H., Etzioni, Amitai, Hansen, Richard A., and Sontag, Marvin (1973). Tolerance for Bureaucratic Structure: Theory and Measurement. *Human Relations,* 26, 775–86.

Bakke, E. Wight (1950). *Bonds of Organization.* New York: Harper.

Bazigos, Michael N., and Burke, W. Warner (1997). Theory Orientations of Organization Development (OD) Practitioners. *Group & Organization Management,* 22, 384–408.

Bryman, Alan (1976). Structure in Organizations: A Reconsideration. *Journal of Occupational Psychology,* 49, 1–9.

Clegg, Stewart R., and Kornberger, Martin (2003). Modernism, Postmodernism, Management and Organization Theory. In Edwin A. Locke (Ed.), *Postmodernism and Management: Pros, Cons and the Alternative.* Oxford, UK: Elsevier Science, 57–88.

Crossan, Mary (2003). Altering Theories of Learning and Action: An Interview with Chris Argyris. *Academy of Management Executive,* 17(2), 40–46.

Dachler, H. Peter (1994). Review of Argyris and Schön's *On Organizational Learning. Organization Studies,* 15, 460–64.

Diamond, Michael A. (1986). Resistance to Change: A Psychoanalytic Critique of Argyris and Schön's Contributions to Organization Theory and Intervention. *Journal of Management Studies,* 23, 543–62.

Fulmer, Robert M,. and Keys, J. Bernard (1998). A Conversation with Chris Argyris: The Father of Organizational Learning. *Organizational Dynamics,* 27(2), 21–32.

Gordon, Leonard V. (1970). Measurement of Bureaucratic Orientation. *Personnel Psychology,* 23, 1–11.

James, Lawrence P., and Jones, Allan P. (1976). Organizational Structure: A Review of Structural Dimensions and Their Conceptual Relationships with Individual Attitudes and Behavior. *Organizational Behavior and Human Performance,* 16, 74–113.

Kowalski, Rita, Harmon, Joel, Yorks, Lyle, and Kowalski, Dan (2003). Reducing Workplace Stress and Aggression: An Action Research Project at the U.S. Department of Veterans Affairs. *Human Resource Planning,* 26(2), 39–53.

Lichtenstein, Benyamin M.B. (2000). Generative Knowledge and Self-Organized Learning—Reflecting on Don Schön's Research. *Journal of Management Inquiry,* 9, 47–54.

Lipshitz, Raanan (2000). Chic, Mystique, and Misconception: Argyris and Schön and the Rhetoric of Organizational Learning. *Journal of Applied Behavioral Science,* 36, 456–73.

Lipshitz, Raanan, Popper, Micha, and Friedman, Victor J. (2002). A Multifacet Model of Organizational Learning. *Journal of Applied Behavioral Science,* 38, 78–98.

Miner, John B. (2002a). *Organizational Behavior: Foundations, Theories, and Analyses.* New York: Oxford University Press.

———. (2002b). The Role Motivation Theories of Organizational Leadership. In Bruce J. Avolio and Francis J. Yammarino (Eds.), *Transformational and Charismatic Leadership: The Road Ahead.* Oxford, UK: Elsevier Science, 309–38.

———. (2005). *Organizational Behavior 1: Essential Theories of Motivation and Leadership.* Armonk, NY: M.E. Sharpe.

Porter, Lyman W. (1989). A Retrospective Review: Argyris's *Personality and Organization. Academy of Management Review,* 14, 284–85.

Putnam, Robert (1995). A Biography of Chris Argyris. *Journal of Applied Behavioral Science,* 31, 253–55.

Roth, George, and Kleiner, Art (2000). *Car Launch: The Human Side of Managing Change.* New York: Oxford University Press.

Seo, Myeong-Gu (2003). Overcoming Emotional Barriers, Political Obstacles, and Control Imperatives in the Action-Science Approach to Individual and Organizational Learning. *Academy of Management Learning and Education,* 2, 7–21.

Stinchcombe, Arthur L. (1974). *Creating Efficient Industrial Administrations.* New York: Academic Press.

Sugarman, Barry (2001). A Learning-Based Approach to Organizational Change: Some Results and Guidelines. *Organizational Dynamics,* 30(1), 62–76.

Tan, Tay Keong, and Heracleous, Loizos (2001). Teaching Old Dogs New Tricks: Implementing Organizational Learning in an Asian National Police Force. *Journal of Applied Behavioral Science,* 37, 361–80.

CHAPTER 18

ORGANIZATIONAL CULTURE THEORY AND PROCESS CONSULTATION

EDGAR SCHEIN

Importance rating	★ ★ ★ ★
Estimated validity	★ ★
Estimated usefulness	★ ★ ★ (★)
Decade of origin	1960s

The origins of organization development were in a humanist antibureaucracy/classical management philosophy that is clearly manifest in the theory initially expounded by Argyris (Chapter 17). The theory considered in this chapter is organizational in nature, but is tied to more micro level leadership theories as well.

Edgar Schein's initial concern was with the change process and with his own particular approach to organization development (process consultation). Only as it became evident that this approach would benefit from a broader theoretical perspective did he delve into the area of leadership and its role in influencing organizational culture (Schein 1985). In the end what emerged was a comprehensive culture theory in which top managers were significant actors. In this theory culture served in a number of respects as a substitute for hierarchy (and thus bureaucracy). Thus Schein's theory offers an alternative to bureaucracy not only in its early and continuing focus on organization development, but in its subsequent elaboration of the culture construct as a tool for human organization that can in certain respects replace aspects of bureaucracy.

Edgar Schein was influenced in his approach to practice and in his theoretical thinking by a number of people, but among these he gives special credit to certain specific sources. First among these is Douglas McGregor (see Miner 2002), who was in many respects his mentor in the early days at MIT (Schein 1975; Luthans 1989). The second source singled out is what is referred to as the Chicago school of sociology by which Schein (1989a) says he means Everett Hughes, Melville Dalton, and Erving Goffman. These people tried to articulate a clinical approach to their work during the late 1950s, emphasizing careful observation, sensemaking, and theories built on observational underpinnings. Schein was much impressed by this approach, which he tried to emulate in his own work.

BACKGROUND

Edgar Schein is another of those who escaped to the United States from a Hitler-dominated Europe. He was born in Switzerland in 1928 and lived in several European countries before moving to the United States in 1938. He attended the University of Chicago, graduating in 1947. Then, after receiving a master's degree from Stanford University in 1949, he went to Harvard University, where he obtained a doctorate in social and clinical psychology in 1952. From Harvard he moved to the Walter Reed Institute of Research for a stint in the military that included an opportunity to study released prisoners who had been brainwashed during the Korean War.

In 1956 Schein joined the faculty of the newly formed Graduate School of Management at MIT. He was hired by Douglas McGregor, who also introduced him to T-groups (T for training) at the Bethel, Maine, center of the National Training Laboratories and to consulting work (Schein 1993a). He remained at MIT throughout his career, served on the Bethel faculty during the summer months for many years, and continues as an active consultant, although he is now emeritus from MIT.

The interrelationships among the various areas of Schein's interest, and his publishing, are important to an understanding of the ideas to be discussed. His initial work was the study of how prisoners were influenced by the Chinese communists to do and say things that, without coercion, would have been out of the question for them (Schein 1957; Schein, Schneier, and Barker 1961). Taking up the issue of organizational participants' reactions to influences exerted on them by their organizations, Schein next studied the effects of companies on MIT graduates as they moved into the labor force. This concern with processes of organizational socialization continued for some time (Schein 1968; Van Maanen and Schein 1979). Gradually it merged into the subsequent formulations regarding organizational cultures, and into a broader concern with career dynamics and career anchors (Schein 1978, 1987a, 1996a), which became a distinct theoretical thrust of its own.

However, Schein is best known for his contributions in the areas of process consultation and organizational culture (Luthans 1989), and it is these that are given primary attention here. The process consultation ideas represent a direct contribution to practice and they came first. They were an outgrowth of Schein's early experience with laboratory training, but were colored by other influences as well (Schein and Bennis 1965). The theory of organizational culture, and leadership influences on it, came later. The latter reflects Schein's desire to provide a broader underpinning for the process consultation ideas and was in addition a natural outgrowth of his work on socialization. Schein was also influenced by an intense exposure to other cultures worldwide through a series of visiting appointments and consulting engagements (Schein 1993a).

PROCESS CONSULTATION AND ORGANIZATIONAL PRACTICE

The approach to practice that Schein developed was in its origins initially antibureaucracy simply because the laboratory training movement was of that nature. However, the idea of helping the client system to help itself rapidly became central to process consulting, and with this there developed a more accepting approach to organizations in their current forms (Schein 1990a). Yet bits and pieces of humanism and antibureaucracy continued to manifest themselves in Schein's work. There are references to bureaucracy as ineffective (Schein 1981a), to the need to empower employees and eliminate dependence on the hierarchy (Schein 1995), and to the uselessness of studying bureaucratic structural variables such as centralization and formalization (Luthans 1989). Humanistic values are frequently noted as a guiding force, although not always with positive consequences (see Schein 1990b). The possibility of abandoning hierarchy in the world of the future is given serious consideration (Schein 1989b).

Early Process Consultation

The initial public presentation of process consultation (Schein 1969) had a long history in the author's existing consulting practice, but not a long gestation period. The 1969 book was a first attempt to explain what was already an established approach. The definition of process consulting, along with the assumptions behind it, which derive from laboratory training, are as follows:

> *Definition.* Process consulting is a set of activities on the part of the consultant which help the client to perceive, understand, and act upon process events which occur in the client's environment.
>
> 1. Managers often do not know what is wrong and need special help in diagnosing what their problems actually are.
> 2. Managers often do not know what kinds of help consultants can give to them.
> 3. Most managers have a constructive intent to improve things, but need help in identifying what to improve and how to improve it.
> 4. Most organizations can be more effective if they learn to diagnose their own strengths and weaknesses. . . . every . . . organization will have some weaknesses.
> 5. A consultant could probably not . . . learn enough about the culture . . . to suggest reliable new courses of action . . . he must work jointly with members of the organization who do know the culture.
> 6. One of the process consultant's roles is to provide new and challenging alternatives . . . Decision-making . . . must, however, remain in the hands of the client.
> 7. It is of prime importance that the process consultant be expert in how to *diagnose* and . . . *establish effective helping relationships* with clients. Effective process consultation involves passing on . . . these skills. (Schein 1969, 8–9)

The human processes involved here that contribute to organizational effectiveness include communication, member roles and functions in groups, group problem-solving, group norms and growth, leadership and authority, and intergroup cooperation or competition. The approach clearly operates primarily at the group level.

The stages of process consultation tend to overlap one another. However, they may be specified as follows:

1. Initial contact with the client organization—indication of the perceived problem.
2. Defining the relationship, including the formal and psychological contract—focus on how the group gets its work done.
3. Selecting a setting (what and when to observe, as near the top of the organization as possible, one in which it is easy to observe group processes, one in which real work is involved) and a method of work (as congruent as possible with process consultation values, thus making the consultant maximally visible to develop trust).
4. Data gathering and diagnosis, which inevitably are interventions—use of observation and interviews, but not questionnaires and survey measures, which are too impersonal.
5. Intervention—in declining order of likelihood, the use of agenda-setting interventions, feedback of observations or data, coaching or counseling, and structural suggestions (which occur rarely).
6. Evaluation and disengagement—looking for evidence of changes in values as related to concern for human problems and process issues, as well as in interpersonal skills. (Schein 1969, 78)

Throughout, efforts are concentrated on helping the organization to become aware of organizational processes and to engage in self-diagnosis. Much of what is described represents extending laboratory training to the real working groups of an ongoing organization.

Process Consultation in Maturity

While Schein's first presentation was intended largely to tell his colleagues what he did out in the corporate world, his initial writing in the 1980s was directed much more at managers. The intent was to show them how they could exert influence without resort to power and authority (Schein 1987b) and thus to demonstrate the value of assuming the same helping role that process consultants assume. When this happens, the organization achieves its goals, and subordinates are helped to grow and develop. In discussing these process interventions Schein (1987b, 52) has the following to say:

1. Process is always to be favored as an intervention focus over content.
2. Task process is always to be favored over interpersonal process.
3. Structural interventions are in principle the most powerful . . . but they are also likely to be most resisted.

The list of human processes that contribute to organizational effectiveness is extended to include intrapsychic processes, cultural rules of interaction, and change processes as epitomized by Lewin's unfreezing-moving-refreezing model (see Miner 2005). The intervention process is expounded in much greater detail; four basic types are noted: exploratory interventions (What do you have in mind?), diagnostic interventions (Why is this more of a problem now?), action alternative interventions (Have you considered either of these alternatives?), confrontive interventions (It sounds to me like you feel angry at this person, is that right?). Also a variety of techniques that may be built into process consultation with the assistance of key client members are noted: intergroup exercises, survey feedback, role-playing, educational interventions, responsibility-charting, and many others. Schein suggests that in dealing with structural issues, process consultants should limit themselves to raising questions that make structural options clear.

In a small book written in this period Schein (1987c) makes a distinction between the clinical perspective that characterizes process consultation and the ethnographic perspective of the cultural anthropologist. The former focuses on helping and producing change while the latter is concerned with obtaining valid data for science while leaving the system undisturbed. To really understand an organization, he argues that both approaches must be combined in some manner.

Schein (1988) is a redo of the 1969 volume with considerable expansion of the discussion. The definition of process consultation noted previously is amended by adding the phrase "in order to improve the situation as defined by the client" (11). A chapter is added on performance appraisal and feedback on the grounds that both appraisal and process consultation require skills in giving feedback. The general structure of this book, however, is much the same as that of its predecessor.

Revisitation

In returning one more time to the topic of process consultation, Schein (1999a) covers many of the same matters that were considered in previous volumes. But he makes additional points as well. For instance, he likens process consultation to Argyris's double loop learning, in that the intent is to increase the client system's capacity for learning. Furthermore, he sets forth a set of principles with the intent of providing guidance to the process consultant:

1. Always try to be helpful.
2. Always stay in touch with the current reality.
3. Access your ignorance.
4. Everything you do is an intervention.
5. It is the client who owns the problem and the solution.
6. Go with the flow.
7. Timing is crucial.
8. Be constructively opportunistic with confrontive interventions.
9. Everything is a source of data; errors will occur and are the prime source of learning.
10. When in doubt, share the problem. (Schein 1999a, 60)

Although these principles are amplified with much more specific detail, their listing here helps to provide a feeling for what process consultation entails. Schein has applied these principles in consulting engagements with Digital, General Foods, Royal Dutch Shell, BP, and Ciba-Geigy (Coutu 2002).

Schein (1999a) now places considerable stress on a technique called dialogue, which may be used with quite large groups and which he contrasts with the sensitivity training approach that came more directly out of the laboratory training at Bethel. The following quotes reflect a certain distancing from the positions Schein took in the 1960s:

> Sensitivity training is focused more on hearing others' *feelings* and tuning in on all the levels of communication; dialogue is focused more on the *thinking* process and how our perceptions and cognitions are preformed by our past experiences. (203)

> In the typical sensitivity-training workshop, participants explore relationships . . . through giving and receiving deliberate feedback. . . . In dialogue, the participants explore *all* the complexities of thinking and language. (203–4)

In sensitivity training the goal is to use the group process to develop our *individual* interpersonal skills, whereas dialogue aims to build a group that can think generatively, creatively, and most importantly *together*. . . . Dialogue is thus a potential vehicle for creative problem identification and problem solving. (204)

It is this latter feature that makes dialogue particularly attractive for use within the context of process consultation; it now appears to have taken center stage (see Quick and Gavin 2000).

THE THEORY OF ORGANIZATIONAL CULTURE AND LEADERSHIP

The concept of organizational culture can be found in Schein's earlier writings, but in the 1980s it became a topic that suffused the field of organizational behavior. Schein was at the forefront of this onslaught, starting with a number of articles that dealt with components of his theory. These often derived from his work on socialization and careers, but they were also informed by the author's experiences as a process consultant (Schein 1981b; 1983; 1984a, b). This all came together in a subsequent book that represents Schein's most comprehensive theoretical statement (Schein 1985). This book is the primary source for the discussion that follows.

Basic Statement

Leadership comes in the front door of any discussion of culture because what leaders actually do, as distinct from managers, is to create and change cultures. Culture, in turn, means—

> . . . a pattern of basic assumptions—invented, discovered, or developed by a given group as it learns to cope with its problems of external adaptation and internal integration—that has worked well enough to be considered valid and, therefore, to be taught to new members as the correct way to perceive, think, and feel in relation to those problems." (Schein 1985, 9)

Figure 18.1 depicts the levels of culture; the essence of organizational culture is at the level of basic assumptions. These assumptions set limits on corporate strategies; if the alignment is not appropriate the strategies cannot be implemented. Thus, cultures, like structures, are a means to strategic implementation and, in fact, cultures incorporate structures as one of their components.

Schein's knowledge of cultures and his ideas about them derive primarily from his clinical experience with them, and thus from process consultation. This may be a limited perspective in certain respects, but it is a rich source as well. However, just as Schein's consulting has been focused at the group level, his concept of culture has a similar focus:

> . . . [C]ulture formation is . . . identical with the process of group formation in that the very essence of "groupness" or group identity—the shared patterns of thought, belief, feelings, and values that result from shared experience and common learning—is what we ultimately end up calling the "culture" of that group. . . . So group growth and culture formation can be seen as two sides of the same coin, and both are the result of leadership activities.

What we need to understand, then, is how the *individual* intentions of the founders, leaders, or conveners of a new group or organization, their own definitions of the situation,

Figure 18.1 **The Levels of Culture**

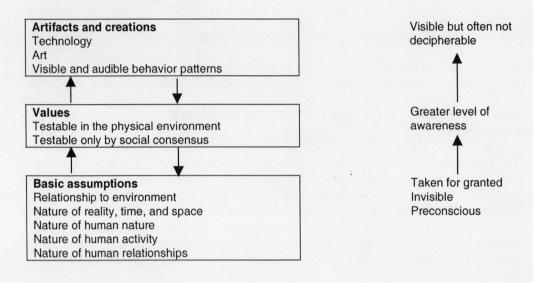

Source: Schein (1985, 14). Copyright © 1985 by Jossey-Bass. Reprinted with permission of Jossey-Bass, Inc., a subsidiary of John Wiley & Sons, Inc.

their assumptions and values, come to be a *shared, consensually validated* set of definitions that are passed on to new members as "the correct way to define the situation." (Schein 1985, 50)

Cultures are interrelated sets of assumptions and thus multidimensional. They are far superior to typologies, such as those involving bureaucracy, as bases for understanding organizations; two organizations with the same structures may otherwise have totally different cultures.

The recommended approach to deciphering culture is observation and interviews. Artifacts are used only to check hypotheses derived from other sources. Culture questionnaires are not recommended because they get at espoused values at best. They do not tap the basic assumptions that represent the essence of culture. Also Schein has serious doubts about the efficacy of feeding back written culture descriptions to the organization involved. To do this is often interpreted as akin to an invasion of privacy. It may remove the defenses against anxiety that the culture provides for its members and thus leave them emotionally exposed.

Culture and Leadership

Culture is the result of group learning experiences in which a number of people face a problem and work out a solution together. To the extent the solution is effective, it and the factors associated with it become embedded in the emerging culture. Variations in cultures reflect differences in the personalities of leaders and members and the circumstances of early problem solutions. It is assumed that all organizations start as small groups, and that therefore organizational cultures inevitably have their origins in the development of group norms.

Both at the level of the initial group and as organizational dynamics are added with growth, founders and leaders are a key ingredient of culture formation. Founders have a vision for the organization and they bring in others who share this vision. Founders also have strong assumptions in the areas noted in Figure 18.1, and many of these assumptions survive in the culture, because they contribute to effective problem solutions. If this is not the case, the venture fails. As certain founder assumptions prove effective, they reduce the anxieties of members, and this reinforces learning of specific ways of thinking and doing things. Thus a process of cultural embedding occurs.

The primary mechanisms for embedding are: (1) the things leaders pay attention to, measure, and control; (2) leader reaction to critical incidents or crises; (3) deliberate leader role modeling and teaching; (4) the criteria for allocation of rewards and status applied; and (5) the criteria for recruitment, selection, promotion, and termination applied. In addition, there are certain secondary mechanisms for embedding, which work only if they are logically consistent with the primary ones. In order to obtain this reinforcing effect, leaders attempt to control these secondary mechanisms. They are: (1) organizational structure and design, (2) organizational procedures and systems, (3) the design of buildings and physical space, (4) stories and myths regarding important people and events, and (5) formal statements of organizational philosophies and missions (Schein 1985, 224–25, 237).

The cultures thus constructed can be very strong, so that much change can occur within an organization even though the basic culture remains unmoved. When culture change does become an issue, however, the change mechanisms mobilized and the unfreezing forces operating appear to be a function of the firm's age. How the growth stages of an organization influence culture changes is set forth in Figure 18.2.

At both stages I and II, organizational theory and development are noted as change mechanisms on the ground that culture is in part a defense mechanism to protect against anxiety, and consequently these approaches should be appropriate to helping organizations change themselves. Organization development, although not totally of a therapeutic nature, does start with therapeutic interventions intended to promote self-insight. To achieve change it is necessary to bring the buried assumptions of culture to the surface in such a way that they are confronted and evaluated; this is rare.

In closing the 1985 discussion, Schein emphasizes various "do nots" for managers. Such concepts as values, climate, and corporate philosophy are determined by culture, but managers should not assume that they *are* the culture; culture operates at a deeper level. Assuming that culture applies to the human side of the organization only is also a mistake; products, markets, missions, and the like are also important aspects of culture. Culture cannot easily be manipulated, and to assume otherwise can produce trouble; managers are controlled by culture much more than they control it. No culture should be assumed to be inherently better than others, and strong cultures are not better than weak ones. Do not assume that culture relates only to the matter of organizational effectiveness; it is much more than that.

Subcultures and the Learning Leader

Schein (1992,) says in the preface of his second edition, "The major changes are in dropping various materials that were peripheral to culture and in adding a number of chapters on

Figure 18.2 **Growth Stages, Functions of Culture, and Change Mechanisms**

Growth stage	Function of culture/issue
I. Birth and early growth Founder domination, possible family domination	1. Culture is a distinctive competence and source of identity. 2 Culture is the "glue" that holds organization together. 3. Organization strives toward more integration and clarity. 4. Heavy emphasis on socialization as evidence of commitment.
Succession phase	1. Culture becomes battleground between conservatives and liberals. 2. Potential successors are judged on whether they will preserve or change cultural elements.
Change mechanisms 1. Natural evolution 2. Self-guided evolution through organizational therapy 3. Managed evolution through hybrids 4. Managed "revolution" through outsiders	
II. Organizational midlife 1. Expansion of products/markets. 2. Vertical integration 3. Geographical expansion 4. Acquisitions, mergers	1. Cultural integration declines as new subcultures are spawned. 2. Loss of key goals, values, and assumptions creates crisis of identity. 3. Opportunity to manage direction of cultural change is provided.
Change mechanisms 5. Planned change and organization development 6. Technological seduction 7. Change through scandal, explosion of myths 8. Incrementalism 9. Coercive persuasion 10. Turnaround 11. Reorganization, destruction, rebirth	
III. Organizational maturity 1. Maturity or decline of markets. 2. Increasing internal stability and/or stagnation. 3. Lack of motivation to change.	1. Culture becomes a constraint on innovation. 2. Culture preserves the glories of the past, hence is valued as a source of self-esteem, defense.
Transformation option	1. Culture change is necessary and inevitable, but not all elements of culture can or must change. 2. Essential elements of culture must be identified, preserved. 3. Culture change can be managed or simply allowed to evolve.
Destruction option 1. Bankruptcy and reorganization. 2. Takeover and reorganization. 3. Merger and assimilation.	1. Culture changes at fundamental paradigm levels. 2. Culture changes through massive replacement of key people.
Change mechanisms 9. Coercive Persuasion 10. Turnaround 11. Reorganization, destruction, rebirth	

Source: Schein (1985, 271, 272). Copyright © 1985 by Jossey-Bass. Reprinted with permission of Jossey-Bass, Inc., a subsidiary of John Wiley & Sons, Inc.

Table 18.1

Assumptions Required for a Perpetually Learning Culture

1. Regarding relationships to the environment—organization dominant
2. Regarding the nature of reality (truth)—pragmatic
3. Regarding the nature of time—near-future oriented, medium units of time
4. Regarding the nature of human nature—basically good, mutable
5. Regarding the nature of human activity—proactive
6. Regarding the nature of human relationships—blend of groupism–individualism, blend of authoritative–collegial
7. Regarding information and communication—fully connected
8. Regarding subcultural uniformity vs. diversity—high diversity
9. Regarding task vs. relationship orientation—blend of task and relationship orientation
10. Regarding linear vs. systemic field logic—systemic thinking

Source: Adapted from Schein (1992, 364–72).

subculture, culture deciphering, and the learning leader and culture" (xvii). There is less attention to theory and more concern with subcultures.

The method of deciphering culture proposed represents a considerable extension of the procedures noted previously. It starts with establishing the commitment of leadership to deal with some problem (usually strategic) assumed to require culture change. A group of up to fifty members from the culture is then constituted and the process consultant works with them by giving an initial lecture on the nature of culture, eliciting values, and probing into the area of shared underlying assumptions. This latter process involves looking for disparities between artifacts identified and values proclaimed. Next, the large group is split into subgroups, which if possible represent subcultures within the whole. These subgroups work on identifying more assumptions and on categorizing assumptions as to whether they will help or hinder solution of the problem at hand. The subgroups report back to the whole, where consensus is ironed out. The change process is then initiated with a lecture on that subject, new subgroups, and the development of a change strategy by the whole.

Subcultures tend to form around areas of differentiation within the organization—functional units, geographical divisions, acquisitions, and the like. Usually the people in these components carry with them an outside culture that becomes melded into the prevailing organizational culture to form a subculture. Professional identifications, geographical variations, customer characteristics, and such may thus intrude into the culture formation process. Subcultures also form at various levels of the managerial hierarchy, influenced by the types of tasks to be performed. Sometimes subcultures arise that are deliberately countercultural vis-à-vis the main culture; diversity on ethnic, racial, gender, and other such grounds can also be a source of subcultures. A particularly salient subculture at present often develops around the information technology component.

An especially intriguing challenge for leadership is to develop a learning organization that can continue to make its own diagnoses and self-manage the change process. Such a culture institutionalizes learning and innovation. Schein's (1992) theory of the assumptions inherent in such a culture is set forth in Table 18.1. This is a very difficult type of culture to establish and maintain.

As stated previously, leadership is the capacity to understand and change cultures; this applies to subcultures as well as main cultures. Different stages of organizational development (see Figure 18.2) require different approaches to handling culture, as do different strategic issues. Dealing with cultural transformations requires a leader who is a perpetual learner. Leaders of this kind must possess:

1. New levels of perception and insight into the realities of the world and also into themselves.
2. Extraordinary levels of motivation to go through the inevitable pain of learning and change.
3. The emotional strength to manage their own and others' anxiety as learning and change become more and more a way of life.
4. New skills in analyzing and changing cultural assumptions.
5. The willingness and ability to involve others and elicit their participation.
6. The ability to learn the assumptions of a whole new organizational culture. (Schein 1992, 391–92)

Schein (1996b) provides a particularly insightful analysis of how leaders can create and nurture an organizational culture, with special reference to the role Singapore's Economic Development Board has played in the economic success of that country.

Cultural Learning and Change

More recently Schein has concentrated on giving his theory wider exposure and on fine-tuning some of the ideas. A small book (Schein 1999b) is the major vehicle for these latter purposes, although there are several significant theoretical extensions noted there also. Among these is a treatment of the anxiety associated with learning, and particularly with the learning that occurs during culture change. This learning anxiety, which is the basis for resistance to change, can be manifested in passive-aggressive behavior (McIlduff and Coghlan 2000). It can be disruptive, and accordingly leaders must create a sense of psychological safety by providing a compelling positive vision, formal training such as team building, involvement of the learner, practice opportunities and feedback, positive role models, support groups, and consistent systems and structures. Without these conditions, change programs will fail. Survival anxiety is the feeling that unless something is learned, the organization will fail; it is a necessary but not sufficient condition for change (Quick and Gavin 2000).

Culture change normally requires establishing a temporary parallel learning system where new assumptions are practiced and learned in comparative safety. The establishment of various groups to foster change is inherent in this parallel learning procedure. The steps involved are: (1) to ensure that before anything else the leaders have learned something new, (2) for the leaders to create a change management group or steering committee, (3) for this steering committee to go through its own learning process, (4) for the steering committee to design the organizational learning process to include various task forces focused on the major issues, (5) for these task forces to learn how to learn, (6) for the task forces to create specific change programs, (7) for the steering committee to maintain communication through the change process, and, finally, (8) for the steering committee to develop mechanisms for continuous learning (Schein 1993b). Process consultants work with these various groups to facilitate the learning and change processes.

Previously we have considered the dialogue approach as it relates to process consultation. Schein (1993c, 1996c, 1999b) also introduces the dialogue concept into his discussion of culture. He feels it is a particularly appropriate technique for bridging the gaps between organizational cultures when companies are joined via merger and acquisition, or when subcultures are in conflict. Among the latter situations are those involving different levels of the management hierarchy, and the perennial disparities between the executive, engineering, and operating cultures in manufacturing firms. Dialogue is the method of choice for dealing with differences extending across culture boundaries, especially differences that need to be ironed out during periods of culture change.

EVALUATION AND IMPACT

Schein (in Luthans 1989) notes that somewhere in the 1960s he largely gave up on experimentation because he felt work of this kind was not adequate to explain the real world variables with which he was dealing in process consultation. The result has been that he has neither carried out research to evaluate the results of his process consulting engagements nor conducted tests of his culture and leadership theory. In fact there is little by way of discussion of research in Schein's writing on these subjects; he appears to perceive himself as a clinician, not a researcher, and at times he seems to be unsure as to whether he is a theorist either. Yet he has contrived a logically tight and compelling theory, as well as methods of approaching the measurement of many of its variables. It is simply that he prefers to leave the whole matter of conducting related research to others, if they feel that is what is needed, or possible. He, himself, has not published research in the scholarly literature since the 1960s, although he has made contributions of other kinds to this literature (see, for example, Schein 1996d). For a statement of his current thinking on research, which is basically unchanged, see Schein (2000).

Status of Research on Process Consultation

As so often happens, the author of this approach to organization development has served as a role model for others in the field of organizational behavior. His failure to conduct research on process consultation has been emulated by others. There is no research to my knowledge that one can point to and say "this is a test of the effectiveness of Schein's procedure for carrying out organization development." Schein does not mention any such studies. There are, however, investigations that attempt to assess procedures of a *human processual* nature, to include team building, T-groups, and other techniques that Schein has used on occasion, and we will consider these shortly. The problem is that, without specific guidance on the matter, it is impossible to determine whether a given application was carried out in a manner that Schein would accept as an appropriate instance of his process consultation. Thus, a particular study may or may not be suitable for consideration as a test. Schein is considered by many to be the father of process consulting, and most, if not all, organization development practitioners are said to use process consulting in their work to some degree (Kahnweiler 2002). Yet "empirical" research on the effectiveness of process consulting is "sorely lacking" (160).

There is some evidence that relates to the viability and impact of process consultation, however. A study conducted by Church, Burke, and Van Eynde (1994) indicates that process consultation ranks fifth among twenty-two interventions and activities considered.

Another study (McMahan and Woodman 1992) uses broader categories of analysis and focuses only on internal organization development consultants, but seems to indicate that these individuals devote roughly a third of their time to something that would pass as process consultation. Roughly half of organization development practitioners appear to be advocates of some approach that is akin to process consultation (Worley and Feyerherm 2003).

A final point is made in a discussion of the use of organization development approaches in relatively small entrepreneurial firms. Dyer (1997), who has had considerable experience with process consultation, reports that, in his experience, these firms require content consulting in addition to a process approach. This focus on both the content of the problem and the process used to solve it appears to be spreading to applications in larger firms as well. Relying entirely on the knowledge base of the firm involved in the manner of process consultation would appear to be on the decline; as a result some see process consulting as being replaced in part by an expert model (Church, Waclawski, and Berr 2002).

Status of Research on Culture and Leadership Theory

Here too there is a dearth of solid research testing the theory, but not for the same reasons. The often unconscious or preconscious nature of cultural assumptions, combined with the fact that the study of culture has its origins in clinical and ethnographic approaches that are primarily based in anthropological observations, has made for a situation where qualitative procedures far outweigh the quantitative. As a result, numerous theories of organizational culture have emerged, often with diverse viewpoints (Martin 1992), but little by way of quantitative testing. Thus, Schein's theory is in the position of being merely one among many such theories whose validity is unknown, even though it was received with considerable acclaim and appears to have substantial potential.

The study of organizational culture has been described as in a state of chaos (Martin and Frost 1996), and with good reason. There is no science to sort out truth from fantasy, and stridency of protestation becomes the major criterion for fleeting acceptance. This state of affairs appears to be primarily attributable to the strong qualitative orientation of the field, which is readily evident from a reading of edited volumes on organizational culture (see, for example, Frost, Moore, Louis, Lundberg, and Martin 1991). Case studies are rampant (see Carter, Giber, and Goldsmith 2001).

Although many have argued that organizational culture is not amenable to quantitative research, and some view it as outside the realm of science as well, these positions do not seem tenable. Just as projective techniques can be used to get at unconscious motivation in micro organizational behavior, they can be used to get at cultural assumptions in macro organizational behavior. The Thematic Apperception Test has been proposed as particularly applicable for this purpose (Trice 1991). Furthermore, observations and field notes can be categorized and scored to get at dimensions of culture and these procedures can be repeated to determine reliability of measurement. My point is that techniques are available to test the hypotheses of culture theories. The preference of those who work in the field for producing what amounts to fiction (Trice 1991) cannot be an excuse for leaving theories untested. Unfortunately, the theory of organizational culture and leadership that Schein has proposed has become caught up in all this.

However, data do exist that have some relevance for assessing the usefulness of process consultation as an organization development intervention when cultural factors are involved. Research by Nohria, Joyce, and Roberson (2003) finds that building the right culture, one that champions high-level performance and ethical behavior, is crucial to superior corporate performance. Other evidence supports this conclusion (see Lee and Yu 2004). Also, demonstration projects, such as the one conducted by Bate, Khan, and Pye (2000), although not designed specifically to test Schein's theory, have utilized aspects of process consultation and cultural constructs to achieve significant cultural and structural changes. Thus, there is some reason to believe that Schein's theorizing may be on the right track in providing an understanding of how and when organizations can achieve successful change.

Effectiveness of Organization Development in the Early Period

Organization development comes in many colors, as we have seen. In addition, researchers in the field have not always described in sufficient detail either the techniques used or the theories underlying these efforts. Thus, reviews of the research literature often provide a good indication of the effectiveness of organization development as a whole, while leaving the specifics of what changed what, and what theory worked best, rather uncertain. Nevertheless, by looking at these reviews we can reach some conclusions about the effectiveness of the various approaches and theories considered in this and the prior chapter, and particularly those of Edgar Schein.

Roughly 75 percent of the early studies, and by that I mean those conducted prior to the mid-1970s, utilized procedures related to laboratory training at some point in the overall process and thus had something in common with process consultation. There clearly have been major changes in the nature of organization development practice over the years (Sanzgiri and Gottlieb 1992), which were particularly pronounced during the 1970s, as T-groups and sensitivity training fell into disrepute. Thus, it is appropriate to separate the reviews conducted before and after the middle of that decade; they deal with different types of interventions.

An analysis by Bowers (1973) of data from organization development programs carried out in twenty-three organizations revealed that laboratory training had a predominantly negative impact using the system 4 oriented Survey of Organizations variables (see Chapter 8 in this volume). Related approaches along the lines of process consultation yield somewhat more positive results, or at least somewhat less negative results. Overall, the results are not favorable to the kinds of interventions we have been considering. On the other hand, all these studies were carried out in conjunction with the Survey Research Center at the University of Michigan and relied entirely on a single change measure dealing primarily with climate.

Analyses that cast a wider net tend to yield somewhat more favorable results. The results of a research survey by Porras and Berg (1978) indicate a high frequency of change in performance indexes as contrasted with factors such as individual job satisfaction. Overall, the data suggest that positive results can be anticipated approximately half the time and that organizationally significant factors such as profits, performance, and output are most likely to be affected.

An additional review by Smith (1975), which focuses on the effects of laboratory training as well as its use in organization development, concludes:

> Of the studies reviewed in this article, 100 permit the drawing of a conclusion as to whether or not an effect of training was obtained. Of these studies, 78 did show an increase in one or more scores after training which was significantly greater than any change the controls may have shown. . . . Only 31 studies permitted the drawing of a conclusion as to persistence of change at follow-up. Of these 21 did show persistence of change. (Smith 1975, 615)

Within organization development these results tend to be somewhat mitigated due to the variety of historical and cultural factors operating.

More Recent Studies of Organization Development Effectiveness

As we move beyond the 1970s both the number of studies and the number of reviews increase. However, the most pronounced change is in the diversity of types of interventions introduced. There clearly has been a shift to other approaches beyond process consultation.

A review by Sashkin and Burke (1990) deals with publications of the 1980s. They conclude that there can be little doubt that organization development overall has major positive effects on performance measures. However, there is also some evidence that these results may be obtained at the cost of performance pressures, which in turn create negative satisfaction and attitude changes. They note that team building using established employee groups has become a key ingredient of practice, and that organizational culture is increasingly discussed in the literature, although with little by way of systematic research to support it. No theory of organization development processes was found to have achieved consensus support within the field.

Porras and Robertson (1992) carry out a literature review that permits breakdown by several types of interventions. What they call social factor interventions, which include process consultation, indicate the highest proportion of positive outcomes, at 51 percent (only 6 percent were negative). These results for social factor interventions may be contrasted with the figure of 38 percent obtained for organization development interventions of all types. Porras and Silvers (1991) provide an extensive review of the literature up to that point, including several meta-analyses conducted during the 1980s. Their conclusions are consistently positive, except that organization development does not appear to work well in professional contexts; it works best within the bureaucratic confines that it was originally intended to supplant.

Team building has been a feature of many process consultation interventions over the years. The research evidence has generally indicated a positive influence on satisfaction and attitudes, but has been somewhat mixed insofar as improved productivity is concerned. A meta-analytic review was undertaken with the specific intent of dealing with the latter issue (Svyantek, Goodman, Benz, and Gard 1999). The conclusion was that team building did have a significant positive impact on productivity, whether measured in objective or subjective terms.

Actually, references to the effectiveness of change initiatives range from 30 percent (Beer and Nohria 2000) to over 70 percent (Golembiewski 2003). A frequent figure is 50 percent (Farias and Johnson 2000), but Burke (2002), in providing an overview of reviews of organizational change research, fails to reach any conclusion as to effectiveness levels. The problem that creates this diversity is what should be included in the definition of a change initiative. For present purposes this would appear to narrow down to organization development interventions of a process nature, given that data on Schein's process consultation do not exist. The best source of information bearing on that purpose is a recent book by Golembiewski (2003).

Golembiewski (2003) reviews a wide range of studies with origins in the United States and other parts of the world, more studies than anyone else has considered; his overall conclusion is that success rates are quite high. Thus the percentage of studies with "highly positive and intended effects" runs in the low 40s, and the percentage with a "definite balance of positive and intended effects" adds at least an equal number of studies and probably 5 percent more than that. These types of success rates are maintained for a variety of approaches that appear to approximate what occurs in process consultation. They have held at least through the 1990s, are not subject to any appreciable effect derived from the sophistication level of the research design, apply internationally, hold for both hard criteria and soft, and do not differ as between published versus unpublished sources.

A more focused analysis identified a class of interventions, labeled as *human processual,* that appears to include much of process consultation, but extends beyond it as well. "Highly positive" support comes from 69 percent of the cases of this kind, with an added 22 percent having a "balance of positive" (qualified support) cases. These recently established findings, when added to other near-term results mentioned previously, make a strong case for the benefits of something that looks very similar to, if not identical with, process consultation (Golembiewski 2003).

Alpha, Beta, and Gamma Change

Golembiewski has developed with others a theory of the change process that occurs as organization development programs are implemented; this theory is important for Schein's views and for other approaches to organization development.

Golembiewski received his doctorate from Yale in political science in 1958 and, having been introduced to laboratory training as a result of a visiting appointment at Yale arranged by Argyris, began to concentrate in the area of organization development (Golembiewski 1992). He has continued to work in that area since, primarily as a faculty member at the University of Georgia, where he has remained for many years. His approach to practice appears to be similar to Schein's in many respects, and in fact he endorsed process consultation in its early applications.

Out of his work reviewing the related literature emerged a question as to what really changes as a result of organization development interventions. The major contribution to answering this question was an article describing alpha, beta, and gamma change (Golembiewski, Billingsley, and Yeager 1976); numerous statements have followed, including, most recently, Golembiewski (2003). The definitions of the three types of change are as follows:

> *Alpha change* involves a variation in the level of some existential state, given a constantly calibrated measuring instrument related to a constant conceptual domain.
> *Beta change* involves a variation in the level of some existential state, complicated by the fact that some intervals of the measurement continuum associated with a constant conceptual domain have been recalibrated.
> *Gamma change* involves a redefinition or reconceptualization of some domain, a major change in the perspective or frame-of-reference within which phenomena are perceived and classified, in what is taken to be relevant in some slice of reality. (Golembiewski, Billingsley, and Yeager 1976, 134–35)

Alpha changes, then, occur along relatively stable dimensions defined in terms of discrete and constant intervals. Beta changes are characterized by shifts in the intervals used and involve restandardization of a measure in the mind of the respondent. Gamma changes involve a redefining of the psychological space covered by a measure, such as shifting from one construct to another or expanding the domain envisaged by a given construct; thus new meanings are introduced.

Alpha change is what we normally assume to occur across the process of an intervention when we repeat measurements over time. Yet there is convincing evidence that beta and gamma changes can occur as well, and usually without their effects being evident to the researcher; thus we have a potential source of error.

This potentiality for error is particularly pronounced in organization development evaluations for three reasons. First, most interventions are intended to produce gamma change, and probably beta change as well. Organization development is typically viewed as a process for introducing a new social order or a new culture. It intends to change values and ways of perceiving; concepts of ideal states are expected to shift. If these changes do not occur, then the effort is likely to be considered ineffectual, but if they do occur, beta and gamma changes are introduced, which in turn confound the measurement process.

Second, beta and gamma changes are factors that are most likely to influence self-report measures where meanings and standards within the individual tend to determine the data; this is in contrast to projective measures or hard data outcome measures of productivity. These self-reports are often used to evaluate the results of organization development interventions, either in the form of survey questionnaires or, less often, standardized interviews. To the extent these approaches are used, conclusions regarding organization development success rates are placed in jeopardy.

Third, procedures of various kinds aimed at detecting beta and gamma changes have been developed; some are statistical in nature and some involve innovations in research design. There are numerous remaining problems in this regard but procedures do exist (Porras and Robertson 1992). The problem is that, beyond the research employed to develop them, they are not used in the actual conduct of evaluation studies (Sashkin and Burke 1990, Porras and Silvers 1991). Thus, in spite of the substantial increase in knowledge that has occurred as a result of Golembiewski's theory of change processes, there has been little impact on evaluation practice.

What then does Golembiewski's theory mean for the success rates noted previously, which are predicated on the incorrect assumption that all change is alpha in nature? The original instigation for the theory came from a deviant case, when an evaluation by the usual self-report methods indicated failure, as indicated by no change from pretest to posttest. Yet participants in the intervention insisted on its overall success. This type of situation would suggest that the research reports may represent underestimates. Others, including Golembiewski (2003), have reached this same conclusion.

One solution to the problems thus identified is to utilize measures other than those of a self-report nature. This has been done with measures of performance, including productivity, absenteeism, turnover, and the like; positive results have been obtained with these kinds of measures, thus providing confidence in the success rates reported. Another alternative would be to utilize projective measures, which call for individuals to provide responses that are interpreted by the researcher, not the individuals themselves, as in the self-report techniques; this approach has not been used to my knowledge.

There is also the question of whether beta and gamma changes, if they do operate to decrease the amount of recognized change, do so to a meaningful degree. Some beta change and most gamma change would seem to require basic cultural changes before their mechanisms are activated. Yet Schein contends that such changes are difficult to achieve and probably occur rarely; most interventions produce their results within the flexibility allowed by the existing culture. If this is the case, we are dealing with a real phenomenon, yet one that has only minimal effects on the results obtained. Clearly there remains a great deal for research to tell us. However, it does appear that if the variables of the tripartite theory do have a meaningful influence, it is to increase the size of positive success findings in most instances. Since the effects of approaches akin to process consultation are often evaluated using self-report measures, this would seem to provide increased support for this type of approach to organization development.

CONCLUSIONS

A look at the box at the beginning of this chapter reveals a rather strange situation. Without the (★) added to estimated usefulness, the stars add up only to nine and the total is not sufficient in itself to justify an essential designation. With the new star, this changes dramatically—the usefulness rating rises to a level sufficient to warrant essential status, four stars. This occurs because of findings published in the past few years, and since my evaluations were made originally. The dominant consideration here is the Golembiewski (2003) review, which provides a new and more solid grounding for process consultation.

Given the two-star evaluation on estimated validity, what this state of affairs seems to indicate is that practice has outdistanced theory, that organization development practitioners are mixing approaches and adapting techniques to situations so as to get better results than the basic theory would warrant. The theories may in some cases be better than this, but until they are more adequately tested we cannot be sure. Anyway, organization development seems to be progressing nicely. What we need now is a theory that will catch up with practice, and provide the driving force for a new round of advances in practice. In the mean time, we have the unexpected situation that Schein's theory of organizational culture and leadership is given an importance rating of 4.85 by his peers, while process consultation is rated 4.02, almost a full point difference, in the reverse direction, of the validity and usefulness findings. This appears to reflect one of the ironies of organization development that Golembiewski (2003) discusses.

We now move from theories underpinning organization development to types of theories that have come to dominate modern sociological theorizing in the more recent period.

REFERENCES

Bate, Paul, Khan, Raza, and Pye, Annie (2000). Towards a Culturally Sensitive Approach to Organization Structuring: Where Organization Design Meets Organization Development. *Organization Science,* 11, 197–211.

Beer, Michael, and Nohria, Nitin (2000). Cracking the Code of Change. *Harvard Business Review,* 78(3), 133–41.

Bowers, David G. (1973). OD Techniques and Their Results in 23 Organizations: The Michigan ICL Study. *Journal of Applied Behavioral Science,* 9, 21–43.

Burke, W. Warner (2002). *Organization Change: Theory and Practice.* Thousand Oaks, CA: Sage.

Carter, Louis, Giber, David, and Goldsmith, Marshall (2001). *Best Practices in Organization Development and Change.* San Francisco, CA: Jossey-Bass.

Church, Allan H., Burke, W. Warner, and Van Eynde, Donald F. (1994). Values, Motives, and Interventions of Organization Development Practitioners. *Group and Organization Management,* 19, 5–50.

Church, Allan H., Waclawski, Janine, and Berr, Seth A. (2002). Voices from the Field: Future Directions for Organization Development. In Janine Waclawski and Allan H. Church (Eds.), *Organization Development: A Data-Driven Approach to Organizational Change.* San Francisco, CA: Jossey-Bass, 321–36.

Coutu, Dianne L. (2002). The Anxiety of Learning. *Harvard Business Review,* 80(3), 100–6.

Dyer, W. Gibb (1997). Organization Development in the Entrepreneurial Firm. *Journal of Applied Behavioral Science, 33,* 190–208.

Farias, Gerard, and Johnson, Homer (2000). Organizational Development and Change Management: Setting the Record Straight. *Journal of Applied Behavioral Science, 36,* 376–79.

Frost, Peter J., Moore, Larry F., Louis, Meryl R., Lundberg, Craig C., and Martin, Joanne (1991). *Reframing Organizational Culture.* Newbury Park, CA: Sage.

Golembiewski, Robert T. (1992). Mid-Career Perspectives. In Arthur G. Bedeian (Ed.), *Management Laureates: A Collection of Autobiographical Essays,* Vol. I. Greenwich, CT: JAI Press, 371–416.

———. (2003). *Ironies in Organizational Development.* New York: Marcel Dekker.

Golembiewski, Robert T., Billingsley, Keith, and Yeager, Samuel (1976). Measuring Change and Persistence in Human Affairs: Types of Change Generated by OD Designs. *Journal of Applied Behavioral Science, 12,* 133–57.

Kahnweiler, William M. (2002). Process Consultation: A Cornerstone of Organization Development Practice. In Janine Waclawski and Allan H. Church (Eds.), *Organization Development: A Data-Driven Approach to Organizational Change.* San Francisco, CA: Jossey-Bass, 149–63.

Lee, Siew K.J., and Yu, Kelvin (2004). Corporate Culture and Organizational Performance. *Journal of Managerial Psychology, 19,* 340–59.

Luthans, Fred (1989). Conversation with Edgar H. Schein. *Organizational Dynamics, 17*(4), 60–76.

Martin, Joanne (1992). *Cultures in Organizations: Three Perspectives.* New York: Oxford University Press.

Martin, Joanne, and Frost, Peter (1996). The Organizational Culture War Games: A Struggle for Intellectual Dominance. In Stewart R. Clegg, Cynthia Hardy, and Walter R. Nord (Eds.), *Handbook of Organization Studies.* London: Sage, 599–621.

McIlduff, Edward, and Coghlan, David (2000). Understanding and Contending with Passive-Aggressive Behavior in Teams and Organizations. *Journal of Managerial Psychology, 15,* 716–32.

McMahan, Gary C., and Woodman, Richard W. (1992). The Current Practice of Organization Development Within the Firm. *Group and Organization Management, 17,* 117–34.

Miner, John B. (2002). *Organizational Behavior: Foundations, Theories, and Analyses.* New York: Oxford University Press.

———. (2005). *Organizational Behavior 1: Essential Theories of Motivation and Leadership.* Armonk, NY: M.E. Sharpe.

Nohria, Nitin, Joyce, William, and Roberson, Bruce (2003). What Really Works. *Harvard Business Review, 81*(7), 43–52.

Porras, Jerry I., and Berg, Per O. (1978). The Impact of Organization Development. *Academy of Management Review, 3,* 249–66.

Porras, Jerry I., and Robertson, Peter J. (1992). Organization Development: Theory, Practice, and Research. In Marvin D. Dunnette and Leaetta M. Hough (Eds.), *Handbook of Industrial and Organizational Psychology,* Vol. 3. Palo Alto, CA: Consulting Psychologists Press, 719–822.

Porras, Jerry I., and Silvers, Robert C. (1991). Organization Development and Transformation. *Annual Review of Psychology, 42,* 51–78.

Quick, James C., and Gavin, Joanne H. (2000). The Next Frontier: Edgar Schein on Organizational Therapy. *Academy of Management Executive, 14,* 31–44.

Sanzgiri, Jyotsna, and Gottlieb, Jonathan Z. (1992). Philosophic and Pragmatic Influences on the Practice of Organization Development, 1950–2000. *Organizational Dynamics, 21*(2), 57–69.

Sashkin, Marshall, and Burke, W. Warner (1990). Organization Development in the 1980s. *Advances in Organization Development, 1,* 315–46.

Schein, Edgar H. (1957). Patterns of Reactions to Severe Chronic Stress in American Army Prisoners of War of the Chinese. In *Symposium No. 4—Methods of Forceful Indoctrination: Observations and Interviews.* New York: Group for the Advancement of Psychiatry, 253–69.

———. (1968). Organizational Socialization and the Profession of Management. *Sloan Management Review, 9*(2), 1–16.

———. (1969). *Process Consultation: Its Role in Organization Development.* Reading, MA: Addison-Wesley.

———. (1975). The Hawthorne Group Studies Revisited: A Defense of Theory Y. In Eugene L. Cass and Frederick G. Zimmer (Eds.), *Man and Work in Society.* New York: Van Nostrand Reinhold, 78–94.

———. (1978). *Career Dynamics: Matching Individual and Organizational Needs.* Reading, MA: Addison-Wesley.

————. (1981a). Improving Face-to-Face Relationships. *Sloan Management Review,* 22(2), 43–52.

————. (1981b). Does Japanese Management Style Have a Message for American Managers? *Sloan Management Review,* 23(1), 55–68.

————. (1983). The Role of the Founder in Creating Organizational Culture. *Organizational Dynamics,* 12(1), 13–28.

————. (1984a). Culture as an Environmental Context for Careers. *Journal of Occupational Behavior,* 5, 71–81.

————. (1984b). Coming to a New Awareness of Organizational Culture. *Sloan Management Review,* 25(2), 3–16.

————. (1985). *Organizational Culture and Leadership: A Dynamic View.* San Francisco, CA: Jossey-Bass.

————. (1987a). Individuals and Careers. In Jay W. Lorsch (Ed.), *Handbook of Organizational Behavior.* Englewood Cliffs, NJ: Prentice Hall, 155–71.

————. (1987b). *Process Consultation, Volume II: Lessons for Managers and Consultants.* Reading, MA: Addison-Wesley.

————. (1987c). *The Clinical Perspective in Fieldwork.* Newbury Park, CA: Sage.

————. (1988). *Process Consultation, Volume I: Its Role in Organization Development.* Reading, MA: Addison-Wesley.

————. (1989a). A Social Psychologist Discovers Chicago Sociology. *Academy of Management Review,* 14, 103–4.

————. (1989b). Reassessing the "Divine Rights" of Managers. *Sloan Management Review,* 30(2), 63–68.

————. (1990a). Back to the Future: Recapturing the OD Vision. *Advances in Organization Development,* 1, 13–26.

————. (1990b). A General Philosophy of Helping: Process Consultation. *Sloan Management Review,* 31(3), 57–64.

————. (1992). *Organizational Culture and Leadership, Second Edition.* San Francisco, CA: Jossey-Bass.

————. (1993a). The Academic as Artist: Personal and Professional Roots. In Arthur G. Bedeian (Ed.), *Management Laureates: A Collection of Autobiographical Essays,* Vol. 3. Greenwich, CT: JAI Press, 31–62.

————. (1993b). How Can Organizations Learn Faster? The Challenge of Entering the Green Room. *Sloan Management Review,* 34(2), 85–92.

————. (1993c). On Dialogue, Culture, and Organizational Learning. *Organizational Dynamics,* 22(2), 40–51.

————. (1995). Process Consultation, Action Research and Clinical Inquiry: Are They the Same? *Journal of Managerial Psychology,* 10(6), 14–19.

————. (1996a). Career Anchors Revisited: Implications for Career Development in the 21st Century. *Academy of Management Executive,* 10(4), 80–88.

————. (1996b). *Strategic Pragmatism: The Culture of Singapore's Economic Development Board.* Cambridge, MA: MIT Press.

————. (1996c). Three Cultures of Management: The Key to Organizational Learning. *Sloan Management Review,* 38(1), 9–20.

————. (1996d). Culture: The Missing Concept in Organization Studies. *Administrative Science Quarterly,* 41, 229–40.

————. (1999a). *Process Consultation Revisited: Building the Helping Relationship.* Reading, MA: Addison-Wesley.

————. (1999b). *The Corporate Culture Survival Guide: Sense and Nonsense About Culture Change.* San Francisco, CA: Jossey-Bass.

————. (2000). When Will We Learn? In Art Kleiner and George Roth (Eds.), *Oil Change: Perspectives on Corporate Transformation.* New York: Oxford University Press, 189–98.

Schein, Edgar H., and Bennis, Warren G. (1965). *Personal and Organizational Change Through Group Methods: The Laboratory Approach.* New York: Wiley.

Schein, Edgar H., Schneier, Inge, and Barker, Curtis H. (1961). *Coercive Persuasion.* New York: W.W. Norton.

Smith, Peter B. (1975). Controlled Studies of the Outcome of Sensitivity Training. *Psychological Bulletin,* 82, 597–622.

Svyantek, Daniel J., Goodman, Scott A., Benz, Lori L., and Gard, Julia A. (1999). The Relationship Between Organizational Characteristics and Team Building Success. *Journal of Business and Psychology,* 14, 265–83.

Trice, Harrison M. (1991). Comments and Discussion. In Peter J. Frost, Larry F. Moore, Meryl R. Louis, Craig C. Lundberg, and Joanne Martin (Eds.), *Reframing Organizational Culture.* Newbury Park, CA: Sage, 298–308.

Van Maanen, John, and Schein, Edgar H. (1979). Toward a Theory of Organizational Socialization. *Research in Organizational Behavior,* 1, 209–64.

Worley, Christopher G., and Feyerherm, Ann E. (2003). Reflections on the Future of Organization Development. *Journal of Applied Behavioral Science,* 39, 97–115.

PART V

SOCIOLOGICAL CONCEPTS
OF ORGANIZATION

CHAPTER 19

EXTERNAL CONTROL OF ORGANIZATIONS— RESOURCE DEPENDENCE PERSPECTIVE

JEFFREY PFEFFER
GERALD SALANCIK

Importance rating	★ ★ ★ ★ ★
Estimated validity	★ ★ ★ ★ ★
Estimated usefulness	★ ★ ★
Decade of origin	1970s

Pfeffer's work on resource dependence theory does not appear to have had major roots in prior writings. It is not related to the resource-based view that has its origins in economics (see Barney 2001). Pfeffer labels his autobiography "Taking the Road Less Traveled" (Pfeffer 1996) and describes a process of theory development that represents a break with existing positions. Presumably as a result of this iconoclastic bent, he had difficulty initially getting his theoretical ideas accepted for publication, although his empirical work had much better success. As a result, although the first statements of the theory were contained in his 1971 dissertation, it was not until seven years later that a full and formal published version appeared (Pfeffer and Salancik 1978). This presentation, which now included a collaboration with Gerald Salancik, represents a considerable refinement of the earlier views.

BACKGROUND

Pfeffer received his undergraduate and master's degrees at the same time in industrial administration from Carnegie Mellon University in Pittsburgh. That was in 1968. Subsequently he entered the doctoral program in business at Stanford University from which he obtained a

Ph.D. in 1971. Next came a sojourn in the business school at the University of Illinois, where he joined forces with Salancik, who arrived there at the same time. This stint together, in fact, lasted only two years, before Pfeffer moved back west to the University of California at Berkeley. From there, in 1979, he shifted to his alma mater, Stanford, where he has remained since. His entire career has been in the business schools, and in organizational behavior.

Salancik came to resource dependence theory after considerable theoretical and empirical work had been completed on the subject, but at a point when the theory itself was going nowhere; in fact its author had largely given up on attempting to publish the theory (Pfeffer 1996). Salancik brought to this endeavor a master's degree in journalism from Northwestern University, a doctorate in social psychology from Yale University (in 1970), skills as an effective writer and editor, and a questioning mind, which paid little deference to the status quo (Leblebici and Porac 1997). Salancik remained at Illinois for a number of years after Pfeffer left, but ultimately moved on to the School of Industrial Administration at Carnegie Mellon. He died in 1996 at the age of 53.

RESOURCE DEPENDENCE THEORY

Resource dependence theory is in fact one among several outgrowths of a somewhat more fundamental perspective. This position is set forth in a paper by Pfeffer (1990) originally presented on the occasion of the fiftieth anniversary of the publication of Chester Barnard's *The Functions of the Executive*. This basic perspective utilizes the assumptions that (1) organizations and their people are interdependent with other organizations and people, and (2) consequent to this interdependence and the social relationships involved, understanding is much better served by investigating the effects and the constraints emanating from the social contexts; this is true of both individual and organizational behavior. We have already seen some of the outgrowths of this perspective in Part I of this book, specifically Pfeffer's views on the dispositions versus situations controversy and his treatment of consensus in science.

In the discussion that follows I focus directly on Pfeffer's resource dependence formulations, and do not follow other outgrowths of his more fundamental perspective. The major source here is the book with Salancik (1978). However, there were earlier abbreviated theoretical statements, including Aldrich and Pfeffer (1976) and Pfeffer (1978).

The External Perspective

The approach to theorizing utilized is essentially that of open systems, in that the focus is on external social constraints on organizational action. In addition, the discussion draws heavily on the ideas of other organizational behavior theorists, many of them treated in prior chapters of this book. Among these are Katz and Kahn's social psychology of organizations (Chapter 9), Trist and Emery's sociotechnical systems approach (Chapter 10), Thompson's sociological open systems theory (Chapter 11), Blau's theory of differentiation (Chapter 16), the contributions of Simon, Cyert, and March on organizational decision making (Chapters 3 and 4), and Weick's views on organizing and sensemaking (Chapter 6). Furthermore, the strategic contingencies theory of intraorganizational power (Hickson, Hinings, Lee, Schneck, and Pennings 1971), which had close ties to the Aston studies (Chapter 15), is utilized extensively. These reference points provide some indication of the domain within which the Pfeffer and Salancik theory operates.

The theory is largely concerned with how managers attempt to ensure organizational survival.

> ... [O]rganizations survive to the extent that they are effective. Their effectiveness derives from the management of demands, particularly the demands of interest groups upon which the organizations depend for resources and support. ... The key to organizational survival is the ability to acquire and maintain resources. ... Organizations must transact with other elements in their environment to acquire needed resources. (Pfeffer and Salancik 1978, 2)

Environments can change and resources can become scarce; environmental demands and constraints are constantly shifting. *Effectiveness* is the ability to create outcomes and actions that meet the external standards determining how well the organization meets the demands of environmental interests concerned with its activities. *Environments* are important to know about and understand because that is where judgments about organizational effectiveness reside. *Constraints* operate whenever one response to a situation, rather than being random, is more probable than other responses. Because behavior is widely, if not exclusively, constrained, individuals actually account for relatively little variation in organizational behavior. A major function of managers is to serve as symbols, thus enhancing feelings of predictability and control; yet there are in addition many important possibilities for managerial action, often aimed at adjusting to and altering the social context.

Organizations must operate as parts of coalitions that contribute resources and support if they are to survive. Coalition participants that contribute more needed or valued inputs tend to have greater influence and control, and thus these factors become part of the exchange. Participants may institute inconsistent criteria and conflicting demands; any one participant will contribute only a proportion of its behavior. The boundary of an organization is established by the point at which the discretion to control an activity is less than the discretion of some other entity. In contrast to effectiveness, which is an external judgment, efficiency is the extent to which an organization accomplishes objectives given the resources used. The managerial task is to manage the coalition to ensure continued support and survival of the organization (Pfeffer and Salancik 1978).

Interdependence

Whenever one actor does not fully control all conditions for achieving an action or obtaining the desired outcome, *interdependence* exists. This interdependence varies with the scarcity of resources, characterizes transactions within the same environment, and is a consequence of the open-systems nature of organizations; it is virtually inevitable. The extent to which an organization is subject to control under these circumstances varies with the extent that:

1. The focal organization is aware of the demands.
2. The focal organization obtains some resources from the social actor making the demands.
3. The resource is a critical or important part of the focal organization's operation.
4. The social actor controls the allocation, access, or use of the resource; alternative sources for the resource are not available to the focal organization.
5. The focal organization does not control the allocation, access, or use of other resources critical to the social actor's operation and survival.

Figure 19.1 **Relationships Among the Dimensions of Organizational Environments**

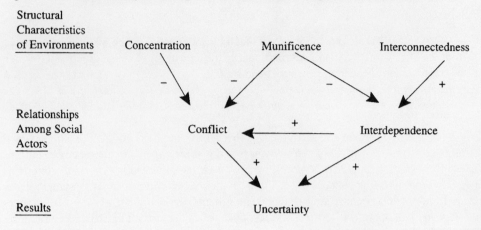

Source: Pfeffer and Salancik (1978, 68). Copyright © 1978 by Jeffrey Pfeffer and Gerald R. Salancik. Reprinted by permission of Pearson Education, Inc.

6. The actions or inputs of the focal organization are visible and can be assessed by the social actor to judge whether the actions comply with its demands.
7. The focal organization's satisfaction of the social actor's requests are not in conflict with the satisfaction of demands from other components of the environment with which it is interdependent.
8. The focal organization does not control the determination, formulation, or expression of the social actor's demands.
9. The focal organization is capable of developing actions or outcomes that will satisfy the external demands.
10. The organization desires to survive. (Pfeffer and Salancik 1978, 44)

External control becomes increasingly likely as more of these conditions exist. Vulnerability in this regard depends on the importance of the resource exchange (both the relative magnitude and the criticality) and on the degree of discretion over the allocation of the resource existing in some other social actor. Bases for control over a resource include possession, actual use, and the ability to regulate resource possession and use.

Dependence is the product of the importance of an input or output to an organization and the degree to which it is controlled by a few organizations. For dependence to operate, there must be asymmetry of exchange, so that some net power exists in the hands of the less dependent participant.

Knowing the Environment

Three levels of environment may be distinguished: the entire system created by an organization's transactions; those features with which the organization directly interacts; and the organization's enacted environment, created by its processes of perception and attention.

Figure 19.1 sets forth the strategic dimensions of organizational environments and the relationships among them. *Concentration* is the extent to which power is concentrated or dispersed in the environment. *Munificence* is the availability or scarcity of critical resources.

Figure 19.2 **A Methodology for Evaluating the Effectiveness of Actions**

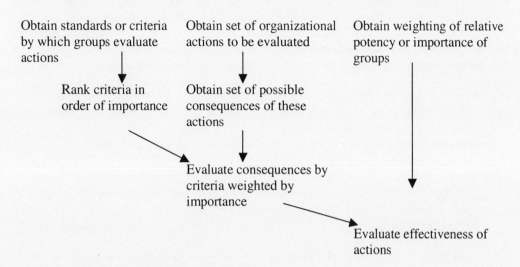

Source: Pfeffer and Salancik (1978,87). Copyright © 1978 by Jeffrey Pfeffer and Gerald R. Salancik. Reprinted by permission of Pearson Education, Inc.

Interconnectedness is the number and pattern of linkages among relevant organizations. If the interconnectedness is high, the environment of the focal organization tends to be more uncertain; if the system is loosely coupled, disturbances have a chance to be absorbed and certainty increases. Because of government actions, organizations are now experiencing greater interconnectedness.

Since environments are enacted as organizations respond to them, organizations tend to be in a lag position, reacting to what has been important in the past. Organizations may also misread interdependence, either by underestimating their dependence in certain respects, or even by failing to perceive the complex relationships that exist with other elements of their environments. A problem also exists when an organization is recognized as a potent influence, but the demands or criterion involved are misinterpreted. Then there is the matter of balancing competing demands. A procedure for determining the effectiveness of actions in the face of these problems in environmental enactment is outlined in Figure 19.2.

Managing the Organization's Environment

Managers cope with environmental constraints and demands in various ways: compliance, adaptation, avoidance, and so forth. An organization that permits itself to be subjected to long-term, successful influence attempts may well find its survival threatened. Thus, some method of managing the dependence becomes necessary. Perhaps most effective for this purpose is to find some way to avoid those conditions that demand compliance. This, in turn, may well require a resort to secrecy or the restriction of information.

Merger and growth are related ways of restructuring and increasing influence within environmental relationships. Organizations would be expected to merge into industries that create their greatest problems. Diversification is similarly motivated by a desire to avoid interdependence. Attempts to reduce sales in certain areas, or of particular product lines, can also serve to remove dependencies. Growth, on the other hand, can provide greater power over environmental factors and enhance an organization's prospects for survival.

Coordination with external organizations serves to manage interdependence. Included here are co-optation, trade associations, cartels, reciprocal agreements, coordinating councils, advisory boards, interlocking boards of directors, joint ventures, and social norms that govern interdependent parties. The latter are particularly common among professionals. Boards of directors are commonly used to co-opt external organizations with which important interdependencies exist. In all of these approaches there is the attempt to border on collusion without invoking legal actions.

Finally, another class of strategies may be used to manage interdependence:

> When dependence is not capable of being managed by negotiating stable structures of interorganizational action, . . . organizations seek to use the greater power of . . . government to eliminate the difficulties or provide for their needs. The organization . . . may seek direct cash subsidies, market protection, or may seek to reduce competitive uncertainty by charging competitors with antitrust violations. . . . The courts and the government are increasingly replacing the market in determining which organizations will survive and prosper. (Pfeffer and Salancik 1978, 189)

Executive Succession

The basic proposition with regard to succession is that environmental contingencies influence the selection and replacement of top managers in such a way as to place the organization in greater alignment with environmental requirements. One possible model of adaptation along these lines is given in Figure 19.3, which shows that organizational actions are a result of political processes within organizations, not a direct consequence of environmental requirements; the coupling is loose, with power as an intervening variable.

Power is conceptualized according to the strategic contingencies theory (Hickson, Hinings, Lee, Schneck, and Pennings 1971), which involves:

1. The ability of a subunit to cope with organizational uncertainties or contingencies.
2. The substitutability of the subunit's capabilities—these capabilities must be relatively unique.
3. The pervasiveness or importance of the contingency and uncertainty to the organization. (220–22)

Such power may become institutionalized, and subunit power serves to resolve political contests over administrative succession.

Top executives tend to be recruited from competitors if interfirm coordination appears to be an appropriate strategy. Turnover at the top is most likely when the contingencies faced are ones that present managers cannot handle. Thus, the theory is not one of direct environmental determinism.

Three managerial roles are posited: symbolic, responsive, and discretionary. The *symbolic* role has already been noted, and administrative succession may be invoked to change appearances in this manner. But it is typically the responsive and discretionary roles that contribute to whatever variance in outcomes does stem from managerial activity. In the

Figure 19.3 **A Model of Organizational Adaptation to Environmental Constraints Via Succession**

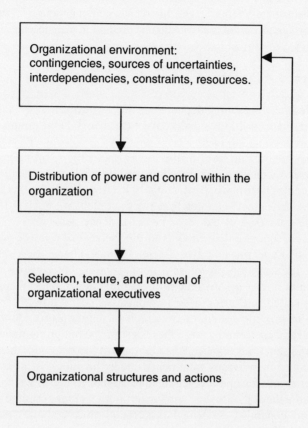

Source: Adapted from Pfeffer and Salancik (1978, 229) and Pfeffer (1982, 203).

responsive role, a manager assesses the organizational context, determines how to cope with it, and implements that process; these are adaptive processes. In the *discretionary* role, a manager goes beyond adaptation in taking action to modify the environment and to alter the existing system of constraints and dependencies.

The implications of the theory for organizational design relate to the design of environmental scanning systems, designs intended to loosen dependencies, designs for managing conflicting demands, and designs to modify chief executive positions. Clearly knowing the environment well and creating mechanisms to accomplish this are a central focus of the resource dependence perspective. Loosening dependencies is best achieved through diversification, as by a resort to many small suppliers. Structural differentiation is introduced, in this view, not as a direct means to cope with size, but as a method of coping with conflicting demands, bringing them together in order to concentrate a specific structure on them. Finally, an approach to the chief executive position that involves multiple chief executives to cope with varied demands is recommended.

This scenario does not suggest an increase in decentralized, participative management structures as a result of turbulent organizational environments. Rather, we would suggest that uncertainty will result in greater efforts at coordination, which require the concentration of power and decision discretion. . . . If turbulence and uncertainty is perceived as stress or pressure, then centralization is a more correct prediction than decentralization. (Pfeffer and Salancik 1978, 285–86)

Further on Power

Several recapitulations of resource dependence theory have appeared since the basic statement in 1978. These are short, intended to place the theory in the context of organizational behavior theory as a whole, and add little if anything that is new. Pfeffer (1982) describes the theory as operating at the level of the total organization and taking a perspective on action that is externally constrained and controlled. In these respects, the theory is grouped with population ecology theory (Chapter 21). In Pfeffer (1997) the theory is described as a social model of behavior and is related to network models of organizations, which are said to have in a sense arisen out of the resource dependence perspective.

The primary subsequent enhancements to the theory came in the area of power, however, with most of them presented in Pfeffer (1981). That book contains an extensive treatment of the literature on power as a nonpsychological construct, and only limited attention is given to power in the context of resource dependence theory.

The theory as stated in Pfeffer (1981) emphasizes social power of a kind that derives from the ability to provide resources on which the organization depends. Accordingly, power may be organized around a large set of resources, including money, prestige, legitimacy, rewards and sanctions, expertise, and the ability to deal with uncertainty. The latter had been considered in previous treatments under the rubric of strategic contingencies theory. The other resources operate in a manner similar to the way strategic contingencies formulations handle the ability to deal with uncertainty. Within resource dependence theory, uncertainty coping capability is defined as a crucial resource within an organization.

Although the ability to bring in crucial resources or to cope with critical uncertainties is important to power attainment, this is not the whole story. Power also accrues from a person's ability to affect some part of the decision process. The capacity to affect the decision premises or underlying values is particularly important; so too is control over the decision alternatives considered, or over information bearing on alternatives. Clearly a person's position in the communication network has a great deal to do with individual power.

With regard to the symbolic role of managers, Pfeffer (1981) holds that the task of symbolic activity (and political language) is to rationalize and to justify decisions that have been reached on the basis of power, so as to make these results more acceptable and legitimate. Thus the exercise of power is facilitated. The theoretical position is that power derived from resource-based considerations is employed partly in the definition of social realities and justifications for behaviors that are consistent with the basic positions held by those with power.

In Pfeffer (1981) very little is said about "individual differences in ability, political skill, and the willingness to use those skills and abilities in contests within the organization" (131). The literature on these psychological matters is skimmed over lightly and power motivation is not considered at all. Subsequently, in Pfeffer (1992), written primarily as a text on power, this coverage of psychological factors is expanded somewhat, but is still incomplete. What treatment there is is couched in terms of criticism, largely on the grounds that research in the area does not give sufficient attention to contextual factors surrounding and preceding the manifestation of power motivation.

EVALUATION AND IMPACT

Almost all of the research bearing on resource dependence theory in the 1970s and 1980s was produced by the theory's authors. A considerable amount of this research was published, particularly in the period during the 1970s preceding the emergence of Pfeffer and Salancik (1978). The impact of this research on the field of organizational behavior was sizable. Its ties to the published theory are subject to some debate in that these research results clearly did influence specific formulations on occasion. Nevertheless, it is apparent that much of the theory preceded the research, and certainly the fundamental perspective regarding the role of interdependence and context did; thus it is appropriate to view the early research by the authors in a general sense as providing tests of theory.

Research by the Theory's Authors in the 1970s

As indicated, the body of research in this category is sizable, with over twenty-five studies reported. Among these I will focus on some of the more significant, in an attempt to show the diversity of findings marshaled behind the theory. These publications began to appear immediately after Pfeffer completed his doctorate and initially were based on his dissertation.

Pfeffer (1972a) dealt with the use of cooptation as a tactic for managing interdependence, and like so many of the other studies, utilized public data for purposes of analysis. The research was concerned with corporate board composition and size, and demonstrated that these factors are systematically related to the organization's need to deal with important environmental components—the percentage of board members from financial institutions was related to the firm's need for external capital, for instance. Eight out of nine such hypotheses were confirmed.

Pfeffer (1972b) utilized interview data collected from managers in Israel by a nonauthor. The data showed how the companies involved were influenced by their dependence on government particularly, but on banks as well. Managers' attitudes, time allocations, and advancements were all related to these external contingencies, although the correlations obtained were generally rather low.

Next Pfeffer (1972c) turned to merger activity. A strong association between mergers and patterns of resource exchange was found, accounting for about one half of the variance in merger behavior. Mergers were found to consistently reduce interdependence by allowing acquisition of competitors, suppliers, and customers or allowing diversification into new areas so that reliance on an existing set of organizations was reduced.

Research on hospitals provided further evidence of environmental interdependence. Boards of directors were influenced by such factors as the need to raise money, the relationship to government, the importance of influence in the community, political connections, and the like (Pfeffer 1973). The size of the board was influenced by the need for co-optation, supporting prior conclusions. An analysis focused on the tenure and characteristics of hospital administrators indicated that here too variables descriptive of the external context played an important role (Pfeffer and Salancik 1977).

Pfeffer and Leblebici (1973) studied how such environmental factors as the number of organizations in the industry, growth in industry sales, technological change, and average firm size relate to the movement of executives between firms. A number of associations between the environmental context and executive recruitment were established, in particular those involving the promotion from within of the chief executive.

Other studies were conducted relating power indexes to resource considerations in a university context, specifically at the University of Illinois. In the first of these, a department's power was found to be positively related to the proportion of the university budget received; workload and student demand had little influence (Pfeffer and Salancik 1974). Subsequently it was found that departmental power was most highly correlated with the ability to bring in funds through grants and contracts, and somewhat less with indicators of national prestige (Salancik and Pfeffer 1974). In one way or another power was a function of the ability to provide needed resources.

In an investigation using Federal Trade Commission data Pfeffer and Nowak (1976) documented that joint venture activity was consistently supportive of a number of hypotheses tying joint ventures to the process of managing interdependencies. However, the findings were not strong and accounted for only a small proportion of the variance in joint venture formation.

Finally, an analysis of United Fund distributions to member agencies indicated that the amount so designated was greater if the agency could raise more money outside the fund, and thus had greater ability to withdraw from United Fund participation (Pfeffer and Leong 1977). If the fund was more dependent on the particular agency for visibility and fundraising credibility, the relationship between outside support and fund allocation was particularly strong. Again resource dependence was key.

Author Research in the 1980s

Research by the authors on resource dependence propositions generally trailed off in the 1980s, and appears nonexistent after that. Among the more significant studies from this period are several dealing with a university context other than the University of Illinois (Pfeffer and Moore 1980a, b). Average tenure of department heads (and thus little succession) was positively related to level of paradigm consensus in the field and negatively related to department size. Both of these effects were more pronounced when resource scarcity in a monetary sense was greater. Paradigm consensus is assumed to reflect both shared beliefs internally and an external constraint system. This research also found support for the previous University of Illinois findings regarding departmental power, budget allocations, and contract funding. However, paradigm consensus as a characteristic of the field was now added to this mix, contributing to both budget allocations, and grants and contracts. It appears that paradigm considerations contribute to power, which in turn facilitates resource advocacy.

A study of the development of internal labor markets, which were defined as favoring promotion from within and having a limited number of ports of entry into the organization, tested the hypothesis that greater labor scarcity (recruitment difficulties) will create more internalized markets. This was the only one of ten research hypotheses that was based on resource dependence formulations. It was not supported by the data (Pfeffer and Cohen 1984).

Pfeffer and Davis-Blake (1987) reported on a test of resource dependence and power that compared the salaries paid to certain incumbents in public and private universities. In public universities, community services, student placement, and athletics were found to be more prevalent and thus presumably more important; in private universities, the more important functions were development, admissions, and alumni affairs. The relative salaries of the directors of these various functions in the two sectors were determined, and were generally found (with a few exceptions) to be higher in the context where the activities involved were viewed as more important, again supporting the Pfeffer and Salancik (1978) theory.

Replications and Expansions

Although the bulk of the research on resource dependence theory has been done by the authors, and a considerable body of research of a tangential nature has been invoked in its support, there have been a few studies by others that bear directly on the theory and require discussion.

One of the earliest of these studies involved a replication of the Pfeffer and Leong (1977) work on power relationships in United Fund activities (Provan, Beyer, and Kruytbosch 1980). The results generally supported those found previously and thus support resource dependency theory. There was, however, some discrepancy in the interpretation of the findings. Without further data, it cannot be determined if these discrepancies represent a significant consideration. In any event, it is clear that units that obtain more resources externally also are in a position to extract more internally. The study did not obtain this same result using alternative power measures, but did yield replication when the Pfeffer and Leong (1977) measure was used. The problem appears to be a lack of construct validity among the various power indexes, none of which dealt with power motivation and individual difference measures. Had the latter been included, they may well have helped to explain the disparities.

Research by Finkelstein (1997) provided a replication of the Pfeffer (1972c) analysis of corporate merger activity, but with a more precise methodology. Again, the results were consistent with the prior findings. Although significant results were found, however, the magnitudes of association and of explained variance were considerably less than previous research would have indicated, suggesting that resource dependence theory may have rather limited explanatory power. Clearly other factors have a lot to do with merger activity, especially mergers across industries.

Hillman, Cannella, and Paetzold (2000) conducted a study intended to determine how boards of directors change when confronted with drastic shifts in environmental context. The research focused on the airline industry in the United States, pre- and postderegulation. As hypothesized, board composition did change, with appointments being made more frequently from insiders and support specialists during regulation, and, with deregulation, shifting to a greater emphasis on business experts and, in particular, on community influentials. These findings are interpreted as supporting resource dependence expectations.

Data bearing on the Pfeffer and Davis-Blake (1987) conclusion that compensation levels are often geared to the importance of the work and the power of the incumbent comes from a study of pay strategies applied to sales personnel (Tremblay, Côté, and Balkin 2003). The findings tend to support resource dependence theory, with the various hypotheses all supported to some degree. On balance, however, the statistical results are such that the theory does not yield very strong predictions of the amount of the salary component, as opposed to the incentive component in sales pay.

In four different areas, these studies provide results that are entirely consistent with predictions from the Pfeffer/Salancik theory and from the authors' earlier investigations.

Looking at the Research

Overall, the evidence in support of research dependence theory appears to be varied and quite convincing. Some of the findings do not appear to explain a great deal of variance in dependent variables, but nevertheless the phenomenon is robust enough to cross-validate in new samples and contexts. The major criticisms seem to involve a call for research in areas of the theory not considered to date, rather than attacks on existing research or a serious deficiency in research overall. Pfeffer, and Salancik later on, have done an exemplary job of providing examples of what research on the theory and its variables should look like. In the process they have confirmed the theory in many of its aspects as well.

Pfeffer's (1989) own specifications regarding needed research relate to the succession process:

> . . . [N]ew people are brought in and a new perspective on the organization and its issues comes to occupy more and more positions in the organization—perhaps until that power becomes institutionalized, the organization fails to adapt, and the process begins anew. (387)

Later he says:

> None of these assertions tying operation of power to succession and adjustment to environmental contingencies has, in fact, been adequately tested. So there is the question of to what extent succession actually reflects considerations of power and . . . the consequences of this for the organization. (392)

The Hillman, Cannella, and Paetzold (2000) study of board succession deals with this issue in part, but much more longitudinal study along these lines is clearly needed, as Pfeffer indicates.

Another perspective on gaps in the research argues for more studies dealing with the role of groups such as cartels, trade associations, oligopolies, coalitions of consumer organizations, and the like within the resource dependence perspective (Galaskiewicz 1985). Similarly, there is a call for research on variations in the resource environment—rich or lean, stable or unstable, homogeneous or heterogeneous, concentrated or dispersed—as these influence managing interdependencies. The point is that major parts of the theory have not been studied at all. This appears to reflect the fact that these areas have not been the subject of research by the authors, and consequently lack the specific delineation that such research can provide.

Looking at the Theory

A major criticism that has been directed specifically at the Pfeffer/Salancik theory is that it intentionally utilizes linguistic ambiguity to increase the range of phenomena covered. Thus what is really a rather narrow gauge theory comes to be extended to a much broader framework, where studies that are in fact very tangential become applicable. Advocates of this view argue that the three central concepts of the theory—power, resource dependence, and organizational coalitions—are so general and ambiguous in meaning that they are virtually incapable of refutation (Astley and Zammuto 1992).

This critique has some validity in that the theory does appear to be relatively narrow in its application, given the limited amount of variance often accounted for in research and the failure to deal with internal organizational dynamics. Furthermore, the level of ambiguity of the theoretical statements is sufficient to accommodate citations to a literature that on other grounds would not seem appropriate. But the key consideration is that, when variables are operationalized and research is actually conducted, things become much less ambiguous. Thus in a sense the authors' research keeps the theory honest. Without the research, the theory might be considered to manifest excessive generality, but with the research, a large number of the theory's aspects achieve considerable precision.

An example of how this process works may be derived from looking at the theory, plus the research testing it that was conducted by Pfeffer and Davis-Blake (1987). Based on this background, Balkin and Bannister (1993) developed a set of propositions to predict the use of special pay forms (executive incentives, commissions, team bonuses) for certain types of positions. Thus strategic employee groups and political considerations in pay decisions were encompassed. In this instance, the theory, when adequately amplified by author research, proved sufficiently precise to serve as a building block for an applied theoretical extension. Adding precision to theory through research design is not the recommended approach to theory construction, but it appears to have worked well in this instance.

A different type of theoretical concern relates to the open systems nature of the resource dependence formulations, and the consequent stress on *survival* in the face of environmental constraints as the essential intended result of organizational efforts (Hall 1987). In endorsing this perspective, Pfeffer and Salancik (1978) bypass any view of organizational goals as factors in decision processes. Yet simply including internal goals as additional types of constraints (see Chapters 3 and 4 in this volume) to be considered in the mix with external environmental constraints when managerial decisions are under consideration would make the theory much more powerful, and closer to reality. To ignore profit considerations, for example, seems shortsighted.

This type of resort to blinders on the theory seems to represent an unnecessary limitation. There are other examples of this same type of problem, which seems to result from a doctrinaire commitment to avoiding any mention of the internal processes that guide organizational actors (see Jongbloed and Frost 1985; Campling and Michelson 1998). If the theory could be opened up in this manner, what is now a useful but constrained theory could become much more broadly valuable.

An example of this point can be provided with reference to Pfeffer's handling of the power variable. Pfeffer (1992) argues that treatments of power motivation and related individual differences are deficient because they do not consider external contextual factors, and that for this reason such micro variables should not be incorporated in his theory. Thus he is left with a structural approach that amounts to an extended version of strategic contingencies theory. Yet House (1988) has set forth a set of propositions that clearly do exactly what Pfeffer says individual differences theory does not do, thus bringing together micro and macro theories in the area. Elsewhere House (1991, 44) says of resource dependence theory:

> . . . [T]here are several reasons why the theory is likely to make rather weak predictions. That is, there are several reasons why correlations between the variables are likely to be substantially less than unity. First, the theory appears to apply more to organic than mechanistic organizations. Second, the theory appears to be more relevant to the long term than the short term. Third, the theory appears to apply to non-institutionalized organizations and

organizations not embedded in a larger institutionalized network of organizational relation-ships. Fourth, theoretical predictions of the theory are substantially weakened when the chief operating officer or the dominant coalition has a high degree of power relative to the board of directors, owners, or external agencies intended to exercise stewardship over the organization.

In fact the predictions often are weak, and the theory would seem to be in a position to benefit from incorporating additional types of individualized power constructs. Yet Pfeffer does not do this because these constructs are viewed as impure; thus he makes exactly the same type of error that micro organizational behaviorists are accused of making. The theory would benefit from a more open approach that lets individual differences in, and thus could explain more variance. The problem is that, as Pfeffer consistently illustrates in his recent writings, he exhibits a continuing opposition to individual differences, and to sources that might contribute to the emergence of such differences (Pfeffer 2000, 2001; Pfeffer and Fong 2002).

Certainly a theorist has the right to define the domain of a theory as that person sees fit, and thus Pfeffer cannot be faulted in that regard. However, his theory, though certainly not trivial, is more trivial than it could be. At a time when macro organizational behavior is extending its domain to include micro variables increasingly (see Baum 2002), Pfeffer re-mains adamant against this development, and the benefits it can produce.

Other criticisms have been leveled against resource dependence theory (see, for instance, Donaldson 2001; Vibert 2004), but these are often couched in terms that present a countervailing theoretical argument or are equivocal. The point that needs to be emphasized is that the theory does have substantial research support. Hall (2001), in spite of his concern about resource dependency theory's treatment of goals, views the theory as a useful contri-bution to the understanding of organizational resource acquisition and of how organizations deal with environmental contingencies. Organizational behavior generally has accepted this conclusion.

CONCLUSIONS

Resource dependence theory has an importance rating of five stars, with the exact figure at 5.29. This is an impressive showing. It is entirely consistent with the estimated validity of five stars. This is a theory that has been researched by its authors, and by others as well, and is consistently found to possess considerable validity. There are some theoretical areas that have not been studied, some departures from hypothesized results have occurred, and the findings obtained have been less than might be expected on occasion, although still signifi-cant. Yet the weight of the evidence is distinctly supportive of the theory. Plus, the research designs used appear to be fully adequate to the task.

On the usefulness dimension, the evaluation given is three stars. The theory itself is some-what ambiguous, too much so to permit immediate application. However, the operationaliza-tions of variables used in the research are much more precise. This appears to be a theory that could be converted to practical endeavors, using the research to provide guidelines, rather readily. This has been accomplished in the compensation area, and it could be done in other areas as well, although the authors have not done this. The estimated usefulness rating reflects this unfulfilled promise, as well as what has been done to convert the theory to practice.

In the next chapter I take up a group of theories focused on the same subject matter, an area that has received a great deal of attention in sociology and organizational behavior: neoinstitutional theory. Neoinstitutional theory presumes a prior institutional theory—and rightly so. It replaces and embellishes on a long theoretical tradition in sociology. I will emphasize primarily three versions of neoinstitutional theory, although I will consider other treatments as well.

REFERENCES

Aldrich, Howard E., and Pfeffer, Jeffrey (1976). Environments of Organizations. *Annual Review of Sociology,* 2, 79–105.

Astley, W. Graham, and Zammuto, Raymond F. (1992). Organizational Science, Managers, and Language Games. *Organization Science,* 3, 443–60.

Balkin, David B., and Bannister, Brendan D. (1993). Explaining Pay Forms for Strategic Employee Groups in Organizations: A Resource Dependence Perspective. *Journal of Occupational and Organizational Psychology,* 66, 139–51.

Barney, Jay B. (2001). Resource-Based Theories of Competitive Advantage: A Ten-Year Retrospective on the Resource-Based View. *Journal of Management,* 27, 643–50.

Baum, Joel A.C. (2002). *The Blackwell Companion to Organizations.* Malden, MA: Blackwell.

Campling, John T., and Michelson, Grant (1998). A Strategic Choice-Resource Dependence Analysis of Union Mergers in the British and Australian Broadcasting and Film Industries. *Journal of Management Studies,* 35, 579–600.

Donaldson, Lex (2001). *The Contingency Theory of Organizations.* Thousand Oaks, CA: Sage.

Finkelstein, Sydney (1997). Interindustry Merger Patterns and Resource Dependence: A Replication and Extension of Pfeffer (1972). *Strategic Management Journal,* 18, 787–810.

Galaskiewicz, Joseph (1985). Interorganizational Relations. *Annual Review of Sociology,* 11, 281–304.

Hall, Richard H. (1987). Organizational Behavior: A Sociological Perspective. In Jay W. Lorsch (Ed.), *Handbook of Organizational Behavior.* Englewood Cliffs, NJ: Prentice Hall, 84–95.

———. (2001). *Organizations: Structures, Processes, and Outcomes.* Upper Saddle River, NJ: Prentice Hall.

Hickson, David J., Hinings, C. Robert, Lee, C.A., Schneck, R.H., and Pennings, Johannes M. (1971). A Strategic Contingencies' Theory of Intraorganizational Power. *Administrative Science Quarterly,* 16, 216–29.

Hillman, Amy J., Cannella, Albert A., and Paetzold, Ramona L. (2000). The Resource Dependence Role of Corporate Directors: Strategic Adaptation of Board Composition in Response to Environmental Change. *Journal of Management Studies,* 37, 235–55.

House, Robert J. (1988). Power and Personality in Complex Organizations. *Research in Organizational Behavior,* 10, 305–57.

———. (1991). The Distribution and Exercise of Power in Complex Organizations: A Meso Theory. *Leadership Quarterly,* 2, 23–58.

Jongbloed, Lyn, and Frost, Peter J. (1985). Pfeffer's Model of Management: An Expansion and Modification. *Journal of Management,* 11, 97–110.

Leblebici, Huseyin, and Porac, Joseph (1997). Memorial for Gerald R. Salancik: 1.29.1943–7.24.1996. *Journal of Management Inquiry,* 6, 256–61.

Pfeffer, Jeffrey (1972a). Size and Composition of Corporate Boards of Directors: The Organization and Its Environment. *Administrative Science Quarterly,* 17, 218–28.

———. (1972b). Interorganizational Influence and Managerial Attitudes. *Academy of Management Journal,* 15, 317–30.

———. (1972c). Merger as a Response to Organizational Interdependence. *Administrative Science Quarterly,* 17, 382–94.

———. (1973). Size, Composition, and Function of Hospital Boards of Directors: A Study of Organization-Environment Linkage. *Administrative Science Quarterly,* 18, 349–64.

———. (1978). *Organizational Design.* Arlington Heights, IL: AHM Publishing.

———. (1981). *Power in Organizations.* Marshfield, MA: Pitman.

————. (1982). *Organizations and Organization Theory.* Marshfield, MA: Pitman.

————. (1989). A Political Perspective on Careers: Interests, Networks, and Environments. In Michael B. Arthur, Douglas T. Hall, and Barbara S. Lawrence (Eds.), *Handbook of Career Theory.* Cambridge, UK: Cambridge University Press, 380–96.

————. (1990). Incentives in Organizations: The Importance of Social Relations. In Oliver E. Williamson (Ed.), *Organization Theory: From Chester Barnard to the Present and Beyond.* New York: Oxford University Press, 72–97.

————. (1992). *Managing with Power: Politics and Influence in Organizations.* Boston, MA: Harvard Business School Press.

————. (1996). Taking the Road Less Traveled: Serendipity and the Influence of Others in a Career. In Arthur G. Bedeian (Ed.), *Management Laureates: A Collection of Autobiographical Essays,* Vol. 4. Greenwood, CT: JAI Press, 201–33.

————. (1997). *New Directions for Organization Theory: Problems and Prospects.* New York: Oxford University Press.

————. (2000). Governance of the Employment Relationship—From Rhetoric to Public Policy. In Carrie R. Leana and Denise M. Rousseau (Eds.), *Relational Wealth: The Advantages of Stability in a Changing Economy.* New York: Oxford University Press, 247–60.

————. (2001). Fighting the War for Talent Is Hazardous to Your Organization's Health. *Organizational Dynamics,* 29, 248–59.

Pfeffer, Jeffrey, and Cohen, Yinon (1984). Determinants of Internal Labor Markets in Organizations. *Administrative Science Quarterly,* 29, 550–72.

Pfeffer, Jeffrey, and Davis-Blake, Alison (1987). Understanding Organizational Wage Structures: A Resource Dependence Approach. *Academy of Management Journal,* 30, 437–55.

Pfeffer, Jeffrey, and Fong, Christina T. (2002). The End of Business Schools? Less Success Than Meets the Eye. *Academy of Management Learning and Education,* 1, 78–95.

Pfeffer, Jeffrey, and Leblebici, Huseyin (1973). Executive Recruitment and the Development of Interfirm Organizations. *Administrative Science Quarterly,* 18, 449–61.

Pfeffer, Jeffrey, and Leong, A. (1977). Resource Allocation in United Funds: An Examination of Power and Dependence. *Social Forces,* 55, 775–90.

Pfeffer, Jeffrey, and Moore, William L. (1980a). Average Tenure of Academic Department Heads: The Effects of Paradigm, Size, and Departmental Demography. *Administrative Science Quarterly,* 25, 387–406.

————. (1980b). Power in University Budgeting: A Replication and Extension. *Administrative Science Quarterly,* 25, 637–53.

Pfeffer, Jeffrey, and Nowak, Phillip (1976). Joint Ventures and Interorganizational Interdependence. *Administrative Science Quarterly,* 21, 398–418.

Pfeffer, Jeffrey, and Salancik, Gerald R. (1974). Organizational Decision Making as a Political Process: The Case of a University Budget. *Administrative Science Quarterly,* 19, 135–51.

————. (1977). Organizational Context and the Characteristics and Tenure of Hospital Administrators. *Academy of Management Journal,* 20, 74–88.

————. (1978). *The External Control of Organizations: A Resource Dependence Perspective.* New York: Harper and Row.

Provan, Keith G., Beyer, Janice M., and Kruytbosch, Carlos (1980). Environmental Linkages and Power in Resource-Dependence Relations between Organizations. *Administrative Science Quarterly,* 25, 200–225.

Salancik, Gerald R., and Pfeffer, Jeffrey (1974). The Bases and Uses of Power in Organizational Decision Making: The Case of a University. *Administrative Science Quarterly,* 19, 453–73.

Tremblay, Michel, Côté, Jérôme, and Balkin, David B. (2003). Explaining Sales Pay Strategy Using Agency, Transaction Cost and Resource Dependence Theories. *Journal of Management Studies,* 40, 1651–82.

Vibert, Conor (2004). *Theories of Macro Organizational Behavior: A Handbook of Ideas and Explanations.* Armonk, NY: M.E. Sharpe.

CHAPTER 20

NEOINSTITUTIONAL THEORY

JOHN MEYER AND RICHARD SCOTT
LYNNE ZUCKER
PAUL DIMAGGIO AND WALTER POWELL

Meyer/Scott Variant	
Importance rating	★ ★ ★ ★
Estimated validity	★ ★ ★ ★ ★
Estimated usefulness	★ ★ ★
Decade of origin	1970s

Zucker Variant	
Importance rating	★ ★ ★ ★
Estimated validity	★ ★ ★ ★
Estimated usefulness	★ ★
Decade of origin	1970s

DiMaggio/Powell Variant	
Importance rating	★ ★ ★ ★ ★
Estimated validity	★ ★ ★
Estimated usefulness	★ ★
Decade of origin	1980s

As it originally emerged, neoinstitutional theory was a fragmented array of positions with some common ground, but many differences as well (Scott 1987). By far the most fully developed of these positions, and apparently the first, was that of John Meyer and Richard Scott, who were both at Stanford University. A second position in a somewhat similar vein was that of Lynne Zucker at the University of California at Los Angeles (UCLA), which appeared at roughly the same time in the 1970s. Somewhat later a variant was developed jointly by Paul DiMaggio and Walter Powell, then at Yale University. I will focus primarily on the Meyer/Scott approach, but devote some attention to the other two, to provide a feel for the diversity. These three are generally considered to be the major current neoinstitutional theories, although there are other versions as well.

BACKGROUND

John Meyer received his Ph.D. in sociology from Columbia University. He has been on the sociology faculty at Stanford University for many years and was at one point chairman of that department. In addition he has held appointments in the School of Education at Stanford, where he has been engaged in research on various educational subjects throughout much of his career. This educational research preceded and was closely intertwined with the development of neoinstitutional theory.

Richard Scott has also spent his career in the sociology department at Stanford and served a stint as its chairman. He was born in 1932. His Ph.D. in sociology from the University of Chicago in 1961 followed undergraduate and master's work at the University of Kansas. He too has been active in the field of educational research and has held an appointment in Stanford's School of Education, but his organizational orientation has been somewhat broader, extending to medicine and business, areas in which he has held joint appointments as well. He is now emeritus from Stanford. Before beginning to develop neoinstitutional theory, he was concerned with the nature of professional work, with authority systems, and with issues related to organizational effectiveness. His academic career has been coterminous with the development of the field of organizational sociology (Scott 2004). Scott and Meyer developed their ideas on institutional processes together, publishing jointly on occasion, but independently as well.

Lynne Zucker was a graduate student at Stanford with Meyer, but has spent most of her career, beginning in 1974, at UCLA in sociology, with joint appointments in education and industrial relations. She was born in 1945. Paul DiMaggio and Walter Powell started out together in the School of Organization and Management at Yale University, where they began their collaboration on neoinstitutional theory; Powell is now in the School of Education (with additional appointments in organizational behavior, sociology, and communications) at Stanford University, and DiMaggio holds a position in the sociology department at Princeton University.

THE MEYER/SCOTT PERSPECTIVE

Neoinstitutional implies that there was some type of institutional emphasis preceding, and there was. This "old institutionalism" spread across many of the social sciences in a rather loose form, but within the study of organizations it is best manifested in the writings of the sociologist Philip Selznick (1949, 1957), who continues to reassert his position (Selznick 2000). That this old version is not entirely dead or displaced is evident from a recent attack on the new upstarts as being impoverished by Arthur Stinchcombe, a student of Selznick's at Berkeley. His views will provide a useful backdrop against which to present the theoretical ideas to follow:

> . . . [T]he trouble with the new institutionalism is that it does not have the guts of institutions in it. The guts of institutions is that somebody somewhere cares to hold an organization to

the standards and is often paid to do that. Sometimes that somebody is inside the organization, maintaining its competence. Sometimes it is an accrediting body. . . . [S]ometimes that somebody . . . is lacking, in which case the center cannot hold, and mere anarchy is loosed upon the world. (Stinchcombe 1997, 17–18)

Institutionalized Organizations: Formal Structures as Myth and Ceremony

Neoinstitutional theory began with an article by Meyer and Rowan (1977), which had the above title. This article was reprinted in a book (Meyer and Scott 1983) that contains a number of previously published articles by the authors and a number of newly written pieces as well. I refer to this latter source in the following discussion.

Organizational structures are said to develop in highly institutionalized contexts. Thus, they are influenced to take on the practices and procedures that are defined by prevailing rationalized ideas about organizational work held in society. When they do this they increase their legitimacy and their chances of survival. However, these societal expectations are really myths and may well conflict with criteria of efficiency. Formal structures and the rules that govern them are in fact reflections of the institutional environment. These institutional effects are quite apart from the effects produced by networks of social behavior and relationships within and around a particular organization. Examples of institutionalized processes are professional rules, business functions, and established technologies. Following these approaches is viewed as being appropriate and displays responsibility and avoids charges of negligence.

These ideas are followed by a series of propositions interspersed with commentary:

1. As rationalized institutional rules arise in given domains of work activity, formal organizations form and expand by incorporating these rules as structural elements.
   1a. As institutionalized myths define new domains of rationalized activity, formal organizations emerge in these domains.
   1b. As rationalized institutional myths arise in existing domains of activity, extant organizations expand their formal structures so as to become isomorphic [of similar form] with these new myths.
2. The more modernized the society, the more extended the rationalized institutional structure in given domains and the greater the number of domains containing rationalized institutions.
   2a. Formal organizations are more likely to emerge in more modernized societies, even with the complexity of immediate relational networks held constant.
   2b. Formal organizations in a given domain of activity are likely to have more elaborated structures in more modernized societies, even with the complexity of immediate relational networks held constant.

Isomorphism with environmental institutions has some crucial consequences: (a) incorporation of elements that are legitimated externally, rather than because they are efficienct; (b) employing external or ceremonial assessment criteria to define the value of structural elements; and (c) dependence on externally fixed institutions, which reduces turbulence and maintains stability.

3. Organizations that incorporate societally legitimated rationalized elements in their formal structures maximize their legitimacy and increase their resources and survival capabilities.

Organizations may be ordered on a continuum from . . . production organizations under strong output controls . . . to institutionalized organizations whose success depends on the confidence and stability achieved by isomorphism with institutional rules.

Two problems face organizations of the latter type: (a) technical activities and demands for efficiency create conflicts and inconsistencies in an institutionalized organization's efforts to conform to the ceremonial rules of production and (b) because these ceremonial rules are transmitted by myths that may arise from different parts of the environment, the rules may conflict with one another.

4. Because attempts to control and coordinate activities in institutionalized organizations lead to conflicts and loss of legitimacy, elements of structure are decoupled from activities and from each other.
5. The more an organization's structure is derived from institutionalized myths, the more it maintains elaborate displays of confidence, satisfaction, and good faith, internally and externally.
6. Institutionalized organizations seek to minimize inspection and evaluation by both internal managers and external constituents.

These propositions and arguments lead to three theses for research attention:

1. Environments and environmental domains that have institutionalized a greater number of rational myths generate more formal organization.
2. Organizations that incorporate institutionalized myths are more legitimate, successful, and likely to survive.
3. Organizational control efforts, especially in highly institutionalized contexts, are devoted to ritual conformity, both internally and externally. (Meyer and Scott 1983, 26–44)

Further to Organizational Environments

Organizational structures are expected to be generated as technologies and environmental interactions foster the development of bureaucratic systems (this is the technological side); they are also generated in that institutional structures operate to define roles and programs as being rational and legitimate (this is the institutional side).

The following propositions deal with what is involved:

1. Organizations evolving in environments with complex technologies create structures that coordinate and control technical work.
2. Organizations with complex technologies buffer their technical activities from the environment.
3. Organizations with efficient production and coordination structures tend to succeed in environments with complex technologies.
4. Organizations evolving in environments with elaborated institutional rules create structures that conform to those rules.
5. Organizations in institutional environments buffer their organizational structures from their technical activities.
6. Organizations with structures that conform to institutional rules tend to succeed in environments with elaborated institutional structures. (Meyer and Scott 1983, 47–48)

These propositions are straightforward enough as long as technology and institutions remain separate, but as the authors say, ambiguity enters into the theory when, for instance, technologies become institutionalized—as medical technologies do in hospitals. The ambiguities involved here are not resolved.

Societal sectors are said to include all organizations that supply a particular type of product or service, together with the suppliers, financial sources, regulators, and the like within the organizational set. The theory then attempts to develop hypotheses as to the effects of sector characteristics on organizational forms:

1. Organizations in technical sectors will attempt to control and coordinate their production activities, buffering them from environmental influences.
2. Organizations in technical sectors will succeed to the extent that they develop efficient production activities and effective coordination structures.
3. Organizations in institutional sectors will not attempt to closely control or coordinate their production activities, but will seek to buffer or decouple these activities from organizational structures.
4. Organizations in institutional sectors will succeed to the extent that they are able to acquire types of personnel and to develop structural arrangements and production processes that conform to the specifications of that sector.
5. Organizations functioning in sectors that are highly developed both institutionally and technically will develop more complex and elaborate administrative systems and will experience higher levels of internal conflict.
6. Organizations functioning in sectors that are not highly developed technically or institutionally are expected to be relatively small in size and weak in terms of their capacity for survival.
7. Organizations located in more complex and uncertain environments develop more complex internal structures (holding constant the complexity of work processes).
8. Within public sectors in the United States, funding decisions are more highly centralized than are programmatic decisions and programmatic decisions are more highly centralized than are instrumental decisions.
9. The more highly professionalized a sector, the more likely that instrumental and programmatic decisions will be decentralized.
10. The centralization of decision making concerning funding, in the absence of centralized programmatic or instrumental decision making, is associated with the development of vertical interlevel controls exercised through accounting mechanisms.
11. Liberal political regimes that encourage a pluralistic approach to decision making and that emphasize the separation of powers within nation-state structures are likely to exhibit higher levels of fragmentation of decision making within sectors, as well as between sectors.
12. Organizations operating in sectors characterized by centralized, unified, and concentrated programmatic decision making are expected to be tightly coupled across levels and to exhibit relatively small administrative components at each level.
13. Organizations operating in sectors characterized by fragmented or federalized programmatic decision making are expected to exhibit complex linkages across levels and elaborated and enlarged administrative components at each level.

14. The more centralized, unified, and concentrated is the programmatic decision making within a sector, the greater is the extent to which organizations within that sector will be limited and specific in the types of functional activities they perform.

15. The more centralized, unified, and concentrated is the decision making within a sector, the smaller is the number of different organization forms within the sector and the greater is the variance between them.

16. Organizations functioning in sectors that are highly developed technically but not institutionally will be subjected primarily to interlevel controls emphasizing outcomes.

17. Organizations functioning in sectors that are highly developed institutionally but not technically will be subjected primarily to interlevel controls emphasizing structural measures.

18. Organizations functioning in sectors in which decision making is centralized but fragmented or federalized are likely to be subjected primarily to interlevel controls emphasizing processes.

19. The exercise of structural controls is more compatible with the loose coupling of administrative to production tasks than is the exercise of process controls, and the exercise of process controls is more so than the exercise of outcome controls. (Meyer and Scott 1983, 141–49)

Elsewhere Scott (1990) has reemphasized that, in sectors where both technical and institutional environments are not well developed, the organizations tend to be small and weak.

Institutional Environments and Organizations

The preceding theoretical statements wrap up what the authors refer to as the first wave. The second wave is reflected in a book with the same title as this section, which again contains a balance of previously published articles (1986 to 1993) and original papers (Scott and Meyer 1994).

Here *institutions* are defined as cultural rules giving collective meaning (in terms of the collective purposes of progress and justice) and value to particular entities and activities, integrating them into the larger schemes. *Institutionalization,* accordingly, is the process through which a given set of units and a pattern of activities come to be normatively and cognitively held in place, so that they are taken for granted to be lawful (either as a result of formal law, custom, or knowledge). In this view, action is not a matter of individual choice but of broad social scripts; individualism loses out in large part to "the massive institutional features of the social system." These features in turn are part of the culture.

The term *rationalization* is used to refer to purposive or instrumental processes that structure everyday life within impersonal rules that constitute social organization and lead to collective purpose. Institutions embody universalized claims tied closely to moral purpose and the rules of nature; consequently, specific institutional claims and definitions tend to be much the same throughout most of the world.

The essential themes here are:

1. Rationalization . . . leads to the formation of an extraordinary array of legitimated actors reified as purposive and rational—individuals, associations, classes, organizations, ethnic groups, nation-states.

2. Collective actors command greater legitimacy and authority if they are founded on a theory of individual membership and activity, such as the nation-state or the rationalized firm.

3. Organizational entities that are tied into the theories of justice and progress gain special standing above all others.

4. Because they derive from universalistic cultural ideology, dominant organizational forms, including the structure and boundaries of collective action, are relatively standardized across societies. (Scott and Meyer 1994, 26–27)

Subsequently a general institutional model is set forth as follows:

1. Macro sociological processes—origins of environmental rationalization
↓

2. Dimensions of the rationalized environment—boundaries not clearly delineated
↓

3. Institutionalized elements in the environment—mechanisms influencing organizations
↓

4. The extant set of organizations:
   • identities
   • structures
   • activity patterns

Of these four, the first two are less developed in either a theoretical or research sense; 3 and 4 are the primary sources of attention. Figure 20.1 focuses on this interaction. The processes through which behavior is shaped noted there may be specified as follows:

• Representational rules that involve shared logics or modes of reasoning that help to create shared understandings of reality that are "taken for granted."
• Constitutive rules that create social actors—that is, identities linked to specified behaviors and action routines.
• Normative rules that stipulate expectations for behavior that are both internalized by actors and reinforced by the beliefs and actions of those with whom they interact.
• Enforcement mechanisms, both formal and informal, involving surveillance, assessment, and the application of sanctions rewarding conformity and punishing deviance. (Scott and Meyer 1994, 67)

Working from this perspective, institutions are now defined as symbolic and behavioral systems containing representational, constitutive, and normative rules together with regulatory mechanisms that define a common meaning system and give rise to distinctive actors and action routines. To this is added somewhat later that institutions operate at a variety of levels, and their elements can be embodied in and carried by cultures, regimes, and formal organizations.

Interpreting Neoinstitutionalism

Scott (1987, 2001) has not only been a contributor to neoinstitutional theory but a purveyor of its history and an interpreter of its development. Much of this is not relevant for present purposes except to show the diversity of approaches. However, a discussion of the role of

Figure 20.1 **A Layered Model of Institutional Process**

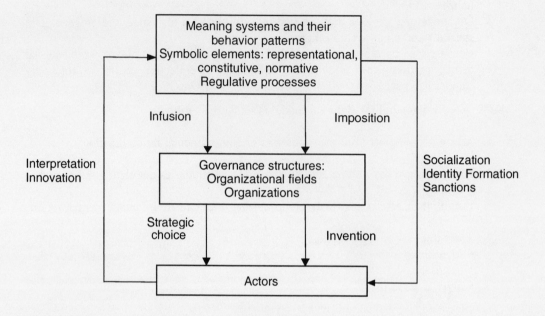

Source: Adapted from Scott and Meyer (1994, 57).

cognitive, normative, and regulative structures and activities in influencing social behavior provides an addition to what was said previously on this score. This discussion is summarized in Table 20.1.

ALTERNATIVE THEORETICAL VERSIONS

Now we turn to two other ways of considering institutional processes in this new period, ways that differ considerably from those just considered, and from one another.

The Zucker Perspective

The primary statement of the neoinstitutional perspective set forth by Zucker (1977) is in fact an introduction to three experiments conducted to test that perspective. Institutionalization is defined as both a process, through which actors transmit what is socially considered to be real, and a property existing at any point in the process, where the meaning of an act can be said to be a taken-for-granted part of the social reality. Such institutionalized acts must be perceived as *objective* (potentially repeatable) and *exterior,* in that they are viewed as part of the world external to the individual.

Objectification and exteriority vary together, so that increasing one causes an increase in the other; thus institutionalization can vary from low to high, and acts can possess different degrees of institutionalization. Acts that have ready-made accounts are institutionalized acts.

Table 20.1

The Roles and Workings of Cognitive, Normative, and Regulative Processes

	Structure and activities		
	Cognitive	Normative	Regulative
Characteristics			
Basis of compliance	Taken for granted	Social obligation	Expedience
Mechanisms	Imitation	Normative	Coercive
Logic	Orthodoxy	Appropriateness	Instrumentality
Indicators	Prevalence	Certification	Rules
	Isomorphism	Accreditation	Laws
			Sanctions
Basis of legitimacy	Culturally supported	Morally governed	Legally sanctioned
	Conceptually correct		
Carriers			
Cultures	Categories	Values	Rules
	Typifications	Expectations	Laws
Social structures	Isomorphism	Regimes	Government systems
	Identities	Authority systems	Power systems
Routines	Performance programs	Conformity	Protocols
	Scripts	Performance of duty	Standard procedures

Source: Adapted from Scott (2001, 52, 77).

These accounts are socially created and function as objective rules in the absence of direct social control. In fact, the invoking of incentives or sanctions may serve to deinstitutionalize the acts involved. Acts performed by occupants of an organizational office tend to be seen as highly objective and exterior, thus institutionalized.

Institutionalization affects three aspects of cultural persistence: transmission, maintenance, and resistance to change. *Transmission* is the process by which cultural understandings are communicated to a succession of actors. The more the objectification and exteriority, the greater the transmission; continuity of the transmission process fosters institutionalization.

The basic assumption is that the fact of transmission of acts that are highly institutionalized will be sufficient to cause the *maintenance* of these acts. The institutionalization process serves to define a social reality that will be transmitted, and then maintained, as fact.

Acts high on institutionalization will exhibit *resistance to change,* and attempts to change them through personal influence will face resistance simply because they are viewed as external facts. Failures of influence efforts in such circumstances may well extend to redefining the actor rather than the act.

The higher the level of institutionalization, the higher the transmission, maintenance, and resistance to change of cultural understanding hypothesized. This expectation, which is essentially one of cultural persistence, was tested in the research that we will take up shortly.

Zucker's (1977) theoretical statement is essentially presented at the micro level. Subsequently, she began to move toward a theory of organizations as institutions in which organizational power is based not on the control of resources, but on control of institutional structure and process (Zucker 1983). This effort, however, resulted only in the presentation of "the basic outlines which such a theory might take" (37). The objective was to stimulate others to work on a general theory of institutionalization.

Figure 20.2 **Origins and Maintenance of Institutional Patterns**

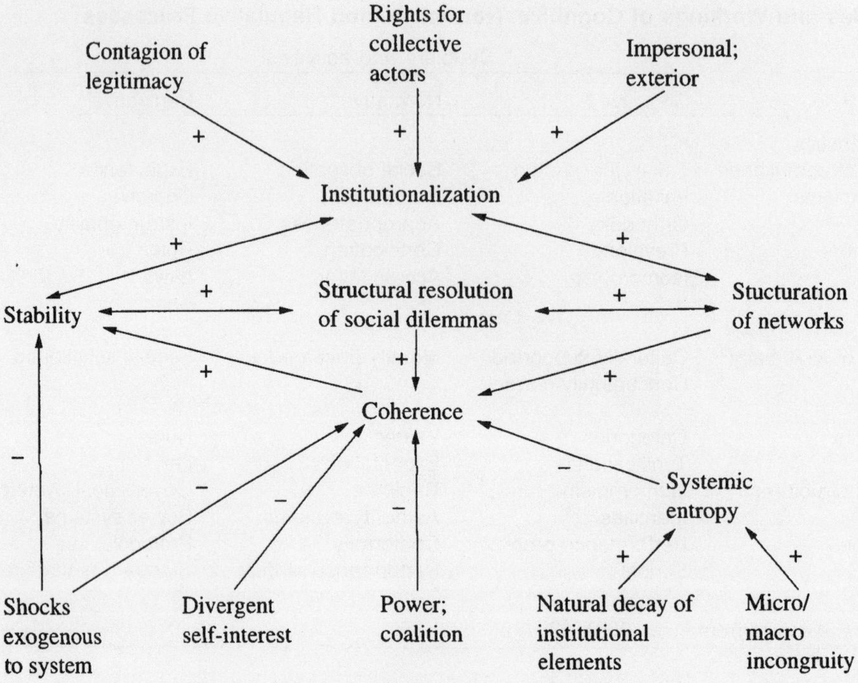

Source: Zucker (1988, 45). Copyright © 1988 by Lynne G. Zucker. Reprinted with permission.

In another, later approach to macro level theorizing Zucker (1988) set forth a view in which the starting principles are that social entropy threatens organizational stability, the organization of the social system is characterized by coherence and interconnectedness, the primary change agents are the formally organized collectivity and the power of organizations, institution building is a continual process to foster maintenance, and the key problem is maintaining a degree of stability. The net effect of this effort is the set of relationships in Figure 20.2, in which coherence is critical to the stability of the social system, but is continually threatened by systemic entropy as well as other factors. This approach too is considered to be "not yet either well developed or tightly interconnected" (45), and is offered in the hope of stimulating the theoretical work of others.

The DiMaggio/Powell Perspective

The seminal publication on this perspective, like Meyer and Rowan (1977) and Zucker (1977) for those perspectives, is DiMaggio and Powell (1983). The primary concern of this view is with the mechanisms of institutional isomorphic change, said to be either *coercive* isomorphism (stemming from political influence and the problem of legitimacy), *mimetic* isomorphism (resulting from standard, imitative responses to uncertainty), or *normative* isomorphism (associated with professionalization).

A series of hypotheses is presented, dealing with the predictors of isomorphic change, first those operating at the organizational level and then those operating at the field level.

Organizational:

1. The greater the dependence of an organization on another organization, the more similar it will become to that organization in structure, climate, and behavioral focus.
2. The greater the centralization of organization A's resource supply, the greater the extent to which organization A will change isomorphically to resemble the organization on which it depends for resources.
3. The more uncertain the relationship between means and ends, the greater the extent to which an organization will model itself after organizations it perceives to be successful.
4. The more ambiguous the goals of an organization, the greater the extent to which the organization will model itself after organizations it perceives to be successful.
5. The greater the reliance on academic credentials in choosing managerial and staff personnel, the greater the extent to which an organization will become like other organizations in its field.
6. The greater the participation of organizational managers in trade and professional associations, the more likely the organization will be, or will become, like other organizations in the field.

Field:

7. The greater the extent to which an organizational field is dependent upon a single (or several similar) source(s) of support for vital resources, the higher the level of the isomorphism.
8. The greater the extent to which the organizations in a field transact with agencies of the state, the greater the extent of isomorphism in the field as a whole.
9. The fewer the number of visible alternative organizational models in a field, the faster the rate of isomorphism in that field.
10. The greater the extent to which technologies are uncertain or goals are ambiguous within a field, the greater the rate of isomorphic change.
11. The greater the extent of professionalization in a field, the greater the amount of institutional isomorphic change.
12. The greater the extent of structuration in a field, the greater the degree of isomorphics. (DiMaggio and Powell 1983, 154–56)

The authors note that they have not attempted to develop measures of the variables they propose.

Subsequently DiMaggio (1988) attempted to deal theoretically with what he viewed as the failure of institutional theory to handle the matter of self-interest. His central thesis to this end is that:

> . . . [I]nstitutionalization is a product of the political efforts of actors to accomplish their ends, and the success of an institutionalization project and the form that the institution takes depend on the relative power of the actors who support, oppose, or otherwise strive to influence it . . . the success of an institutionalization process creates new sets of legitimated actors who, in the course of pursuing distinct interests, tend to delegitimate and deinstitutionalize aspects of the institutional forms to which they owe their own autonomy

and legitimacy. . . . Institutionalization as an *outcome* places organizational structures and practices beyond the reach of interest and politics. By contrast, institutionalization as a *process* is profoundly political. (DiMaggio 1988, 13)

Beyond the writings already noted, both of the theory's authors have contributed in various ways to the literature on institutionalism, but not in the form of concerted theoretical formulations. Rather the tendency has been to argue for further development and broadening of the institutional perspective in various ways (see, for example, Powell and DiMaggio 1991) and in various contexts (see DiMaggio, Hargittai, Neuman, and Robinson 2001).

Modeling Institutional Development

As an instance of such broadening, Greenwood, Suddaby, and Hinings (2002) have distilled from the literature a model of how institutional change processes operate. An adaptation of that model should facilitate understanding of how the various concepts fit together. This model of institutional development establishes a series of stages:

I. *Destabilization*—established practices are subjected to perceived crises, felt needs, and precipitating jolts arising out of technological disruptions, competitive discontinuities, social upheavals, or regulatory changes.
↓

II. *Deinstitutionalization*—new players emerge, existing actors ascend to new statuses, and institutional entrepreneurship is mobilized, thus disturbing any existing consensus in the established institutional field.
↓

III. *Preinstitutionalization*—organizations and individuals innovate on their own with a view to introducing solutions that are technically viable in response to local problems.
↓

IV. *Theorization*—abstract categories are developed and specified, and cause-effect chains are elaborated, so that local deviations can be made available for wider adoption; thus specifying a failing of the status quo and justifying a replacement.
↓

V. *Diffusion*—what were once local innovations are spread by becoming objectified, gaining consensus, and achieving legitimacy based on their assumed pragmatic value.
↓

VI. *Full institutionalization*—cognitive legitimacy is attained as a function of the density of adoption, with the result that the ideas are taken for granted as natural and to be expected, thus uncritically accepted. (59–61)

Some will recognize in this stage model the various elements of Kurt Lewin's (see Miner 2005) unfreezing-moving-freezing model of change in group life. In this formulation, the beginning is a quasi-stationary social equilibrium, where the forces favoring change and those resisting it are stabilized. This equilibrium is then disturbed or destabilized, usually by external forces. Social habits represent internal resistances to change. These habits are then unfrozen through some process that modifies group standards, with the result that individual group members move to stay close to the new standards (conform). As a sense of belonging develops in the newly constituted group with its new standards, refreezing occurs, and a new equilibrium is stabilized.

EVALUATION AND IMPACT

Research on neoinstitutional theory presents a number of difficulties for those searching for tests of the theory. First, much of it is oriented to the "old" institutionalism, not the new, and consequently may or may not be relevant in any given instance. Second, there is extensive use of qualitative studies to adduce support for theory, a practice that relies much more on the writer's particular interpretation and version of the story than on science. Third, although numerous reviews of the theories have been written, most tend to deal primarily with matters of logical consistency and speculative concerns, rather than with a comprehensive, objective coverage of the research evidence per se. Fourth, much of the research tends to use institutional measures that could be interpreted as reflecting the operation of some other theoretical perspective; the support for institutional theory is often not as specifically focused on institutional variables as one might wish.

Research Involving the Authors of the Meyer/Scott Theory

The Meyer/Scott theory arose out of studies of educational administration, and this is the area we will focus on here. In Meyer and Scott (1983), data from surveys conducted within schools in the San Francisco Bay area were presented as typical of what has been found elsewhere. As expected, there was a high level of agreement across organizations on matters of policy, and school location accounted for only a small part of any variance. This homogeneity is viewed as evidence of institutional effects. Also, the high levels of satisfaction found among various stakeholders is interpreted as consistent with maintaining institutional rules. A second set of findings relate to loose coupling. The professional system, consisting primarily of teachers, was found to be decoupled from the administrative system, thus permitting the two types of institutional processes to operate together.

Other relevant studies by Meyer and Scott, working with others, are reported in Zucker (1988). One study dealt with the institutionalization of grievance procedures and affirmative action in organizations. These processes appeared to be fostered by public visibility and linkages to government as well as size and the more modern period in which the processes operated. Another study, again dealing with education, also obtained indexes over time (forty years). A rapid expansion in bureaucratization was apparent, reflecting the dominance of a national educational culture. This move to a particular organizational structure is attributed to a complex institutional system rather than to the rise of a dominating organizational center.

The 1994 book by Scott and Meyer contains several other studies that the authors conducted. One compared data on private and public school systems and found substantial differences, with the public schools exhibiting much more elaborate organizational structures commensurate with their more complex environmental demands. Other studies suggest that the complex and fragmented environments of public schools, and not centralization in the hands of the federal government, result in greatly expanded administrative activities. Further data are also reported on the increasing bureaucratization of the educational system, attributed to a national institutional structure, not to control by the central bureaucratic state. In another arena, internal labor markets within organizations are explained in terms of institutional processes in the environment rather than firm self-interest. All of these studies utilize data of some kind, mostly archival, to substantiate, but not in fact to prove their theses.

A recent example of this approach involved an analysis of the antecedents and effects of legitimacy (as reflected in accreditation procedures) in San Francisco hospitals. Legitimacy clearly increases survival chances (Ruef and Scott 1998). Evidence is presented to the effect that the logic of the surrounding institutional environment plays an important role. This work on the changes that have occurred in the institutionalization of health care organizations has been set forth in expanded form in a book on the research (Scott, Ruef, Mendel, and Caronna 2000).

It is important to note that none of this research is directly coupled with the specific theoretical propositions and hypotheses noted previously; in no instance is there said to be a direct test of a given hypothesis from the prior theory. The research is only loosely coupled with the theory.

Research Involving the Authors of Alternative Theories

As indicated previously, Zucker's (1977) theorizing introduced a set of research investigations. These were laboratory studies utilizing the autokinetic effect, in which the degree of institutionalization was manipulated by introducing various organizational conditions. The effects on the perceived movement of a light under otherwise darkroom circumstances were obtained for transmission, maintenance, and resistance to change conditions. Institutionalization clearly had the anticipated impact under all three conditions; the hypothesized relationships between degree of institutionalization and cultural persistence were supported.

Subsequently Zucker (1983) reported several other investigations that provide evidence for the effects of institutional environments on organizations. An analysis of the spread of civil service reform over a fifty-five-year period showed a gradual institutionalizing process. Although city characteristics were good predictors in the early years, these correlations disappeared later and adoption came to be expected even if not functional for a specific city. An analysis of the establishment of evaluation units in school systems showed a similar development as a function of state regulation and funding. An analysis of city responses to state-wide budget cuts in California indicated that institutional forces established parameters for local responses.

In a particularly interesting study Zucker and Kreft (1994) used archival data to study the effects of strike activity on founding rates of union locals. They concluded that institutions (unions) form in response to demand and social conflict (strikes). Thus, institutional development does *not* appear always to be a consequence of institutional isomorphism, as prior theories had proposed; variance may be added, at least initially, and homogeneity decreased. The data also suggest that institutional structures do not just happen. They evolve over a period of time as a consequence of human agency and demand, and are maintained as resources to keep them going become available.

Finally, Zucker was involved in analyses of organizations that were inefficient but survived for long periods on the basis of their institutional status. Of this work she says, "The notion that organizations could survive despite very low objective performance implied the possibility of permanently failing organizations (Meyer and Zucker 1989), that is organizations that survive despite evident inefficiencies that logically should cause them to fail" (Tolbert and Zucker 1996, 178).

The Powell/DiMaggio perspective has not been the subject of significant quantitative research by its authors. There have been qualitative studies, referred to by the authors as case studies, dealing with institutional processes as they relate to book publishing, public television, art museums, and the like (see, for example, their articles in Zucker 1988 and Powell and DiMaggio 1991), but these cannot be considered tests of either their theory or any other institutional theory. This situation exists in spite of the fact that both of these authors have conducted quantitative research in other areas.

Significant Outside Research in the Early Period

Much of the early research, during the late 1970s and the 1980s, was conducted by either Meyer and Scott or Zucker. Yet there were other studies conducted outside this nexus in this period. Some of the more significant of these require discussion.

One such study looked at institutionalization (in terms of industry norms and traditions) as it relates to sales compensation practices (Eisenhardt 1988). The findings indicated that, although institutional theory did contribute to an understanding of these practices, this effect was only partial, operating most strongly in relation to founding conditions and industry traditions. Agency theory from economics was shown to operate jointly with institutional theory to provide the most complete understanding; this conjoint effect has been found more recently as well (Young, Stedham, and Beekum 2000). Another, similar study utilized variables from institutional and ecological theory (see Chapter 21 in this volume) to analyze relationships involving vital measures in voluntary organizations in Toronto, using an event-history approach (Singh, Tucker, and Meinhard in Powell and DiMaggio 1991). Both theoretical orientations proved to have a significant, complementary effect in explaining foundings, deaths, and organizational changes. Such a combined operation of ecological and institutional theory has been documented in studies since, as well (see Lee and Pennings 2002). That institutional theory provides only a partial explanation of dependent variables seems now to be well established.

Tolbert (in Zucker 1988) studied institutional factors in the operation of large U.S. law firms, specifically the establishment of structures to ensure the socialization of new members. The results clearly showed that professional organizations are affected by institutional processes, as various theorists had indicated previously.

Another area of institutional interest has been the diversification of large firms. Fligstein (in Powell and DiMaggio 1991) studied this process among the hundred largest United States companies from 1919 to 1979. He found that diversification put companies in the top 100, but failure to diversify led to a more rapid exit. Diversification also institutionalized an elevated role for financial executives (Zorn 2004). In the early period, diversification appeared to follow from chief executive characteristics, but this correlation disappeared in the later years. The best index in this later period was the proportion of firms already diversified. The data lend good support to institutional theory and its imitative processes.

Embellishments on the Imitative Theme

Within neoinstitutional theory the process that received by far the greatest research attention from 1985 to 1995, and to some extent beyond, is that labeled as imitative, or mimetic, following on the DiMaggio and Powell (1983) nomenclature (Mizruchi and Fein 1999). One study looked into the diversification strategy that Fligstein had analyzed previously for the period up to 1979 (Davis, Diekmann, and Tinsley 1994). The data, extended through the period up to 1990, showed a marked deinstitutionalization, with many firms merging and having their diversified components sold off, and many others shunning the conglomerate growth pattern. Evidence is presented that this change occurred abruptly, was influenced by pressure from Wall Street, and appeared to reflect an underlying institutional shift. How these changes can be better understood and predicted remains a challenge to theory, but clearly market forces do interject themselves, at least in the business world. A similar effect is apparent in the deinstitutionalization of permanent employment occasioned by downsizing in Japan (Ahmadjian and Robinson 2001); economic pressures were a distinct consideration.

Other studies in the business context (and apart from the prevailing educational context) raise similar problems. For example, Haunschild and Miner (1997) studied acquisitions and investment banker decisions and found three different imitation modes operating. Furthermore, these three modes may affect different components of a firm in different ways, producing variety in the company overall, not homogeneity. Thus, the usual predicted effects of imitative processes may well not occur in the manner theory anticipates. How often this sort of thing may occur is an open question.

An analysis of the adoption of total quality management programs by hospitals found that early adopters tended to customize the approach to meet their particular efficiency needs, while later adopters accepted the programs in standard form to gain legitimacy (Westphal, Gulati, and Shortell 1997). Thus, mimicking the normative model seems to be a late-stage process; before that, efficiency concerns may well exert considerable impact, producing variability, not homogeneity. Another study, also in the hospital setting, dealt with the decision to undertake cesarean births, studied as a hospital-level phenomenon (Goodrick and Salancik 1996). It was found that institutional forces set boundaries on the use of discretion in decisions. When risk was intermediate, and thus uncertainty the greatest, the characteristics of individual hospitals exerted the most influence on cesarean rates and thus hospital-level discretion was exercised. When risks were either high or low, institutionalized practices tended to prevail. Thus institutionalized actions do not emerge as direct mandates, but as frameworks within which technical forces may operate, setting the limits, as it were.

In a study undertaken to establish the domain limitations on neoinstitutional theory, Kraatz and Zajac (1996) considered longitudinal data on a large number of private liberal arts colleges from 1971 to 1986. What they found was a substantial and pervasive move to professional and vocational curricula, a loss of homogeneity, and a failure to imitate the more prestigious institutions of this type. All this appears to have occurred in response to market conditions, and with positive consequences for enrollments and survival. In 1986 38 percent of all degrees granted were professional in nature, as contrasted with a comparable figure of 11 percent in 1971, but note that the majority still remain of a liberal arts nature. This study is interpreted as indicating a failure of neoinstitutional theory in a context that should be highly institutionalized; it also reflects the conjoint operation of factors that are probably best described in resource dependence terms (see Chapter 19 in this volume).

An interpretation of these results within institutional theory is also possible, however (see Stryker 2000), if an expanded version of the institutional domain is accepted. Furthermore, subsequent research indicates that a major factor in the adoption of professional programs was the advent of decisions by new presidents who migrated from colleges that had had professional programs (Kraatz and Moore 2002).

Evidence on Different Versions

Many of the studies noted previously have supported neoinstitutional theory while at the same time pointing up certain deficiencies or limitations. Yet evidence of a more comprehensive nature is available also.

In support of the Meyer/Scott theory Laurila and Ropponen (2003) find that foreign expansion can turn into an institutional requirement that directs the development of firms in part irrespective of the economic aspects involved. Other studies reinforce the role of managerial cognition, myth, and symbolism inherent in the Meyer/Scott perspective (see, for example, Labianca, Fairbank, Thomas, Gioia, and Umphress 2001; Glynn and Abzug 2002). That firms do not necessarily choose certain techniques because they are technologically the best or most efficient is now widely apparent; rather, external legitimacy or reputation enter strongly into the equation (Staw and Epstein 2000).

The Zucker perspective, as reflected in the use of laboratory studies where institutionalization is introduced as an experimental manipulation, continues to receive some support (Lucas 2003), although micro research of this kind is not found commonly in the institutional literature. The DiMaggio/Powell perspective has been promoted mostly through case studies and qualitative research, rather than through more robust quantitative analyses. A case in point is a qualitative study intended to provide evidence for the existence of institutional entrepreneurship in the sponsorship of a particular technology by Sun Microsystems (Garud, Jain, and Kumaraswamy 2002).

Critiques

As indicated previously, it is difficult to find good critiques of neoinstitutional theory that do not deviate considerably from the dictates of objectivity. There are the devotees of the "old" institutionalism (see, for example, Stinchcombe 1997), the adherents of some version of the "new" theory (see, for example, Scott 2001), the advocates of alternative positions altogether (see, for example, Donaldson 1995, 2001 and Greve 2003), as well as those operating from an alternative philosophy, such as postmodernism (see Bowring 2000 and Hasselbladh and Kallinikos 2000). All have something to say, but what they say does not always represent a balanced position. Yet there does appear to be a certain consensus that "institutional theory is clearly the leading perspective among organizational sociologists in the United States" (Mizruchi and Fein 1999, 678).

In this context it may be helpful to explore some of the critiques in more depth to see what they do say. Tolbert and Zucker (1996) are critical of the Meyer and Rowan (1977) views on the grounds that there is an inherent ambiguity in their definition of institutionalization as opposed to the idea that institutionalized structures are often decoupled from behavior. They feel that this leads to a confounding of institutional and resource dependence theory, a combination regarding which Zucker (1989) previously indicated considerable reservations; others, however, have found this to be a useful theoretical marriage (see Sherer and Lee 2002). It is evident from the Tolbert and Zucker (1996) review that a certain amount of controversy does exist, not only vis-à-vis other types of macro theories, but within the neoinstitutional camp as well.

Another point made in this review is that more direct measures of institutionalization are needed to document when institutionalized structures are and are not present. Such measures could derive from survey research and from content analysis of written materials. This is a point well taken. It becomes particularly important where conflicting institutional streams may be operative, as in the case of the liberal arts colleges (Kraatz and Zajac 1996). The use of such measures would also facilitate separating different alternative theoretical explanations of the same phenomena from one another. More often than not the research simply assumes the operation of institutional processes under certain circumstances; more definitive evidence in the form of clear operationalizations of constructs is needed.

A final point is that institutional theory offers good reasons why and how bounded rationality and satisficing occur (see Chapter 3 in this volume). Understanding in this regard, and the scope of both theories, would benefit from further theoretical development dealing with this issue.

A quite different theoretical and research review, and one of the most negative that I have seen, is that of Donaldson (1995). This is part of his basic advocacy of structural contingency theory (see Chapter 16 in this volume) and his attempt to vitiate the influence of competing theories. He concludes that only the coercive isomorphism aspect of institutional theory can lay claim to unequivocal support from research. He offers numerous criticisms both of theory (usually as lacking logical consistency) and of early research (as inappropriately conceived and conducted). He makes some good points and some clear errors as well, and demonstrates a considerable amount of emotionality, and what many would consider overkill, in his zeal to negate institutional formulations. Overall, the net effect is no more detrimental to neoinstitutional theory than are his similar attacks on population ecology theory (Chapter 21 in this volume) and resource dependence theory (Chapter 19 in this volume). However, he raises useful questions regarding the conduct and interpretation of certain specific research studies, particularly the early ones.

On balance, my own view is that the theory has a great deal of promise. It needs to deal more effectively with what appear to be changes away from institutionalization, as in the Davis, Diekmann, and Tinsley (1994) and Kraatz and Zajac (1996) studies, but it is not true that such changes are not considered by the theory. DiMaggio (1988) develops the role of political process in both institutionalization and deinstitutionalization at length. The theory needs to attain greater precision in this area and probably to do so it will need to move to a treatment of dynamic processes within individual organizations, and even within individual personalities, including the sources of their interests; thus it will need to deal more explicitly with micro sociology (Hargadon 2002). The importance of developing measures of theoretical variables that Tolbert and Zucker (1996) stress would seem to put emphasis on a crucial consideration for the conduct of research that will move the theory beyond its present bounds. Furthermore, neoinstitutional theory in its present forms serves to describe phenomena that result in variance suppression across organizations; the theory does not handle factors, such as innovation, that produce increased variance (Bettis 2000). Thus its domain is limited, and this limitation needs to be recognized. On occasion the theoretical domain has been expanded beyond what the theoretical framework will support. This overextension has been noted by Hall (2001). Finally, informal institutions consisting of rules based on implicit understandings (social norms, routines, and political processes) need to be more fully integrated into theory (Zenger, Lazzarini, and Poppo 2002).

CONCLUSIONS

All of the three variants on neoinstitutional theory have high importance ratings. But there are differences. The DiMaggio/Powell approach is viewed the most positively, with a five-star rating at 5.22. The other theories both fall into the four-star range—the Meyer/Scott variant is at 4.79 and the Zucker at 4.51. Like resource dependence theory, this is clearly a well-regarded theoretical orientation.

The evaluations of the validity of the three variants do not follow the importance ratings. The Meyer/Scott theory is at five stars, the Zucker theory is at four stars, and the DiMaggio/ Powell theory at three stars. These differences are tied to the quantity and quality of the research on each approach, epitomized by the research conducted by the authors themselves. The Meyer/Scott theory is buttressed by extensive research by the authors, primarily in education and health care. Zucker's theory also has strong research backing, which is distinctive in its micro orientation, but the theory itself is incomplete in ways that the author recognizes. Overall, the research in support of the Zucker theory is not as abundant as that behind the Meyer/Scott variant. The DiMaggio/Powell theory is in several respects more comprehensive than the other two, and probably the appeal of this accounts for the somewhat higher importance rating; it does seem that citations to DiMaggio/Powell are more frequent. Yet, what in my judgment brings this variant down in its validity is the heavy reliance on qualitative research, which has proven productive in generating theory, but is clearly lacking insofar as proving validity is concerned.

None of the theories are rated particularly high on estimated usefulness. Recognizing that institutionalization may be operative in a given situation is clearly an important matter for managers. They may want to weight legitimacy more, or less, strongly than performance, but to do so they need to be aware that institutionalization is at issue, and how it operates. Although the Meyer/Scott theory does something in this regard (thus its rating is three stars), the matter is not featured. The other variants do very little (both are at two stars). A management development program dealing with how and when institutionalization works would help a great deal in sensitizing managers to the phenomenon. Whether such a program would have any effect in breaking down individual predispositions remains to be seen.

Now we turn to the final major sociological theory of organization that is of more recent vintage.

REFERENCES

Ahmadjian, Christina L., and Robinson, Patricia (2001). Safety in Numbers: Downsizing and the Deinstitutionalization of Permanent Employment in Japan. *Administrative Science Quarterly*, 46, 622–54.

Bettis, Richard A. (2000). The Iron Cage Is Emptying: The Dominant Logic No Longer Dominates. *Advances in Strategic Management*, 17, 167–74.

Bowring, Michèle A. (2000). De/constructing Theory: A Look at the Institutional Theory That Positivism Built. *Journal of Management Inquiry*, 9, 258–70.

Davis, Gerald F., Diekmann, Kristina A., and Tinsley, Catherine H. (1994). The Decline and Fall of the Conglomerate Firm in the 1980s: The Deinstitutionalization of an Organizational Form. *American Sociological Review*, 59, 547–70.

DiMaggio, Paul J. (1988). Interest and Agency in Institutional Theory. In Lynne G. Zucker (Ed.), *Institutional Patterns and Organizations: Culture and Environment*. Cambridge, MA: Ballinger, 3–21.

DiMaggio, Paul, Hargittai, Eszter, Neuman, W. Russell, and Robinson, John P. (2001). Social Implications of the Internet. *Annual Review of Sociology*, 27, 307–36.

DiMaggio, Paul J., and Powell, Walter W. (1983). The Iron Cage Revisited: Institutional Isomorphism and Collective Rationality in Organizational Fields. *American Sociological Review*, 48, 147–60.

Donaldson, Lex (1995). *American Anti-Management Theories of Organization: A Critique of Paradigm Proliferation*. Cambridge, UK: Cambridge University Press.

———. (2001). *The Contingency Theory of Organizations*. Thousand Oaks, CA: Sage.

Eisenhardt, Kathleen M. (1988). Agency- and Institutional-Theory Explanations: The Case of Retail Sales Compensation. *Academy of Management Journal,* 31, 488–511.

Garud, Raghu, Jain, Sanjay, and Kumaraswamy, Arun (2002). Institutional Entrepreneurship in the Sponsorship of Common Technological Standards: The Case of Sun Microsystems and Java. *Academy of Management Journal,* 45, 196–214.

Glynn, Mary Ann, and Abzug, Rikki (2002). Institutionalizing Identity: Symbolic Isomorphism and Organizational Names. *Academy of Management Journal,* 45, 267–80.

Goodrick, Elizabeth, and Salancik, Gerald R. (1996). Organizational Discretion in Responding to Institutional Practices: Hospitals and Cesarean Births. *Administrative Science Quarterly,* 41, 1–28.

Greenwood, Royston, Suddaby, Roy, and Hinings, C.R. (2002). Theorizing Change: The Role of Professional Associations in the Transformation of Institutionalized Fields. *Academy of Management Journal,* 45, 58–79.

Greve, Henrich R. (2003). *Organizational Learning from Performance Feedback: A Behavioral Perspective on Innovation and Change.* Cambridge, UK: Cambridge University Press.

Hall, Richard H. (2001). *Organizations: Structures, Processes, and Outcomes.* Upper Saddle River, NJ: Prentice Hall.

Hargadon, Andrew B. (2002). Brokering Knowledge: Linking Learning and Innovation. *Research in Organizational Behavior,* 24, 41–85.

Hasselbladh, Hans, and Kallinikos, Jannis (2000). The Project of Rationalization: A Critique and Reappraisal of Neo-Institutionalism in Organization Studies. *Organization Studies,* 21, 697–720.

Haunschild, Pamela R., and Miner, Anne S. (1997). Modes of Interorganizational Imitation: The Effects of Outcome Salience and Uncertainty. *Administrative Science Quarterly,* 42, 472–500.

Kraatz, Matthew S., and Moore, James H. (2002). Executive Migration and Institutional Change. *Academy of Management Journal,* 45, 120–43.

Kraatz, Matthew S., and Zajac, Edward J. (1996). Exploring the Limits of the New Institutionalism: The Causes and Consequences of Illegitimate Organizational Change. *American Sociological Review,* 61, 812–36.

Labianca, Giuseppe, Fairbank, James F., Thomas, James B., Gioia, Dennis A., and Umphress, Elizabeth E. (2001). Emulation in Academia: Balancing Structure and Identity. *Organization Science,* 12, 312–30.

Laurila, Juha, and Ropponen, Minna (2003). Institutional Conditioning of Foreign Expansion: Some Evidence from Finnish-Based Paper Industry Firms, 1994–2000. *Journal of Management Studies,* 40, 725–51.

Lee, Kyungmook, and Pennings, Johannes M. (2002). Mimicry and the Market: Adoption of a New Organizational Form. *Academy of Management Journal,* 45, 144–62.

Lucas, Jeffrey W. (2003). Status Processes and the Institutionalization of Women as Leaders. *American Sociological Review,* 68, 464–80.

Meyer, John W., and Rowan, Brian (1977). Institutionalized Organizations: Formal Structure as Myth and Ceremony. *American Journal of Sociology,* 83, 340–63.

Meyer, John W., and Scott, W. Richard (1983). *Organizational Environments: Ritual and Rationality.* Beverly Hills, CA: Sage.

Meyer, Marshall W., and Zucker, Lynne G. (1989). *Permanently Failing Organizations.* Newbury Park, CA: Sage.

Miner, John B. (2005). *Organizational Behavior 1: Essential Theories of Motivation and Leadership.* Armonk, NY: M.E. Sharpe.

Mizruchi, Mark S., and Fein, Lisa C. (1999). The Social Construction of Organizational Knowledge: A Study of the Uses of Coercive, Mimetic, and Normative Isomorphism. *Administrative Science Quarterly,* 44, 653–83.

Powell, Walter W., and DiMaggio, Paul J. (Eds.) (1991). *The New Institutionalism in Organizational Analysis.* Chicago, IL: University of Chicago Press.

Ruef, Martin, and Scott, W. Richard (1998). A Multidimensional Model of Organizational Legitimacy: Hospital Survival in Changing Institutional Environments. *Administrative Science Quarterly,* 43, 877–904.

Scott, W. Richard (1987). The Adolescence of Institutional Theory. *Administrative Science Quarterly,* 32, 493–511.

———. (1990). Symbols and Organizations: From Barnard to the Institutionalists. In Oliver E. Williamson (Ed.), *Organization Theory: From Chester Barnard to the Present and Beyond.* New York: Oxford University Press, pp. 38–55.

————. (2001). *Institutions and Organizations.* Thousand Oaks, CA: Sage.

————. (2004). Reflections on a Half-century of Organizational Sociology. *Annual Review of Sociology,* 30, 1–21.

Scott, W. Richard, and Meyer, John W. (1994). *Institutional Environments and Organizations: Structural Complexity and Individualism.* Thousand Oaks, CA: Sage.

Scott, W. Richard, Ruef, Martin, Mendel, Peter J., and Caronna, Carol A. (2000). *Institutional Change and Healthcare Organizations: From Professional Dominance to Managed Care.* Chicago, IL: University of Chicago Press.

Selznick, Philip (1949). *TVA and the Grass Roots.* Berkeley: University of California Press.

————. (1957). *Leadership in Administration: A Sociological Interpretation.* Berkeley: University of California Press.

————. (2000). On Sustaining Research Agendas: Their Moral and Scientific Basis. *Journal of Management Inquiry,* 9, 277–82.

Sherer, Peter D., and Lee, Kyungmook (2002). Institutional Change in Large Law Firms: A Resource Dependency and Institutional Perspective. *Academy of Management Journal,* 45, 102–19.

Staw, Barry M., and Epstein, Lisa D. (2000). What Bandwagons Bring: Effects of Popular Management Techniques on Corporate Performance, Reputation, and CEO Pay. *Administrative Science Quarterly,* 45, 523–56.

Stinchcombe, Arthur L. (1997). On the Virtues of the Old Institutionalism. *Annual Review of Sociology,* 23, 1–18.

Stryker, Robin (2000). Legitimacy Processes as Institutional Politics: Implications for Theory and Research in the Sociology of Organizations. *Research in the Sociology of Organizations,* 17, 179–223.

Tolbert, Pamela S., and Zucker, Lynne G. (1996). The Institutionalization of Institutional Theory. In Stewart R. Clegg, Cynthia Hardy, and Walter R. Nord (Eds.), *Handbook of Organizations.* London: Sage, 175–90.

Westphal, James D., Gulati, Ranjay, and Shortell, Stephen M. (1997). Customization or Conformity? An Institutional and Network Perspective on the Content and Consequences of TQM Adoption. *Administrative Science Quarterly,* 42, 366–94.

Young, Gary J., Stedham, Yvonne, and Beekum, Rafik I. (2000). Boards of Directors and the Adoption of a CEO Performance Evaluation Process: Agency- and Institutional-Theory Perspectives. *Journal of Management Studies,* 37, 277–95.

Zenger, Todd R., Lazzarini, Sergio G., and Poppo, Laura (2002). Informal and Formal Organization in New Institutional Economics. *Advances in Strategic Management,* 19, 277–305.

Zorn, Dirk M. (2004). Here a Chief, There a Chief: The Rise of the CFO in the American Firm. *American Sociological Review,* 69, 345–64.

Zucker, Lynne G. (1977). The Role of Institutionalization in Cultural Persistence. *American Sociological Review,* 42, 726–43.

————. (1983). Organizations as Institutions. *Research in the Sociology of Organizations,* 2, 1–47.

————. (Ed.) (1988). *Institutional Patterns and Organizations: Culture and Environment.* Cambridge, MA: Ballinger.

————. (1989). Combining Institutional Theory and Population Ecology: No Legitimacy, No History. *American Sociological Review,* 54, 542–45.

Zucker, Lynne G., and Kreft, Ita G.G. (1994). The Evolution of Socially Contingent Rational Action: Effects of Labor Strikes on Change in Union Founding in the 1880s. In Joel A.C. Baum and Jitendra V. Singh (Eds.), *Evolutionary Dynamics of Organizations.* New York: Oxford University Press, 294–313.

CHAPTER 21

ORGANIZATIONAL ECOLOGY
AND DEMOGRAPHY

MICHAEL HANNAN
JOHN FREEMAN
GLENN CARROLL

Importance rating	★ ★ ★ ★
Estimated validity	★ ★ ★ (★)
Estimated usefulness	★ (★)
Decade of origin	1970s

In its early years organizational behavior gave little attention to biological perspectives. The two visible exceptions were a paper by Mason Haire (1959), then at the University of California at Berkeley, and the work of Donald Campbell (see Baum and McKelvey 1999) at Northwestern University. Neither sparked either research or theoretical development subsequently within organizational behavior, in spite of the use of both mathematical models and biological analogies to growth. In contrast, the later development of a similar approach, based on an established underpinning in sociology, by Michael Hannan (Stanford) and John Freeman (Berkeley) provoked a major impact, and an outpouring of research. The role of timing and the zeitgeist seem important here, but so does the power of the ideas themselves.

BACKGROUND

Both Hannan and Freeman received their doctorates in sociology from the University of North Carolina. Both moved on to California in sociology; Hannan at Stanford University and Freeman at the University of California at Riverside. Subsequently Freeman shifted to the business school at Berkeley. Both spent a considerable period at Cornell University, Hannan in the sociology department from 1984 to 1991, and Freeman in the business school, where he served as editor of the *Administrative Science Quarterly* from 1985 to 1993. Both ultimately returned to their former positions in California, although Hannan now has taken a major appointment in the business school at the age of 56.

At North Carolina both authors were strongly influenced by the ideas of Amos Hawley (1968), a long-term contributor to the sociological work dealing with human ecology. Another major contributor to their thinking and to the development of the theory was Arthur Stinchcombe (1965). Although statements of the theory draw on numerous sources, mostly within sociology and biology, these two people appear to have exerted the most influence as the theory evolved.

Glenn Carroll came to ecological and demographic theory somewhat later, as a student of Hannan's at Stanford. From there he went to the University of California at Berkeley in the business school, but with a joint appointment in sociology. In 2001 he moved back to Stanford, with an appointment similar to the one he had held at Berkeley. In the past few years he has seemed to take Freeman's role as a major theorist, with special emphasis now on the demographic aspects.

THE HANNAN/FREEMAN THEORY OF ECOLOGY

Organizational ecology theory was first published, although in a less than finished form, in the latter 1970s, as a journal article and as a chapter in a book to which many of the theorists considered in this chapter contributed (Hannan and Freeman 1977, 1978). During the 1980s there were a number of articles in the sociological literature, mostly jointly authored; these were brought together and supplemented to produce a book (Hannan and Freeman 1989). In addition I have utilized two book chapters that contain abbreviated and somewhat simplified versions of this same theory (Hannan and Freeman 1988; Hannan and Carroll 1995a). Although both Hannan and Freeman contributed to the ecological literature subsequent to the late 1980s, their collaboration was no longer in evidence. Hannan has in fact been the major contributor of the two during the 1990s and after.

Theoretical Context

The theory seeks to answer the question Why are there so many (or so few) kinds of organizations? This requires indicating both the sources of increasing diversity, such as new forms, and the sources of decreasing diversity, such as competitive exclusion. The theory thus attempts to achieve an understanding of the rates of new organization and new form founding, the rates of organizational change, and the rates at which organizations and their forms die.

When there are only a few forms of organizations, society faces major problems when environments change. Diversity also provides more work opportunities for individuals with varied skills and characteristics.

A basic assumption is that organizational variation is a function primarily of the creation of new organizations and forms, and the demise of others; actual change within organizations is rare, slow moving, and occurs early in their histories, if at all. Environments change, but inertia prevails within organizations. Examination of such matters involves three levels of complexity:

1. The *demography of organizations*—founding rates, merger rates, disbanding rates.
2. The *population ecology of organizations*—how the existence and density of other populations of organizations affect a focal population.
3. The *community ecology of organizations*—a set of interacting populations, for example, firms, their labor unions, and relevant regulatory agencies. (Hannan and Freeman 1989, 14–15)

The current diversity of organizational forms is a consequence of a long history of variation and selection (founding, mortality, and merger processes). Selection processes have general properties that hold across long historical periods. Yet the theory is only partial in its evolutionary treatment of organizational change; it focuses primarily on selection within organizational populations. The theory assumes that change:

... is more Darwinian than Lamarckian. It argues that inertial pressures prevent most organizations from radically changing strategies and structures. Only the most concrete features of technique can be easily copied and inserted into ongoing organizations. Moreover, there are density-dependent constraints on adaptation by individual organizations: although it may be in the interests of the leaders of many organizations to adopt a certain strategy, the carrying capacity for organizations with that strategy is often quite limited. Only a few can succeed in exploiting such a strategy, and those in the vanguard ... have decided advantages.

Even when actors strive to cope with their environments, action may be random with respect to adaptation as long as the environments are highly uncertain or the connections between means and ends are not well understood. It is the *match* between action and environmental outcomes that must be random on the average for selection models to apply. In a world of high uncertainty, adaptive efforts by individuals may turn out to be essentially random with respect to future value. (Hannan and Freeman 1989, 22)

This is a quite different approach than that of the Pfeffer/Salancik theory. Here selection is based on the importance of randomness to success; selection processes do not necessarily favor efficiency, and in fact they treat managerial action in distinctly antiheroic ways—as romanticized myth.

Four factors are posited that limit managerial potential to create change:

1. The organizations form, which is not easily changed.
2. The scarcity of resources, which provides little slack to devote to change.
3. The competitive pressures, which magnify the effects of other factors.
4. The limitations on rationality, which have been emphasized by decision theorists. (Hannan and Freeman 1989, 41)

Boundaries of Forms and Populations

Organizational ecology theory assumes that populations of organizations can be defined in ways that involve very similar environmental dependencies, and that consequently there exist sizable discontinuities within the world of organizations. Furthermore, these populations can be identified a priori, based on information dealing with organizational structures and social boundaries. However, the theory does not draw upon anything approaching an organizational genetics approach to this problem of classification.

Organizational forms are defined by technological factors, differences in transaction costs, the closure of social networks, successful collective action, and institutional processes. These segregating processes serve to establish boundaries, which are, however, also subject to blending processes that serve to break down their influences; thus boundaries across organizational forms do change.

In spite of considerable discussion by Hannan and Freeman (1989) of the factors that might be used to build a theoretical typology of organizational forms, and their recognition that further theoretical work in this area will be needed, the authors finally settle upon the "conventional wisdom" of participants and observers to define forms. These "native" classifications appear to have had particular appeal because the data needed for research tend to come bundled in this manner. Thus, at least operationally, the theory is rather unsophisticated in its handling of the types of organizational forms, and the boundaries among them. Because the conventional wisdom can change and even be a matter of some dispute, a degree of ambiguity is in fact built into an otherwise quite sophisticated theory at this point.

Structural Inertia

As previously noted, a substantial inertia in structure and in other characteristics that define membership in an organizational population is assumed. Selection processes tend to favor organizations that exhibit this inertia in their core structures; thus inertia can be explained as a consequence of evolutionary processes and as a result of certain constraints on structural change. Among these are: investments in assets not easily shifted to other uses, the limitations on information held by decision makers, internal political forces that act to thwart change, and the effects of normative agreements built into organizational histories. There are as well external constraints on change, such as legal and financial barriers, environmental restraints on the availability of information, and legitimacy claims on the part of important stakeholders.

The authors recognize that this emphasis on a limited potential for structural change (a change in form) is at variance with the mainstream position. Inertia does not mean that organizations never change, however, only that they respond rather slowly. The faster the speed with which organizations may be founded, the greater the inertia of the established structure. Selection favors organizations that can demonstrate *reliability* and *accountability*. Structures of roles and communications need to be reproducible, and this becomes achievable by creating processes of institutionalization and standardized routines, and thus resistance to change. Structural inertia increases directly with age, and organizational mortality rates decrease with age. Thus, newness is a liability, as Stinchcombe (1965) had proposed. Attempting reorganization serves to decrease reliability and increases mortality rates; it sets the liability of newness back toward zero, with all the risks thus entailed.

Once a *complex organization* begins change, the process will be longer lasting; thus to complexity contributes to a greater mortality risk. The ability to react quickly to new opportunities conflicts with the ability to perform with reliability and accountability here. Thus inertia is not always a plus for selection. The theory, although it states a number of specific hypotheses related to inertia and similar matters as noted above, has a tendency to respond with statements such as "it is not clear," "is indeterminate in our theory," and "is an open question" at other points. The authors' willingness to admit the limits of their theoretical capabilities is admirable at these points, but logical consistency tends to be lost and ambiguity often prevails (Hannan and Freeman 1989).

Competition and the Niche

The theory as applied to niches focuses on interactions within and between populations of organizations. The argument starts with Hawley's (1968) principle of isomorphism: "Units subjected to the same environmental conditions or to environmental conditions as mediated through a given key unit, acquire a similar form of organization. They must submit to standard terms of communication and to standard procedures in consequence of which they develop similar internal arrangements within limits imposed by their respective sizes." Thus, organizational diversity results from the diversity of agents controlling resources. Hawley's principle does not apply when a large number of resources are involved, however, as is typically the case. Accordingly, the theory turns to niche theory and the processes of competition and legitimation in search of a solution.

The niche of an organization form consists of the social arrangements whereby a population can grow. To this the theory adds the process of *interaction* among populations, a process that occurs when one population affects the growth rate of others. At this point the discussion moves to a series of mathematical equations derived from bioecology. These deal with the carrying capacity of the environment for a given population, the intrinsic growth rate (the speed with which a population grows when there are no resource constraints), and competition coefficients that indicate how the carrying capacity for each population declines with the density of a competitor. The equations involved, however, do not have a known solution, although competition coefficients can be estimated from data; the number of coexisting populations is constrained by the number of resources and constraints operating.

A related approach is to obtain estimates of competition from the overlap of niches and from niche width, which is the variance of the niche's resource utilization. Specialist organizations have less slack and thus less excess capacity than generalists, but they also are more vulnerable to uncertainty and changing environments. Thus stable environments favor populations of specialists, but under many conditions variable environments favor generalists. Talking about selection on the basis of niche width has the advantage that it takes into account the degree of specialism.

Dynamics of Organizational Populations

Population growth rates may be treated in terms of:

1. Intrinsic speed of expansion.
2. General environmental limits on growth or carrying capacities.

3. Specific competition within and between populations. (Hannan and Freeman 1989, 117)

Speed of expansion varies markedly across organizational forms. Life-history strategies may vary from *opportunistic*, with many organizational foundings and resources spread thinly, to the opposite, with few foundings and heavy resource investments in each. Life chances vary accordingly, but even so, environments with rapid changes and high uncertainty favor the opportunistic approach. Populations with forms that foster high founding rates tend to continue to exist even though individual organizations do not survive long.

Both speed of founding and carrying capacities, which are set by time-varying social and material processes, are joined by density dependence in determining vital rates. *Density* serves as a surrogate for features of the social and material environment. *Legitimacy*, which increases as a particular form becomes more prevalent, produces a positive relationship between founding rates and density, while competition produces a negative relationship. Dense environments are characterized by limited resources and packed markets. Legitimacy processes dominate when N (population size) is small and competition processes when N is large, so that the function as a whole is nonmonotonic (does change). The authors developed formulas to show this. Disbanding rates fall with increasing density, up to the limits set by carrying capacity, after which they begin to rise. Merger processes, however, are more complicated, and are beyond the capabilities of the theory to explain (Hannan and Freeman 1989, 139).

The 1992 Restatement

In many respects, organizational ecology as treated by Hannan and Freeman is not so much an integrated theory as an exercise in applying a rich variety of formal models to the subject matter. One such area for formal modeling is the dynamics of organizational populations as treated in the prior section. This area has been reworked and restated several times; the Hannan and Carroll (1992) restatement is of particular interest because it is more precisely developed.

The propositions set forth are as follows:

1. The founding rate of an organizational population at time t, $\lambda(t)$, is inversely proportional to the intensity of competition within the population at that time, C_t. That is, $\lambda(t) \alpha C_t^{-1}$.
2. The mortality rate of organizations in a population at time t, $\mu(t)$, is directly proportional to the intensity of competition within the population at the time (contemporaneous competition). That is, $\mu(t) \alpha C_t$.
3. The mortality rate at time t of organizations founded at time f, $\mu(t,f)$, is directly proportional (at any age) to the intensity of competition at the time of founding, C_f. That is, $\mu(t,f) \alpha C_f$.
4. The founding rate in an organizational population at time t is directly proportional to the legitimation of its organizational form at that time, L_t. That is, $\lambda(t) \alpha L_t$.
5. The mortality rate in an organizational population at time t is inversely proportional to the legitimation of its organizational form at that time. That is, $\mu(t) \alpha L_t^{-1}$.
6. The intensity of contemporaneous competition, C_t, increases with density, N_t, at an increasing rate. That is, $C_t = \varphi(N_t)$; and $\varphi' > 0$ and $\varphi'' > 0$.

7. The intensity of competition at the time of founding, C_f, increases at an increasing rate with density at the time of founding, N_f. That is, $C_f = \psi (N_f)$, with $\psi'>0$ and $\psi''>0$.

8. Legitimation increases with density at a decreasing rate. That is,

$$L_t = \vartheta(N_t); \text{ and } \vartheta' > 0, \text{ and } \vartheta'' < 0.$$

9. The relationship between density and legitimation is positive with a point of inflection $(\tilde{N}_\lambda)$ such that legitimation increases at an increasing rate with density to some point (the inflection point) beyond which legitimation grows with density at a decreasing rate. That is, $L_t = v(N_t)$; and $v'>0$, and

$$v'' \quad \text{is} \quad \begin{cases} >0 & \text{if } N_t < \tilde{N}_\lambda; \\ <0 & \text{if } N_t > \tilde{N}_\lambda. \end{cases}$$

10. Legitimation is stronger than competition at very low densities. In particular,

$$\vartheta(N_t) > \varphi(N_t), \text{ and } v(N_t) > \varphi(N_t)$$

when $N_t<2$.

From propositions 1, 4, 6, 8, and 10:

Theorem 1. Density dependence in founding rates is nonmonotonic,

$$\lambda(t) \propto \frac{L_t}{C_t} = \frac{\varphi(N_t)}{\vartheta(N_t)},$$

and

$$\lambda(t)' \equiv \frac{d\lambda(t)}{dN_t} \quad \text{is} \quad \begin{cases} >0, & \text{if } N_t < N_\lambda^*; \\ <0, & \text{if } N_t > N_\lambda^*, \end{cases}$$

where N_λ^* denotes the turning point in the relationship.

From propositions 1, 4, 6, 9, and 10:

Theorem 2. Density dependence in founding rates is nonmonotonic,

$$\lambda(t) \propto \frac{L_t}{C_t} = \frac{v(N_t)}{\vartheta(N_t)},$$

and

$$\lambda(t)' \equiv \frac{d\lambda(t)}{dN_t} \quad \text{is} \quad \begin{cases} >0, & \text{if } N_t < N_\lambda^*; \\ <0, & \text{if } N_t > N_\lambda^*. \end{cases}$$

From propositions 2, 5, 6, 8, and 10:

Theorem 3. Contemporaneous density dependence in mortality rates is nonmonotonic,

$$\mu(t) \propto \frac{C_t}{L_t} = \frac{\vartheta(N_t)}{\varphi(N_t)},$$

and

$$\mu(t)' \equiv \frac{d\mu(t)}{dN_t} \quad \begin{cases} < 0, & \text{if } N_t < N_\mu^*; \\ > 0, & \text{if } N_t > N_\mu^*. \end{cases}$$

From propositions 3, 5, and 7:

Theorem 4. Density at founding permanently increases mortality rates. That is, the mortality rate at time t of organizations founded at time f is proportional to the density at that time,

$$\mu(t, f) \propto C_f = \psi(N_f);$$

and

$$\mu(t, f)' \equiv \frac{d\mu(t, f)}{dN_f} > 0; \quad \mu(t, f)'' > 0.$$

(Hannan and Carroll 1992, 31–46)

THE CARROLL/HANNAN THEORY OF DEMOGRAPHY

The shift from a theoretical focus on ecology to a focus on demography occurred at the turn of the century (Carroll and Hannan 2000a, 2000b). It brought with it new constructs and new emphases, but the result has been primarily a continuation of the prior approach to theory development. Many of the additions within the demography thrust represent attempts to rectify previous theoretical shortcomings; in this regard the new theory has been eminently successful.

Extensions to Prior Theory

The Carroll and Hannan (2000b) book contains at least five major extensions of the theory. These five are recognized by Rao (2002) as follows:

1. The established axiom of age dependence in death rates is reconsidered in a fresh light with the use of logical formalization, a powerful new weapon in the arsenal of organizational ecology. Carroll and Hannan lucidly discuss how initial endowments, imprinting effects, and positional advantage underlie age dependence in death rates and formalize the scope conditions of the liabilities of newness, adolescence, obsolescence, and senescence. . . .

2. Carroll and Hannan revisit the nettlesome issue of organizational forms and outline a new account of organizational forms. *Organizational Ecology* emphasized the boundaries of forms and directed attention to segregating and blending mechanisms. By contrast Carroll and Hannan assert that forms are organizational identities based on genetic and penal codes that are enforced by external and internal observers who respond to code violations with sanctions. . . . Industry persistence may conceal extraordinary turnover in organizational forms.

3. There is a striking difference in the two books' accounts of segregating processes. While *Organizational Ecology* gave prominence to how institutional processes were critical in the segregation of organizations, Carroll and Hannan depict resource partitioning and size-localized competition as segregating processes, but they are careful to show how resource partitioning may be premised on identity movements and institutional dynamics.

4. *The Demography of Corporations and Industries* describes the effects of corporate demography on the social structure of individual careers and, in particular, the effects of vital rates on job creation, dissolution, and individual mobility. In doing so, it opens up promising avenues for invigorating contact between corporate demography and the study of labor markets and inequality.

5. *Organizational Ecology* presents theory discursively, but Carroll and Hannan present theory through the adroit use of logical formalization. (585)

Quite evidently Rao (2002) is much enamored of these new contributions to theory.

The distinction that Carroll and Hannan (2000b) now make within their theoretical domain should also be noted:

> *Organizational demography*—processes that apply at the levels of populations of organizations.
> *Population ecology*—interactions between localized sets of populations.
> *Community ecology*—processes that follow from the full set of population interactions in some system. (xx)

Forms and Populations Revisited

In the reconstructed theory of organizational forms, Carroll and Hannan (2000b) posit that forms and identities are closely related concepts. A form is a recognizable pattern that acquires rulelike qualities. It is based on judgments made by outsiders and it involves both *cognitive recognition* and *imperative standing*. Thus it is a cultural aspect. An identity becomes a form only if certain conditions apply:

1. The identity applied to and was satisfied by a form-specific constant number of organizations at the beginning of the interval.
2. Violation of the applicable identity causes the outsider evaluation functions to drop sharply. (73)

Defining forms in this way still permits the use of the same research data as previously, but it is somewhat more precise. Ideally it would call for an operationalization that relies upon the actual judgments of outsiders who reflect the culture.

Nothing has changed in the definition of organizational populations, except as implied by the new way of establishing forms. Accordingly, an organizational population is now established "as the set consisting of the organizations defined by a given minimal external identity in a bounded system in some period" (75). This concept of population, embedded in an identity-based theory of form, is explained further and illustrated in an article by McKendrick, Jaffee, Carroll, and Khessina (2003). There it is shown that disk array production does not attain the "minimal external identity" necessary to constitute an organizational form.

Segregating Processes and Resource Partitioning

Among the theoretical developments stressed in the Carroll and Hannan (2000b) volume is the concept of resource partitioning, which appears to have been introduced in large part to explain certain inconsistencies in prior theory when subjected to research test. Resource partitioning says that differences in niche width come to play a determining role in that specialist forms react differently to competition than large generalist forms. In the later stages of population age a segregating process sets in that produces discontinuity on some dimension such as size, niche width, or status. A set of hypotheses is generated to deal with these phenomena as follows:

1. Under conditions of resource partitioning, as market concentration rises, the founding rates of specialist organizations will rise and the mortality rates of specialists will fall. (266)
2. Under conditions of resource partitioning, as the number of dimensions in resource space increases, the founding rates of specialist organizations will rise and the mortality rates of specialist organizations will decline. (268)
3. Under such competition, the greater the aggregate distance of larger competitors, the higher the generalist mortality rate. (271)
4. Under resource partitioning based on identity, the legitimating effects of specialist organizational identity depend on (a) the normative status of the specialist form and (b) the social visibility of the specialist form. (274)

Generally, small specialist organizations do not compete with one another; however, intense competition among large generalist organizations tends to be characteristic. As a result, specialists proliferate and generalists are few in number.

These views are elaborated further in a subsequent publication (Carroll, Dobrev, and Swaminathan 2002) and the following hypotheses are proposed:

1. An organization's hazard of mortality increases as a function of its position distance away from the market center. (13)
2. Among scale-based (generalist) competitors within an organizational population, the greater the sum of distances of a firm from each of its larger (generalist) competitors, the higher its mortality hazard. (14)
3. As market concentration rises, the mean amount of resource space covered by surviving individual generalists will expand. (15)
4. As market concentration rises, the amount of unique resource space covered by the combination of all generalist organizations contracts. (16)
5. The more concentrated the environmental resource distribution, the more concentrated the scale-based organizations serving the market. (16)

6. As market concentration rises, the total amount of resource space open to specialist organizations expands. (17)
7. As the number of dimensions in resource space increases, the total amount of space open to specialist organizations expands. (18)
8. As the resource space open to specialists expands, the founding rates of specialist organizations will rise. (18)
9. As the resource space open to specialists expands, the mortality rates of specialist organizations will fall. (18)

These hypotheses place primary emphasis on the location of an organization in resource space. Other factors, such as customization, anti-mass-production cultural sentiment, and conspicuous status consumption may operate in the same manner, however (Carroll, Dobrev, and Swaminathan 2002).

Initial Mobilizing

Most start-ups of new organizations involve a period of planning and, in many cases, preproduction operation that result either in failure or mobilization prior to actual entry into production. Hypotheses have been formulated in this regard also:

1. Preproducer density has an inverted-U-shaped relationship with the rate of entry into production.
2. Producer density has a greater impact on the rate of entry into production than does preproducer density.
3. The rate of preproducer initiation has an inverted-U-shaped relationship with the density of producers.
4. The rate of successful movement from preproduction into production declines monotonically with the time spent in (preproduction) organizing mode. (Carroll and Hannan 2000b, 345–46)

These hypotheses represent attempts to tie what happens in the pre-start-up period to the larger body of theory dealing with density dependence.

Organizational Transformation and Inertia

The idea that inertia follows from the theory is modeled in various ways stressing that organizations that are favored by selection tend to be resistant to change. Thus organizations attempting structural transformation should be more predisposed to failure. The models proposed in Carroll and Hannan (2000b) reach this conclusion in new ways, but achieve the same result as in the ecological theory.

An instance of organizational inertia occurs in the case of *environmental imprinting*, under which specific environmental characteristics are mapped onto an organization, thus influencing its subsequent development and life chances. This is particularly likely to occur in the founding period; the imprinted features continue to hold over long periods.

Driven by inconsistent research findings, the theory continues to be elaborated with regard to change and inertia (Hannan, Pólos, and Carroll 2003a, b). The idea thus advanced is that architectural changes in an organization prompt additional alterations that reverberate through the firm, generating what amounts to a cascade of changes. Organizations undergoing change tend to concentrate on the change process, and thus miss opportunities to acquire resources. Consequently, long cascades increase the risk of failure. This risk is accentuated by limited foresight that creates a systematic inclination to underestimate both the length of an organizational transformation and the costs associated with it.

Note that concepts such as inertia and the deleterious effects of cascading change appear to contradict a number of other theoretical positions in the literature. These include the idea that organizations should adapt to environmental changes by transforming themselves in some way (see Chapters 13 and 16 in this volume), the general thrust of organization development (see Chapters 17 and 18 in this volume), and the concept of structural modulation, whereby efficiency is fostered by frequent changes, even in the absence of environmental prompting (see Nickerson and Zenger 2002).

EVALUATION AND IMPACT

The preferred approach to conducting research on organizational ecology and demography theory is to collect information on the life histories of organizational populations and, in particular, on the occurrence of certain theory-relevant events of the type discussed previously such as foundings, mergers, disbandings, and the like; thus to use a kind of event-history procedure (Hannan and Tuma 1979). This retrospective approach differs from the modal methodology used in organizational behavior by emphasizing populations rather than focal organizations and longitudinal analyses extending over extended time periods. It has been at the core of research on the Hannan/Freeman/Carroll theory from the beginning, although there are both major benefits and some drawbacks associated with it.

The benefits are that using archival data, events in the life histories of organizations of a given form and in a particular niche can be reconstructed. The only readily apparent alternatives are to start at the founding of the first organization and collect data forward until the last such organization dies (not a very parsimonious or perhaps even tenable procedure, although some truncation at the extremes might prove feasible) and to develop and run simulations of the processes involved (not the kind of approach one would want to rely on exclusively for evidence regarding a subject). Thus, the event-history procedure clearly does lend itself to testing this type of theory.

The problem is that events and theoretical constructs do not always match perfectly. For instance, archival data may differ in the way organizational foundings are defined, thus resulting in construct invalidity (Hannan and Freeman 1989). Other features of organizations may be used in different ways in different studies because the available information differs. Published histories and data sources may vary in the precision used to define events. Certain types of information may be unavailable for periods of time or even completely lacking on a particular population (see Carroll and Hannan 2000b for an extended discussion of these issues).

These difficulties in conducting research with archival, retrospective data sources constructed for purposes completely different from the theory they are used to test are enough of a problem. However, there is an even greater threat in that a theory constructed to be tested in this way might be driven in both its definition of variables and its specification of relationships by a knowledge of the available research data sets. That Hannan and Freeman (1989) often note their inability to formulate theory on a particular subject suggests that they are not forcing theory in this way, and gives reason for optimism on this score. However, the real test is to look into studies conducted at a time and by researchers far removed from the original theorists. But first we need to consider the research that has involved participation by Hannan, Freeman, and Carroll themselves.

Initial Studies by the Theory Authors

The book *Organizational Ecology* (Hannan and Freeman 1989) draws upon three primary organizational populations to test its theory. These are all populations that had been utilized and discussed to some extent in previous publications during the 1980s. They are:

1. The 479 U.S. labor unions founded in the period 1836–1985; foundings/year were close to 0 until the Civil War. (see also Hannan and Freeman 1987)
2. The 1,197 entries into the semiconductor manufacturing industry between 1946 and 1984; a number were new entries that had a prior organizational existence. (see also Brittain and Freeman 1980)
3. The 2,170 newspapers founded in the San Francisco Bay area in the 1840–1975 period; this is part of a wider study of seven urban newspaper populations in the United States. (see Carroll 1987)

For all three populations, founding rates were related to density, usually rising with increasing density to a point and then declining with further increases in density. This theoretically specified, nonmonotonic pattern was characteristic of all but the independent foundings in the semiconductor industry; the latter do not appear to have encountered a carrying capacity in the same way as the other organizations. As predicted, failure rates were consistently a monotonic function of age, the liability of newness phenomenon (see also Freeman, Carroll, and Hannan 1983). Mortality rates were also a function of density, with rates falling with increasing density to a point and then rising. This consistency across populations was not maintained for the effects of competition on mortality rates; competitive pressures were particularly pronounced for the unions. Overall, across three very different populations, the theory received extensive, but not universal, support.

The Subsequent Hannan/Carroll Research

Hannan has continued to published research with a variety of coauthors focusing on a multipopulation approach similar to that used in the initial studies. One such analysis used three populations of newspapers, the San Francisco Bay population noted previously, an Irish population for the 1800 to 1975 period, and an Argentinean population from 1800 to 1900, as well as the U.S. labor union data and a population of brewing firms in the United States, covering the period from 1633 to 1988 (Carroll and Hannan 1989). The question to be resolved was whether density at founding affects mortality rates. The conclusion was that it does, in all five instances. However, whether this was a function primarily of resource scarcity or niche packing remains unresolved, requiring size-related data for its solution.

A subsequent study by Ranger-Moore, Banaszak-Holl, and Hannan (1991) extended the density dependence research to Manhattan banks (1791–1980) and American life insurance companies (1759–1937). The nonmonotonic function involving legitimacy and competition noted previously was again attained, confirming the theory in both instances. Furthermore, these data indicate that the theory is not merely applicable to small firms that are relatively free of regulation.

All of the populations discussed to this point, except the semiconductor firms, which did not match the theory as to entry, were used in the Hannan and Carroll (1992) analysis. That the results reported tended to support the theory is as expected, but it is also worth noting that certain computer simulations were attempted and produced results consistent with theoretical expectations.

More recently, Hannan and his colleagues have become involved in event-history studies of the automobile industry, particularly for the 1886 to 1981 period in Europe (Hannan, Carroll, Dundon, and Torres 1995). Again, the predictions of the theory hold, and for all five countries studied, insofar as density dependence is concerned. In addition, there is evidence that the legitimation process is driven by density in Europe as a whole, while competition is a function of specific country densities. The generality of this apparently industry-specific finding is unclear.

One failure in this long list of research successes, other than what has been noted previously, involves the role of organizational size. This has been an area of considerable theoretical uncertainty and attempts to deal with it, using the bank and insurance company data, have proved to be only partially effective (Hannan, Ranger-Moore, and Banaszak-Holl 1990). Some theoretical developments to deal with these matters are contained in Carroll and Hannan (2000b).

The same volume presents reports on other research of interest. One such study dealt with initial mobilizing in the U.S. automobile industry from 1886 to 1982, where data on the subject were available. The results indicated some weak support for the first hypothesis on the inverted-U-shaped relationship between preproducer density and the rate of entry into production, and much stronger support for the effect of producer density in this regard. The other two hypotheses noted previously do not appear to have been confirmed.

Also the Carroll and Hannan (2000b) book contains a summary of studies on the effects of organizational change on mortality. Some fifteen investigations are noted, two of which involved Carroll as an author; the types of changes considered spread over a wide range. The two studies with Carroll as author supported theory in indicating a positive relationship between change and mortality, but a number of studies did not. As indicated, "the pattern of findings is far from uniform" (370). There are some indications of design problems in certain of the nonconfirming studies. Yet all in all the theory is not consistently supported by this line of research.

However, Dobrev, Kim, and Carroll (2003), working with the automobile industry data, continue to find that change elevates the potential for failure. The fact that instances of change that do not have these negative effects occur is also acknowledged, and explained using the niche width of generalist organizations as a moderator. It becomes increasingly evident that the theory of organizational transformation and inertia holds only under certain circumstances and that relationships in this area are exceedingly complex (see Dobrev, Kim, and Carroll 2002).

The Subsequent Freeman Research

Among Freeman's contributions subsequent to his collaboration with Hannan has been a study of rural cooperative banks in Italy over the period since 1948, when the banks were legalized (Freeman and Lomi 1994). The data show a positive linear density effect on foundings. The competition effects usually associated with carrying capacity were not in evidence. There are reasons to believe, however, that this particular situation may not be typical and may not be the most appropriate for testing theory. This study, as have others, also raises the question of the effects of population definition on the results obtained; regional analyses, for instance, produce certain findings that differ significantly from those at the national level. The theory needs to be specific in providing a priori guidance in this regard.

Freeman also coauthored a study (Barnett and Freeman 2001) showing that when companies introduce multiple new products all at once, rather than introducing them incrementally, the result is very likely to be disruptive change and, ultimately, failure. The exit rate was over 40 percent for simultaneous product innovations. "The greater the number of such changes occurring at once, the more we multiply the agony" (556). Unfortunately this study did not produce evidence as to how, within the internal dynamics of individual firms, this result comes about, although it is attributed to coordination difficulties. Clearly the most recent theory is confirmed.

In the past few years Freeman's writing has as often been concerned with institutional matters as with ecological (see Freeman 2000; Jaffee and Freeman 2002).

Findings That Give Reason for Pause

The research involving the authors provides considerable positive evidence in support of the theory. There are points at which exceptions appear, but these are commonly attributed to imperfections in the research data. Carroll's (1987) analysis of various newspaper populations, a particularly propitious setting for the conduct of event-histories, provides a good example of this positive set of findings. Numerous studies by others yield an equally positive picture.

Yet there are findings that introduce problems for the theory. I will start with a treatment of research on the theory of ecology. A study of voluntary social service organizations in Toronto from 1970 to 1982 obtained information on organizational changes from interviews (Singh, House, and Tucker 1986). The data indicated that changes did not necessarily result in an increase in organizational death rates. Ecological theory best described core changes, but peripheral changes were best described by an adaptation perspective: thus a truly comprehensive theory of change would require the incorporation of both selection and adaptation processes. A subsequent study of the same population focused on specialist and generalist organizations and found substantial differences between the two forms (Tucker, Singh, and Meinhard 1990). Both ecological dynamics and institutional changes appeared to influence specialists more.

An analysis of organizational failures in the California wine industry between 1940 and 1985 fails to support the Hannan/Freeman ecological theory (Delacroix, Swaminathan, and Solt 1989). That theory, as it applies to the density dependence of mortality, consistently overstates the negative effects of a lack of legitimacy. In a number of instances, overcrowding was avoided by migrating to a new niche or by enlarging the initial niche. A follow-up analysis of information from the wine industry indicated that both businesses founded in the table wine niche and those that diversified into it had lower failure rates (Swaminathan and Delacroix 1991). Organizations appear to be more flexible in a strategic sense and environments less rigid than the density dependence concept of organizational demise would indicate.

An event-history analysis of newspapers in Finland over the period from 1771 to 1963 indicated that certain factors reduced failures, increased organizational transformations, and changed the chances of failure subsequent to transformation (Miner, Amburgey, and Stearns 1990). These factors operated in conjunction with interorganizational linkages, which served to buffer against failure, influence the likelihood of organizational transformation, and change the effects of transformation on failure. Thus, interorganizational linkages introduced a degree of flexibility in avoiding failures.

Petersen and Koput (1991) provide evidence that the decreasing mortality rate in the early part of a population's history is not necessarily a function of increasing legitimacy, but can be explained as a result of unresolved heterogeneity. Thus there appears no need to invoke the process of legitimation, and if legitimacy is to be invoked, direct measures are needed to support it, rather than the inferential procedures of the Hannan/Freeman theory. These findings are based on various simulations and accordingly are not definitive, but they do underscore the need for hard measures of legitimacy rather than proxies more readily derivable from archival data.

Taken as a whole, the research prior to 2000 emphasizes greater adaptability and flexibility on the part of organizations than the Hannan/Freeman theory seems to permit. It also raises questions as to whether the event-history approach to research alone is adequate to the task of validating the theory.

With the publication of the Carroll and Hannan (2000b) volume, and the theoretical extensions contained therein, however, a number of the earlier questions are given theoretical answers. In particular, the advent of resource partitioning theory helps to explain the differential between generalist and specialist organizations. Swaminathan (2001) presents further evidence from the wine industry that yields considerable support for resource partitioning, and accordingly places that industry in much closer alignment with the revised demographic theory. Also this study indicates that identity plays an important role in the evolution of specialist forms, thus adding credibility to the new definition of organizational form.

On the other hand, research continues to emphasize the importance of adaptability and flexibility. Analyses of Spanish savings and loan organizations:

> support the validity of the different evolutionary patterns of the model and reveal the existence of different strategies for organizational adaptation in the population studied. In some cases, SS&L institutions resorted to strategic adjustment (internal adaptation), whereas in other cases, they stood inert or disappeared. . . . [W]e also arrived at the following conclusion: on the one hand, business strategy is capable of leading organizational evolution and, on the other hand, the firm and its environment are clearly interrelated. . . . [W]e found that organizational resources conditioned the path of organizational evolution. In short, organizational resources and routines linked to expansion policies clearly determined whether an institution died or adapted to the new competitive environment. . . . In summary, our results highlight the existence of different ways in which organizational evolutionary processes may operate. (Alvarez and Merino 2003, 1449–50)

Critiques from Other Disciplines

Organizational ecology theory overlaps with several other disciplines and has as a result elicited comments from representatives of these fields. One such instance comes from mathematics and computer science, which have contributed a formal logical analysis of the theory (Péli, Bruggeman, Masuch, and Ó Nualláin 1994). The conclusion is that the theory is logically consistent, except that a clear distinction needs to be made between organizations under reorganization and those free of such conditions. Certain reductions in the domain of the theory to make it less general are recommended as well, and a number of instances of ambiguity in statement, some of which I have noted previously, are pointed out. All in all, however, the theory fares well at the hands of this analysis by formal logic.

Such is not the case at the hands of a biologist and a mathematician (Low and Simon 1995). Their comment on reading the edited volume by Baum and Singh (1994) is that the terms from biology are utilized incorrectly; that "contradictory usages are rife and coherence is absent;" and that the evolutionary analogy "adds little, is frequently pushed too far, and in fact contributes confusion" (738–40). These judgments would seem to apply to the approach taken by organizational ecology in general, since the book contains some twenty-eight selections ranging over a wide selection of subject matter within the field. Certainly Hannan and Freeman have every right to develop their theory as they see fit, borrowing from biology as they go, but it would appear from this reaction that the resort to biological analogy has not contributed to the legitimacy of their ideas, at least within the biological community. Perhaps the theory would benefit from a major change in terminology that served to remove it from the biological context completely. This might serve to eliminate ambiguities and to open up new domains for consideration as well. On this point it might be noted that other organizational writers in the evolutionary-ecology vein have had terminological problems as well (see Aldrich 1999). The appeal to biology may well have contributed to the legitimacy of the theory at an earlier point, but at present this appeal would seem to be no longer needed.

Critiques from Within Macro Organizational Behavior

Most critiques have not come from other disciplines, or even from within organizational behavior as a whole, but from macro theorists and researchers, often with an organizational ecology orientation. One of the macro critiques derives from a review symposium, again dealing with the Baum and Singh (1994) volume. Here, both authors, Davis and Swaminathan (1996), come down hard on the theory for failing to deal effectively with the concept of organizational form, which is basic to all that follows. The problem is that the Hannan/Freeman theory is based on a research methodology that forces researchers to use groupings of organizations for which archival data sources are available. These groupings then become the forms of which populations are composed. The forms and their populations are thus made up anew for each study, depending on the requirements of those who created the data, not the theorists. There is no overarching typology; the theory simply accepts what is given in whatever grouping is available. Accordingly, there is not an unambiguous statement of what constitutes a form; nor is there any basis for determining when an organization changes its form and enters another population. The idea that organizations of considerable size might contain within them multiple forms is simply not entertained. This is not an issue that has been given much attention since Hannan and Freeman (1989), but that needs to be addressed.

Pfeffer (1997) indicates that the liability of newness, and of size as well, is no longer much in dispute. However, Baum (1996) raises certain issues in this regard. If one controls for organizational size, failure rates do not decline with age. Thus, the question becomes a matter of establishing whether such a correction is appropriate. Carroll and Hannan (2000b) recognize this difficulty, however, and give it considerable attention.

The Role of Density Dependence

To this point I have not considered issues related to density dependence. Yet this is the area where criticism has been the most intense, and the research most extensive. A number of the early attacks on ecology theory, in the 1980s when it first began to attract attention, were with regard to this aspect. These early arguments have been in many cases discredited; a few have survived into the present. I will concentrate our discussion on positions that are currently viable. It should be recognized, however, that when organizational ecology came on the scene it was a major innovation and drew a considerable amount of heat, some warranted, but certainly a great deal that was not.

In a review of Hannan and Carroll's (1992) *Dynamics of Organizational Populations,* Miner (1993) says:

> I believe the book provides convincing evidence that the negative effect of founding density on mortality is quite robust, and that predicted nonmonotonic effects of contemporaneous density on foundings and failures are common if not universal. But the reader must make demanding leaps of inferential faith to conclude that this is strong evidence for the specific processes of legitimation and competition proposed to generate these results. (365)

> One cannot rule out the authors' theory . . . but one also cannot rule out several other very plausible theories nor point to substantial collaborative evidence for the authors' theories. (363)

In particular, the legitimacy interpretation, as to both individual organizations and forms, has been the subject of continuing controversy (see Amburgey and Rao 1996). The problem is that even if the density dependence curve is valid, there is no measured evidence that legitimacy is part of the process; the concept of legitimacy appears to have been imposed "ex post facto and without direct measurement on empiricist findings that would otherwise remain unexplained" (Delacroix and Rao 1994, 258). Furthermore, the evidence most frequently cited in support of the Hannan/Freeman theory and its interpretation comes from organizations (labor unions, newspapers, breweries) that are particularly subject to legitimacy problems. Other organizations may well not exhibit the same type of effect.

These questions of course require analyses of the research literature for an answer. Baum and Powell (1995), as part of a substantial challenge to the legitimacy interpretation, start to bring evidence to bear in this regard. They cite a large number of studies to the effect that founding studies support the theory's predictions 74 percent of the time and failure studies 55 percent of the time. Hannan and Carroll (1995b) challenge these data on several grounds, and otherwise provide a rebuttal to the Baum and Powell (1995) thesis.

Yet, as we have seen, there are a number of studies extending back into the 1980s that do serve to question the density dependence formulations. Even if we accept the legitimacy and competition labeling, the density curve itself does not always take the expected form. Not all of these departures from theory can be attributed to the effects of truncation, or censoring, as it is called in event-history analysis, on the left or right sides of the distribution, although some of the studies do appear to be rather short term in nature for the purposes intended. Baum (1996) continues to provide substantial evidence that although a majority of the research is aligned with theoretical expectations, much of it is not. Again, the Carroll and Hannan (2000b) formulations under the demography banner do much to correct the disparities, and there is new evidence in support of these views (Dobrev 2001).

Applications

Pfeffer (1997) notes that organizational ecology, in its denial of substantial effects to managerial choice and strategic action, "is in its present versions reasonably far from a theory that permits knowledge to be translated into action" (169). There is little that can actually be put to use by a practitioner simply because the theory deals primarily with causal processes that are beyond the control of those who occupy positions in organizations. This consequently places a damper on the attractiveness of the theory for those seeking information on how to manage better. Again, since adaptive response does retain credibility based on the research, this inflexibility seems to operate to unnecessarily restrict the practical value of the theory. If, as Donaldson (1995) indicates, the theory is viewed as antimanagement, that would serve to restrict it even further.

This pessimistic position, derived from the Hannan/Freeman ecological theory, improves only slightly when applications are viewed through the lens of the Carroll/Hannan theory. The last section of Carroll and Hannan (2000b) contains material on applications, thus breaking with past presentations. This material is introduced as describing: "some preliminary ideas about connections between organizational population structure and issues related to employment patterns, public policies, and industrial outcomes. Many of these notions are not yet highly developed and almost all of them need stronger empirical validation" (42).

A number of these proposals deal with regulatory matters, such as policies regarding competition and deregulation; others consider job mobility, career paths, and various employment considerations. The high proportion of unemployment that results from business failures caused by demographic processes is emphasized. The recommendations tend to stress the need for research related to career dynamics and government policy. Little is said about managerial practice, and certainly nothing that would specify guidelines derived from theory.

CONCLUSIONS

All three theories discussed in this part have substantial evidence of validity. Thus, it is not surprising that there would be consideration of combining certain of these theories, if only because they represent some of macro organizational behavior's best. Also, these theories tend to emerge as partial in their coverage of their domains.

The merger that one hears about most, although not necessarily the one that involves the most compelling logic, is between the organizational ecology view and some version of neoinstitutionalism (see Chapter 20 in this volume). Such a convergence has been given considerable attention, with various degrees of approximation to a full theoretical statement (Carroll, Delacroix, and Goodstein 1988; Singh and Lumsden 1990). The common ground, of course, is the role of legitimacy as an overlapping construct, although that construct plays somewhat different roles in the two theories. Legitimacy could bring resource dependence theory (see Chapter 19 in this volume) in under the same large tent, but there it is not a key concept, being handled as only one among many organizational resources (Stryker 2000). Legitimacy would have to be given an enlarged role in resource dependence formulations to serve as a bridge into the other theories. Certainly the common origins of the three theories and their overlapping constituencies suggest that some type of merger may occur eventually.

Yet another possibility suggests itself. All three theories seem to exhibit key lacunae of much the same kind—a space into which some type of formulation from micro organizational behavior might be placed to mutual advantage. Examples would be power motivation in resource dependence theory, group decision making and leadership in organizational ecology and demography, and various motivational constructs in neoinstitutional theory. I am sure that many would demur at this point on the ground that this would require leaving the discipline of sociology and entering the domain of psychology. Realistically, for a sociologist this might represent a problem, both in terms of values and knowledge constraints. There are rational reasons for compartmentalizing knowledge to foster specialization and permit definitive identification of disciplinary participants. But the important consideration here is that for organizational behavior, with its professional school locus and its penchant for following problems wherever they may lead, such a disciplinary convergence presents no difficulties at all; meso theorizing and research of this kind are at the heart of the discipline.

As I move now to the evaluations of organizational ecology and demography theory, something needs to be said about the assessment by others of the theory in its demography phase. Although much has been written about the pros and cons of the ecology aspects of the theory, much less is available on the Carroll/Hannan extensions, largely because the time since emergence is short. I have already noted that Rao (2002) indicates a very positive view of the Carroll and Hannan (2000b) book. An editorial by van Witteloostuijn (2000), introducing a journal special issue on the theory, is consistently laudatory, using terms such as "here to stay," "successful," "well-communicated and well-established," and "in a very healthy state." To date, at least, the theory as a whole that we have been considering appears to have been very favorably received.

The original evaluations of this theory were done without benefit of access to the Carroll and Hannan (2000b) volume. Still, the importance rating is 4.88—not in the five-star range that characterizes several of the theories considered in this part, but very close to it.

Estimated validity was initially established at three stars, but was raised to four stars based on the content of the Carroll and Hannan (2000b) book and the articles that followed it. Theoretical elaborations, such as the new handling of the organizational forms construct and the resource partitioning formulations, represent considerable advances. The new confirming evidence is also impressive. Yet the theory, even in its recently developed form, remains lacking in certain areas; in particular, the inertia formulations appear deficient. Thus, a move up to five stars does not seem warranted. Nevertheless, the rise to four stars shifts the theory of organizational ecology and demography into a category consistent with the *essential* designation, and it is for that reason that the theory is included in this book.

The fact that the theory of organizational demography contains some effort to deal with applications raises the estimated usefulness rating from one to two stars. The treatment on this score is limited, unsupported by research, and presents applications to career dynamics or public policy, not managerial practice. Yet the fact that three chapters of the Carroll and Hannan (2000b) book are devoted to implications is worthy of some recognition. This change, of course, is not associated with any alteration in the essential designation.

REFERENCES

Aldrich, Howard E. (1999). *Organizations Evolving.* London: Sage.

Alvarez, Valle S., and Merino, Teresa G. (2003). The History of Organizational Renewal: Evolutionary Models of Spanish Savings and Loans Institutions. *Organization Studies,* 24, 1437–61.

Amburgey, Terry L., and Rao, Hayagreeva (1996). Organizational Ecology: Past, Present, and Future Directions. *Academy of Management Journal,* 39, 1265–86.

Barnett, William P., and Freeman, John (2001). Too Much of a Good Thing? Product Proliferation and Organizational Failure. *Organization Science,* 12, 539–58.

Baum, Joel A.C. (1996). Organizational Ecology. In Stewart R. Clegg, Cynthia Hardy, and Walter R. Nord (Eds.), *Handbook of Organization Studies.* London: Sage, 77–114.

Baum, Joel A.C., and McKelvey, Bill (1999). *Variations in Organization Science: In Honor of Donald T. Campbell.* Thousand Oaks, CA: Sage.

Baum, Joel A.C., and Powell, Walter W. (1995). Cultivating an Institutional Ecology of Organizations: Comment on Hannan, Carroll, Dundon, and Torres. *American Sociological Review,* 60, 529–38.

Baum, Joel A.C., and Singh, Jitendra V. (1994). *Evolutionary Dynamics of Organizations.* New York: Oxford University Press.

Brittain, Jack W., and Freeman, John H. (1980). Organizational Proliferation and Density Dependent Selection. In John R. Kimberly and Robert H. Miles (Eds.), *The Organizational Life Cycle: Issues in the Creation, Transformation, and Decline of Organizations.* San Francisco, CA: Jossey-Bass, 291–338.

Carroll, Glenn R. (1987). *Publish and Perish: The Organizational Ecology of Newspaper Industries.* Greenwich, CT: JAI Press.

Carroll, Glenn R., Delacroix, Jacques, and Goodstein, Jerry (1988). The Political Environments of Organizations: An Ecological View. *Research in Organizational Behavior,* 10, 359–92.

Carroll, Glenn R., Dobrev, Stanislav D., and Swaminathan, Anand (2002). Organizational Processes of Resource Partitioning. *Research in Organizational Behavior,* 24, 1–40.

Carroll, Glenn R., and Hannan, Michael T. (1989). Density Delay in the Evolution of Organizational Populations: A Model and Five Empirical Tests. *Administrative Science Quarterly,* 34, 411–30.

———. (2000a). Why Corporate Demography Matters: Policy Implications of Organizational Diversity. *California Management Review,* 42(3), 148–63.

———. (2000b). *The Demography of Corporations and Industries.* Princeton, NJ: Princeton University Press.

Davis, Gerald F., and Swaminathan, Anand (1996). Review Symposium—*Evolutional Dynamics of Organizations. Administrative Science Quarterly,* 41, 538–50.

Delacroix, Jacques, and Rao, Hayagreeva (1994). Externalities and Ecological Theory: Unbundling Density Dependence. In Joel A.C. Baum and Jitendra V. Singh (Eds.), *Evolutionary Dynamics of Organizations.* New York: Oxford University Press, 255–68.

Delacroix, Jacques, Swaminathan, Anand, and Solt, Michael E. (1989). Density Dependence versus Population Dynamics: An Ecological Study of Failings in the California Wine Industry. *American Sociological Review,* 54, 245–62.

Dobrev, Stanislav D. (2001). Revisiting Organizational Legitimation: Cognitive Diffusion and Sociopolitical Factors in the Evolution of Bulgarian Newspaper Enterprises, 1846–1992. *Organization Studies,* 22, 419–44.

Dobrev, Stanislav D., Kim, Tai-Young, and Carroll, Glenn R. (2002). The Evolution of Organizational Niches: U.S. Automobile Manufacturers, 1885–1981. *Administrative Science Quarterly,* 47, 233–64.

———. (2003). Shifting Gears, Shifting Niches: Organizational Inertia and Change in the Evolution of the U.S. Automobile Industry, 1995–1981. *Organization Science,* 14, 264–82.

Donaldson, Lex (1995). *American Anti-Management Theories of Organization: A Critique of Paradigm Proliferation.* Cambridge, UK: Cambridge University Press.

Freeman, John (2000). Differentiation in Business Organizations. *Advances in Strategic Management,* 17, 95–102.

Freeman, John, Carroll, Glenn R., and Hannan, Michael T. (1983). The Liability of Newness: Age Dependence in Organizational Death Rates. *American Sociological Review,* 48, 692–710.

Freeman, John, and Lomi, Alessandro (1994). Resource Partitioning and Foundings of Banking Cooperatives in Italy. In Joel A.C. Baum and Jitendra V. Singh (Eds.), *Evolutionary Dynamics of Organizations.* New York: Oxford University Press, 269–93.

Haire, Mason (1959). *Modern Organization Theory.* New York: Wiley, 272–306.

Hannan, Michael T., and Carroll, Glenn R. (1992). *Dynamics of Organizational Populations: Density, Legitimation, and Competition.* New York: Oxford University Press.

———. (1995a). An Introduction to Organizational Ecology. In Glenn R. Carroll and Michael T. Hannan (Eds.), *Organizations in Industry: Strategy, Structure, and Selection.* New York: Oxford University Press, 17–31.

———. (1995b). Theory Building and Cheap Talk about Legitimation: Reply to Baum and Powell. *American Sociological Review,* 60, 539–44.

Hannan, Michael T., Carroll, Glenn R., Dundon, Elizabeth A., and Torres, John C. (1995). Organizational Evolution in a Multinational Context: Entries of Automobile Manufacturers in Belgium, Britain, France, Germany, and Italy. *American Sociological Review,* 60, 509–28.

Hannan, Michael T., and Freeman, John H. (1977). The Population Ecology of Organizations. *American Journal of Sociology,* 82, 929–64.

———. (1978). The Population Ecology of Organizations. In Marshall W. Meyer and Associates (Eds.), *Environments and Organizations.* San Francisco, CA: Jossey-Bass, 131–71.

———. (1987). The Ecology of Organizational Founding: American Labor Unions, 1836–1985. *American Journal of Sociology,* 92, 910–43.

———. (1988). Density Dependence in the Growth of Organizational Populations. In Glenn R. Carroll (Ed.), *Ecological Models of Organizations.* Cambridge, MA: Ballinger, 7–31.

———. (1989). *Organizational Ecology.* Cambridge, MA: Harvard University Press.

Hannan, Michael T., Pólos, László, and Carroll, Glenn R. (2003a). Cascading Organizational Change. *Organization Science,* 14, 463–82.

———. (2003b). The Fog of Change: Opacity and Asperity in Organizations. *Administrative Science Quarterly,* 48, 399–432.

Hannan, Michael T., Ranger-Moore, James, and Banaszak-Holl, Jane (1990). Competition and the Evolution of Organizational Size Distributions. In Jitendra V. Singh (Ed.), *Organizational Evolution: New Directions.* Newbury Park, CA: Sage, 246–68.

Hannan, Michael T., and Tuma, Nancy B. (1979). Methods for Temporal Analysis. *Annual Review of Sociology,* 5, 303–28.

Hawley, Amos (1968). Human Ecology. In David Sills (Ed.), *International Encyclopedia of the Social Sciences,* Vol .4. New York: Free Press, 328–37.

Jaffee, Jonathan, and Freeman, John (2002). Institutional Change in Real Time: The Development of Employee Stock Options for German Venture Capital. *Advances in Strategic Management,* 19, 219–46.

Low, Bobbi S., and Simon, Carl P. (1995). Review of Baum and Singh's *Evolutionary Dynamics of Organizations. Academy of Management Review,* 20, 735–41.

McKendrick, David G., Jaffee, Jonathan, Carroll, Glenn R., and Khessina, Olga M. (2003). In the Bud? Disk Array Producers as a (Possibly) Emergent Organizational Form. *Administrative Science Quarterly,* 48, 69–93.

Miner, Anne S. (1993). Review of Hannan and Carroll's *Dynamics of Organizational Populations. Academy of Management Review,* 18, 355–67.

Miner, Anne S., Amburgey, Terry L., and Stearns, Timothy M. (1990). Interorganizational Linkages and Population Dynamics: Buffering and Transformational Shields. *Administrative Science Quarterly,* 35, 689–713.

Nickerson, Jack A., and Zenger, Todd R. (2002). Being Efficiently Fickle: A Dynamic Theory of Organizational Choice. *Organization Science,* 13, 547–66.

Péli, Gábor, Bruggeman, Jeroen, Masuch, Michael, and Ó Nualláin, Breanndán (1994). A Logical Approach to Formalizing Organizational Ecology. *American Sociological Review,* 59, 571–93.

Peterson, Trond, and Koput, Kenneth W. (1991). Density Dependence in Organizational Mortality: Legitimacy or Unobserved Heterogeneity? *American Sociological Review,* 56, 399–409.

Pfeffer, Jeffrey (1997). *New Directions for Organization Theory: Problems and Prospects.* New York: Oxford University Press.

Ranger-Moore, James, Banaszak-Holl, Jane, and Hannan, Michael T. (1991). Density-Dependent Dynamics in Regulated Industries: Founding Rates of Banks and Life Insurance Companies. *Administrative Science Quarterly,* 36, 36–65.

Rao, Hayagreeva (2002). Review of Carroll and Hannan's *The Demography of Corporations and Industries. Administrative Science Quarterly,* 47, 584–86.

Singh, Jitendra V., House, Robert J., and Tucker, David J. (1986). Organizational Change and Organizational Mortality. *Administrative Science Quarterly,* 31, 587–611.

Singh, Jitendra V., and Lumsden, Charles J. (1990). Theory and Research in Organizational Ecology. *Annual Review of Sociology,* 16, 161–95.

Stinchcombe, Arthur L. (1965). Social Structure and Organizations. In James G. March (Ed.), *Handbook of Organizations.* Chicago, IL: Rand McNally, 153–93.

Stryker, Robin (2000). Legitimacy Processes as Institutional Politics: Implications for Theory and Research in the Sociology of Organizations. *Research in the Sociology of Organizations,* 17, 179–223.

Swaminathan, Anand (2001). Resource Partitioning and the Evolution of Specialist Organizations: The

Role of Location and Identity in the U.S. Wine Industry. *Academy of Management Journal,* 44, 1169–85.

Swaminathan, Anand, and Delacroix, Jacques (1991). Differentiation Within an Organizational Population: Additional Evidence from the Wine Industry. *Academy of Management Journal,* 34, 679–92.

Tucker, David J., Singh, Jitendra V., and Meinhard, Agnes G. (1990). Organizational Form, Population Dynamics, and Institutional Change: The Founding Patterns of Voluntary Organizations. *Academy of Management Journal,* 33, 151–78.

van Witteloostuijn, Argen (2000). Organizational Ecology Has a Bright Future. *Organization Studies,* 21, v–xiv.

NAME INDEX

SUBJECT INDEX

ABOUT THE AUTHOR

John B. Miner currently has a professional practice in Eugene, Oregon. He held the Donald S. Carmichael Chair in Human Resources at the State University of New York–Buffalo and was faculty director of the Center for Entrepreneurial Leadership there. Previously he was Research Professor of Management at Georgia State University. He has written fifty-three books and over 140 other publications.